OMNIBUS
VOLUME 1

MEEP!
MEEP!

DOCTOR WHO CLASSICS

OMNIBUS
VOLUME 1

Original Series Edits by Dez Skinn, Paul Neary, Alan McKenzie,
Sheila Cranna, and Richard Starkings

Series Edits by Chris Ryall and Denton J. Tipton

Collection Edits by Justin Eisinger and Mariah Huehner

Collection Design by Shawn Lee

Cover by Joe Corroney

Special Thanks to Gary Russell, David Turbitt and Guy Lamont
at BBC Worldwide, and Mike Riddell and Tom Spilsbury at
Panini Publishing Limited for their invaluable assistance.

www.IDWpublishing.com   ISBN: 978-1-60010-622-4   13 12 11 10   1 2 3 4

Operations: Ted Adams, Chief Executive Officer • Greg Goldstein, Chief Operating Officer • Matthew Ruzicka, CPA, Chief Financial Officer • Alan Payne, VP of Sales • Lorelei Bunjes, Dir. of Digital Services • AnnaMaria White, Marketing & PR Manager • Marci Hubbard, Executive Assistant • Alonzo Simon, Shipping Manager • Angela Loggins, Staff Accountant • Editorial: Chris Ryall, Publisher/Editor-in-Chief • Scott Dunbier, Editor, Special Projects • Andy Schmidt, Senior Editor • Bob Schreck, Senior Editor • Justin Eisinger, Editor • Kris Oprisko, Editor/Foreign Lic. • Denton J. Tipton, Editor • Tom Waltz, Editor • Mariah Huehner, Associate Editor • Carlos Guzman, Editorial Assistant • Design: Robbie Robbins, EVP/Sr. Graphic Artist • Neil Uyetake, Art Director • Chris Mowry, Graphic Artist • Amauri Osorio, Graphic Artist • Gilberto Lazcano, Production Assistant • Shawn Lee, Production Assistant

Originally published as DOCTOR WHO CLASSICS Issues # 1-10, GRANT MORRISON'S DOCTOR WHO Issues # 1-2, and DOCTOR WHO CLASSICS Series 2 Issues #1-3.

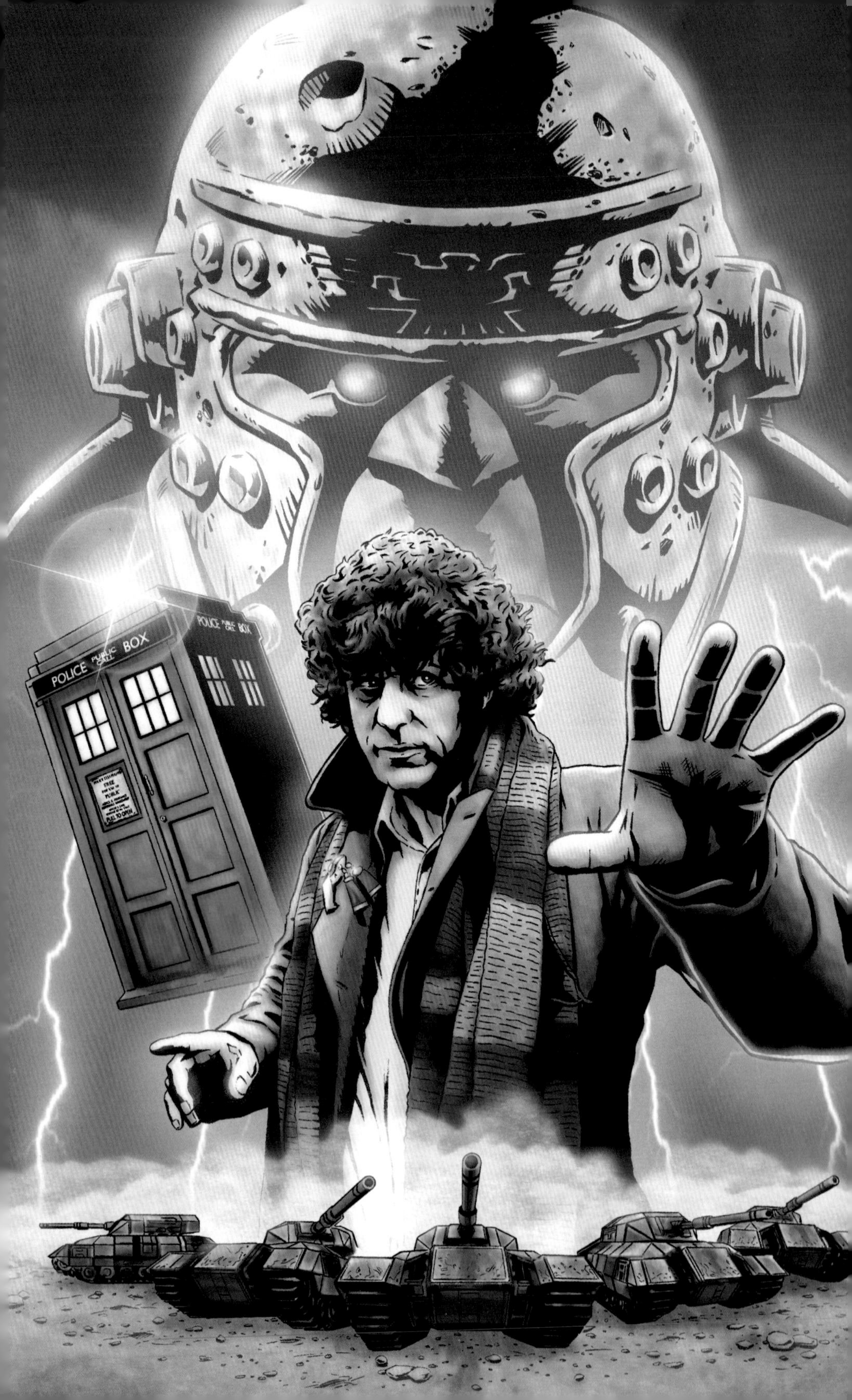
POLICE PUBLIC CALL BOX
POLICE PUBLIC CALL BOX

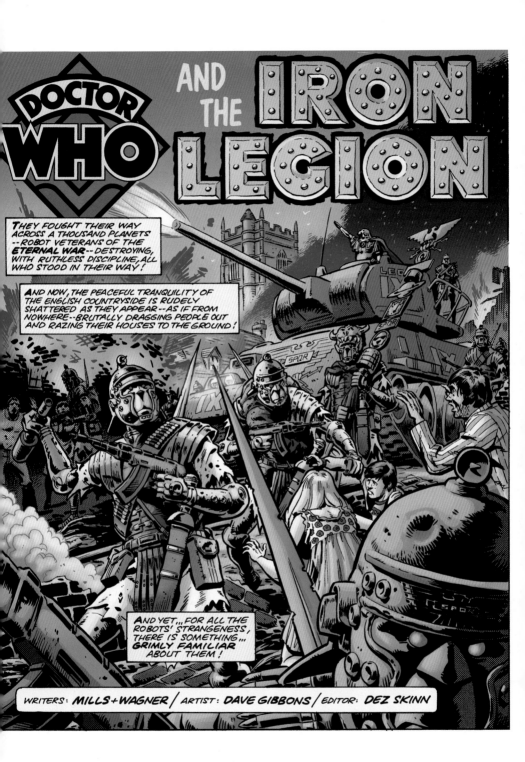

DOCTOR WHO AND THE IRON LEGION

THEY FOUGHT THEIR WAY ACROSS A THOUSAND PLANETS --ROBOT VETERANS OF THE **ETERNAL WAR**--DESTROYING, WITH RUTHLESS DISCIPLINE, ALL WHO STOOD IN THEIR WAY!

AND NOW, THE PEACEFUL TRANQUILITY OF THE ENGLISH COUNTRYSIDE IS RUDELY SHATTERED AS THEY APPEAR--AS IF FROM NOWHERE--BRUTALLY DRAGGING PEOPLE OUT AND RAZING THEIR HOUSES TO THE GROUND!

AND YET...FOR ALL THE ROBOTS' STRANGENESS, THERE IS SOMETHING... GRIMLY FAMILIAR ABOUT THEM!

WRITERS: **MILLS+WAGNER** / ARTIST: **DAVE GIBBONS** / EDITOR: **DEZ SKINN**

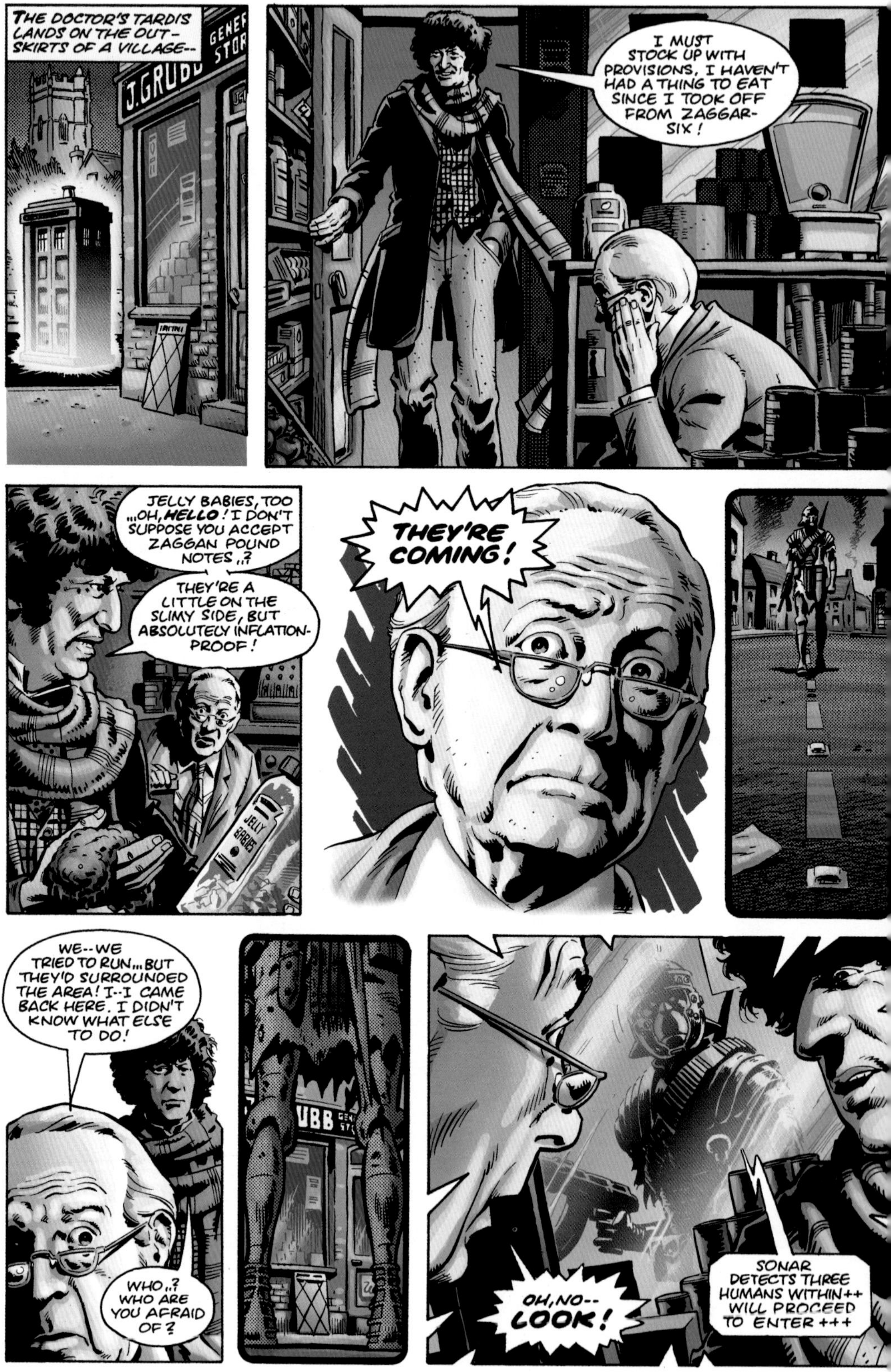
THE DOCTOR'S TARDIS LANDS ON THE OUT-SKIRTS OF A VILLAGE--
J. GRUBB
GENERAL STORE
I MUST STOCK UP WITH PROVISIONS, I HAVEN'T HAD A THING TO EAT SINCE I TOOK OFF FROM ZAGGAR-SIX!
JELLY BABIES, TOO ...OH, HELLO! I DON'T SUPPOSE YOU ACCEPT ZAGGAN POUND NOTES ..?
THEY'RE A LITTLE ON THE SLIMY SIDE, BUT ABSOLUTELY INFLATION-PROOF!
JELLY BABIES
THEY'RE COMING!
WE--WE TRIED TO RUN... BUT THEY'D SURROUNDED THE AREA! I--I CAME BACK HERE. I DIDN'T KNOW WHAT ELSE TO DO!
WHO..? WHO ARE YOU AFRAID OF?
OH, NO-- LOOK!
SONAR DETECTS THREE HUMANS WITHIN++ WILL PROCEED TO ENTER+++

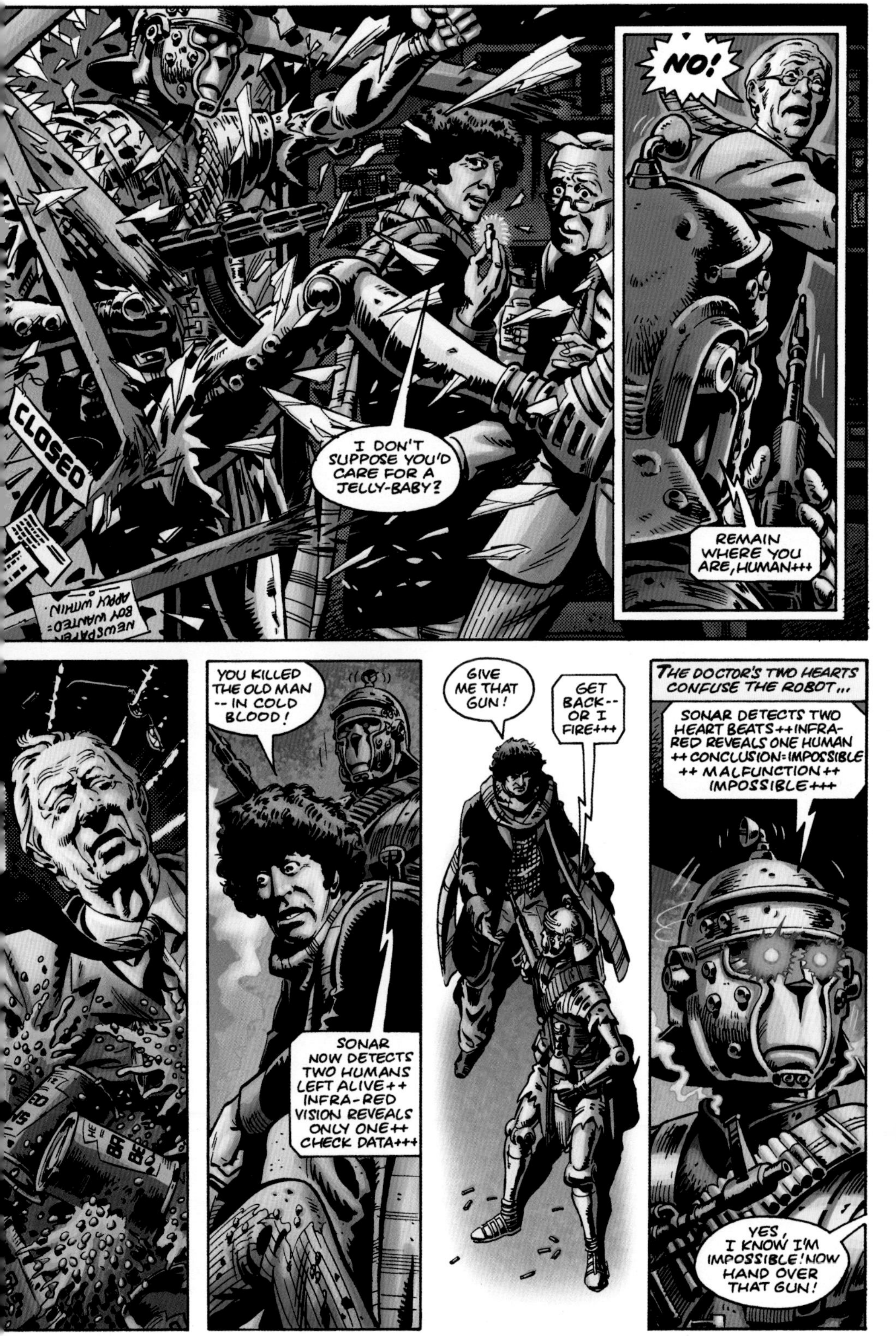
CLOSED
NEWSPAPER BOY WANTED: APPLY WITHIN.
I DON'T SUPPOSE YOU'D CARE FOR A JELLY-BABY?
NO!
REMAIN WHERE YOU ARE, HUMAN+++
YOU KILLED THE OLD MAN -- IN COLD BLOOD!
SONAR NOW DETECTS TWO HUMANS LEFT ALIVE++ INFRA-RED VISION REVEALS ONLY ONE++ CHECK DATA+++
GIVE ME THAT GUN!
GET BACK-- OR I FIRE+++
THE DOCTOR'S TWO HEARTS CONFUSE THE ROBOT...
SONAR DETECTS TWO HEART BEATS++INFRA-RED REVEALS ONE HUMAN ++CONCLUSION=IMPOSSIBLE ++ MALFUNCTION++ IMPOSSIBLE+++
YES, I KNOW I'M IMPOSSIBLE! NOW HAND OVER THAT GUN!

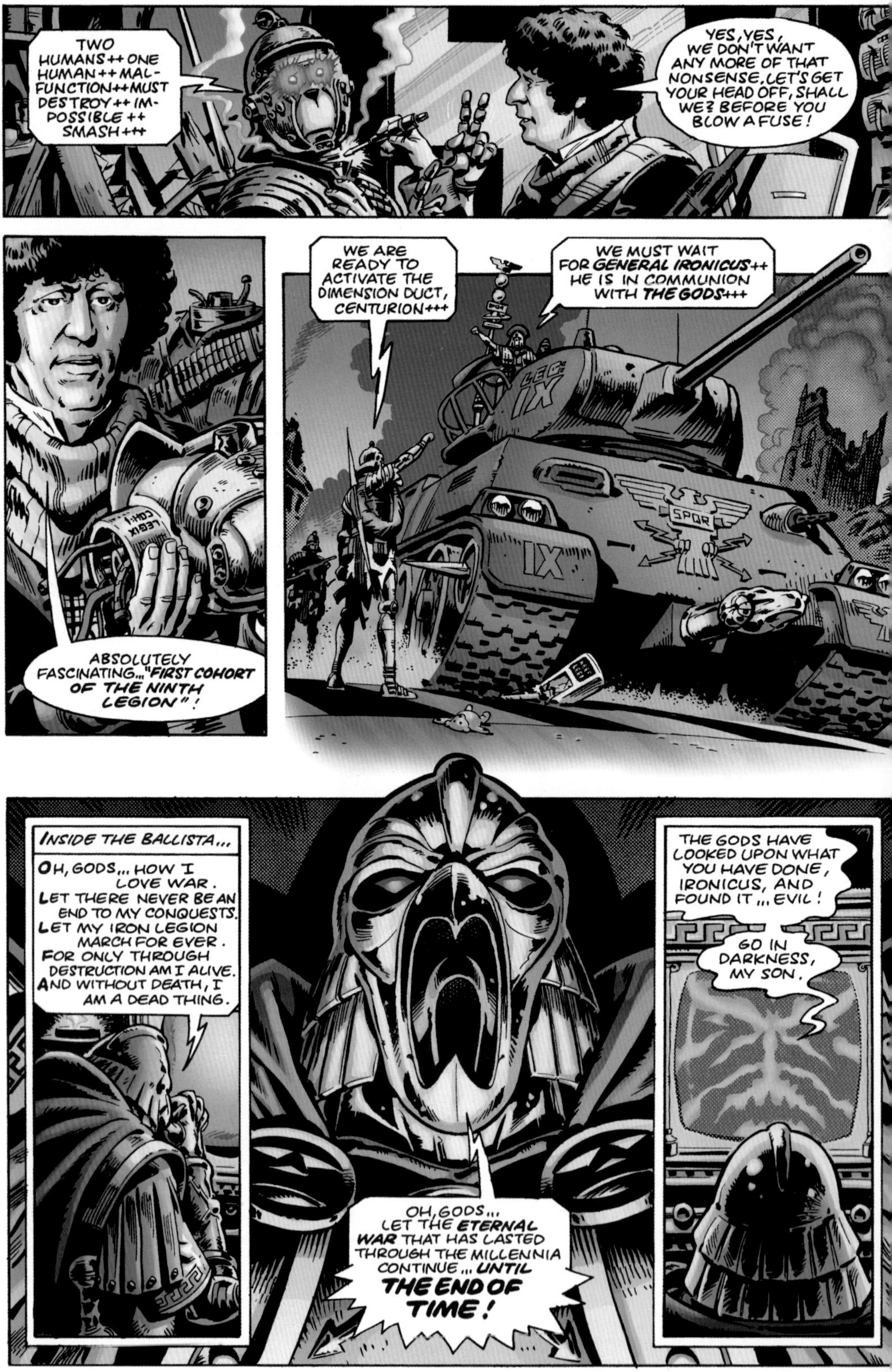
TWO HUMANS ++ ONE HUMAN ++ MAL-FUNCTION ++ MUST DESTROY ++ IM-POSSIBLE ++ SMASH +++
YES, YES, WE DON'T WANT ANY MORE OF THAT NONSENSE, LET'S GET YOUR HEAD OFF, SHALL WE? BEFORE YOU BLOW A FUSE!
WE ARE READY TO ACTIVATE THE DIMENSION DUCT, CENTURION +++
WE MUST WAIT FOR GENERAL IRONICUS ++ HE IS IN COMMUNION WITH THE GODS +++
ABSOLUTELY FASCINATING... "FIRST COHORT OF THE NINTH LEGION"!
SPQR
INSIDE THE BALLISTA...
OH, GODS... HOW I LOVE WAR. LET THERE NEVER BE AN END TO MY CONQUESTS. LET MY IRON LEGION MARCH FOR EVER. FOR ONLY THROUGH DESTRUCTION AM I ALIVE. AND WITHOUT DEATH, I AM A DEAD THING.
OH, GODS... LET THE ETERNAL WAR THAT HAS LASTED THROUGH THE MILLENNIA CONTINUE... UNTIL THE END OF TIME!
THE GODS HAVE LOOKED UPON WHAT YOU HAVE DONE, IRONICUS, AND FOUND IT... EVIL!
GO IN DARKNESS, MY SON.

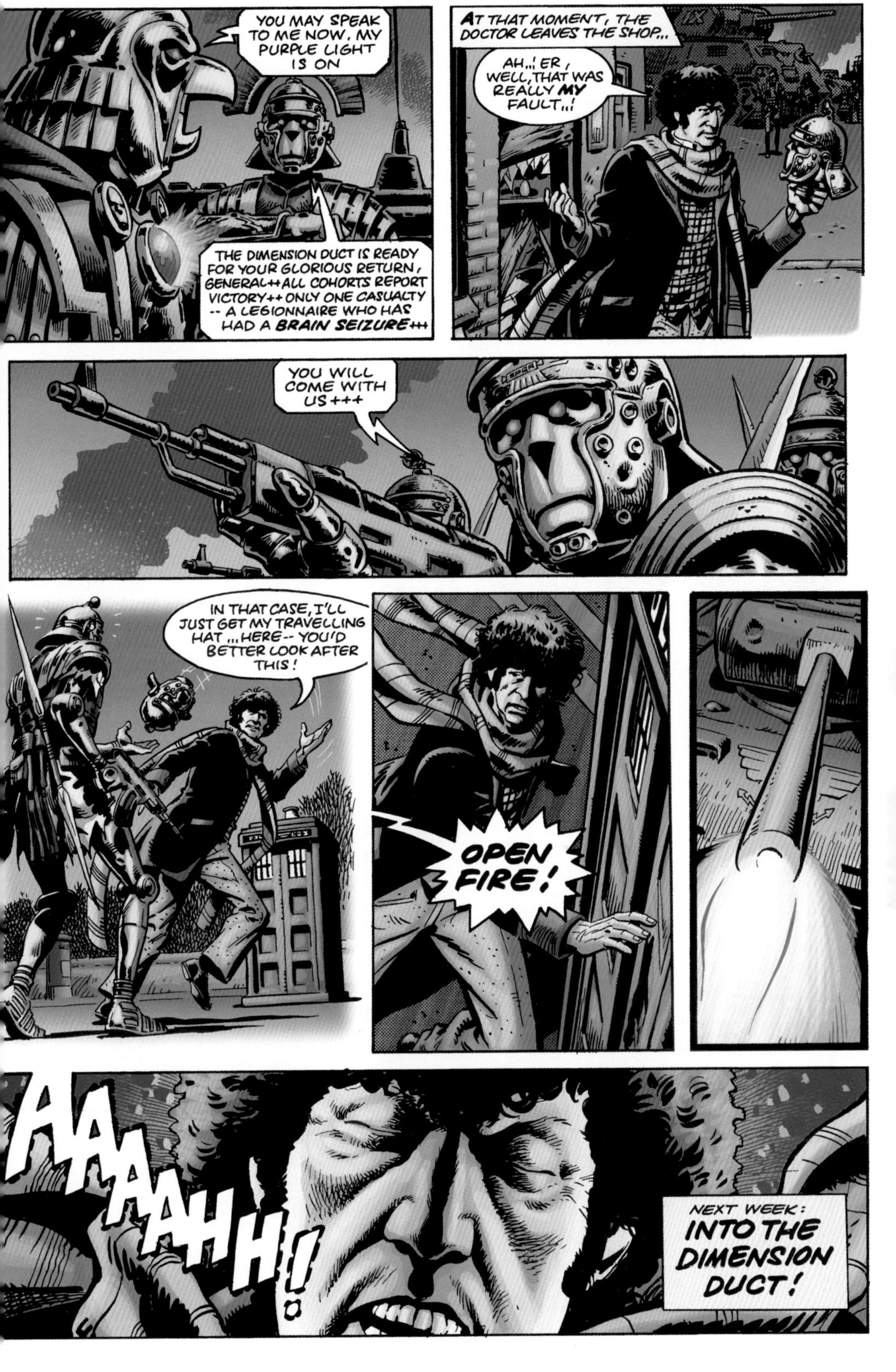
YOU MAY SPEAK TO ME NOW. MY PURPLE LIGHT IS ON
THE DIMENSION DUCT IS READY FOR YOUR GLORIOUS RETURN, GENERAL++ ALL COHORTS REPORT VICTORY++ ONLY ONE CASUALTY -- A LEGIONNAIRE WHO HAS HAD A **BRAIN SEIZURE**+++
AT THAT MOMENT, THE DOCTOR LEAVES THE SHOP...
AH...! ER, WELL, THAT WAS REALLY **MY** FAULT...!
YOU WILL COME WITH US+++
IN THAT CASE, I'LL JUST GET MY TRAVELLING HAT ... HERE-- YOU'D BETTER LOOK AFTER THIS!
OPEN FIRE!
AAAAAHH!
NEXT WEEK:
INTO THE DIMENSION DUCT!

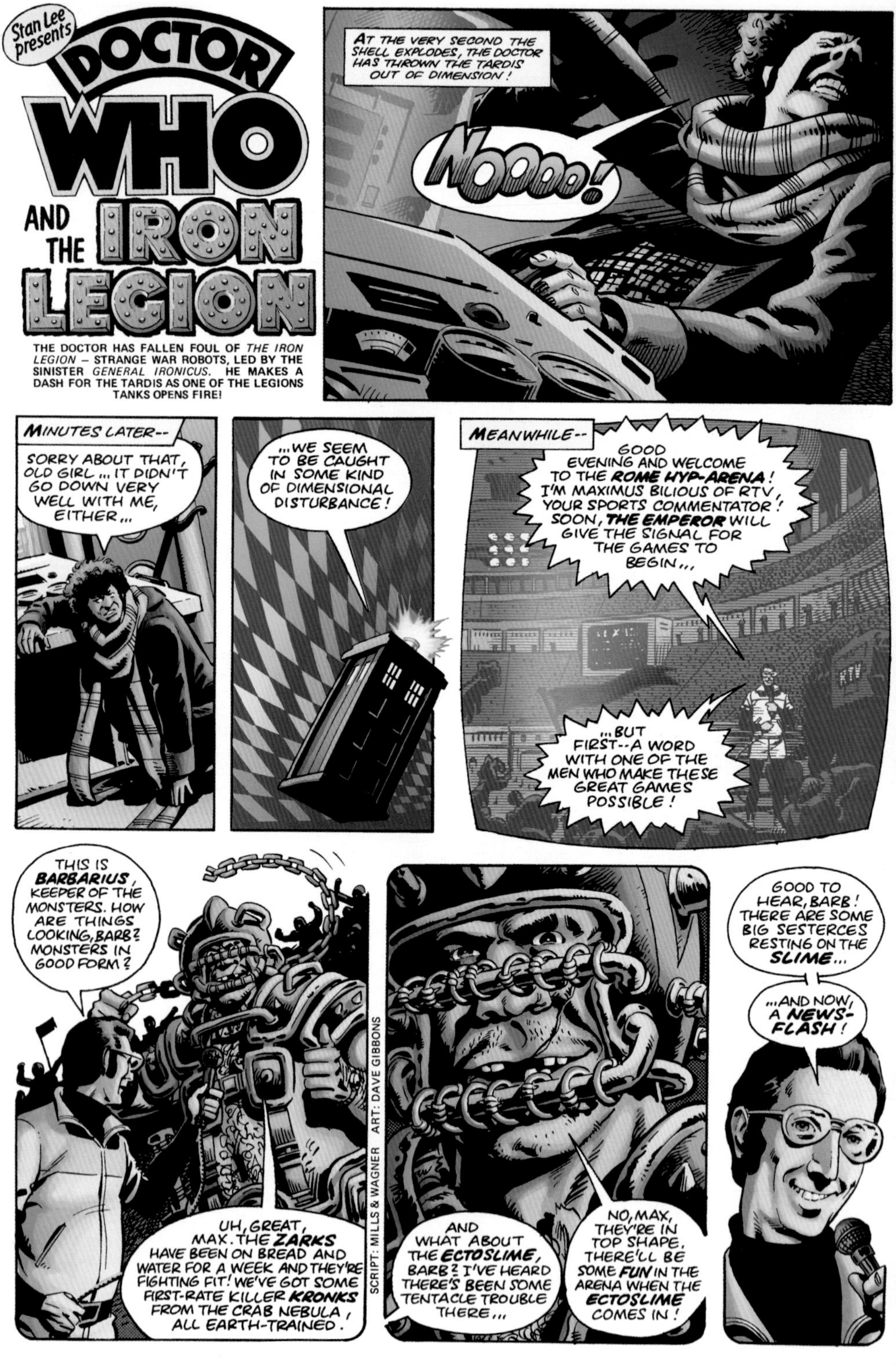
Stan Lee presents
DOCTOR WHO AND THE IRON LEGION
THE DOCTOR HAS FALLEN FOUL OF THE IRON LEGION – STRANGE WAR ROBOTS, LED BY THE SINISTER GENERAL IRONICUS. HE MAKES A DASH FOR THE TARDIS AS ONE OF THE LEGIONS TANKS OPENS FIRE!
AT THE VERY SECOND THE SHELL EXPLODES, THE DOCTOR HAS THROWN THE TARDIS OUT OF DIMENSION!
NOOOOO!
MINUTES LATER--
SORRY ABOUT THAT, OLD GIRL... IT DIDN'T GO DOWN VERY WELL WITH ME, EITHER...
...WE SEEM TO BE CAUGHT IN SOME KIND OF DIMENSIONAL DISTURBANCE!
MEANWHILE--
GOOD EVENING AND WELCOME TO THE ROME HYP-ARENA! I'M MAXIMUS BILIOUS OF RTV, YOUR SPORTS COMMENTATOR! SOON, THE EMPEROR WILL GIVE THE SIGNAL FOR THE GAMES TO BEGIN...
...BUT FIRST--A WORD WITH ONE OF THE MEN WHO MAKE THESE GREAT GAMES POSSIBLE!
THIS IS BARBARIUS, KEEPER OF THE MONSTERS. HOW ARE THINGS LOOKING, BARB? MONSTERS IN GOOD FORM?
UH, GREAT, MAX. THE ZARKS HAVE BEEN ON BREAD AND WATER FOR A WEEK AND THEY'RE FIGHTING FIT! WE'VE GOT SOME FIRST-RATE KILLER KRONKS FROM THE CRAB NEBULA, ALL EARTH-TRAINED.
SCRIPT: MILLS & WAGNER ART: DAVE GIBBONS
AND WHAT ABOUT THE ECTOSLIME, BARB? I'VE HEARD THERE'S BEEN SOME TENTACLE TROUBLE THERE...
NO, MAX, THEY'RE IN TOP SHAPE. THERE'LL BE SOME FUN IN THE ARENA WHEN THE ECTOSLIME COMES IN!
GOOD TO HEAR, BARB! THERE ARE SOME BIG SESTERCES RESTING ON THE SLIME...
...AND NOW, A NEWS-FLASH!

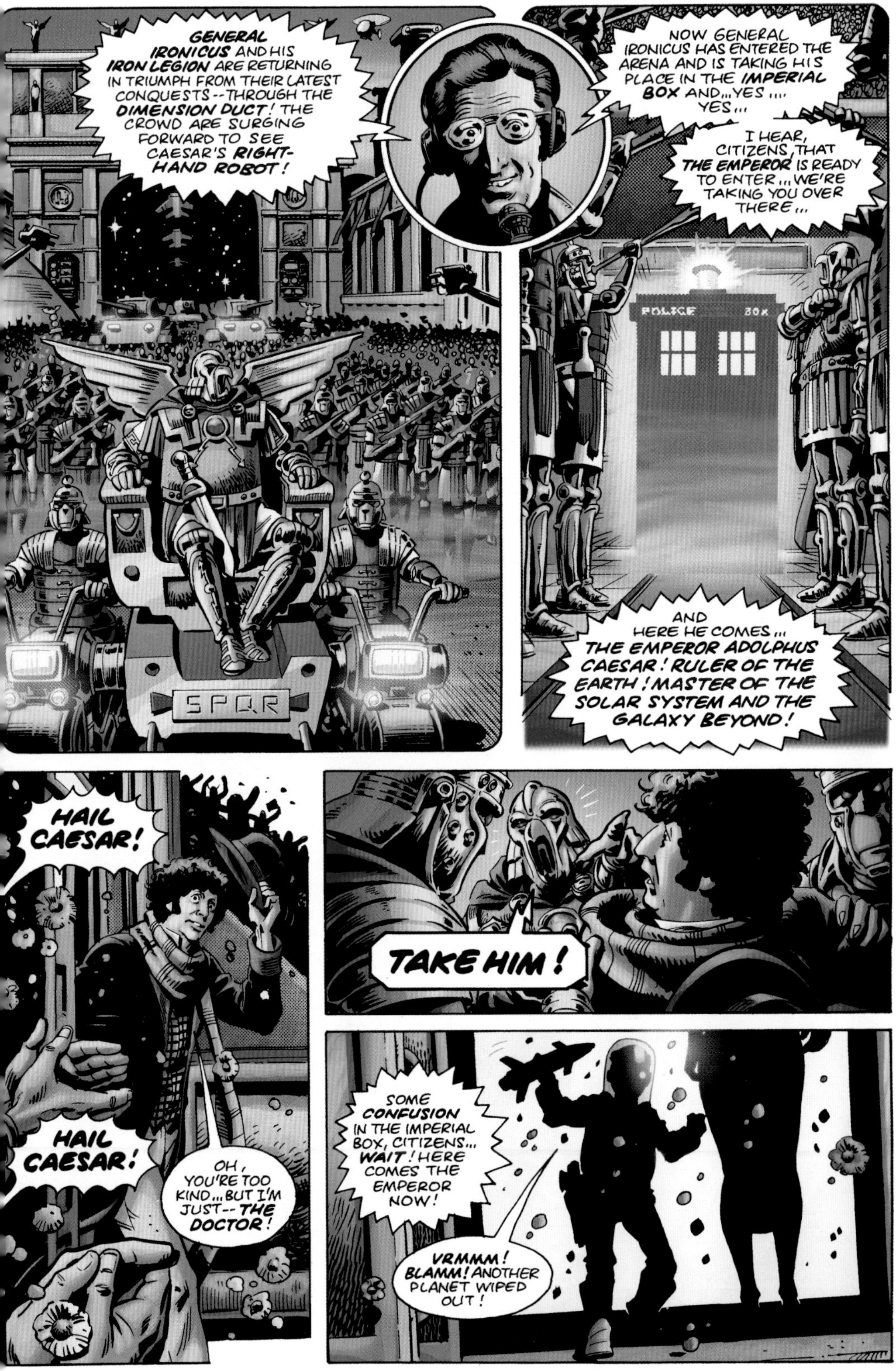
GENERAL IRONICUS AND HIS IRON LEGION ARE RETURNING IN TRIUMPH FROM THEIR LATEST CONQUESTS -- THROUGH THE DIMENSION DUCT! THE CROWD ARE SURGING FORWARD TO SEE CAESAR'S RIGHT-HAND ROBOT!
SPQR
NOW GENERAL IRONICUS HAS ENTERED THE ARENA AND IS TAKING HIS PLACE IN THE IMPERIAL BOX AND... YES .... YES...
I HEAR, CITIZENS, THAT THE EMPEROR IS READY TO ENTER... WE'RE TAKING YOU OVER THERE...
POLICE BOX
AND HERE HE COMES... THE EMPEROR ADOLPHUS CAESAR! RULER OF THE EARTH! MASTER OF THE SOLAR SYSTEM AND THE GALAXY BEYOND!
HAIL CAESAR!
HAIL CAESAR!
OH, YOU'RE TOO KIND... BUT I'M JUST -- THE DOCTOR!
TAKE HIM!
SOME CONFUSION IN THE IMPERIAL BOX, CITIZENS... WAIT! HERE COMES THE EMPEROR NOW!
VRMMM! BLAMM! ANOTHER PLANET WIPED OUT!

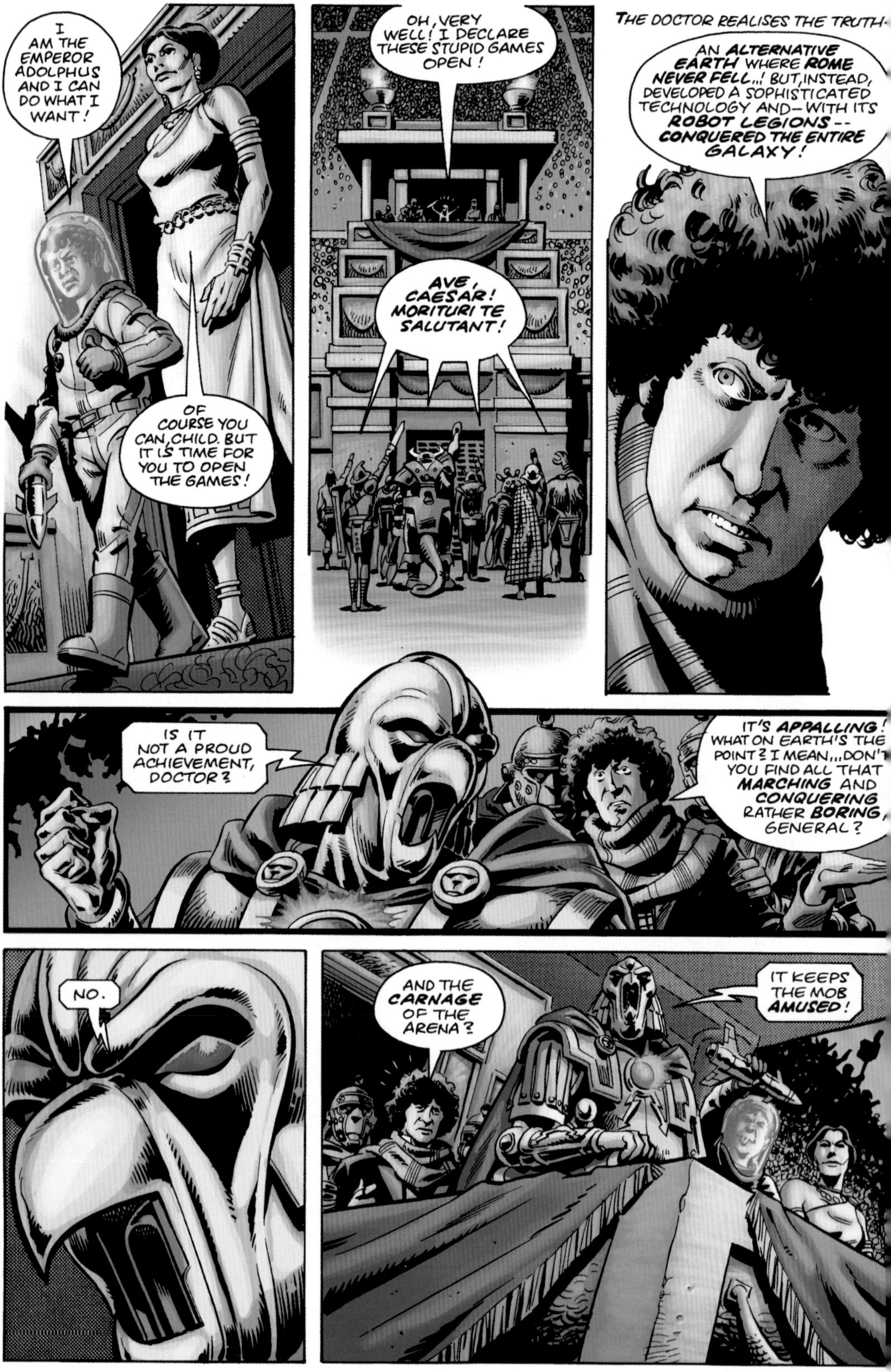
I AM THE EMPEROR ADOLPHUS AND I CAN DO WHAT I WANT!
OF COURSE YOU CAN, CHILD. BUT IT IS TIME FOR YOU TO OPEN THE GAMES!
OH, VERY WELL! I DECLARE THESE STUPID GAMES OPEN!
AVE, CAESAR! MORITURI TE SALUTANT!
THE DOCTOR REALISES THE TRUTH...
AN ALTERNATIVE EARTH WHERE ROME NEVER FELL...! BUT, INSTEAD, DEVELOPED A SOPHISTICATED TECHNOLOGY AND--WITH ITS ROBOT LEGIONS--CONQUERED THE ENTIRE GALAXY!
IS IT NOT A PROUD ACHIEVEMENT, DOCTOR?
IT'S APPALLING! WHAT ON EARTH'S THE POINT? I MEAN... DON'T YOU FIND ALL THAT MARCHING AND CONQUERING RATHER BORING, GENERAL?
NO.
AND THE CARNAGE OF THE ARENA?
IT KEEPS THE MOB AMUSED!

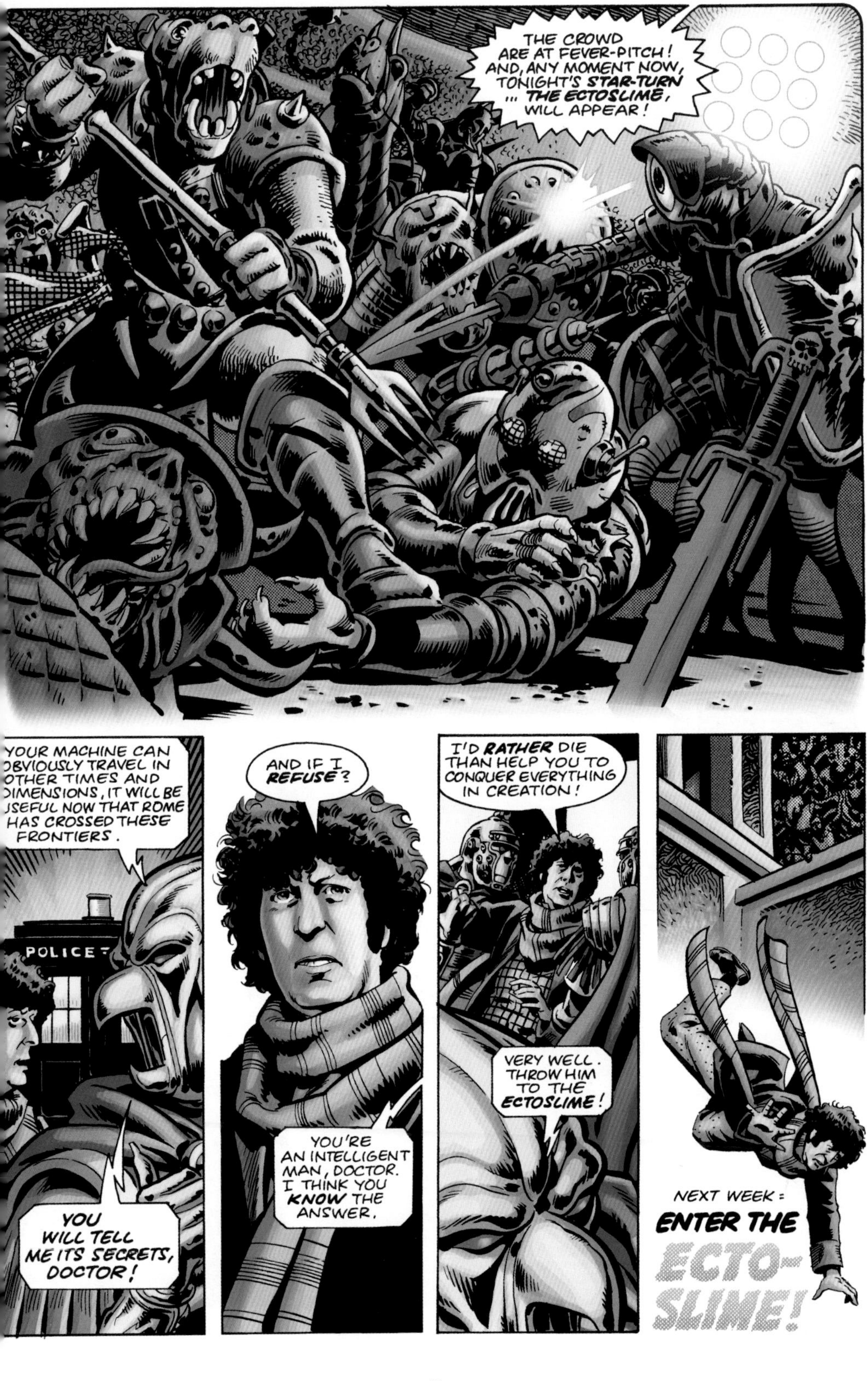
THE CROWD ARE AT FEVER-PITCH! AND, ANY MOMENT NOW, TONIGHT'S **STAR-TURN** ... **THE ECTOSLIME**, WILL APPEAR!
YOUR MACHINE CAN OBVIOUSLY TRAVEL IN OTHER TIMES AND DIMENSIONS. IT WILL BE USEFUL NOW THAT ROME HAS CROSSED THESE FRONTIERS.
POLICE
YOU WILL TELL ME ITS SECRETS, DOCTOR!
AND IF I **REFUSE**?
YOU'RE AN INTELLIGENT MAN, DOCTOR. I THINK YOU **KNOW** THE ANSWER.
I'D **RATHER** DIE THAN HELP YOU TO CONQUER EVERYTHING IN CREATION!
VERY WELL. THROW HIM TO THE **ECTOSLIME**!
NEXT WEEK:
ENTER THE ECTO-SLIME!

Stan Lee presents

DOCTOR WHO AND THE IRON LEGION

THE DOCTOR HAS DISCOVERED AN ALTERNATIVE EARTH WHERE THE ROMAN EMPIRE NEVER FELL ... BUT WENT ON TO CONQUER THE ENTIRE GALAXY! AFTER REFUSING TO REVEAL THE SECRETS OF THE TARDIS TO THE SINISTER GENERAL IRONICUS, THE DOCTOR IS THROWN INTO THE ARENA. . .

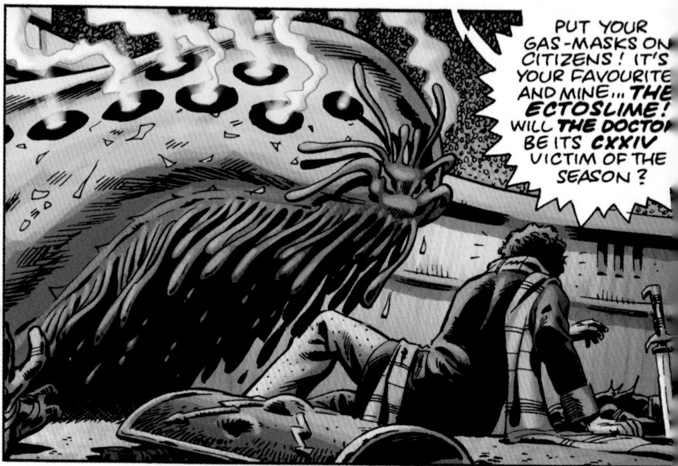
PUT YOUR GAS-MASKS ON CITIZENS! IT'S YOUR FAVOURITE AND MINE... THE ECTOSLIME! WILL THE DOCTOR BE ITS CXXIV VICTIM OF THE SEASON?

SCRIPT: MILLS & WAGNER ART: DAVE GIBBONS

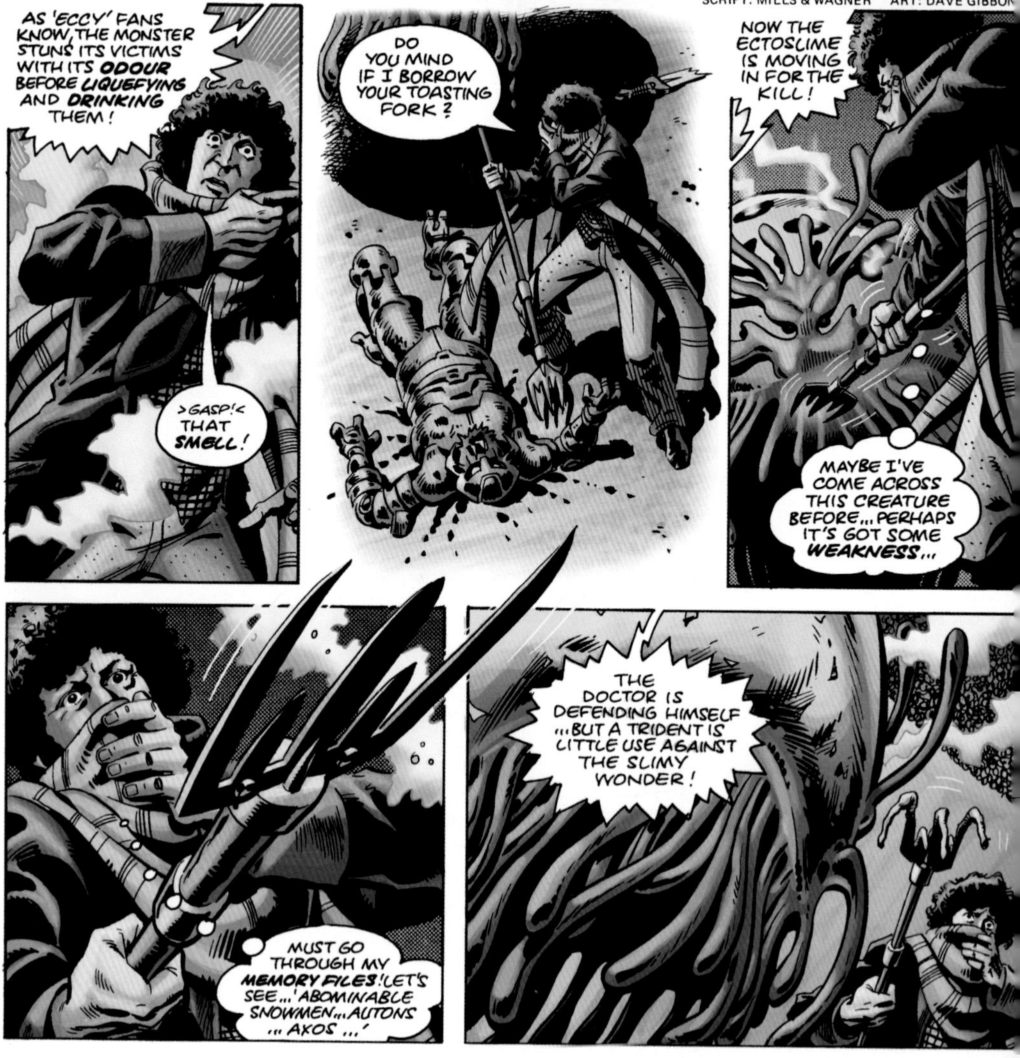
AS 'ECCY' FANS KNOW, THE MONSTER STUNS ITS VICTIMS WITH ITS ODOUR BEFORE LIQUEFYING AND DRINKING THEM!
>GASP!< THAT SMELL!
DO YOU MIND IF I BORROW YOUR TOASTING FORK?
NOW THE ECTOSLIME IS MOVING IN FOR THE KILL!
MAYBE I'VE COME ACROSS THIS CREATURE BEFORE... PERHAPS IT'S GOT SOME WEAKNESS...
MUST GO THROUGH MY MEMORY FILES! LET'S SEE...'ABOMINABLE SNOWMEN... AUTONS ... AXOS ...'
THE DOCTOR IS DEFENDING HIMSELF ...BUT A TRIDENT IS LITTLE USE AGAINST THE SLIMY WONDER!

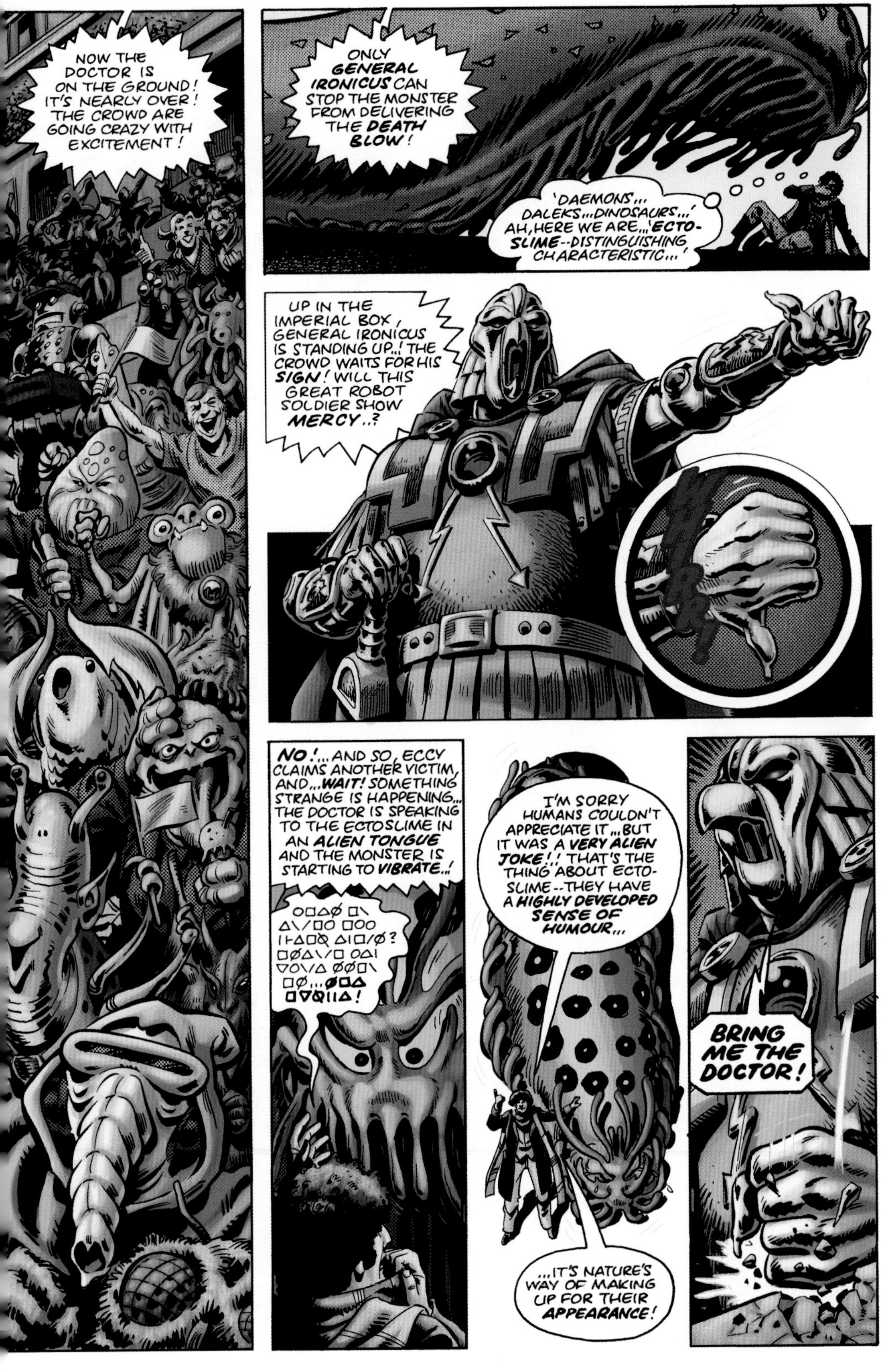
NOW THE DOCTOR IS ON THE GROUND! IT'S NEARLY OVER! THE CROWD ARE GOING CRAZY WITH EXCITEMENT!
ONLY GENERAL IRONICUS CAN STOP THE MONSTER FROM DELIVERING THE DEATH BLOW!
'DAEMONS... DALEKS... DINOSAURS...' AH, HERE WE ARE... 'ECTO-SLIME--DISTINGUISHING CHARACTERISTIC...'
UP IN THE IMPERIAL BOX, GENERAL IRONICUS IS STANDING UP..! THE CROWD WAITS FOR HIS SIGN! WILL THIS GREAT ROBOT SOLDIER SHOW MERCY..?
NO!... AND SO, ECCY CLAIMS ANOTHER VICTIM, AND... WAIT! SOMETHING STRANGE IS HAPPENING... THE DOCTOR IS SPEAKING TO THE ECTOSLIME IN AN ALIEN TONGUE AND THE MONSTER IS STARTING TO VIBRATE..!
I'M SORRY HUMANS COULDN'T APPRECIATE IT... BUT IT WAS A VERY ALIEN JOKE!! THAT'S THE THING ABOUT ECTO-SLIME--THEY HAVE A HIGHLY DEVELOPED SENSE OF HUMOUR...
...IT'S NATURE'S WAY OF MAKING UP FOR THEIR APPEARANCE!
BRING ME THE DOCTOR!

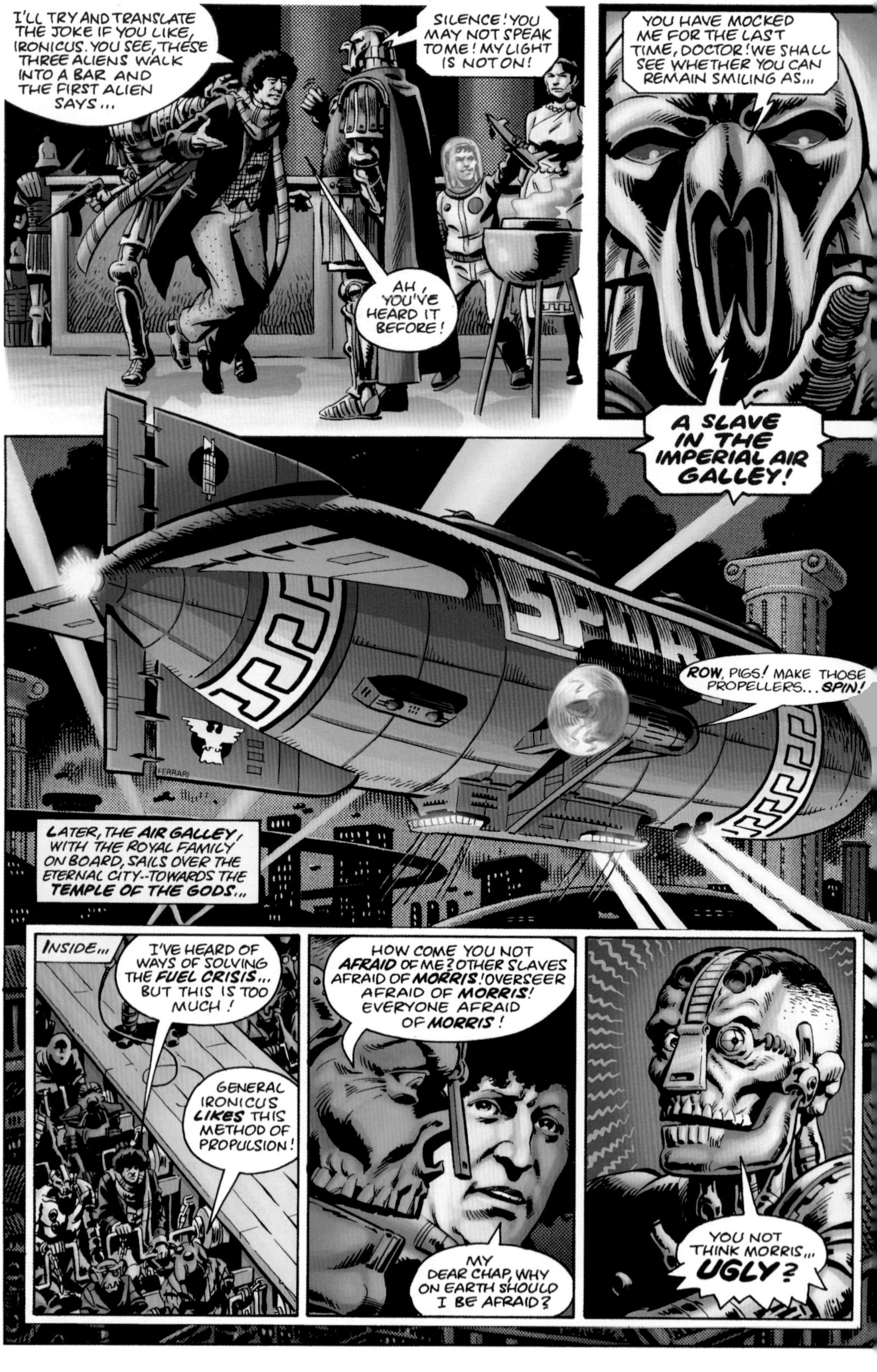

I'LL TRY AND TRANSLATE THE JOKE IF YOU LIKE, IRONICUS. YOU SEE, THESE THREE ALIENS WALK INTO A BAR AND THE FIRST ALIEN SAYS...
SILENCE! YOU MAY NOT SPEAK TO ME! MY LIGHT IS NOT ON!
AH, YOU'VE HEARD IT BEFORE!
YOU HAVE MOCKED ME FOR THE LAST TIME, DOCTOR! WE SHALL SEE WHETHER YOU CAN REMAIN SMILING AS...
A SLAVE IN THE IMPERIAL AIR GALLEY!
SPQR
FERRARI
ROW, PIGS! MAKE THOSE PROPELLERS... SPIN!
LATER, THE AIR GALLEY, WITH THE ROYAL FAMILY ON BOARD, SAILS OVER THE ETERNAL CITY--TOWARDS THE TEMPLE OF THE GODS...
INSIDE...
I'VE HEARD OF WAYS OF SOLVING THE FUEL CRISIS... BUT THIS IS TOO MUCH!
GENERAL IRONICUS LIKES THIS METHOD OF PROPULSION!
HOW COME YOU NOT AFRAID OF ME? OTHER SLAVES AFRAID OF MORRIS! OVERSEER AFRAID OF MORRIS! EVERYONE AFRAID OF MORRIS!
MY DEAR CHAP, WHY ON EARTH SHOULD I BE AFRAID?
YOU NOT THINK MORRIS... UGLY?

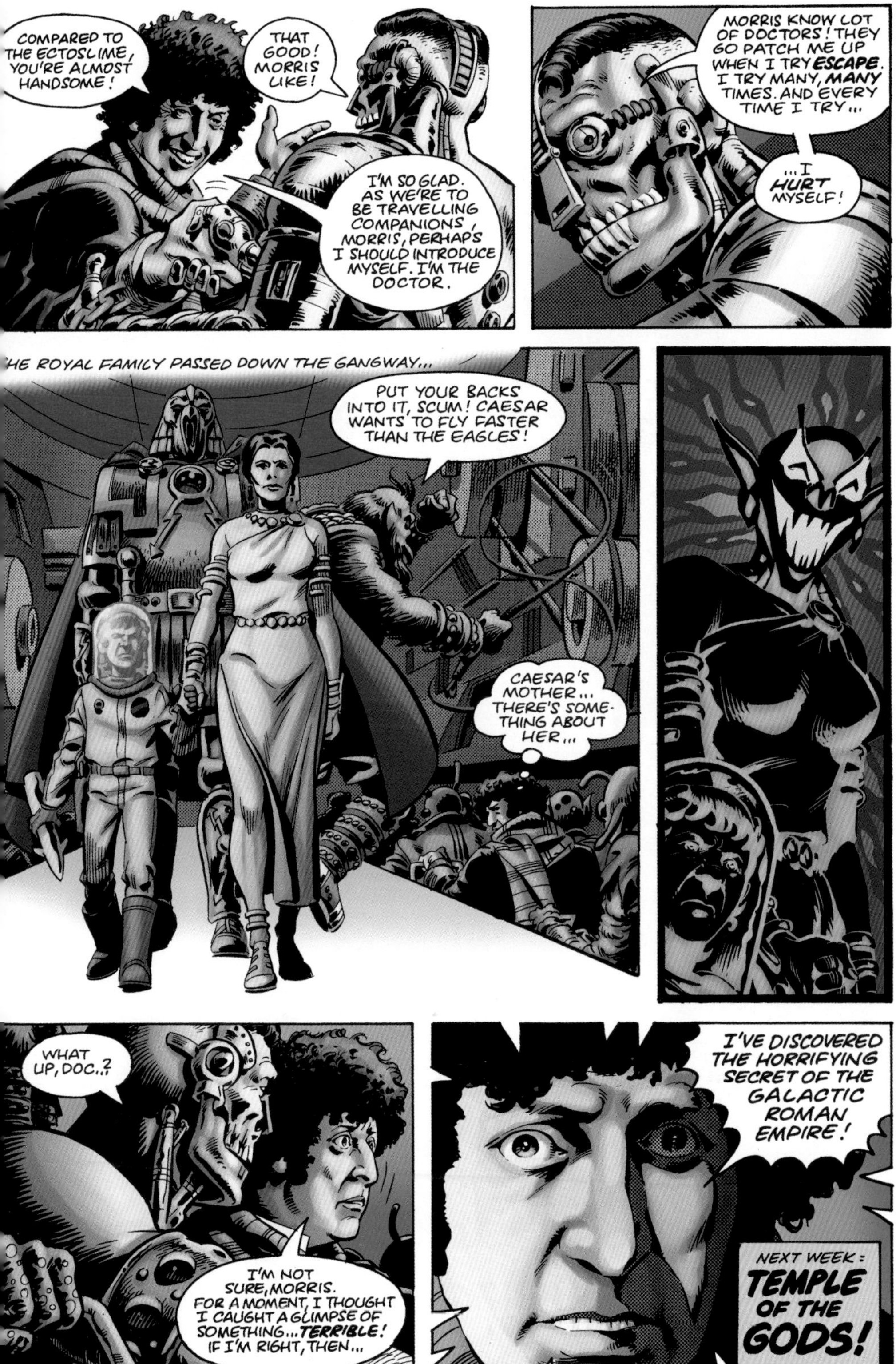
COMPARED TO THE ECTOSLIME, YOU'RE ALMOST HANDSOME!
THAT GOOD! MORRIS LIKE!
I'M SO GLAD. AS WE'RE TO BE TRAVELLING COMPANIONS, MORRIS, PERHAPS I SHOULD INTRODUCE MYSELF. I'M THE DOCTOR.
MORRIS KNOW LOT OF DOCTORS! THEY GO PATCH ME UP WHEN I TRY ESCAPE. I TRY MANY, MANY TIMES. AND EVERY TIME I TRY...
...I HURT MYSELF!
HE ROYAL FAMILY PASSED DOWN THE GANGWAY...
PUT YOUR BACKS INTO IT, SCUM! CAESAR WANTS TO FLY FASTER THAN THE EAGLES!
CAESAR'S MOTHER... THERE'S SOMETHING ABOUT HER...
WHAT UP, DOC..?
I'M NOT SURE, MORRIS. FOR A MOMENT, I THOUGHT I CAUGHT A GLIMPSE OF SOMETHING... TERRIBLE! IF I'M RIGHT, THEN...
I'VE DISCOVERED THE HORRIFYING SECRET OF THE GALACTIC ROMAN EMPIRE!
NEXT WEEK: TEMPLE OF THE GODS!

Stan Lee presents

DOCTOR WHO
AND THE IRON LEGION

THE DOCTOR HAS DISCOVERED AN ALTERNATIVE EARTH WHERE THE ROMAN EMPIRE NEVER FELL... BUT WENT ON TO CONQUER THE GALAXY! AFTER ESCAPING DEATH IN THE ARENA, HE IS SENT TO THE IMPERIAL AIR GALLEY BY THE SINISTER GENERAL IRONICUS.

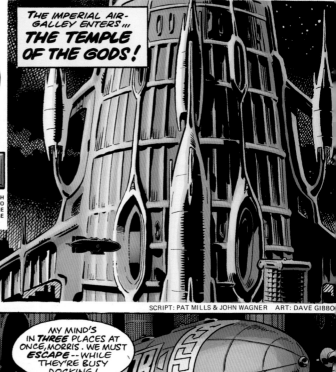

THE IMPERIAL AIR-GALLEY ENTERS... *THE TEMPLE OF THE GODS!*

SCRIPT: PAT MILLS & JOHN WAGNER   ART: DAVE GIBBO[...]

IT'S MORE THAN A TEMPLE ...IT'S AN *ALIEN SPACE-SHIP!*

WHAT UP, DOC..? YOU CAN TELL MORRIS. MORRIS IS YOUR PAL!

MY MIND'S IN *THREE* PLACES AT ONCE, MORRIS. WE MUST *ESCAPE* -- WHILE THEY'RE BUSY DOCKING!

YOU BETCHA, DOC! MORRIS NOT ESCAPED FOR A COUPLE O' WEEKS!

WILL YOUR BIONIC ARM BREAK THESE CHAINS?

YEHHH! MORRIS USED TO BE *GLADIATOR* --UNTIL THEY IMPRISON HIM FOR 'SOUPING-UP' HIS BIONIC ARM CIRCUITS!

WATCH!

YES, I SEE WHAT YOU MEAN!

NOW MORRIS GO GET ...

18

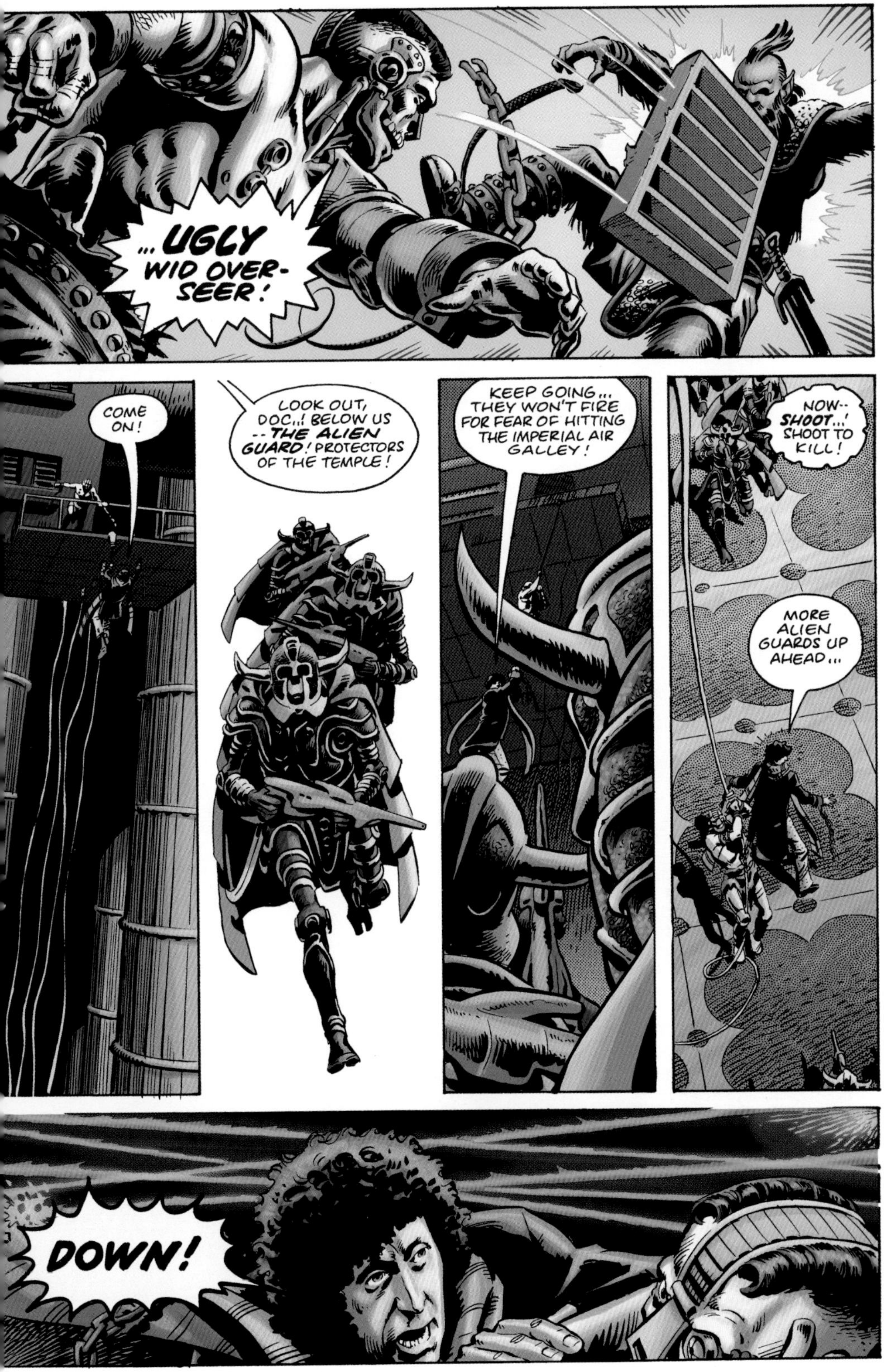

...UGLY WID OVER-SEER!
COME ON!
LOOK OUT, DOC..! BELOW US --THE ALIEN GUARD! PROTECTORS OF THE TEMPLE!
KEEP GOING... THEY WON'T FIRE FOR FEAR OF HITTING THE IMPERIAL AIR GALLEY!
NOW-- SHOOT...! SHOOT TO KILL!
MORE ALIEN GUARDS UP AHEAD...
DOWN!

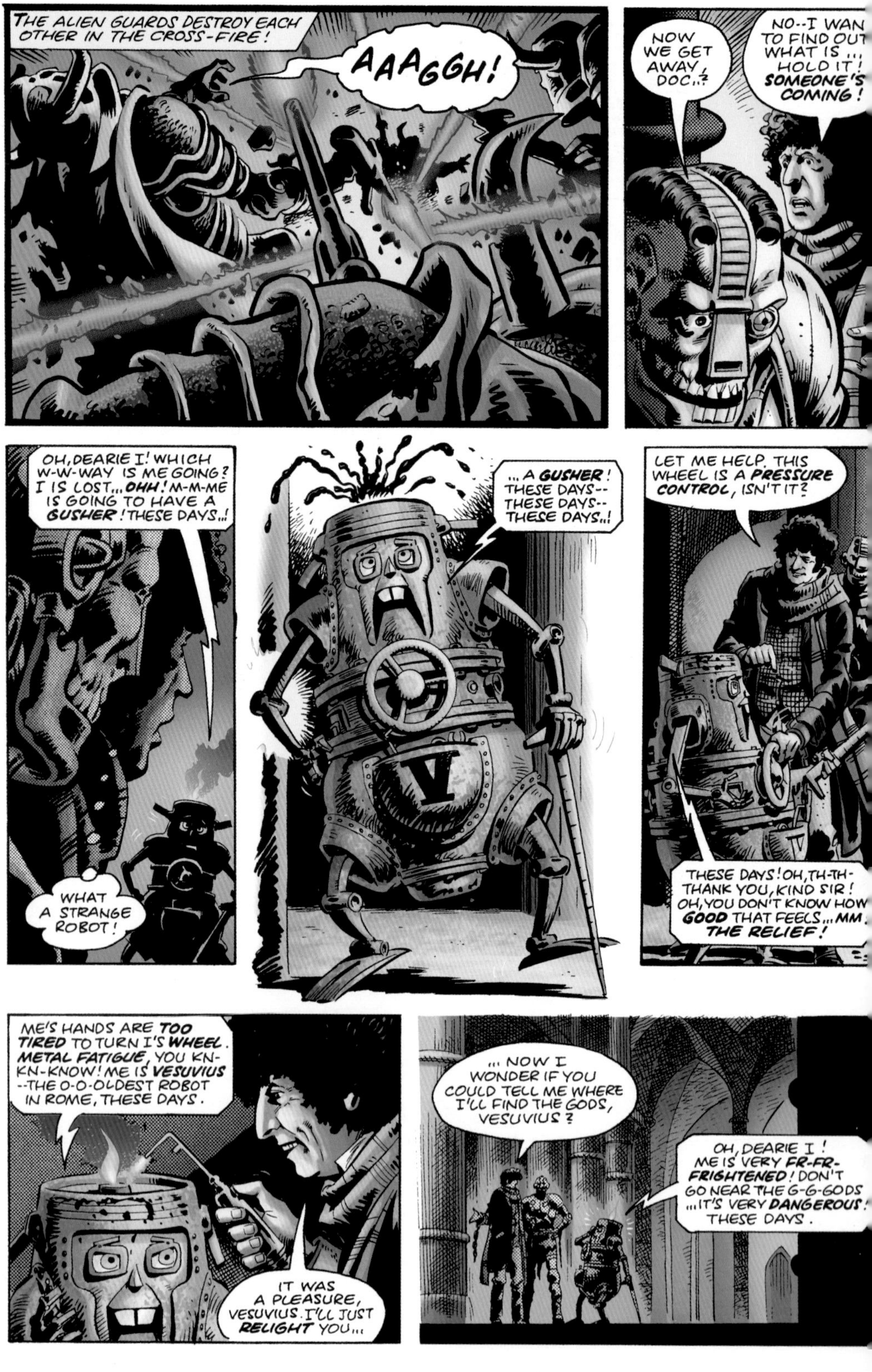
THE ALIEN GUARDS DESTROY EACH OTHER IN THE CROSS-FIRE!
AAAGGH!
NOW WE GET AWAY, DOC..?
NO--I WAN TO FIND OUT WHAT IS ... HOLD IT! SOMEONE'S COMING!
OH, DEARIE I! WHICH W-W-WAY IS ME GOING? I IS LOST... OHH! M-M-ME IS GOING TO HAVE A GUSHER! THESE DAYS...!
WHAT A STRANGE ROBOT!
... A GUSHER! THESE DAYS-- THESE DAYS-- THESE DAYS...!
LET ME HELP. THIS WHEEL IS A PRESSURE CONTROL, ISN'T IT?
THESE DAYS! OH, TH-TH-THANK YOU, KIND SIR! OH, YOU DON'T KNOW HOW GOOD THAT FEELS... MM THE RELIEF!
ME'S HANDS ARE TOO TIRED TO TURN I'S WHEEL. METAL FATIGUE, YOU KN-KN-KNOW! ME IS VESUVIUS --THE O-O-OLDEST ROBOT IN ROME, THESE DAYS.
IT WAS A PLEASURE, VESUVIUS. I'LL JUST RELIGHT YOU...
... NOW I WONDER IF YOU COULD TELL ME WHERE I'LL FIND THE GODS, VESUVIUS?
OH, DEARIE I! ME IS VERY FR-FR-FRIGHTENED! DON'T GO NEAR THE G-G-GODS ...IT'S VERY DANGEROUS! THESE DAYS.

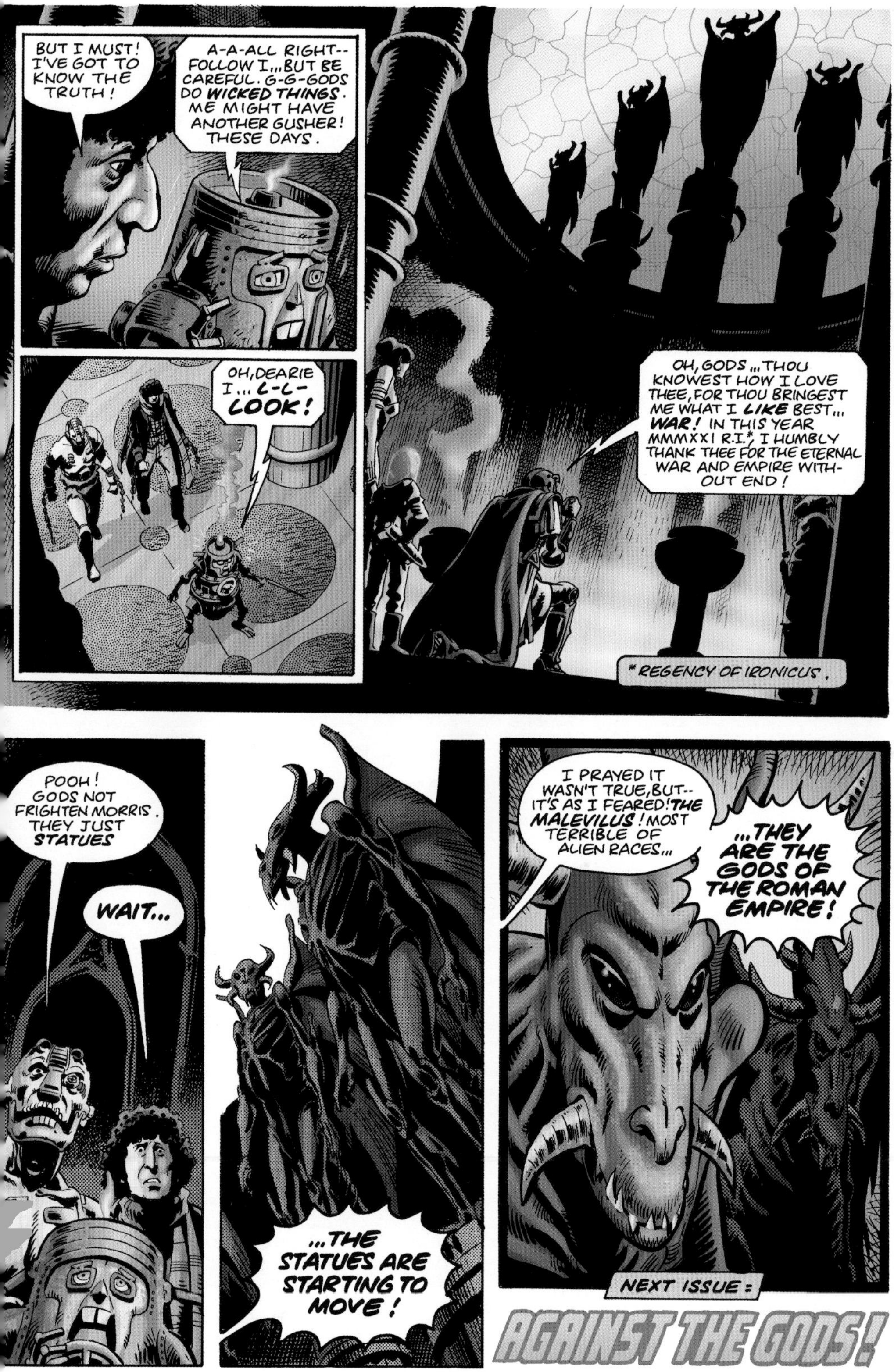

BUT I MUST! I'VE GOT TO KNOW THE TRUTH!
A-A-ALL RIGHT-- FOLLOW I... BUT BE CAREFUL. G-G-GODS DO WICKED THINGS. ME MIGHT HAVE ANOTHER GUSHER! THESE DAYS.
OH, DEARIE I... L-L-LOOK!
OH, GODS... THOU KNOWEST HOW I LOVE THEE, FOR THOU BRINGEST ME WHAT I LIKE BEST... WAR! IN THIS YEAR MMMXXI R.I.*, I HUMBLY THANK THEE FOR THE ETERNAL WAR AND EMPIRE WITHOUT END!
* REGENCY OF IRONICUS.
POOH! GODS NOT FRIGHTEN MORRIS. THEY JUST STATUES
WAIT...
...THE STATUES ARE STARTING TO MOVE!
I PRAYED IT WASN'T TRUE, BUT-- IT'S AS I FEARED! THE MALEVILUS! MOST TERRIBLE OF ALIEN RACES...
...THEY ARE THE GODS OF THE ROMAN EMPIRE!
NEXT ISSUE:
AGAINST THE GODS!

Stan Lee presents

DOCTOR WHO AND THE IRON LEGION

PART FIVE : AGAINST THE GODS!

THE DOCTOR HAS DISCOVERED AN ALTERNATIVE EARTH WHERE ROME NEVER FELL BUT WENT ON TO CONQUER THE GALAXY. NOW THE DOCTOR FINDS HIMSELF IN THE TEMPLE OF THE GODS--AN ALIEN SPACE-SHIP--AND REALISES ...THE HORRIBLE TRUTH ABOUT THE EMPIRE OF THE CAESARS!

GENERAL IRONICUS, ROBOT LEADER. HIS IRON LEGIONS HAVE CONQUERED THE GALAXY.

THE SPOILT EMPEROR ADOLPHUS AND HIS MOTHER, JUNO...THE DOCTOR SUSPECTS HER OF BEING ONE OF THE ALIENS.

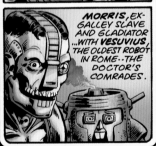

MORRIS, EX-GALLEY SLAVE AND GLADIATOR ...WITH VESUVIUS, THE OLDEST ROBOT IN ROME--THE DOCTOR'S COMRADES.

THE MALEVILUS! MOST TERRIBLE OF ALIEN RACES...THEY ARE THE GODS OF THE ROMAN EMPIRE!

OH GODS...NOW THAT ROME HAS GONE ON TO CONQUER ALL DIMENSIONS, I OFFER YOU THESE HUMANS ...THE FIRST FRUITS OF VICTORY!

WRITERS=MILLS+WAGNER / ARTIST=DAVE GIBBONS / EDITOR=DEZ SKINN

COME, *ADOLPHUS*--WE MUST GO. FOR THOSE WHO ARE NOT *INITIATED*, THE SIGHT OF THE GODS *FEASTING* MAY BE A LITTLE DISTURBING

AWW, MATER!

THE FIRST PRISONERS FROM OTHER DIMENSIONS --THEY'RE GOING TO BE OFFERED IN *THANKSGIVING* TO THE GODS!

MORRIS NOT UNDERSTAND, DOC...WHO ARE THESE GODS?

HIDEOUS FORMS OF ANTI-LIFE! THE MALEVILUS FEED OFF *DEATH*!

RARE AND SUCCULENT DISHES! THIS SACRIFICE IS PLEASING TO US, IRONICUS!

THERE ARE FIVE...*BABIYON*...!*ABISS*...! *EPOK*...!*NEKROS*...! AND THE MOST *FOUL* OF ALL... *MAGOG*!

NOOOO! PLEASE!

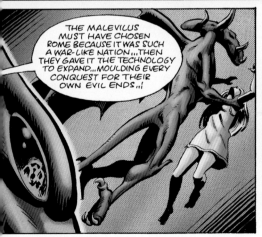

THE MALEVILUS MUST HAVE CHOSEN ROME BECAUSE IT WAS SUCH A WAR-LIKE NATION...THEN THEY GAVE IT THE TECHNOLOGY TO EXPAND...MOULDING EVERY CONQUEST FOR THEIR OWN EVIL ENDS...!

AAAAHH!

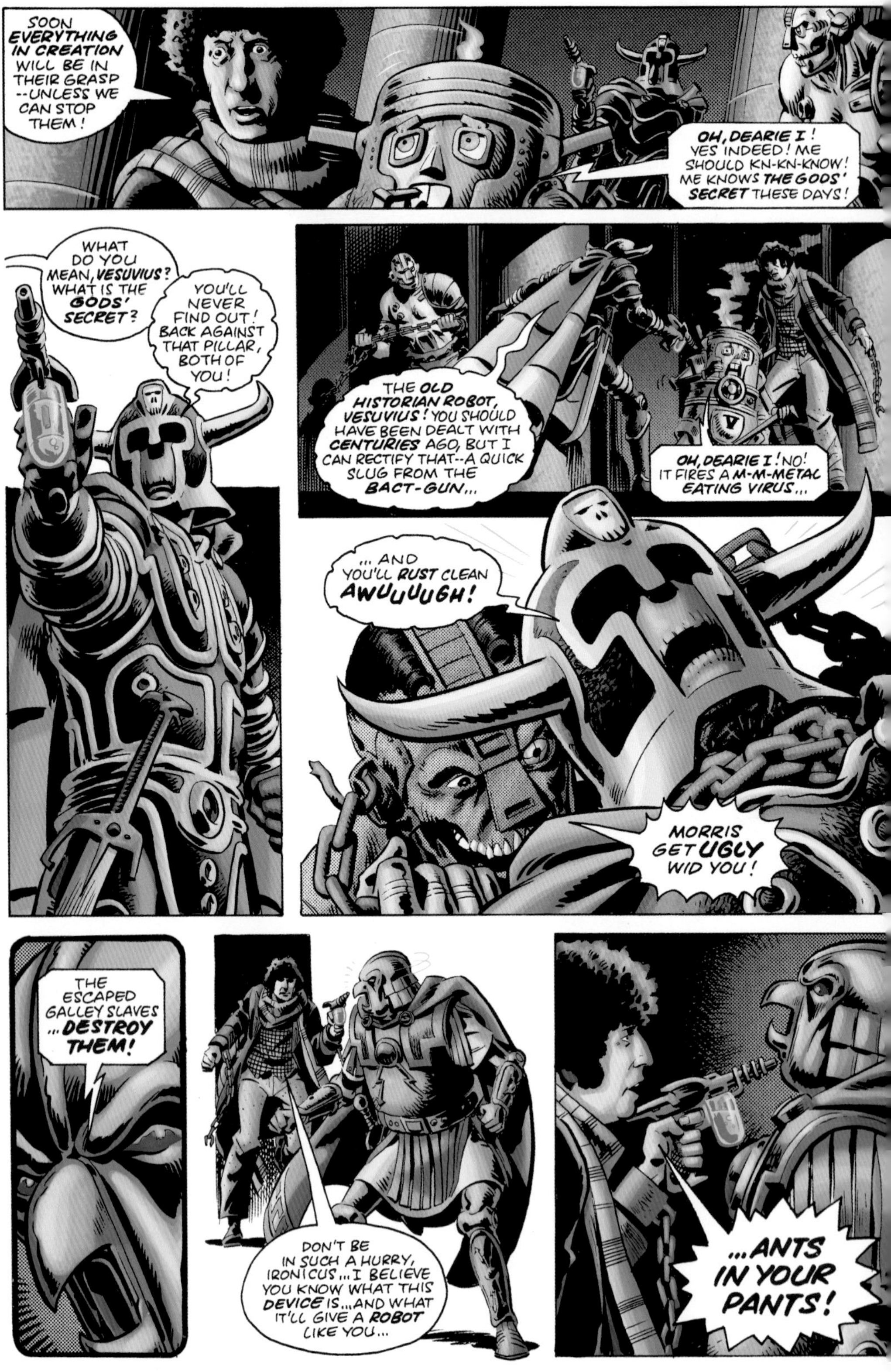

SOON EVERYTHING IN CREATION WILL BE IN THEIR GRASP --UNLESS WE CAN STOP THEM!
OH, DEARIE I! YES INDEED! ME SHOULD KN-KN-KNOW! ME KNOWS THE GODS' SECRET THESE DAYS!
WHAT DO YOU MEAN, VESUVIUS? WHAT IS THE GODS' SECRET?
YOU'LL NEVER FIND OUT! BACK AGAINST THAT PILLAR, BOTH OF YOU!
THE OLD HISTORIAN ROBOT, VESUVIUS! YOU SHOULD HAVE BEEN DEALT WITH CENTURIES AGO, BUT I CAN RECTIFY THAT--A QUICK SLUG FROM THE BACT-GUN...
OH, DEARIE I! NO! IT FIRES A M-M-METAL EATING VIRUS...
... AND YOU'LL RUST CLEAN AWUUUUGH!
MORRIS GET UGLY WID YOU!
THE ESCAPED GALLEY SLAVES ...DESTROY THEM!
DON'T BE IN SUCH A HURRY, IRONICUS... I BELIEVE YOU KNOW WHAT THIS DEVICE IS... AND WHAT IT'LL GIVE A ROBOT LIKE YOU...
...ANTS IN YOUR PANTS!

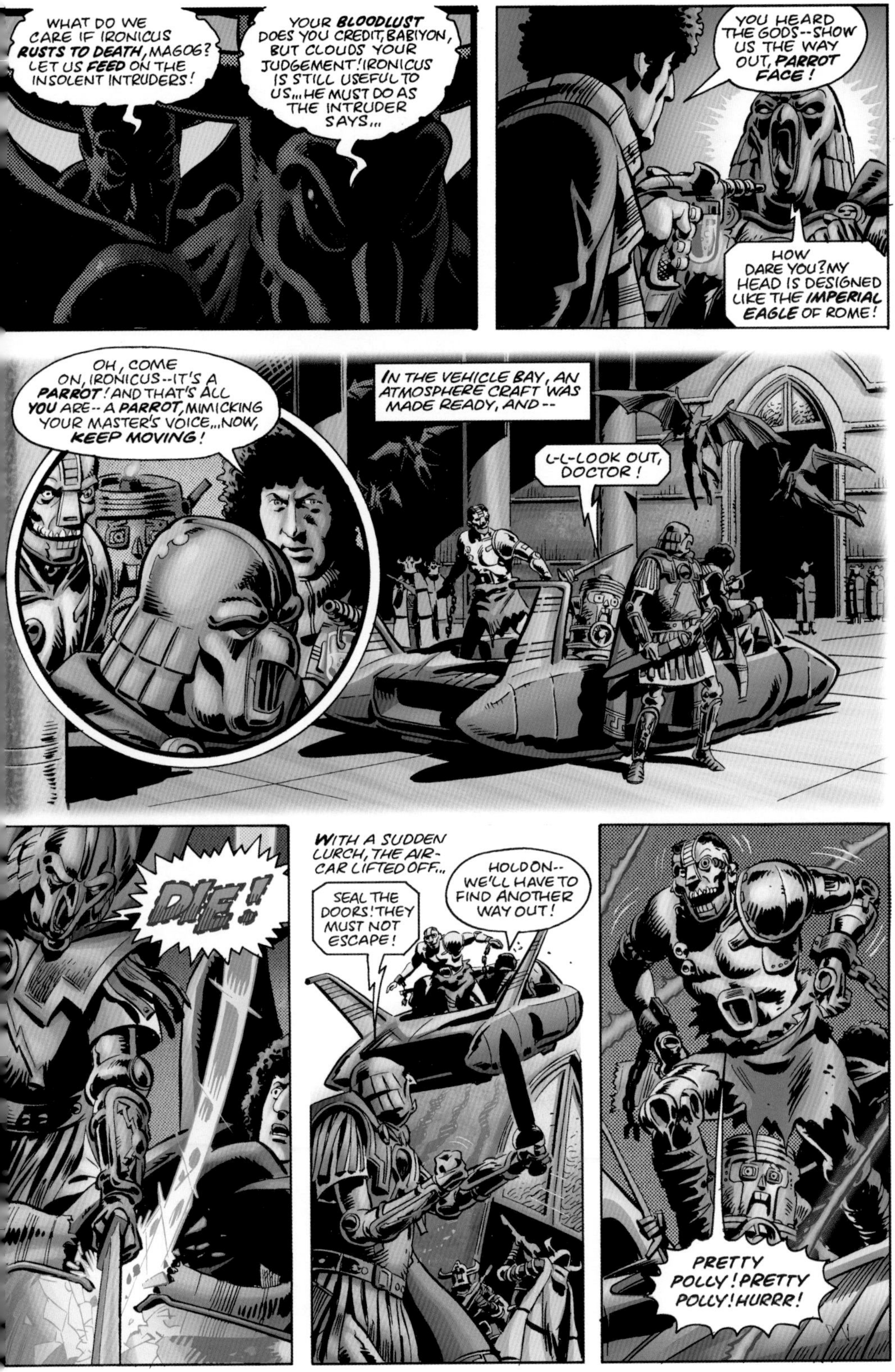
WHAT DO WE CARE IF IRONICUS RUSTS TO DEATH, MAGOG? LET US FEED ON THE INSOLENT INTRUDERS!
YOUR BLOODLUST DOES YOU CREDIT, BABIYON, BUT CLOUDS YOUR JUDGEMENT! IRONICUS IS STILL USEFUL TO US... HE MUST DO AS THE INTRUDER SAYS...
YOU HEARD THE GODS--SHOW US THE WAY OUT, PARROT FACE!
HOW DARE YOU? MY HEAD IS DESIGNED LIKE THE IMPERIAL EAGLE OF ROME!
OH, COME ON, IRONICUS--IT'S A PARROT! AND THAT'S ALL YOU ARE-- A PARROT, MIMICKING YOUR MASTER'S VOICE... NOW, KEEP MOVING!
IN THE VEHICLE BAY, AN ATMOSPHERE CRAFT WAS MADE READY, AND--
L-L-LOOK OUT, DOCTOR!
DIE!
WITH A SUDDEN LURCH, THE AIR-CAR LIFTED OFF...
SEAL THE DOORS! THEY MUST NOT ESCAPE!
HOLD ON-- WE'LL HAVE TO FIND ANOTHER WAY OUT!
PRETTY POLLY! PRETTY POLLY! HURRR!

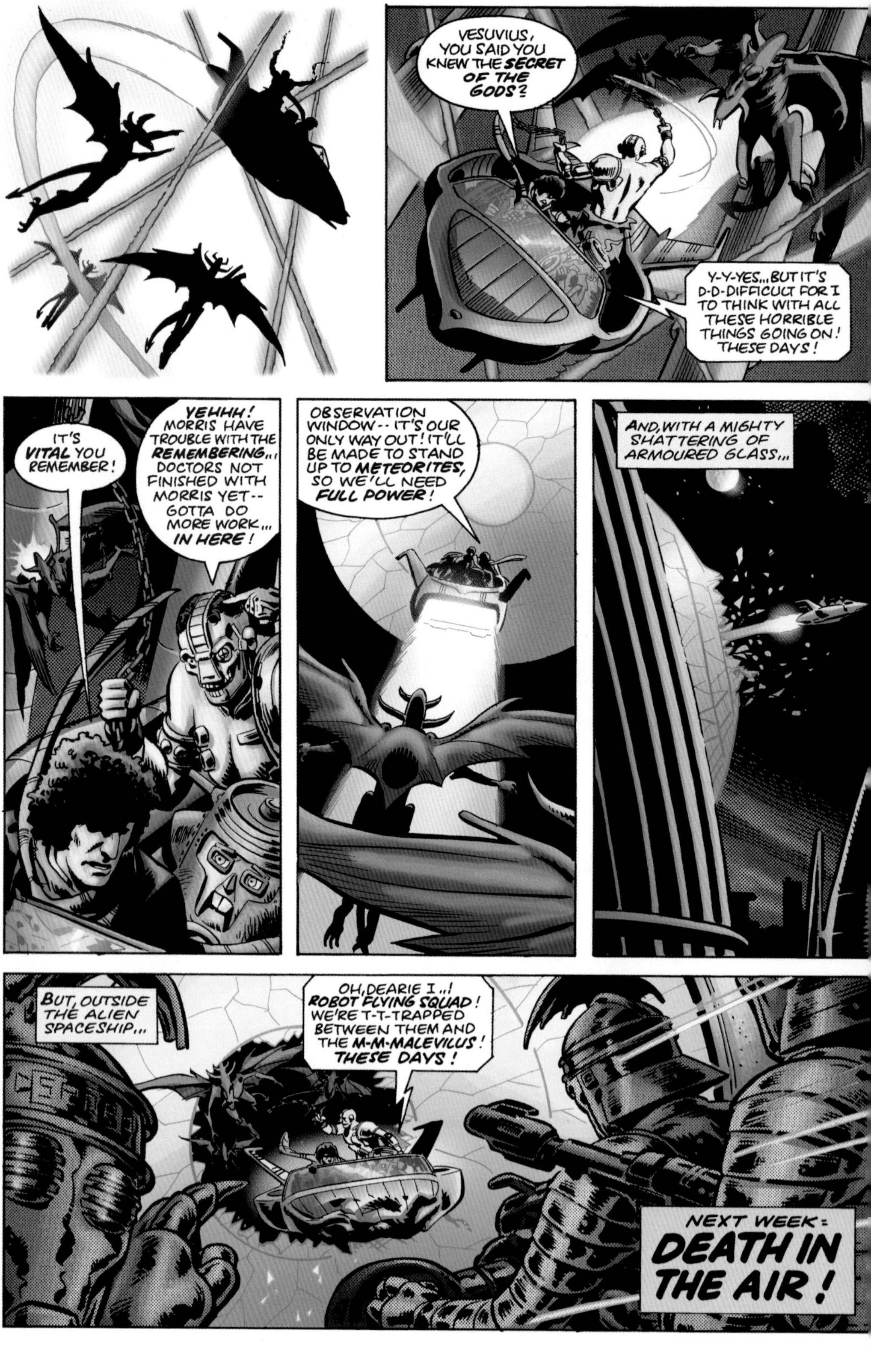
VESUVIUS, YOU SAID YOU KNEW THE SECRET OF THE GODS?
Y-Y-YES... BUT IT'S D-D-DIFFICULT FOR I TO THINK WITH ALL THESE HORRIBLE THINGS GOING ON! THESE DAYS!
IT'S VITAL YOU REMEMBER!
YEHHH! MORRIS HAVE TROUBLE WITH THE REMEMBERING... DOCTORS NOT FINISHED WITH MORRIS YET-- GOTTA DO MORE WORK... IN HERE!
OBSERVATION WINDOW-- IT'S OUR ONLY WAY OUT! IT'LL BE MADE TO STAND UP TO METEORITES, SO WE'LL NEED FULL POWER!
AND, WITH A MIGHTY SHATTERING OF ARMOURED GLASS...
BUT, OUTSIDE THE ALIEN SPACESHIP...
OH, DEARIE I..! ROBOT FLYING SQUAD! WE'RE T-T-TRAPPED BETWEEN THEM AND THE M-M-MALEVILUS! THESE DAYS!
NEXT WEEK: DEATH IN THE AIR!

Stan Lee presents

DOCTOR WHO AND THE IRON LEGION

THE DOCTOR HAS DISCOVERED AN ALTERNATIVE EARTH WHERE ROME NEVER FELL, BUT WENT ON TO CONQUER THE ENTIRE GALAXY! THE DOCTOR AND HIS COMPANIONS ESCAPE FROM THE MALEVILUS. . . THE GODS OF THE ROMAN EMPIRE—ONLY TO FACE ANOTHER THREAT. . .THE ROMAN FLYING SQUAD!

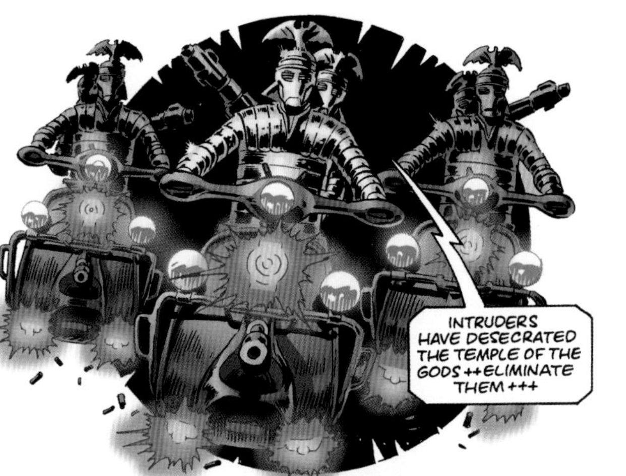

INTRUDERS HAVE DESECRATED THE TEMPLE OF THE GODS ++ELIMINATE THEM+++

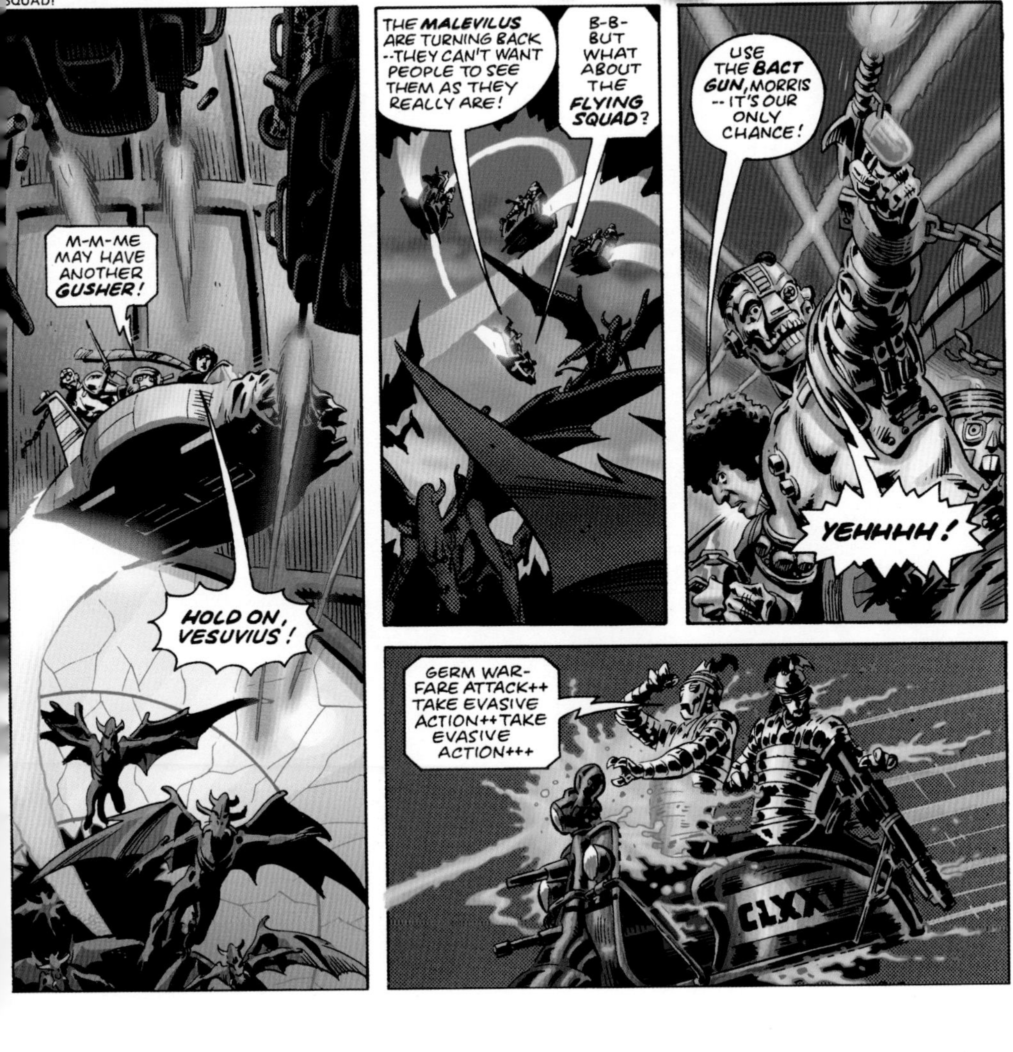

M-M-ME MAY HAVE ANOTHER GUSHER!
HOLD ON, VESUVIUS!
THE MALEVILUS ARE TURNING BACK --THEY CAN'T WANT PEOPLE TO SEE THEM AS THEY REALLY ARE!
B-B-BUT WHAT ABOUT THE FLYING SQUAD?
USE THE BACT GUN, MORRIS --IT'S OUR ONLY CHANCE!
YEHHHH!
GERM WAR-FARE ATTACK++ TAKE EVASIVE ACTION++TAKE EVASIVE ACTION+++
CLXXV

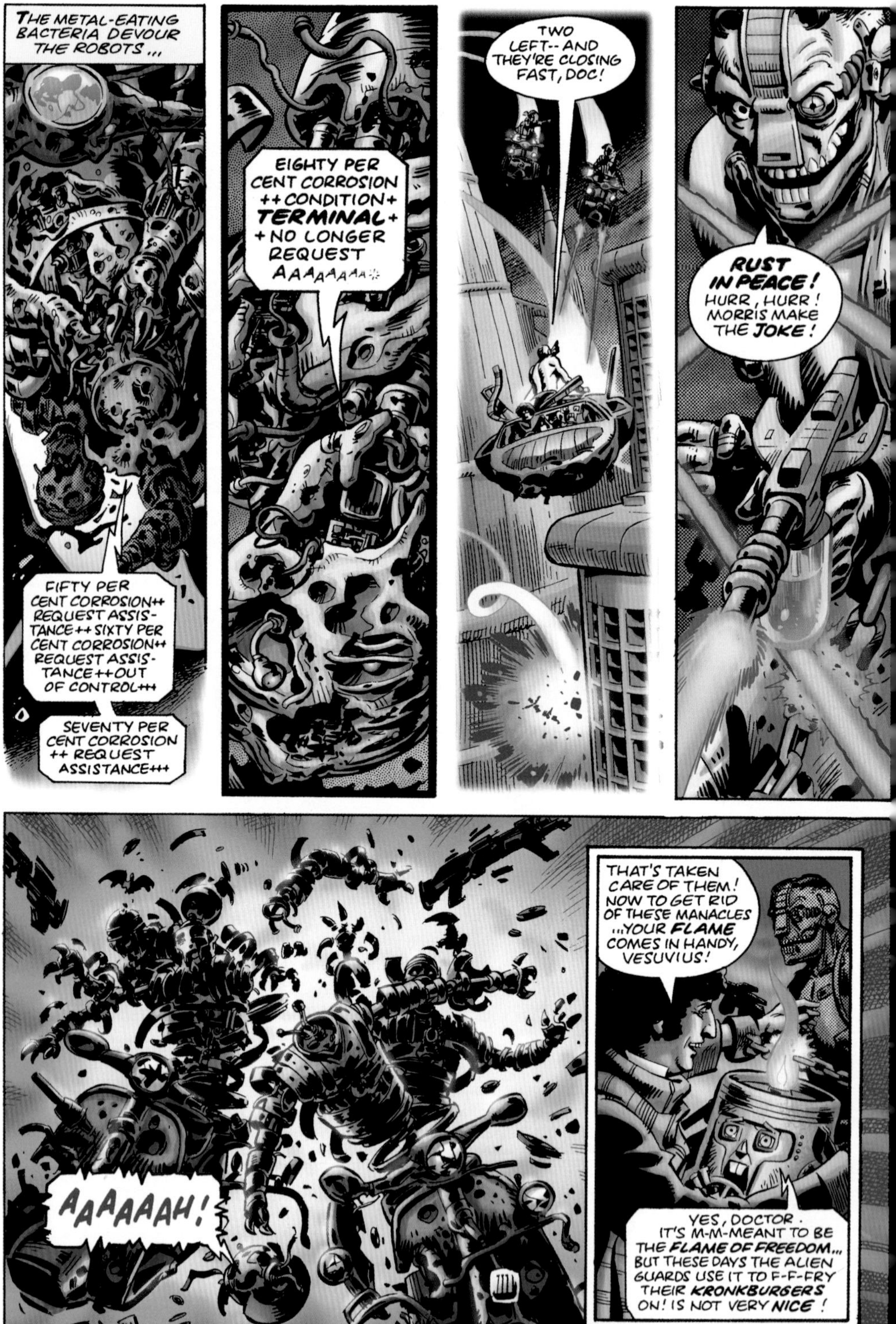
THE METAL-EATING BACTERIA DEVOUR THE ROBOTS...
FIFTY PER CENT CORROSION++ REQUEST ASSIS-TANCE++ SIXTY PER CENT CORROSION++ REQUEST ASSIS-TANCE++OUT OF CONTROL+++
SEVENTY PER CENT CORROSION ++ REQUEST ASSISTANCE+++
EIGHTY PER CENT CORROSION ++CONDITION+ TERMINAL+ +NO LONGER REQUEST AAAAAAAA
TWO LEFT-- AND THEY'RE CLOSING FAST, DOC!
RUST IN PEACE! HURR, HURR! MORRIS MAKE THE JOKE!
AAAAAAH!
THAT'S TAKEN CARE OF THEM! NOW TO GET RID OF THESE MANACLES ...YOUR FLAME COMES IN HANDY, VESUVIUS!
YES, DOCTOR. IT'S M-M-MEANT TO BE THE FLAME OF FREEDOM... BUT THESE DAYS THE ALIEN GUARDS USE IT TO F-F-FRY THEIR KRONKBURGERS ON! IS NOT VERY NICE!

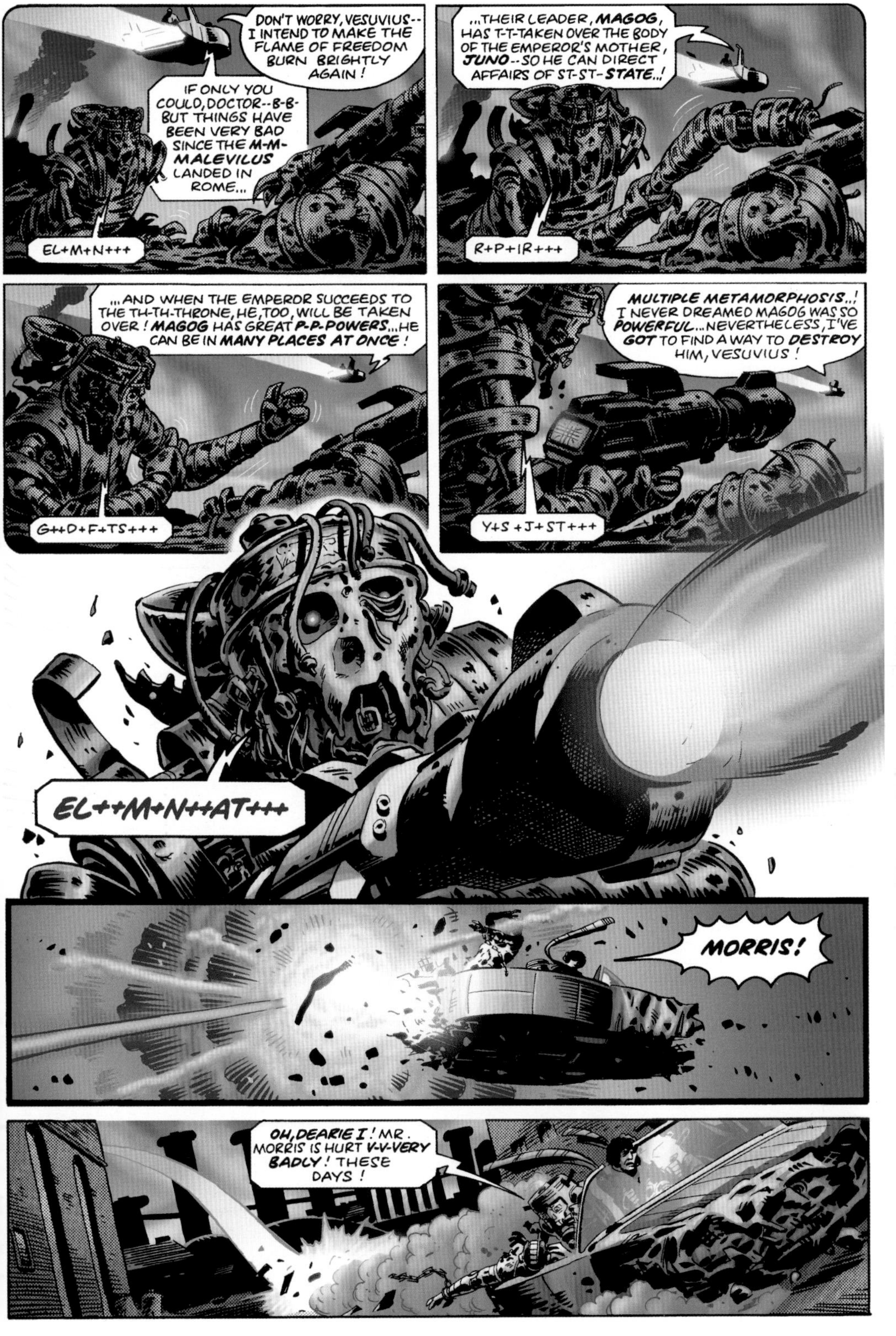
DON'T WORRY, VESUVIUS-- I INTEND TO MAKE THE FLAME OF FREEDOM BURN BRIGHTLY AGAIN!
IF ONLY YOU COULD, DOCTOR--B-B-BUT THINGS HAVE BEEN VERY BAD SINCE THE M-M-MALEVILUS LANDED IN ROME...
EL+M+N+++
...THEIR LEADER, MAGOG, HAS T-T-TAKEN OVER THE BODY OF THE EMPEROR'S MOTHER, JUNO--SO HE CAN DIRECT AFFAIRS OF ST-ST-STATE...!
R+P+IR+++
...AND WHEN THE EMPEROR SUCCEEDS TO THE TH-TH-THRONE, HE, TOO, WILL BE TAKEN OVER! MAGOG HAS GREAT P-P-POWERS... HE CAN BE IN MANY PLACES AT ONCE!
G++D+F+TS+++
MULTIPLE METAMORPHOSIS...! I NEVER DREAMED MAGOG WAS SO POWERFUL... NEVERTHELESS, I'VE GOT TO FIND A WAY TO DESTROY HIM, VESUVIUS!
Y+S+J+ST+++
EL++M+N++AT+++
MORRIS!
OH, DEARIE I! MR. MORRIS IS HURT V-V-VERY BADLY! THESE DAYS!

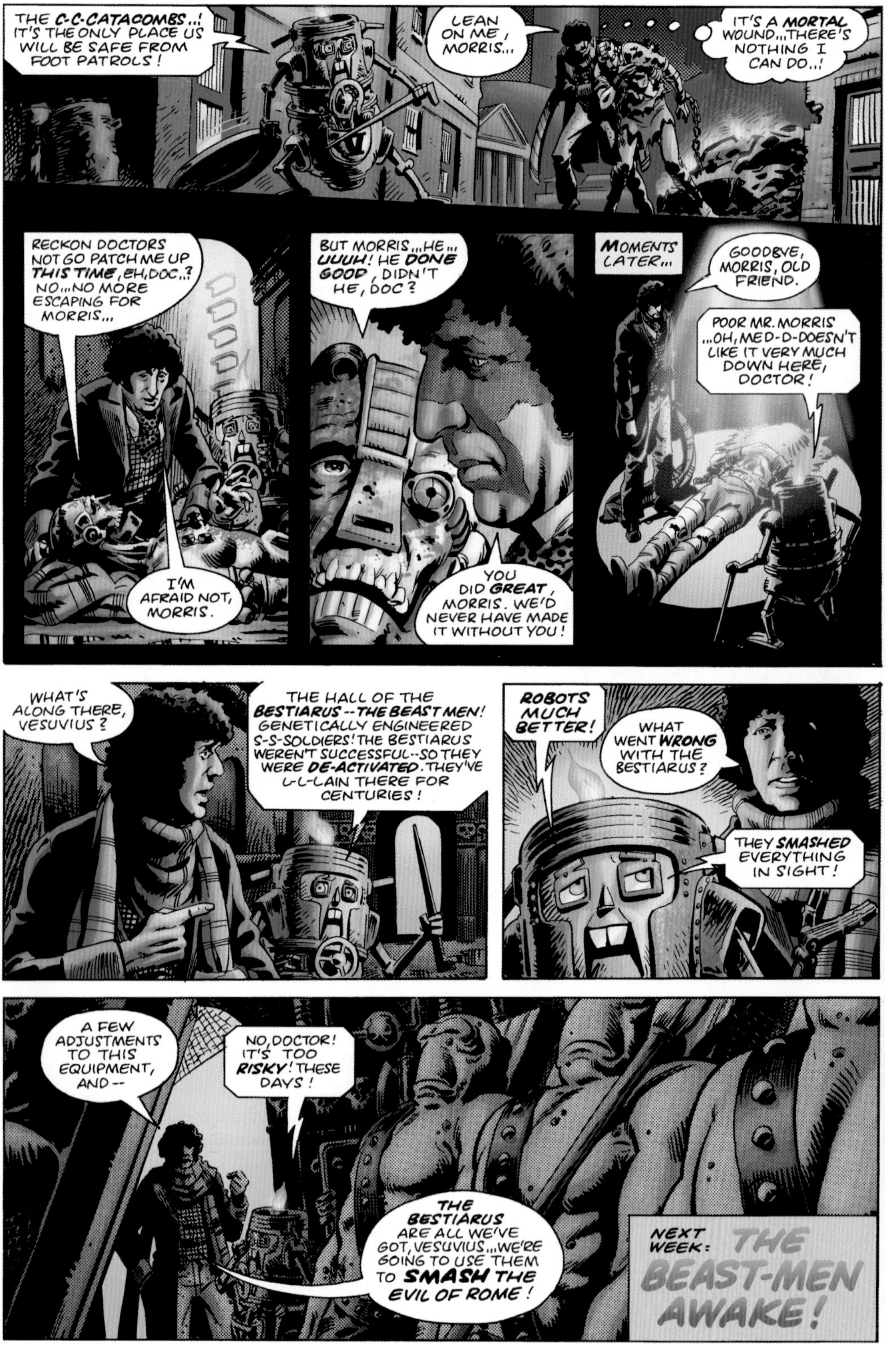

THE C-C-CATACOMBS...! IT'S THE ONLY PLACE US WILL BE SAFE FROM FOOT PATROLS!
LEAN ON ME, MORRIS...
IT'S A MORTAL WOUND... THERE'S NOTHING I CAN DO...!
RECKON DOCTORS NOT GO PATCH ME UP THIS TIME, EH, DOC..? NO... NO MORE ESCAPING FOR MORRIS...
I'M AFRAID NOT, MORRIS.
BUT MORRIS... HE... UUUH! HE DONE GOOD, DIDN'T HE, DOC?
YOU DID GREAT, MORRIS. WE'D NEVER HAVE MADE IT WITHOUT YOU!
MOMENTS LATER...
GOODBYE, MORRIS, OLD FRIEND.
POOR MR. MORRIS ...OH, MED-D-DOESN'T LIKE IT VERY MUCH DOWN HERE, DOCTOR!
WHAT'S ALONG THERE, VESUVIUS?
THE HALL OF THE BESTIARUS -- THE BEAST MEN! GENETICALLY ENGINEERED S-S-SOLDIERS! THE BESTIARUS WEREN'T SUCCESSFUL -- SO THEY WERE DE-ACTIVATED. THEY'VE L-L-LAIN THERE FOR CENTURIES!
ROBOTS MUCH BETTER!
WHAT WENT WRONG WITH THE BESTIARUS?
THEY SMASHED EVERYTHING IN SIGHT!
A FEW ADJUSTMENTS TO THIS EQUIPMENT, AND --
NO, DOCTOR! IT'S TOO RISKY! THESE DAYS!
THE BESTIARUS ARE ALL WE'VE GOT, VESUVIUS... WE'RE GOING TO USE THEM TO SMASH THE EVIL OF ROME!
NEXT WEEK: THE BEAST-MEN AWAKE!

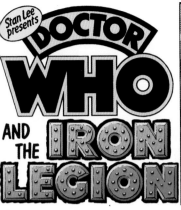

Stan Lee presents
DOCTOR WHO AND THE IRON LEGION

THE DOCTOR REPAIRS THE **CONTROL CONSOLE** AND THEN ... AS **RAW POWER** SURGES THROUGH THE MACHINES ...

...THE BEAST MEN AWAKE!

MILLS/WAGNER + GIBBONS

I'VE PROGRAMMED **THE BESTIARUS** TO FUNCTION FOR TWENTY FOUR HOURS ...THEY'LL USE THE **CATACOMB SYSTEM** TO STRIKE AT **STRATEGIC POINTS** THROUGHOUT **ROME!**

YOU'RE GOING TO START A **REVOLUTION** ...? G-G-GOSH!

WE'VE GOT **TWENTY FOUR HOURS** TO SEIZE AN **EMPIRE!** FOR WHOEVER CONTROLS **ROME...**

...CONTROLS THE **GALAXY!**

WITH GRIM MENACE, THE BESTIARUS LUMBER TOWARDS THEIR **OBJECTIVES** ...

I HOPE YOU KEPT THE BEAST MEN'S INSTRUCTIONS **SIMPLE,** DOCTOR ...ALTHOUGH THEY'RE S-S-SAVAGE **FIGHTERS,** THEY HAVE DIFFICULTY **UNDERSTANDING THINGS!**

YOU MEAN LIKE THE **DIFFERENCE** BETWEEN **DOORS** AND **WALLS**..?

EXACTLY, DOCTOR!

AS THE BEAST MEN DEPART...

BUT WHAT ABOUT **GENERAL IRONICUS** AND **MAGOG**..? THEY'LL BE AT THE **CIRCUS MAXIMUS** THESE DAYS TO WATCH THE **CH-CH-CHARIOT RACES!**

THEN THAT'S WHERE **WE'RE** GOING, VESUVIUS -- FOR A **FINAL CONFRONTATION** WITH MAGOG!

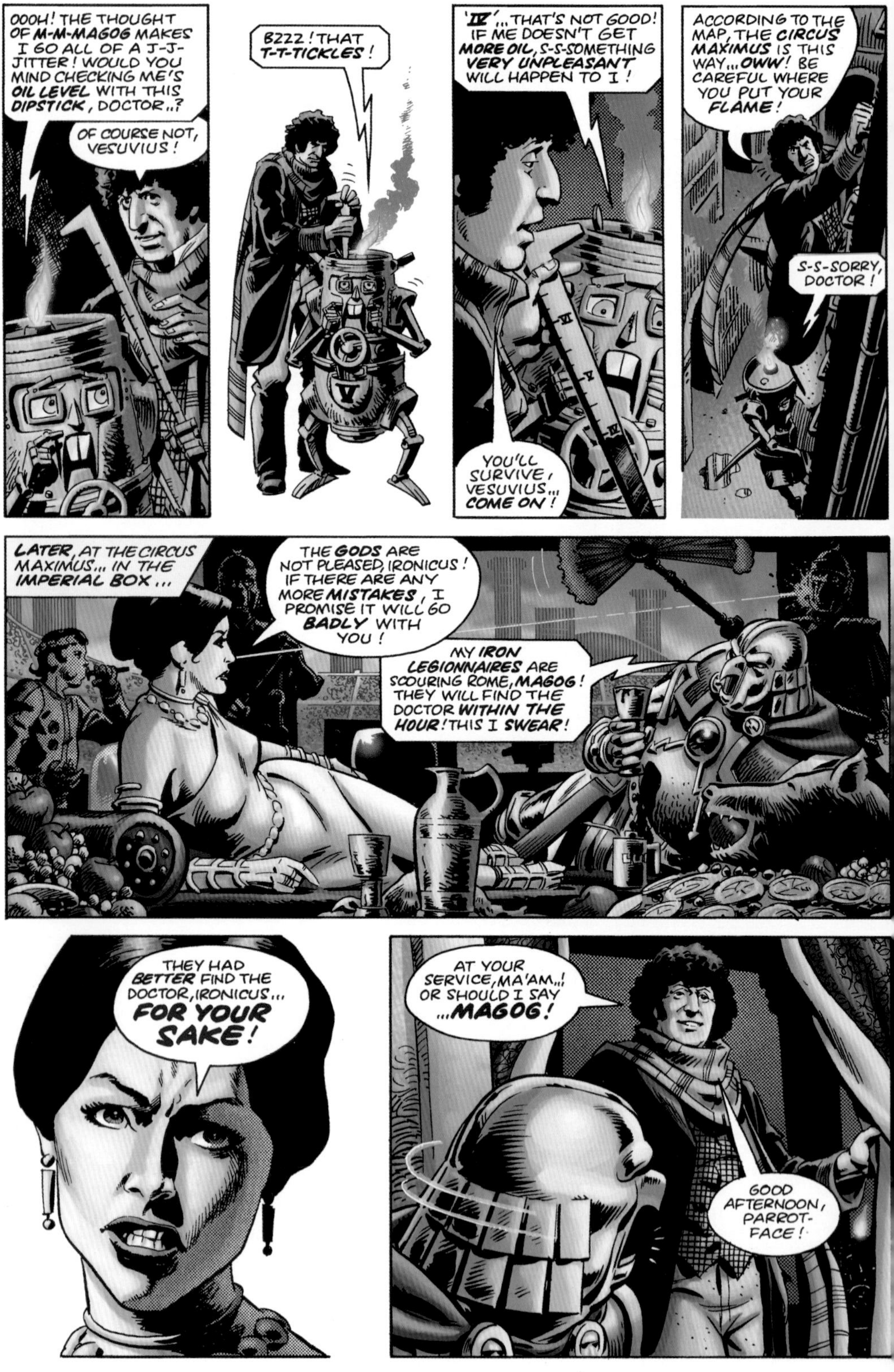
OOOH! THE THOUGHT OF M-M-MAGOG MAKES I GO ALL OF A J-J-JITTER! WOULD YOU MIND CHECKING ME'S OIL LEVEL WITH THIS DIPSTICK, DOCTOR..?
OF COURSE NOT, VESUVIUS!
BZZZ! THAT T-T-TICKLES!
'IV'... THAT'S NOT GOOD! IF ME DOESN'T GET MORE OIL, S-S-SOMETHING VERY UNPLEASANT WILL HAPPEN TO I!
YOU'LL SURVIVE, VESUVIUS... COME ON!
ACCORDING TO THE MAP, THE CIRCUS MAXIMUS IS THIS WAY... OWW! BE CAREFUL WHERE YOU PUT YOUR FLAME!
S-S-SORRY, DOCTOR!
LATER, AT THE CIRCUS MAXIMUS... IN THE IMPERIAL BOX...
THE GODS ARE NOT PLEASED, IRONICUS! IF THERE ARE ANY MORE MISTAKES, I PROMISE IT WILL GO BADLY WITH YOU!
MY IRON LEGIONNAIRES ARE SCOURING ROME, MAGOG! THEY WILL FIND THE DOCTOR WITHIN THE HOUR! THIS I SWEAR!
THEY HAD BETTER FIND THE DOCTOR, IRONICUS... FOR YOUR SAKE!
AT YOUR SERVICE, MA'AM..! OR SHOULD I SAY ...MAGOG!
GOOD AFTERNOON, PARROT-FACE!

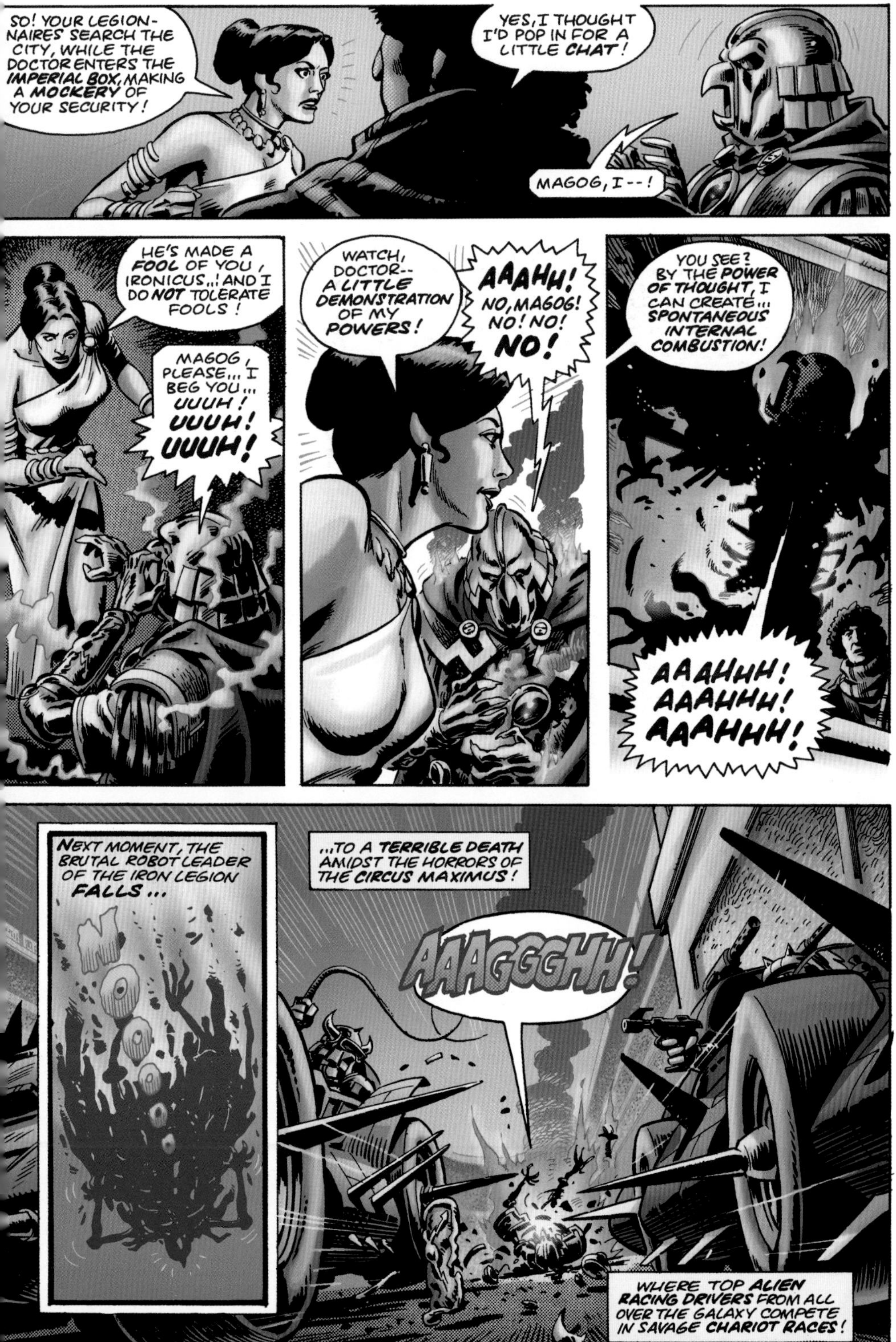

SO! YOUR LEGION-NAIRES SEARCH THE CITY, WHILE THE DOCTOR ENTERS THE IMPERIAL BOX, MAKING A MOCKERY OF YOUR SECURITY!
YES, I THOUGHT I'D POP IN FOR A LITTLE CHAT!
MAGOG, I--!
HE'S MADE A FOOL OF YOU, IRONICUS...! AND I DO NOT TOLERATE FOOLS!
MAGOG, PLEASE... I BEG YOU... UUUH! UUUH! UUUH!
WATCH, DOCTOR-- A LITTLE DEMONSTRATION OF MY POWERS!
AAAHH! NO, MAGOG! NO! NO! NO!
YOU SEE? BY THE POWER OF THOUGHT, I CAN CREATE... SPONTANEOUS INTERNAL COMBUSTION!
AAAHHH! AAAHHH! AAAHHH!
NEXT MOMENT, THE BRUTAL ROBOT LEADER OF THE IRON LEGION FALLS...
...TO A TERRIBLE DEATH AMIDST THE HORRORS OF THE CIRCUS MAXIMUS!
AAAGGGHH!
WHERE TOP ALIEN RACING DRIVERS FROM ALL OVER THE GALAXY COMPETE IN SAVAGE CHARIOT RACES!

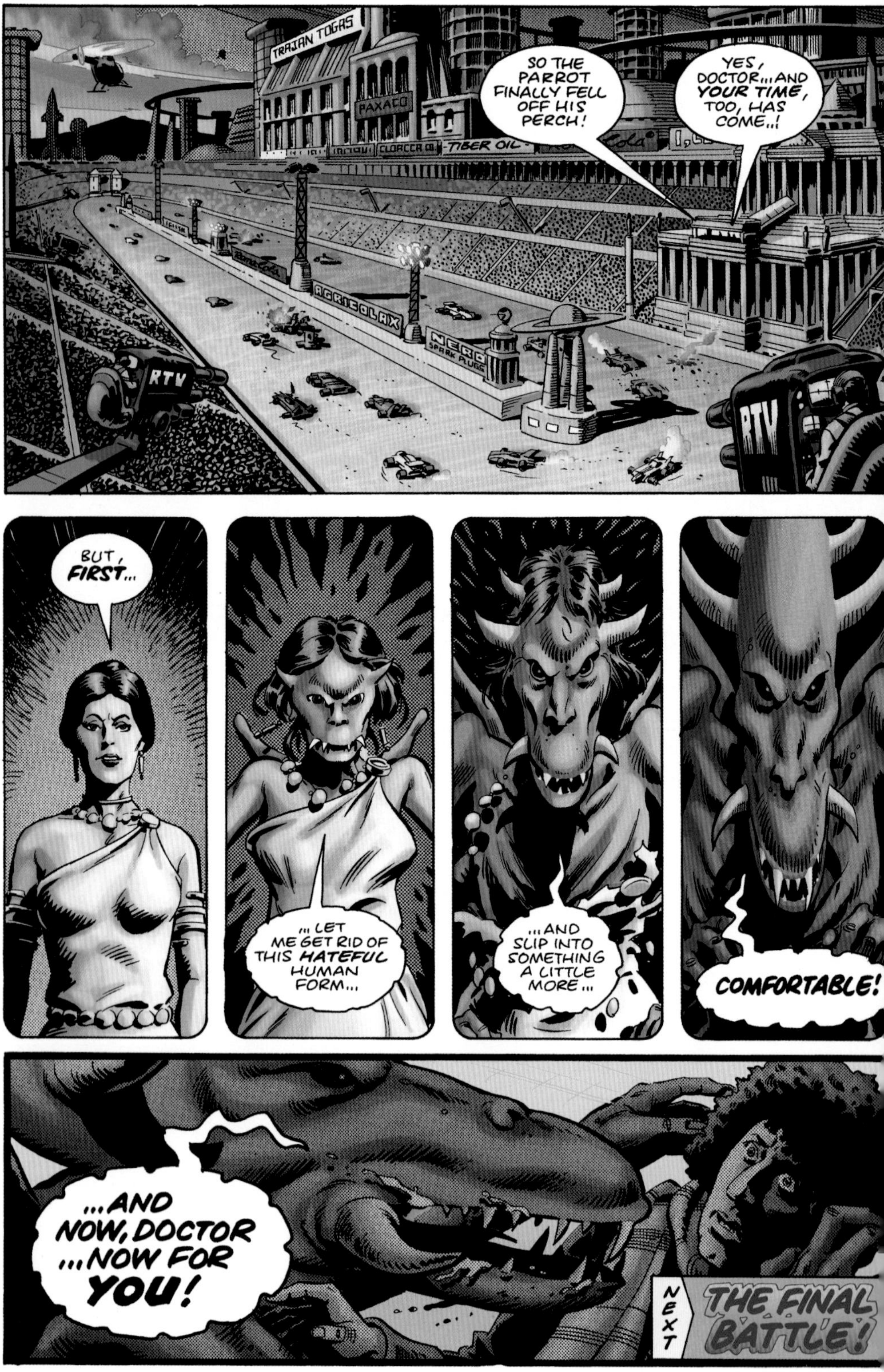
TRAJAN TOGAS
PAXACO
CLOACCA OIL
TIBER OIL
AGRICOLAX
NERO SPARK PLUGS
RTV
SO THE PARROT FINALLY FELL OFF HIS PERCH!
YES, DOCTOR...AND YOUR TIME, TOO, HAS COME..!
BUT, FIRST...
...LET ME GET RID OF THIS HATEFUL HUMAN FORM...
...AND SLIP INTO SOMETHING A LITTLE MORE...
COMFORTABLE!
...AND NOW, DOCTOR ...NOW FOR YOU!
NEXT
THE FINAL BATTLE!

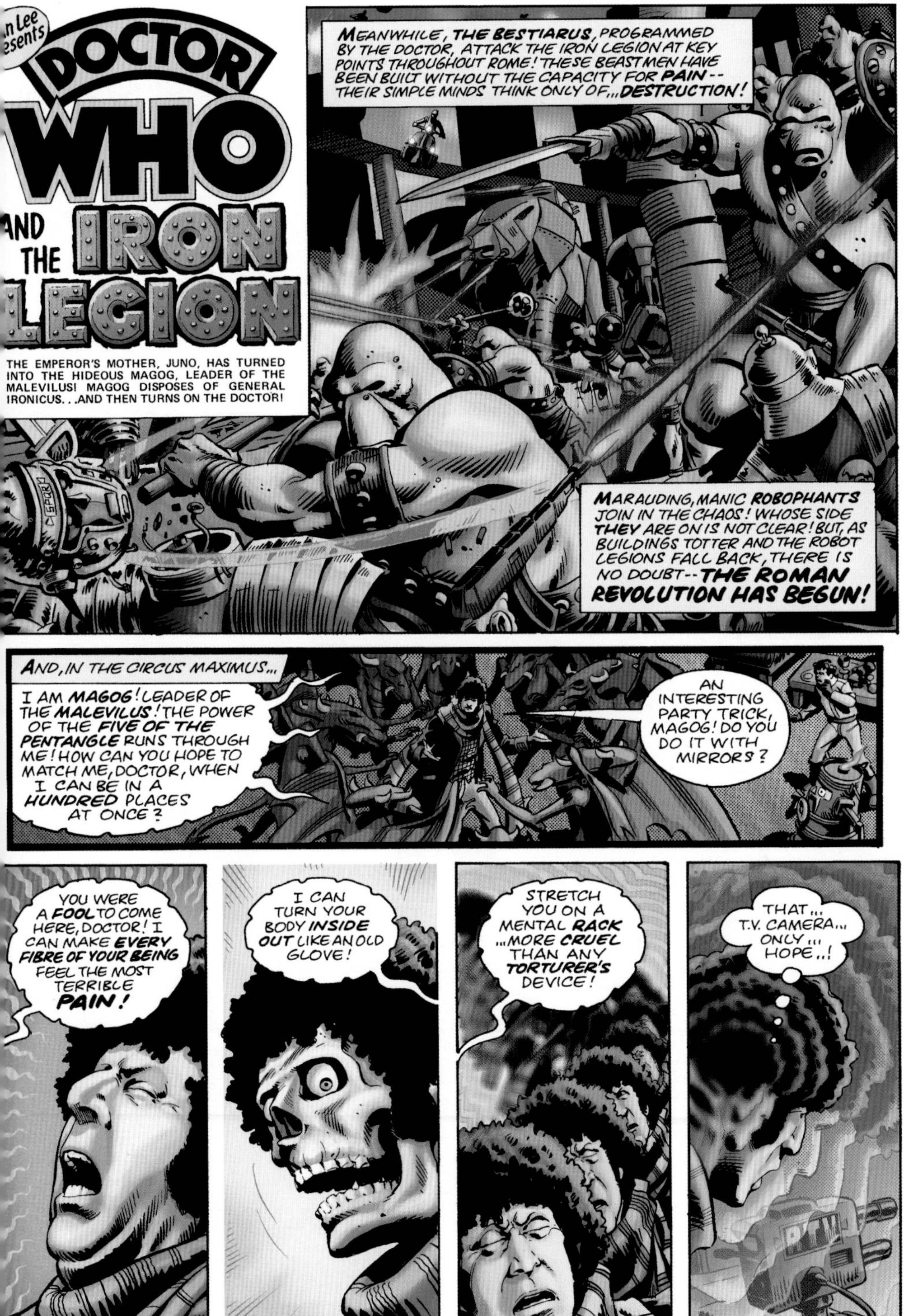

...n Lee
...esents
DOCTOR WHO
AND THE IRON LEGION
THE EMPEROR'S MOTHER, JUNO, HAS TURNED INTO THE HIDEOUS MAGOG, LEADER OF THE MALEVILUS! MAGOG DISPOSES OF GENERAL IRONICUS. . .AND THEN TURNS ON THE DOCTOR!
MEANWHILE, THE BESTIARUS, PROGRAMMED BY THE DOCTOR, ATTACK THE IRON LEGION AT KEY POINTS THROUGHOUT ROME! THESE BEASTMEN HAVE BEEN BUILT WITHOUT THE CAPACITY FOR PAIN-- THEIR SIMPLE MINDS THINK ONLY OF... DESTRUCTION!
MARAUDING, MANIC ROBOPHANTS JOIN IN THE CHAOS! WHOSE SIDE THEY ARE ON IS NOT CLEAR! BUT, AS BUILDINGS TOTTER AND THE ROBOT LEGIONS FALL BACK, THERE IS NO DOUBT--THE ROMAN REVOLUTION HAS BEGUN!
AND, IN THE CIRCUS MAXIMUS...
I AM MAGOG! LEADER OF THE MALEVILUS! THE POWER OF THE FIVE OF THE PENTANGLE RUNS THROUGH ME! HOW CAN YOU HOPE TO MATCH ME, DOCTOR, WHEN I CAN BE IN A HUNDRED PLACES AT ONCE?
AN INTERESTING PARTY TRICK, MAGOG! DO YOU DO IT WITH MIRRORS?
YOU WERE A FOOL TO COME HERE, DOCTOR! I CAN MAKE EVERY FIBRE OF YOUR BEING FEEL THE MOST TERRIBLE PAIN!
I CAN TURN YOUR BODY INSIDE OUT LIKE AN OLD GLOVE!
STRETCH YOU ON A MENTAL RACK ...MORE CRUEL THAN ANY TORTURER'S DEVICE!
THAT... T.V. CAMERA... ONLY... HOPE...!

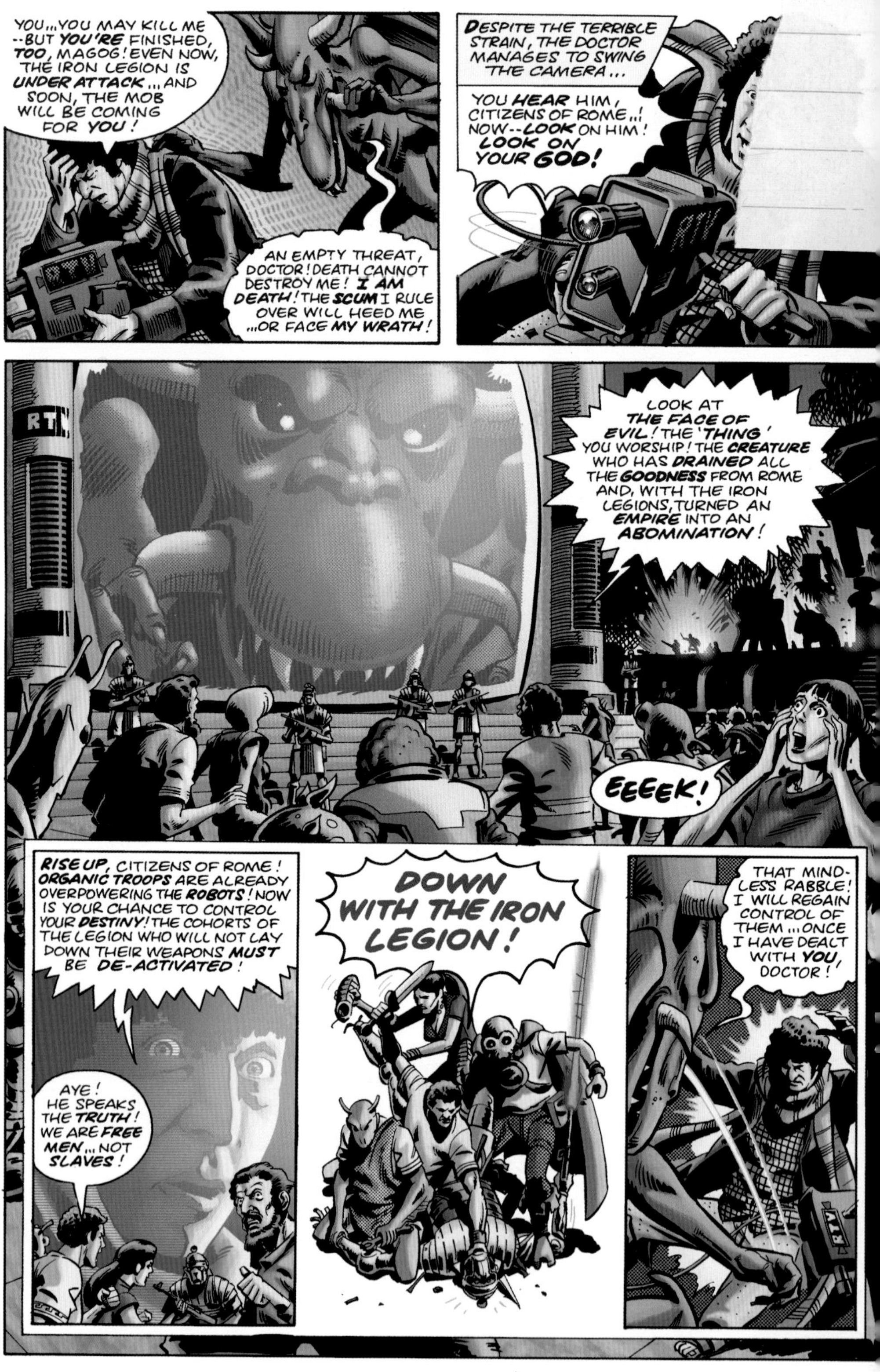

YOU...YOU MAY KILL ME --BUT YOU'RE FINISHED, TOO, MAGOG! EVEN NOW, THE IRON LEGION IS UNDER ATTACK... AND SOON, THE MOB WILL BE COMING FOR YOU!
AN EMPTY THREAT, DOCTOR! DEATH CANNOT DESTROY ME! I AM DEATH! THE SCUM I RULE OVER WILL HEED ME ...OR FACE MY WRATH!
DESPITE THE TERRIBLE STRAIN, THE DOCTOR MANAGES TO SWING THE CAMERA...
YOU HEAR HIM, CITIZENS OF ROME...! NOW--LOOK ON HIM! LOOK ON YOUR GOD!
LOOK AT THE FACE OF EVIL! THE 'THING' YOU WORSHIP! THE CREATURE WHO HAS DRAINED ALL THE GOODNESS FROM ROME AND, WITH THE IRON LEGIONS, TURNED AN EMPIRE INTO AN ABOMINATION!
EEEEK!
RISE UP, CITIZENS OF ROME! ORGANIC TROOPS ARE ALREADY OVERPOWERING THE ROBOTS! NOW IS YOUR CHANCE TO CONTROL YOUR DESTINY! THE COHORTS OF THE LEGION WHO WILL NOT LAY DOWN THEIR WEAPONS MUST BE DE-ACTIVATED!
AYE! HE SPEAKS THE TRUTH! WE ARE FREE MEN... NOT SLAVES!
DOWN WITH THE IRON LEGION!
THAT MINDLESS RABBLE! I WILL REGAIN CONTROL OF THEM... ONCE I HAVE DEALT WITH YOU, DOCTOR!

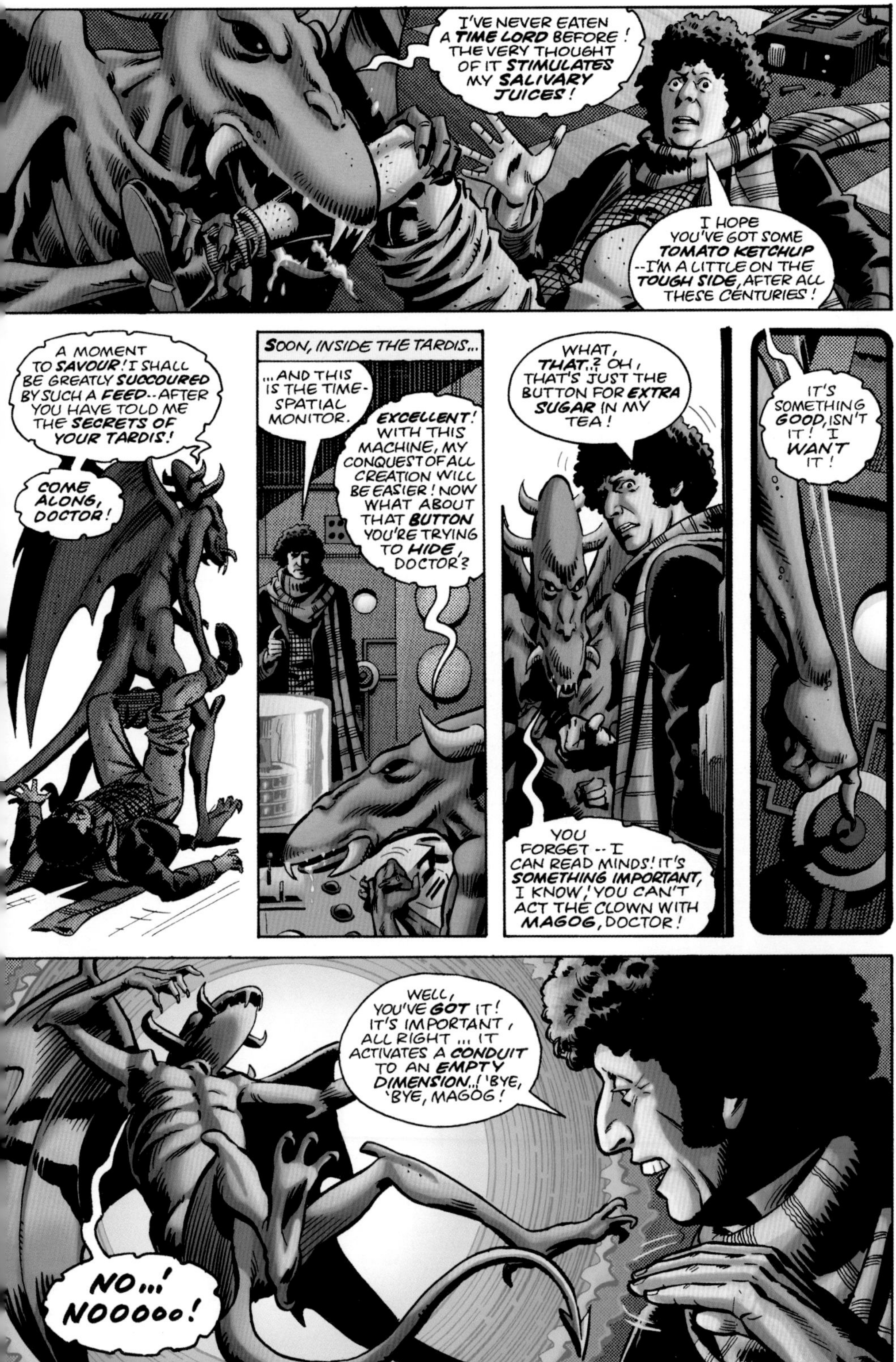
I'VE NEVER EATEN A TIME LORD BEFORE! THE VERY THOUGHT OF IT STIMULATES MY SALIVARY JUICES!
I HOPE YOU'VE GOT SOME TOMATO KETCHUP --I'M A LITTLE ON THE TOUGH SIDE, AFTER ALL THESE CENTURIES!
A MOMENT TO SAVOUR! I SHALL BE GREATLY SUCCOURED BY SUCH A FEED-- AFTER YOU HAVE TOLD ME THE SECRETS OF YOUR TARDIS!
COME ALONG, DOCTOR!
SOON, INSIDE THE TARDIS...
...AND THIS IS THE TIME-SPATIAL MONITOR.
EXCELLENT! WITH THIS MACHINE, MY CONQUEST OF ALL CREATION WILL BE EASIER! NOW WHAT ABOUT THAT BUTTON YOU'RE TRYING TO HIDE, DOCTOR?
WHAT, THAT..? OH, THAT'S JUST THE BUTTON FOR EXTRA SUGAR IN MY TEA!
YOU FORGET -- I CAN READ MINDS! IT'S SOMETHING IMPORTANT, I KNOW! YOU CAN'T ACT THE CLOWN WITH MAGOG, DOCTOR!
IT'S SOMETHING GOOD, ISN'T IT! I WANT IT!
WELL, YOU'VE GOT IT! IT'S IMPORTANT, ALL RIGHT ... IT ACTIVATES A CONDUIT TO AN EMPTY DIMENSION..! 'BYE, 'BYE, MAGOG!
NO...! NOOOOO!

YOU CAN'T *DIE*--BUT YOU *CAN* BE *CAGED!* UNTIL *THE END OF ETERNITY*, YOU'LL RULE A KINGDOM *BEYOND* ALL KINGDOMS, *MAGOG!* FOR NOW, YOU'RE THE *EMPEROR* OF THE EMPTY DIMENSION! LORD OF *NOTHING!* *KING OF THE BIG ZERO!*

MAGOG... WILL.... RETURN!

GOOD JOB EVERY TARDIS CARRIES A *SPARE DIMENSION* AS STANDARD EQUIPMENT!

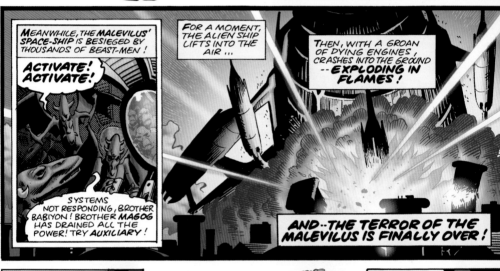

MEANWHILE, THE *MALEVILUS'* SPACE-SHIP IS BESIEGED BY THOUSANDS OF BEAST-MEN!

ACTIVATE! ACTIVATE!

SYSTEMS *NOT RESPONDING*, BROTHER BABIYON! BROTHER *MAGOG* HAS DRAINED ALL THE POWER! TRY *AUXILIARY!*

FOR A MOMENT, THE ALIEN SHIP LIFTS INTO THE AIR ...

THEN, WITH A GROAN OF DYING ENGINES, CRASHES INTO THE GROUND --*EXPLODING IN FLAMES!*

AND--THE TERROR OF THE *MALEVILUS* IS FINALLY OVER!

SOME TIME LATER...

OH, DEARIE I! ROME IS *FREE*, THANKS TO YOU, D-D-DOCTOR! ME IS *SO HAPPY*-- ME COULD *ERUPT!*

IT WAS YOUR DOING, TOO, *VESUVIUS!* THAT'S WHY THE CITIZENS MADE YOU THEIR *NEW EMPEROR!*

OH, YES! OH, G-G-GOSH! SO MANY *IMPORTANT DECISIONS* FOR I TO MAKE THESE DAYS! LIKE WHAT TO DO WITH THE *LAST EMPEROR*, LITTLE *ADOLPHUS!*

THIS ADDRESS MIGHT BE USEFUL, CAESAR ...IT'S A *BOARDING SCHOOL* ON THE *ICE-PLANET CRYOS FOUR*, IN A REMOTE CORNER OF THE GALAXY! RUN BY AN ORDER OF *LUKRONIAN VORKS*--VERY STRICT ON DISCIPLINE, I BELIEVE!

AN EXCELLENT IDEA, DOCTOR! ME WILL WR-WR-WRITE TO THEM IMMEDIATELY!

WELL, *GOOD LUCK*, CAESAR! I'M OFF FOR A *QUIET* HOLIDAY, SOMEWHERE *PEACEFUL!* CHAP I MET SUGGESTED *BENIDORM*...! SUN, SEA, SAND -- AND A LITTLE BIT OF *OLÉ!*

THE END.

NEXT ISSUE = JOIN THE DOCTOR IN ...  CITY of the DAMNED!

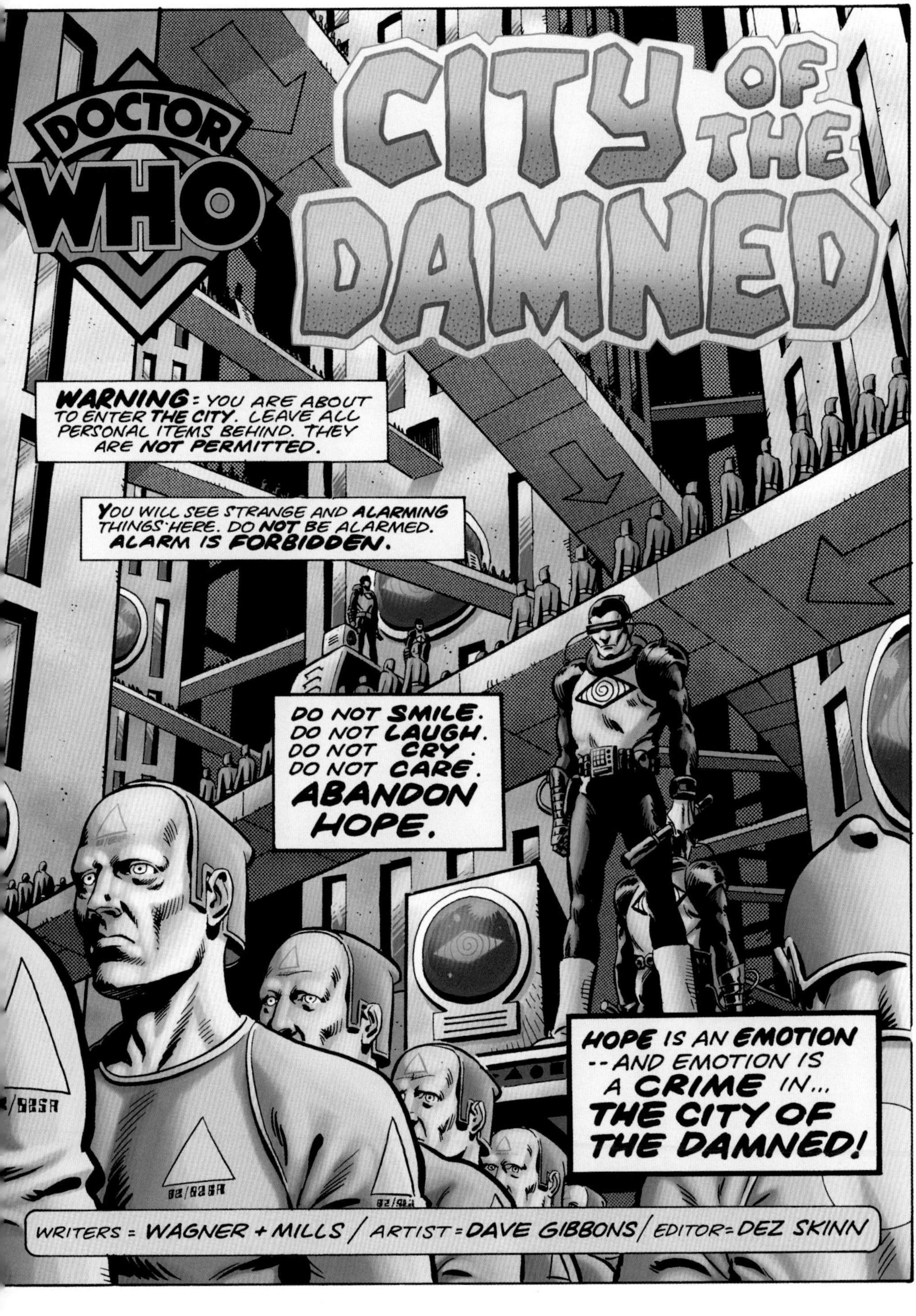
DOCTOR WHO
CITY OF THE DAMNED
WARNING: YOU ARE ABOUT TO ENTER THE CITY. LEAVE ALL PERSONAL ITEMS BEHIND. THEY ARE NOT PERMITTED.
YOU WILL SEE STRANGE AND ALARMING THINGS HERE. DO NOT BE ALARMED. ALARM IS FORBIDDEN.
DO NOT SMILE. DO NOT LAUGH. DO NOT CRY. DO NOT CARE. ABANDON HOPE.
HOPE IS AN EMOTION --AND EMOTION IS A CRIME IN... THE CITY OF THE DAMNED!
WRITERS = WAGNER + MILLS / ARTIST = DAVE GIBBONS / EDITOR = DEZ SKINN

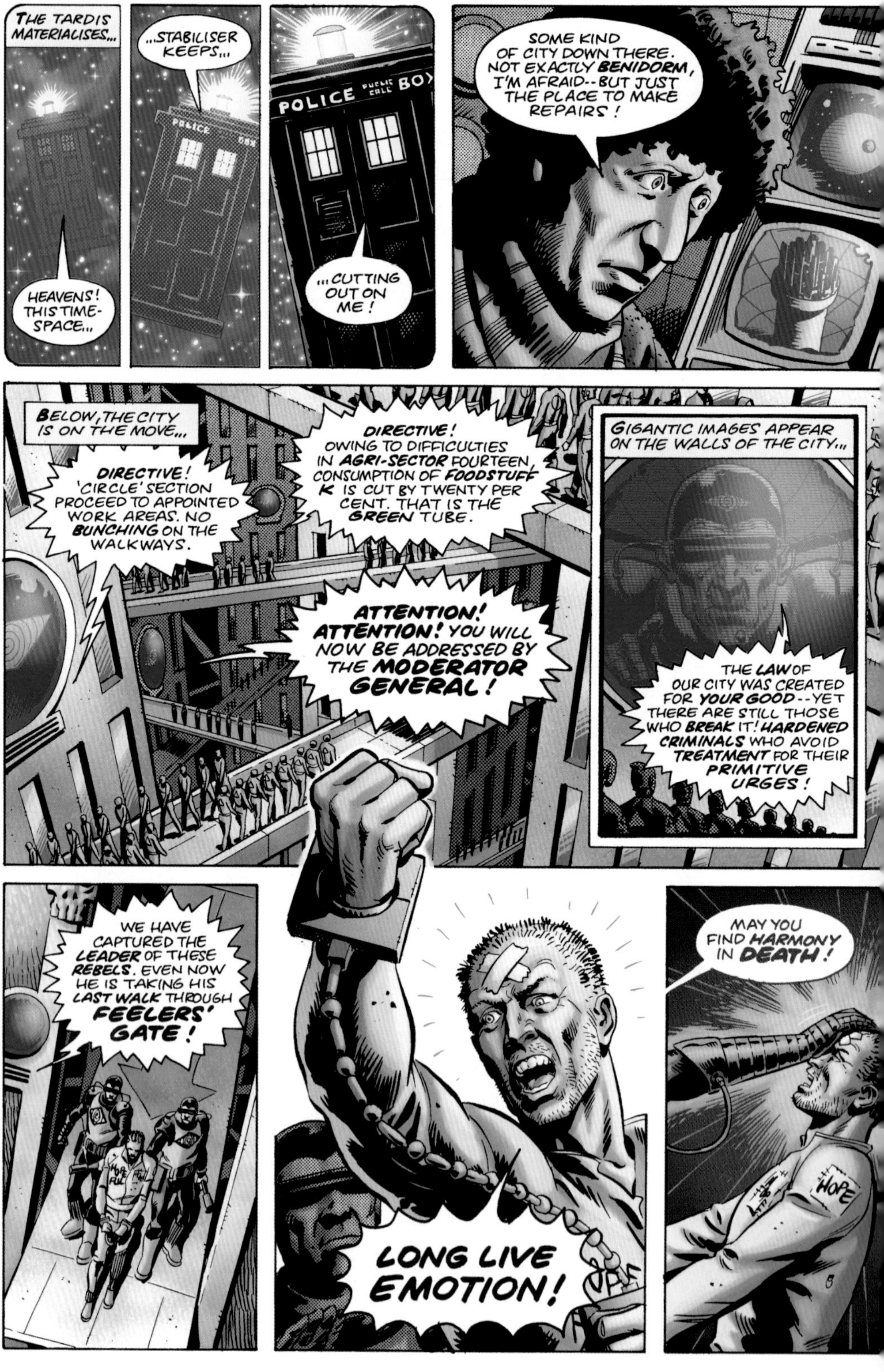
THE TARDIS MATERIALISES...
HEAVENS! THIS TIME-SPACE...
...STABILISER KEEPS...
POLICE
POLICE PUBLIC CALL BOX
...CUTTING OUT ON ME!
SOME KIND OF CITY DOWN THERE. NOT EXACTLY BENIDORM, I'M AFRAID--BUT JUST THE PLACE TO MAKE REPAIRS!
BELOW, THE CITY IS ON THE MOVE...
DIRECTIVE! 'CIRCLE' SECTION PROCEED TO APPOINTED WORK AREAS. NO BUNCHING ON THE WALKWAYS.
DIRECTIVE! OWING TO DIFFICULTIES IN AGRI-SECTOR FOURTEEN, CONSUMPTION OF FOODSTUFF K IS CUT BY TWENTY PER CENT. THAT IS THE GREEN TUBE.
ATTENTION! ATTENTION! YOU WILL NOW BE ADDRESSED BY THE MODERATOR GENERAL!
GIGANTIC IMAGES APPEAR ON THE WALLS OF THE CITY...
THE LAW OF OUR CITY WAS CREATED FOR YOUR GOOD--YET THERE ARE STILL THOSE WHO BREAK IT! HARDENED CRIMINALS WHO AVOID TREATMENT FOR THEIR PRIMITIVE URGES!
WE HAVE CAPTURED THE LEADER OF THESE REBELS. EVEN NOW HE IS TAKING HIS LAST WALK THROUGH FEELERS' GATE!
LONG LIVE EMOTION!
MAY YOU FIND HARMONY IN DEATH!
HOPE

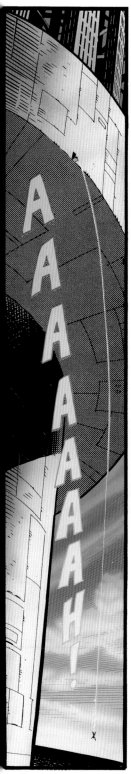

BE **WARNED**! IF YOU FEEL AN EMOTION COMING ON, VISIT YOUR **HARMONY BOOTH** IMMEDIATELY!

LIVE IN HARMONY!

HARMONY!

IN THE LIVING QUARTERS...

THERE IS A STRANGE **BOX** APPEARING IN THE CORNER, 'B'.

YES, 'A'. IGNORE IT. PERHAPS IT WILL GO AWAY.

OH, DEAR, I APPEAR TO HAVE LANDED IN YOUR KITCHEN! WOULD YOU LIKE ME TO MOVE?

DO AS YOU WILL. I DON'T CARE.

LIKES AND DISLIKES ARE NOT PERMITTED.

AH! BREAKFAST, I SEE--

MIND IF I ...

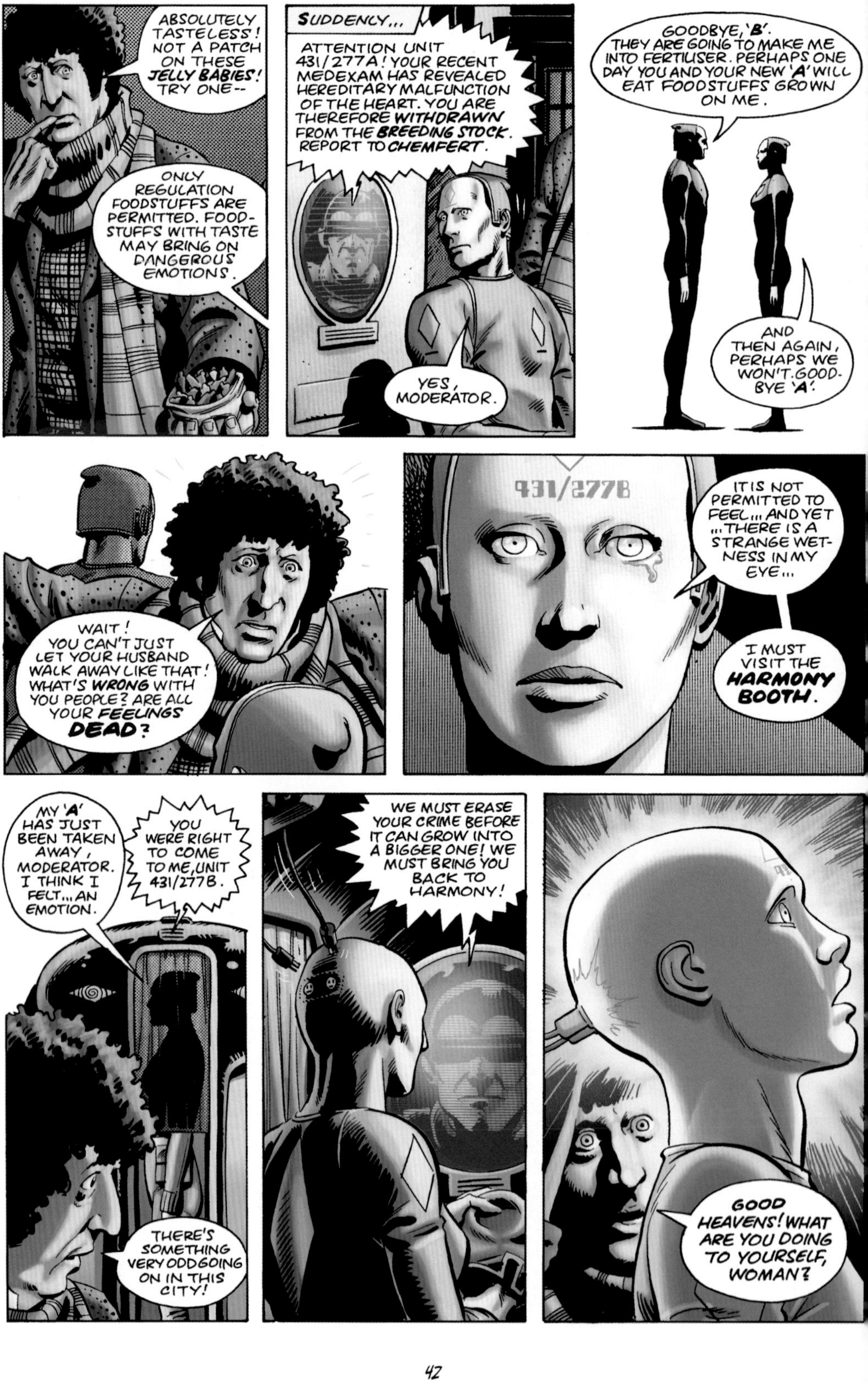
ABSOLUTELY TASTELESS! NOT A PATCH ON THESE JELLY BABIES! TRY ONE--
ONLY REGULATION FOODSTUFFS ARE PERMITTED. FOODSTUFFS WITH TASTE MAY BRING ON DANGEROUS EMOTIONS.
SUDDENLY...
ATTENTION UNIT 431/277A! YOUR RECENT MEDEXAM HAS REVEALED HEREDITARY MALFUNCTION OF THE HEART. YOU ARE THEREFORE WITHDRAWN FROM THE BREEDING STOCK. REPORT TO CHEMFERT.
YES, MODERATOR.
GOODBYE, 'B'. THEY ARE GOING TO MAKE ME INTO FERTILISER. PERHAPS ONE DAY YOU AND YOUR NEW 'A' WILL EAT FOODSTUFFS GROWN ON ME.
AND THEN AGAIN, PERHAPS WE WON'T. GOODBYE 'A'.
WAIT! YOU CAN'T JUST LET YOUR HUSBAND WALK AWAY LIKE THAT! WHAT'S WRONG WITH YOU PEOPLE? ARE ALL YOUR FEELINGS DEAD?
431/277B
IT IS NOT PERMITTED TO FEEL... AND YET ...THERE IS A STRANGE WETNESS IN MY EYE...
I MUST VISIT THE HARMONY BOOTH.
MY 'A' HAS JUST BEEN TAKEN AWAY, MODERATOR. I THINK I FELT... AN EMOTION.
YOU WERE RIGHT TO COME TO ME, UNIT 431/277B.
THERE'S SOMETHING VERY ODD GOING ON IN THIS CITY!
WE MUST ERASE YOUR CRIME BEFORE IT CAN GROW INTO A BIGGER ONE! WE MUST BRING YOU BACK TO HARMONY!
GOOD HEAVENS! WHAT ARE YOU DOING TO YOURSELF, WOMAN?

MODERATOR GENERAL-- THERE IS SOMEONE *INTERFERING* WITH THE *HARMONISATION* PROCESS.

WE WILL INVESTIGATE.

MODERATION SQUAD--'*PORT OUT.*

HMM! MORE ARRIVALS! IT'S LIKE YARGOS CENTRAL SPACEDROME IN HERE!

GOOD DAY! I AM THE DOCTOR. PERHAPS YOU CAN EXPLAIN WHAT'S GOING ON --

MODERATORS DO NOT GIVE EXPLANATIONS. *SCAN HIM.*

FIERCE EMOTIONAL ACTIVITY --THE COMPLETE *E-WAVE* SPECTRUM.

I CAN SEE EVERY COLOUR OF THE RAINBOW AROUND HIM.

WELL, NATURALLY. WE TIME LORDS ARE VERY COLOURFUL CHARACTERS...

SILENCE, CRIMINAL! WE'LL WIPE THAT SMILE OFF YOUR FACE.

FOREVER!

NEXT WEEK = MIND-WIPE!

Stan Lee presents

DOCTOR WHO

CITY OF THE DAMNED

THE DOCTOR HAS ARRIVED IN AN ALIEN CITY WHERE THE INHABITANTS ARE FORBIDDEN TO FEEL EMOTION. THERE HE IS CAPTURED BY THE CITY'S POLICE — THE SINISTER MODERATORS — WHO GRASP HIM WITH STRANGE GAUNTLETS —

DEMATERIALISING!

SCRIPT: MILLS & WAGNER   ART: DAVE GIBBON

THEN...

OHO, HERE WE ARE AGAIN! SOME SORT OF PRIMITIVE *MATTER TRANS- MITTER,* IF I'M NOT MISTAKEN!

YOU REALLY SHOULD HAVE WARNED ME! I LIKE TO SUCK A JELLY BABY IN FLIGHT--STOPS THE EARS POPPING!

SILENCE! YOU ARE IN *THE WATCHTOWER,* WHERE WE MODERATORS WATCH OVER THE CITY!

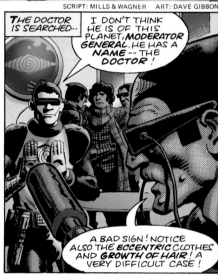

THE DOCTOR IS SEARCHED--

I DON'T THINK HE IS OF THIS PLANET, *MODERATOR GENERAL.* HE HAS A *NAME* -- THE *DOCTOR*!

A BAD SIGN! NOTICE ALSO THE *ECCENTRIC* CLOTHES AND *GROWTH OF HAIR*! A VERY DIFFICULT CASE!

A STRANGE ASSORTMENT OF JUNK COMES FROM THE DOCTOR'S POCKETS...

PILLS?

FOR *SPANISH TUMMY.* I WAS GOING TO BENI- DORM. SEEMS SO LONG AGO NOW...

THAT'S *JUNDIAN* -- SEVENTH PLANET OF THE VORLAG SYSTEM. A *SPEEDING TICKET*-- THOUGH I STILL SAY I WASN'T DOING A *GRUMMA* OVER FORTY!

CAREFUL! THAT WILL *GO OFF* IN YOUR HANDS!

TOO LATE!

COFFEE AND DONUTS! IT'S THE LATEST IN INSTANT FOOD FROM THE PLANET EARTH. DO YOU *DUNK*?

DUNKING IS NOT PERMITTED!

YOUR SENSE OF HUMOUR IS *HIGHLY ILLEGAL*.

EVERYTHING SEEMS TO BE ILLEGAL IN THIS CITY!

THERE IS ONLY *ONE* CRIME --*THE CRIME OF EMOTION!*

YOU ARE AN OUTSIDER, DOCTOR. YOU DO NOT UNDERSTAND THE *MIRACLE* OF OUR SOCIETY...

THE MODERATOR GENERAL EXPLAINS...

LONG AGO, WE OF THE PLANET *ZOM* WERE A *VIOLENT, CRIMINAL* RACE! A RACE *DAMNED* BY OUR OWN PETTY *LOVES* AND *HATES*. OUR *GREED*. OUR *DESIRES*.

THEN OUR RULING *BRAINS TRUST* FOUND THE ANSWER. ALL CRIME WAS CAUSED BY *EMOTION*--THERE-FORE EMOTION ITSELF *MUST BE OUTLAWED!*

'IT WAS A *HUGE* TASK. FIRST, THE CITY OF *ZOMBOS* WAS BUILT, HIGH ABOVE THE DISTURBING INFLUENCES OF THE LAND.

THE PEOPLE DID NOT WANT TO COME HERE, BUT THE MODERATORS KEPT THEM IN LINE. IT WAS FOR THEIR *OWN* GOOD.

IN THE CITY, EMOTION WAS RUTHLESSLY DESTROYED. NAMES WERE REPLACED BY *NUMBERS*. FACIAL EXPRESSION WAS *BANNED*.

MARRIAGES WERE CHOSEN BY MODERATORS TO AVOID THE POSSIBILITY OF *AFFECTION* BETWEEN COUPLES. AND MORE, MUCH MORE.

EVEN THEN, EMOTION WOULD NOT DIE. ZOMBANS WERE PRACTISING IT LATE AT NIGHT IN SECRET PLACES. IT WAS THE *BRAINS TRUST* WHO FOUND THE *FINAL SOLUTION*--

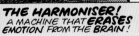

THE HARMONISER! A MACHINE THAT *ERASES* EMOTION FROM THE BRAIN!

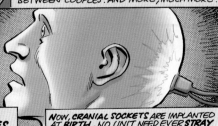

NOW, CRANIAL SOCKETS ARE IMPLANTED AT *BIRTH*. NO UNIT NEED EVER *STRAY* FROM THE *WAY OF HARMONY*.'

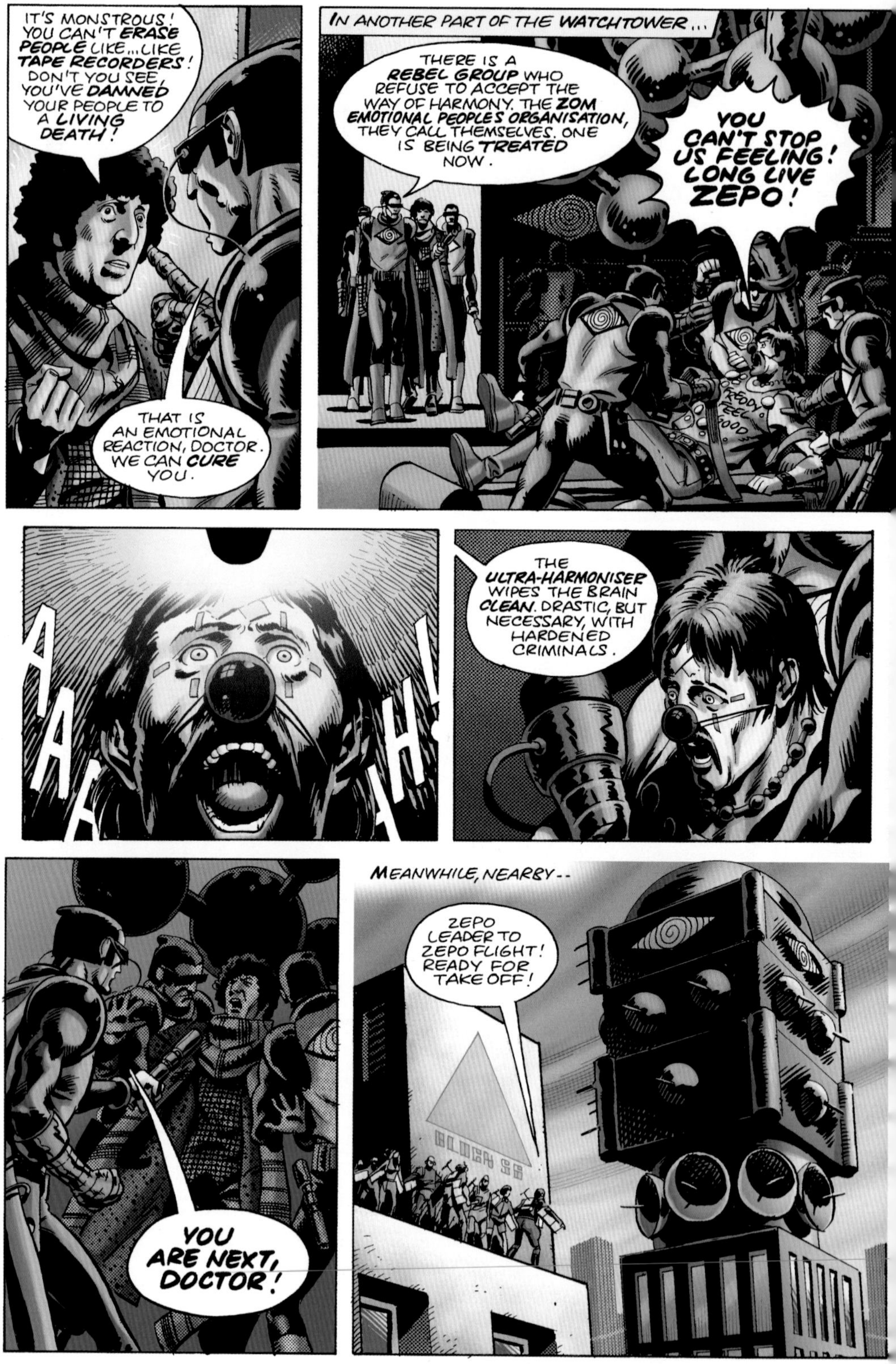

IT'S MONSTROUS! YOU CAN'T ERASE PEOPLE LIKE... LIKE TAPE RECORDERS! DON'T YOU SEE, YOU'VE DANNED YOUR PEOPLE TO A LIVING DEATH!
THAT IS AN EMOTIONAL REACTION, DOCTOR. WE CAN CURE YOU.
IN ANOTHER PART OF THE WATCHTOWER...
THERE IS A REBEL GROUP WHO REFUSE TO ACCEPT THE WAY OF HARMONY. THE ZOM EMOTIONAL PEOPLES ORGANISATION, THEY CALL THEMSELVES. ONE IS BEING TREATED NOW.
YOU CAN'T STOP US FEELING! LONG LIVE ZEPO!
AAAH!
THE ULTRA-HARMONISER WIPES THE BRAIN CLEAN. DRASTIC, BUT NECESSARY, WITH HARDENED CRIMINALS.
YOU ARE NEXT, DOCTOR!
MEANWHILE, NEARBY--
ZEPO LEADER TO ZEPO FLIGHT! READY FOR TAKE OFF!

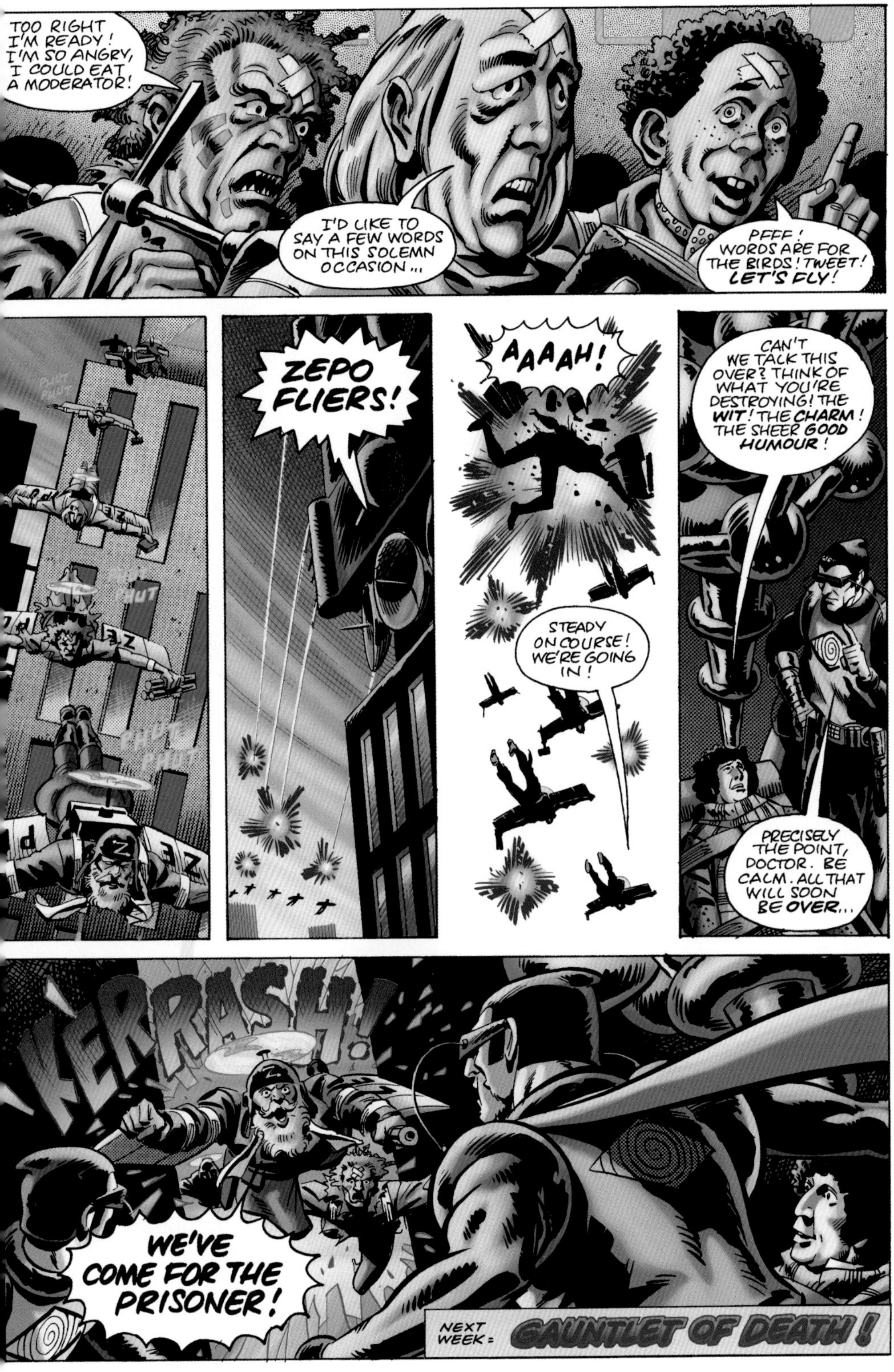
TOO RIGHT I'M READY! I'M SO ANGRY, I COULD EAT A MODERATOR!
I'D LIKE TO SAY A FEW WORDS ON THIS SOLEMN OCCASION...
PFFF! WORDS ARE FOR THE BIRDS! TWEET! LET'S FLY!
PHUT PHUT
PHUT PHUT
PHUT PHUT
ZEPO FLIERS!
AAAAH!
STEADY ON COURSE! WE'RE GOING IN!
CAN'T WE TACK THIS OVER? THINK OF WHAT YOU'RE DESTROYING! THE WIT! THE CHARM! THE SHEER GOOD HUMOUR!
PRECISELY THE POINT, DOCTOR. BE CALM. ALL THAT WILL SOON BE OVER...
KERRASH!
WE'VE COME FOR THE PRISONER!
NEXT WEEK: GAUNTLET OF DEATH!

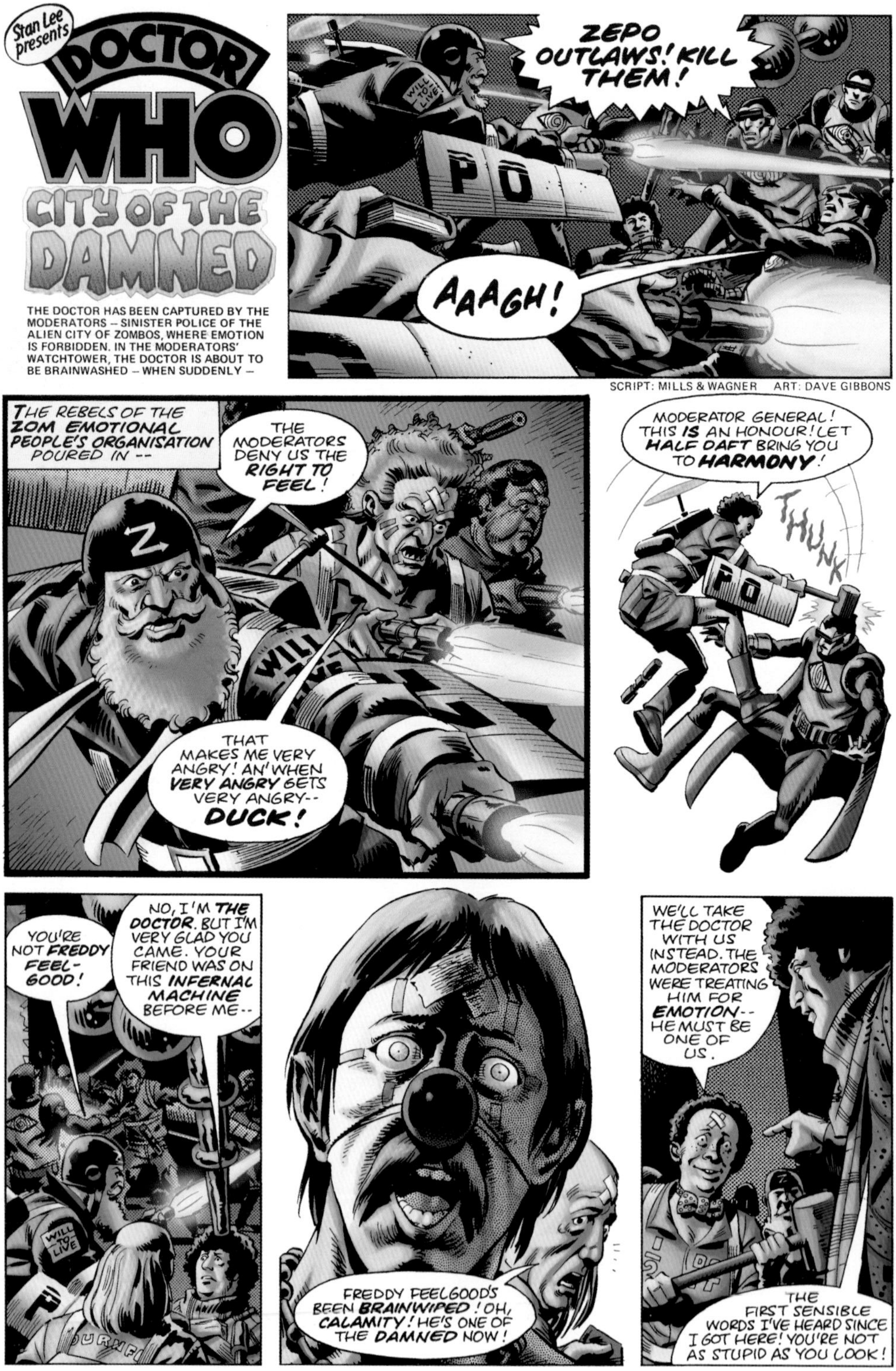
Stan Lee presents
DOCTOR WHO
CITY OF THE DAMNED
THE DOCTOR HAS BEEN CAPTURED BY THE MODERATORS -- SINISTER POLICE OF THE ALIEN CITY OF ZOMBOS, WHERE EMOTION IS FORBIDDEN. IN THE MODERATORS' WATCHTOWER, THE DOCTOR IS ABOUT TO BE BRAINWASHED -- WHEN SUDDENLY --
ZEPO OUTLAWS! KILL THEM!
AAAGH!
SCRIPT: MILLS & WAGNER ART: DAVE GIBBONS
THE REBELS OF THE ZOM EMOTIONAL PEOPLE'S ORGANISATION POURED IN --
THE MODERATORS DENY US THE RIGHT TO FEEL!
THAT MAKES ME VERY ANGRY! AN' WHEN VERY ANGRY GETS VERY ANGRY-- DUCK!
MODERATOR GENERAL! THIS IS AN HONOUR! LET HALF DAFT BRING YOU TO HARMONY!
THUNK
YOU'RE NOT FREDDY FEEL-GOOD!
NO, I'M THE DOCTOR. BUT I'M VERY GLAD YOU CAME. YOUR FRIEND WAS ON THIS INFERNAL MACHINE BEFORE ME--
FREDDY FEELGOOD'S BEEN BRAINWIPED! OH, CALAMITY! HE'S ONE OF THE DAMNED NOW!
WE'LL TAKE THE DOCTOR WITH US INSTEAD. THE MODERATORS WERE TREATING HIM FOR EMOTION-- HE MUST BE ONE OF US.
THE FIRST SENSIBLE WORDS I'VE HEARD SINCE I GOT HERE! YOU'RE NOT AS STUPID AS YOU LOOK!

THE DOCTOR STRAPS A MODERATOR'S MATTER TRANSMITTER TO THE ULTRA-HARMONISER --

THESE **MATTER TRANSMITTERS** GENERATE ONLY A **LIMITED** FIELD. SO WHEN I ACTIVATE IT--

I KNOW, BUT I **TRY.** SOMEDAY I HOPE TO GO **COMPLETELY** CRAZY.

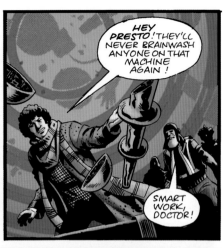

HEY **PRESTO!** THEY'LL NEVER BRAINWASH ANYONE ON THAT MACHINE AGAIN!

SMART WORK, DOCTOR!

PHUT PHUT

WE MUST FLY! YOU HAVE NOT USED HALF DAFT'S **WING** BEFORE...

HALF DAFT! THAT EXPLAINS THE DESIGN! MONSTROSITIES LIKE THIS COULD ONLY WORK ON A **LOW GRAVITY** PLANET.

OH, WELL, I'LL TRY ANYTHING ONCE...!

DOCTOR!

OH DEAR!

THIS ISN'T AS EASY--

AS IT LOOKS!

AH, THAT'S BETTER! GOT TO USE THE FEET LIKE A TAIL!

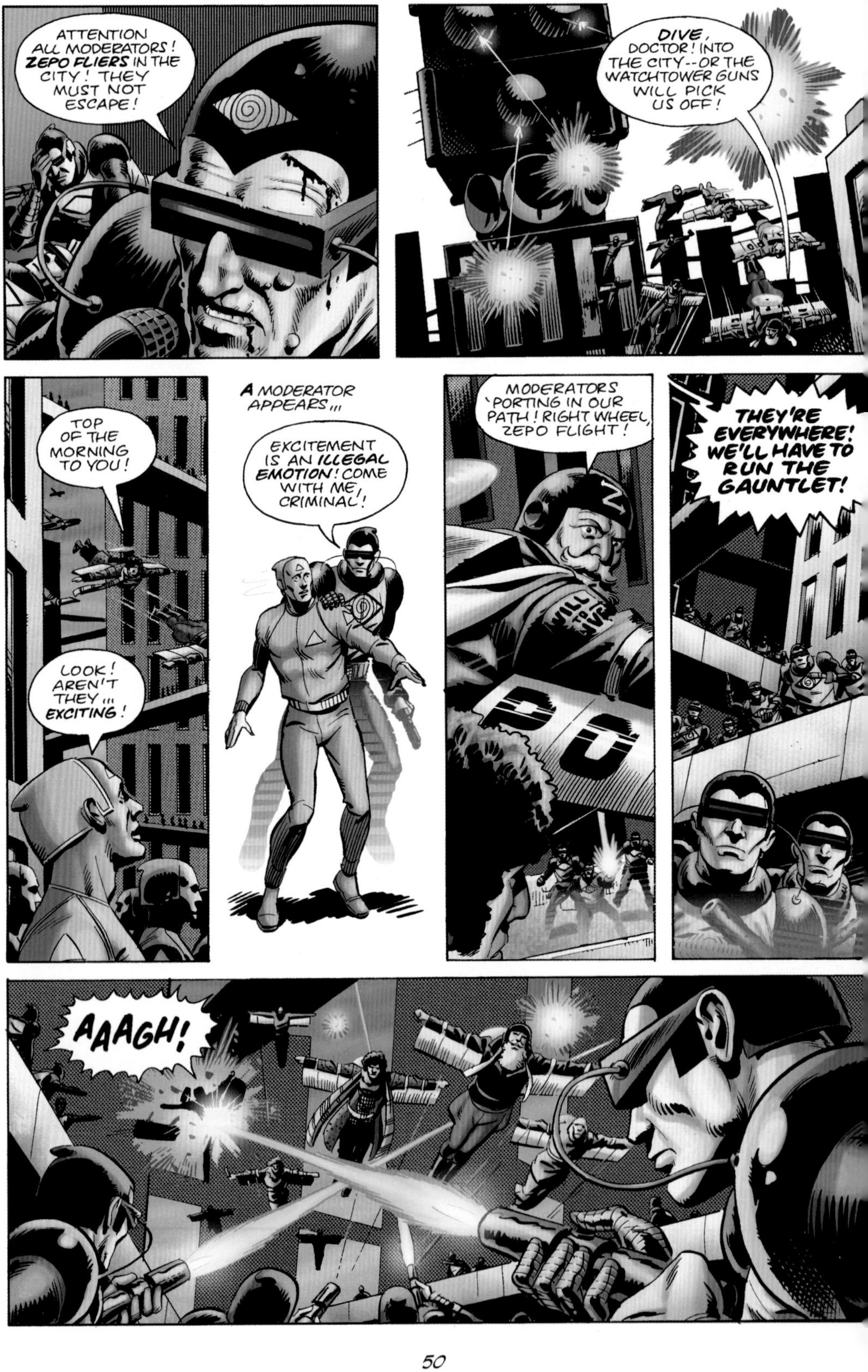
ATTENTION ALL MODERATORS! ZEPO FLIERS IN THE CITY! THEY MUST NOT ESCAPE!
DIVE, DOCTOR! INTO THE CITY--OR THE WATCHTOWER GUNS WILL PICK US OFF!
TOP OF THE MORNING TO YOU!
LOOK! AREN'T THEY... EXCITING!
A MODERATOR APPEARS...
EXCITEMENT IS AN ILLEGAL EMOTION! COME WITH ME, CRIMINAL!
MODERATORS 'PORTING IN OUR PATH! RIGHT WHEEL, ZEPO FLIGHT!
THEY'RE EVERYWHERE! WE'LL HAVE TO RUN THE GAUNTLET!
AAAGH!

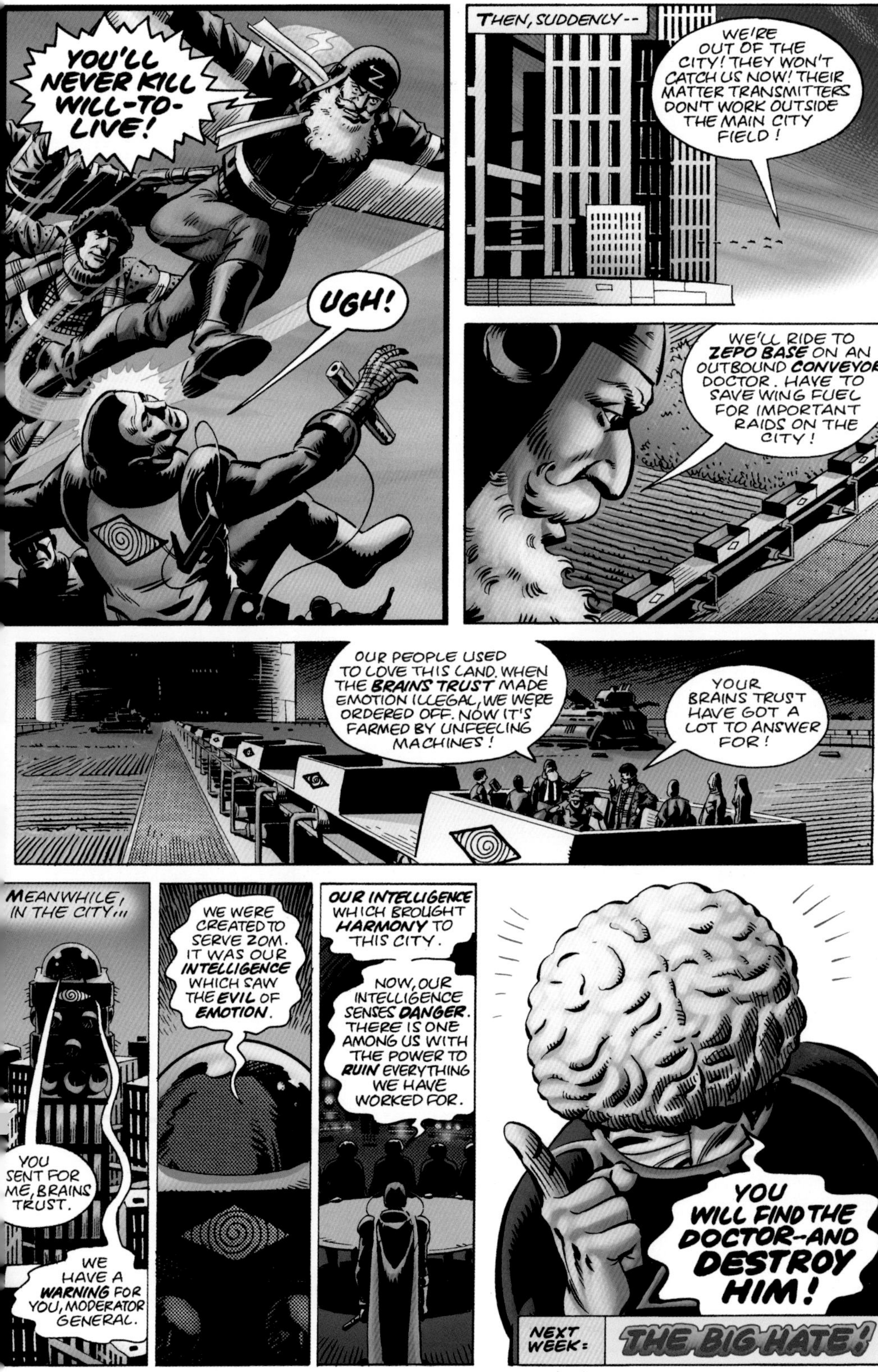

YOU'LL NEVER KILL WILL-TO-LIVE!
UGH!
THEN, SUDDENLY--
WE'RE OUT OF THE CITY! THEY WON'T CATCH US NOW! THEIR MATTER TRANSMITTERS DON'T WORK OUTSIDE THE MAIN CITY FIELD!
WE'LL RIDE TO ZEPO BASE ON AN OUTBOUND CONVEYOR, DOCTOR. HAVE TO SAVE WING FUEL FOR IMPORTANT RAIDS ON THE CITY!
OUR PEOPLE USED TO LOVE THIS LAND. WHEN THE BRAINS TRUST MADE EMOTION ILLEGAL, WE WERE ORDERED OFF. NOW IT'S FARMED BY UNFEELING MACHINES!
YOUR BRAINS TRUST HAVE GOT A LOT TO ANSWER FOR!
MEANWHILE, IN THE CITY...
YOU SENT FOR ME, BRAINS TRUST.
WE HAVE A WARNING FOR YOU, MODERATOR GENERAL.
WE WERE CREATED TO SERVE ZOM. IT WAS OUR INTELLIGENCE WHICH SAW THE EVIL OF EMOTION.
OUR INTELLIGENCE WHICH BROUGHT HARMONY TO THIS CITY.
NOW, OUR INTELLIGENCE SENSES DANGER. THERE IS ONE AMONG US WITH THE POWER TO RUIN EVERYTHING WE HAVE WORKED FOR.
YOU WILL FIND THE DOCTOR--AND DESTROY HIM!
NEXT WEEK: THE BIG HATE!

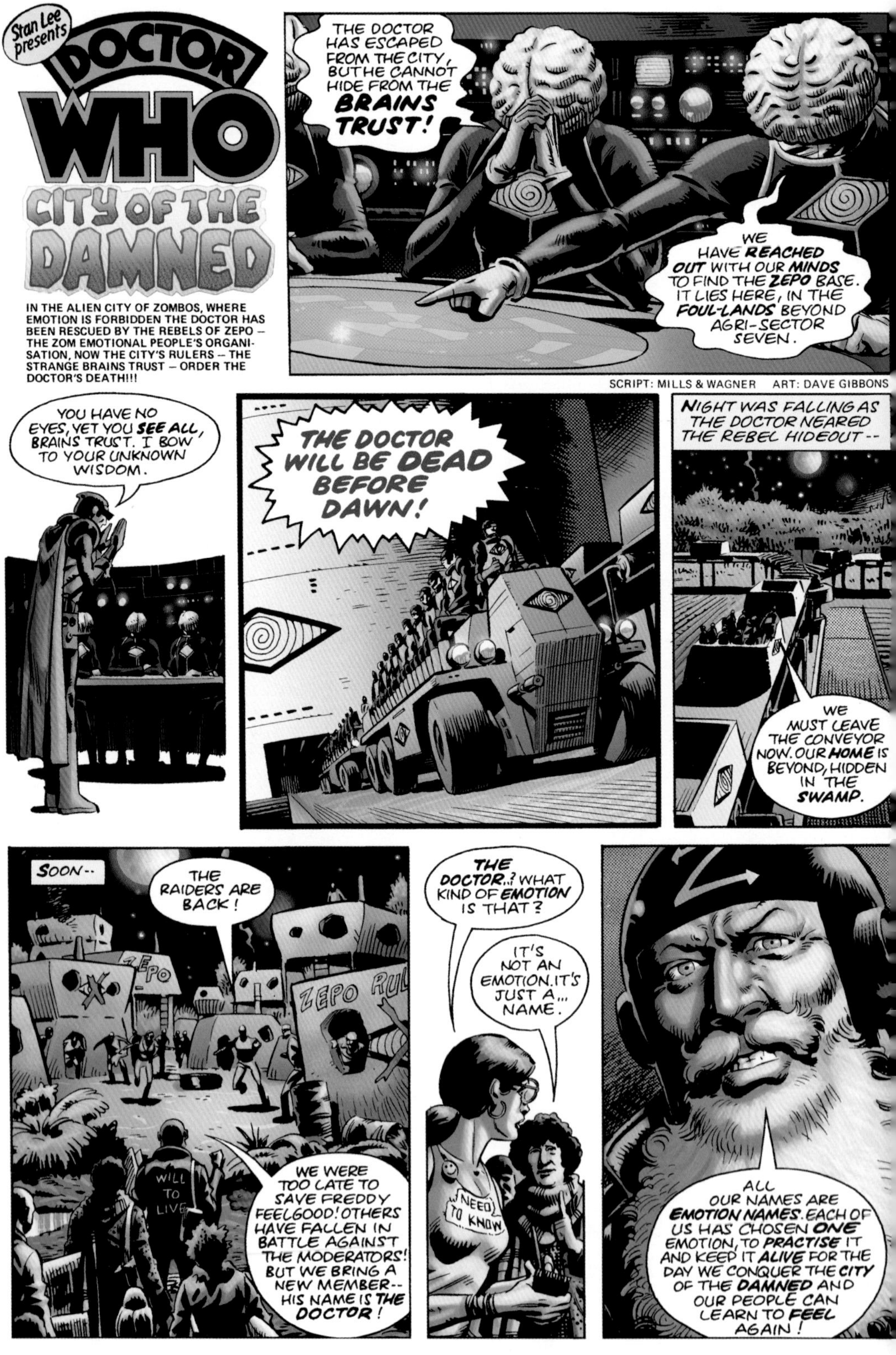
Stan Lee presents
DOCTOR WHO
CITY OF THE DAMNED
IN THE ALIEN CITY OF ZOMBOS, WHERE EMOTION IS FORBIDDEN THE DOCTOR HAS BEEN RESCUED BY THE REBELS OF ZEPO – THE ZOM EMOTIONAL PEOPLE'S ORGANISATION, NOW THE CITY'S RULERS – THE STRANGE BRAINS TRUST – ORDER THE DOCTOR'S DEATH!!!
THE DOCTOR HAS ESCAPED FROM THE CITY, BUT HE CANNOT HIDE FROM THE BRAINS TRUST!
WE HAVE REACHED OUT WITH OUR MINDS TO FIND THE ZEPO BASE. IT LIES HERE, IN THE FOUL-LANDS BEYOND AGRI-SECTOR SEVEN.
SCRIPT: MILLS & WAGNER ART: DAVE GIBBONS
YOU HAVE NO EYES, YET YOU SEE ALL, BRAINS TRUST. I BOW TO YOUR UNKNOWN WISDOM.
THE DOCTOR WILL BE DEAD BEFORE DAWN!
NIGHT WAS FALLING AS THE DOCTOR NEARED THE REBEL HIDEOUT --
WE MUST LEAVE THE CONVEYOR NOW. OUR HOME IS BEYOND, HIDDEN IN THE SWAMP.
SOON --
THE RAIDERS ARE BACK!
ZEPO
ZEPO RUL
WILL TO LIVE
WE WERE TOO LATE TO SAVE FREDDY FEELGOOD! OTHERS HAVE FALLEN IN BATTLE AGAINST THE MODERATORS! BUT WE BRING A NEW MEMBER -- HIS NAME IS THE DOCTOR!
THE DOCTOR..? WHAT KIND OF EMOTION IS THAT?
IT'S NOT AN EMOTION. IT'S JUST A... NAME.
NEED TO KNOW
ALL OUR NAMES ARE EMOTION NAMES. EACH OF US HAS CHOSEN ONE EMOTION, TO PRACTISE IT AND KEEP IT ALIVE FOR THE DAY WE CONQUER THE CITY OF THE DAMNED AND OUR PEOPLE CAN LEARN TO FEEL AGAIN!

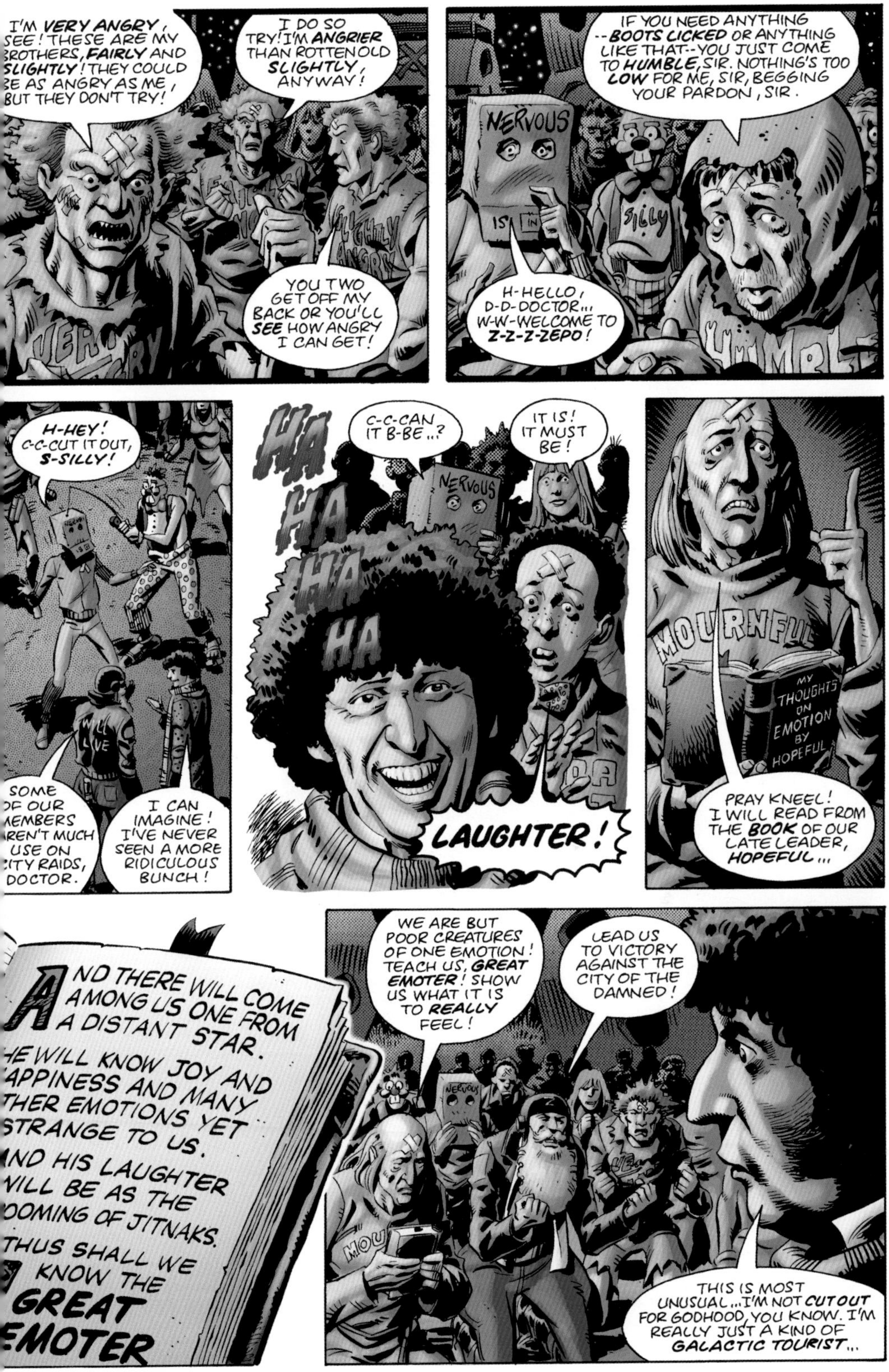
I'M VERY ANGRY, SEE! THESE ARE MY BROTHERS, FAIRLY AND SLIGHTLY! THEY COULD BE AS ANGRY AS ME, BUT THEY DON'T TRY!
I DO SO TRY! I'M ANGRIER THAN ROTTEN OLD SLIGHTLY, ANYWAY!
YOU TWO GET OFF MY BACK OR YOU'LL SEE HOW ANGRY I CAN GET!
IF YOU NEED ANYTHING --BOOTS LICKED OR ANYTHING LIKE THAT--YOU JUST COME TO HUMBLE, SIR. NOTHING'S TOO LOW FOR ME, SIR, BEGGING YOUR PARDON, SIR.
NERVOUS
SILLY
H-HELLO, D-D-DOCTOR... W-W-WELCOME TO Z-Z-Z-ZEPO!
H-HEY! C-C-CUT IT OUT, S-SILLY!
SOME OF OUR MEMBERS AREN'T MUCH USE ON CITY RAIDS, DOCTOR.
I CAN IMAGINE! I'VE NEVER SEEN A MORE RIDICULOUS BUNCH!
HA HA HA HA
C-C-CAN IT B-BE...?
IT IS! IT MUST BE!
LAUGHTER!
MOURNFUL
MY THOUGHTS ON EMOTION BY HOPEFUL
PRAY KNEEL! I WILL READ FROM THE BOOK OF OUR LATE LEADER, HOPEFUL...
AND THERE WILL COME AMONG US ONE FROM A DISTANT STAR.
HE WILL KNOW JOY AND HAPPINESS AND MANY OTHER EMOTIONS YET STRANGE TO US.
AND HIS LAUGHTER WILL BE AS THE COMING OF JITNAKS.
THUS SHALL WE KNOW THE GREAT EMOTER
WE ARE BUT POOR CREATURES OF ONE EMOTION! TEACH US, GREAT EMOTER! SHOW US WHAT IT IS TO REALLY FEEL!
LEAD US TO VICTORY AGAINST THE CITY OF THE DAMNED!
THIS IS MOST UNUSUAL... I'M NOT CUT OUT FOR GODHOOD, YOU KNOW. I'M REALLY JUST A KIND OF GALACTIC TOURIST...

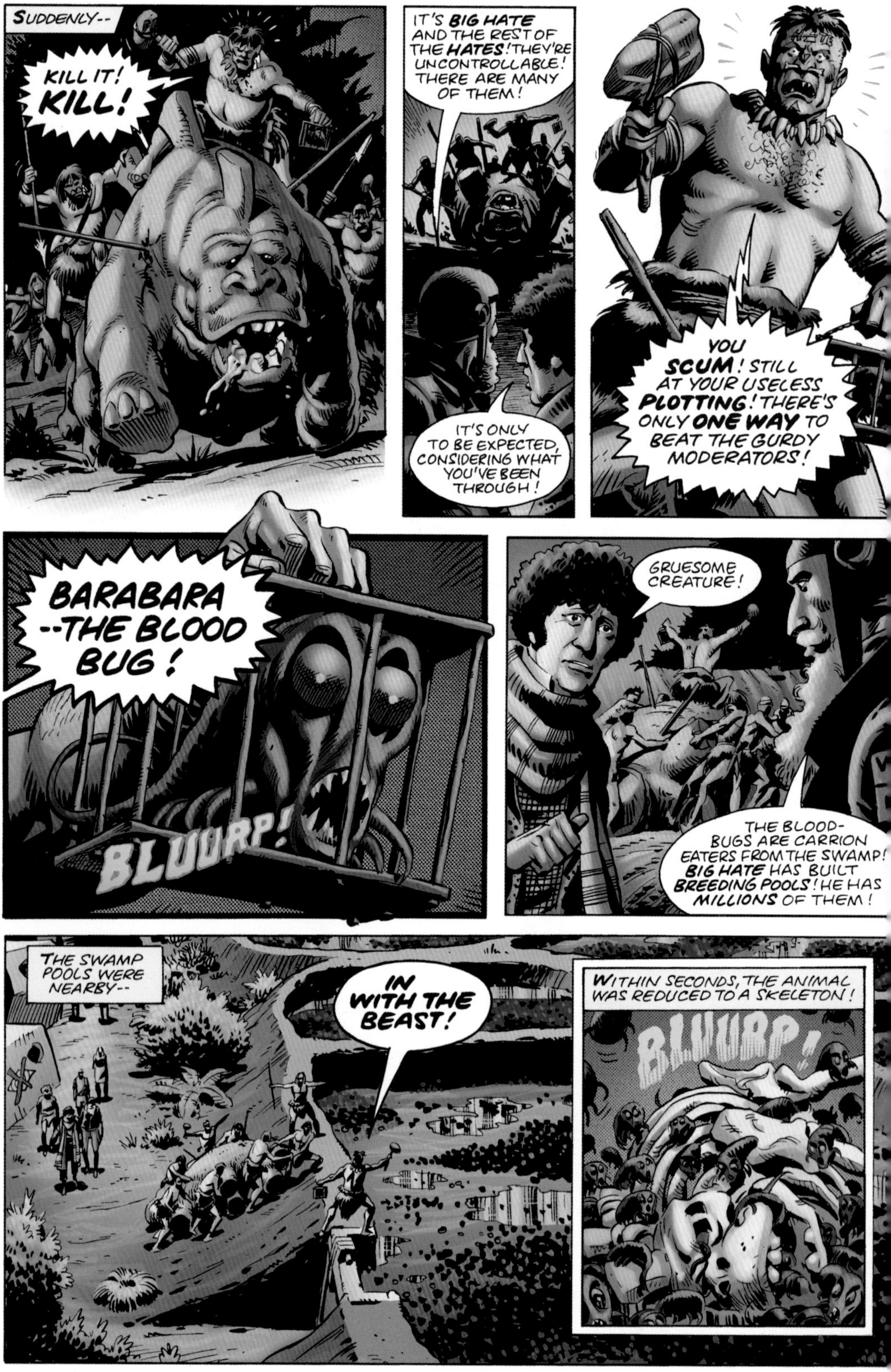

SUDDENLY--
KILL IT! KILL!
IT'S BIG HATE AND THE REST OF THE HATES! THEY'RE UNCONTROLLABLE! THERE ARE MANY OF THEM!
IT'S ONLY TO BE EXPECTED, CONSIDERING WHAT YOU'VE BEEN THROUGH!
YOU SCUM! STILL AT YOUR USELESS PLOTTING! THERE'S ONLY ONE WAY TO BEAT THE GURDY MODERATORS!
BARABARA --THE BLOOD BUG!
BLUURP!
GRUESOME CREATURE!
THE BLOOD-BUGS ARE CARRION EATERS FROM THE SWAMP! BIG HATE HAS BUILT BREEDING POOLS! HE HAS MILLIONS OF THEM!
THE SWAMP POOLS WERE NEARBY--
IN WITH THE BEAST!
WITHIN SECONDS, THE ANIMAL WAS REDUCED TO A SKELETON!
BLUURP!

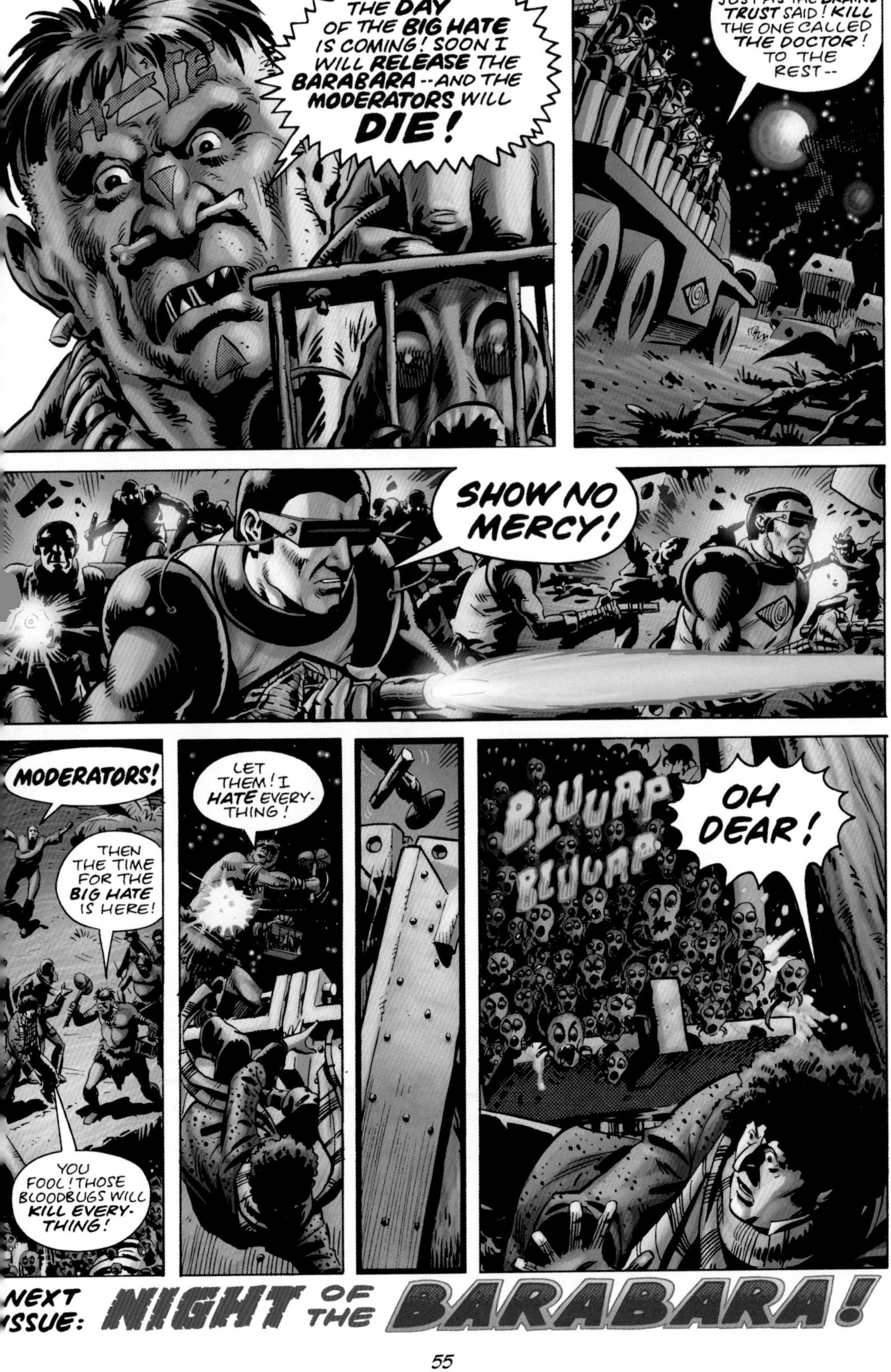
THE DAY OF THE BIG HATE IS COMING! SOON I WILL RELEASE THE BARABARA -- AND THE MODERATORS WILL DIE!
THE REBEL CAMP, JUST AS THE BRAINS TRUST SAID! KILL THE ONE CALLED THE DOCTOR! TO THE REST --
SHOW NO MERCY!
MODERATORS!
THEN THE TIME FOR THE BIG HATE IS HERE!
YOU FOOL! THOSE BLOODBUGS WILL KILL EVERY-THING!
LET THEM! I HATE EVERY-THING!
BLUURP
BLUURP
OH DEAR!

NEXT ISSUE: NIGHT OF THE BARABARA!

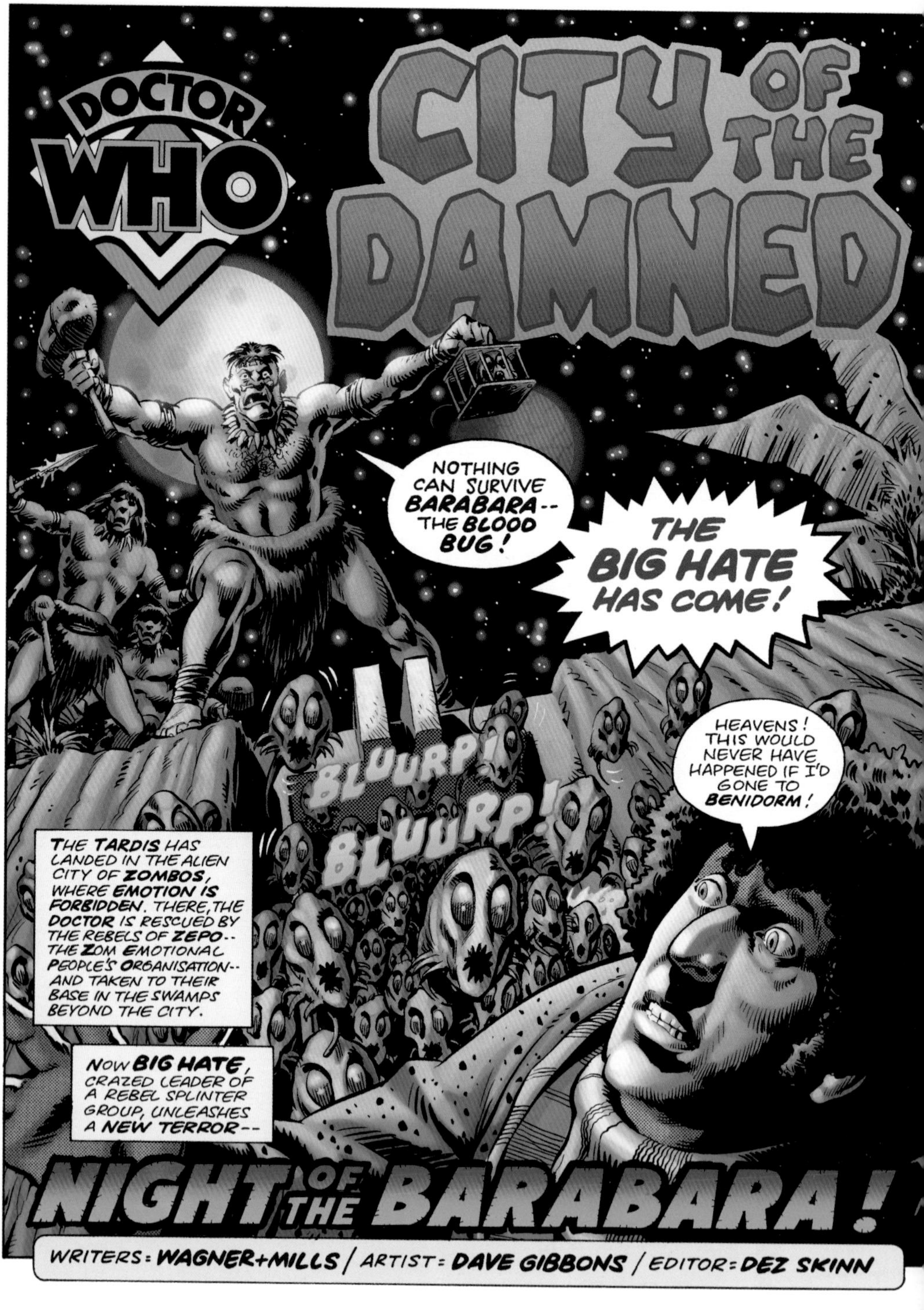

DOCTOR WHO
CITY OF THE DAMNED
NOTHING CAN SURVIVE BARABARA-- THE BLOOD BUG!
THE BIG HATE HAS COME!
BLUURP! BLUURP!
HEAVENS! THIS WOULD NEVER HAVE HAPPENED IF I'D GONE TO BENIDORM!
THE TARDIS HAS LANDED IN THE ALIEN CITY OF ZOMBOS, WHERE EMOTION IS FORBIDDEN. THERE, THE DOCTOR IS RESCUED BY THE REBELS OF ZEPO-- THE ZOM EMOTIONAL PEOPLE'S ORGANISATION-- AND TAKEN TO THEIR BASE IN THE SWAMPS BEYOND THE CITY.
NOW BIG HATE, CRAZED LEADER OF A REBEL SPLINTER GROUP, UNLEASHES A NEW TERROR--
NIGHT OF THE BARABARA!
WRITERS: WAGNER+MILLS / ARTIST: DAVE GIBBONS / EDITOR: DEZ SKINN

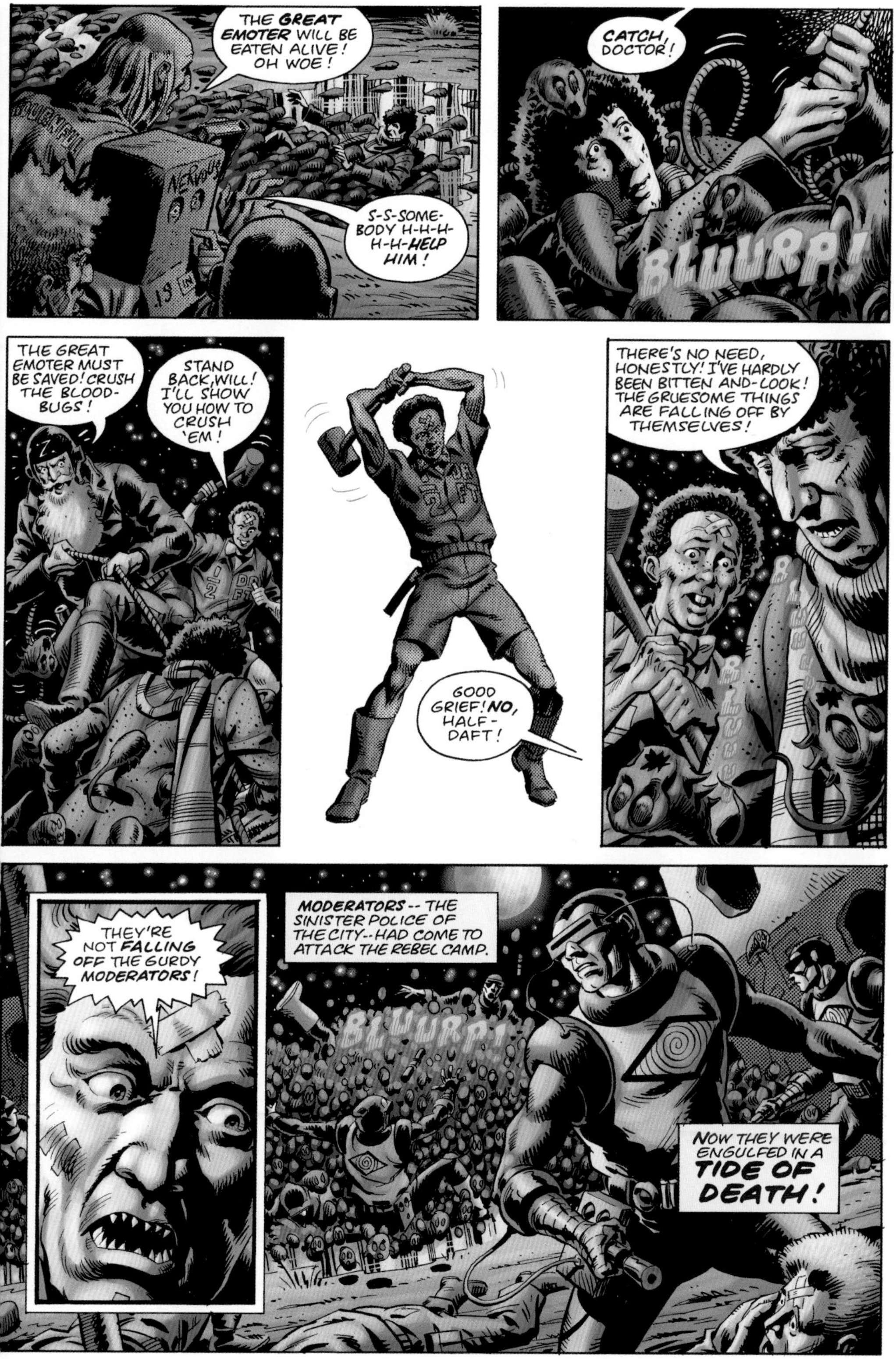
THE GREAT EMOTER WILL BE EATEN ALIVE! OH WOE!
S-S-SOME-BODY H-H-H-H-HELP HIM!
CATCH, DOCTOR!
BLUURP!
THE GREAT EMOTER MUST BE SAVED! CRUSH THE BLOOD-BUGS!
STAND BACK, WILL! I'LL SHOW YOU HOW TO CRUSH 'EM!
GOOD GRIEF! NO, HALF-DAFT!
THERE'S NO NEED, HONESTLY! I'VE HARDLY BEEN BITTEN AND-LOOK! THE GRUESOME THINGS ARE FALLING OFF BY THEMSELVES!
THEY'RE NOT FALLING OFF THE GURDY MODERATORS!
MODERATORS -- THE SINISTER POLICE OF THE CITY--HAD COME TO ATTACK THE REBEL CAMP.
BLUURP!
NOW THEY WERE ENGULFED IN A TIDE OF DEATH!

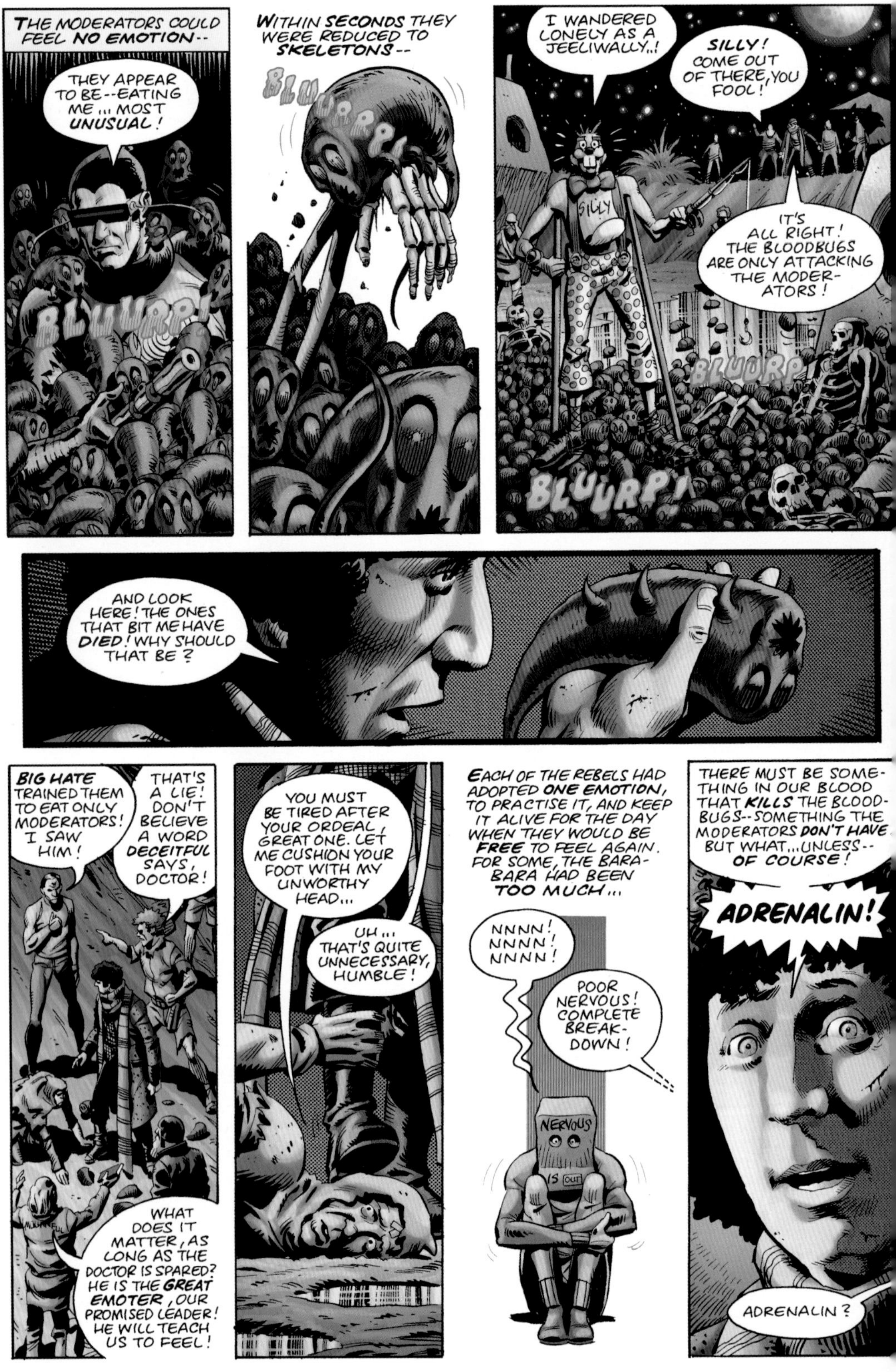

THE MODERATORS COULD FEEL NO EMOTION--
THEY APPEAR TO BE--EATING ME... MOST UNUSUAL!
BLUURP!
WITHIN SECONDS THEY WERE REDUCED TO SKELETONS--
BLUURRP!
I WANDERED LONELY AS A JEELIWALLY..!
SILLY! COME OUT OF THERE, YOU FOOL!
IT'S ALL RIGHT! THE BLOODBUGS ARE ONLY ATTACKING THE MODERATORS!
SILLY
BLUURP
BLUURP!
AND LOOK HERE! THE ONES THAT BIT ME HAVE DIED! WHY SHOULD THAT BE?
BIG HATE TRAINED THEM TO EAT ONLY MODERATORS! I SAW HIM!
THAT'S A LIE! DON'T BELIEVE A WORD DECEITFUL SAYS, DOCTOR!
WHAT DOES IT MATTER, AS LONG AS THE DOCTOR IS SPARED? HE IS THE GREAT EMOTER, OUR PROMISED LEADER! HE WILL TEACH US TO FEEL!
YOU MUST BE TIRED AFTER YOUR ORDEAL, GREAT ONE. LET ME CUSHION YOUR FOOT WITH MY UNWORTHY HEAD...
UH... THAT'S QUITE UNNECESSARY, HUMBLE!
EACH OF THE REBELS HAD ADOPTED ONE EMOTION, TO PRACTISE IT, AND KEEP IT ALIVE FOR THE DAY WHEN THEY WOULD BE FREE TO FEEL AGAIN. FOR SOME, THE BARABARA HAD BEEN TOO MUCH...
NNNN! NNNN! NNNN!
POOR NERVOUS! COMPLETE BREAKDOWN!
NERVOUS
IS OUT
THERE MUST BE SOMETHING IN OUR BLOOD THAT KILLS THE BLOODBUGS--SOMETHING THE MODERATORS DON'T HAVE BUT WHAT... UNLESS-- OF COURSE!
ADRENALIN!
ADRENALIN?

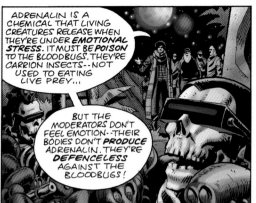

ADRENALIN IS A CHEMICAL THAT LIVING CREATURES RELEASE WHEN THEY'RE UNDER *EMOTIONAL STRESS.* IT MUST BE *POISON* TO THE BLOODBUGS, THEY'RE CARRION INSECTS--NOT USED TO EATING LIVE PREY...

BUT THE MODERATORS DON'T FEEL EMOTION--THEIR BODIES DON'T *PRODUCE* ADRENALIN. THEY'RE *DEFENCELESS* AGAINST THE BLOODBUGS!

AND SO IS THE *WHOLE CITY!* BIG HATE HAS GOT TO BE STOPPED!

BIG HATE AND HIS MEN HAD BEEN *BREEDING* THE BARABARA IN POOLS ABOVE THE CAMP--

YOU'RE TOO LATE, SCUM! NOBODY CAN STOP *THE BIG HATE* NOW!

BIG HATE'S STOLEN ONE OF THE GIANT *FARMING MACHINES!* HE'S SUCKING THE BLOODBUGS UP AND PROCESSING THEM LIKE KRAK-WHEAT!

BLUURP!

BLUURP!

YES, SCUM! I BUILT THAT BELT DOWN TO THE MAIN FOOD CONVEYORS! THEY'LL CARRY THE BLOOD-BUGS RIGHT INTO ZOMBOS! *THE CITY OF THE DAMNED IS DOOMED!*

FIELD SEAL

BLUURP!

HATE HAS TWISTED HIS MIND! WITH ME, *ZEPO!*

FOLLOW THE GREAT EMOTER!

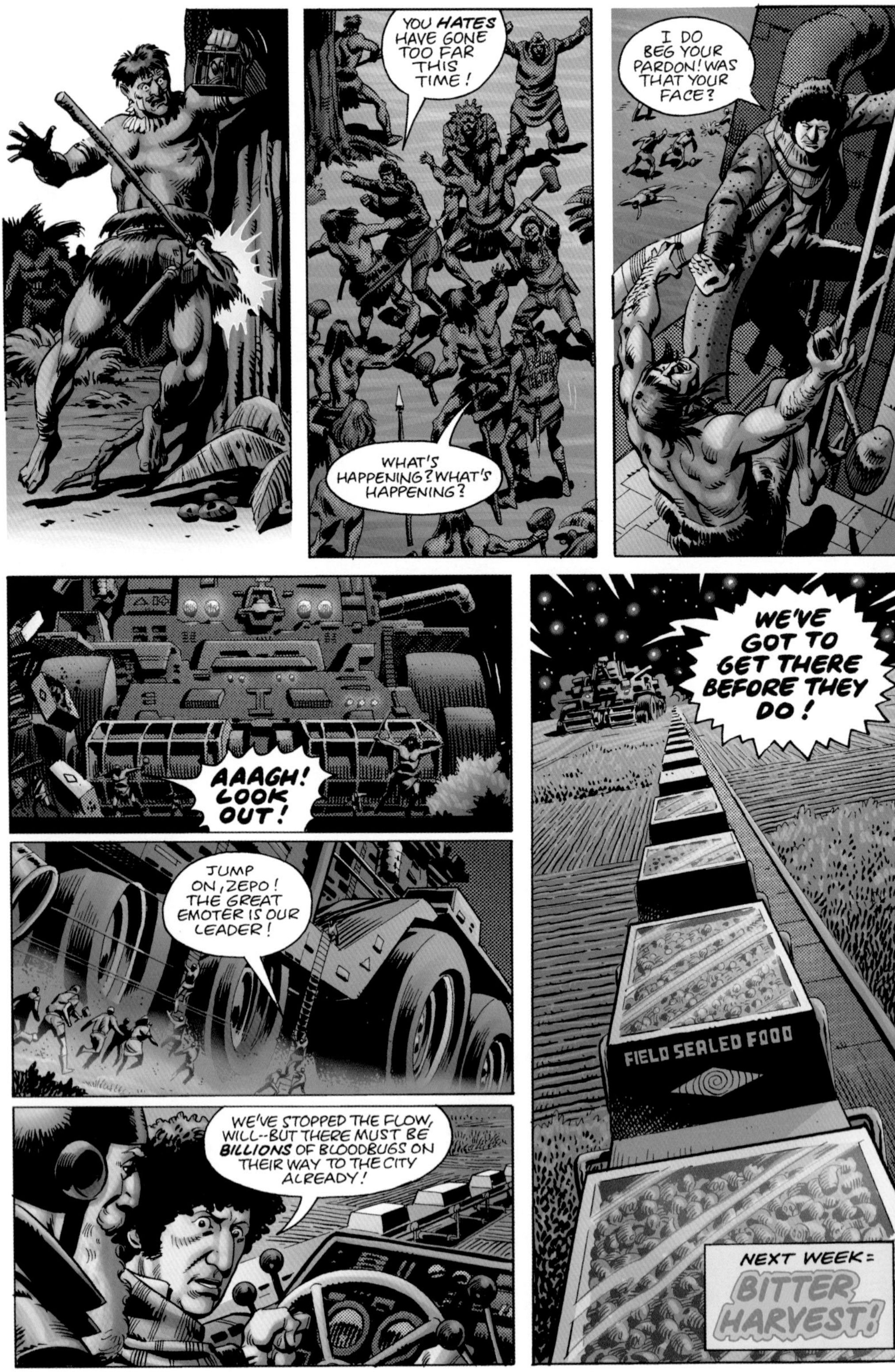
YOU HATES HAVE GONE TOO FAR THIS TIME!
WHAT'S HAPPENING? WHAT'S HAPPENING?
I DO BEG YOUR PARDON! WAS THAT YOUR FACE?
AAAGH! LOOK OUT!
JUMP ON, ZEPO! THE GREAT EMOTER IS OUR LEADER!
WE'VE STOPPED THE FLOW, WILL--BUT THERE MUST BE BILLIONS OF BLOODBUGS ON THEIR WAY TO THE CITY ALREADY!
WE'VE GOT TO GET THERE BEFORE THEY DO!
FIELD SEALED FOOD
NEXT WEEK: BITTER HARVEST!

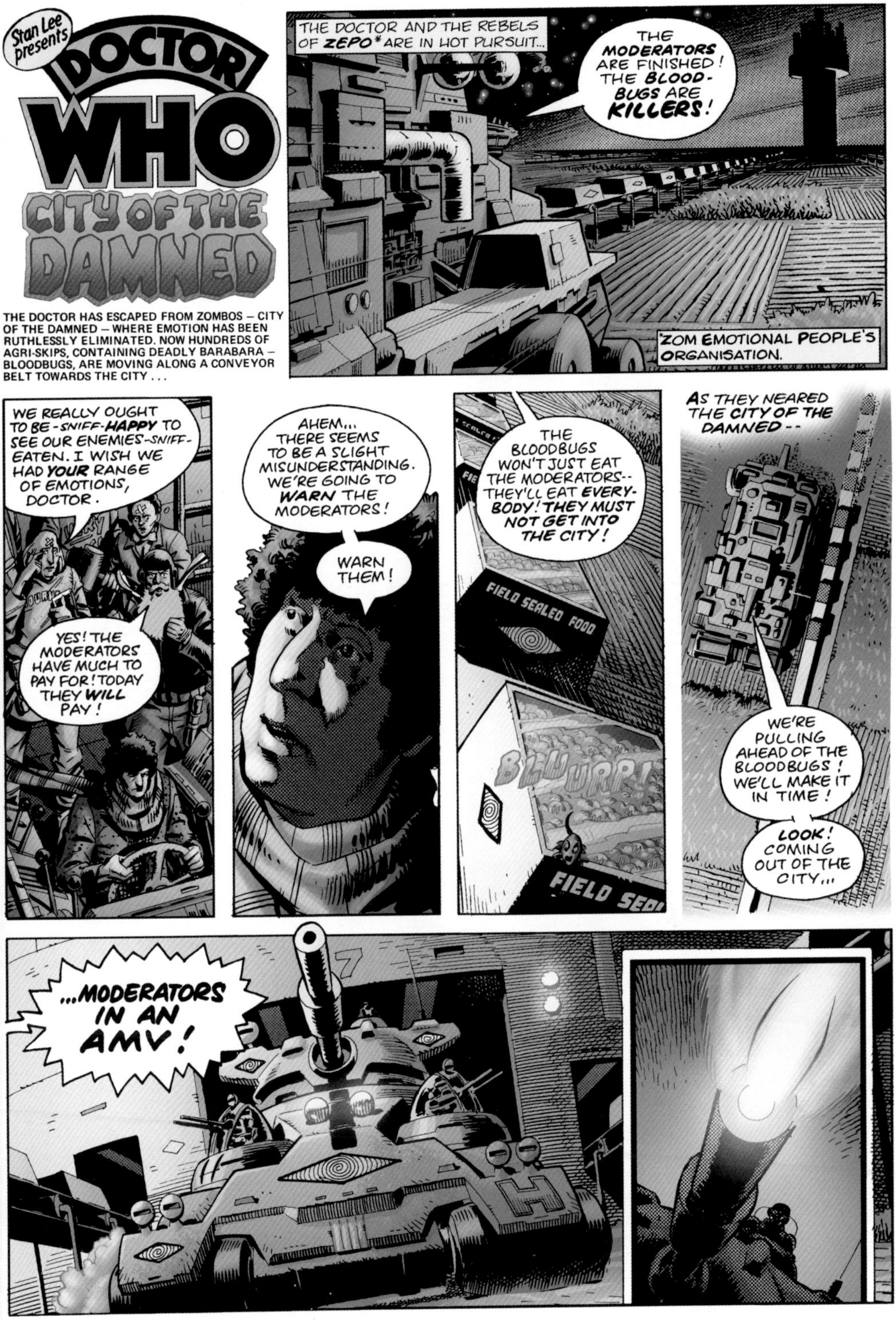
Stan Lee presents
DOCTOR WHO
CITY OF THE DAMNED
THE DOCTOR HAS ESCAPED FROM ZOMBOS – CITY OF THE DAMNED – WHERE EMOTION HAS BEEN RUTHLESSLY ELIMINATED. NOW HUNDREDS OF AGRI-SKIPS, CONTAINING DEADLY BARABARA – BLOODBUGS, ARE MOVING ALONG A CONVEYOR BELT TOWARDS THE CITY . . .
THE DOCTOR AND THE REBELS OF ZEPO* ARE IN HOT PURSUIT...
THE MODERATORS ARE FINISHED! THE BLOOD-BUGS ARE KILLERS!
*ZOM EMOTIONAL PEOPLE'S ORGANISATION.
WE REALLY OUGHT TO BE -SNIFF- HAPPY TO SEE OUR ENEMIES -SNIFF- EATEN. I WISH WE HAD YOUR RANGE OF EMOTIONS, DOCTOR.
YES! THE MODERATORS HAVE MUCH TO PAY FOR! TODAY THEY WILL PAY!
AHEM... THERE SEEMS TO BE A SLIGHT MISUNDERSTANDING. WE'RE GOING TO WARN THE MODERATORS!
WARN THEM!
THE BLOODBUGS WON'T JUST EAT THE MODERATORS-- THEY'LL EAT EVERY-BODY! THEY MUST NOT GET INTO THE CITY!
FIELD SEALED FOOD
BLURRP!
FIELD SEA
AS THEY NEARED THE CITY OF THE DAMNED--
WE'RE PULLING AHEAD OF THE BLOODBUGS! WE'LL MAKE IT IN TIME!
LOOK! COMING OUT OF THE CITY...
...MODERATORS IN AN AMV!

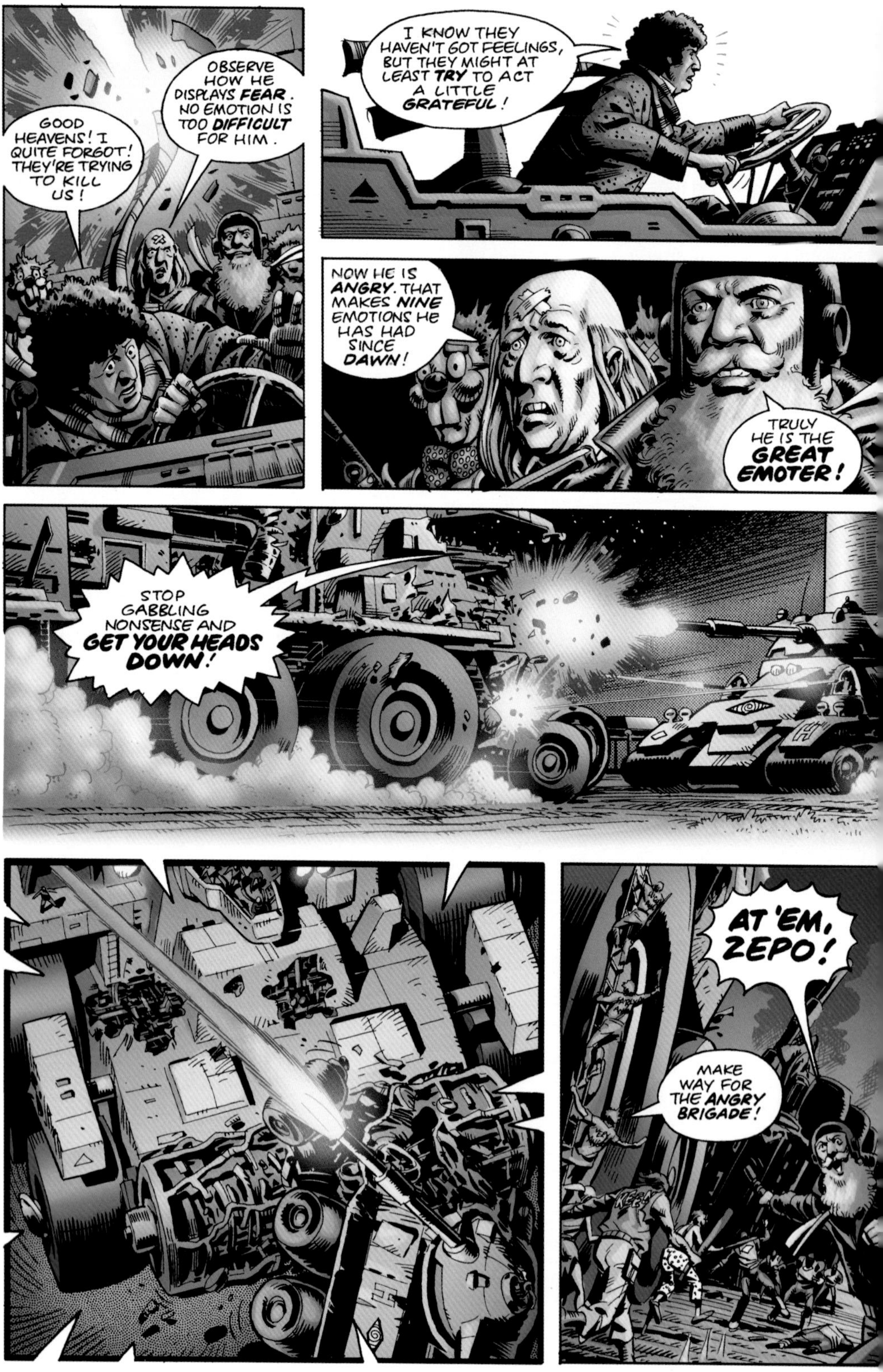
GOOD HEAVENS! I QUITE FORGOT! THEY'RE TRYING TO KILL US!
OBSERVE HOW HE DISPLAYS FEAR. NO EMOTION IS TOO DIFFICULT FOR HIM.
I KNOW THEY HAVEN'T GOT FEELINGS, BUT THEY MIGHT AT LEAST TRY TO ACT A LITTLE GRATEFUL!
NOW HE IS ANGRY. THAT MAKES NINE EMOTIONS HE HAS HAD SINCE DAWN!
TRULY HE IS THE GREAT EMOTER!
STOP GABBLING NONSENSE AND GET YOUR HEADS DOWN!
AT 'EM, ZEPO!
MAKE WAY FOR THE ANGRY BRIGADE!

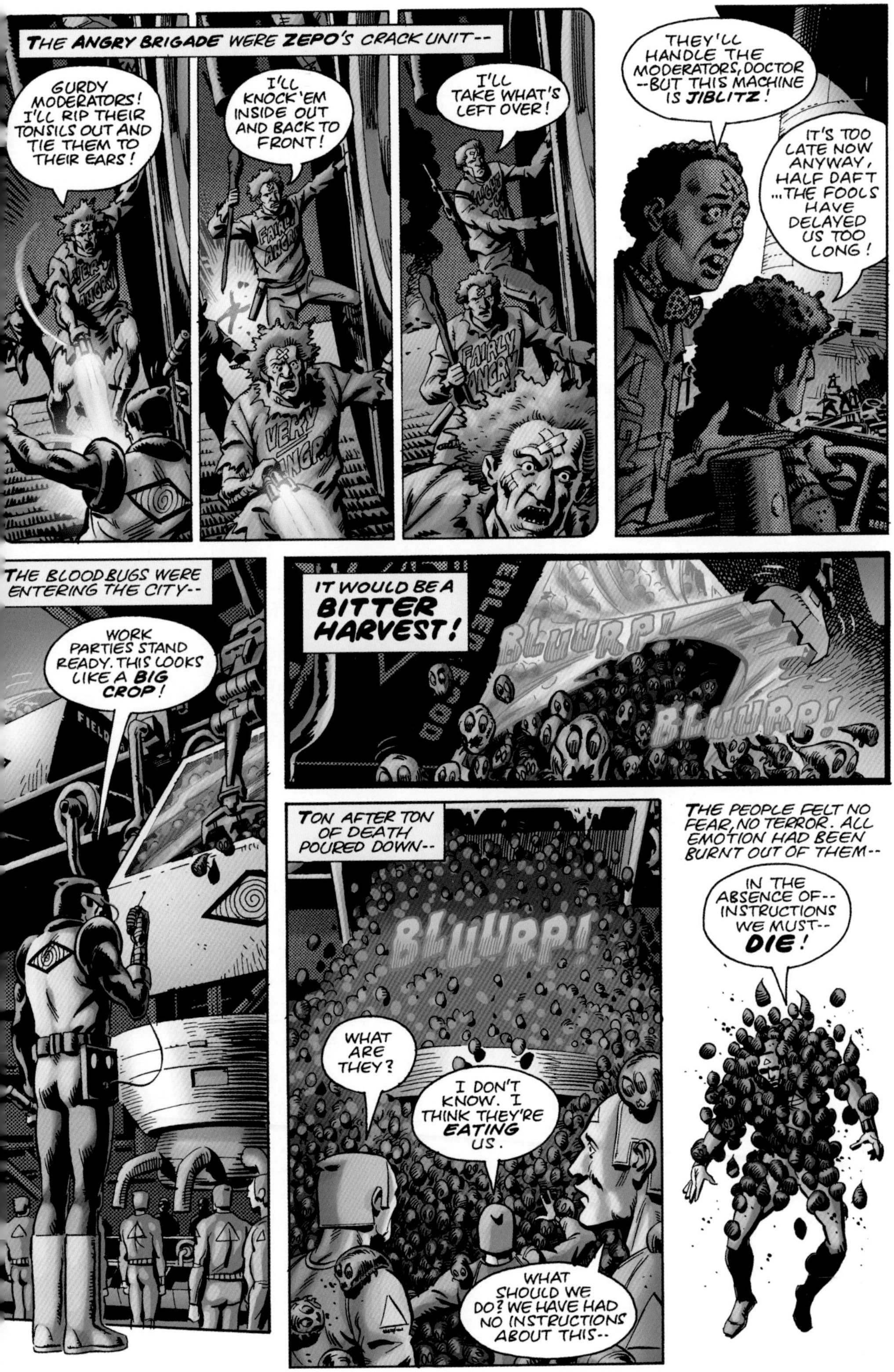
THE ANGRY BRIGADE WERE ZEPO'S CRACK UNIT--
GURDY MODERATORS! I'LL RIP THEIR TONSILS OUT AND TIE THEM TO THEIR EARS!
VERY ANGRY
I'LL KNOCK 'EM INSIDE OUT AND BACK TO FRONT!
FAIRLY ANGRY
VERY ANGRY
I'LL TAKE WHAT'S LEFT OVER!
FAIRLY ANGRY
THEY'LL HANDLE THE MODERATORS, DOCTOR --BUT THIS MACHINE IS JIBLITZ!
IT'S TOO LATE NOW ANYWAY, HALF DAFT ...THE FOOLS HAVE DELAYED US TOO LONG!
THE BLOODBUGS WERE ENTERING THE CITY--
WORK PARTIES STAND READY. THIS LOOKS LIKE A BIG CROP!
IT WOULD BE A BITTER HARVEST!
BLUURP!
BLUURP!
TON AFTER TON OF DEATH POURED DOWN--
BLUURP!
WHAT ARE THEY?
I DON'T KNOW. I THINK THEY'RE EATING US.
WHAT SHOULD WE DO? WE HAVE HAD NO INSTRUCTIONS ABOUT THIS--
THE PEOPLE FELT NO FEAR, NO TERROR. ALL EMOTION HAD BEEN BURNT OUT OF THEM--
IN THE ABSENCE OF-- INSTRUCTIONS WE MUST-- DIE!

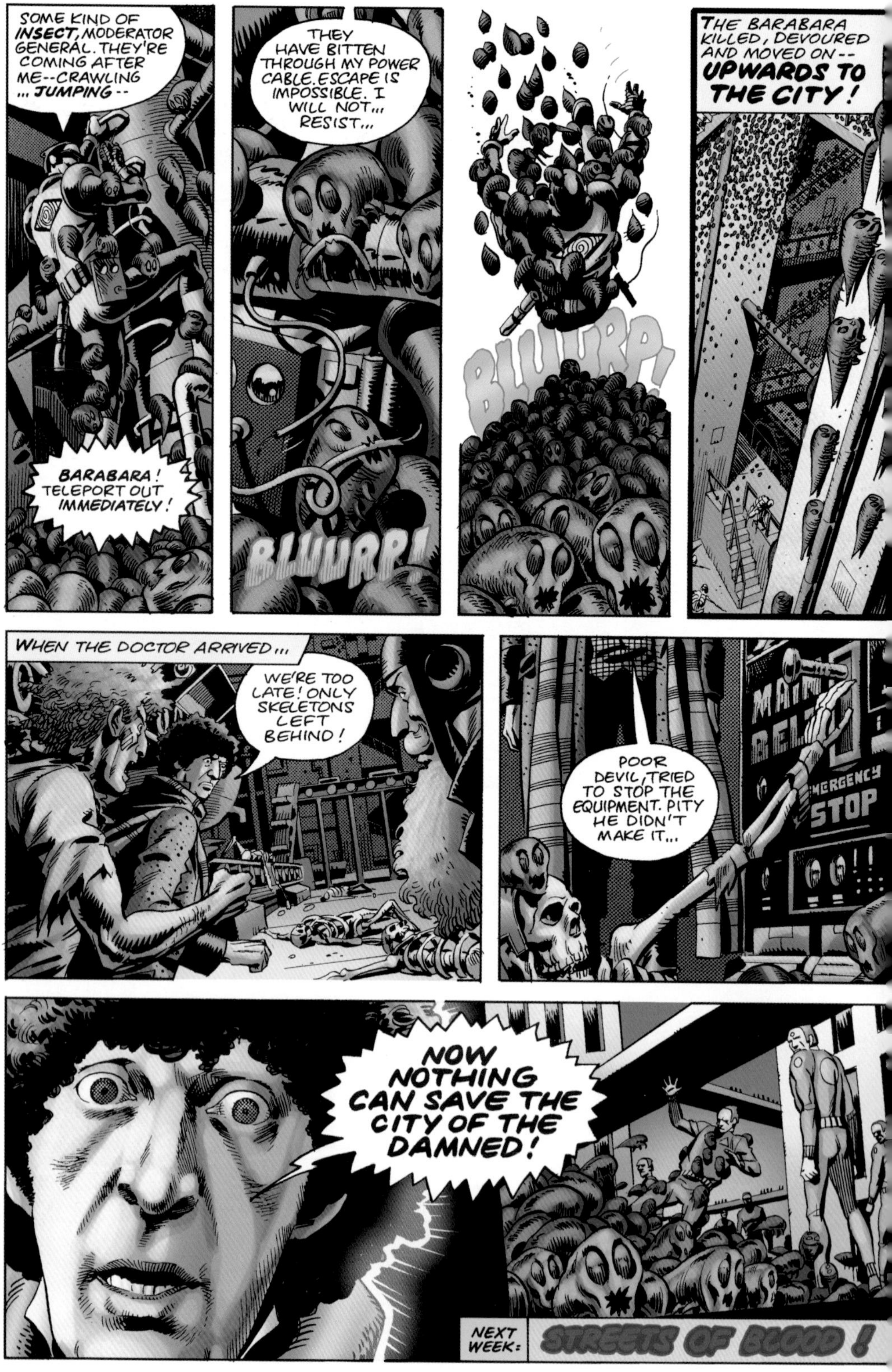

SOME KIND OF INSECT, MODERATOR GENERAL. THEY'RE COMING AFTER ME--CRAWLING ... JUMPING --
BARABARA! TELEPORT OUT IMMEDIATELY!
THEY HAVE BITTEN THROUGH MY POWER CABLE. ESCAPE IS IMPOSSIBLE. I WILL NOT... RESIST...
BLUURP!
BLUURP!
THE BARABARA KILLED, DEVOURED AND MOVED ON -- UPWARDS TO THE CITY!
WHEN THE DOCTOR ARRIVED...
WE'RE TOO LATE! ONLY SKELETONS LEFT BEHIND!
POOR DEVIL, TRIED TO STOP THE EQUIPMENT. PITY HE DIDN'T MAKE IT...
MERGENCY STOP
NOW NOTHING CAN SAVE THE CITY OF THE DAMNED!
NEXT WEEK:
STREETS OF BLOOD!

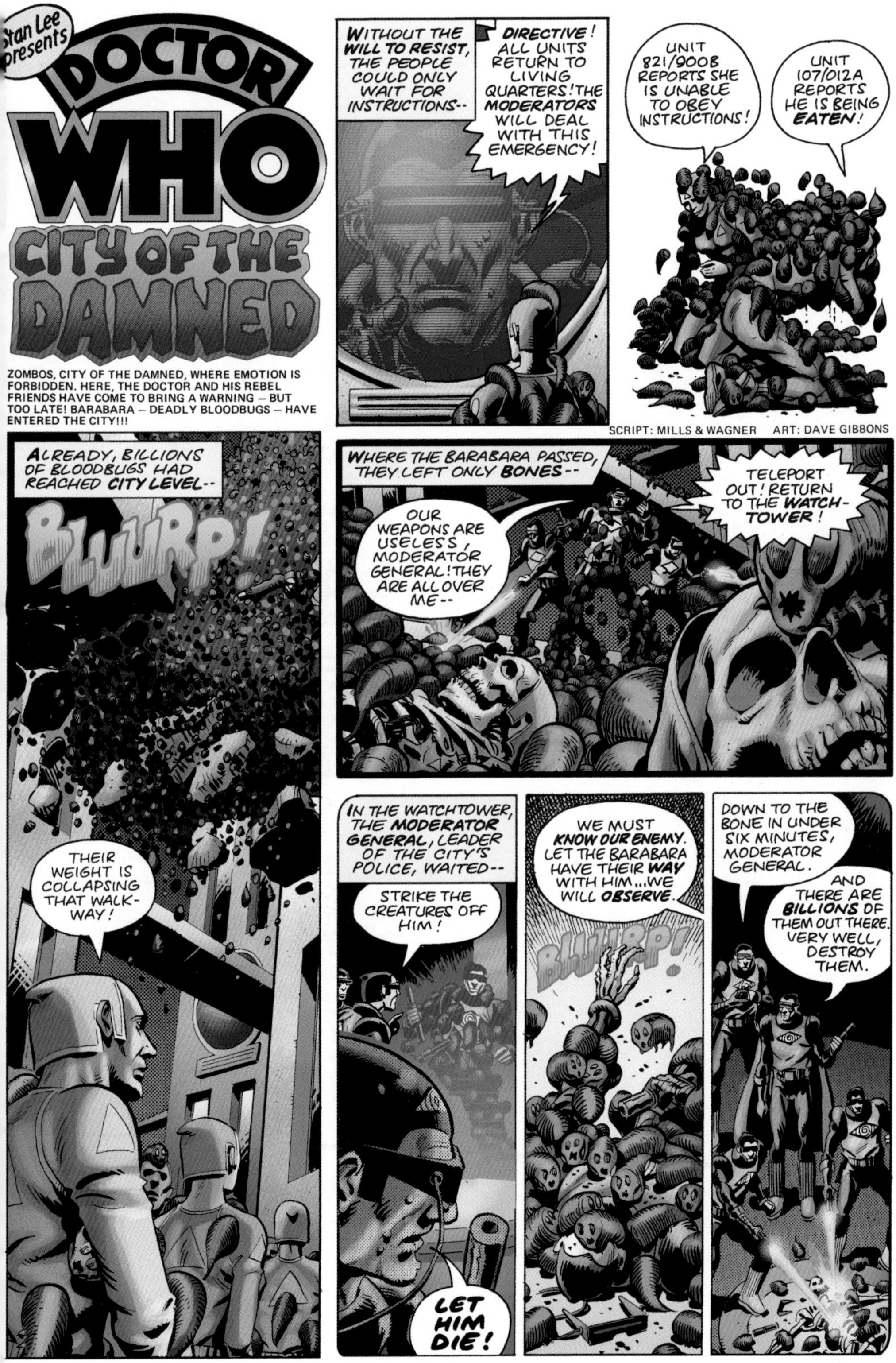

Stan Lee presents
DOCTOR WHO
CITY OF THE DAMNED
ZOMBOS, CITY OF THE DAMNED, WHERE EMOTION IS FORBIDDEN. HERE, THE DOCTOR AND HIS REBEL FRIENDS HAVE COME TO BRING A WARNING — BUT TOO LATE! BARABARA — DEADLY BLOODBUGS — HAVE ENTERED THE CITY!!!
WITHOUT THE WILL TO RESIST, THE PEOPLE COULD ONLY WAIT FOR INSTRUCTIONS--
DIRECTIVE! ALL UNITS RETURN TO LIVING QUARTERS! THE MODERATORS WILL DEAL WITH THIS EMERGENCY!
UNIT 821/900B REPORTS SHE IS UNABLE TO OBEY INSTRUCTIONS!
UNIT 107/012A REPORTS HE IS BEING EATEN!
SCRIPT: MILLS & WAGNER ART: DAVE GIBBONS
ALREADY, BILLIONS OF BLOODBUGS HAD REACHED CITY LEVEL--
BLUURP!
THEIR WEIGHT IS COLLAPSING THAT WALK-WAY!
WHERE THE BARABARA PASSED, THEY LEFT ONLY BONES--
OUR WEAPONS ARE USELESS, MODERATOR GENERAL! THEY ARE ALL OVER ME--
TELEPORT OUT! RETURN TO THE WATCH-TOWER!
IN THE WATCHTOWER, THE MODERATOR GENERAL, LEADER OF THE CITY'S POLICE, WAITED--
STRIKE THE CREATURES OFF HIM!
LET HIM DIE!
WE MUST KNOW OUR ENEMY. LET THE BARABARA HAVE THEIR WAY WITH HIM... WE WILL OBSERVE.
BLUURP!
DOWN TO THE BONE IN UNDER SIX MINUTES, MODERATOR GENERAL.
AND THERE ARE BILLIONS OF THEM OUT THERE. VERY WELL, DESTROY THEM.

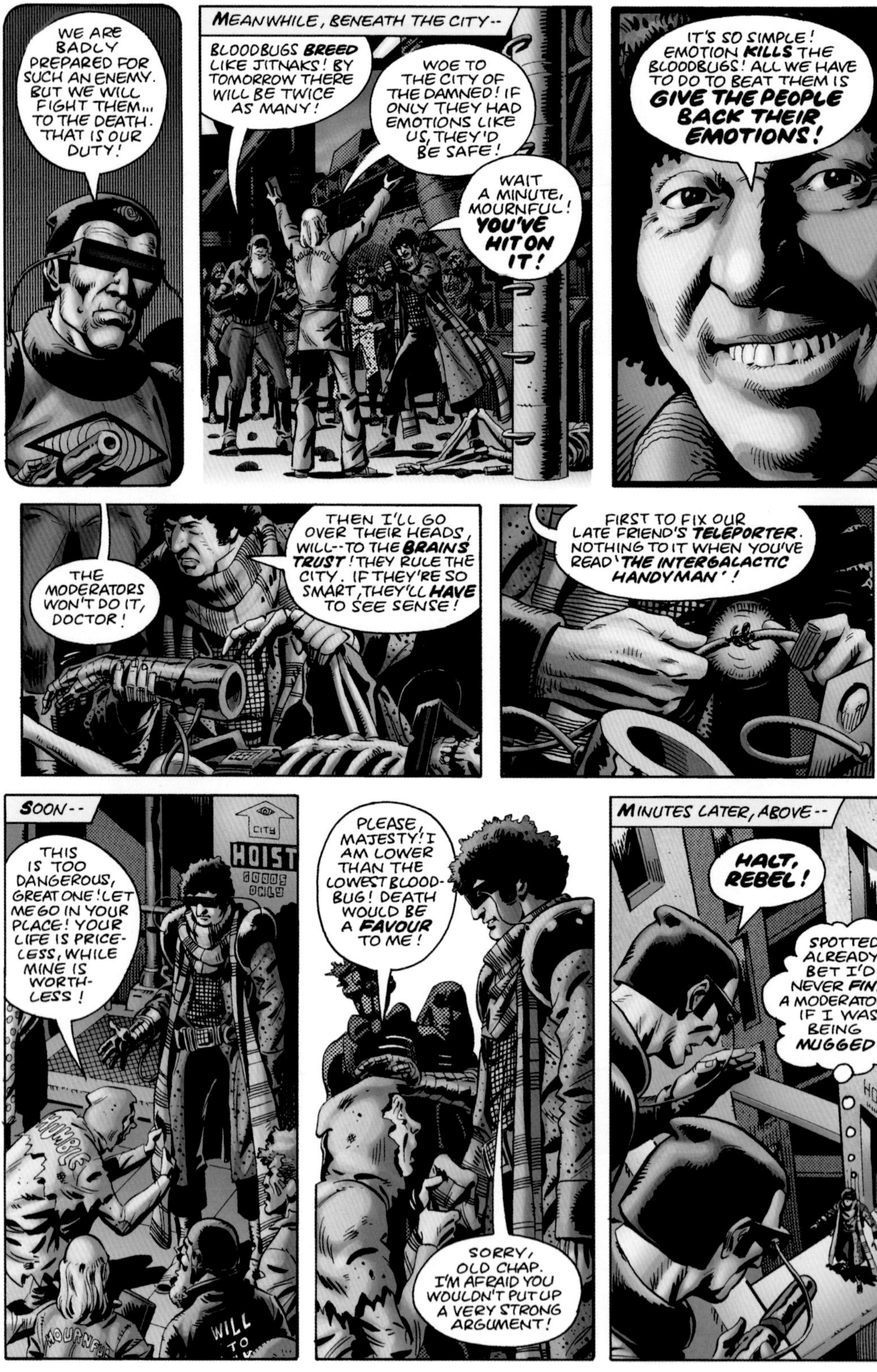
WE ARE BADLY PREPARED FOR SUCH AN ENEMY. BUT WE WILL FIGHT THEM... TO THE DEATH. THAT IS OUR DUTY!
MEANWHILE, BENEATH THE CITY--
BLOODBUGS BREED LIKE JITNAKS! BY TOMORROW THERE WILL BE TWICE AS MANY!
WOE TO THE CITY OF THE DAMNED! IF ONLY THEY HAD EMOTIONS LIKE US, THEY'D BE SAFE!
WAIT A MINUTE, MOURNFUL! YOU'VE HIT ON IT!
IT'S SO SIMPLE! EMOTION KILLS THE BLOODBUGS! ALL WE HAVE TO DO TO BEAT THEM IS GIVE THE PEOPLE BACK THEIR EMOTIONS!
THE MODERATORS WON'T DO IT, DOCTOR!
THEN I'LL GO OVER THEIR HEADS, WILL--TO THE BRAINS TRUST! THEY RULE THE CITY. IF THEY'RE SO SMART, THEY'LL HAVE TO SEE SENSE!
FIRST TO FIX OUR LATE FRIEND'S TELEPORTER. NOTHING TO IT WHEN YOU'VE READ 'THE INTERGALACTIC HANDYMAN'!
SOON--
CITY
HOIST
GOODS ONLY
THIS IS TOO DANGEROUS, GREAT ONE! LET ME GO IN YOUR PLACE! YOUR LIFE IS PRICELESS, WHILE MINE IS WORTHLESS!
PLEASE, MAJESTY! I AM LOWER THAN THE LOWEST BLOODBUG! DEATH WOULD BE A FAVOUR TO ME!
SORRY, OLD CHAP. I'M AFRAID YOU WOULDN'T PUT UP A VERY STRONG ARGUMENT!
MINUTES LATER, ABOVE--
HALT, REBEL!
SPOTTED ALREADY! BET I'D NEVER FIND A MODERATOR IF I WAS BEING MUGGED!

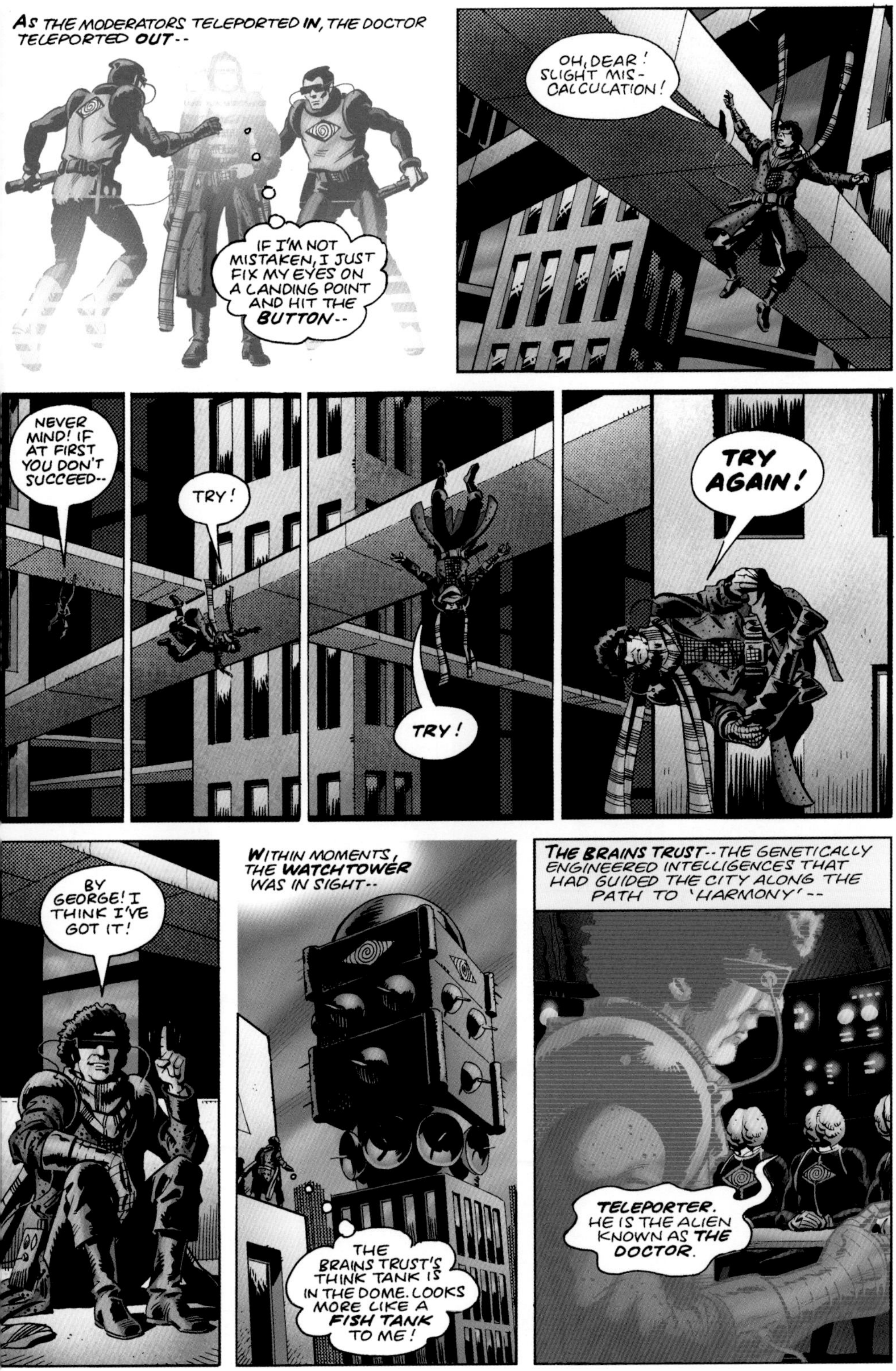
AS THE MODERATORS TELEPORTED IN, THE DOCTOR TELEPORTED OUT--
IF I'M NOT MISTAKEN, I JUST FIX MY EYES ON A LANDING POINT AND HIT THE BUTTON--
OH, DEAR! SLIGHT MIS-CALCULATION!
NEVER MIND! IF AT FIRST YOU DON'T SUCCEED--
TRY!
TRY!
TRY AGAIN!
BY GEORGE! I THINK I'VE GOT IT!
WITHIN MOMENTS, THE WATCHTOWER WAS IN SIGHT--
THE BRAINS TRUST'S THINK TANK IS IN THE DOME. LOOKS MORE LIKE A FISH TANK TO ME!
THE BRAINS TRUST--THE GENETICALLY ENGINEERED INTELLIGENCES THAT HAD GUIDED THE CITY ALONG THE PATH TO 'HARMONY'--
TELEPORTER. HE IS THE ALIEN KNOWN AS THE DOCTOR.

IT IS USELESS TO HARM US. OUR INTELLIGENCE IS ON FILE.

I'M NOT HERE TO HARM YOU! I'VE COME WITH INFORMATION THAT CAN SAVE THE CITY!

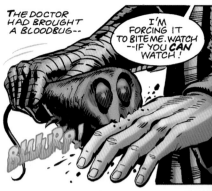

THE DOCTOR HAD BROUGHT A BLOODBUG--

I'M FORCING IT TO BITE ME. WATCH --IF YOU *CAN* WATCH!

BLLURP!

WE DO NOT NEED *EYES* TO SEE. THE CREATURE IS ...*DYING!*

INTERESTING, ISN'T IT? THE *ADRENALIN* IN MY BLOOD IS *POISON* TO IT! ADRENALIN THAT'S PRODUCED BECAUSE OF MY OWN *FEAR* AND *REVULSION* -- MY OWN *EMOTION!*

YOU HAVE THE EQUIPMENT! YOU CAN GIVE YOUR PEOPLE BACK THE EMOTIONS YOU STOLE FROM THEM! IT'S THEIR ONLY CHANCE!

WHAT YOU SAY ...MAKES SENSE. IT MEANS DESTROYING EVERYTHING WE HAVE BUILT...

SO BE IT. BETTER THAT THAN DESTROY OUR OWN PEOPLE.

SEND FOR THE *MODERATOR GENERAL!*

I AM HERE! AND I HAVE BEEN LISTENING, BRAINS TRUST! *I WILL NEVER ABANDON THE WAYS OF HARMONY!*

YOU WILL OBEY US!

WITHOUT EMOTION WE HAVE CREATED A WELL-ORDERED, OBEDIENT POPULATION. THERE IS *NO CRIME, NO STRIFE.* WE LIVE IN *HARMONY-- THE PERFECT SOCIETY!*

BETTER THAT WE *PERISH* THAN RETURN TO THE *EVIL* WAY OF *EMOTION!*

YOU HAVE OUTLIVED YOUR USEFULNESS, BRAINS TRUST! YOUR OWN WORDS HAVE CONVICTED YOU OF *TREASON!*

NO!

NEXT ISSUE: THE LAST HOURS!

68

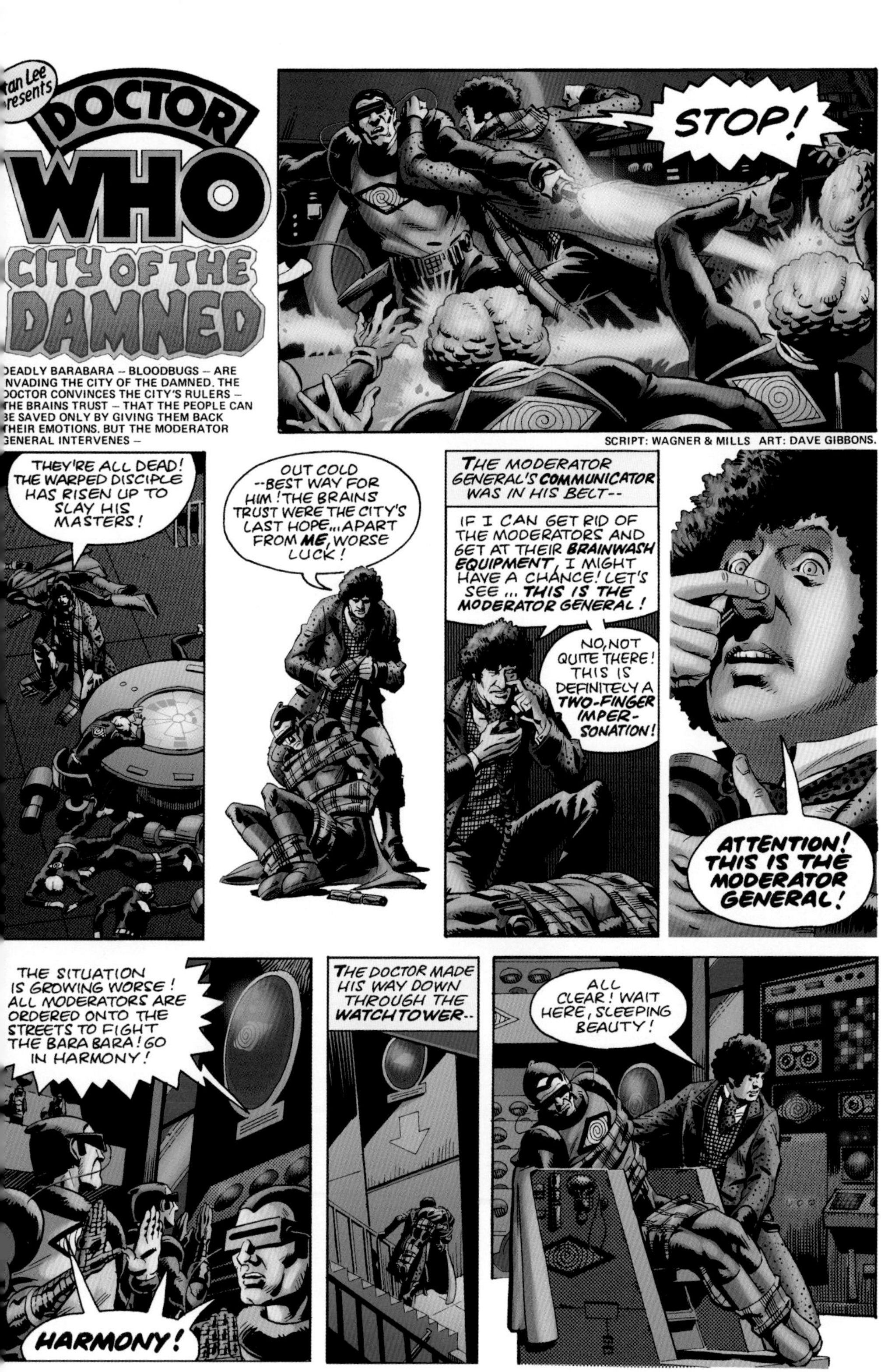
tan Lee
resents
DOCTOR WHO
CITY OF THE DAMNED
DEADLY BARABARA – BLOODBUGS – ARE INVADING THE CITY OF THE DAMNED. THE DOCTOR CONVINCES THE CITY'S RULERS – THE BRAINS TRUST – THAT THE PEOPLE CAN BE SAVED ONLY BY GIVING THEM BACK THEIR EMOTIONS. BUT THE MODERATOR GENERAL INTERVENES –
STOP!
SCRIPT: WAGNER & MILLS ART: DAVE GIBBONS.
THEY'RE ALL DEAD! THE WARPED DISCIPLE HAS RISEN UP TO SLAY HIS MASTERS!
OUT COLD --BEST WAY FOR HIM! THE BRAINS TRUST WERE THE CITY'S LAST HOPE... APART FROM ME, WORSE LUCK!
THE MODERATOR GENERAL'S COMMUNICATOR WAS IN HIS BELT--
IF I CAN GET RID OF THE MODERATORS AND GET AT THEIR BRAINWASH EQUIPMENT, I MIGHT HAVE A CHANCE! LET'S SEE ... THIS IS THE MODERATOR GENERAL!
NO, NOT QUITE THERE! THIS IS DEFINITELY A TWO-FINGER IMPER-SONATION!
ATTENTION! THIS IS THE MODERATOR GENERAL!
THE SITUATION IS GROWING WORSE! ALL MODERATORS ARE ORDERED ONTO THE STREETS TO FIGHT THE BARA BARA! GO IN HARMONY!
HARMONY!
THE DOCTOR MADE HIS WAY DOWN THROUGH THE WATCHTOWER--
ALL CLEAR! WAIT HERE, SLEEPING BEAUTY!

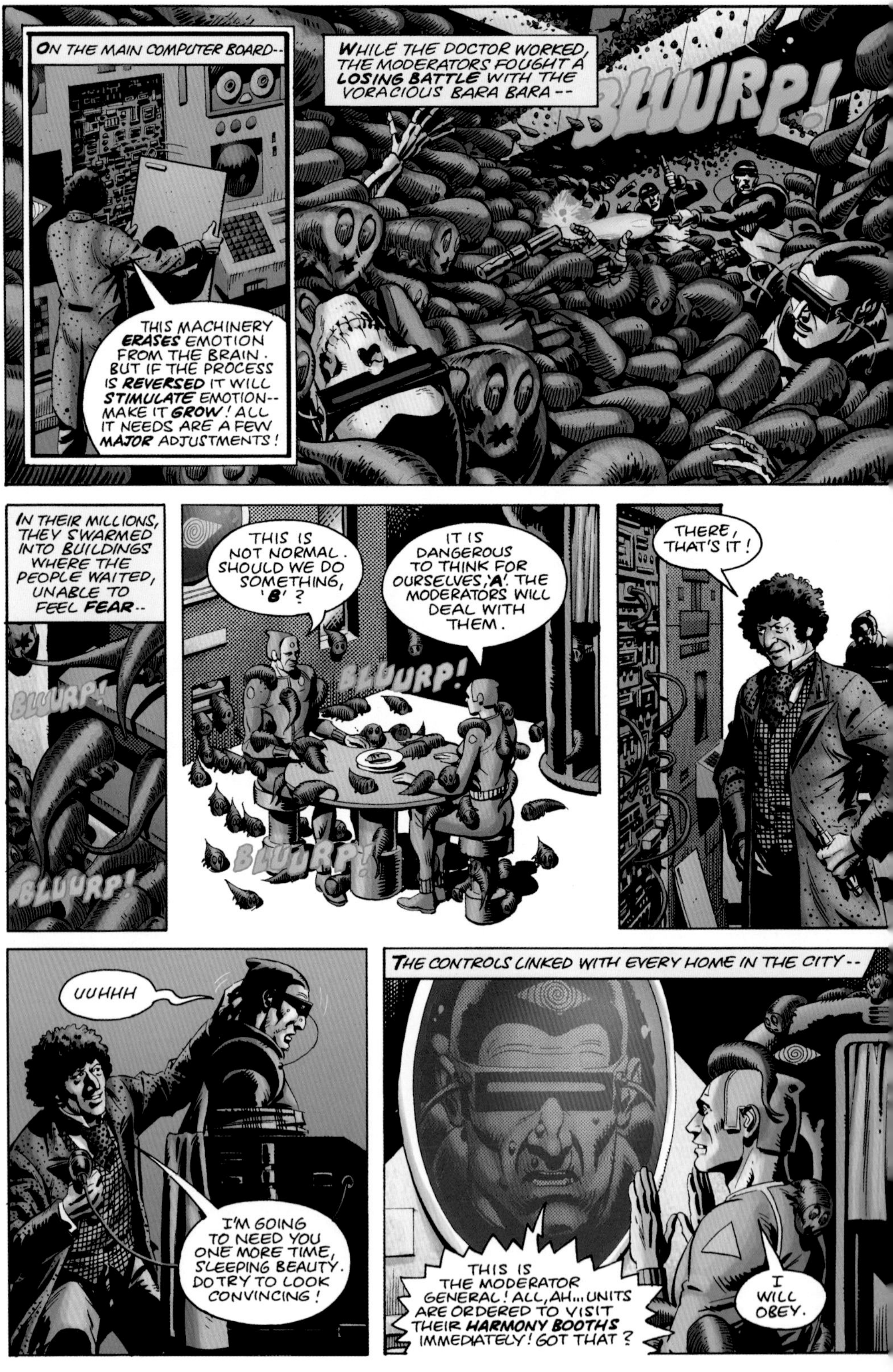

ON THE MAIN COMPUTER BOARD--
THIS MACHINERY ERASES EMOTION FROM THE BRAIN. BUT IF THE PROCESS IS REVERSED IT WILL STIMULATE EMOTION-- MAKE IT GROW! ALL IT NEEDS ARE A FEW MAJOR ADJUSTMENTS!
WHILE THE DOCTOR WORKED, THE MODERATORS FOUGHT A LOSING BATTLE WITH THE VORACIOUS BARA BARA--
BLUURP!
IN THEIR MILLIONS, THEY SWARMED INTO BUILDINGS WHERE THE PEOPLE WAITED, UNABLE TO FEEL FEAR--
BLUURP!
BLUURP!
THIS IS NOT NORMAL. SHOULD WE DO SOMETHING, 'B'?
IT IS DANGEROUS TO THINK FOR OURSELVES, 'A'. THE MODERATORS WILL DEAL WITH THEM.
BLUURP!
BLUURP!
THERE, THAT'S IT!
UUHHH
I'M GOING TO NEED YOU ONE MORE TIME, SLEEPING BEAUTY. DO TRY TO LOOK CONVINCING!
THE CONTROLS LINKED WITH EVERY HOME IN THE CITY--
THIS IS THE MODERATOR GENERAL! ALL, AH... UNITS ARE ORDERED TO VISIT THEIR HARMONY BOOTHS IMMEDIATELY! GOT THAT?
I WILL OBEY.

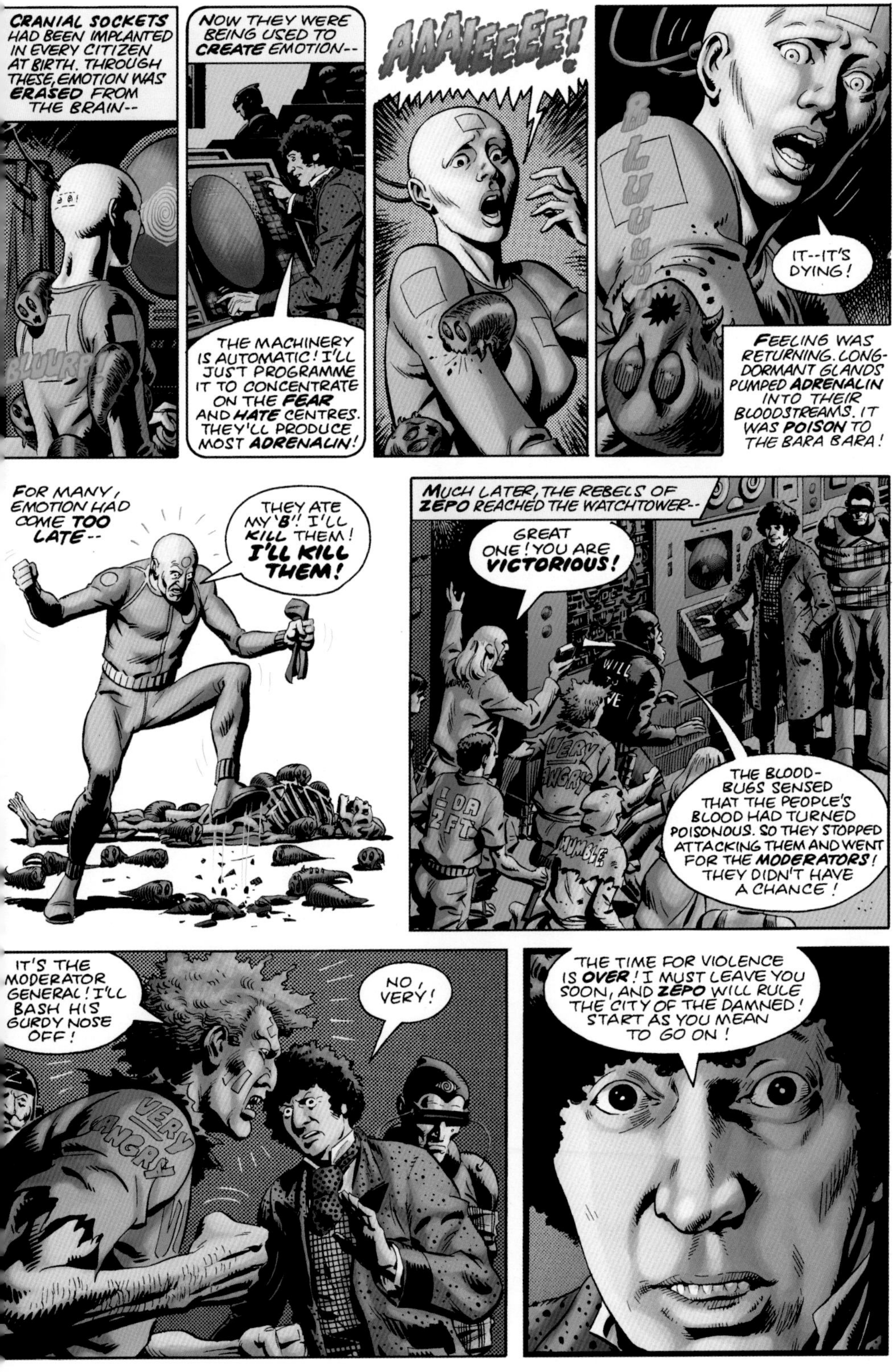
CRANIAL SOCKETS HAD BEEN IMPLANTED IN EVERY CITIZEN AT BIRTH. THROUGH THESE, EMOTION WAS ERASED FROM THE BRAIN--
BLUURP!
NOW THEY WERE BEING USED TO CREATE EMOTION--
THE MACHINERY IS AUTOMATIC! I'LL JUST PROGRAMME IT TO CONCENTRATE ON THE FEAR AND HATE CENTRES. THEY'LL PRODUCE MOST ADRENALIN!
AAAIEEEE!
IT--IT'S DYING!
FEELING WAS RETURNING. LONG-DORMANT GLANDS PUMPED ADRENALIN INTO THEIR BLOODSTREAMS. IT WAS POISON TO THE BARA BARA!
FOR MANY, EMOTION HAD COME TOO LATE--
THEY ATE MY 'B'! I'LL KILL THEM! I'LL KILL THEM!
MUCH LATER, THE REBELS OF ZEPO REACHED THE WATCHTOWER--
GREAT ONE! YOU ARE VICTORIOUS!
THE BLOOD-BUGS SENSED THAT THE PEOPLE'S BLOOD HAD TURNED POISONOUS. SO THEY STOPPED ATTACKING THEM AND WENT FOR THE MODERATORS! THEY DIDN'T HAVE A CHANCE!
IT'S THE MODERATOR GENERAL! I'LL BASH HIS GURDY NOSE OFF!
NO, VERY!
THE TIME FOR VIOLENCE IS OVER! I MUST LEAVE YOU SOON, AND ZEPO WILL RULE THE CITY OF THE DAMNED! START AS YOU MEAN TO GO ON!

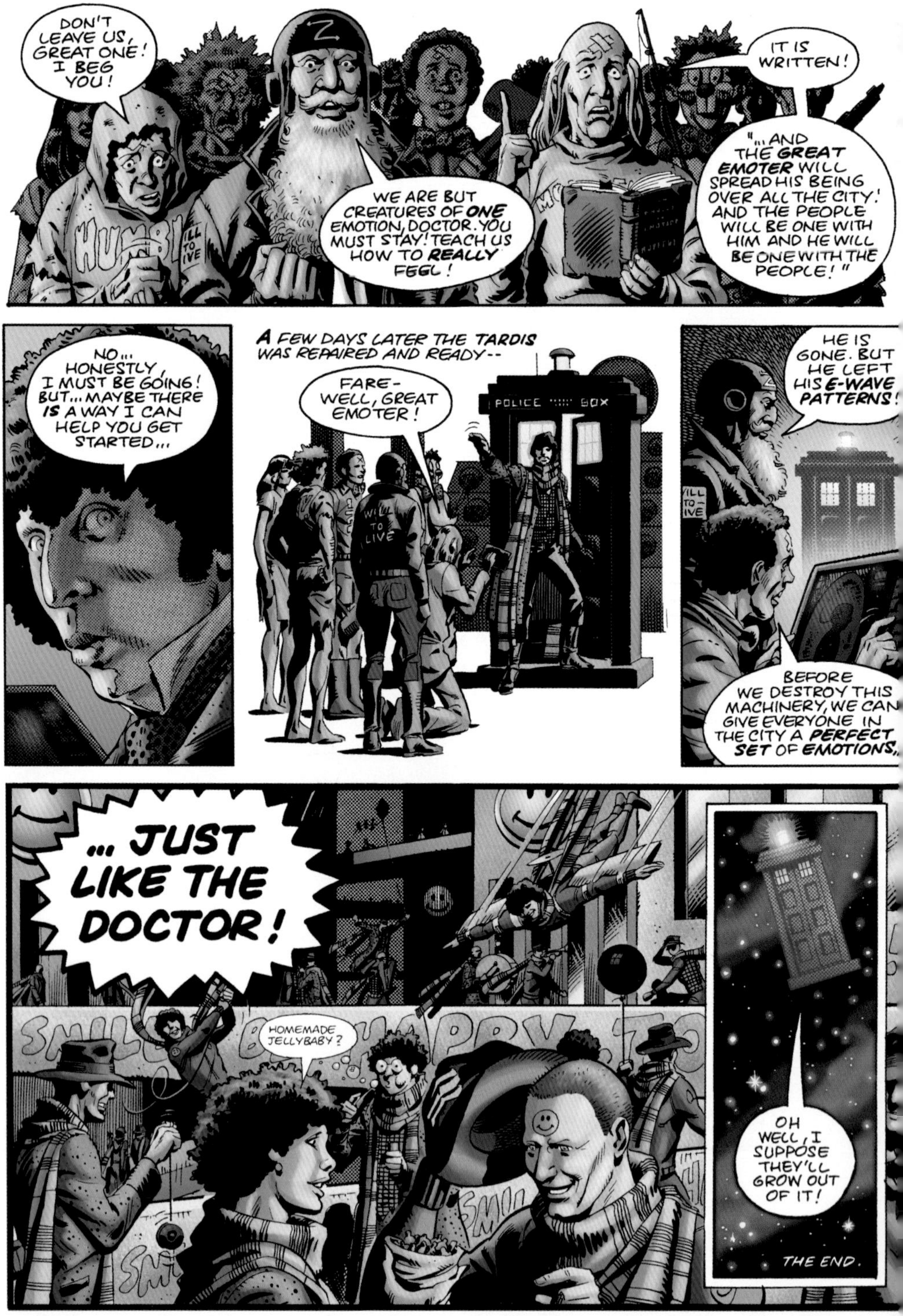
DON'T LEAVE US, GREAT ONE! I BEG YOU!
WE ARE BUT CREATURES OF ONE EMOTION, DOCTOR. YOU MUST STAY! TEACH US HOW TO REALLY FEEL!
IT IS WRITTEN!
"...AND THE GREAT EMOTER WILL SPREAD HIS BEING OVER ALL THE CITY! AND THE PEOPLE WILL BE ONE WITH HIM AND HE WILL BE ONE WITH THE PEOPLE!"
NO... HONESTLY, I MUST BE GOING! BUT... MAYBE THERE IS A WAY I CAN HELP YOU GET STARTED...
A FEW DAYS LATER THE TARDIS WAS REPAIRED AND READY--
FARE-WELL, GREAT EMOTER!
POLICE BOX
WILL TO LIVE
HE IS GONE. BUT HE LEFT HIS E-WAVE PATTERNS!
BEFORE WE DESTROY THIS MACHINERY, WE CAN GIVE EVERYONE IN THE CITY A PERFECT SET OF EMOTIONS...
... JUST LIKE THE DOCTOR!
HOMEMADE JELLYBABY?
OH WELL, I SUPPOSE THEY'LL GROW OUT OF IT!
THE END.

NEXT ISSUE: JOIN THE DOCTOR AND K-9 IN ... TIME-TRAP!

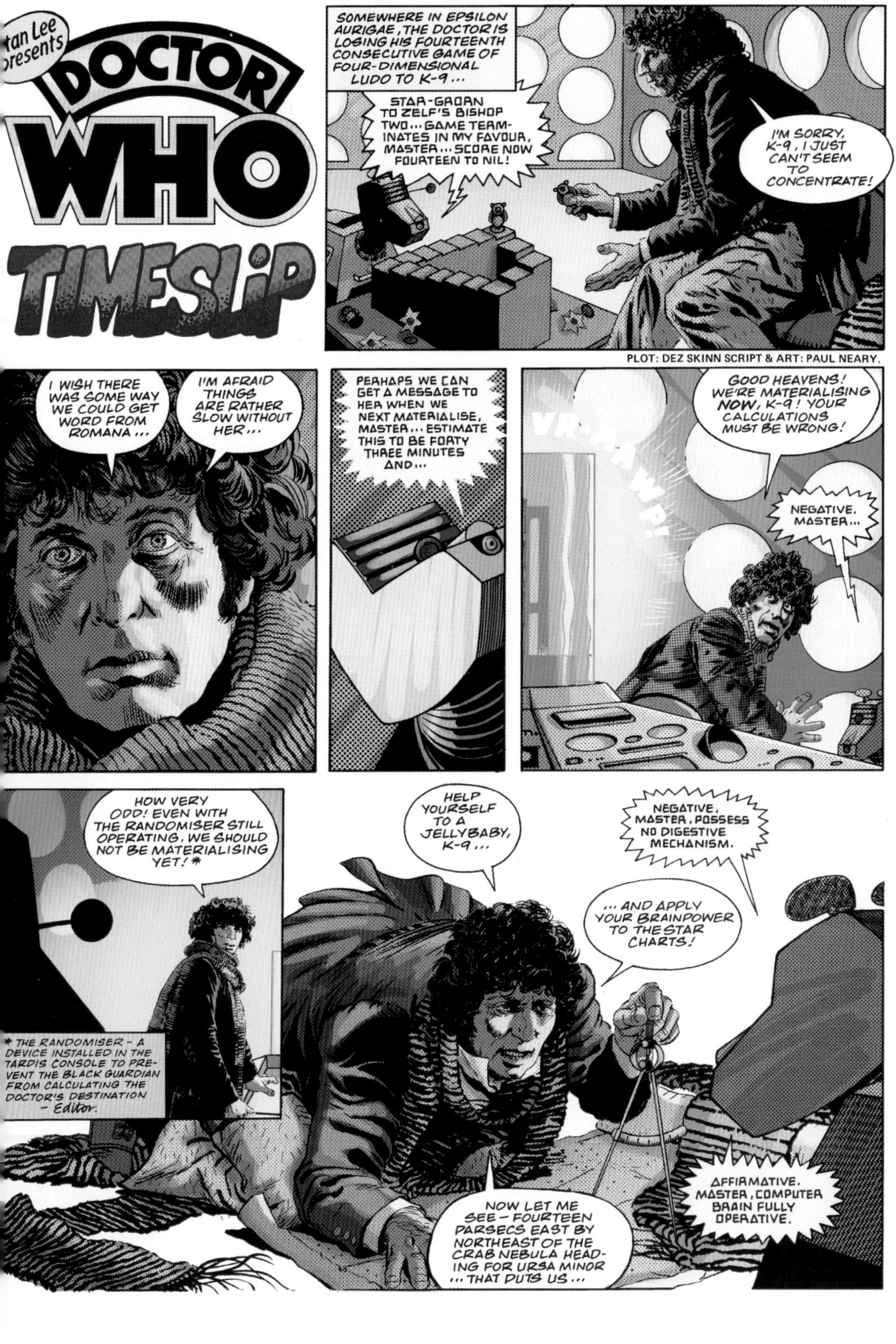

Stan Lee presents
DOCTOR WHO
TIMESLIP
SOMEWHERE IN EPSILON AURIGAE, THE DOCTOR IS LOSING HIS FOURTEENTH CONSECUTIVE GAME OF FOUR-DIMENSIONAL LUDO TO K-9...
STAR-GRORN TO ZELF'S BISHOP TWO... GAME TERMINATES IN MY FAVOUR, MASTER... SCORE NOW FOURTEEN TO NIL!
I'M SORRY, K-9, I JUST CAN'T SEEM TO CONCENTRATE!
PLOT: DEZ SKINN SCRIPT & ART: PAUL NEARY.
I WISH THERE WAS SOME WAY WE COULD GET WORD FROM ROMANA...
I'M AFRAID THINGS ARE RATHER SLOW WITHOUT HER...
PERHAPS WE CAN GET A MESSAGE TO HER WHEN WE NEXT MATERIALISE, MASTER... ESTIMATE THIS TO BE FORTY THREE MINUTES AND...
VR-RRAWP!
GOOD HEAVENS! WE'RE MATERIALISING NOW, K-9! YOUR CALCULATIONS MUST BE WRONG!
NEGATIVE, MASTER...
HOW VERY ODD! EVEN WITH THE RANDOMISER STILL OPERATING, WE SHOULD NOT BE MATERIALISING YET! *
* THE RANDOMISER - A DEVICE INSTALLED IN THE TARDIS CONSOLE TO PREVENT THE BLACK GUARDIAN FROM CALCULATING THE DOCTOR'S DESTINATION - Editor.
HELP YOURSELF TO A JELLYBABY, K-9...
NEGATIVE, MASTER, POSSESS NO DIGESTIVE MECHANISM.
... AND APPLY YOUR BRAINPOWER TO THE STAR CHARTS!
NOW LET ME SEE - FOURTEEN PARSECS EAST BY NORTHEAST OF THE CRAB NEBULA HEADING FOR URSA MINOR ... THAT PUTS US...
AFFIRMATIVE, MASTER, COMPUTER BRAIN FULLY OPERATIVE.

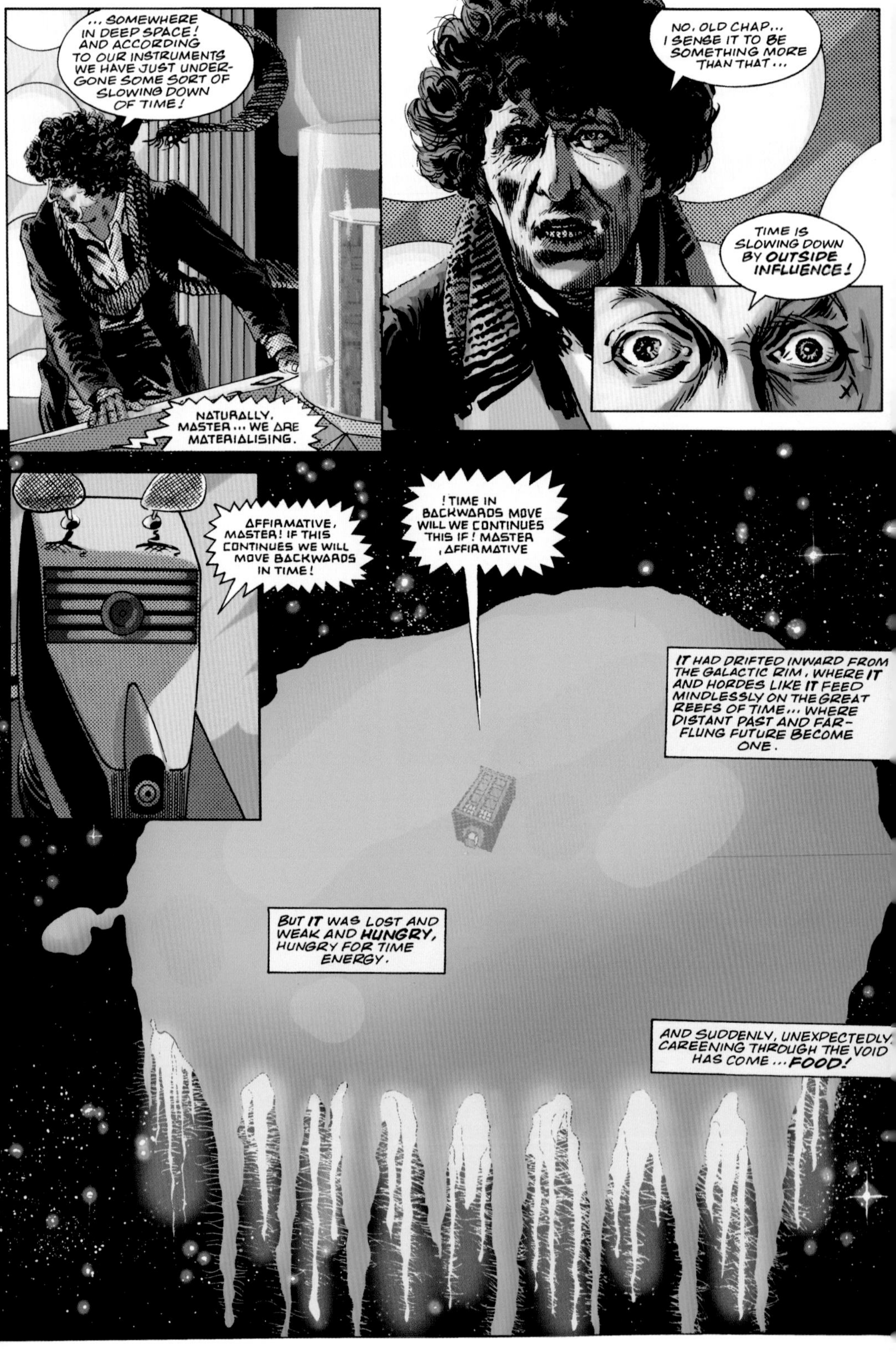

... SOMEWHERE IN DEEP SPACE! AND ACCORDING TO OUR INSTRUMENTS WE HAVE JUST UNDERGONE SOME SORT OF SLOWING DOWN OF TIME!
NATURALLY, MASTER ... WE ARE MATERIALISING.
NO, OLD CHAP... I SENSE IT TO BE SOMETHING MORE THAN THAT...
TIME IS SLOWING DOWN BY OUTSIDE INFLUENCE!
AFFIRMATIVE, MASTER! IF THIS CONTINUES WE WILL MOVE BACKWARDS IN TIME!
! TIME IN BACKWARDS MOVE WILL WE CONTINUES THIS IF ! MASTER ,AFFIRMATIVE
IT HAD DRIFTED INWARD FROM THE GALACTIC RIM, WHERE IT AND HORDES LIKE IT FEED MINDLESSLY ON THE GREAT REEFS OF TIME... WHERE DISTANT PAST AND FAR-FLUNG FUTURE BECOME ONE.
BUT IT WAS LOST AND WEAK AND HUNGRY, HUNGRY FOR TIME ENERGY.
AND SUDDENLY, UNEXPECTEDLY, CAREENING THROUGH THE VOID HAS COME ... FOOD!

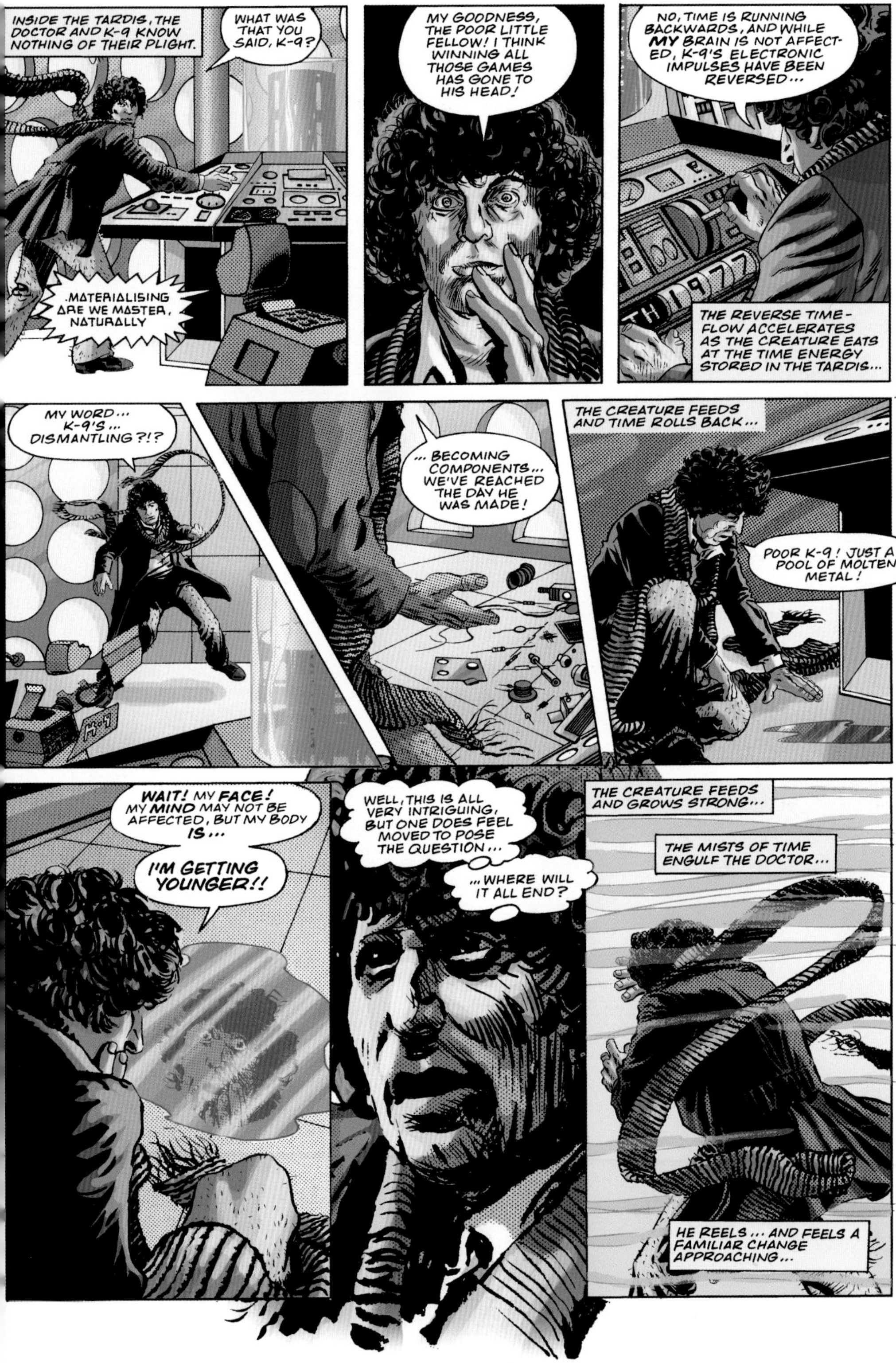

INSIDE THE TARDIS, THE DOCTOR AND K-9 KNOW NOTHING OF THEIR PLIGHT.
WHAT WAS THAT YOU SAID, K-9?
.MATERIALISING ARE WE MASTER, NATURALLY
MY GOODNESS, THE POOR LITTLE FELLOW! I THINK WINNING ALL THOSE GAMES HAS GONE TO HIS HEAD!
NO, TIME IS RUNNING BACKWARDS, AND WHILE MY BRAIN IS NOT AFFECTED, K-9'S ELECTRONIC IMPULSES HAVE BEEN REVERSED...
THE REVERSE TIME-FLOW ACCELERATES AS THE CREATURE EATS AT THE TIME ENERGY STORED IN THE TARDIS...
MY WORD... K-9'S... DISMANTLING?!?
... BECOMING COMPONENTS... WE'VE REACHED THE DAY HE WAS MADE!
THE CREATURE FEEDS AND TIME ROLLS BACK...
POOR K-9! JUST A POOL OF MOLTEN METAL!
WAIT! MY FACE! MY MIND MAY NOT BE AFFECTED, BUT MY BODY IS...
I'M GETTING YOUNGER!!
WELL, THIS IS ALL VERY INTRIGUING, BUT ONE DOES FEEL MOVED TO POSE THE QUESTION...
... WHERE WILL IT ALL END?
THE CREATURE FEEDS AND GROWS STRONG...
THE MISTS OF TIME ENGULF THE DOCTOR...
HE REELS... AND FEELS A FAMILIAR CHANGE APPROACHING...

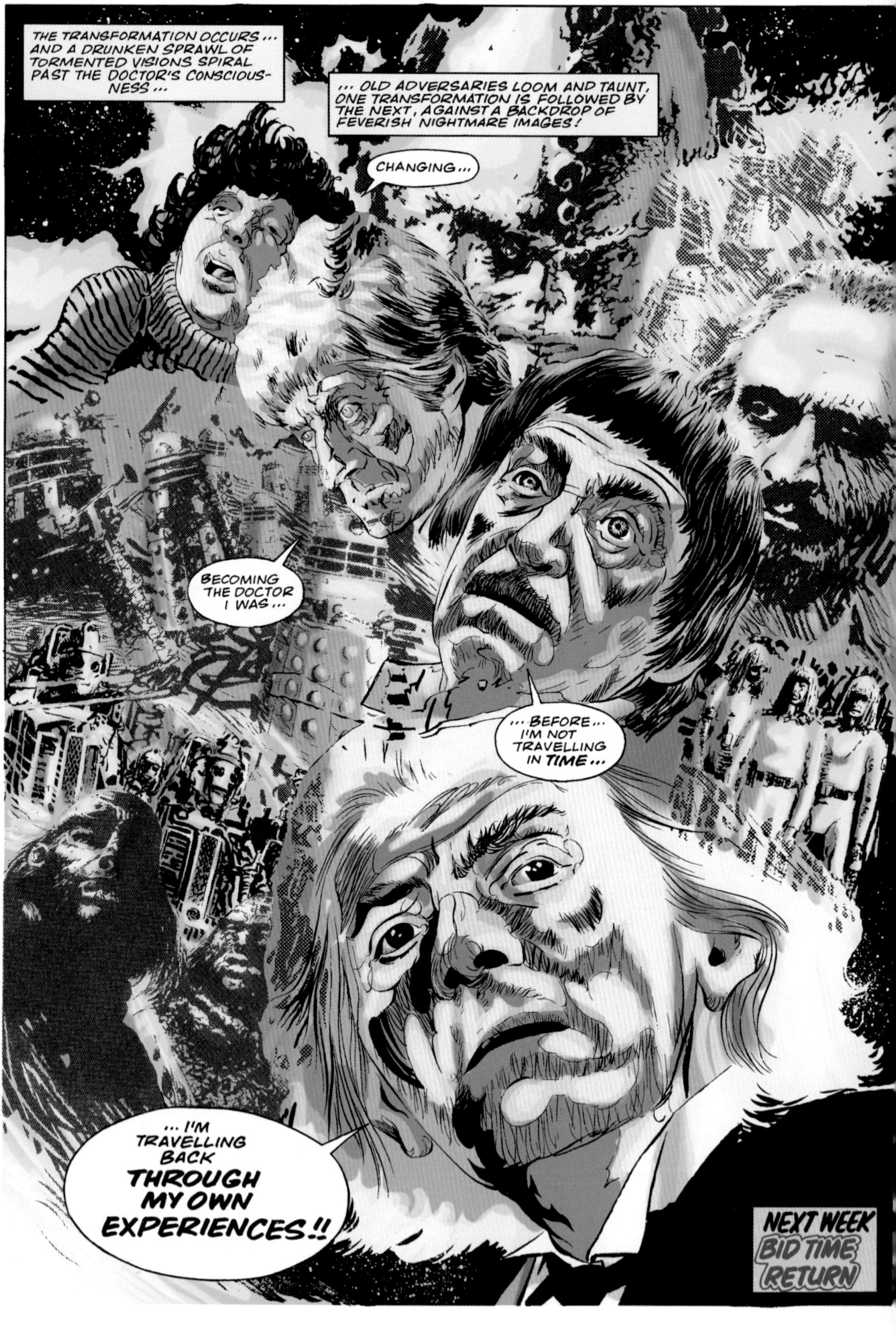

THE TRANSFORMATION OCCURS ... AND A DRUNKEN SPRAWL OF TORMENTED VISIONS SPIRAL PAST THE DOCTOR'S CONSCIOUS-NESS ...
... OLD ADVERSARIES LOOM AND TAUNT, ONE TRANSFORMATION IS FOLLOWED BY THE NEXT, AGAINST A BACKDROP OF FEVERISH NIGHTMARE IMAGES!
CHANGING ...
BECOMING THE DOCTOR I WAS ...
... BEFORE ... I'M NOT TRAVELLING IN TIME ...
... I'M TRAVELLING BACK THROUGH MY OWN EXPERIENCES!!
NEXT WEEK BID TIME RETURN

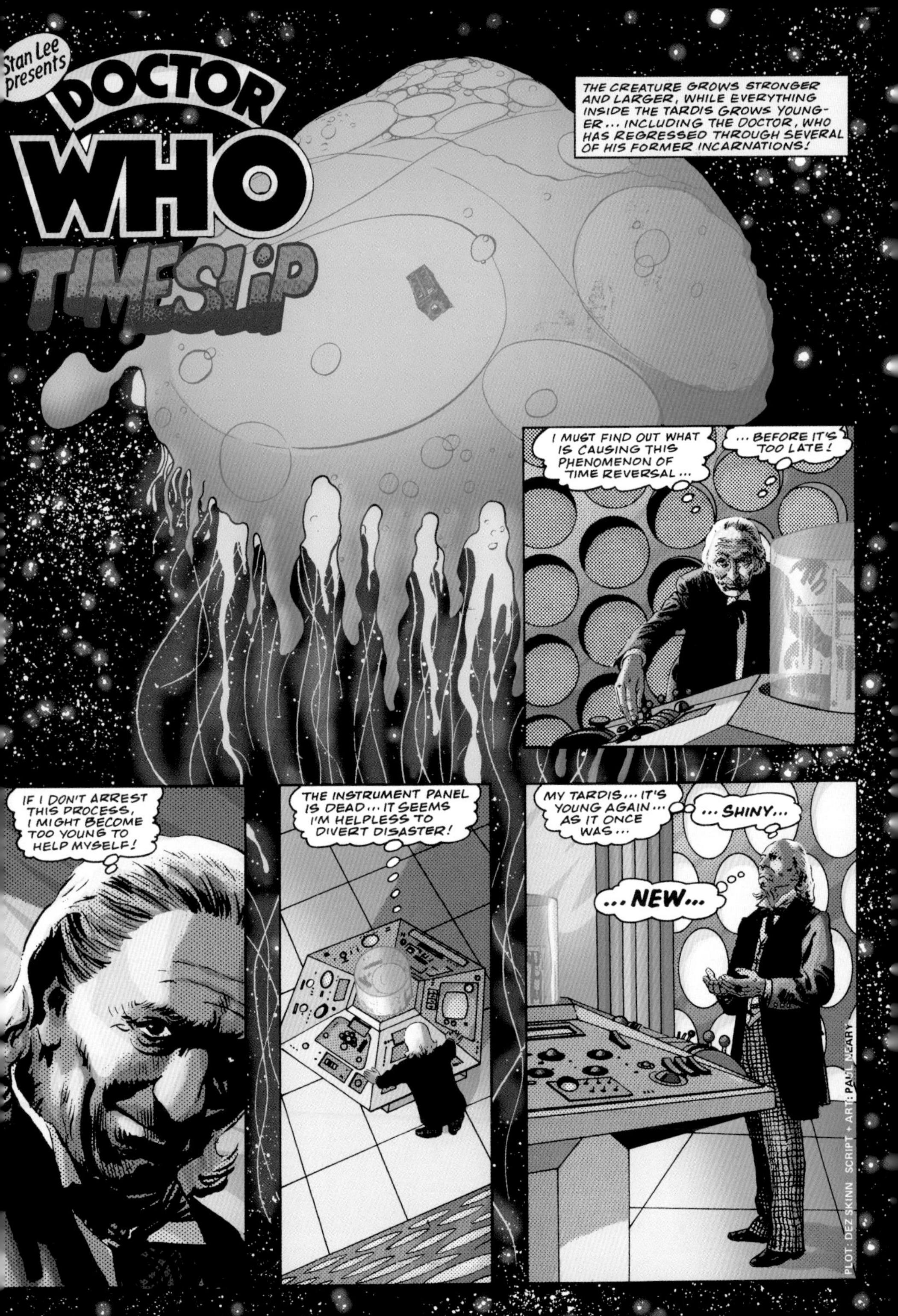
Stan Lee presents
DOCTOR WHO
TIMESLIP
THE CREATURE GROWS STRONGER AND LARGER, WHILE EVERYTHING INSIDE THE TARDIS GROWS YOUNGER... INCLUDING THE DOCTOR, WHO HAS REGRESSED THROUGH SEVERAL OF HIS FORMER INCARNATIONS!
I MUST FIND OUT WHAT IS CAUSING THIS PHENOMENON OF TIME REVERSAL...
... BEFORE IT'S TOO LATE!
IF I DON'T ARREST THIS PROCESS, I MIGHT BECOME TOO YOUNG TO HELP MYSELF!
THE INSTRUMENT PANEL IS DEAD... IT SEEMS I'M HELPLESS TO DIVERT DISASTER!
MY TARDIS... IT'S YOUNG AGAIN... AS IT ONCE WAS...
... SHINY...
... NEW...
PLOT: DEZ SKINN SCRIPT + ART: PAUL NEARY

BUT WE'RE IN TROUBLE NOW, OLD GIRL! IF TIME CONTINUES TO ROLL BACKWARDS, WE'LL BOTH CEASE TO EXIST!

YOUR VIEWSCREEN IS DEAD.... I MUST FIND SOME CLUE TO OUR DILEMMA!

TUT TUT... TIME IS SHORTER THAN I IMAGINED, HERE ARE THE TEST INSTRUMENTS I USED TO CALIBRATE THE CONTROLS IN THE EARLY DAYS...

AS EVENTS UNFOLD, THE DOCTOR FEELS IRRESISTABLY DRAWN TO PERFORM THE FIRST TASK IN THE LIFE OF THE TARDIS...

TIME UNFURLS, THE INSTANT APPROACHES WHEN THE DOCTOR THREW THE LEVER WHICH ACTIVATED THE TARDIS...

THE DOCTOR'S FINGERS CLOSE ABOUT THE LEVER AND MOVE IT INTO THE **OFF** POSITION...

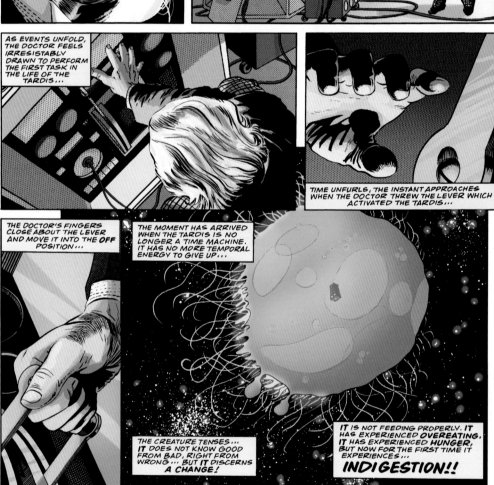

THE MOMENT HAS ARRIVED WHEN THE TARDIS IS NO LONGER A TIME MACHINE. IT HAS NO MORE TEMPORAL ENERGY TO GIVE UP...

THE CREATURE TENSES... IT DOES NOT KNOW GOOD FROM BAD, RIGHT FROM WRONG... BUT IT DISCERNS **A CHANGE!**

IT IS NOT FEEDING PROPERLY. IT HAS EXPERIENCED **OVEREATING**, IT HAS EXPERIENCED **HUNGER**, BUT NOW FOR THE FIRST TIME IT EXPERIENCES...

INDIGESTION!!

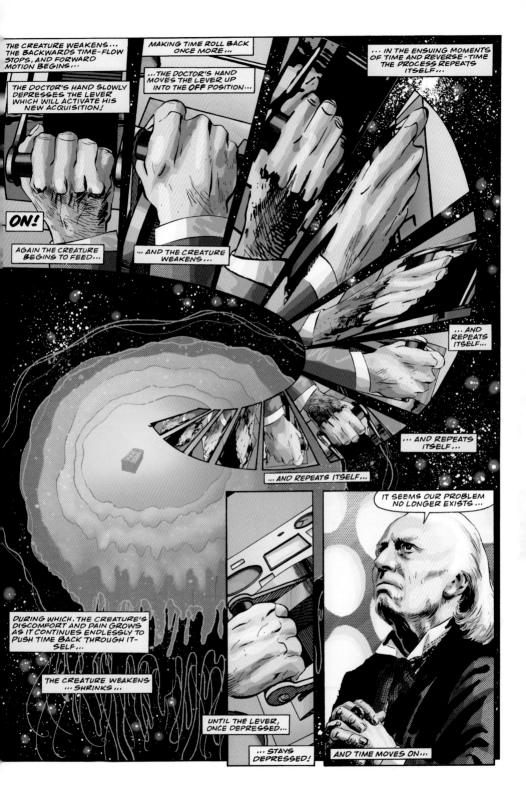

THE CREATURE WEAKENS... THE BACKWARDS TIME-FLOW STOPS, AND FORWARD MOTION BEGINS...

THE DOCTOR'S HAND SLOWLY DEPRESSES THE LEVER WHICH WILL ACTIVATE HIS NEW ACQUISITION!

ON!

AGAIN THE CREATURE BEGINS TO FEED...

MAKING TIME ROLL BACK ONCE MORE...

...THE DOCTOR'S HAND MOVES THE LEVER UP INTO THE OFF POSITION...

... AND THE CREATURE WEAKENS...

... IN THE ENSUING MOMENTS OF TIME AND REVERSE-TIME THE PROCESS REPEATS ITSELF...

... AND REPEATS ITSELF...

... AND REPEATS ITSELF...

... AND REPEATS ITSELF...

DURING WHICH, THE CREATURE'S DISCOMFORT AND PAIN GROWS AS IT CONTINUES ENDLESSLY TO PUSH TIME BACK THROUGH ITSELF...

THE CREATURE WEAKENS ... SHRINKS ...

UNTIL THE LEVER, ONCE DEPRESSED...

... STAYS DEPRESSED!

IT SEEMS OUR PROBLEM NO LONGER EXISTS ...

AND TIME MOVES ON ...

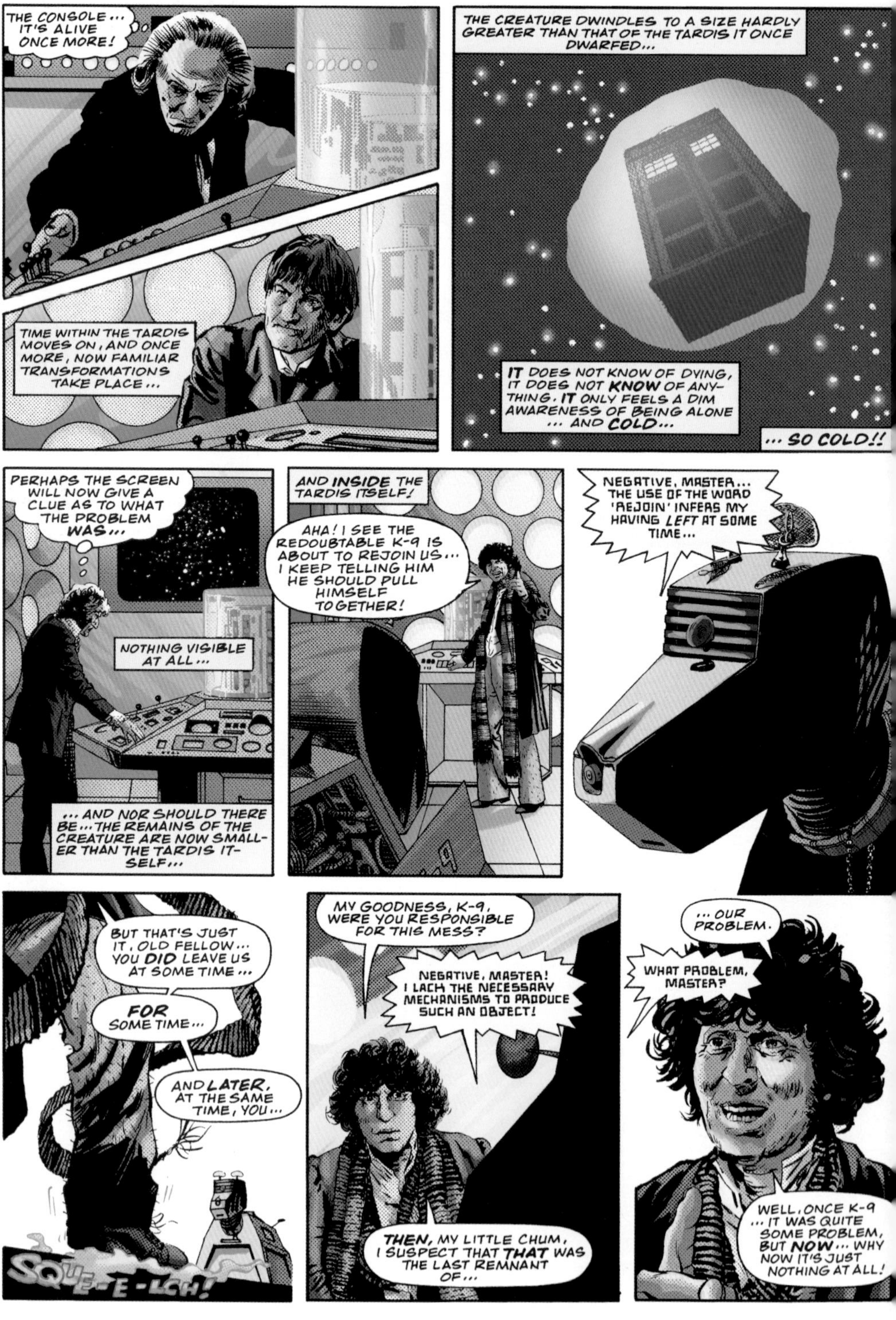
THE CONSOLE... IT'S ALIVE ONCE MORE!
TIME WITHIN THE TARDIS MOVES ON, AND ONCE MORE, NOW FAMILIAR TRANSFORMATIONS TAKE PLACE...
THE CREATURE DWINDLES TO A SIZE HARDLY GREATER THAN THAT OF THE TARDIS IT ONCE DWARFED...
IT DOES NOT KNOW OF DYING, IT DOES NOT KNOW OF ANY-THING. IT ONLY FEELS A DIM AWARENESS OF BEING ALONE ... AND COLD...
... SO COLD!!
PERHAPS THE SCREEN WILL NOW GIVE A CLUE AS TO WHAT THE PROBLEM WAS...
NOTHING VISIBLE AT ALL...
... AND NOR SHOULD THERE BE... THE REMAINS OF THE CREATURE ARE NOW SMALL-ER THAN THE TARDIS IT-SELF...
AND INSIDE THE TARDIS ITSELF!
AHA! I SEE THE REDOUBTABLE K-9 IS ABOUT TO REJOIN US... I KEEP TELLING HIM HE SHOULD PULL HIMSELF TOGETHER!
NEGATIVE, MASTER... THE USE OF THE WORD 'REJOIN' INFERS MY HAVING LEFT AT SOME TIME...
BUT THAT'S JUST IT, OLD FELLOW... YOU DID LEAVE US AT SOME TIME...
FOR SOME TIME...
AND LATER, AT THE SAME TIME, YOU...
SQUE-E-LCH!
MY GOODNESS, K-9, WERE YOU RESPONSIBLE FOR THIS MESS?
NEGATIVE, MASTER! I LACK THE NECESSARY MECHANISMS TO PRODUCE SUCH AN OBJECT!
THEN, MY LITTLE CHUM, I SUSPECT THAT THAT WAS THE LAST REMNANT OF...
... OUR PROBLEM.
WHAT PROBLEM, MASTER?
WELL, ONCE K-9 ... IT WAS QUITE SOME PROBLEM, BUT NOW... WHY NOW IT'S JUST NOTHING AT ALL!

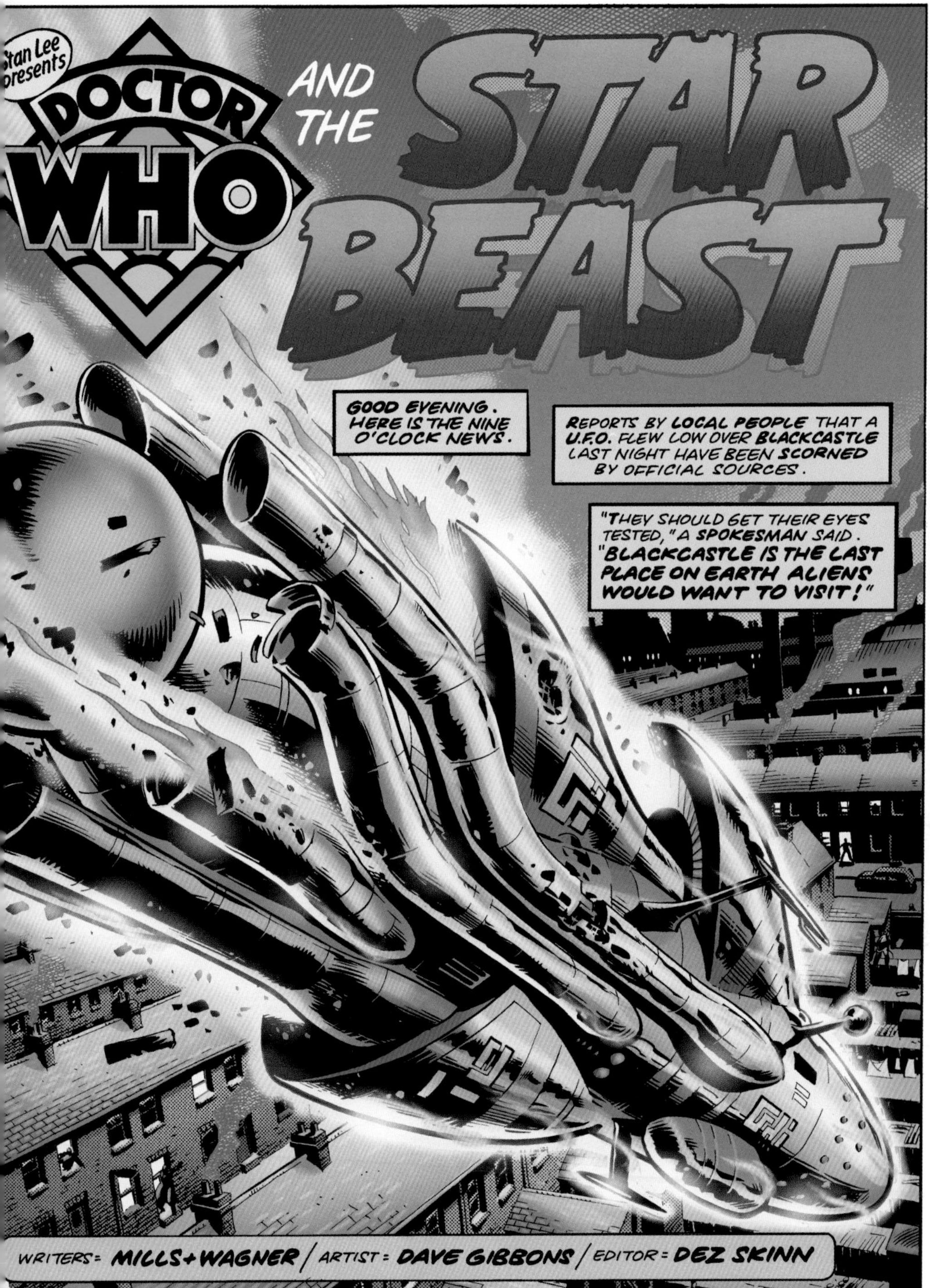
Stan Lee presents
DOCTOR WHO
AND THE
STAR BEAST
GOOD EVENING. HERE IS THE NINE O'CLOCK NEWS.
REPORTS BY LOCAL PEOPLE THAT A U.F.O. FLEW LOW OVER BLACKCASTLE LAST NIGHT HAVE BEEN SCORNED BY OFFICIAL SOURCES.
"THEY SHOULD GET THEIR EYES TESTED," A SPOKESMAN SAID. "BLACKCASTLE IS THE LAST PLACE ON EARTH ALIENS WOULD WANT TO VISIT!"
WRITERS = MILLS+WAGNER / ARTIST = DAVE GIBBONS / EDITOR = DEZ SKINN

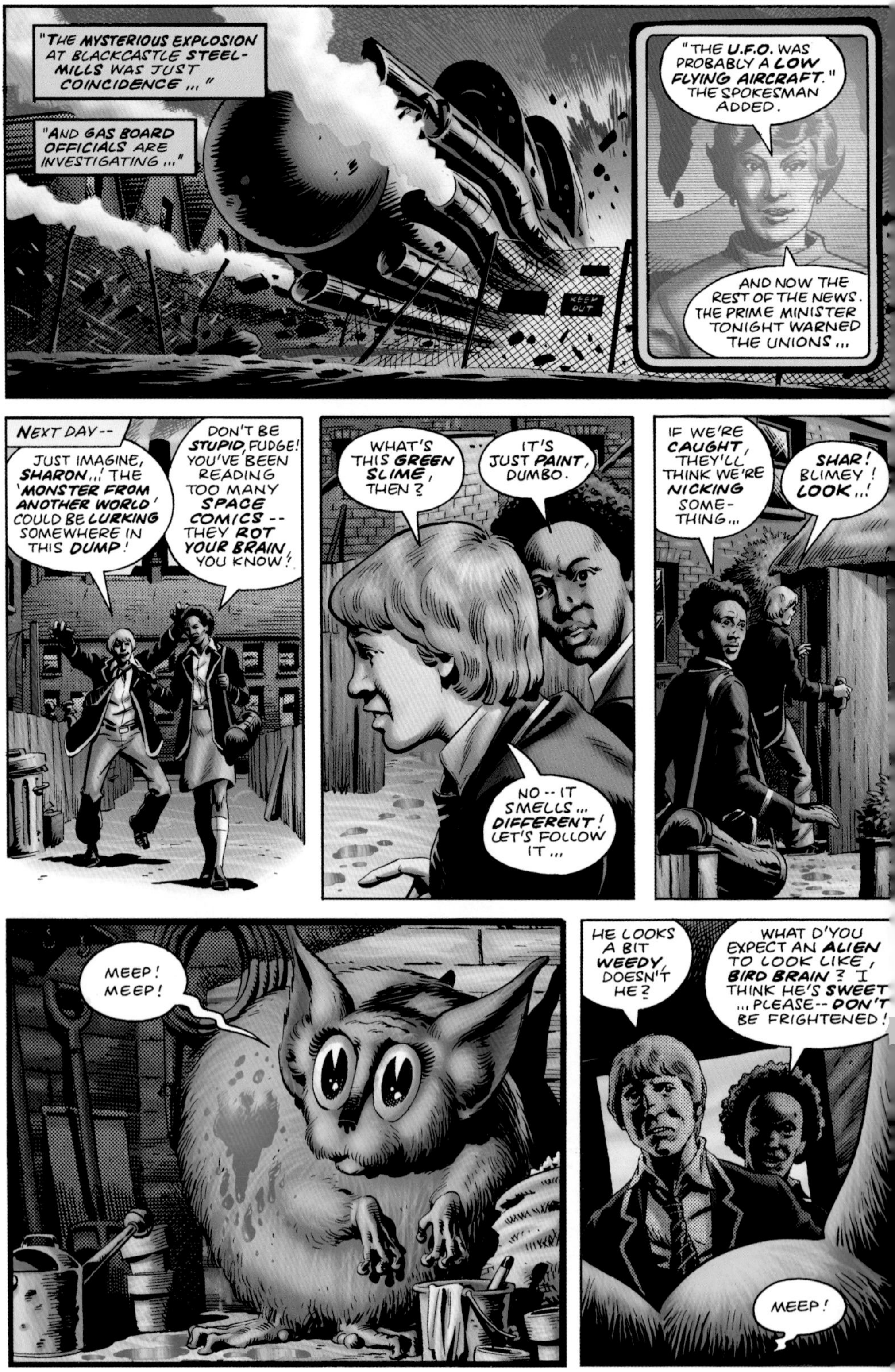
"THE MYSTERIOUS EXPLOSION AT BLACKCASTLE STEEL-MILLS WAS JUST COINCIDENCE ..."
"AND GAS BOARD OFFICIALS ARE INVESTIGATING ..."
KEEP OUT
"THE U.F.O. WAS PROBABLY A LOW FLYING AIRCRAFT." THE SPOKESMAN ADDED.
AND NOW THE REST OF THE NEWS. THE PRIME MINISTER TONIGHT WARNED THE UNIONS ...
NEXT DAY --
JUST IMAGINE, SHARON...! THE 'MONSTER FROM ANOTHER WORLD' COULD BE LURKING SOMEWHERE IN THIS DUMP!
DON'T BE STUPID, FUDGE! YOU'VE BEEN READING TOO MANY SPACE COMICS -- THEY ROT YOUR BRAIN, YOU KNOW!
WHAT'S THIS GREEN SLIME, THEN?
IT'S JUST PAINT, DUMBO.
NO -- IT SMELLS... DIFFERENT! LET'S FOLLOW IT ...
IF WE'RE CAUGHT, THEY'LL THINK WE'RE NICKING SOME-THING...
SHAR! BLIMEY! LOOK...!
MEEP! MEEP!
HE LOOKS A BIT WEEDY, DOESN'T HE?
WHAT D'YOU EXPECT AN ALIEN TO LOOK LIKE, BIRD BRAIN? I THINK HE'S SWEET ... PLEASE-- DON'T BE FRIGHTENED!
MEEP!

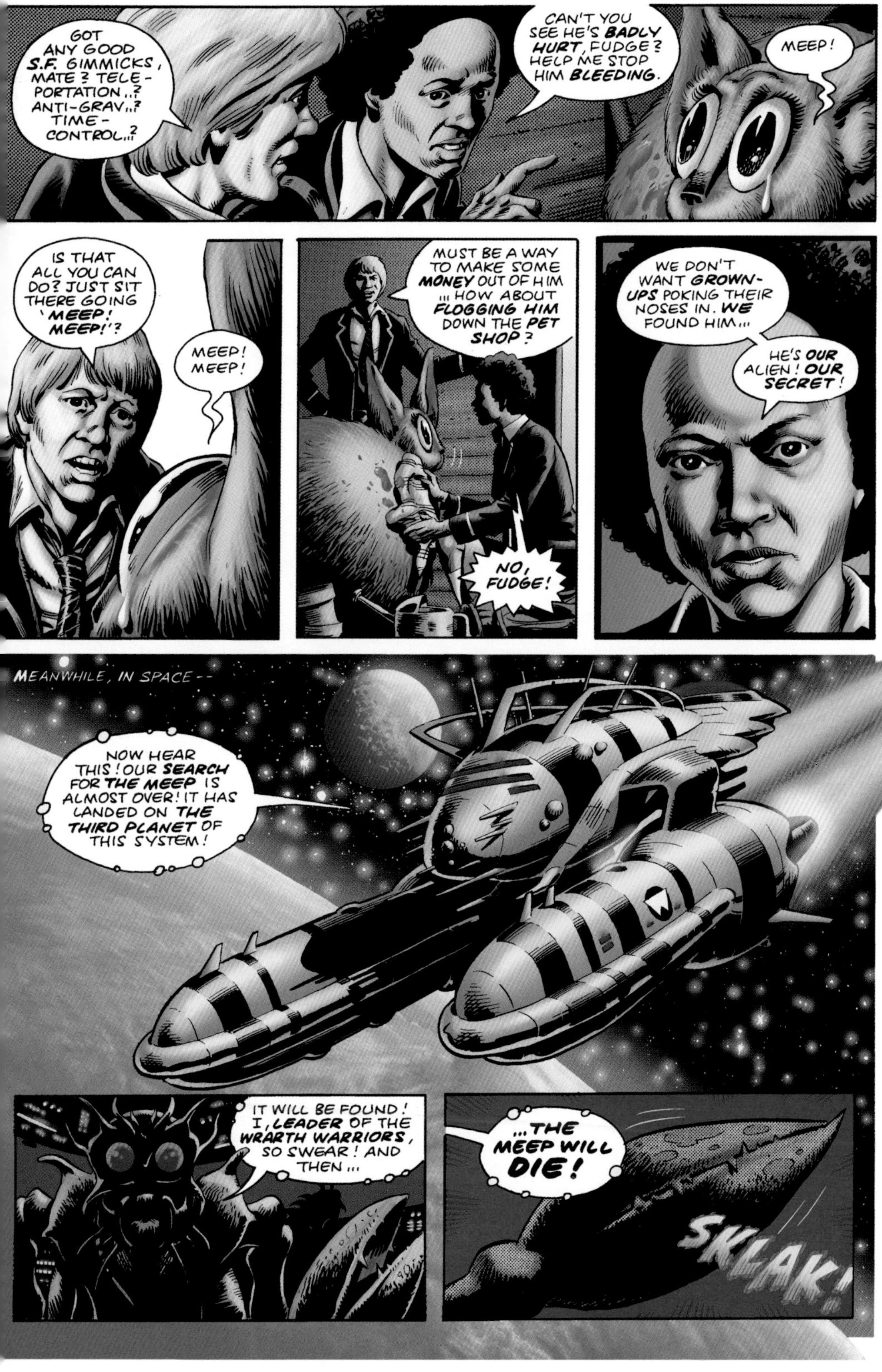
GOT ANY GOOD S.F. GIMMICKS, MATE? TELE-PORTATION..? ANTI-GRAV..? TIME-CONTROL..?
CAN'T YOU SEE HE'S BADLY HURT, FUDGE? HELP ME STOP HIM BLEEDING.
MEEP!
IS THAT ALL YOU CAN DO? JUST SIT THERE GOING 'MEEP! MEEP!'?
MEEP! MEEP!
MUST BE A WAY TO MAKE SOME MONEY OUT OF HIM ... HOW ABOUT FLOGGING HIM DOWN THE PET SHOP?
NO, FUDGE!
WE DON'T WANT GROWN-UPS POKING THEIR NOSES IN. WE FOUND HIM...
HE'S OUR ALIEN! OUR SECRET!
MEANWHILE, IN SPACE--
NOW HEAR THIS! OUR SEARCH FOR THE MEEP IS ALMOST OVER! IT HAS LANDED ON THE THIRD PLANET OF THIS SYSTEM!
IT WILL BE FOUND! I, LEADER OF THE WRARTH WARRIORS, SO SWEAR! AND THEN...
...THE MEEP WILL DIE!
SKLAK!

THE TARDIS MATERIALISES ON BOARD--

♫ ...WE'RE OFF TO SUNNY SPAIN! VIVA ESPAÑA! ♫

THIS ISN'T BENI-DORM, K-9!

CORRECT, MASTER!

IT'S PITCH-BLACK--DEFINITELY NOT THE PLACE FOR A SUN-TAN! WELL, LET'S SEE WHERE THE RANDOMISER HAS LANDED US THIS TIME...

A STAR SHIP OF SOME KIND...BUT WHY IS EVERYTHING IN DARKNESS?

MAYBE THIS IS THE LIGHT-SWITCH...

I'M TERRIBLY SORRY! I DIDN'T REALISE I WAS SQUEEZING YOUR EYE-BALL!

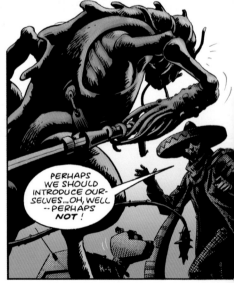

PERHAPS WE SHOULD INTRODUCE OUR-SELVES...OH, WELL --PERHAPS NOT!

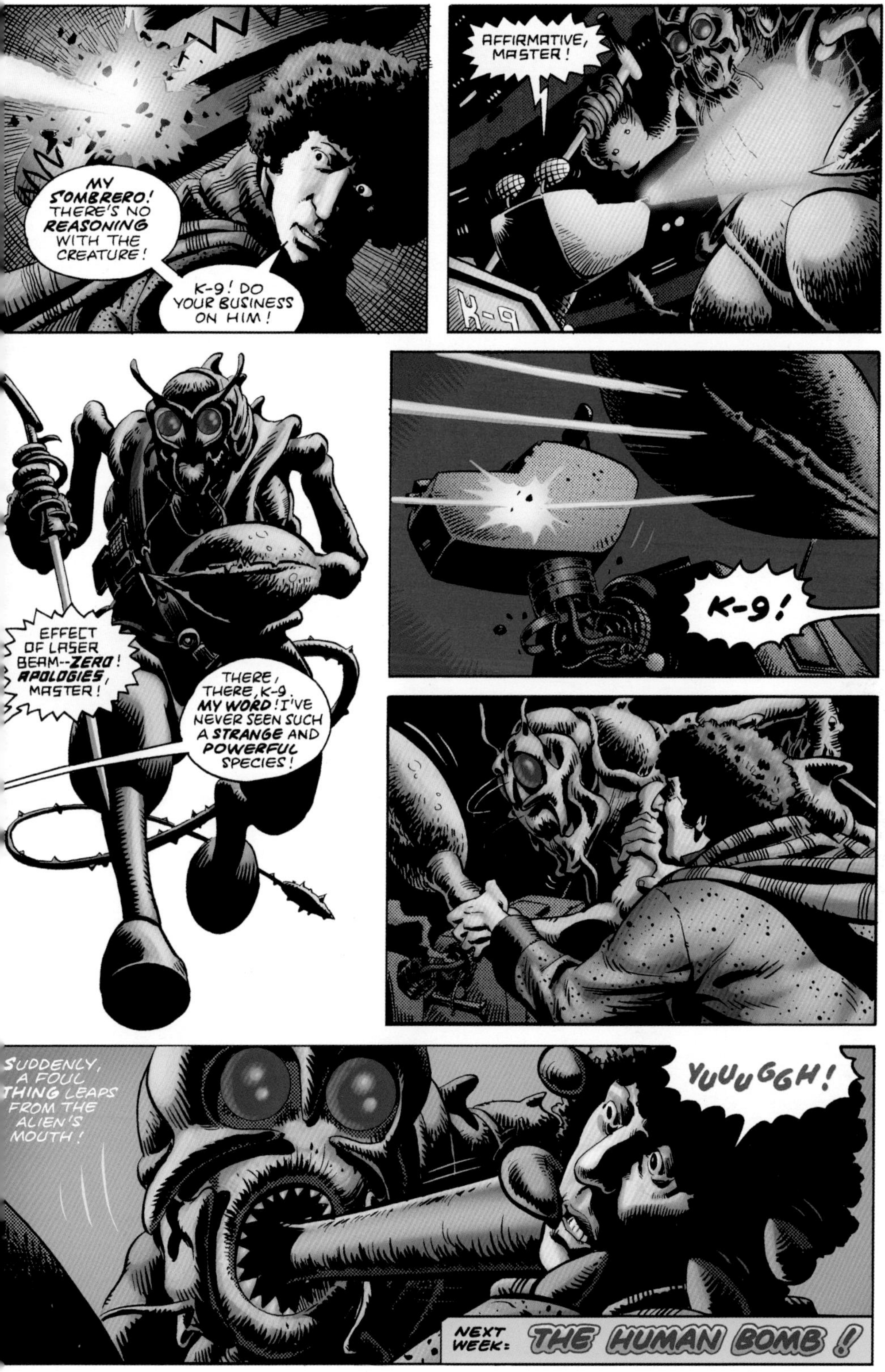
MY SOMBRERO! THERE'S NO REASONING WITH THE CREATURE!
K-9! DO YOUR BUSINESS ON HIM!
AFFIRMATIVE, MASTER!
K-9
EFFECT OF LASER BEAM--ZERO! APOLOGIES, MASTER!
THERE, THERE, K-9. MY WORD! I'VE NEVER SEEN SUCH A STRANGE AND POWERFUL SPECIES!
K-9!
SUDDENLY, A FOUL THING LEAPS FROM THE ALIEN'S MOUTH!
YUUUGGH!
NEXT WEEK: THE HUMAN BOMB!

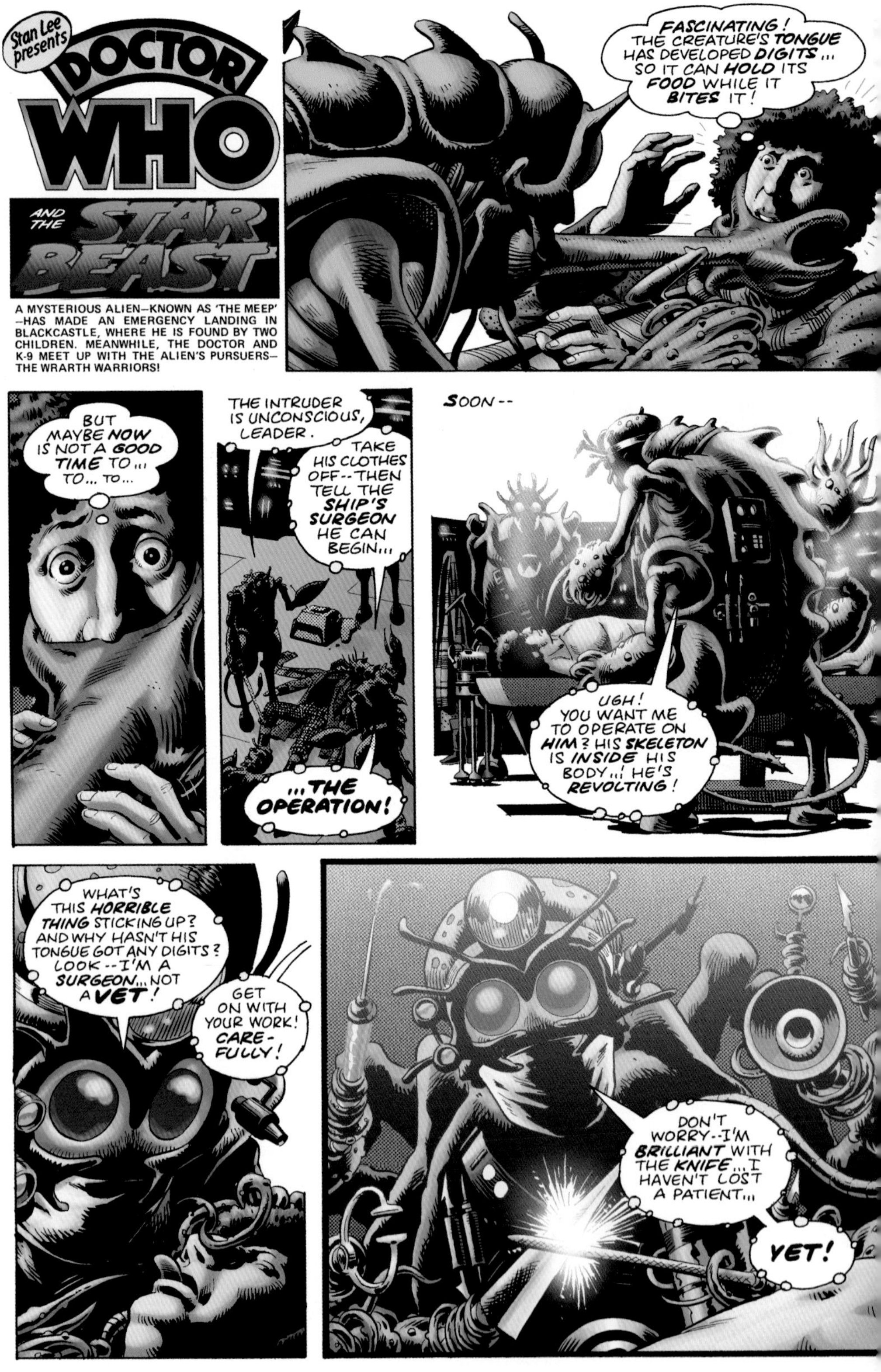

Stan Lee presents
DOCTOR WHO
AND THE STAR BEAST
A MYSTERIOUS ALIEN—KNOWN AS 'THE MEEP' —HAS MADE AN EMERGENCY LANDING IN BLACKCASTLE, WHERE HE IS FOUND BY TWO CHILDREN. MEANWHILE, THE DOCTOR AND K-9 MEET UP WITH THE ALIEN'S PURSUERS— THE WRARTH WARRIORS!
FASCINATING! THE CREATURE'S TONGUE HAS DEVELOPED DIGITS... SO IT CAN HOLD ITS FOOD WHILE IT BITES IT!
BUT MAYBE NOW IS NOT A GOOD TIME TO... TO... TO...
THE INTRUDER IS UNCONSCIOUS, LEADER.
TAKE HIS CLOTHES OFF--THEN TELL THE SHIP'S SURGEON HE CAN BEGIN...
...THE OPERATION!
SOON--
UGH! YOU WANT ME TO OPERATE ON HIM? HIS SKELETON IS INSIDE HIS BODY...! HE'S REVOLTING!
WHAT'S THIS HORRIBLE THING STICKING UP? AND WHY HASN'T HIS TONGUE GOT ANY DIGITS? LOOK--I'M A SURGEON... NOT A VET!
GET ON WITH YOUR WORK! CARE-FULLY!
DON'T WORRY--I'M BRILLIANT WITH THE KNIFE... I HAVEN'T LOST A PATIENT...
YET!

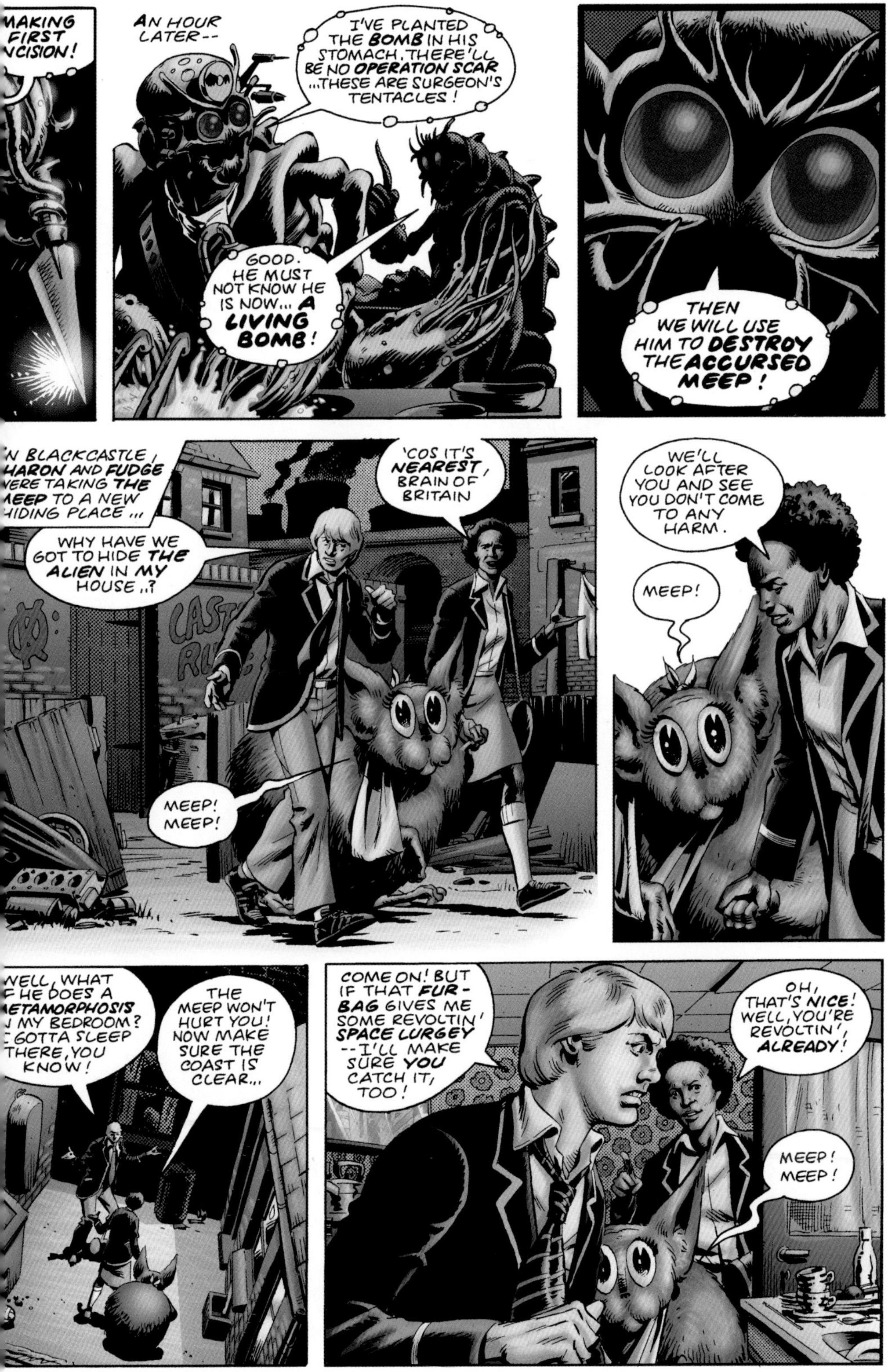
MAKING FIRST NCISION!
AN HOUR LATER--
I'VE PLANTED THE BOMB IN HIS STOMACH. THERE'LL BE NO OPERATION SCAR ...THESE ARE SURGEON'S TENTACLES!
GOOD. HE MUST NOT KNOW HE IS NOW... A LIVING BOMB!
THEN WE WILL USE HIM TO DESTROY THE ACCURSED MEEP!
N BLACKCASTLE, HARON AND FUDGE VERE TAKING THE MEEP TO A NEW HIDING PLACE...
WHY HAVE WE GOT TO HIDE THE ALIEN IN MY HOUSE..?
'COS IT'S NEAREST, BRAIN OF BRITAIN
MEEP! MEEP!
WE'LL LOOK AFTER YOU AND SEE YOU DON'T COME TO ANY HARM.
MEEP!
WELL, WHAT F HE DOES A METAMORPHOSIS N MY BEDROOM? GOTTA SLEEP THERE, YOU KNOW!
THE MEEP WON'T HURT YOU! NOW MAKE SURE THE COAST IS CLEAR...
COME ON! BUT IF THAT FUR-BAG GIVES ME SOME REVOLTIN' SPACE LURGEY --I'LL MAKE SURE YOU CATCH IT, TOO!
OH, THAT'S NICE! WELL, YOU'RE REVOLTIN', ALREADY!
MEEP! MEEP!

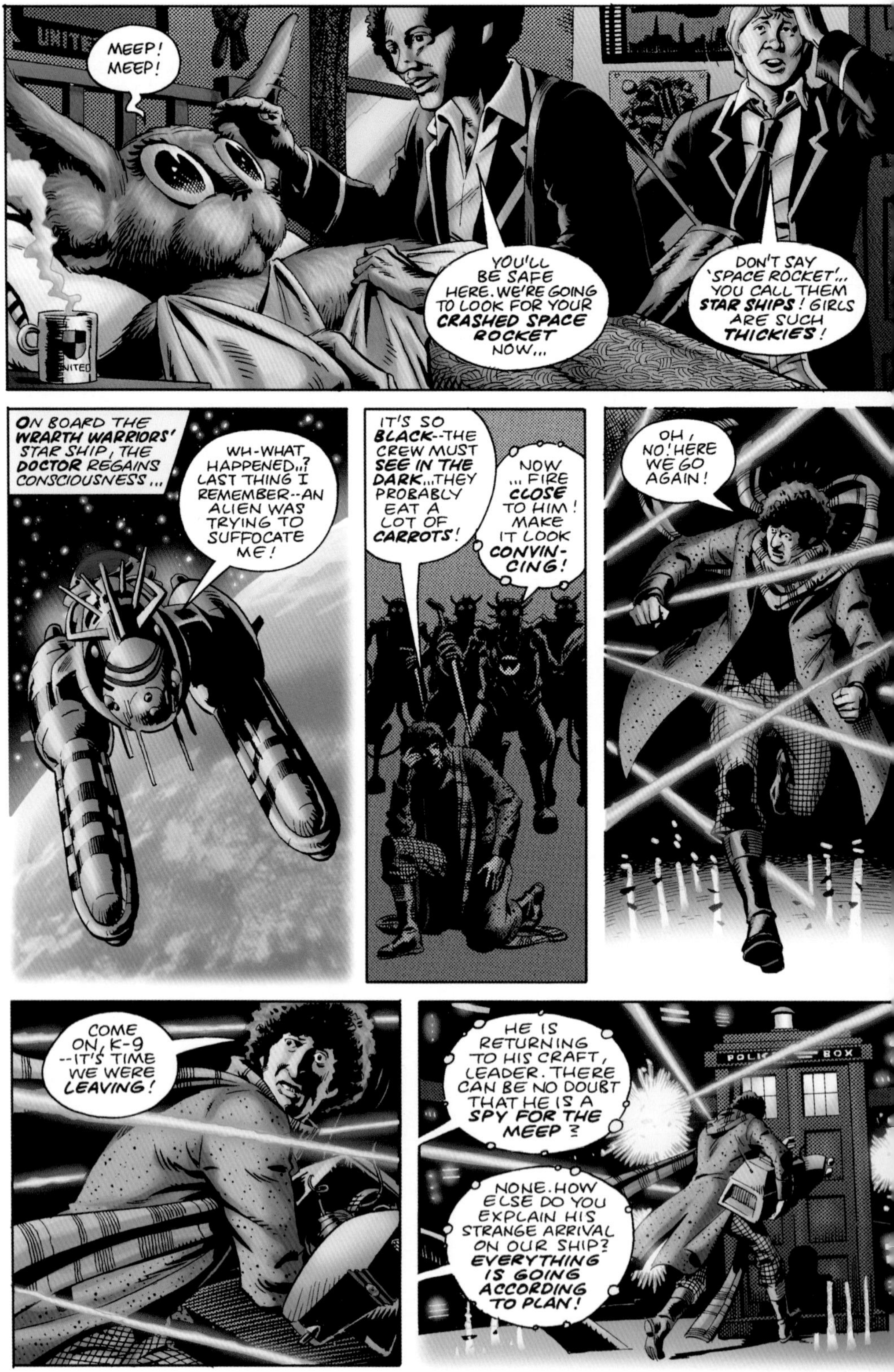
MEEP! MEEP!
YOU'LL BE SAFE HERE. WE'RE GOING TO LOOK FOR YOUR CRASHED SPACE ROCKET NOW...
DON'T SAY 'SPACE ROCKET'... YOU CALL THEM STAR SHIPS! GIRLS ARE SUCH THICKIES!
ON BOARD THE WRARTH WARRIORS' STAR SHIP, THE DOCTOR REGAINS CONSCIOUSNESS...
WH-WHAT HAPPENED..? LAST THING I REMEMBER--AN ALIEN WAS TRYING TO SUFFOCATE ME!
IT'S SO BLACK--THE CREW MUST SEE IN THE DARK...THEY PROBABLY EAT A LOT OF CARROTS!
NOW ... FIRE CLOSE TO HIM! MAKE IT LOOK CONVINCING!
OH, NO! HERE WE GO AGAIN!
COME ON, K-9 --IT'S TIME WE WERE LEAVING!
HE IS RETURNING TO HIS CRAFT, LEADER. THERE CAN BE NO DOUBT THAT HE IS A SPY FOR THE MEEP?
NONE. HOW ELSE DO YOU EXPLAIN HIS STRANGE ARRIVAL ON OUR SHIP? EVERYTHING IS GOING ACCORDING TO PLAN!
POLICE BOX
UNITED

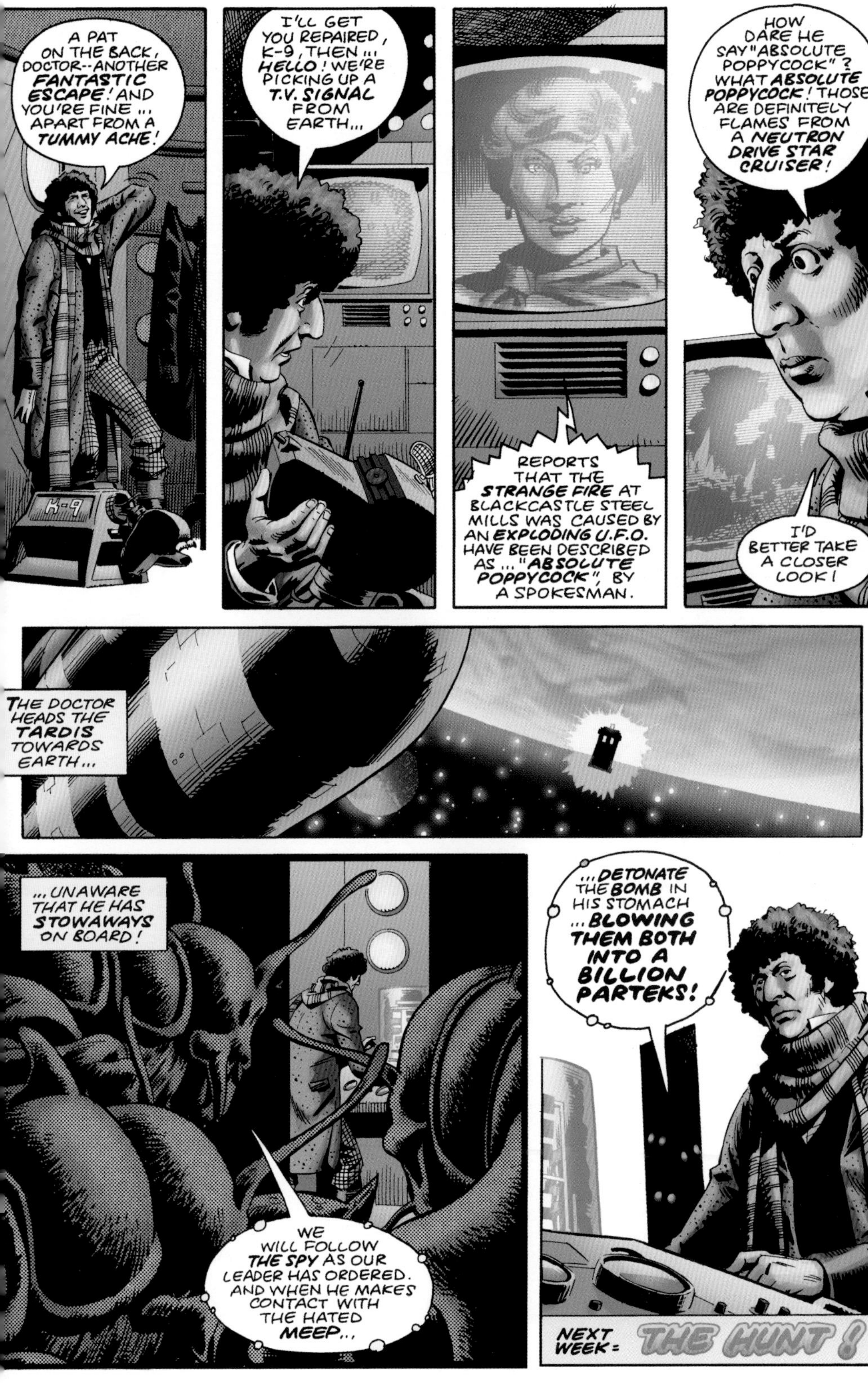
A PAT ON THE BACK, DOCTOR--ANOTHER FANTASTIC ESCAPE! AND YOU'RE FINE ... APART FROM A TUMMY ACHE!
K-9
I'LL GET YOU REPAIRED, K-9, THEN ... HELLO! WE'RE PICKING UP A T.V. SIGNAL FROM EARTH...
REPORTS THAT THE STRANGE FIRE AT BLACKCASTLE STEEL MILLS WAS CAUSED BY AN EXPLODING U.F.O. HAVE BEEN DESCRIBED AS ... "ABSOLUTE POPPYCOCK", BY A SPOKESMAN.
HOW DARE HE SAY "ABSOLUTE POPPYCOCK"? WHAT ABSOLUTE POPPYCOCK! THOSE ARE DEFINITELY FLAMES FROM A NEUTRON DRIVE STAR CRUISER!
I'D BETTER TAKE A CLOSER LOOK!
THE DOCTOR HEADS THE TARDIS TOWARDS EARTH...
...UNAWARE THAT HE HAS STOWAWAYS ON BOARD!
WE WILL FOLLOW THE SPY AS OUR LEADER HAS ORDERED. AND WHEN HE MAKES CONTACT WITH THE HATED MEEP...
...DETONATE THE BOMB IN HIS STOMACH ...BLOWING THEM BOTH INTO A BILLION PARTEKS!
NEXT WEEK = THE HUNT!

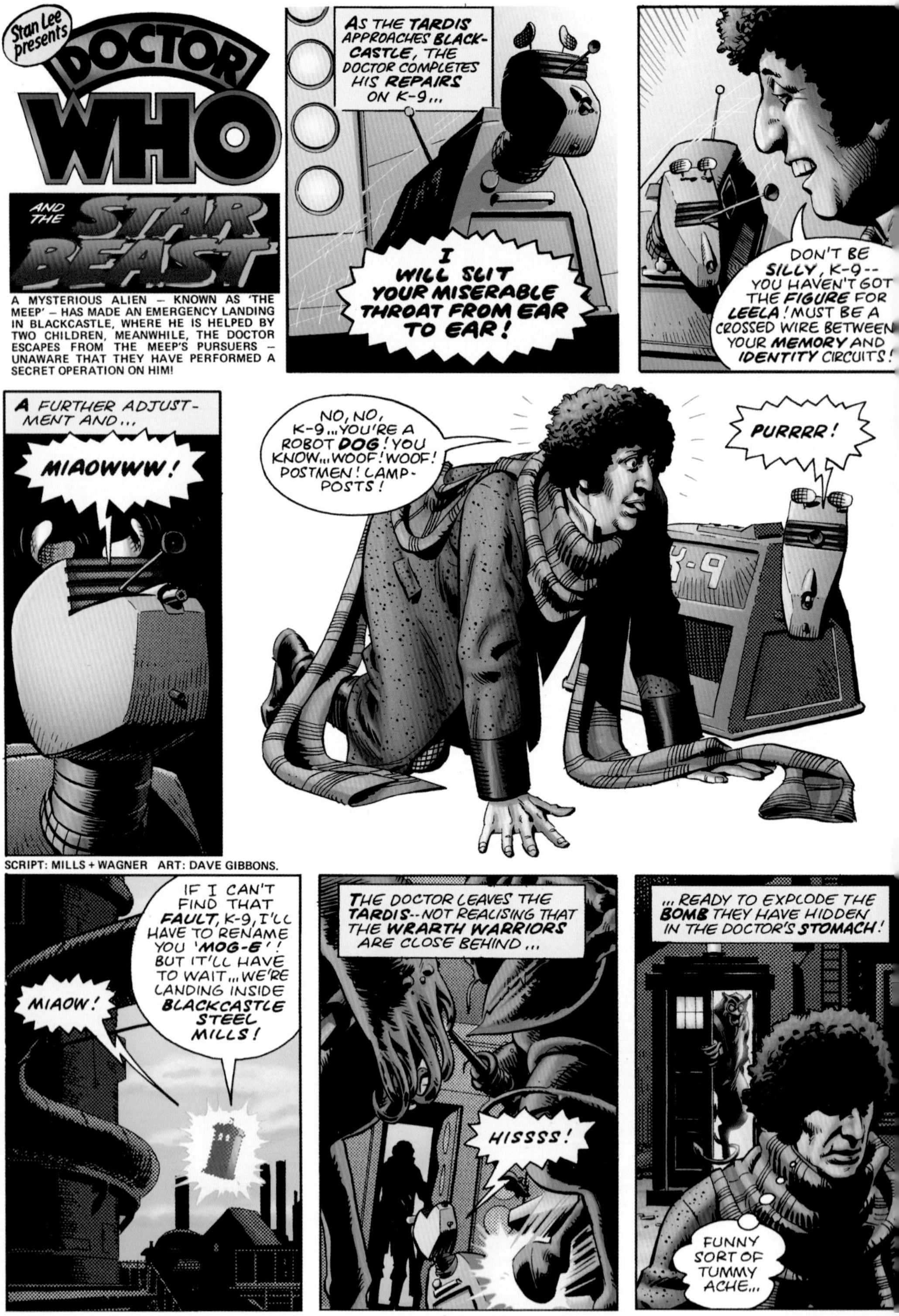
Stan Lee presents
DOCTOR WHO
AND THE STAR BEAST
A MYSTERIOUS ALIEN – KNOWN AS 'THE MEEP' – HAS MADE AN EMERGENCY LANDING IN BLACKCASTLE, WHERE HE IS HELPED BY TWO CHILDREN. MEANWHILE, THE DOCTOR ESCAPES FROM THE MEEP'S PURSUERS – UNAWARE THAT THEY HAVE PERFORMED A SECRET OPERATION ON HIM!
AS THE TARDIS APPROACHES BLACKCASTLE, THE DOCTOR COMPLETES HIS REPAIRS ON K-9...
I WILL SLIT YOUR MISERABLE THROAT FROM EAR TO EAR!
DON'T BE SILLY, K-9-- YOU HAVEN'T GOT THE FIGURE FOR LEELA! MUST BE A CROSSED WIRE BETWEEN YOUR MEMORY AND IDENTITY CIRCUITS!
A FURTHER ADJUSTMENT AND...
MIAOWWW!
NO, NO, K-9... YOU'RE A ROBOT DOG! YOU KNOW... WOOF! WOOF! POSTMEN! LAMP-POSTS!
PURRRR!
K-9
SCRIPT: MILLS + WAGNER ART: DAVE GIBBONS.
IF I CAN'T FIND THAT FAULT, K-9, I'LL HAVE TO RENAME YOU 'MOG-E'! BUT IT'LL HAVE TO WAIT... WE'RE LANDING INSIDE BLACKCASTLE STEEL MILLS!
MIAOW!
THE DOCTOR LEAVES THE TARDIS--NOT REALISING THAT THE WRARTH WARRIORS ARE CLOSE BEHIND...
HISSSS!
...READY TO EXPLODE THE BOMB THEY HAVE HIDDEN IN THE DOCTOR'S STOMACH!
FUNNY SORT OF TUMMY ACHE...

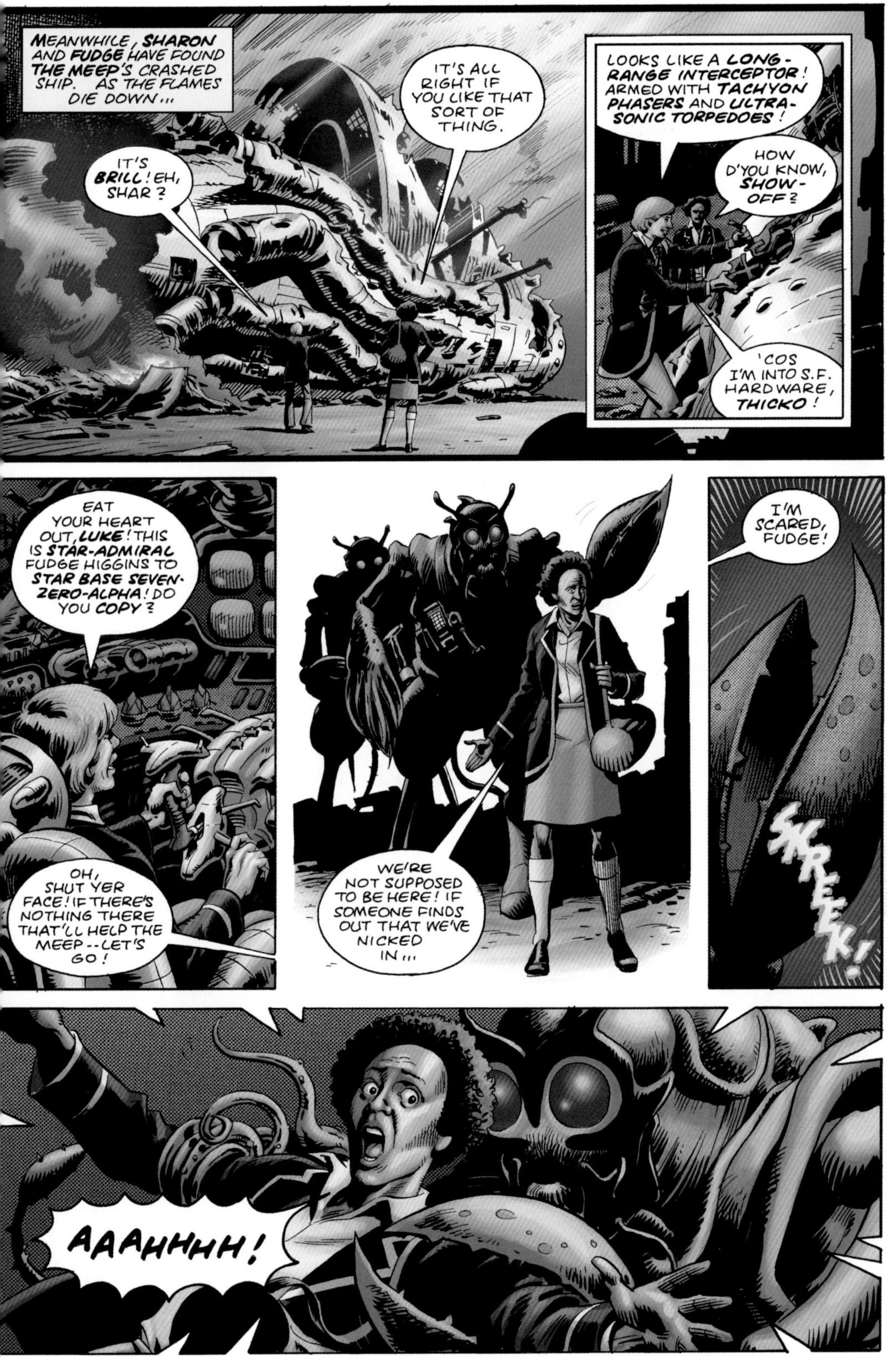
MEANWHILE, SHARON AND FUDGE HAVE FOUND THE MEEP'S CRASHED SHIP. AS THE FLAMES DIE DOWN...
IT'S BRILL! EH, SHAR?
IT'S ALL RIGHT IF YOU LIKE THAT SORT OF THING.
LOOKS LIKE A LONG-RANGE INTERCEPTOR! ARMED WITH TACHYON PHASERS AND ULTRA-SONIC TORPEDOES!
HOW D'YOU KNOW, SHOW-OFF?
'COS I'M INTO S.F. HARDWARE, THICKO!
EAT YOUR HEART OUT, LUKE! THIS IS STAR-ADMIRAL FUDGE HIGGINS TO STAR BASE SEVEN-ZERO-ALPHA! DO YOU COPY?
OH, SHUT YER FACE! IF THERE'S NOTHING THERE THAT'LL HELP THE MEEP--LET'S GO!
WE'RE NOT SUPPOSED TO BE HERE! IF SOMEONE FINDS OUT THAT WE'VE NICKED IN...
I'M SCARED, FUDGE!
SKREEEK!
AAAHHHH!

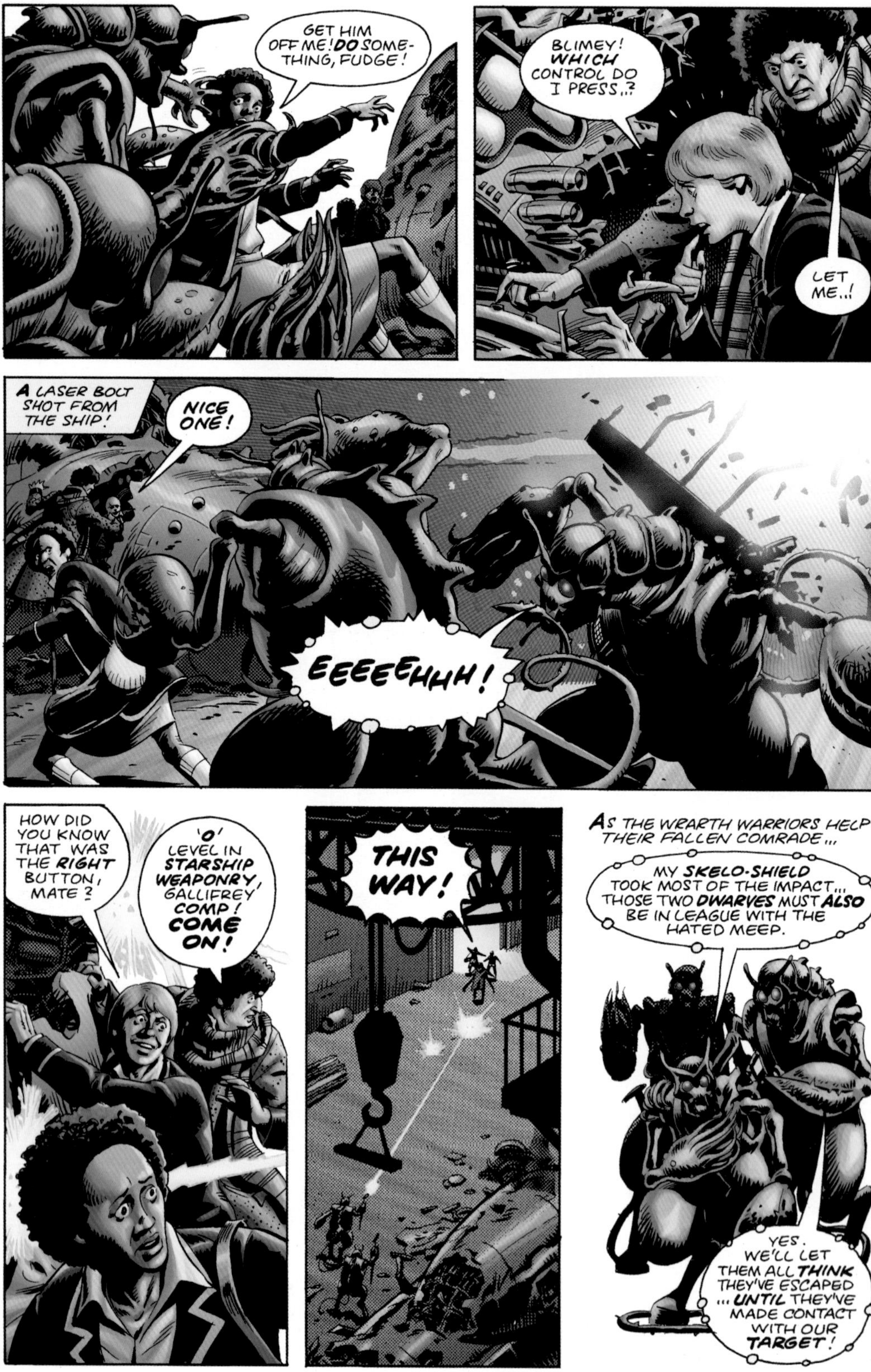

GET HIM OFF ME! DO SOME-THING, FUDGE!
BLIMEY! WHICH CONTROL DO I PRESS..?
LET ME..!
A LASER BOLT SHOT FROM THE SHIP!
NICE ONE!
EEEEEHHH!
HOW DID YOU KNOW THAT WAS THE RIGHT BUTTON, MATE?
'O' LEVEL IN STARSHIP WEAPONRY, GALLIFREY COMP! COME ON!
THIS WAY!
AS THE WRARTH WARRIORS HELP THEIR FALLEN COMRADE...
MY SKELO-SHIELD TOOK MOST OF THE IMPACT... THOSE TWO DWARVES MUST ALSO BE IN LEAGUE WITH THE HATED MEEP.
YES. WE'LL LET THEM ALL THINK THEY'VE ESCAPED ...UNTIL THEY'VE MADE CONTACT WITH OUR TARGET!

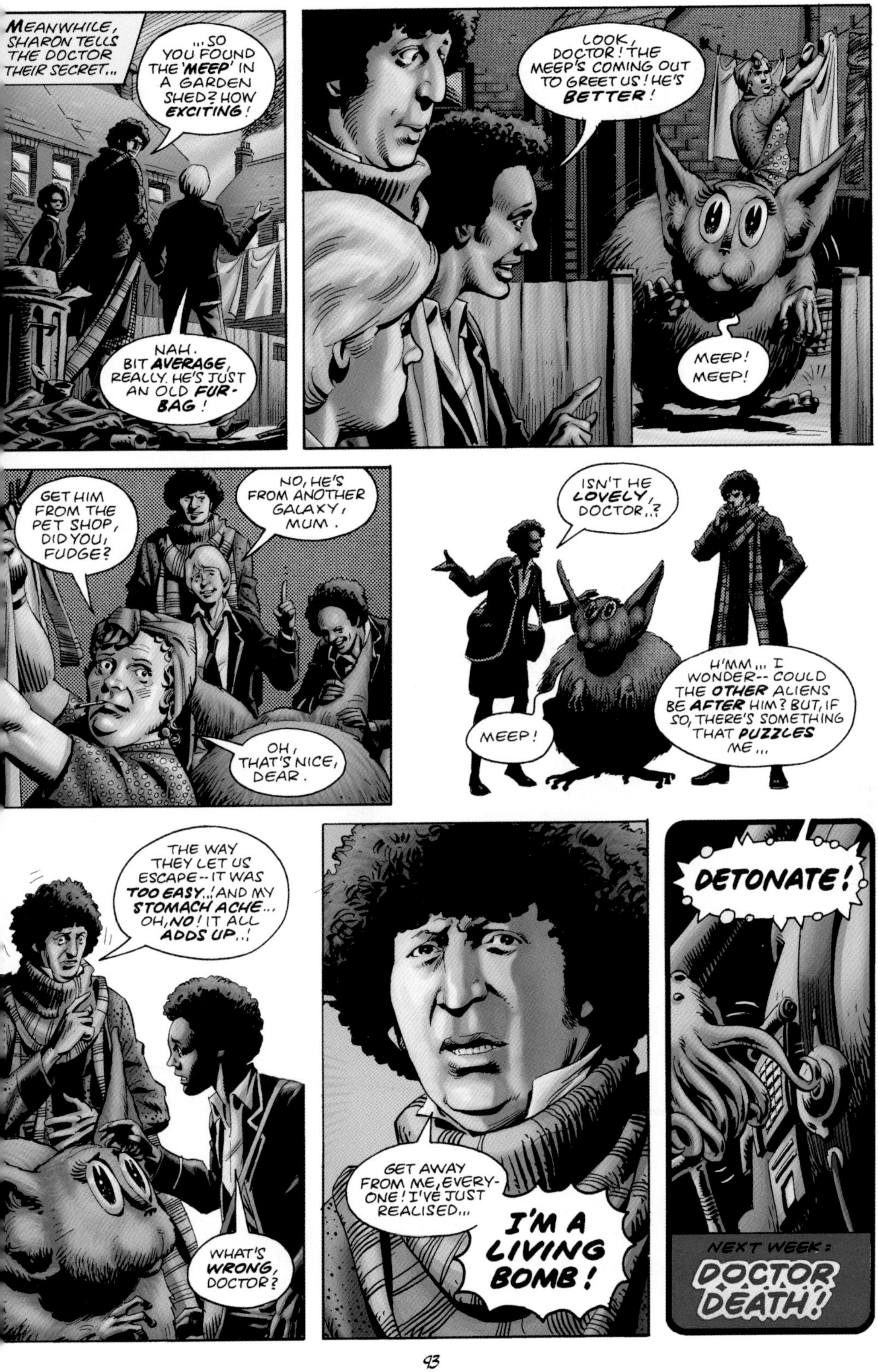
MEANWHILE, SHARON TELLS THE DOCTOR THEIR SECRET...
...SO YOU FOUND THE 'MEEP' IN A GARDEN SHED? HOW EXCITING!
NAH. BIT AVERAGE, REALLY. HE'S JUST AN OLD FUR-BAG!
LOOK, DOCTOR! THE MEEP'S COMING OUT TO GREET US! HE'S BETTER!
MEEP! MEEP!
GET HIM FROM THE PET SHOP, DID YOU, FUDGE?
NO, HE'S FROM ANOTHER GALAXY, MUM.
OH, THAT'S NICE, DEAR.
ISN'T HE LOVELY, DOCTOR..?
MEEP!
H'MM... I WONDER-- COULD THE OTHER ALIENS BE AFTER HIM? BUT, IF SO, THERE'S SOMETHING THAT PUZZLES ME...
THE WAY THEY LET US ESCAPE--IT WAS TOO EASY..! AND MY STOMACH ACHE... OH, NO! IT ALL ADDS UP..!
WHAT'S WRONG, DOCTOR?
GET AWAY FROM ME, EVERY-ONE! I'VE JUST REALISED...
I'M A LIVING BOMB!
DETONATE!
NEXT WEEK: DOCTOR DEATH!

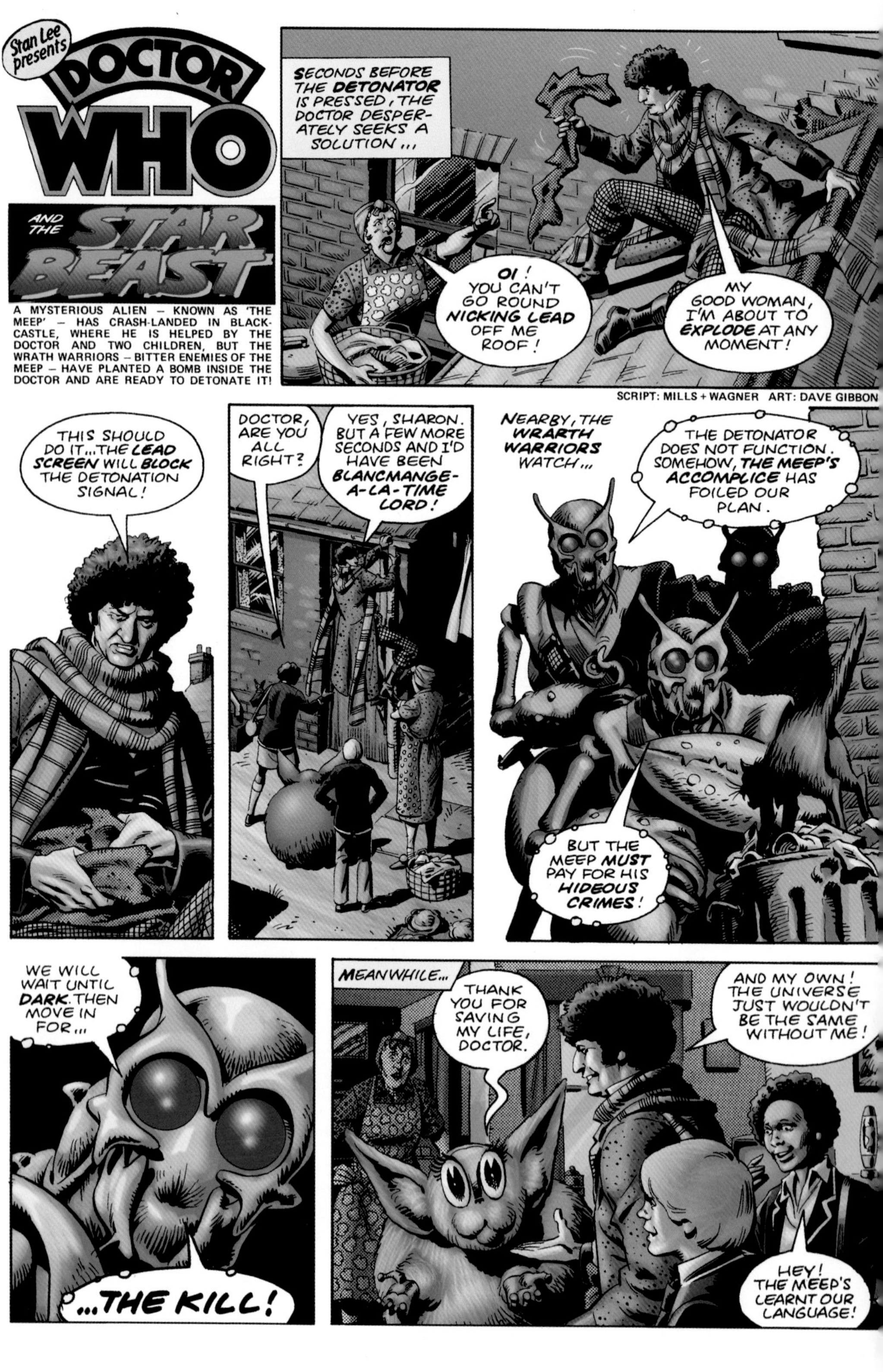
Stan Lee presents
DOCTOR WHO
AND THE STAR BEAST
A MYSTERIOUS ALIEN – KNOWN AS 'THE MEEP' – HAS CRASH-LANDED IN BLACKCASTLE, WHERE HE IS HELPED BY THE DOCTOR AND TWO CHILDREN, BUT THE WRATH WARRIORS – BITTER ENEMIES OF THE MEEP – HAVE PLANTED A BOMB INSIDE THE DOCTOR AND ARE READY TO DETONATE IT!
SECONDS BEFORE THE DETONATOR IS PRESSED, THE DOCTOR DESPERATELY SEEKS A SOLUTION...
OI! YOU CAN'T GO ROUND NICKING LEAD OFF ME ROOF!
MY GOOD WOMAN, I'M ABOUT TO EXPLODE AT ANY MOMENT!
SCRIPT: MILLS + WAGNER ART: DAVE GIBBON
THIS SHOULD DO IT... THE LEAD SCREEN WILL BLOCK THE DETONATION SIGNAL!
DOCTOR, ARE YOU ALL RIGHT?
YES, SHARON. BUT A FEW MORE SECONDS AND I'D HAVE BEEN BLANCMANGE-A-LA-TIME LORD!
NEARBY, THE WRARTH WARRIORS WATCH...
THE DETONATOR DOES NOT FUNCTION. SOMEHOW, THE MEEP'S ACCOMPLICE HAS FOILED OUR PLAN.
BUT THE MEEP MUST PAY FOR HIS HIDEOUS CRIMES!
WE WILL WAIT UNTIL DARK. THEN MOVE IN FOR...
...THE KILL!
MEANWHILE...
THANK YOU FOR SAVING MY LIFE, DOCTOR.
AND MY OWN! THE UNIVERSE JUST WOULDN'T BE THE SAME WITHOUT ME!
HEY! THE MEEP'S LEARNT OUR LANGUAGE!

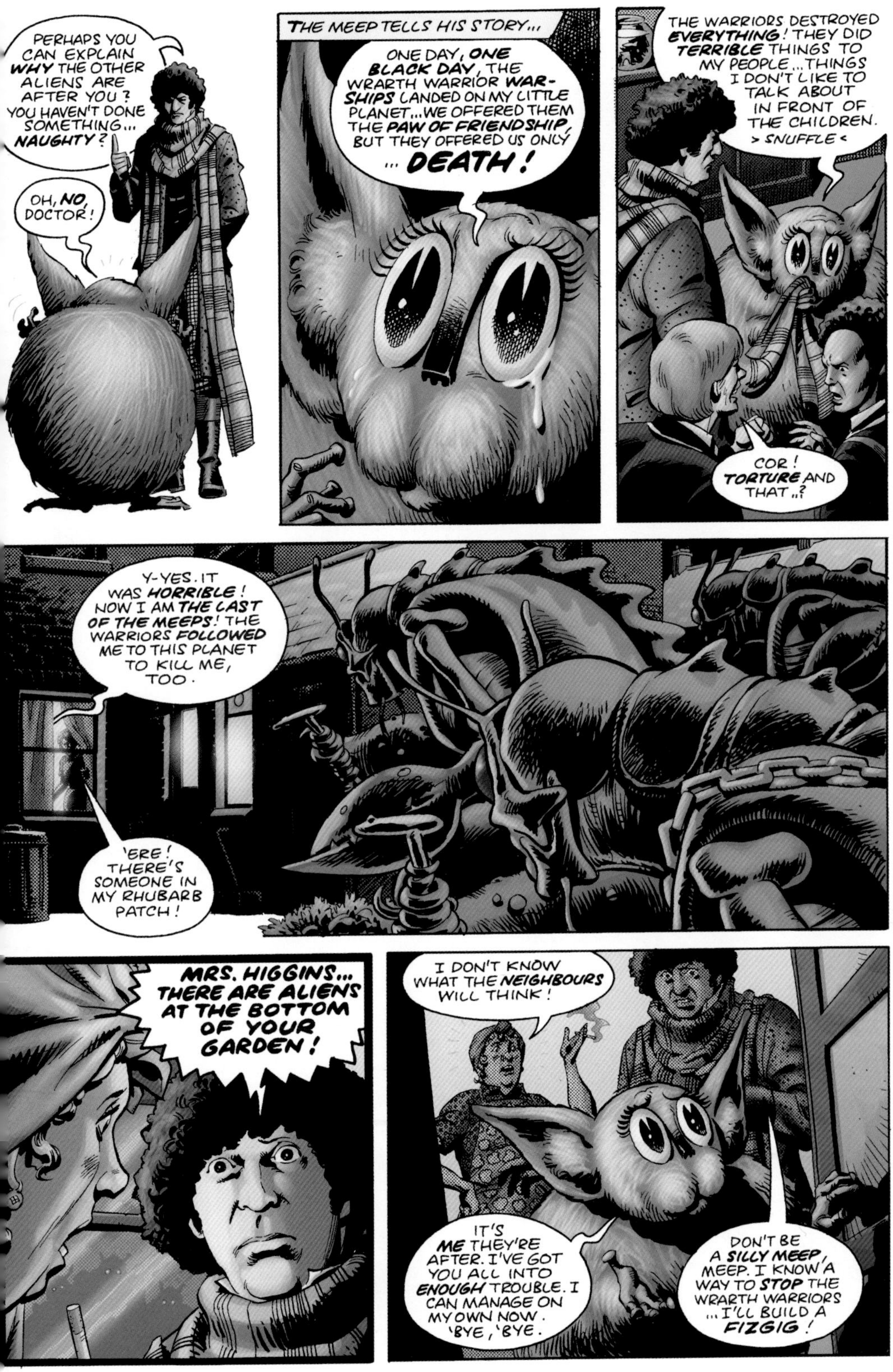
PERHAPS YOU CAN EXPLAIN **WHY** THE OTHER ALIENS ARE AFTER YOU? YOU HAVEN'T DONE SOMETHING... **NAUGHTY**?
OH, **NO**, DOCTOR!
THE MEEP TELLS HIS STORY...
ONE DAY, **ONE BLACK DAY**, THE WRARTH WARRIOR **WAR-SHIPS** LANDED ON MY LITTLE PLANET... WE OFFERED THEM THE **PAW OF FRIENDSHIP**, BUT THEY OFFERED US ONLY ... **DEATH!**
THE WARRIORS DESTROYED **EVERYTHING**! THEY DID **TERRIBLE** THINGS TO MY PEOPLE... THINGS I DON'T LIKE TO TALK ABOUT IN FRONT OF THE CHILDREN. >SNUFFLE<
COR! **TORTURE** AND THAT..?
Y-YES. IT WAS **HORRIBLE**! NOW I AM **THE LAST OF THE MEEPS**! THE WARRIORS **FOLLOWED** ME TO THIS PLANET TO KILL ME, TOO.
'ERE! THERE'S SOMEONE IN MY RHUBARB PATCH!
MRS. HIGGINS... THERE ARE ALIENS AT THE BOTTOM OF YOUR GARDEN!
I DON'T KNOW WHAT THE **NEIGHBOURS** WILL THINK!
IT'S **ME** THEY'RE AFTER. I'VE GOT YOU ALL INTO **ENOUGH** TROUBLE. I CAN MANAGE ON MY OWN NOW. 'BYE, 'BYE.
DON'T BE A **SILLY MEEP**, MEEP. I KNOW A WAY TO **STOP** THE WRARTH WARRIORS ... I'LL BUILD A **FIZGIG**!

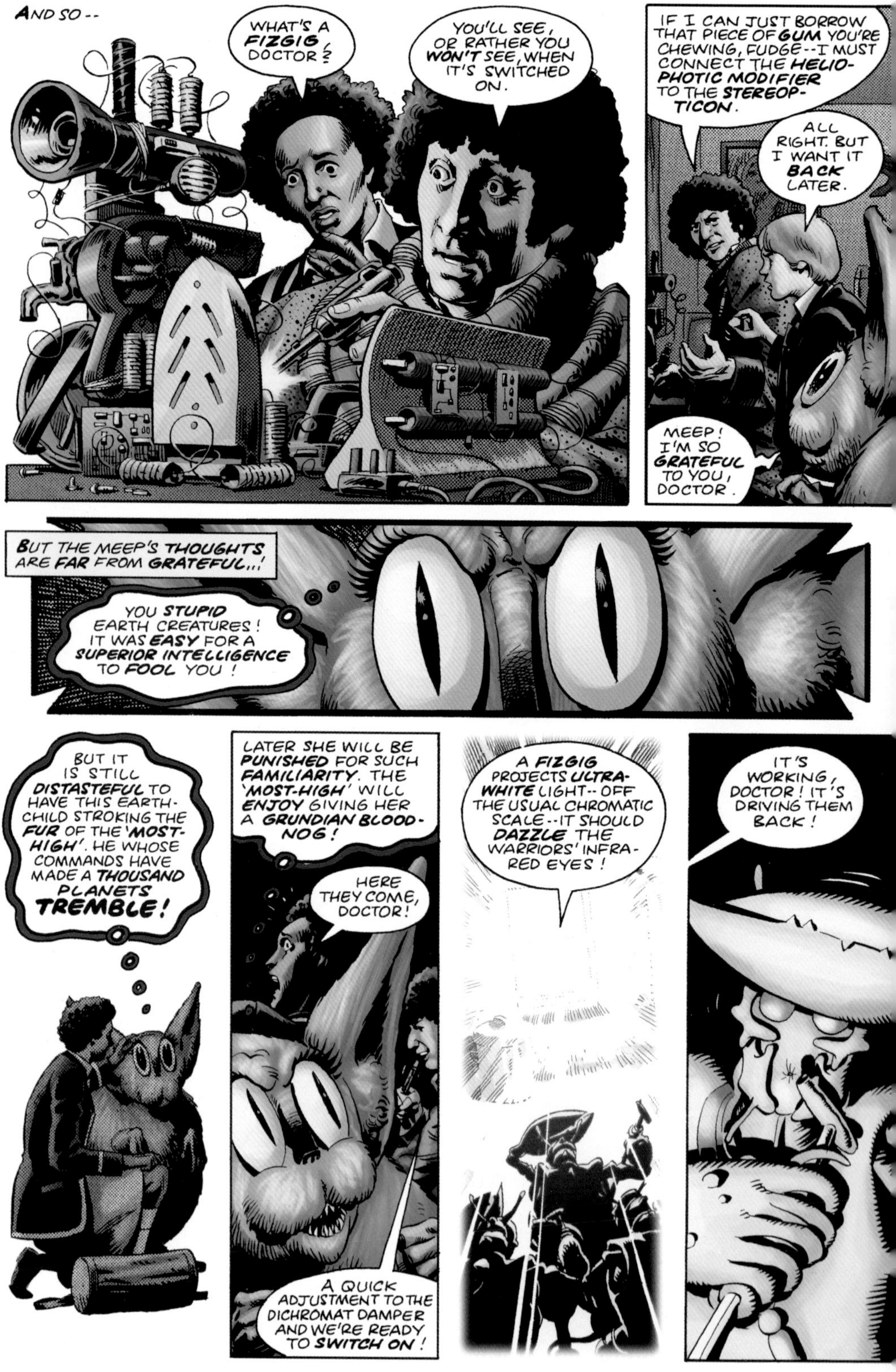

AND SO --
WHAT'S A FIZGIG, DOCTOR?
YOU'LL SEE, OR RATHER YOU WON'T SEE, WHEN IT'S SWITCHED ON.
IF I CAN JUST BORROW THAT PIECE OF GUM YOU'RE CHEWING, FUDGE -- I MUST CONNECT THE HELIO-PHOTIC MODIFIER TO THE STEREOP-TICON.
ALL RIGHT. BUT I WANT IT BACK LATER.
MEEP! I'M SO GRATEFUL TO YOU, DOCTOR.
BUT THE MEEP'S THOUGHTS ARE FAR FROM GRATEFUL...!
YOU STUPID EARTH CREATURES! IT WAS EASY FOR A SUPERIOR INTELLIGENCE TO FOOL YOU!
BUT IT IS STILL DISTASTEFUL TO HAVE THIS EARTH-CHILD STROKING THE FUR OF THE 'MOST-HIGH'. HE WHOSE COMMANDS HAVE MADE A THOUSAND PLANETS TREMBLE!
LATER SHE WILL BE PUNISHED FOR SUCH FAMILIARITY. THE 'MOST-HIGH' WILL ENJOY GIVING HER A GRUNDIAN BLOOD-NOG!
HERE THEY COME, DOCTOR!
A QUICK ADJUSTMENT TO THE DICHROMAT DAMPER AND WE'RE READY TO SWITCH ON!
A FIZGIG PROJECTS ULTRA-WHITE LIGHT -- OFF THE USUAL CHROMATIC SCALE -- IT SHOULD DAZZLE THE WARRIORS' INFRA-RED EYES!
IT'S WORKING, DOCTOR! IT'S DRIVING THEM BACK!

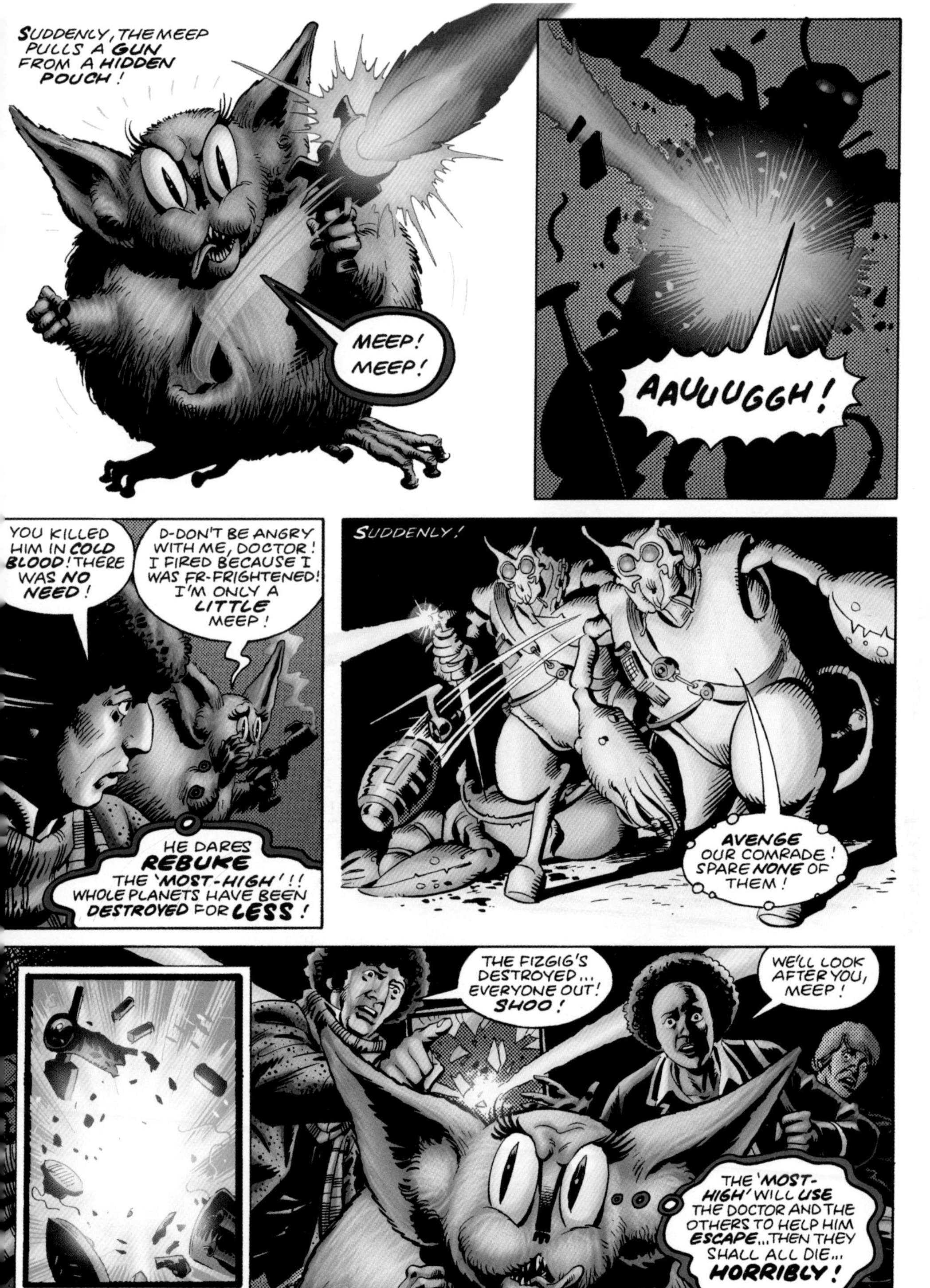
SUDDENLY, THE MEEP PULLS A GUN FROM A HIDDEN POUCH!
MEEP! MEEP!
AAUUUGGH!
YOU KILLED HIM IN COLD BLOOD! THERE WAS NO NEED!
D-DON'T BE ANGRY WITH ME, DOCTOR! I FIRED BECAUSE I WAS FR-FRIGHTENED! I'M ONLY A LITTLE MEEP!
HE DARES REBUKE THE 'MOST-HIGH'!! WHOLE PLANETS HAVE BEEN DESTROYED FOR LESS!
SUDDENLY!
AVENGE OUR COMRADE! SPARE NONE OF THEM!
THE FIZGIG'S DESTROYED... EVERYONE OUT! SHOO!
WE'LL LOOK AFTER YOU, MEEP!
THE 'MOST-HIGH' WILL USE THE DOCTOR AND THE OTHERS TO HELP HIM ESCAPE... THEN THEY SHALL ALL DIE... HORRIBLY!

NEXT ISSUE: REVENGE of WRARTH!

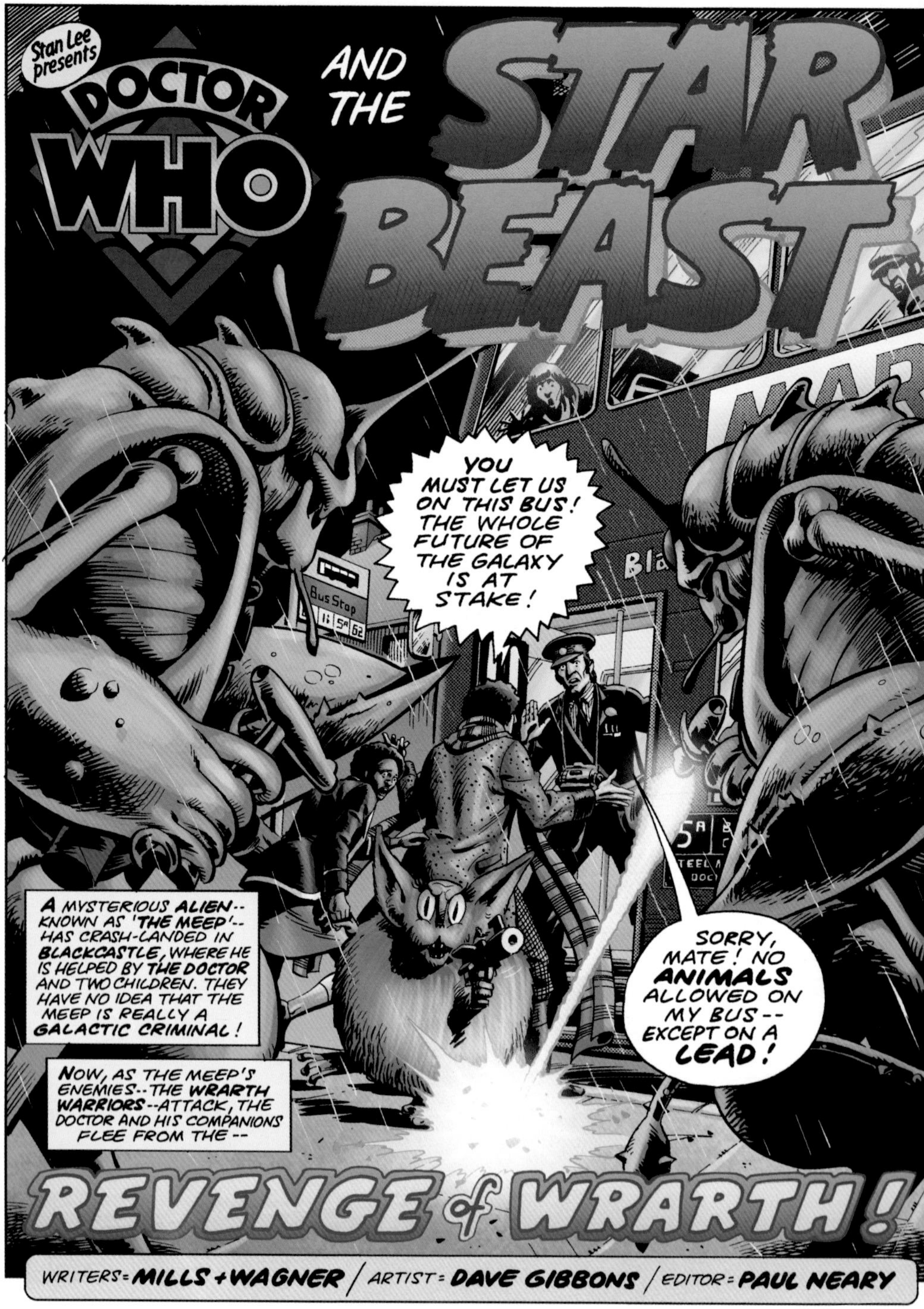
Stan Lee presents
DOCTOR WHO
AND THE
STAR BEAST
YOU MUST LET US ON THIS BUS! THE WHOLE FUTURE OF THE GALAXY IS AT STAKE!
Bus Stop
A MYSTERIOUS ALIEN-- KNOWN AS 'THE MEEP'-- HAS CRASH-LANDED IN BLACKCASTLE, WHERE HE IS HELPED BY THE DOCTOR AND TWO CHILDREN. THEY HAVE NO IDEA THAT THE MEEP IS REALLY A GALACTIC CRIMINAL!
SORRY, MATE! NO ANIMALS ALLOWED ON MY BUS-- EXCEPT ON A LEAD!
NOW, AS THE MEEP'S ENEMIES--THE WRARTH WARRIORS--ATTACK, THE DOCTOR AND HIS COMPANIONS FLEE FROM THE--
REVENGE of WRARTH!
WRITERS= MILLS + WAGNER / ARTIST= DAVE GIBBONS / EDITOR= PAUL NEARY

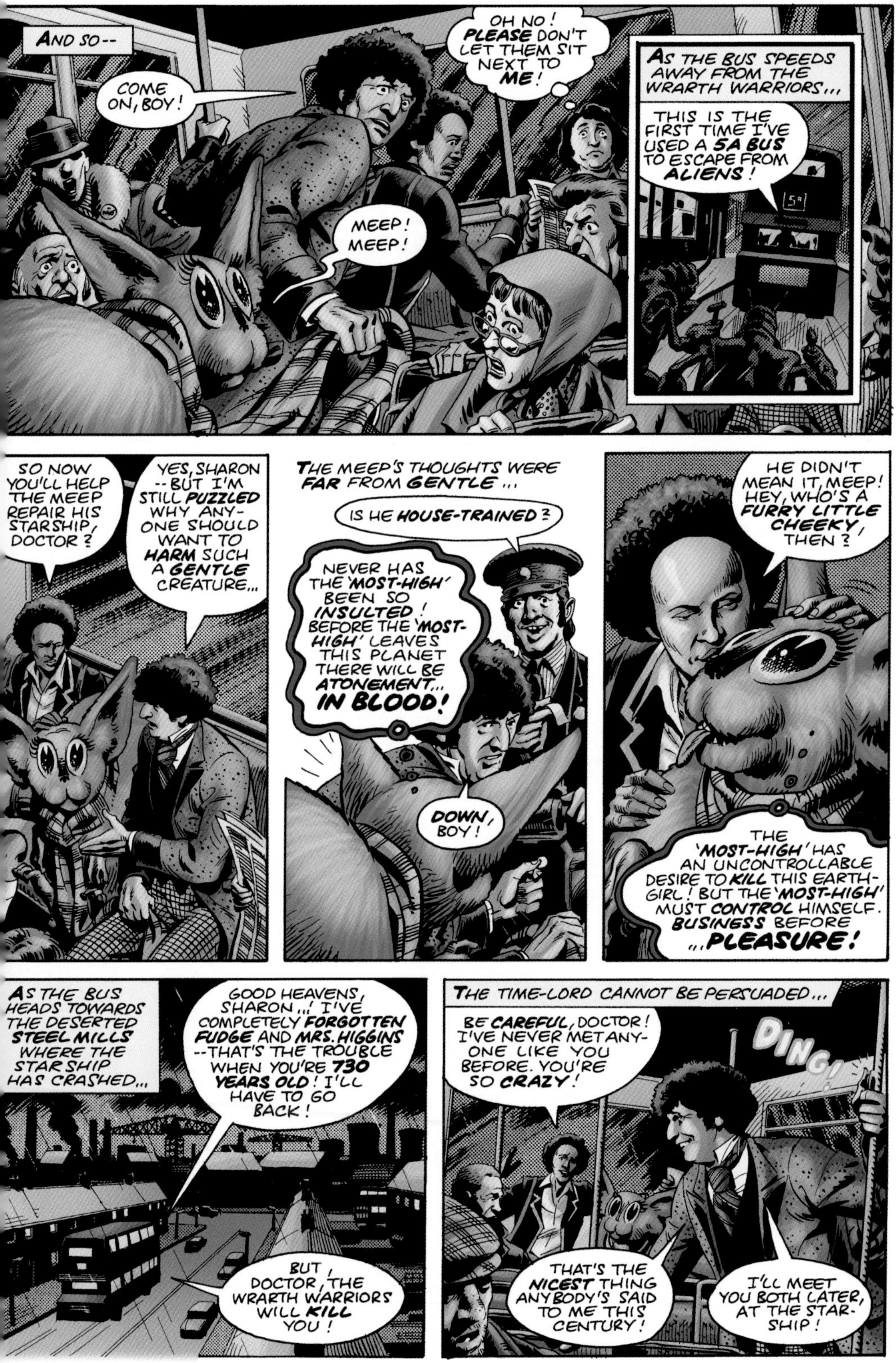

AND SO--
COME ON, BOY!
OH NO! PLEASE DON'T LET THEM SIT NEXT TO ME!
AS THE BUS SPEEDS AWAY FROM THE WRARTH WARRIORS...
THIS IS THE FIRST TIME I'VE USED A 5A BUS TO ESCAPE FROM ALIENS!
MEEP! MEEP!
SO NOW YOU'LL HELP THE MEEP REPAIR HIS STARSHIP, DOCTOR?
YES, SHARON --BUT I'M STILL PUZZLED WHY ANYONE SHOULD WANT TO HARM SUCH A GENTLE CREATURE...
THE MEEP'S THOUGHTS WERE FAR FROM GENTLE...
IS HE HOUSE-TRAINED?
NEVER HAS THE 'MOST-HIGH' BEEN SO INSULTED! BEFORE THE 'MOST-HIGH' LEAVES THIS PLANET THERE WILL BE ATONEMENT... IN BLOOD!
DOWN, BOY!
HE DIDN'T MEAN IT, MEEP! HEY, WHO'S A FURRY LITTLE CHEEKY, THEN?
THE 'MOST-HIGH' HAS AN UNCONTROLLABLE DESIRE TO KILL THIS EARTH-GIRL! BUT THE 'MOST-HIGH' MUST CONTROL HIMSELF. BUSINESS BEFORE ...PLEASURE!
AS THE BUS HEADS TOWARDS THE DESERTED STEEL MILLS WHERE THE STARSHIP HAS CRASHED...
GOOD HEAVENS, SHARON...! I'VE COMPLETELY FORGOTTEN FUDGE AND MRS. HIGGINS --THAT'S THE TROUBLE WHEN YOU'RE 730 YEARS OLD! I'LL HAVE TO GO BACK!
BUT, DOCTOR, THE WRARTH WARRIORS WILL KILL YOU!
THE TIME-LORD CANNOT BE PERSUADED...
BE CAREFUL, DOCTOR! I'VE NEVER MET ANYONE LIKE YOU BEFORE. YOU'RE SO CRAZY!
DING!
THAT'S THE NICEST THING ANYBODY'S SAID TO ME THIS CENTURY!
I'LL MEET YOU BOTH LATER, AT THE STARSHIP!

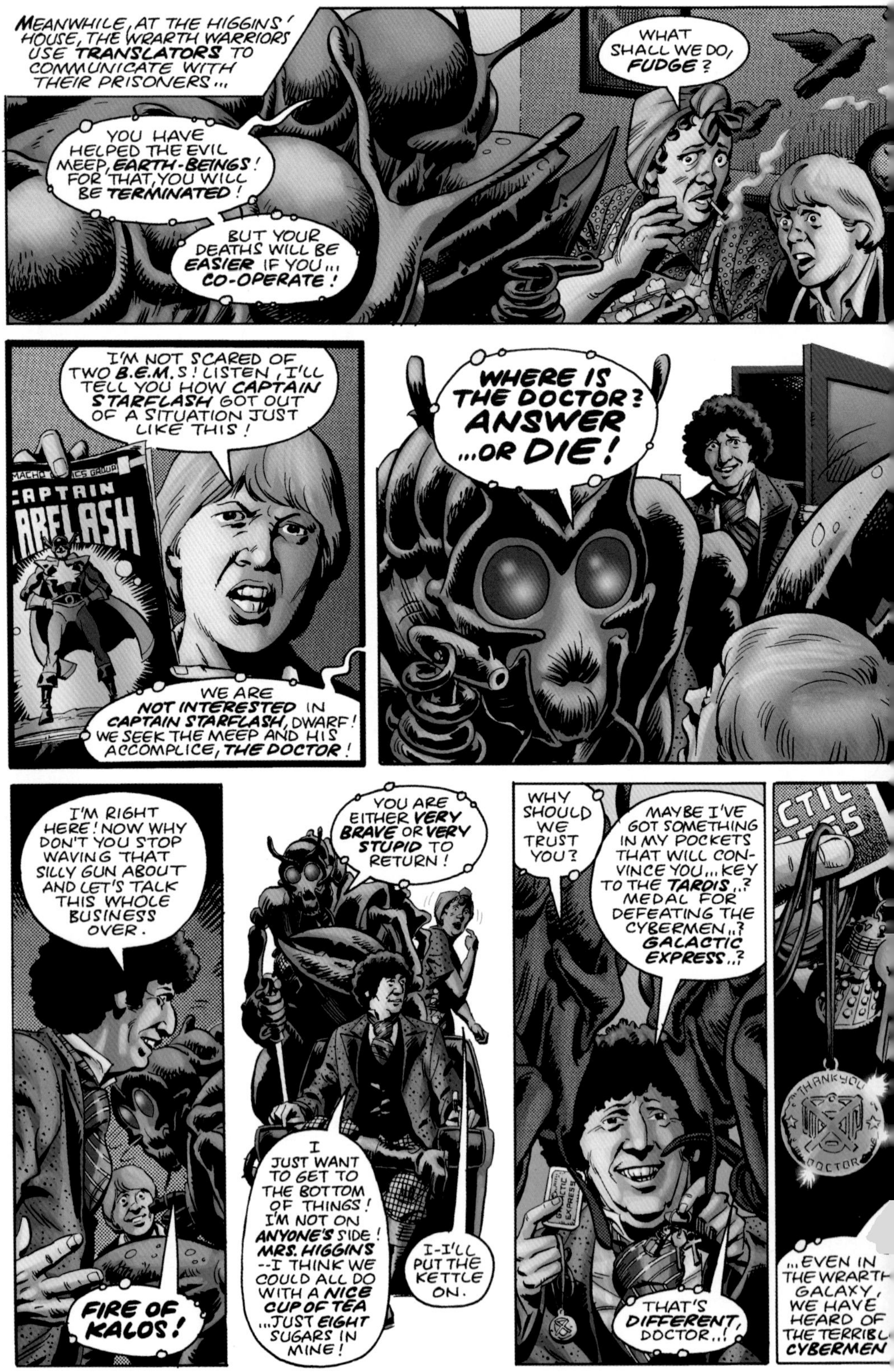

MEANWHILE, AT THE HIGGINS' HOUSE, THE WRARTH WARRIORS USE TRANSLATORS TO COMMUNICATE WITH THEIR PRISONERS...
WHAT SHALL WE DO, FUDGE?
YOU HAVE HELPED THE EVIL MEEP, EARTH-BEINGS! FOR THAT, YOU WILL BE TERMINATED!
BUT YOUR DEATHS WILL BE EASIER IF YOU... CO-OPERATE!
I'M NOT SCARED OF TWO B.E.M.S! LISTEN, I'LL TELL YOU HOW CAPTAIN STARFLASH GOT OUT OF A SITUATION JUST LIKE THIS!
CAPTAIN ARFLASH
WE ARE NOT INTERESTED IN CAPTAIN STARFLASH, DWARF! WE SEEK THE MEEP AND HIS ACCOMPLICE, THE DOCTOR!
WHERE IS THE DOCTOR? ANSWER ...OR DIE!
I'M RIGHT HERE! NOW WHY DON'T YOU STOP WAVING THAT SILLY GUN ABOUT AND LET'S TALK THIS WHOLE BUSINESS OVER.
FIRE OF KALOS!
YOU ARE EITHER VERY BRAVE OR VERY STUPID TO RETURN!
I JUST WANT TO GET TO THE BOTTOM OF THINGS! I'M NOT ON ANYONE'S SIDE! MRS. HIGGINS --I THINK WE COULD ALL DO WITH A NICE CUP OF TEA ...JUST EIGHT SUGARS IN MINE!
I-I'LL PUT THE KETTLE ON.
WHY SHOULD WE TRUST YOU?
MAYBE I'VE GOT SOMETHING IN MY POCKETS THAT WILL CONVINCE YOU... KEY TO THE TARDIS..? MEDAL FOR DEFEATING THE CYBERMEN..? GALACTIC EXPRESS..?
THAT'S DIFFERENT, DOCTOR..!
THANK YOU DOCTOR
...EVEN IN THE WRARTH GALAXY, WE HAVE HEARD OF THE TERRIBL CYBERMEN

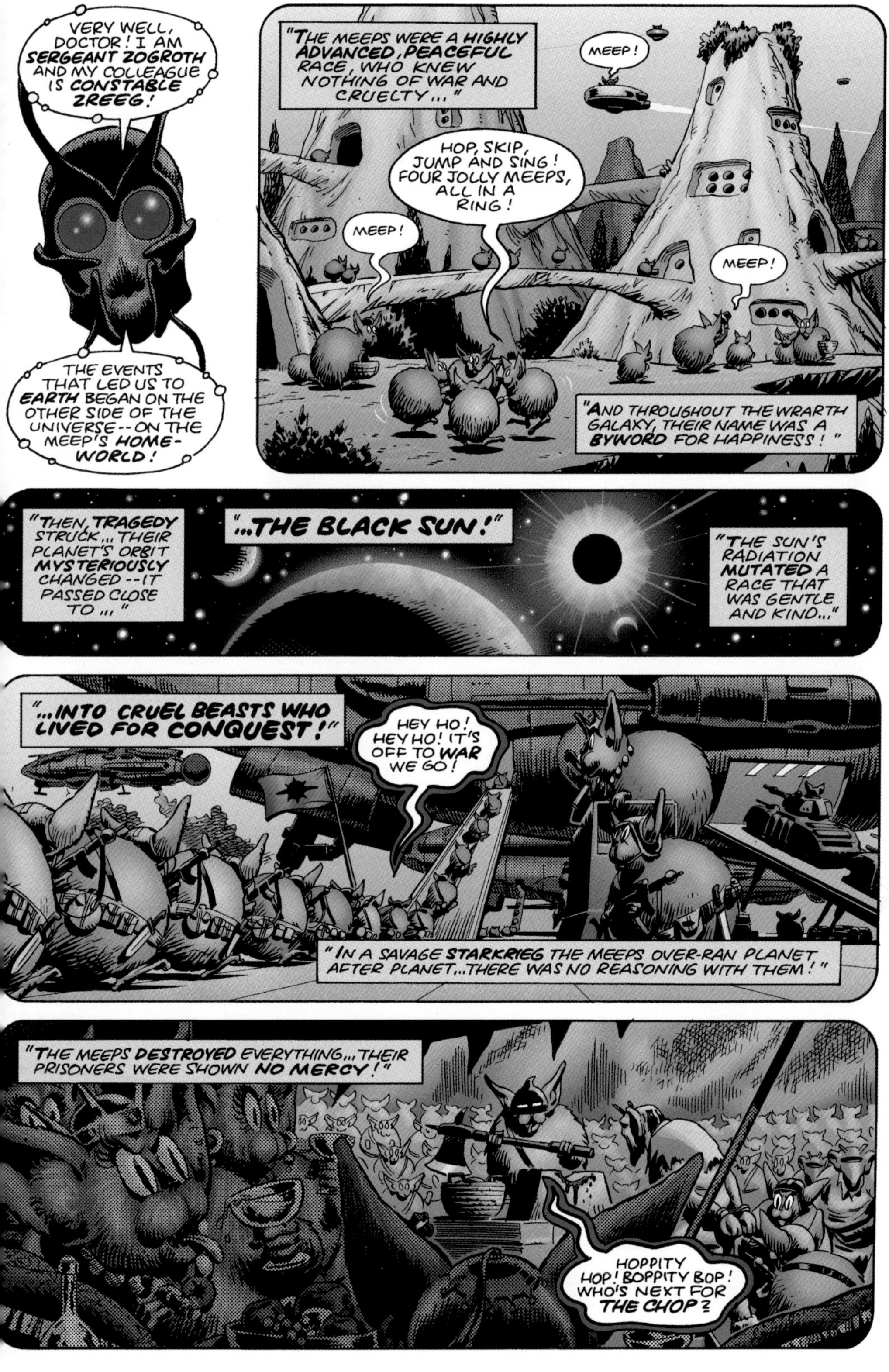
VERY WELL, DOCTOR! I AM SERGEANT ZOGROTH AND MY COLLEAGUE IS CONSTABLE ZREEG!
THE EVENTS THAT LED US TO EARTH BEGAN ON THE OTHER SIDE OF THE UNIVERSE--ON THE MEEP'S HOME-WORLD!
"THE MEEPS WERE A HIGHLY ADVANCED, PEACEFUL RACE, WHO KNEW NOTHING OF WAR AND CRUELTY..."
MEEP!
HOP, SKIP, JUMP AND SING! FOUR JOLLY MEEPS, ALL IN A RING!
MEEP!
MEEP!
"AND THROUGHOUT THE WRARTH GALAXY, THEIR NAME WAS A BYWORD FOR HAPPINESS!"
"THEN, TRAGEDY STRUCK... THEIR PLANET'S ORBIT MYSTERIOUSLY CHANGED --IT PASSED CLOSE TO..."
"...THE BLACK SUN!"
"THE SUN'S RADIATION MUTATED A RACE THAT WAS GENTLE AND KIND..."
"...INTO CRUEL BEASTS WHO LIVED FOR CONQUEST!"
HEY HO! HEY HO! IT'S OFF TO WAR WE GO!
"IN A SAVAGE STARKRIEG THE MEEPS OVER-RAN PLANET AFTER PLANET...THERE WAS NO REASONING WITH THEM!"
"THE MEEPS DESTROYED EVERYTHING... THEIR PRISONERS WERE SHOWN NO MERCY!"
HOPPITY HOP! BOPPITY BOP! WHO'S NEXT FOR THE CHOP?

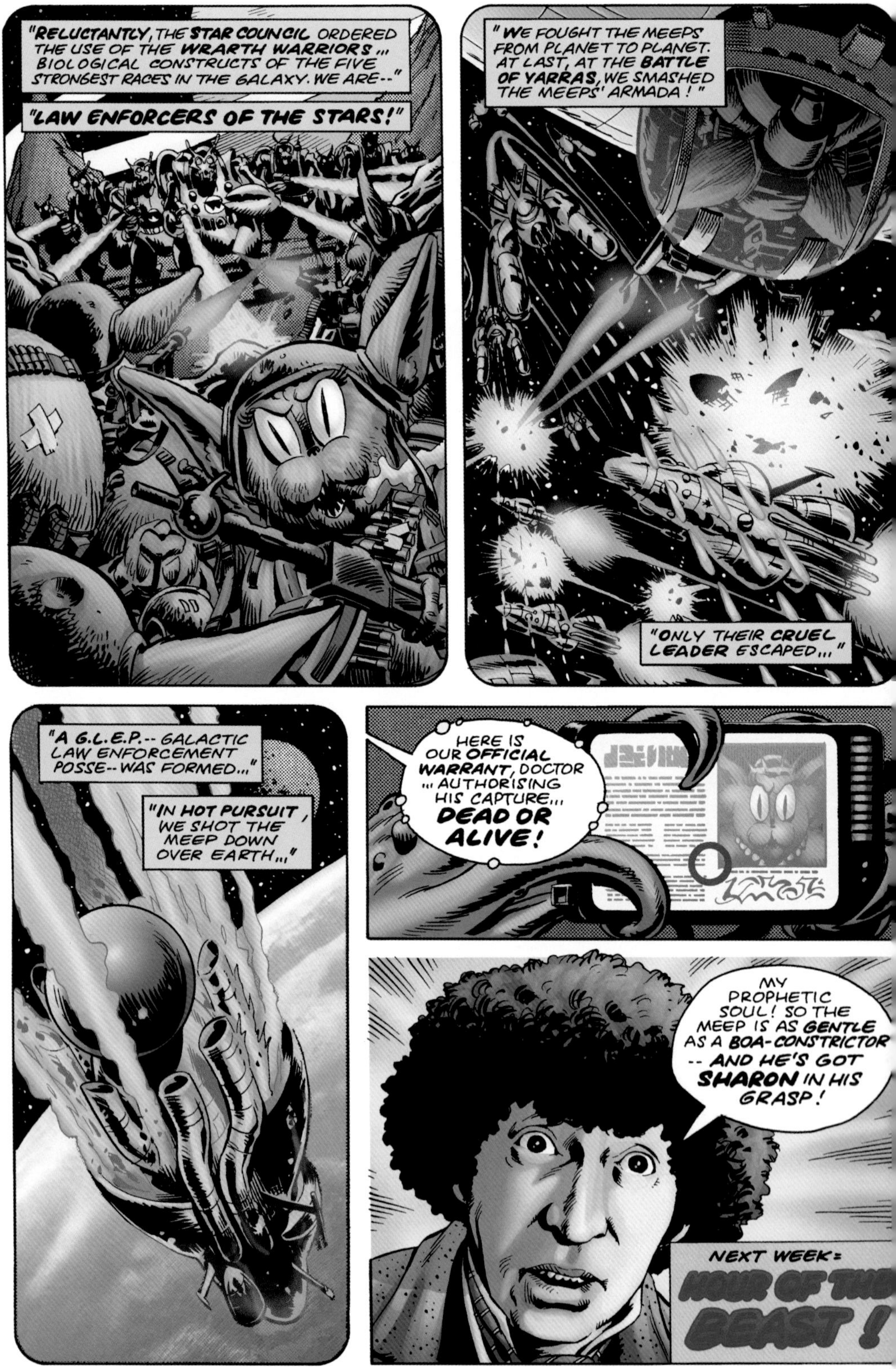
"RELUCTANTLY, THE STAR COUNCIL ORDERED THE USE OF THE WRARTH WARRIORS... BIOLOGICAL CONSTRUCTS OF THE FIVE STRONGEST RACES IN THE GALAXY. WE ARE--"
"LAW ENFORCERS OF THE STARS!"
"WE FOUGHT THE MEEPS FROM PLANET TO PLANET. AT LAST, AT THE BATTLE OF YARRAS, WE SMASHED THE MEEPS' ARMADA!"
"ONLY THEIR CRUEL LEADER ESCAPED..."
"A G.L.E.P.-- GALACTIC LAW ENFORCEMENT POSSE--WAS FORMED..."
"IN HOT PURSUIT, WE SHOT THE MEEP DOWN OVER EARTH..."
HERE IS OUR OFFICIAL WARRANT, DOCTOR ...AUTHORISING HIS CAPTURE... DEAD OR ALIVE!
MY PROPHETIC SOUL! SO THE MEEP IS AS GENTLE AS A BOA-CONSTRICTOR -- AND HE'S GOT SHARON IN HIS GRASP!
NEXT WEEK:
HOUR OF THE BEAST!

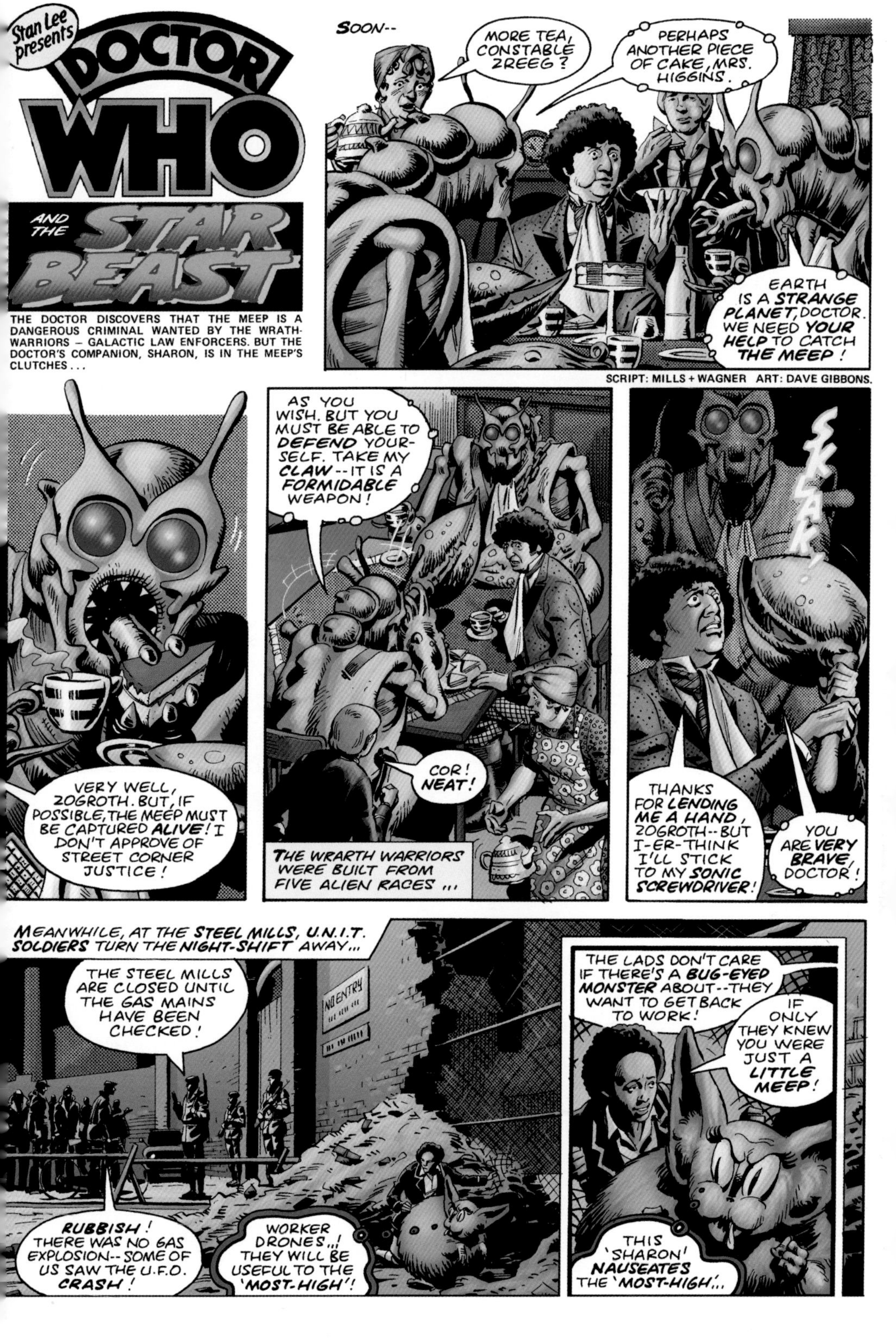
Stan Lee presents
DOCTOR WHO
AND THE STAR BEAST
THE DOCTOR DISCOVERS THAT THE MEEP IS A DANGEROUS CRIMINAL WANTED BY THE WRATH-WARRIORS – GALACTIC LAW ENFORCERS. BUT THE DOCTOR'S COMPANION, SHARON, IS IN THE MEEP'S CLUTCHES . . .
SOON--
MORE TEA, CONSTABLE ZREEG?
PERHAPS ANOTHER PIECE OF CAKE, MRS. HIGGINS.
EARTH IS A STRANGE PLANET, DOCTOR. WE NEED YOUR HELP TO CATCH THE MEEP!
SCRIPT: MILLS + WAGNER ART: DAVE GIBBONS.
VERY WELL, ZOGROTH. BUT, IF POSSIBLE, THE MEEP MUST BE CAPTURED ALIVE! I DON'T APPROVE OF STREET CORNER JUSTICE!
AS YOU WISH. BUT YOU MUST BE ABLE TO DEFEND YOUR-SELF. TAKE MY CLAW --IT IS A FORMIDABLE WEAPON!
COR! NEAT!
THE WRAATH WARRIORS WERE BUILT FROM FIVE ALIEN RACES ...
SKLAK!
THANKS FOR LENDING ME A HAND, ZOGROTH--BUT I-ER-THINK I'LL STICK TO MY SONIC SCREWDRIVER!
YOU ARE VERY BRAVE, DOCTOR!
MEANWHILE, AT THE STEEL MILLS, U.N.I.T. SOLDIERS TURN THE NIGHT-SHIFT AWAY...
THE STEEL MILLS ARE CLOSED UNTIL THE GAS MAINS HAVE BEEN CHECKED!
NO ENTRY
RUBBISH! THERE WAS NO GAS EXPLOSION-- SOME OF US SAW THE U.F.O. CRASH!
WORKER DRONES..! THEY WILL BE USEFUL TO THE 'MOST-HIGH'!
THE LADS DON'T CARE IF THERE'S A BUG-EYED MONSTER ABOUT--THEY WANT TO GET BACK TO WORK!
IF ONLY THEY KNEW YOU WERE JUST A LITTLE MEEP!
THIS 'SHARON' NAUSEATES THE 'MOST-HIGH'...

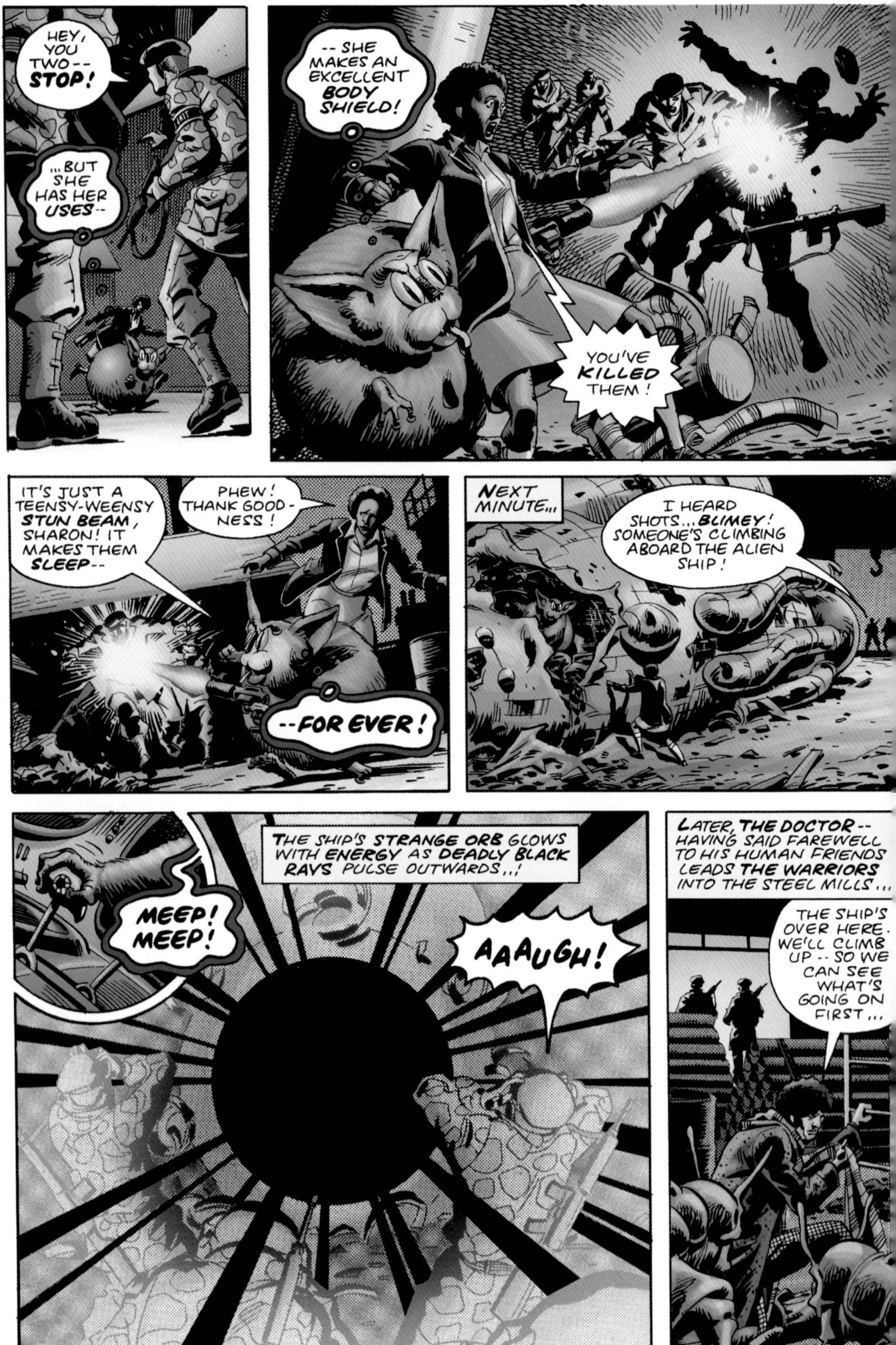
HEY, YOU TWO -- STOP!
...BUT SHE HAS HER USES--
-- SHE MAKES AN EXCELLENT BODY SHIELD!
YOU'VE KILLED THEM!
IT'S JUST A TEENSY-WEENSY STUN BEAM, SHARON! IT MAKES THEM SLEEP--
PHEW! THANK GOOD-NESS!
--FOR EVER!
NEXT MINUTE...
I HEARD SHOTS... BLIMEY! SOMEONE'S CLIMBING ABOARD THE ALIEN SHIP!
THE SHIP'S STRANGE ORB GLOWS WITH ENERGY AS DEADLY BLACK RAYS PULSE OUTWARDS...!
MEEP! MEEP!
AAAUGH!
LATER, THE DOCTOR -- HAVING SAID FAREWELL TO HIS HUMAN FRIENDS LEADS THE WARRIORS INTO THE STEEL MILLS...
THE SHIP'S OVER HERE. WE'LL CLIMB UP -- SO WE CAN SEE WHAT'S GOING ON FIRST...

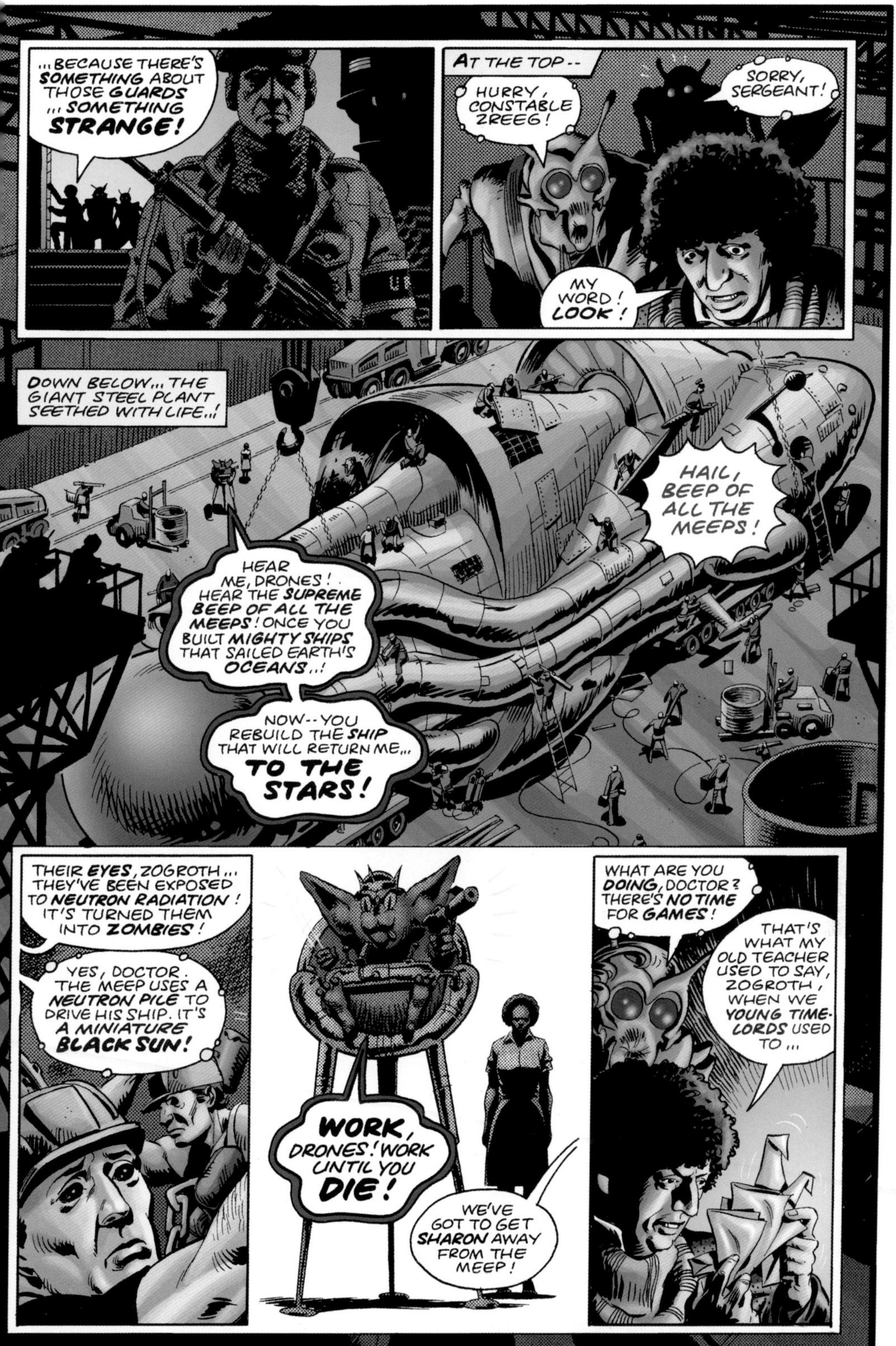
...BECAUSE THERE'S SOMETHING ABOUT THOSE GUARDS ... SOMETHING STRANGE!
AT THE TOP --
HURRY, CONSTABLE ZREEG!
SORRY, SERGEANT!
MY WORD! LOOK!
DOWN BELOW... THE GIANT STEEL PLANT SEETHED WITH LIFE...!
HAIL, BEEP OF ALL THE MEEPS!
HEAR ME, DRONES! HEAR THE SUPREME BEEP OF ALL THE MEEPS! ONCE YOU BUILT MIGHTY SHIPS THAT SAILED EARTH'S OCEANS...!
NOW--YOU REBUILD THE SHIP THAT WILL RETURN ME... TO THE STARS!
THEIR EYES, ZOGROTH... THEY'VE BEEN EXPOSED TO NEUTRON RADIATION! IT'S TURNED THEM INTO ZOMBIES!
YES, DOCTOR. THE MEEP USES A NEUTRON PILE TO DRIVE HIS SHIP. IT'S A MINIATURE BLACK SUN!
WORK, DRONES! WORK UNTIL YOU DIE!
WE'VE GOT TO GET SHARON AWAY FROM THE MEEP!
WHAT ARE YOU DOING, DOCTOR? THERE'S NO TIME FOR GAMES!
THAT'S WHAT MY OLD TEACHER USED TO SAY, ZOGROTH, WHEN WE YOUNG TIME-LORDS USED TO ...

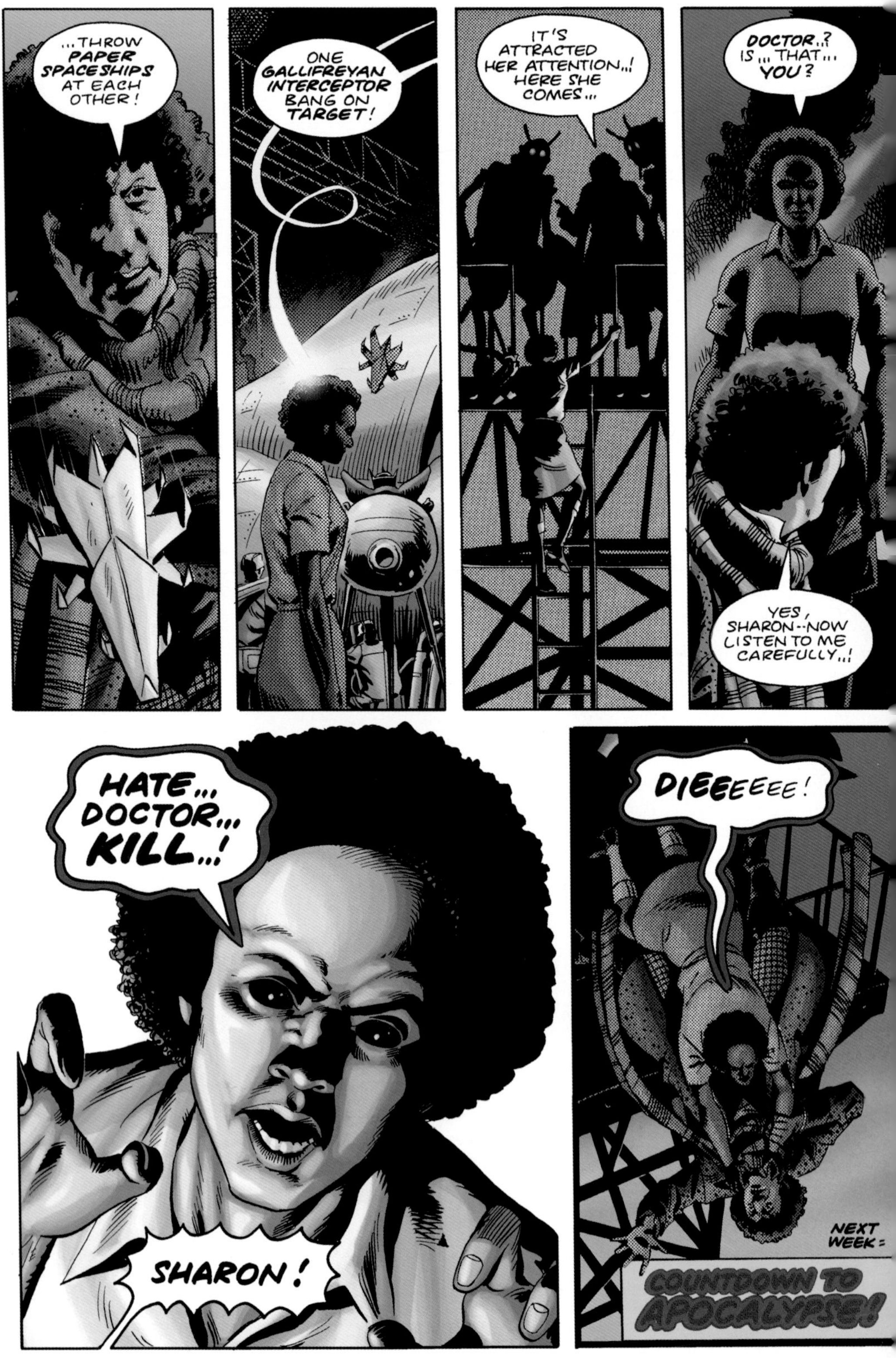
...THROW PAPER SPACESHIPS AT EACH OTHER!
ONE GALLIFREYAN INTERCEPTOR BANG ON TARGET!
IT'S ATTRACTED HER ATTENTION..! HERE SHE COMES...
DOCTOR..? IS... THAT... YOU?
YES, SHARON--NOW LISTEN TO ME CAREFULLY..!
HATE... DOCTOR... KILL...!
SHARON!
DIEEEEEE!
NEXT WEEK=
COUNTDOWN TO APOCALYPSE!

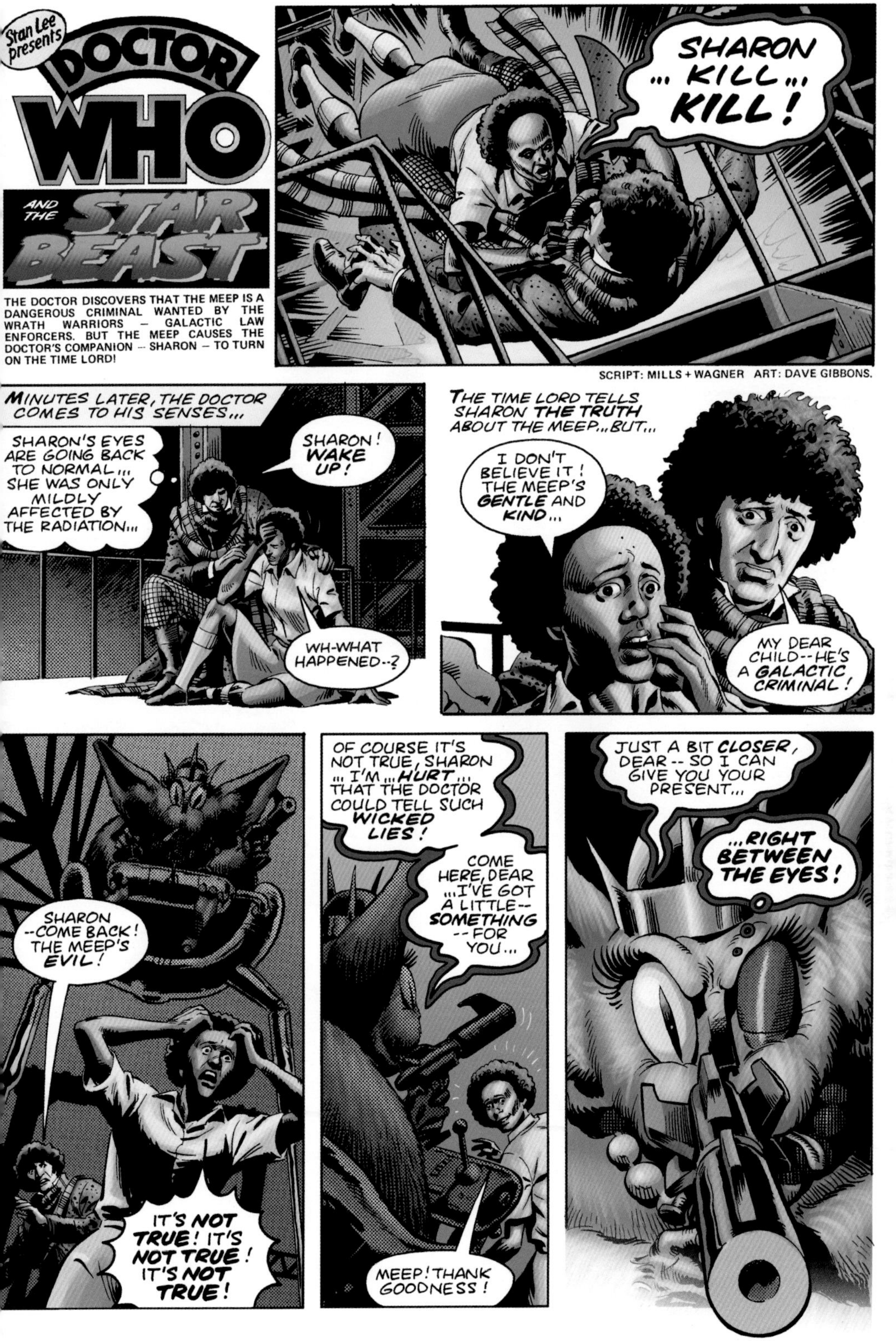
Stan Lee presents
DOCTOR WHO
AND THE STAR BEAST
THE DOCTOR DISCOVERS THAT THE MEEP IS A DANGEROUS CRIMINAL WANTED BY THE WRATH WARRIORS — GALACTIC LAW ENFORCERS. BUT THE MEEP CAUSES THE DOCTOR'S COMPANION -- SHARON — TO TURN ON THE TIME LORD!
SHARON ... KILL ... KILL!
SCRIPT: MILLS + WAGNER ART: DAVE GIBBONS.
MINUTES LATER, THE DOCTOR COMES TO HIS SENSES...
SHARON'S EYES ARE GOING BACK TO NORMAL... SHE WAS ONLY MILDLY AFFECTED BY THE RADIATION...
SHARON! WAKE UP!
WH-WHAT HAPPENED--?
THE TIME LORD TELLS SHARON THE TRUTH ABOUT THE MEEP... BUT...
I DON'T BELIEVE IT! THE MEEP'S GENTLE AND KIND...
MY DEAR CHILD--HE'S A GALACTIC CRIMINAL!
SHARON --COME BACK! THE MEEP'S EVIL!
IT'S NOT TRUE! IT'S NOT TRUE! IT'S NOT TRUE!
OF COURSE IT'S NOT TRUE, SHARON ... I'M ... HURT ... THAT THE DOCTOR COULD TELL SUCH WICKED LIES!
COME HERE, DEAR ... I'VE GOT A LITTLE-- SOMETHING --FOR YOU...
MEEP! THANK GOODNESS!
JUST A BIT CLOSER, DEAR -- SO I CAN GIVE YOU YOUR PRESENT...
...RIGHT BETWEEN THE EYES!

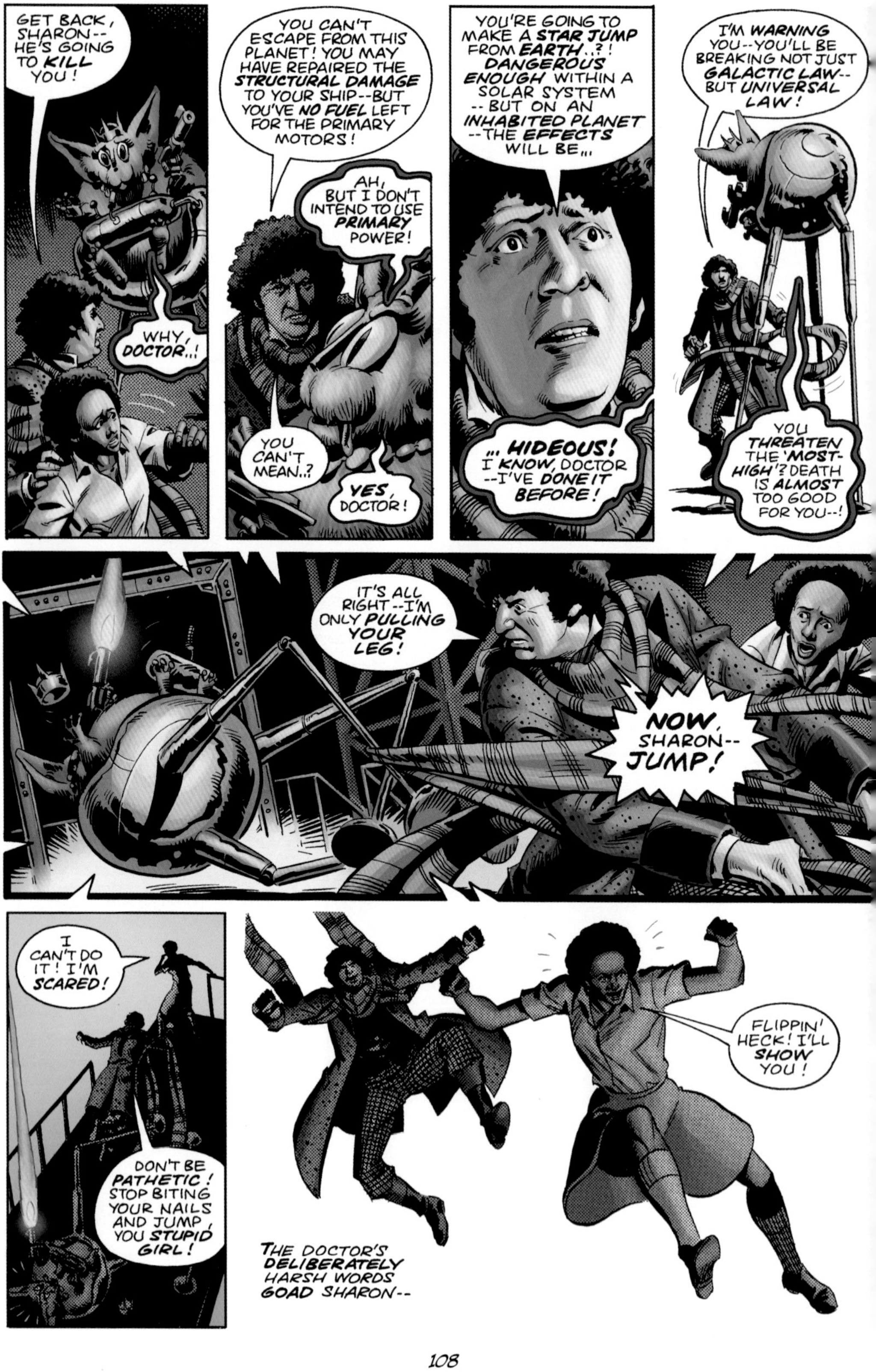
GET BACK, SHARON-- HE'S GOING TO KILL YOU!
WHY, DOCTOR..!
YOU CAN'T ESCAPE FROM THIS PLANET! YOU MAY HAVE REPAIRED THE STRUCTURAL DAMAGE TO YOUR SHIP--BUT YOU'VE NO FUEL LEFT FOR THE PRIMARY MOTORS!
AH, BUT I DON'T INTEND TO USE PRIMARY POWER!
YOU CAN'T MEAN..?
YES, DOCTOR!
YOU'RE GOING TO MAKE A STAR JUMP FROM EARTH..?! DANGEROUS ENOUGH WITHIN A SOLAR SYSTEM --BUT ON AN INHABITED PLANET --THE EFFECTS WILL BE...
...HIDEOUS! I KNOW, DOCTOR --I'VE DONE IT BEFORE!
I'M WARNING YOU--YOU'LL BE BREAKING NOT JUST GALACTIC LAW-- BUT UNIVERSAL LAW!
YOU THREATEN THE 'MOST-HIGH'? DEATH IS ALMOST TOO GOOD FOR YOU--!
IT'S ALL RIGHT--I'M ONLY PULLING YOUR LEG!
NOW, SHARON-- JUMP!
I CAN'T DO IT! I'M SCARED!
DON'T BE PATHETIC! STOP BITING YOUR NAILS AND JUMP, YOU STUPID GIRL!
THE DOCTOR'S DELIBERATELY HARSH WORDS GOAD SHARON--
FLIPPIN' HECK! I'LL SHOW YOU!

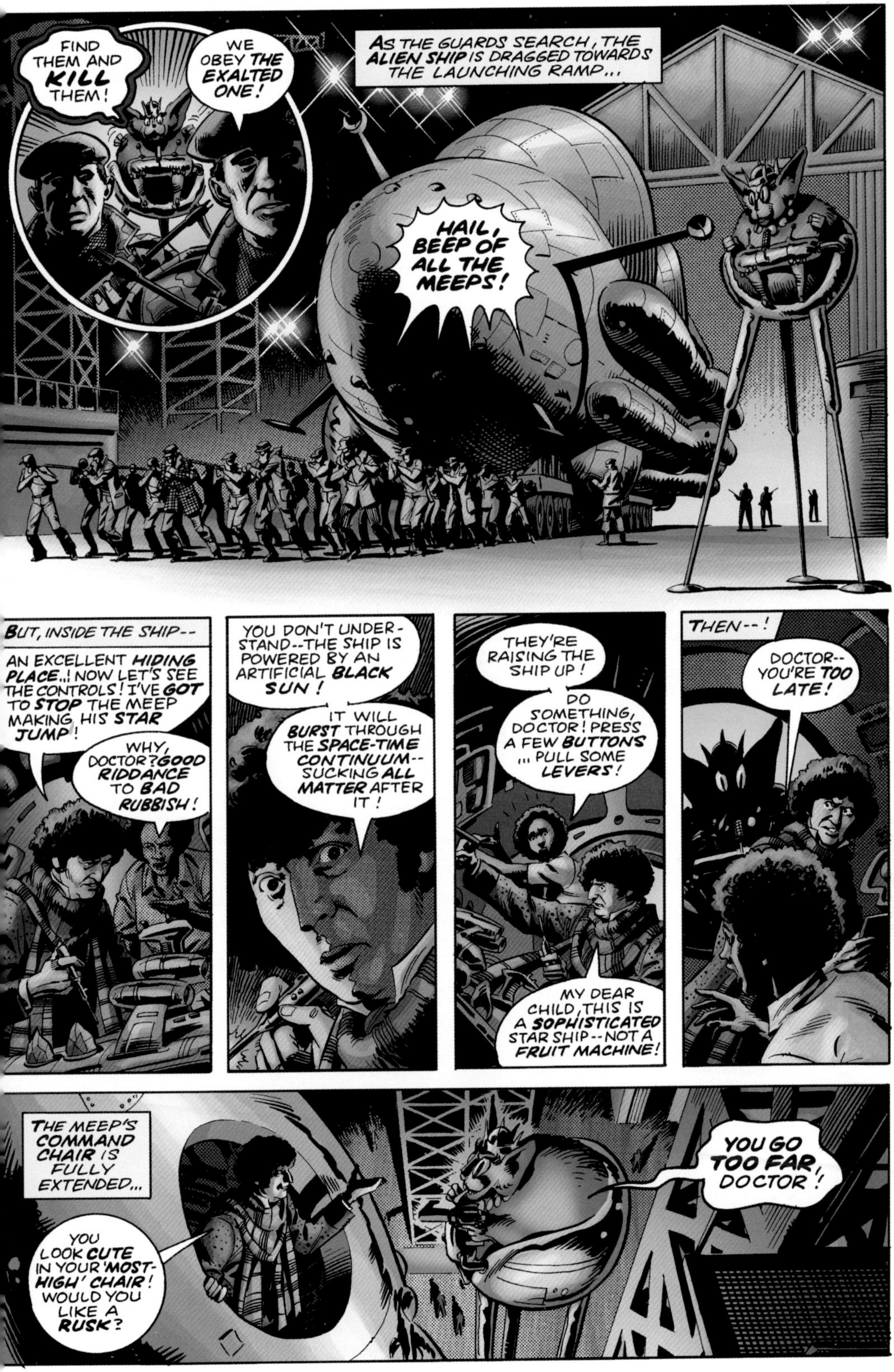

FIND THEM AND KILL THEM!
WE OBEY THE EXALTED ONE!
AS THE GUARDS SEARCH, THE ALIEN SHIP IS DRAGGED TOWARDS THE LAUNCHING RAMP...
HAIL, BEEP OF ALL THE MEEPS!
BUT, INSIDE THE SHIP--
AN EXCELLENT HIDING PLACE..! NOW LET'S SEE THE CONTROLS! I'VE GOT TO STOP THE MEEP MAKING HIS STAR JUMP!
WHY, DOCTOR? GOOD RIDDANCE TO BAD RUBBISH!
YOU DON'T UNDERSTAND--THE SHIP IS POWERED BY AN ARTIFICIAL BLACK SUN!
IT WILL BURST THROUGH THE SPACE-TIME CONTINUUM--SUCKING ALL MATTER AFTER IT!
THEY'RE RAISING THE SHIP UP!
DO SOMETHING, DOCTOR! PRESS A FEW BUTTONS ... PULL SOME LEVERS!
MY DEAR CHILD, THIS IS A SOPHISTICATED STAR SHIP--NOT A FRUIT MACHINE!
THEN--!
DOCTOR--YOU'RE TOO LATE!
THE MEEP'S COMMAND CHAIR IS FULLY EXTENDED...
YOU LOOK CUTE IN YOUR 'MOST-HIGH' CHAIR! WOULD YOU LIKE A RUSK?
YOU GO TOO FAR, DOCTOR!

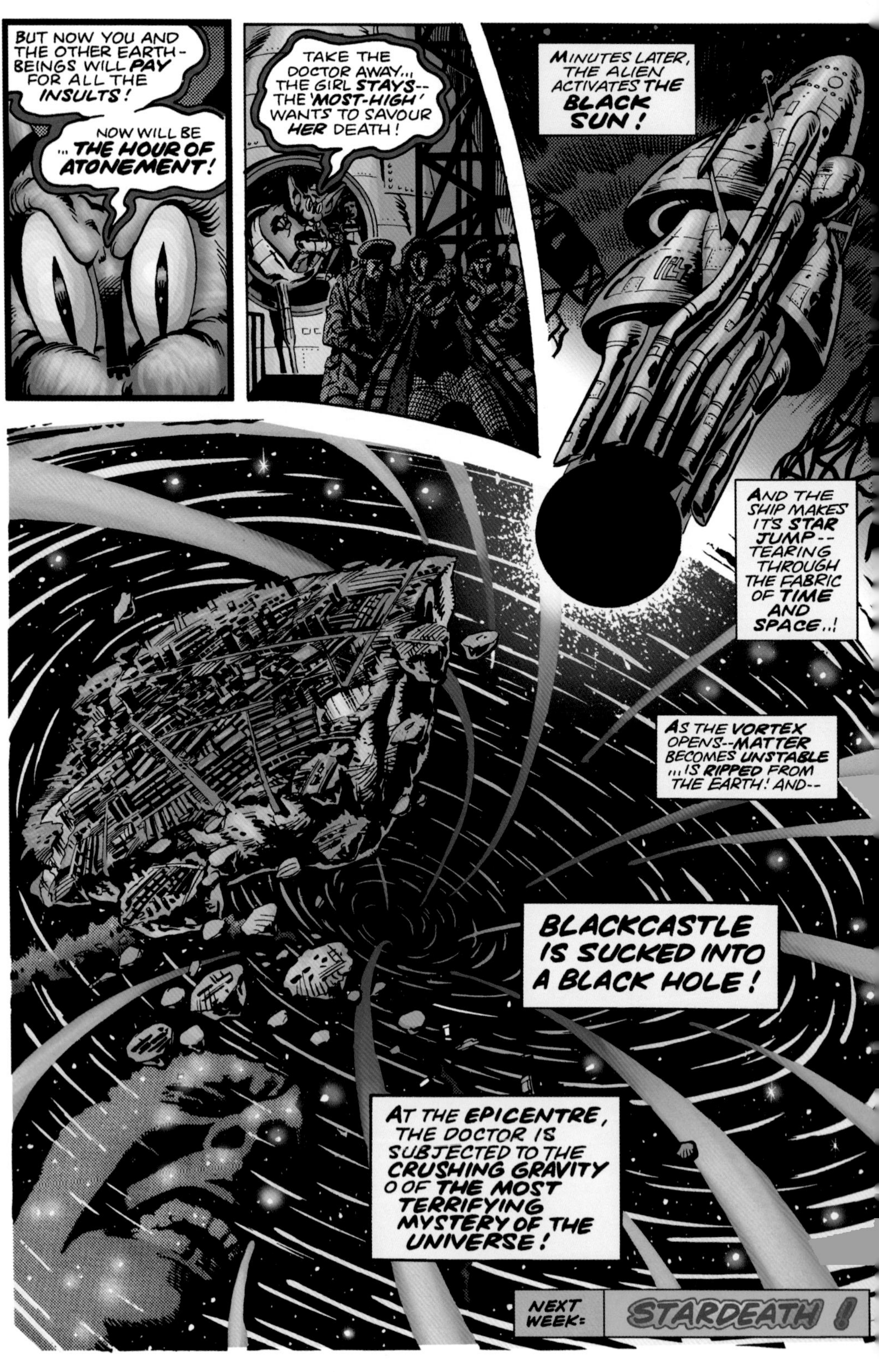
BUT NOW YOU AND THE OTHER EARTH-BEINGS WILL PAY FOR ALL THE INSULTS!
NOW WILL BE ...THE HOUR OF ATONEMENT!
TAKE THE DOCTOR AWAY... THE GIRL STAYS-- THE 'MOST-HIGH' WANTS TO SAVOUR HER DEATH!
MINUTES LATER, THE ALIEN ACTIVATES THE BLACK SUN!
AND THE SHIP MAKES ITS STAR JUMP-- TEARING THROUGH THE FABRIC OF TIME AND SPACE..!
AS THE VORTEX OPENS--MATTER BECOMES UNSTABLE ...IS RIPPED FROM THE EARTH! AND--
BLACKCASTLE IS SUCKED INTO A BLACK HOLE!
AT THE EPICENTRE, THE DOCTOR IS SUBJECTED TO THE CRUSHING GRAVITY OF THE MOST TERRIFYING MYSTERY OF THE UNIVERSE!
NEXT WEEK: STARDEATH!

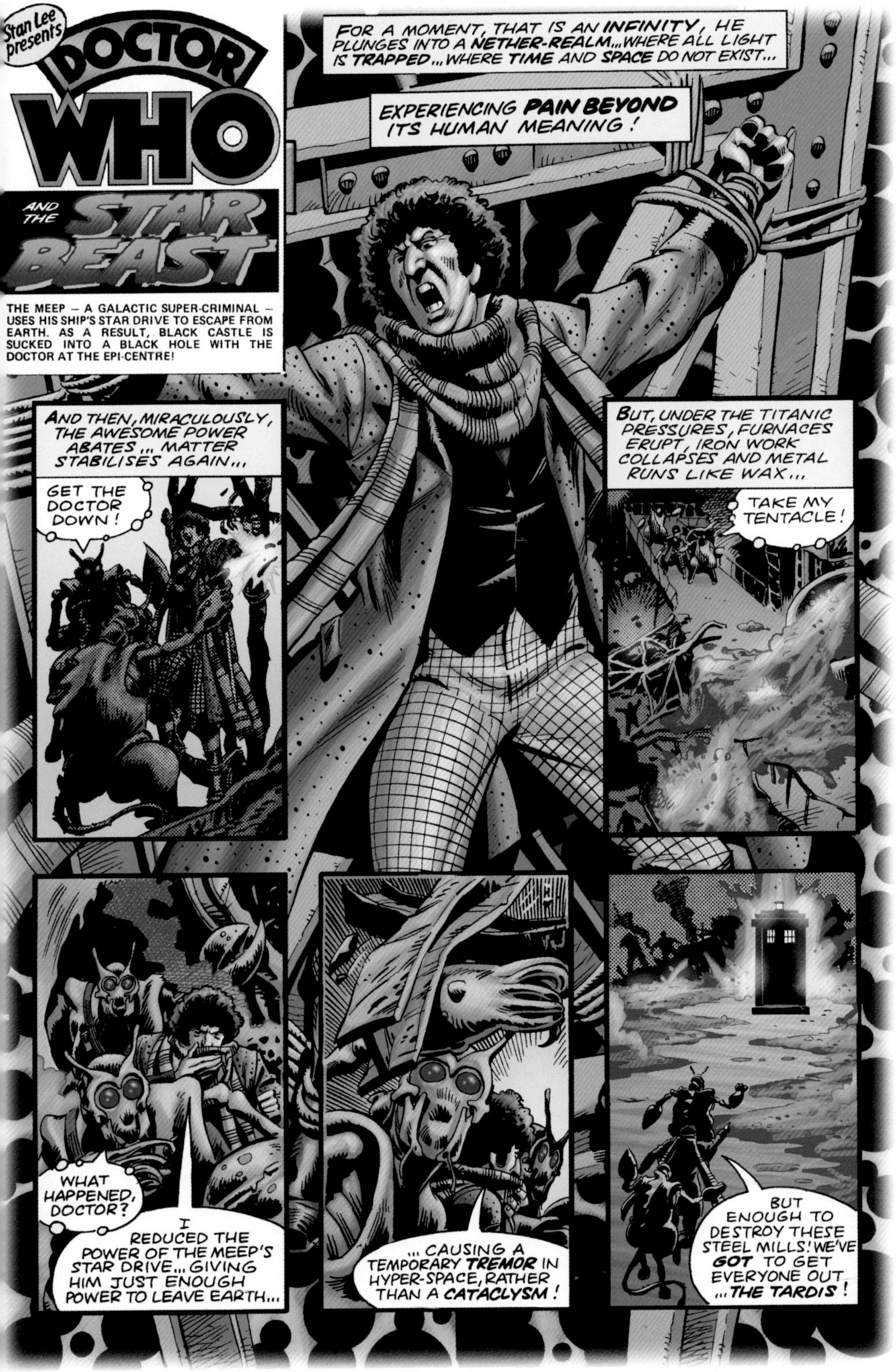
Stan Lee presents
DOCTOR WHO
AND THE STAR BEAST
THE MEEP – A GALACTIC SUPER-CRIMINAL – USES HIS SHIP'S STAR DRIVE TO ESCAPE FROM EARTH. AS A RESULT, BLACK CASTLE IS SUCKED INTO A BLACK HOLE WITH THE DOCTOR AT THE EPI-CENTRE!
FOR A MOMENT, THAT IS AN INFINITY, HE PLUNGES INTO A NETHER-REALM... WHERE ALL LIGHT IS TRAPPED... WHERE TIME AND SPACE DO NOT EXIST...
EXPERIENCING PAIN BEYOND ITS HUMAN MEANING!
AND THEN, MIRACULOUSLY, THE AWESOME POWER ABATES... MATTER STABILISES AGAIN...
GET THE DOCTOR DOWN!
BUT, UNDER THE TITANIC PRESSURES, FURNACES ERUPT, IRON WORK COLLAPSES AND METAL RUNS LIKE WAX...
TAKE MY TENTACLE!
WHAT HAPPENED, DOCTOR?
I REDUCED THE POWER OF THE MEEP'S STAR DRIVE... GIVING HIM JUST ENOUGH POWER TO LEAVE EARTH...
... CAUSING A TEMPORARY TREMOR IN HYPER-SPACE, RATHER THAN A CATACLYSM!
BUT ENOUGH TO DESTROY THESE STEEL MILLS! WE'VE GOT TO GET EVERYONE OUT ...THE TARDIS!

AS THE RADIATION WEARS OFF THE BEWILDERED WORKERS, AN EVACUATION BEGINS...

WE CAN'T ALL FIT IN A POLICE BOX!

PLENTY OF ROOM INSIDE! BUT NOT THE SECOND DOOR ON THE LEFT -- THAT'S MY BEDROOM!

PURRR!

HELLO, K-9 -- I MUST GET ROUND TO REPAIRING YOU, OLD CHAP!

...EXCUSE ME -- IF I CAN JUST GET TO MY CONTROLS!...

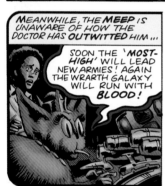

MEANWHILE, THE MEEP IS UNAWARE OF HOW THE DOCTOR HAS OUTWITTED HIM...

SOON THE 'MOST-HIGH' WILL LEAD NEW ARMIES! AGAIN THE WRARTH GALAXY WILL RUN WITH BLOOD!

FOR I AM THE SAVIOUR OF MY RACE! I WILL SAVE THEM FROM THE SENILITY OF PEACE! THE DECAY OF HAPPINESS!

WHAT'S WRONG WITH BEING HAPPY?

HAPPINESS IS A STAGNANT POND! TRUE JOY CAN ONLY BE FOUND THROUGH INFLICTING PAIN, EARTH GIRL!

NO!

SUDDENLY!

NOW HEAR THIS! YOU ARE UNDER ARREST! ANY RESISTANCE AND WE BLOW YOU OUT OF THE COSMOS!

MEEP! MEEP!

THE MEEP'S CRAFT IS SECURED -- A *BOARDING TUBE* SNAKES OUT...

THE *WRARTH WARRIORS!* B-BUT I SHOULD BE ON THE OTHER SIDE OF THE UNIVERSE!

AS THE AIRLOCK DOOR IS CUT THROUGH...

THEY WON'T TAKE ME ALIVE! I'LL--

NO, YOU DON'T!

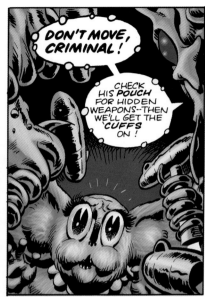

DON'T MOVE, CRIMINAL!

CHECK HIS *POUCH* FOR HIDDEN WEAPONS--THEN WE'LL GET THE *'CUFFS* ON!

SOON AFTER, THE *TARDIS'* MATERIALISES ... AND THE DOCTOR -- HAVING DELIVERED THE WORKERS TO *SAFETY* -- ALIGHTS...

DOCTOR!

I DO BELIEVE THIS IS WHERE WE CAME IN, K-9!

WHAT WILL HAPPEN TO THE MEEP, ZOGROTH?

HE WILL BE GIVEN A FAIR TRIAL, ACCORDING TO THE LAWS OF WRARTH! WE WILL ASK FOR ...*THE SUPREME PENALTY!*

HISSS!

PLEASE, SHARON -- I DON'T WANT TO DIE! I KNOW I'VE BEEN A BAD MEEP -- BUT I'LL BE GOOD IN FUTURE!

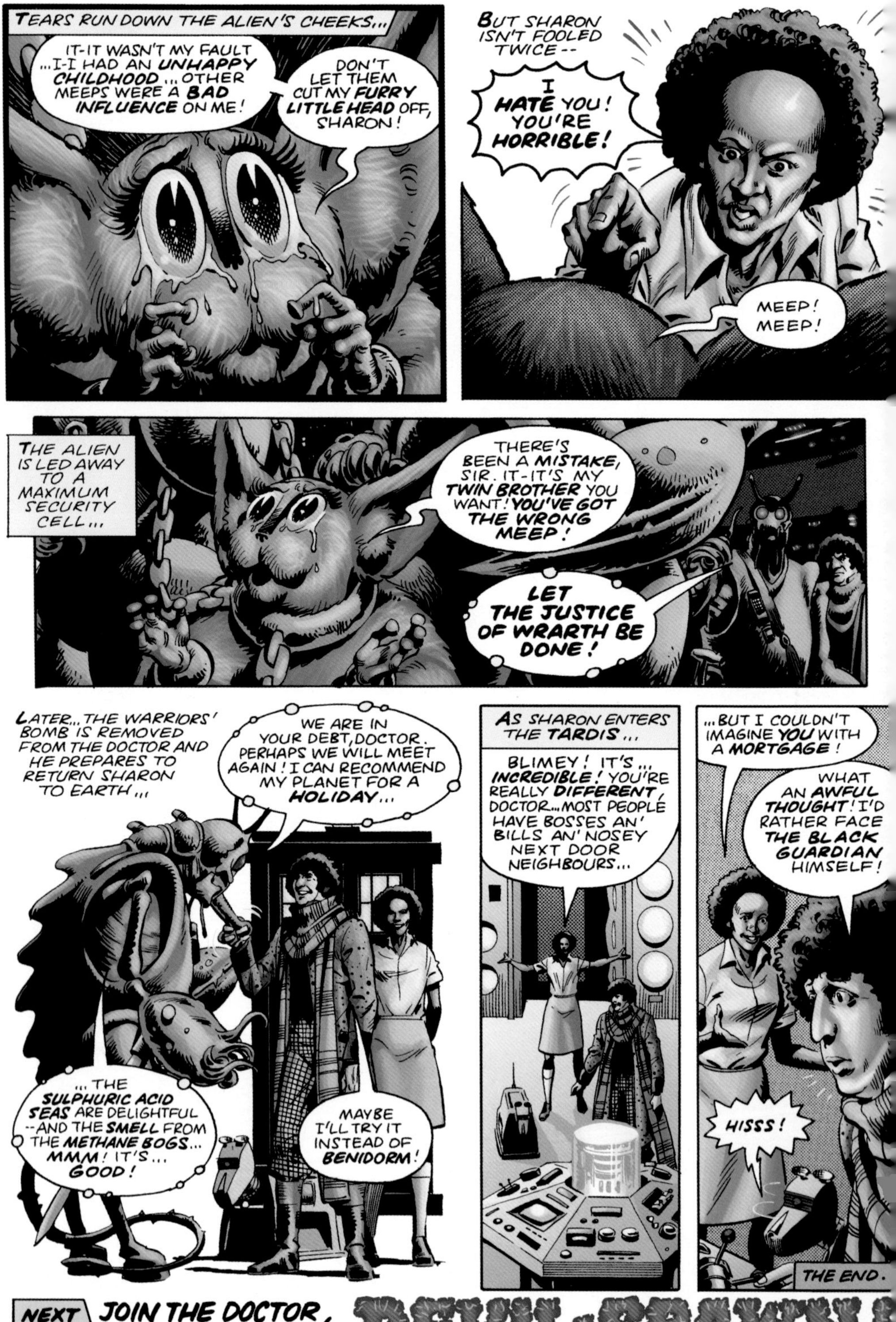
TEARS RUN DOWN THE ALIEN'S CHEEKS...
IT-IT WASN'T MY FAULT ...I-I HAD AN UNHAPPY CHILDHOOD ... OTHER MEEPS WERE A BAD INFLUENCE ON ME!
DON'T LET THEM CUT MY FURRY LITTLE HEAD OFF, SHARON!
BUT SHARON ISN'T FOOLED TWICE --
I HATE YOU! YOU'RE HORRIBLE!
MEEP! MEEP!
THE ALIEN IS LED AWAY TO A MAXIMUM SECURITY CELL...
THERE'S BEEN A MISTAKE, SIR. IT-IT'S MY TWIN BROTHER YOU WANT! YOU'VE GOT THE WRONG MEEP!
LET THE JUSTICE OF WRARTH BE DONE!
LATER... THE WARRIORS' BOMB IS REMOVED FROM THE DOCTOR AND HE PREPARES TO RETURN SHARON TO EARTH...
WE ARE IN YOUR DEBT, DOCTOR. PERHAPS WE WILL MEET AGAIN! I CAN RECOMMEND MY PLANET FOR A HOLIDAY...
... THE SULPHURIC ACID SEAS ARE DELIGHTFUL --AND THE SMELL FROM THE METHANE BOGS... MMM! IT'S... GOOD!
MAYBE I'LL TRY IT INSTEAD OF BENIDORM!
AS SHARON ENTERS THE TARDIS...
BLIMEY! IT'S... INCREDIBLE! YOU'RE REALLY DIFFERENT, DOCTOR... MOST PEOPLE HAVE BOSSES AN' BILLS AN' NOSEY NEXT DOOR NEIGHBOURS...
...BUT I COULDN'T IMAGINE YOU WITH A MORTGAGE!
WHAT AN AWFUL THOUGHT! I'D RATHER FACE THE BLACK GUARDIAN HIMSELF!
HISSS!
THE END.

NEXT ISSUE JOIN THE DOCTOR, SHARON AND K-9 IN... DEVIL-SPAWN!

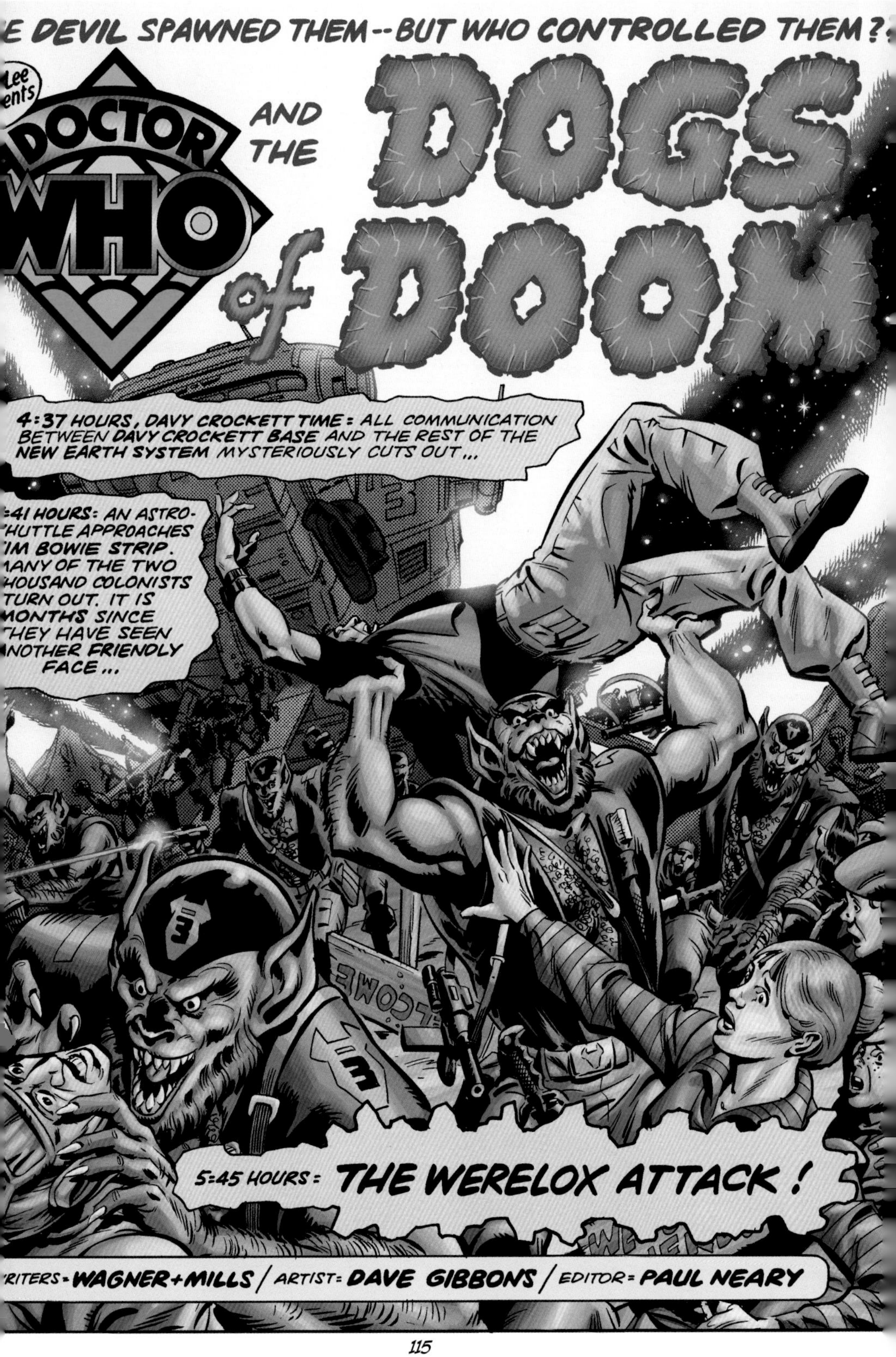

E DEVIL SPAWNED THEM--BUT WHO CONTROLLED THEM?
DOCTOR WHO AND THE DOGS OF DOOM
4:37 HOURS, DAVY CROCKETT TIME: ALL COMMUNICATION BETWEEN DAVY CROCKETT BASE AND THE REST OF THE NEW EARTH SYSTEM MYSTERIOUSLY CUTS OUT...
:41 HOURS: AN ASTRO-HUTTLE APPROACHES IM BOWIE STRIP. MANY OF THE TWO HOUSAND COLONISTS TURN OUT. IT IS MONTHS SINCE THEY HAVE SEEN NOTHER FRIENDLY FACE...
5:45 HOURS: THE WERELOX ATTACK!
RITERS: WAGNER+MILLS / ARTIST: DAVE GIBBONS / EDITOR: PAUL NEARY

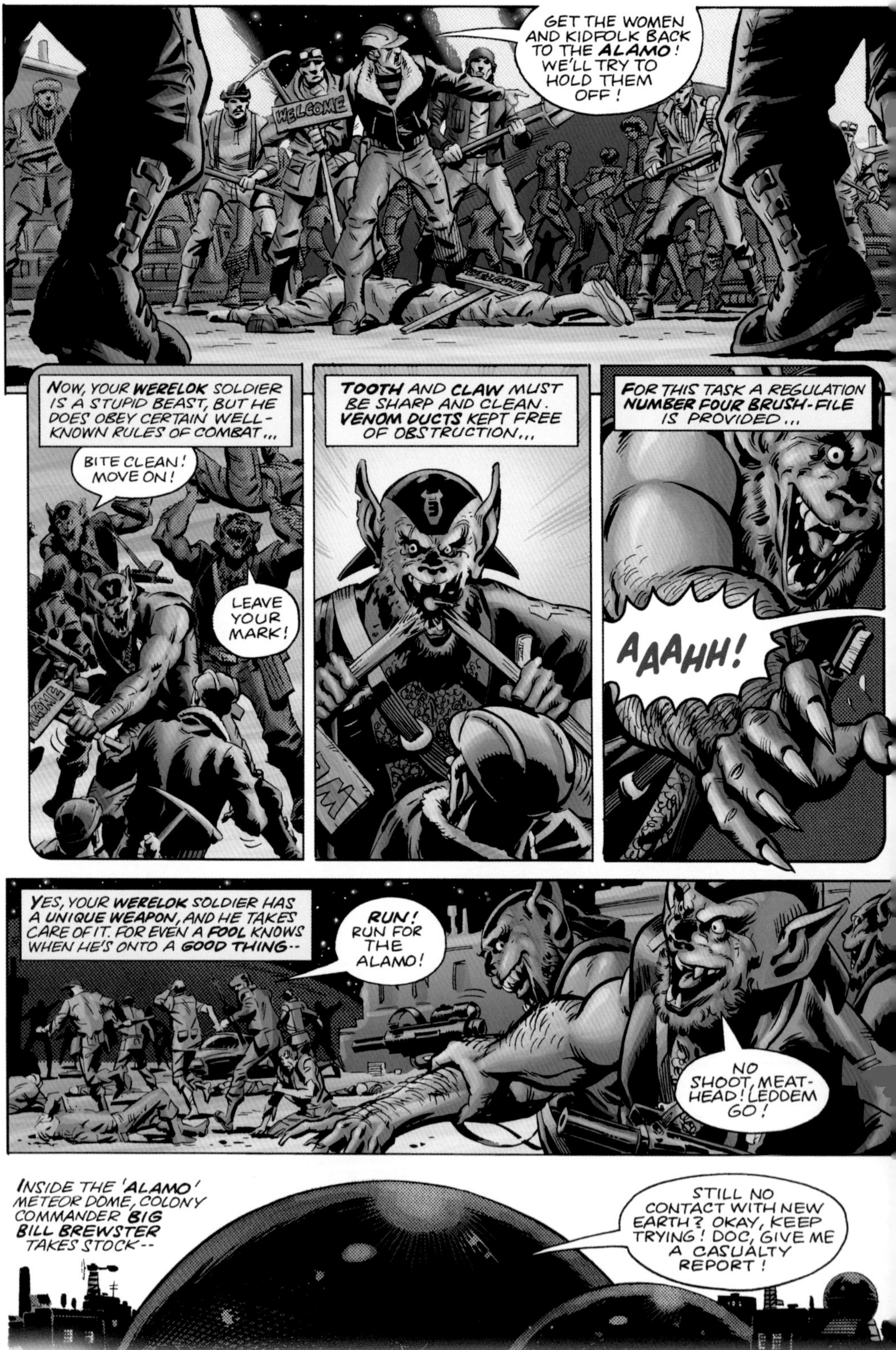
GET THE WOMEN AND KIDFOLK BACK TO THE ALAMO! WE'LL TRY TO HOLD THEM OFF!
WELCOME
NOW, YOUR WERELOK SOLDIER IS A STUPID BEAST, BUT HE DOES OBEY CERTAIN WELL-KNOWN RULES OF COMBAT...
BITE CLEAN! MOVE ON!
LEAVE YOUR MARK!
TOOTH AND CLAW MUST BE SHARP AND CLEAN. VENOM DUCTS KEPT FREE OF OBSTRUCTION...
FOR THIS TASK A REGULATION NUMBER FOUR BRUSH-FILE IS PROVIDED...
AAAHH!
YES, YOUR WERELOK SOLDIER HAS A UNIQUE WEAPON, AND HE TAKES CARE OF IT. FOR EVEN A FOOL KNOWS WHEN HE'S ONTO A GOOD THING--
RUN! RUN FOR THE ALAMO!
NO SHOOT, MEAT-HEAD! LEDDEM GO!
INSIDE THE 'ALAMO' METEOR DOME, COLONY COMMANDER BIG BILL BREWSTER TAKES STOCK--
STILL NO CONTACT WITH NEW EARTH? OKAY, KEEP TRYING! DOC, GIVE ME A CASUALTY REPORT!

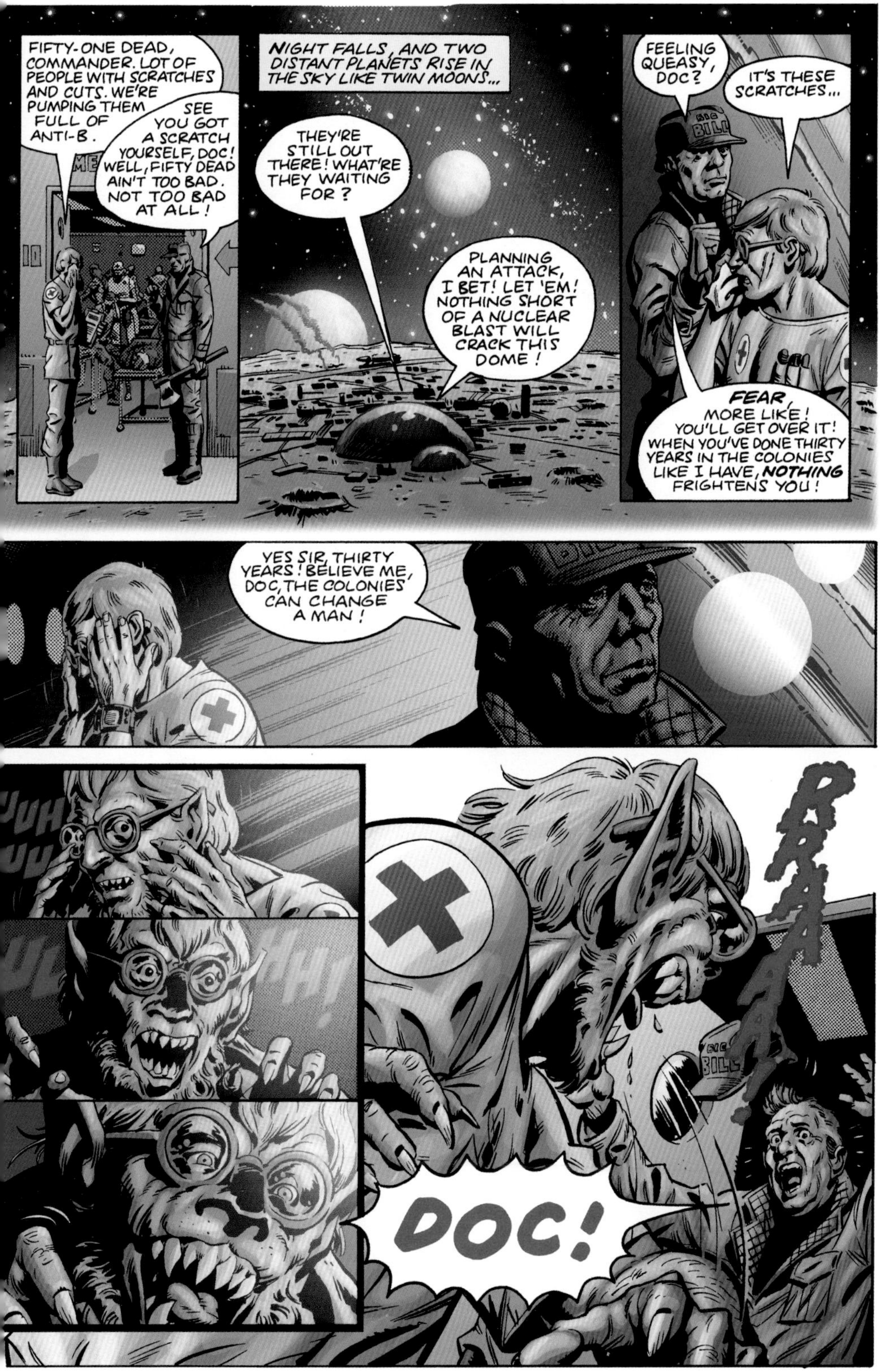
FIFTY-ONE DEAD, COMMANDER. LOT OF PEOPLE WITH SCRATCHES AND CUTS. WE'RE PUMPING THEM FULL OF ANTI-B.
SEE YOU GOT A SCRATCH YOURSELF, DOC! WELL, FIFTY DEAD AIN'T TOO BAD. NOT TOO BAD AT ALL!
NIGHT FALLS, AND TWO DISTANT PLANETS RISE IN THE SKY LIKE TWIN MOONS...
THEY'RE STILL OUT THERE! WHAT'RE THEY WAITING FOR?
PLANNING AN ATTACK, I BET! LET 'EM! NOTHING SHORT OF A NUCLEAR BLAST WILL CRACK THIS DOME!
FEELING QUEASY, DOC?
IT'S THESE SCRATCHES...
FEAR, MORE LIKE! YOU'LL GET OVER IT! WHEN YOU'VE DONE THIRTY YEARS IN THE COLONIES LIKE I HAVE, NOTHING FRIGHTENS YOU!
YES SIR, THIRTY YEARS! BELIEVE ME, DOC, THE COLONIES CAN CHANGE A MAN!
DOC!

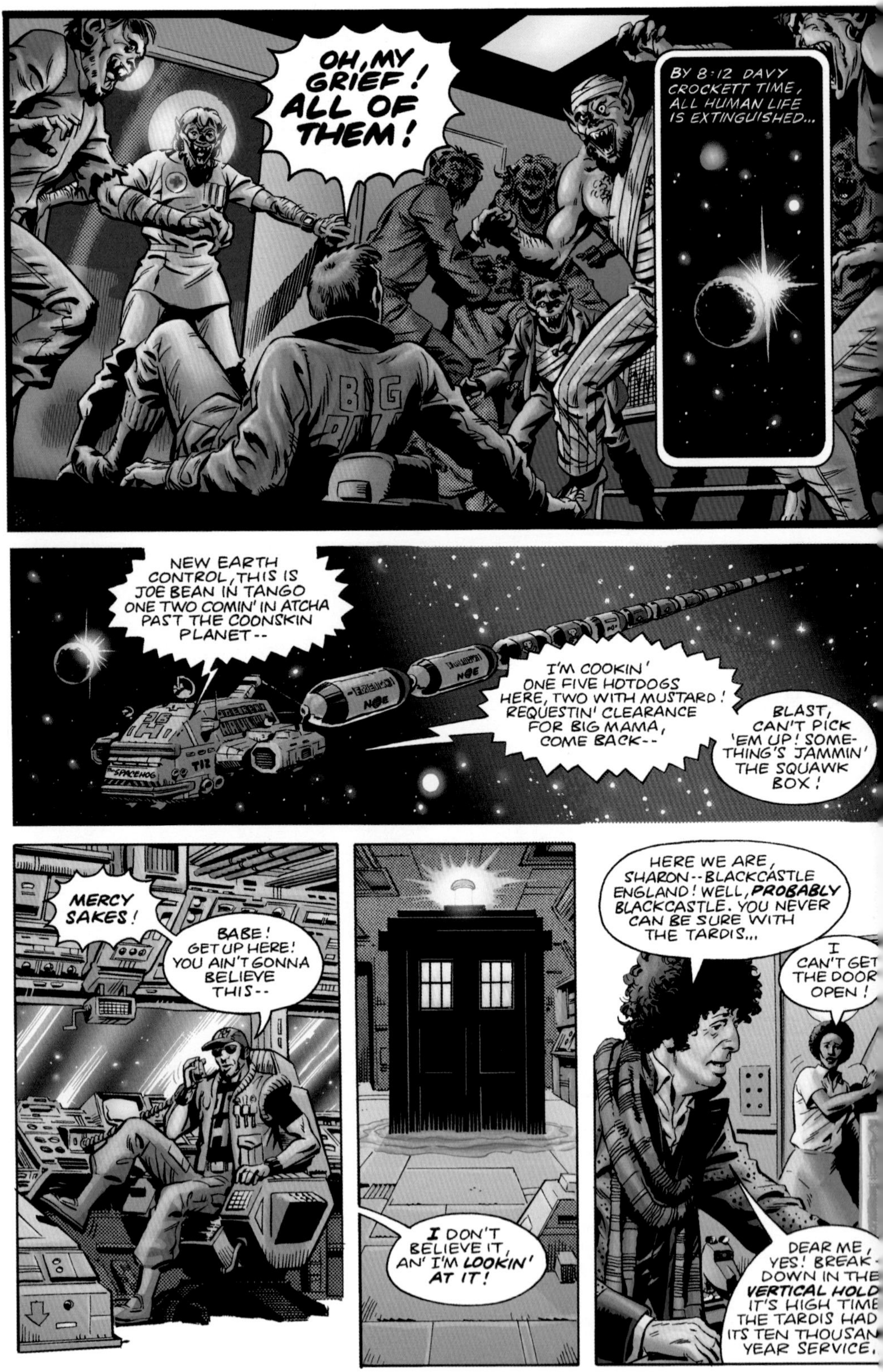
OH, MY GRIEF! ALL OF THEM!
BY 8·12 DAVY CROCKETT TIME, ALL HUMAN LIFE IS EXTINGUISHED...
NEW EARTH CONTROL, THIS IS JOE BEAN IN TANGO ONE TWO COMIN' IN ATCHA PAST THE COONSKIN PLANET--
I'M COOKIN' ONE FIVE HOTDOGS HERE, TWO WITH MUSTARD! REQUESTIN' CLEARANCE FOR BIG MAMA, COME BACK--
BLAST, CAN'T PICK 'EM UP! SOME-THING'S JAMMIN' THE SQUAWK BOX!
MERCY SAKES!
BABE! GET UP HERE! YOU AIN'T GONNA BELIEVE THIS--
I DON'T BELIEVE IT, AN' I'M LOOKIN' AT IT!
HERE WE ARE, SHARON--BLACKCASTLE ENGLAND! WELL, PROBABLY BLACKCASTLE. YOU NEVER CAN BE SURE WITH THE TARDIS...
I CAN'T GET THE DOOR OPEN!
DEAR ME, YES! BREAK-DOWN IN THE VERTICAL HOLD IT'S HIGH TIME THE TARDIS HAD ITS TEN THOUSAN YEAR SERVICE.

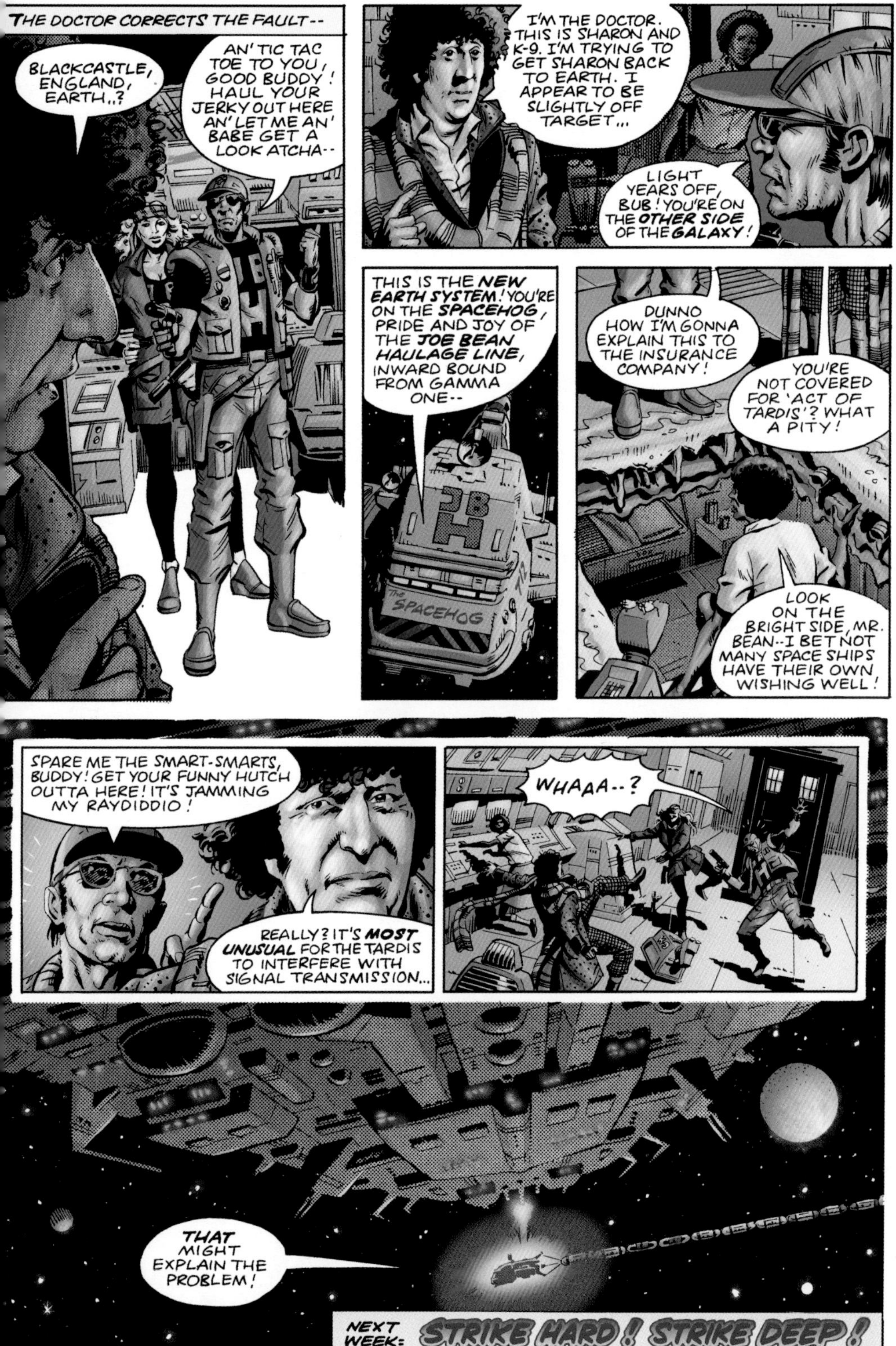

THE DOCTOR CORRECTS THE FAULT--
BLACKCASTLE, ENGLAND, EARTH..?
AN' TIC TAC TOE TO YOU, GOOD BUDDY! HAUL YOUR JERKY OUT HERE AN' LET ME AN' BABE GET A LOOK ATCHA--
I'M THE DOCTOR. THIS IS SHARON AND K-9. I'M TRYING TO GET SHARON BACK TO EARTH. I APPEAR TO BE SLIGHTLY OFF TARGET...
LIGHT YEARS OFF, BUB! YOU'RE ON THE OTHER SIDE OF THE GALAXY!
THIS IS THE NEW EARTH SYSTEM! YOU'RE ON THE SPACEHOG, PRIDE AND JOY OF THE JOE BEAN HAULAGE LINE, INWARD BOUND FROM GAMMA ONE--
The SPACEHOG
DUNNO HOW I'M GONNA EXPLAIN THIS TO THE INSURANCE COMPANY!
YOU'RE NOT COVERED FOR 'ACT OF TARDIS'? WHAT A PITY!
LOOK ON THE BRIGHT SIDE, MR. BEAN--I BET NOT MANY SPACE SHIPS HAVE THEIR OWN WISHING WELL!
SPARE ME THE SMART-SMARTS, BUDDY! GET YOUR FUNNY HUTCH OUTTA HERE! IT'S JAMMING MY RAYDIDDIO!
REALLY? IT'S MOST UNUSUAL FOR THE TARDIS TO INTERFERE WITH SIGNAL TRANSMISSION...
WHAAA--?
THAT MIGHT EXPLAIN THE PROBLEM!
NEXT WEEK: STRIKE HARD! STRIKE DEEP!

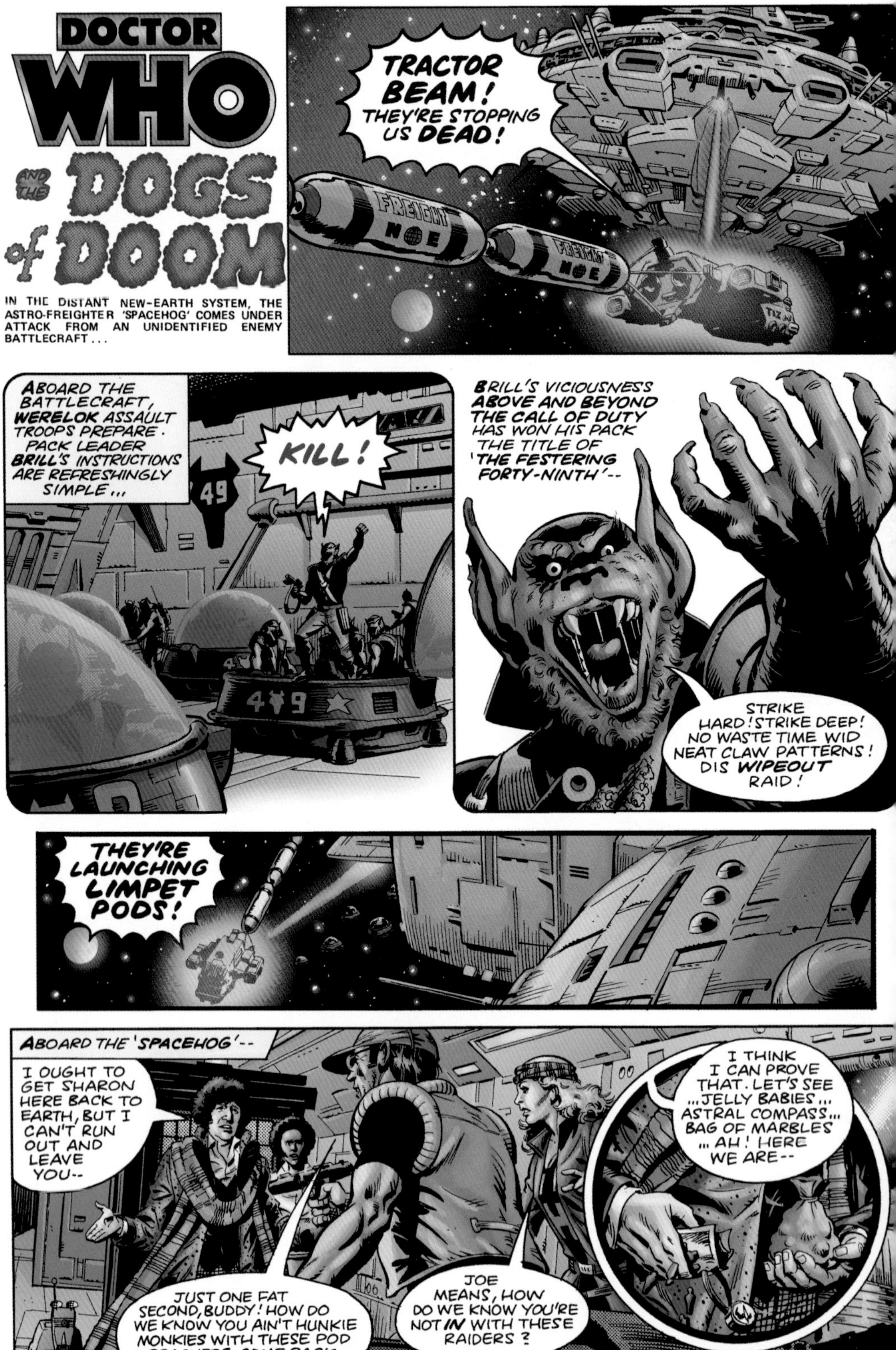
DOCTOR WHO
AND THE DOGS of DOOM
IN THE DISTANT NEW-EARTH SYSTEM, THE ASTRO-FREIGHTER 'SPACEHOG' COMES UNDER ATTACK FROM AN UNIDENTIFIED ENEMY BATTLECRAFT...
TRACTOR BEAM! THEY'RE STOPPING US DEAD!
FREIGHT NOE
ABOARD THE BATTLECRAFT, WERELOK ASSAULT TROOPS PREPARE. PACK LEADER BRILL'S INSTRUCTIONS ARE REFRESHINGLY SIMPLE...
KILL!
49
BRILL'S VICIOUSNESS ABOVE AND BEYOND THE CALL OF DUTY HAS WON HIS PACK THE TITLE OF 'THE FESTERING FORTY-NINTH'--
STRIKE HARD! STRIKE DEEP! NO WASTE TIME WID NEAT CLAW PATTERNS! DIS WIPEOUT RAID!
THEY'RE LAUNCHING LIMPET PODS!
ABOARD THE 'SPACEHOG'--
I OUGHT TO GET SHARON HERE BACK TO EARTH, BUT I CAN'T RUN OUT AND LEAVE YOU--
JUST ONE FAT SECOND, BUDDY! HOW DO WE KNOW YOU AIN'T HUNKIE MONKIES WITH THESE POD POACHERS, COME BACK...
JOE MEANS, HOW DO WE KNOW YOU'RE NOT IN WITH THESE RAIDERS?
I THINK I CAN PROVE THAT. LET'S SEE ...JELLY BABIES... ASTRAL COMPASS... BAG OF MARBLES ...AH! HERE WE ARE--

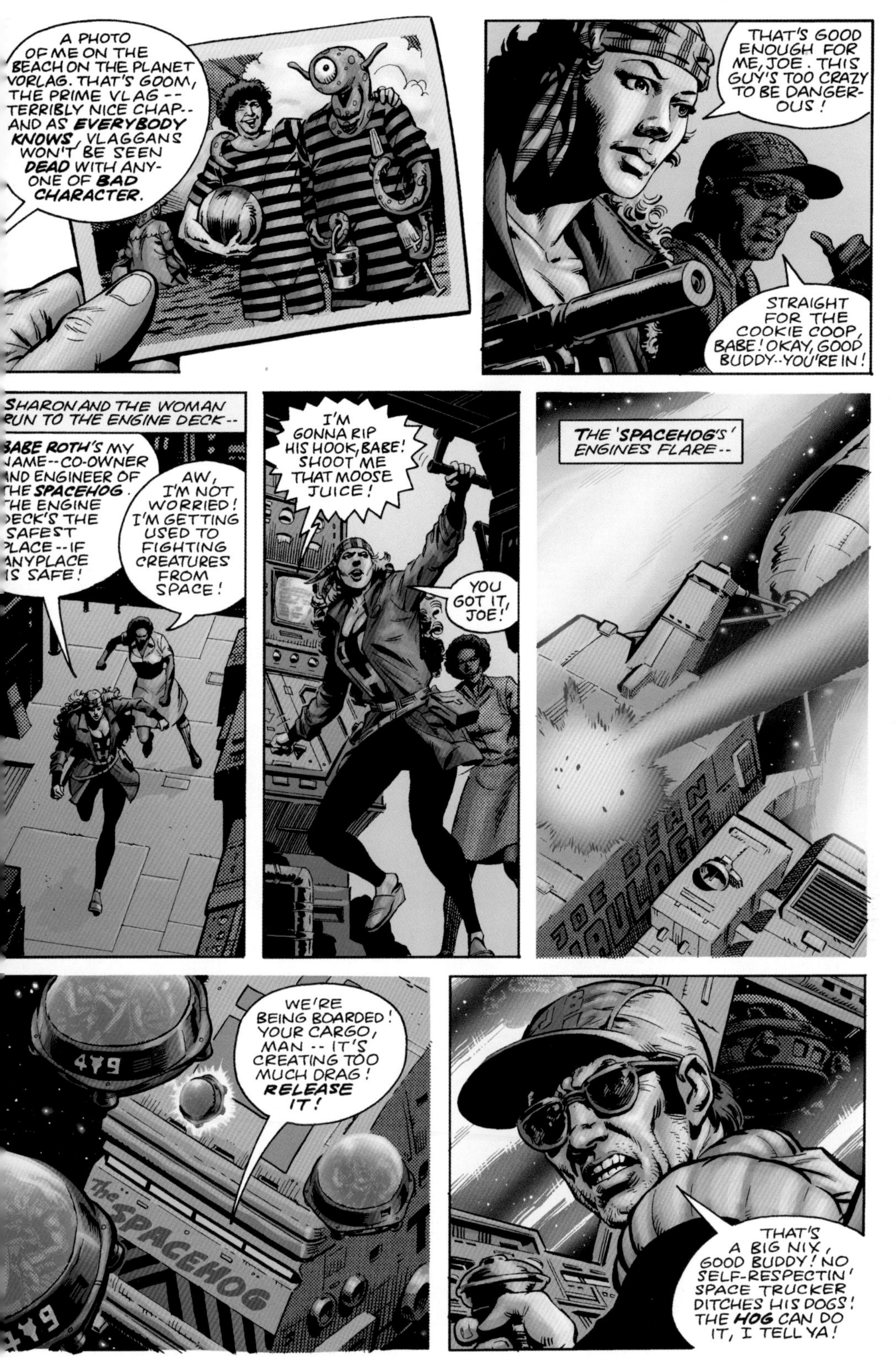

A PHOTO OF ME ON THE BEACH ON THE PLANET VORLAG. THAT'S GOOM, THE PRIME VLAG -- TERRIBLY NICE CHAP -- AND AS **EVERYBODY KNOWS**, VLAGGANS WON'T BE SEEN **DEAD** WITH ANYONE OF **BAD CHARACTER**.
THAT'S GOOD ENOUGH FOR ME, JOE. THIS GUY'S TOO CRAZY TO BE DANGEROUS!
STRAIGHT FOR THE COOKIE COOP, BABE! OKAY, GOOD BUDDY -- YOU'RE IN!
SHARON AND THE WOMAN RUN TO THE ENGINE DECK --
BABE ROTH'S MY NAME -- CO-OWNER AND ENGINEER OF THE **SPACEHOG**. THE ENGINE DECK'S THE SAFEST PLACE -- IF ANYPLACE IS SAFE!
AW, I'M NOT WORRIED! I'M GETTING USED TO FIGHTING CREATURES FROM SPACE!
I'M GONNA RIP HIS HOOK, BABE! SHOOT ME THAT MOOSE JUICE!
YOU GOT IT, JOE!
THE '**SPACEHOG'S**' ENGINES FLARE --
479
The SPACEHOG
WE'RE BEING BOARDED! YOUR CARGO, MAN -- IT'S CREATING TOO MUCH DRAG! **RELEASE IT**!
THAT'S A BIG NIX, GOOD BUDDY! NO SELF-RESPECTIN' SPACE TRUCKER DITCHES HIS DOGS! THE **HOG** CAN DO IT, I TELL YA!

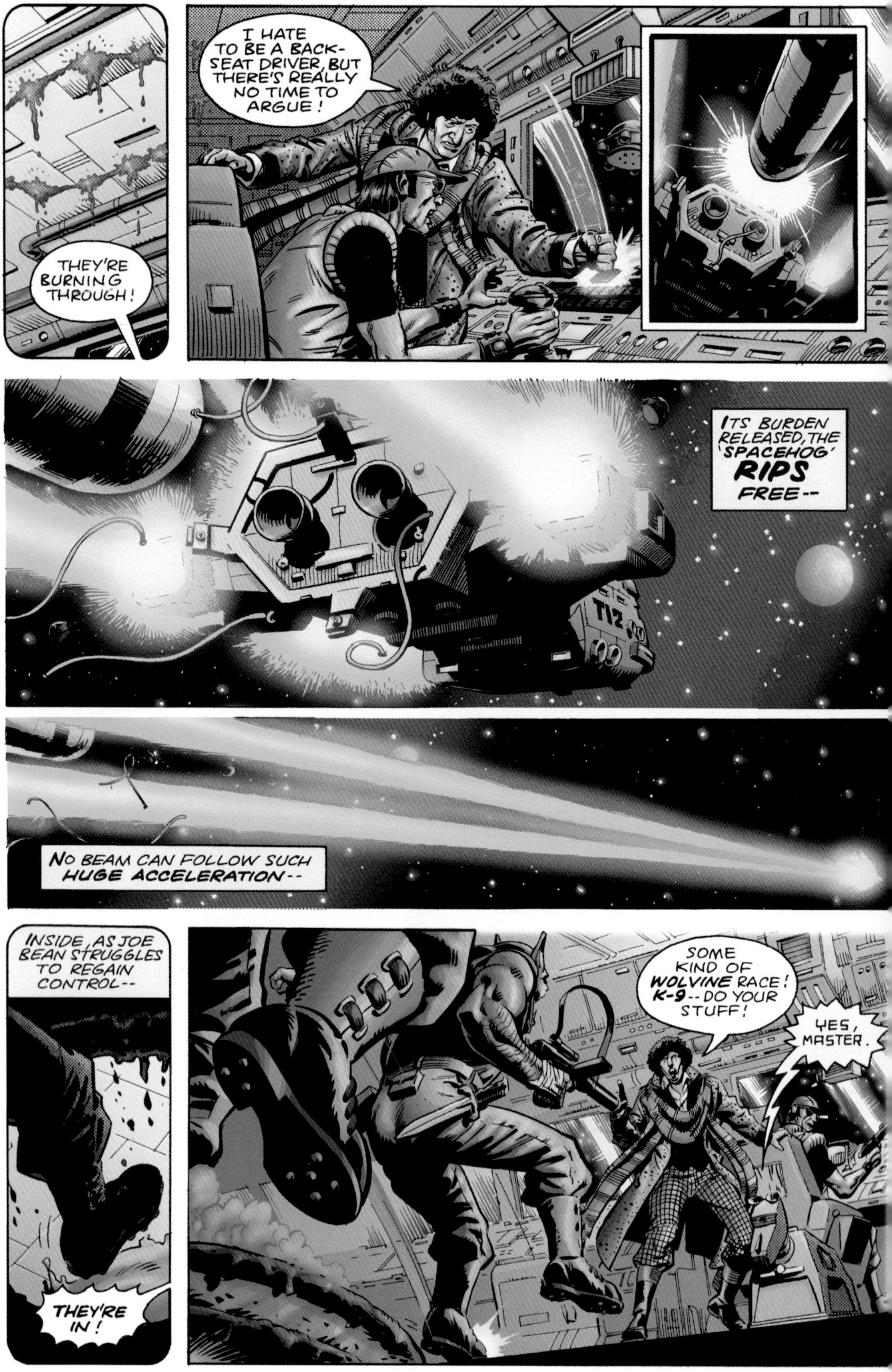
THEY'RE BURNING THROUGH!
I HATE TO BE A BACK-SEAT DRIVER, BUT THERE'S REALLY NO TIME TO ARGUE!
RELEASE
ITS BURDEN RELEASED, THE 'SPACEHOG' RIPS FREE--
T12
NO BEAM CAN FOLLOW SUCH HUGE ACCELERATION--
INSIDE, AS JOE BEAN STRUGGLES TO REGAIN CONTROL--
THEY'RE IN!
SOME KIND OF WOLVINE RACE! K-9--DO YOUR STUFF!
YES, MASTER.

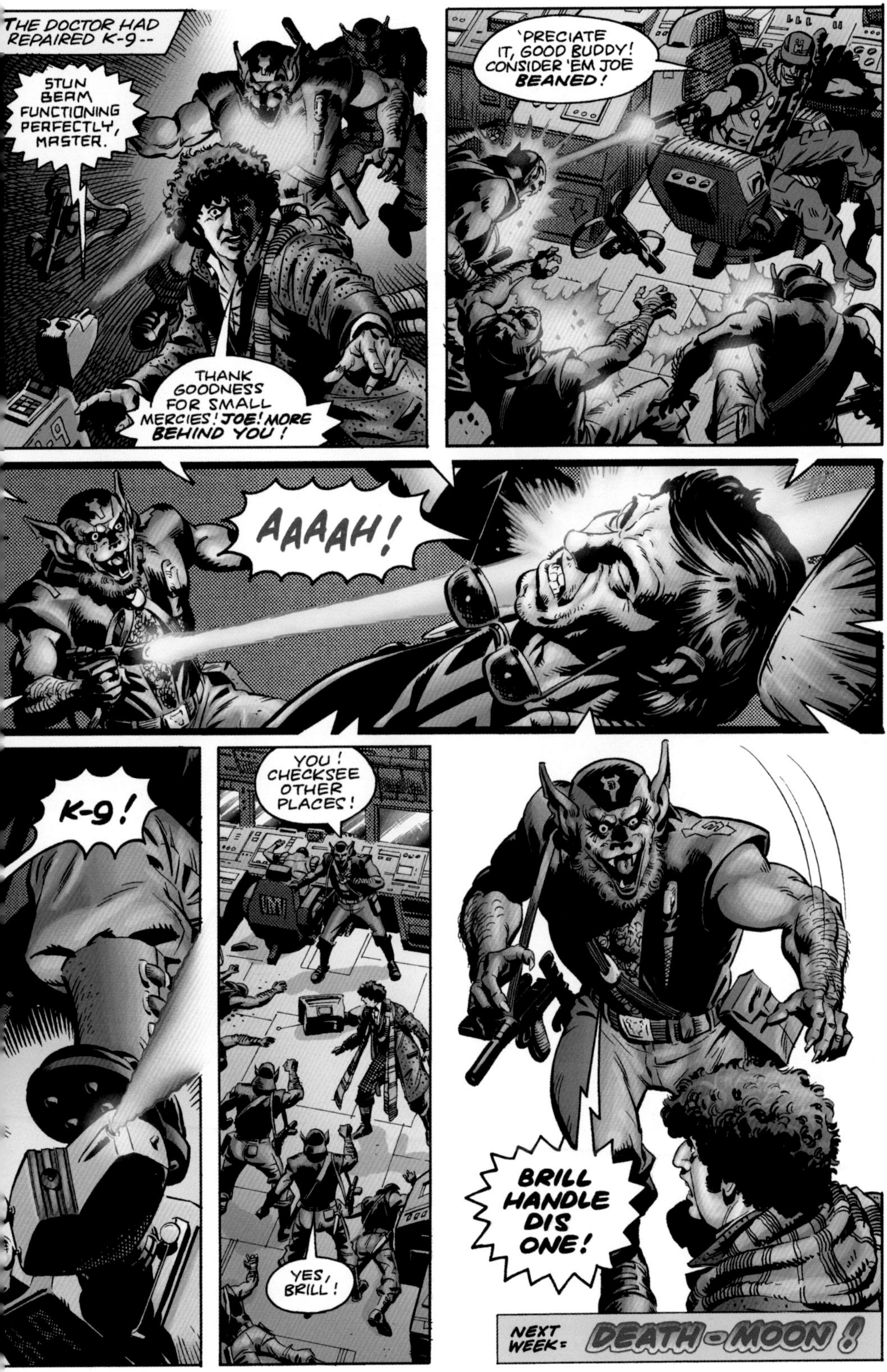
THE DOCTOR HAD REPAIRED K-9--
STUN BEAM FUNCTIONING PERFECTLY, MASTER.
THANK GOODNESS FOR SMALL MERCIES! JOE! MORE BEHIND YOU!
'PRECIATE IT, GOOD BUDDY! CONSIDER 'EM JOE BEANED!
AAAAH!
K-9!
YOU! CHECKSEE OTHER PLACES!
YES, BRILL!
BRILL HANDLE DIS ONE!
NEXT WEEK: DEATH-MOON!

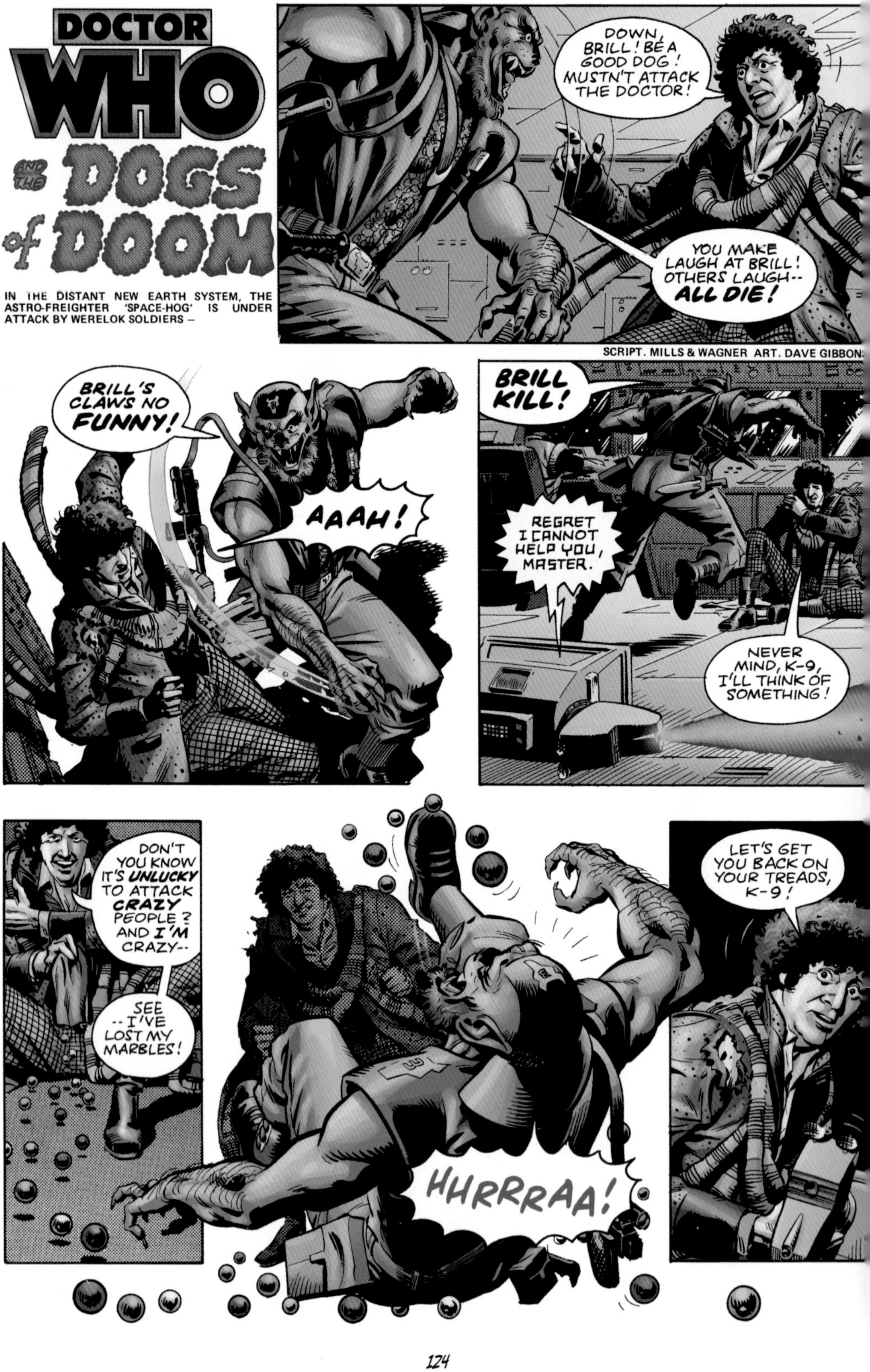

DOCTOR WHO AND THE DOGS of DOOM
IN THE DISTANT NEW EARTH SYSTEM, THE ASTRO-FREIGHTER 'SPACE-HOG' IS UNDER ATTACK BY WERELOK SOLDIERS –
DOWN, BRILL! BE A GOOD DOG! MUSTN'T ATTACK THE DOCTOR!
YOU MAKE LAUGH AT BRILL! OTHERS LAUGH-- ALL DIE!
SCRIPT. MILLS & WAGNER ART. DAVE GIBBONS
BRILL'S CLAWS NO FUNNY!
AAAH!
BRILL KILL!
REGRET I CANNOT HELP YOU, MASTER.
NEVER MIND, K-9, I'LL THINK OF SOMETHING!
DON'T YOU KNOW IT'S UNLUCKY TO ATTACK CRAZY PEOPLE? AND I'M CRAZY--
SEE -- I'VE LOST MY MARBLES!
HHRRRAA!
LET'S GET YOU BACK ON YOUR TREADS, K-9!

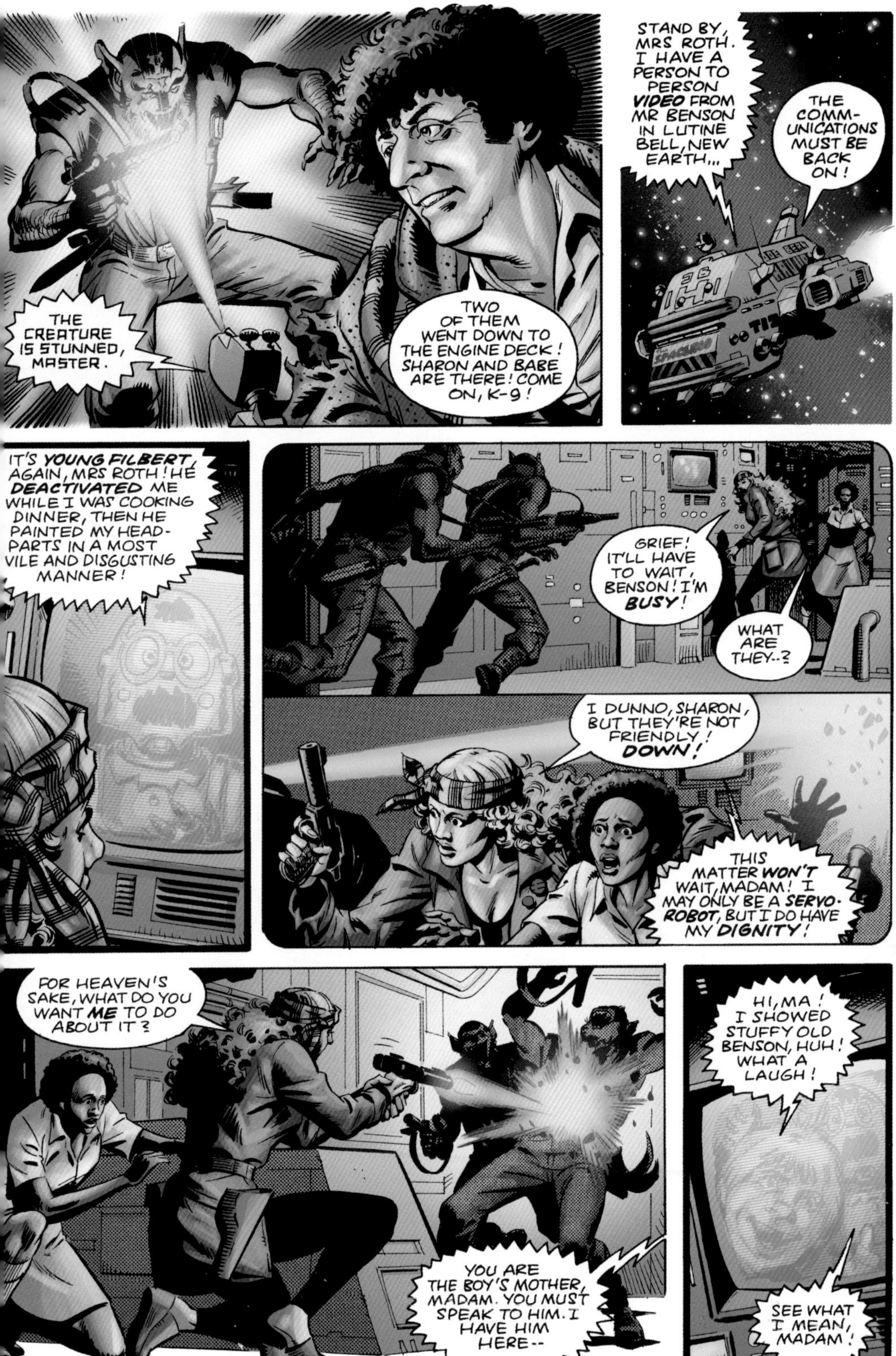
THE CREATURE IS STUNNED, MASTER.
TWO OF THEM WENT DOWN TO THE ENGINE DECK! SHARON AND BABE ARE THERE! COME ON, K-9!
STAND BY, MRS ROTH. I HAVE A PERSON TO PERSON VIDEO FROM MR BENSON IN LUTINE BELL, NEW EARTH...
THE COMMUNICATIONS MUST BE BACK ON!
IT'S YOUNG FILBERT, AGAIN, MRS ROTH! HE DEACTIVATED ME WHILE I WAS COOKING DINNER, THEN HE PAINTED MY HEAD-PARTS IN A MOST VILE AND DISGUSTING MANNER!
GRIEF! IT'LL HAVE TO WAIT, BENSON! I'M BUSY!
WHAT ARE THEY..?
I DUNNO, SHARON, BUT THEY'RE NOT FRIENDLY! DOWN!
THIS MATTER WON'T WAIT, MADAM! I MAY ONLY BE A SERVO-ROBOT, BUT I DO HAVE MY DIGNITY!
FOR HEAVEN'S SAKE, WHAT DO YOU WANT ME TO DO ABOUT IT?
YOU ARE THE BOY'S MOTHER, MADAM. YOU MUST SPEAK TO HIM. I HAVE HIM HERE--
HI, MA! I SHOWED STUFFY OLD BENSON, HUH! WHAT A LAUGH!
SEE WHAT I MEAN, MADAM!

I JUST HAVEN'T GOT TIME FOR THIS! *FILBERT!* YOU STOP MISTREATING BENSON OR I'LL PUNCH YOUR SNOOT WHEN I GET HOME! NOW *GOOD-BYE!*

I SEE WE'RE NOT NEEDED HERE!

BABE FIXED THEM, DOCTOR! SHE'S A REAL *SUPER-MUM!*

ON THE FLIGHT DECK, JOE BEAN IS RECOVERING --

LUCKY THEM LAZ-BURPS ONLY GREASED MY GURNEY OR I'D BE *TRUCKIN' HOTSIDE!* BETTER GET ON THE SQUAWK BOX TO BIG MAMA, FILL 'EM IN ON THE BEAN SCENE --

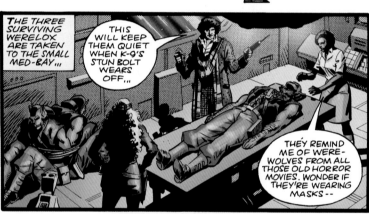

THE THREE SURVIVING WERELOX ARE TAKEN TO THE SMALL MED-BAY...

THIS WILL KEEP THEM QUIET WHEN K-9'S STUN BOLT WEARS OFF...

THEY REMIND ME OF WERE-WOLVES FROM ALL THOSE OLD HORROR MOVIES. WONDER IF THEY'RE WEARING MASKS --

ENOUGH! I'VE GOT THE SCRATCHES TO PROVE IT! NOW IF YOU'LL LEAVE ME IN PEACE, I MAY BE ABLE TO DISCOVER MORE ABOUT THEM!

I EXPECT YOU'D LIKE TO CHANGE INTO SOMETHING MORE COMFORTABLE, SHARON. MY DAUGHTER LEFT SOME CLOTHES ON BOARD -- THEY SHOULD FIT YOU.

WISH I COULD GET AN EXCITING JOB LIKE YOURS, BABE!

I DIDN'T HAVE MUCH CHOICE. MY HUSBAND BEN WAS THE ENGINEER, BUT HE GOT KILLED -- FREAK ACCIDENT. I WAS LEFT WITH TWO KIDFOLK TO BRING UP AND HALF THE *SPACEHOG...*

IN BABE'S QUARTERS --

I'VE NEVER BEEN ON ANOTHER PLANET. WHAT'S *NEW EARTH* LIKE?

A LOT SMALLER THAN *YOUR* EARTH. AND OF COURSE THERE ARE LESS THAN A MILLION PEOPLE IN THE WHOLE SYSTEM. WE'VE ONLY BEEN SETTLED HERE FOR FIFTY YEARS -- SINCE 2380, OLD EARTH TIME.

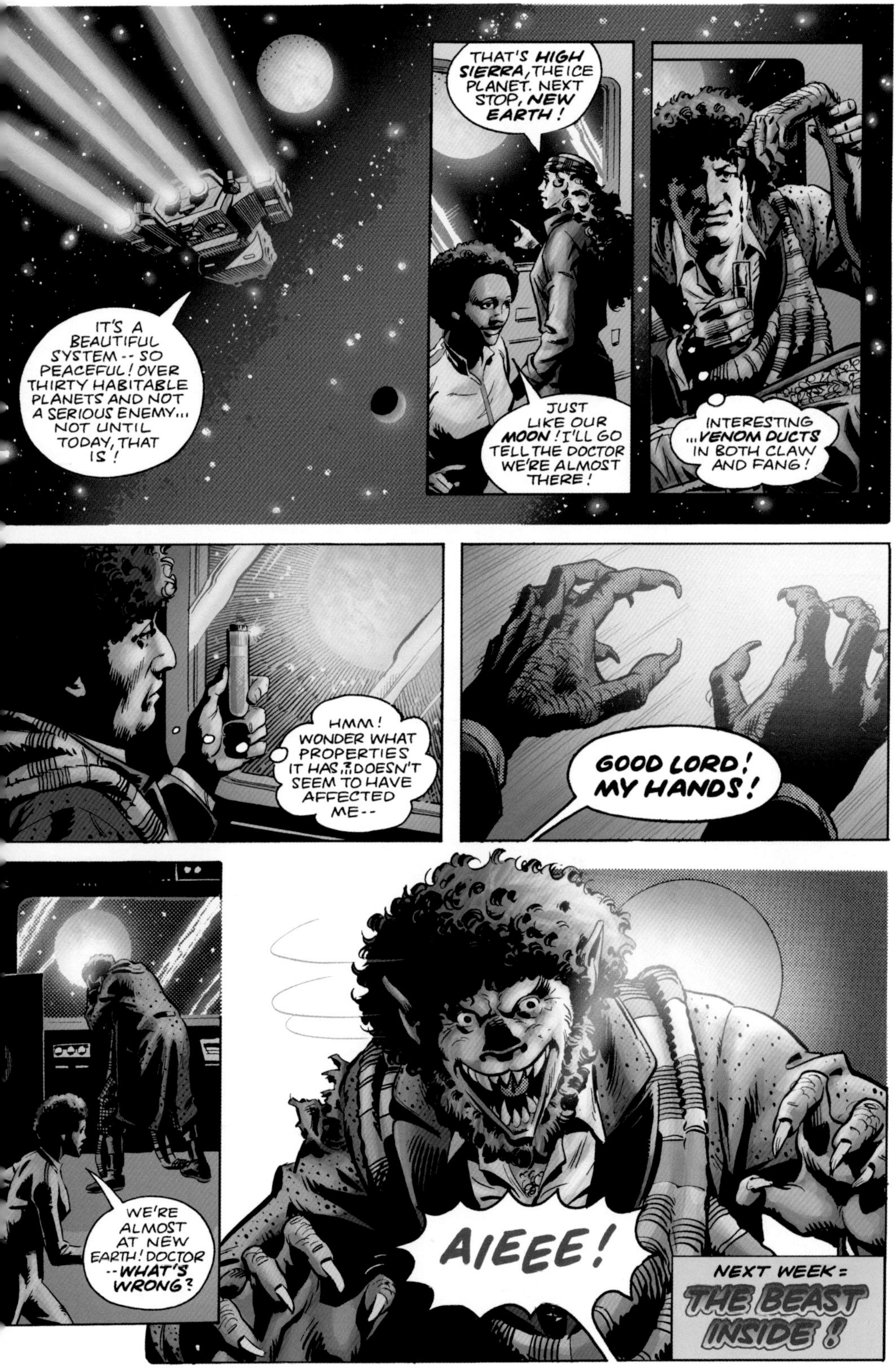
IT'S A BEAUTIFUL SYSTEM -- SO PEACEFUL! OVER THIRTY HABITABLE PLANETS AND NOT A SERIOUS ENEMY... NOT UNTIL TODAY, THAT IS!
THAT'S HIGH SIERRA, THE ICE PLANET. NEXT STOP, NEW EARTH!
JUST LIKE OUR MOON! I'LL GO TELL THE DOCTOR WE'RE ALMOST THERE!
INTERESTING ...VENOM DUCTS IN BOTH CLAW AND FANG!
HMM! WONDER WHAT PROPERTIES IT HAS... DOESN'T SEEM TO HAVE AFFECTED ME--
GOOD LORD! MY HANDS!
WE'RE ALMOST AT NEW EARTH! DOCTOR --WHAT'S WRONG?
AIEEE!
NEXT WEEK: THE BEAST INSIDE!

DOCTOR WHO
and the DOGS of DOOM

ON THE ASTRO-FREIGHTER 'SPACEHOG' AN ATTACK BY WERELOK RAIDERS IS FOILED. BUT THE DOCTOR RECEIVES A SCRATCH FROM A WERELOK CLAW, AND LATER A FRIGHTENING CHANGE TAKES PLACE —

DOCTOR! WH--WHAT'S HAPPENED TO YOU?

PLEASE! DON'T HURT ME!

SCRIPT. MILLS & WAGNER ART. DAVE GIBBONS

NRAAA!

ON THE FLIGHT DECK--

MERCY SAKES! THE BOW-WOW BOYS IS BACK!

DON'T SHOOT, MR BEAN! IT'S THE DOCTOR!

STAY AWAY FROM ME! CAN'T-- CONTROL MYSELF!

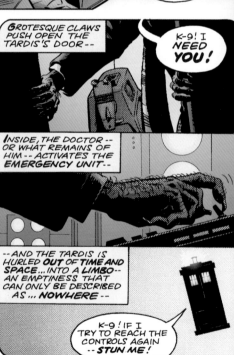

GROTESQUE CLAWS PUSH OPEN THE TARDIS'S DOOR--

K-9! I NEED YOU!

INSIDE, THE DOCTOR -- OR WHAT REMAINS OF HIM -- ACTIVATES THE EMERGENCY UNIT--

--AND THE TARDIS IS HURLED OUT OF TIME AND SPACE...INTO A LIMBO-- AN EMPTINESS THAT CAN ONLY BE DESCRIBED AS ...NOWHERE --

K-9! IF I TRY TO REACH THE CONTROLS AGAIN --STUN ME!

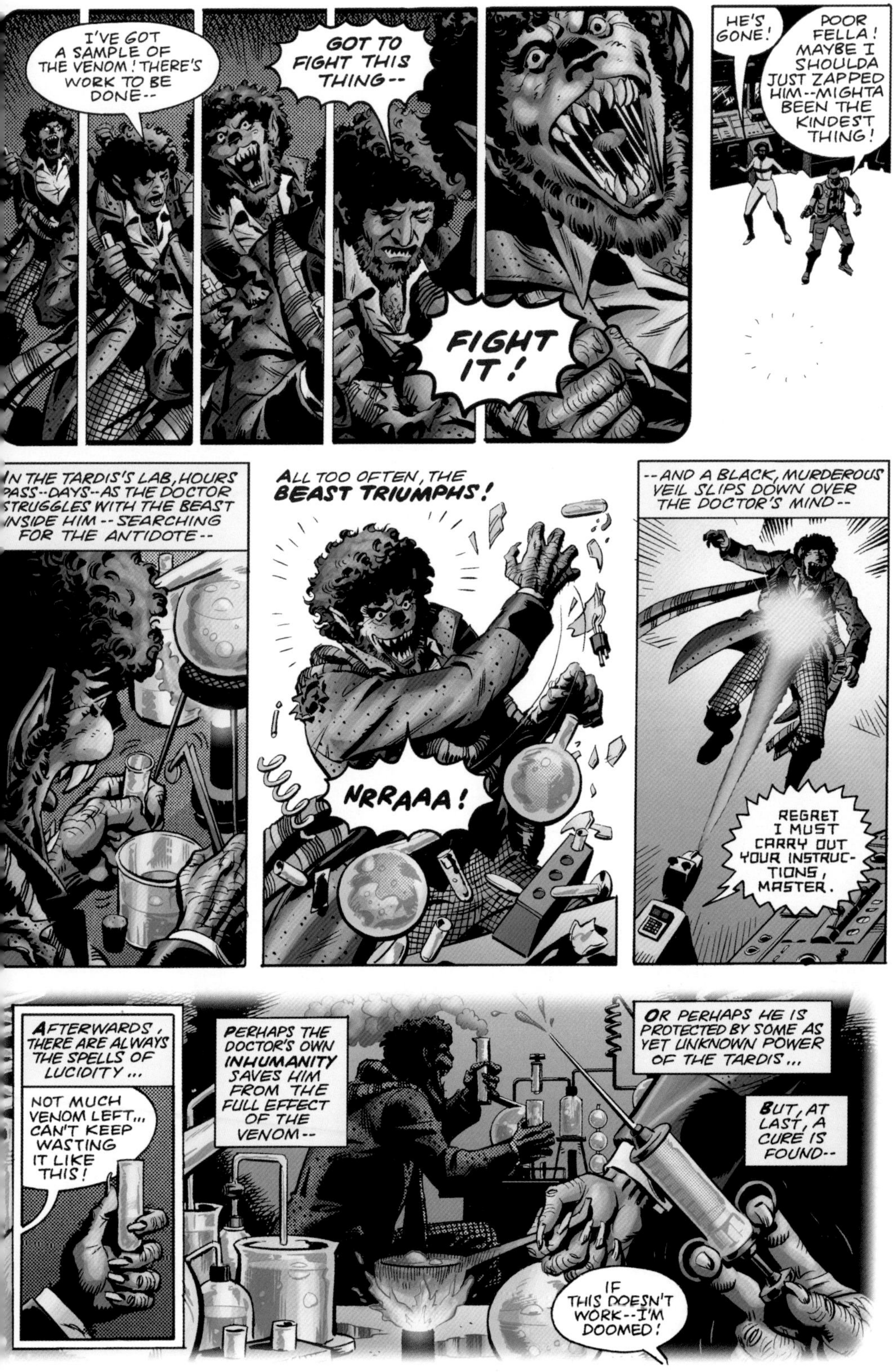
I'VE GOT A SAMPLE OF THE VENOM! THERE'S WORK TO BE DONE--
GOT TO FIGHT THIS THING--
FIGHT IT!
HE'S GONE!
POOR FELLA! MAYBE I SHOULDA JUST ZAPPED HIM--MIGHTA BEEN THE KINDEST THING!
IN THE TARDIS'S LAB, HOURS PASS--DAYS--AS THE DOCTOR STRUGGLES WITH THE BEAST INSIDE HIM--SEARCHING FOR THE ANTIDOTE--
ALL TOO OFTEN, THE BEAST TRIUMPHS!
NRRAAA!
--AND A BLACK, MURDEROUS VEIL SLIPS DOWN OVER THE DOCTOR'S MIND--
REGRET I MUST CARRY OUT YOUR INSTRUCTIONS, MASTER.
AFTERWARDS, THERE ARE ALWAYS THE SPELLS OF LUCIDITY...
NOT MUCH VENOM LEFT... CAN'T KEEP WASTING IT LIKE THIS!
PERHAPS THE DOCTOR'S OWN INHUMANITY SAVES HIM FROM THE FULL EFFECT OF THE VENOM--
OR PERHAPS HE IS PROTECTED BY SOME AS YET UNKNOWN POWER OF THE TARDIS...
BUT, AT LAST, A CURE IS FOUND--
IF THIS DOESN'T WORK--I'M DOOMED!

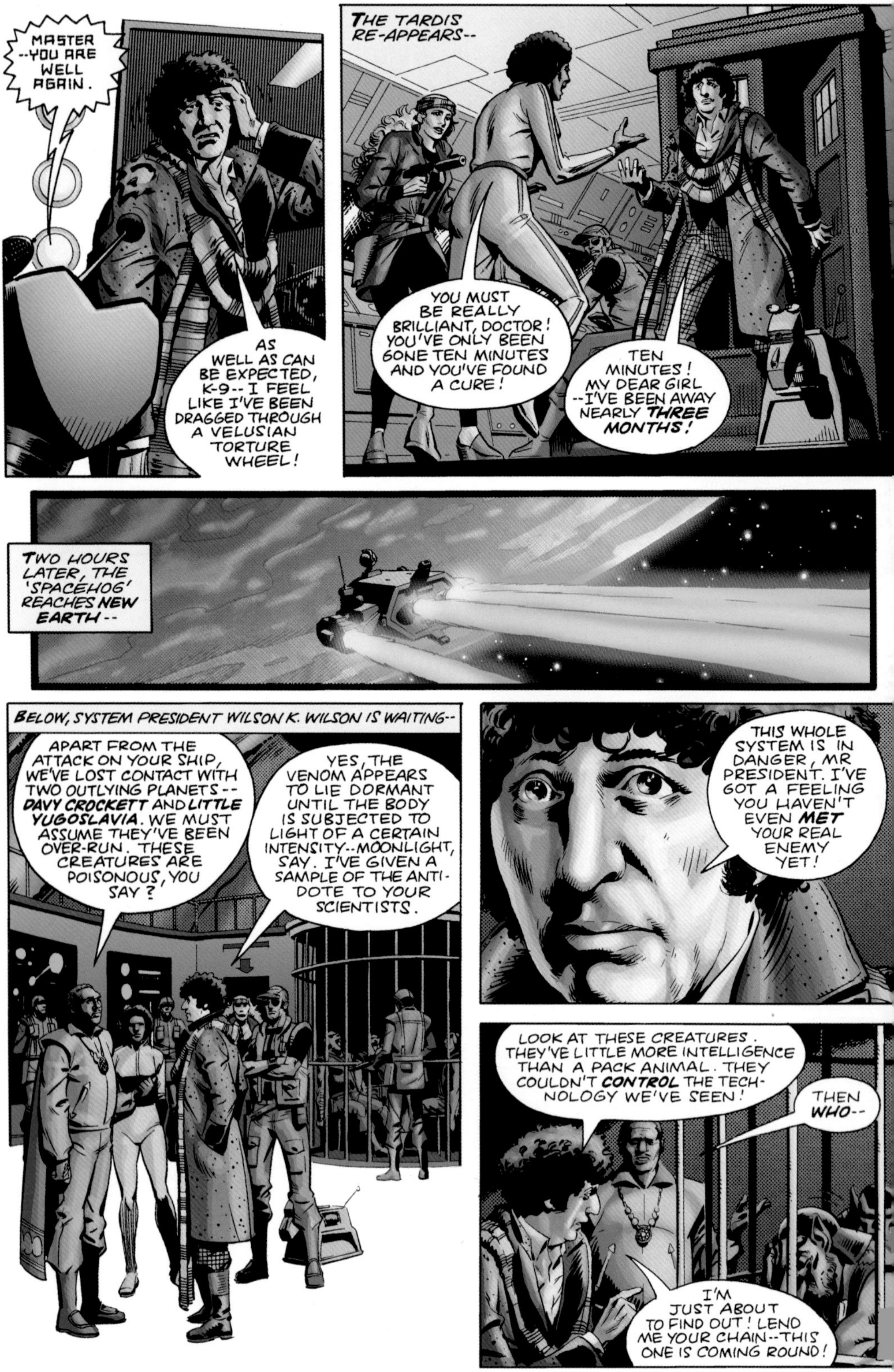

MASTER --YOU ARE WELL AGAIN.
AS WELL AS CAN BE EXPECTED, K-9-- I FEEL LIKE I'VE BEEN DRAGGED THROUGH A VELUSIAN TORTURE WHEEL!
THE TARDIS RE-APPEARS--
YOU MUST BE REALLY BRILLIANT, DOCTOR! YOU'VE ONLY BEEN GONE TEN MINUTES AND YOU'VE FOUND A CURE!
TEN MINUTES! MY DEAR GIRL --I'VE BEEN AWAY NEARLY THREE MONTHS!
TWO HOURS LATER, THE 'SPACEHOG' REACHES NEW EARTH--
BELOW, SYSTEM PRESIDENT WILSON K. WILSON IS WAITING--
APART FROM THE ATTACK ON YOUR SHIP, WE'VE LOST CONTACT WITH TWO OUTLYING PLANETS -- DAVY CROCKETT AND LITTLE YUGOSLAVIA. WE MUST ASSUME THEY'VE BEEN OVER-RUN. THESE CREATURES ARE POISONOUS, YOU SAY?
YES, THE VENOM APPEARS TO LIE DORMANT UNTIL THE BODY IS SUBJECTED TO LIGHT OF A CERTAIN INTENSITY--MOONLIGHT, SAY. I'VE GIVEN A SAMPLE OF THE ANTI-DOTE TO YOUR SCIENTISTS.
THIS WHOLE SYSTEM IS IN DANGER, MR PRESIDENT. I'VE GOT A FEELING YOU HAVEN'T EVEN MET YOUR REAL ENEMY YET!
LOOK AT THESE CREATURES. THEY'VE LITTLE MORE INTELLIGENCE THAN A PACK ANIMAL. THEY COULDN'T CONTROL THE TECH-NOLOGY WE'VE SEEN!
THEN WHO--
I'M JUST ABOUT TO FIND OUT! LEND ME YOUR CHAIN--THIS ONE IS COMING ROUND!

WATCH THE PRETTY CHAIN, BRILL--

UHHNN

YOU ARE GETTING SLEEPY... VERY SLEEPY... YOU CAN HARDLY KEEP THOSE HAIRY EYE-LIDS OPEN...

BRILL TALKS--

I BRILL, LEADER OF FORTY-NINTH WERELOK PACK. I TAKE ORDERS FROM FOUR-PACKER DRAKK--

GO ABOVE HIM, BRILL! TELL ME ABOUT YOUR BIG BOSSES. THERE ARE SOME WHO AREN'T OF YOUR RACE, AREN'T THERE?

YES, WE CALL THEM... THE EVIL ONES! THEY ARE BAD--MORE BAD THAN WERELOX. MAKE EVEN BRILL AFRAID.

THE EVIL ONES NOT LIKE LIVING THINGS--THEY MORE LIKE ROBOT. MAKE WERE-LOX SERVE THEM SAY EXTERMINATE! EXTERMINATE WHOLE SYSTEM!

NO! THAT WORD--EXTER-MINATE!

WHAT IS IT, DOCTOR?

THE WORST NEWS POSSIBLE! YOU'RE DEALING WITH THE MOST EVIL RACE I HAVE EVER ENCOUNTERED ...THE DALEKS!

EXTERMINATE!

NEXT ISSUE · THE DALEK MASTERS!

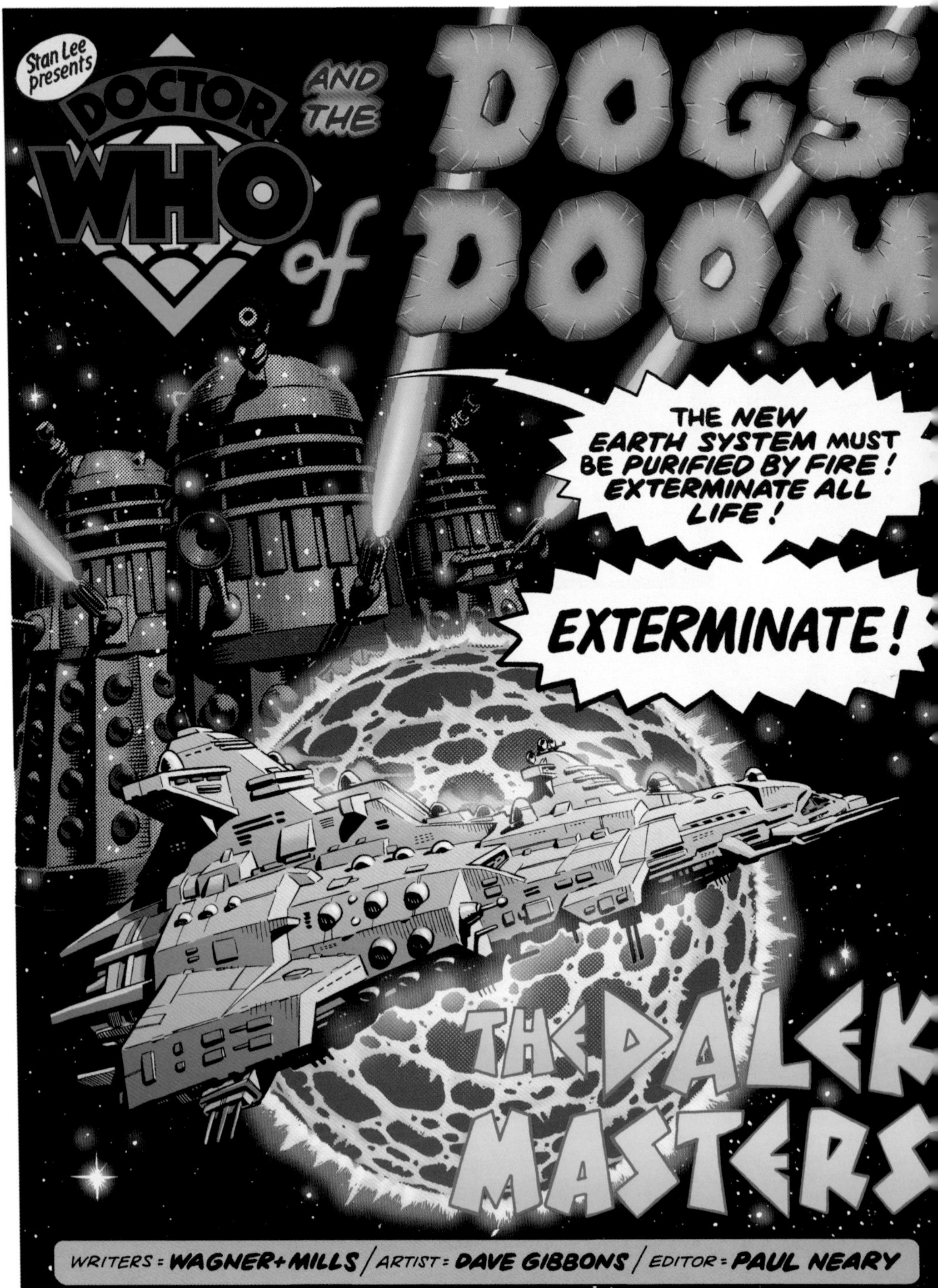

Stan Lee presents
DOCTOR WHO
AND THE
DOGS of DOOM
THE NEW EARTH SYSTEM MUST BE PURIFIED BY FIRE! EXTERMINATE ALL LIFE!
EXTERMINATE!
THE DALEK MASTERS
WRITERS = WAGNER + MILLS / ARTIST = DAVE GIBBONS / EDITOR = PAUL NEARY

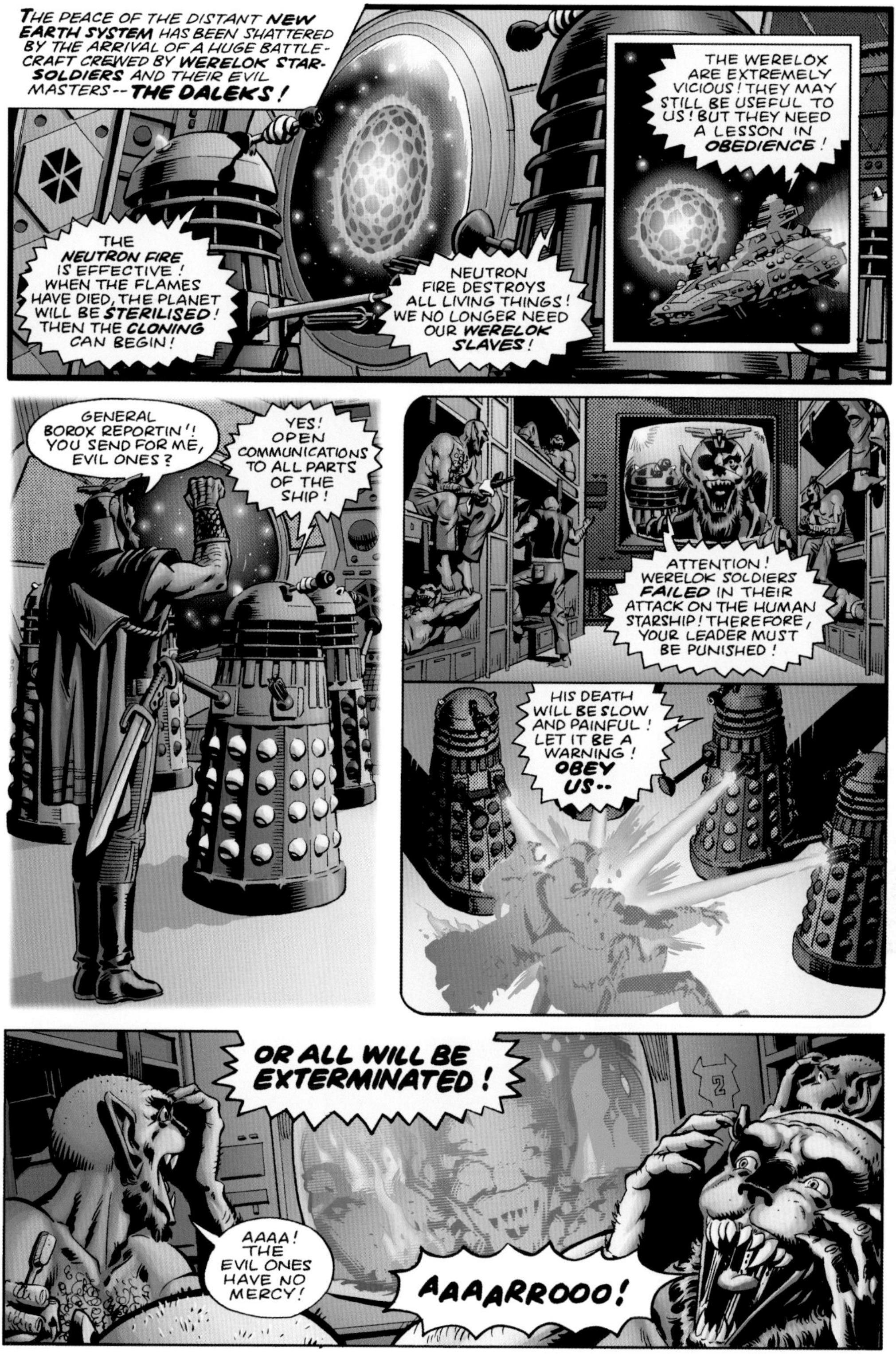

THE PEACE OF THE DISTANT NEW EARTH SYSTEM HAS BEEN SHATTERED BY THE ARRIVAL OF A HUGE BATTLE-CRAFT CREWED BY WERELOK STAR-SOLDIERS AND THEIR EVIL MASTERS -- THE DALEKS!
THE NEUTRON FIRE IS EFFECTIVE! WHEN THE FLAMES HAVE DIED, THE PLANET WILL BE STERILISED! THEN THE CLONING CAN BEGIN!
NEUTRON FIRE DESTROYS ALL LIVING THINGS! WE NO LONGER NEED OUR WERELOK SLAVES!
THE WERELOX ARE EXTREMELY VICIOUS! THEY MAY STILL BE USEFUL TO US! BUT THEY NEED A LESSON IN OBEDIENCE!
GENERAL BOROX REPORTIN'! YOU SEND FOR ME, EVIL ONES?
YES! OPEN COMMUNICATIONS TO ALL PARTS OF THE SHIP!
ATTENTION! WERELOK SOLDIERS FAILED IN THEIR ATTACK ON THE HUMAN STARSHIP! THEREFORE, YOUR LEADER MUST BE PUNISHED!
HIS DEATH WILL BE SLOW AND PAINFUL! LET IT BE A WARNING! OBEY US..
OR ALL WILL BE EXTERMINATED!
AAAA! THE EVIL ONES HAVE NO MERCY!
AAAARROOO!

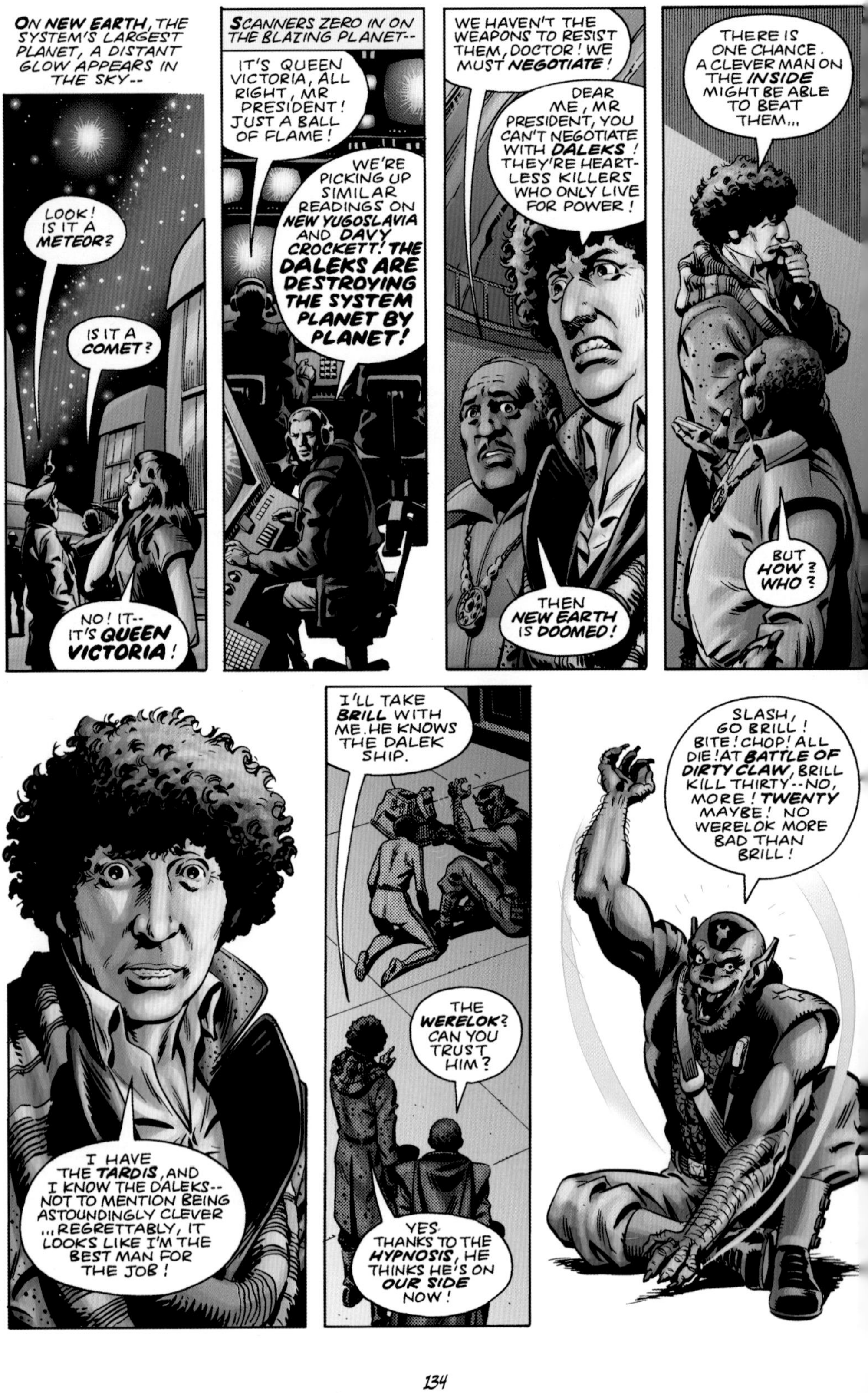

ON NEW EARTH, THE SYSTEM'S LARGEST PLANET, A DISTANT GLOW APPEARS IN THE SKY--
LOOK! IS IT A METEOR?
IS IT A COMET?
NO! IT-- IT'S QUEEN VICTORIA!
SCANNERS ZERO IN ON THE BLAZING PLANET--
IT'S QUEEN VICTORIA, ALL RIGHT, MR PRESIDENT! JUST A BALL OF FLAME!
WE'RE PICKING UP SIMILAR READINGS ON NEW YUGOSLAVIA AND DAVY CROCKETT! THE DALEKS ARE DESTROYING THE SYSTEM PLANET BY PLANET!
WE HAVEN'T THE WEAPONS TO RESIST THEM, DOCTOR! WE MUST NEGOTIATE!
DEAR ME, MR PRESIDENT, YOU CAN'T NEGOTIATE WITH DALEKS! THEY'RE HEART-LESS KILLERS WHO ONLY LIVE FOR POWER!
THEN NEW EARTH IS DOOMED!
THERE IS ONE CHANCE. A CLEVER MAN ON THE INSIDE MIGHT BE ABLE TO BEAT THEM...
BUT HOW? WHO?
I HAVE THE TARDIS, AND I KNOW THE DALEKS-- NOT TO MENTION BEING ASTOUNDINGLY CLEVER ...REGRETTABLY, IT LOOKS LIKE I'M THE BEST MAN FOR THE JOB!
I'LL TAKE BRILL WITH ME. HE KNOWS THE DALEK SHIP.
THE WERELOK? CAN YOU TRUST HIM?
YES. THANKS TO THE HYPNOSIS, HE THINKS HE'S ON OUR SIDE NOW!
SLASH, GO BRILL! BITE! CHOP! ALL DIE! AT BATTLE OF DIRTY CLAW, BRILL KILL THIRTY--NO, MORE! TWENTY MAYBE! NO WERELOK MORE BAD THAN BRILL!

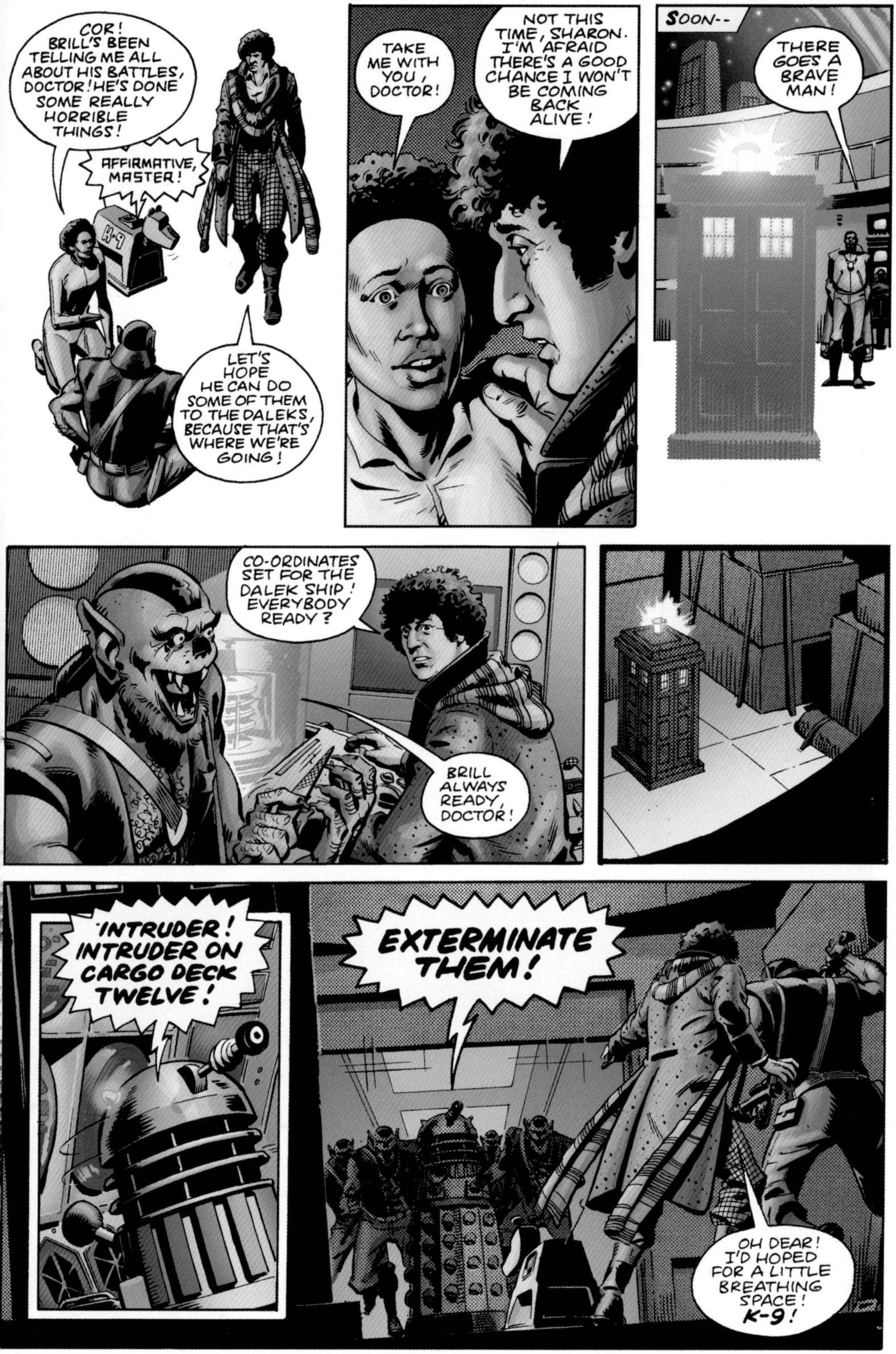
COR! BRILL'S BEEN TELLING ME ALL ABOUT HIS BATTLES, DOCTOR! HE'S DONE SOME REALLY HORRIBLE THINGS!
AFFIRMATIVE, MASTER!
LET'S HOPE HE CAN DO SOME OF THEM TO THE DALEKS, BECAUSE THAT'S WHERE WE'RE GOING!
TAKE ME WITH YOU, DOCTOR!
NOT THIS TIME, SHARON. I'M AFRAID THERE'S A GOOD CHANCE I WON'T BE COMING BACK ALIVE!
SOON--
THERE GOES A BRAVE MAN!
CO-ORDINATES SET FOR THE DALEK SHIP! EVERYBODY READY?
BRILL ALWAYS READY, DOCTOR!
INTRUDER! INTRUDER ON CARGO DECK TWELVE!
EXTERMINATE THEM!
OH DEAR! I'D HOPED FOR A LITTLE BREATHING SPACE! K-9!

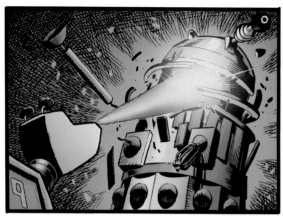

AAIIAAA! IT BRILL! BRILL OF THE FORTY NINTH!

WITH FRIGHTENING EFFICIENCY, BRILL METES OUT *DEATH*--

ENEMY WIPED OUT! WHO YOU WANT BRILL KILL NEXT?

COULD YOU PERHAPS START WITH THE PEANUT GALLERY UP THERE..?

THE EVIL ONES!

HELLO THERE! I'M AFRAID YOU'VE MISSED THE FIRST ACT! CAN YOU COME BACK TOMORROW?

EXTERMINATE!

I GUESS THAT MEANS NO!

NEXT= ALIEN ZOO!

136

DOCTOR WHO AND THE DOGS of DOOM

EXTERMINATE!

THE DALEKS AND THEIR WERELOK HENCHMEN
ARE ATTACKING THE NEW EARTH SYSTEM. THE
DOCTOR, K-9 AND A TAME WERELOK, BRILL, USE
THE TARDIS TO BOARD THE DALEK BATTLE
CRAFT -- RIGHT INTO TROUBLE!

RUN!

NO! BRILL
FEAR EVIL
ONES, BUT BRILL
NEVER RUN!

AAIAA!
MAYBE RUN
JUST THIS
ONCE!

THIS
DOOR'S
LOCKED!

THAT
IS ROOM
OF MANY
CENTURIES!
IT IS FOR-
BIDDEN -- EVEN
TO OTHER
EVIL
ONES!

IT SEALED
FROM INSIDE!
EVIL ONES IN
THERE NEVER
COME OUT --
NEVER!

HEAVY
SECURITY,
EVEN FOR
DALEKS'!
INTER-
ESTING!

DALEKS
CLOSING IN,
MASTER!

DEAR
ME! WHAT-
EVER ELSE
YOU MIGHT
SAY ABOUT
THEM, THEY'RE
PERSISTENT!

THERE
OTHER WAY!
COME!

I WILL
DELAY THEM,
MASTER!

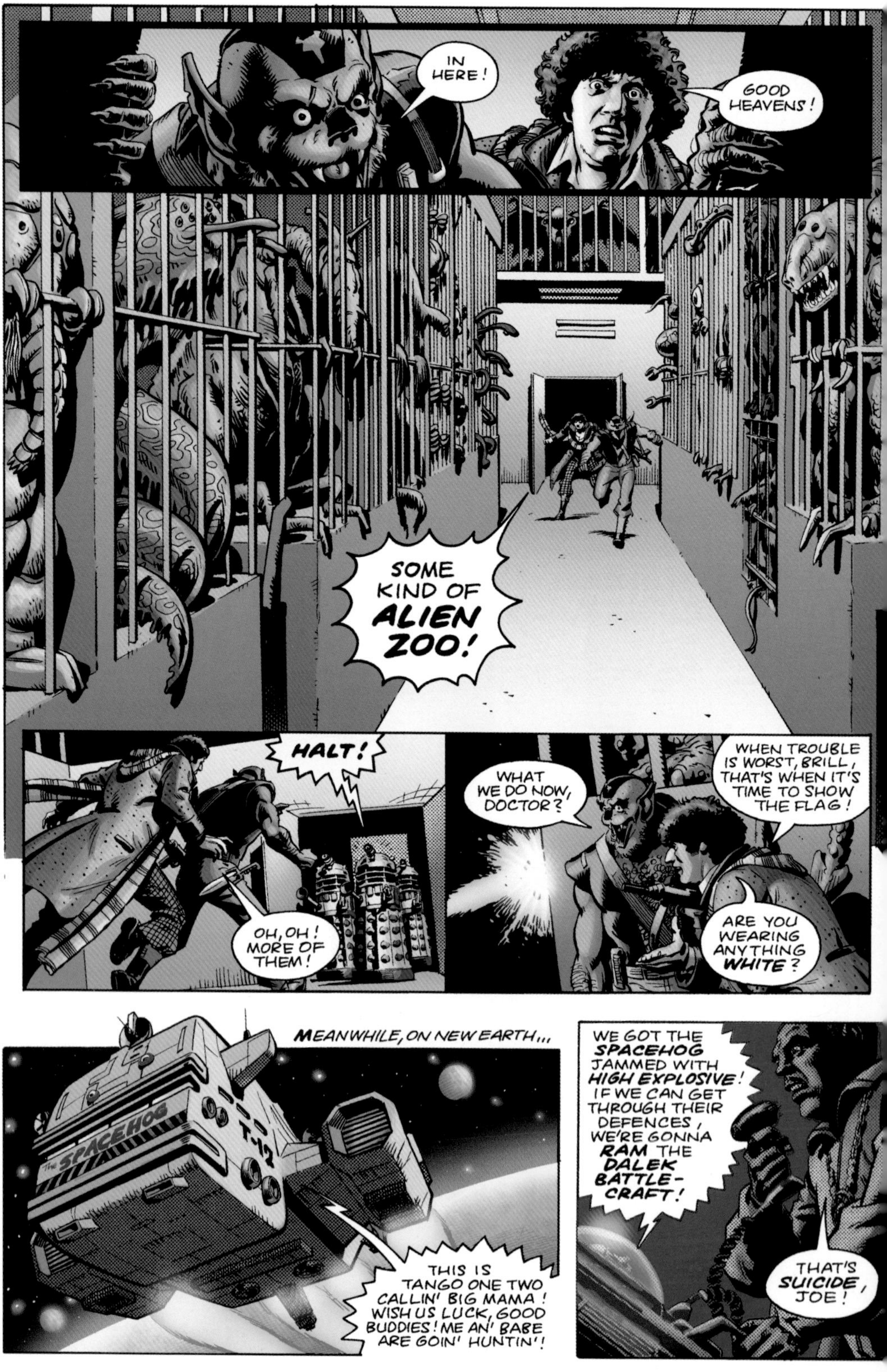
IN HERE!
GOOD HEAVENS!
SOME KIND OF ALIEN ZOO!
HALT!
OH, OH! MORE OF THEM!
WHAT WE DO NOW, DOCTOR?
WHEN TROUBLE IS WORST, BRILL, THAT'S WHEN IT'S TIME TO SHOW THE FLAG!
ARE YOU WEARING ANYTHING WHITE?
MEANWHILE, ON NEW EARTH...
THE SPACEHOG
T-12
THIS IS TANGO ONE TWO CALLIN' BIG MAMA! WISH US LUCK, GOOD BUDDIES! ME AN' BABE ARE GOIN' HUNTIN'!
WE GOT THE SPACEHOG JAMMED WITH HIGH EXPLOSIVE! IF WE CAN GET THROUGH THEIR DEFENCES, WE'RE GONNA RAM THE DALEK BATTLE-CRAFT!
THAT'S SUICIDE, JOE!

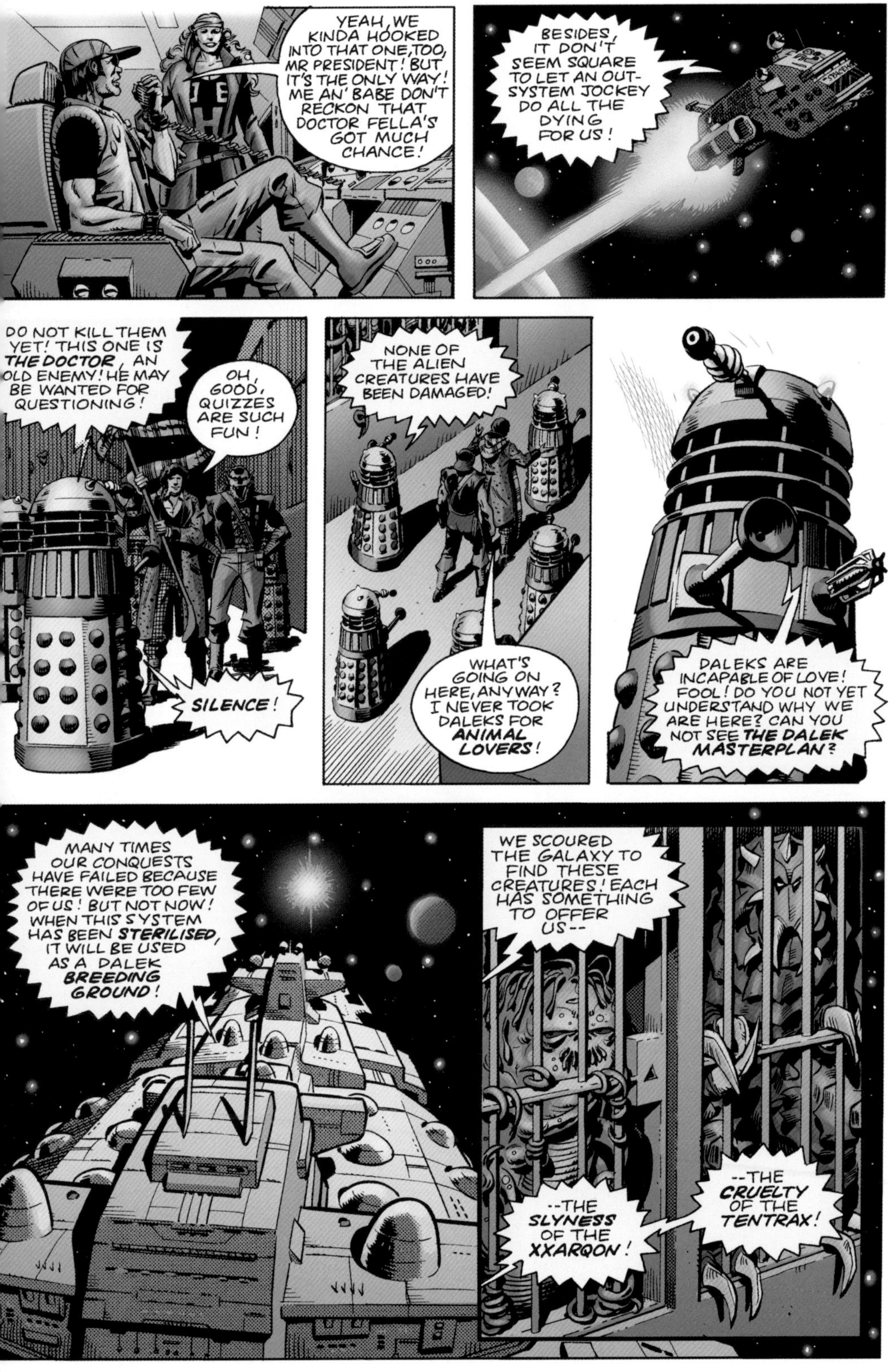
YEAH, WE KINDA HOOKED INTO THAT ONE, TOO, MR PRESIDENT! BUT IT'S THE ONLY WAY! ME AN' BABE DON'T RECKON THAT DOCTOR FELLA'S GOT MUCH CHANCE!
BESIDES, IT DON'T SEEM SQUARE TO LET AN OUT-SYSTEM JOCKEY DO ALL THE DYING FOR US!
DO NOT KILL THEM YET! THIS ONE IS THE DOCTOR, AN OLD ENEMY! HE MAY BE WANTED FOR QUESTIONING!
OH, GOOD, QUIZZES ARE SUCH FUN!
SILENCE!
NONE OF THE ALIEN CREATURES HAVE BEEN DAMAGED!
WHAT'S GOING ON HERE, ANYWAY? I NEVER TOOK DALEKS FOR ANIMAL LOVERS!
DALEKS ARE INCAPABLE OF LOVE! FOOL! DO YOU NOT YET UNDERSTAND WHY WE ARE HERE? CAN YOU NOT SEE THE DALEK MASTERPLAN?
MANY TIMES OUR CONQUESTS HAVE FAILED BECAUSE THERE WERE TOO FEW OF US! BUT NOT NOW! WHEN THIS SYSTEM HAS BEEN STERILISED, IT WILL BE USED AS A DALEK BREEDING GROUND!
WE SCOURED THE GALAXY TO FIND THESE CREATURES! EACH HAS SOMETHING TO OFFER US--
--THE SLYNESS OF THE XXARQON!
--THE CRUELTY OF THE TENTRAX!

THE INSANE HATRED OF THE SHRIEKING GLAROSUS!

HEEEEEE

DELIGHTFUL!

THESE EXCELLENT QUALITIES WILL BE ISOLATED AND *CLONED* INTO EACH NEW DALEK!

EMERGENCY+ MASTER IN DANGER++

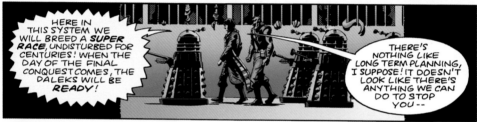

HERE IN THIS SYSTEM WE WILL BREED A *SUPER RACE*, UNDISTURBED FOR CENTURIES! WHEN THE DAY OF THE FINAL CONQUEST COMES, THE DALEKS WILL BE *READY*!

THERE'S NOTHING LIKE LONG TERM PLANNING, I SUPPOSE! IT DOESN'T LOOK LIKE THERE'S ANYTHING WE CAN DO TO STOP YOU--

GET DOWN, MASTER!

WELL DONE, K-9!

I *THINK*!

NEXT: *REVOLT OF THE BEASTS!*

140

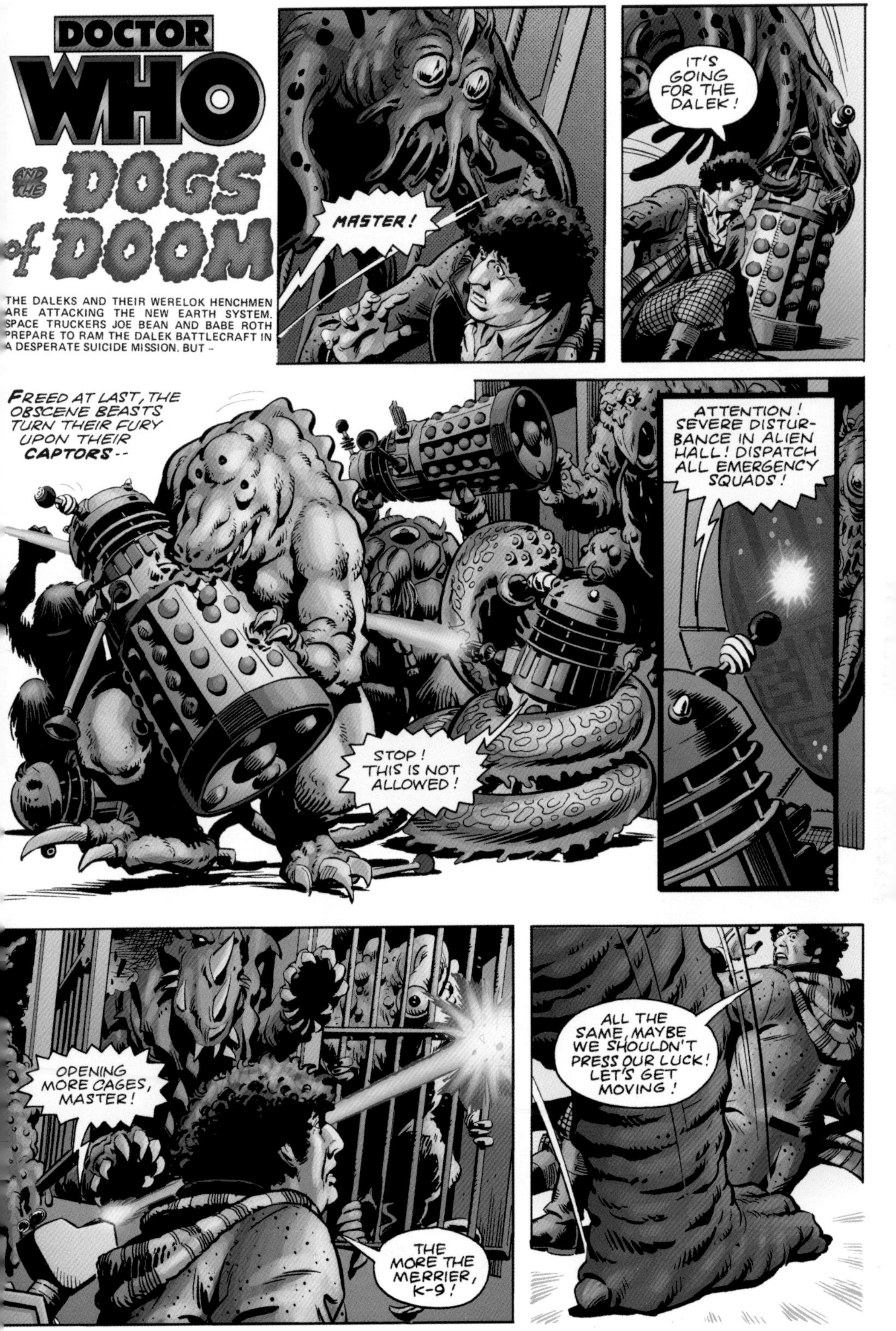
DOCTOR WHO AND THE DOGS OF DOOM
THE DALEKS AND THEIR WERELOK HENCHMEN ARE ATTACKING THE NEW EARTH SYSTEM. SPACE TRUCKERS JOE BEAN AND BABE ROTH PREPARE TO RAM THE DALEK BATTLECRAFT IN A DESPERATE SUICIDE MISSION. BUT –
MASTER!
IT'S GOING FOR THE DALEK!
FREED AT LAST, THE OBSCENE BEASTS TURN THEIR FURY UPON THEIR CAPTORS --
ATTENTION! SEVERE DISTURBANCE IN ALIEN HALL! DISPATCH ALL EMERGENCY SQUADS!
STOP! THIS IS NOT ALLOWED!
OPENING MORE CAGES, MASTER!
THE MORE THE MERRIER, K-9!
ALL THE SAME, MAYBE WE SHOULDN'T PRESS OUR LUCK! LET'S GET MOVING!

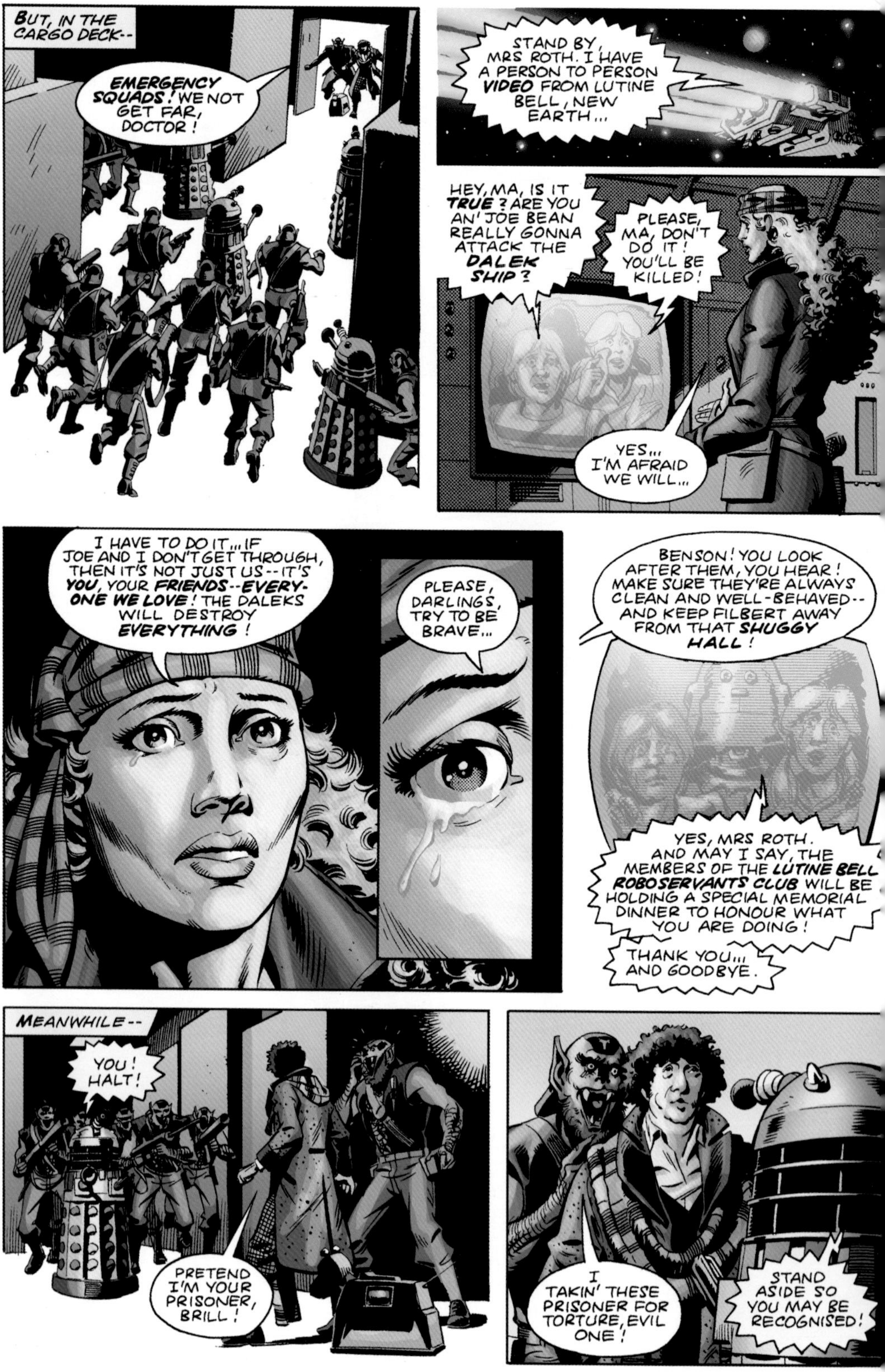
BUT, IN THE CARGO DECK--
EMERGENCY SQUADS! WE NOT GET FAR, DOCTOR!
STAND BY, MRS ROTH. I HAVE A PERSON TO PERSON VIDEO FROM LUTINE BELL, NEW EARTH...
HEY, MA, IS IT TRUE? ARE YOU AN' JOE BEAN REALLY GONNA ATTACK THE DALEK SHIP?
PLEASE, MA, DON'T DO IT! YOU'LL BE KILLED!
YES... I'M AFRAID WE WILL...
I HAVE TO DO IT... IF JOE AND I DON'T GET THROUGH, THEN IT'S NOT JUST US--IT'S YOU, YOUR FRIENDS--EVERYONE WE LOVE! THE DALEKS WILL DESTROY EVERYTHING!
PLEASE, DARLINGS, TRY TO BE BRAVE...
BENSON! YOU LOOK AFTER THEM, YOU HEAR! MAKE SURE THEY'RE ALWAYS CLEAN AND WELL-BEHAVED--AND KEEP FILBERT AWAY FROM THAT SHUGGY HALL!
YES, MRS ROTH. AND MAY I SAY, THE MEMBERS OF THE LUTINE BELL ROBOSERVANTS CLUB WILL BE HOLDING A SPECIAL MEMORIAL DINNER TO HONOUR WHAT YOU ARE DOING!
THANK YOU... AND GOODBYE.
MEANWHILE--
YOU! HALT!
PRETEND I'M YOUR PRISONER, BRILL!
I TAKIN' THESE PRISONER FOR TORTURE, EVIL ONE!
STAND ASIDE SO YOU MAY BE RECOGNISED!

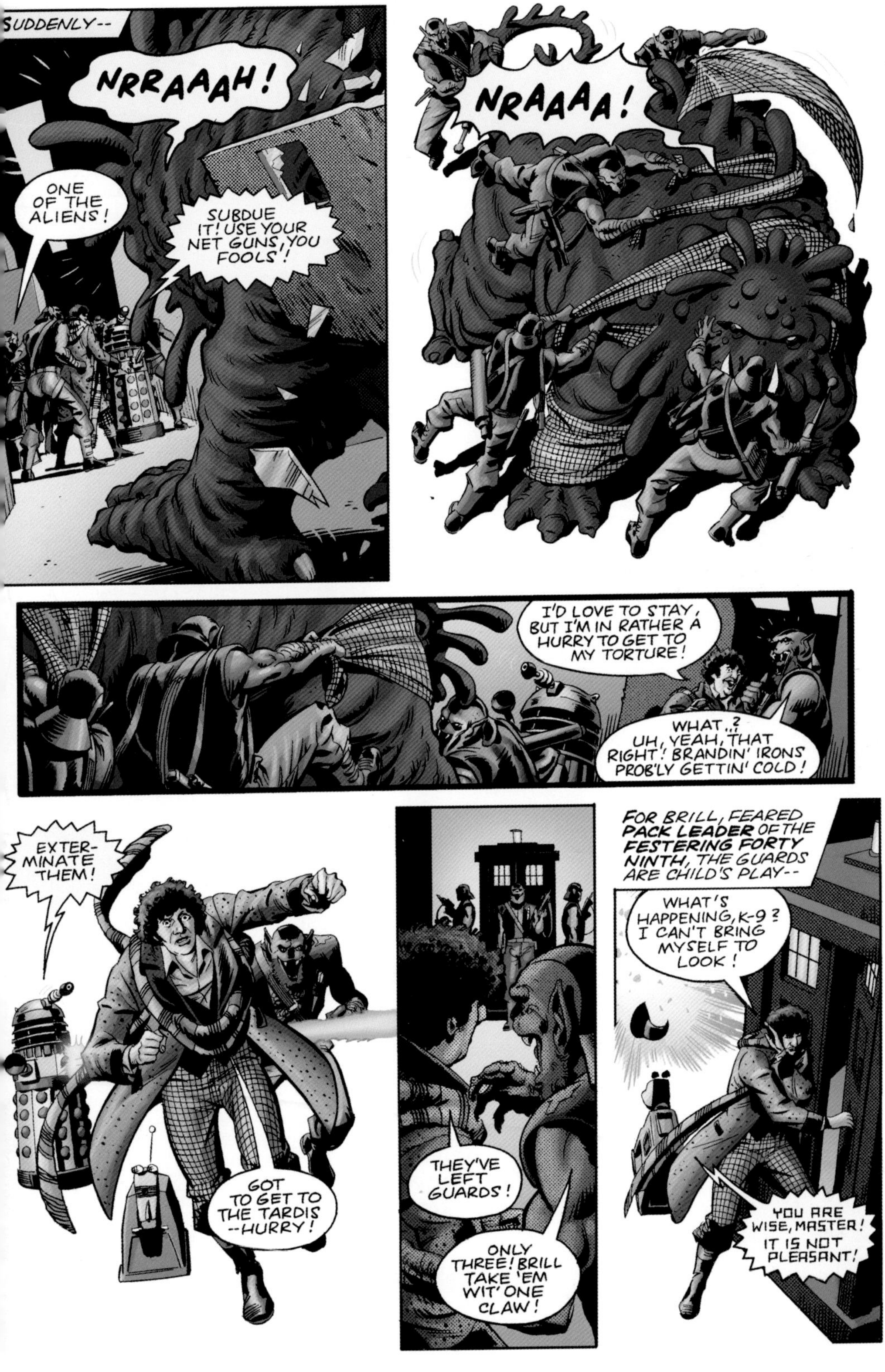
SUDDENLY--
NRRAAAH!
ONE OF THE ALIENS!
SUBDUE IT! USE YOUR NET GUNS, YOU FOOLS!
NRAAAA!
I'D LOVE TO STAY, BUT I'M IN RATHER A HURRY TO GET TO MY TORTURE!
WHAT..? UH, YEAH, THAT RIGHT! BRANDIN' IRONS PROB'LY GETTIN' COLD!
EXTER- MINATE THEM!
GOT TO GET TO THE TARDIS --HURRY!
THEY'VE LEFT GUARDS!
ONLY THREE! BRILL TAKE 'EM WIT' ONE CLAW!
FOR BRILL, FEARED PACK LEADER OF THE FESTERING FORTY NINTH, THE GUARDS ARE CHILD'S PLAY--
WHAT'S HAPPENING, K-9? I CAN'T BRING MYSELF TO LOOK!
YOU ARE WISE, MASTER! IT IS NOT PLEASANT!

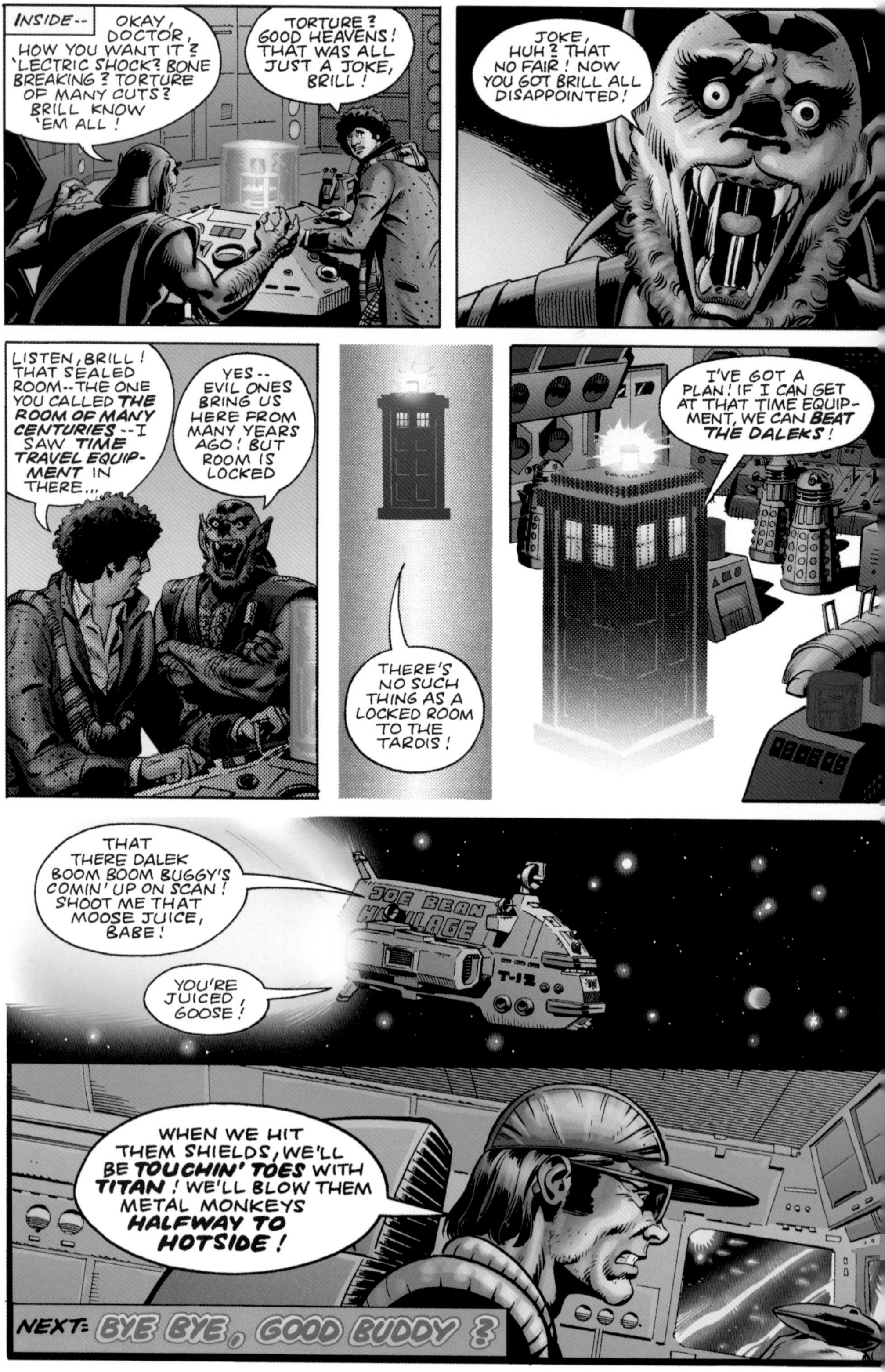
INSIDE--
OKAY, DOCTOR, HOW YOU WANT IT? 'LECTRIC SHOCK? BONE BREAKING? TORTURE OF MANY CUTS? BRILL KNOW 'EM ALL!
TORTURE? GOOD HEAVENS! THAT WAS ALL JUST A JOKE, BRILL!
JOKE, HUH? THAT NO FAIR! NOW YOU GOT BRILL ALL DISAPPOINTED!
LISTEN, BRILL! THAT SEALED ROOM--THE ONE YOU CALLED THE ROOM OF MANY CENTURIES--I SAW TIME TRAVEL EQUIPMENT IN THERE...
YES-- EVIL ONES BRING US HERE FROM MANY YEARS AGO! BUT ROOM IS LOCKED
THERE'S NO SUCH THING AS A LOCKED ROOM TO THE TARDIS!
I'VE GOT A PLAN! IF I CAN GET AT THAT TIME EQUIPMENT, WE CAN BEAT THE DALEKS!
THAT THERE DALEK BOOM BOOM BUGGY'S COMIN' UP ON SCAN! SHOOT ME THAT MOOSE JUICE, BABE!
JOE BEAN HAULAGE
T-12
YOU'RE JUICED, GOOSE!
WHEN WE HIT THEM SHIELDS, WE'LL BE TOUCHIN' TOES WITH TITAN! WE'LL BLOW THEM METAL MONKEYS HALFWAY TO HOTSIDE!
NEXT: BYE BYE, GOOD BUDDY?

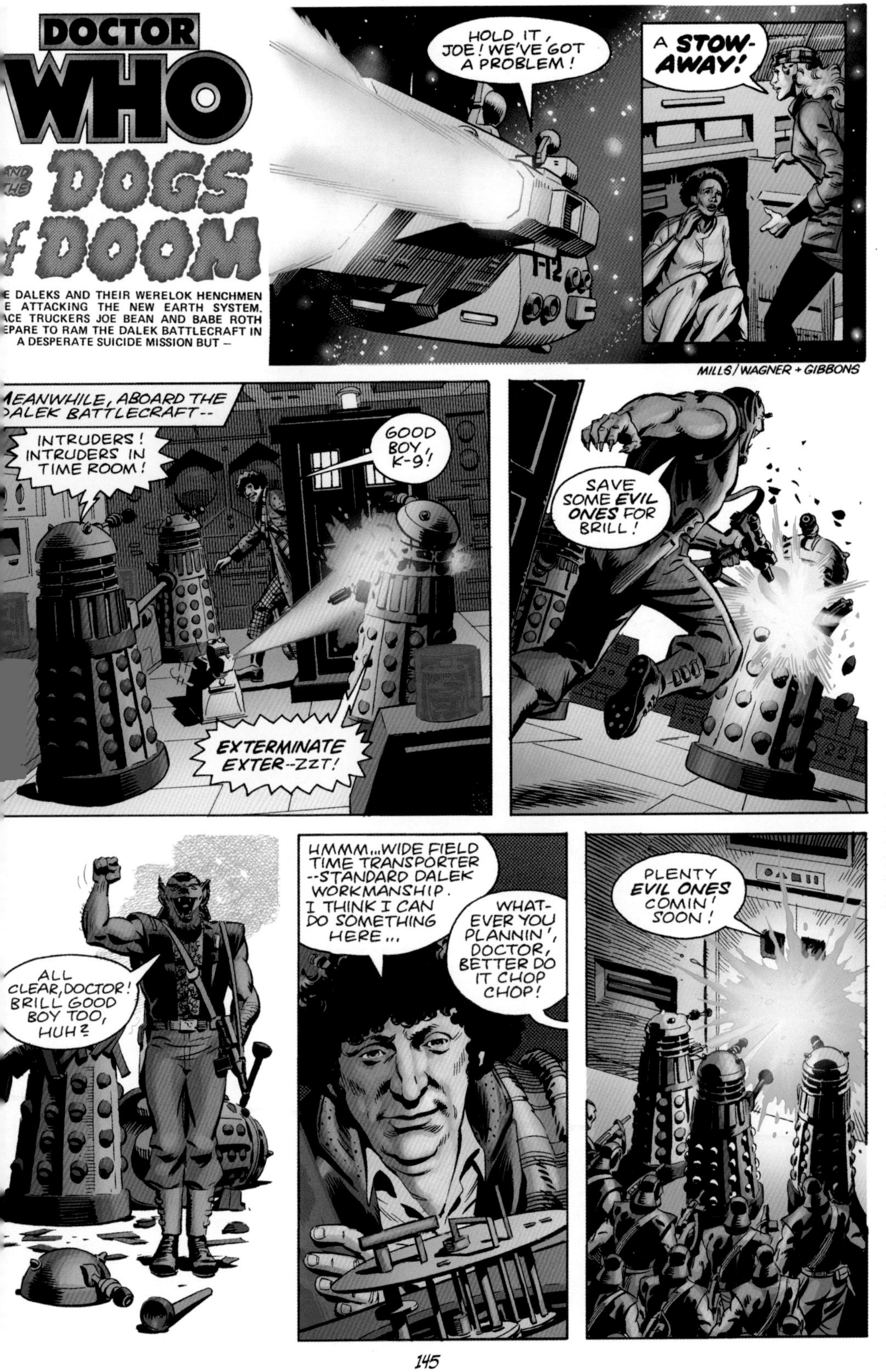
DOCTOR WHO
AND THE DOGS OF DOOM
E DALEKS AND THEIR WERELOK HENCHMEN E ATTACKING THE NEW EARTH SYSTEM. ACE TRUCKERS JOE BEAN AND BABE ROTH EPARE TO RAM THE DALEK BATTLECRAFT IN A DESPERATE SUICIDE MISSION BUT –
HOLD IT, JOE! WE'VE GOT A PROBLEM!
A STOW-AWAY!
MILLS/WAGNER + GIBBONS
MEANWHILE, ABOARD THE DALEK BATTLECRAFT--
INTRUDERS! INTRUDERS IN TIME ROOM!
GOOD BOY, K-9!
EXTERMINATE EXTER--ZZT!
SAVE SOME EVIL ONES FOR BRILL!
ALL CLEAR, DOCTOR! BRILL GOOD BOY TOO, HUH?
HMMM... WIDE FIELD TIME TRANSPORTER --STANDARD DALEK WORKMANSHIP. I THINK I CAN DO SOMETHING HERE...
WHAT-EVER YOU PLANNIN', DOCTOR, BETTER DO IT CHOP CHOP!
PLENTY EVIL ONES COMIN' SOON!

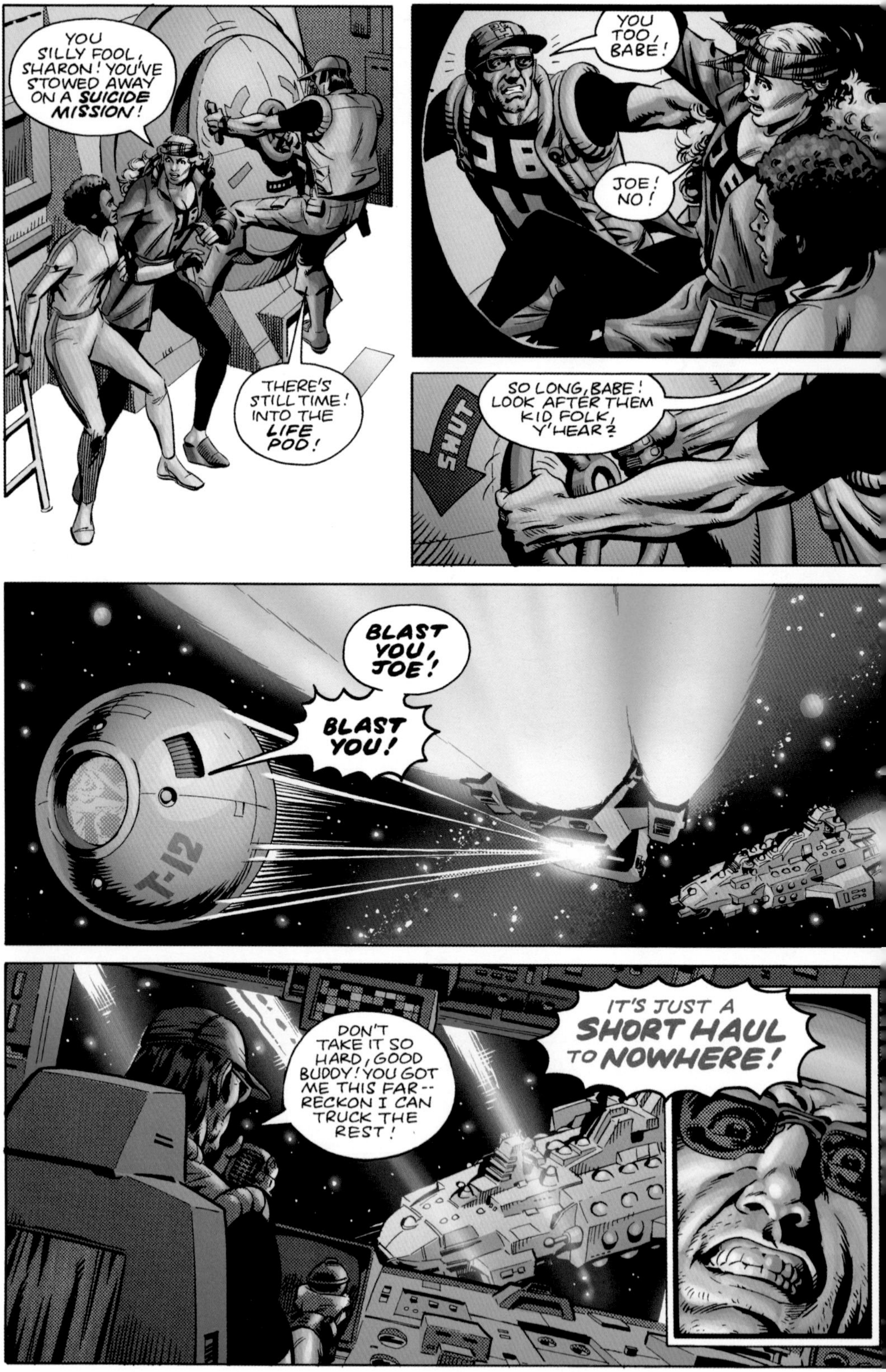
YOU SILLY FOOL, SHARON! YOU'VE STOWED AWAY ON A SUICIDE MISSION!
THERE'S STILL TIME! INTO THE LIFE POD!
YOU TOO, BABE!
JOE! NO!
SO LONG, BABE! LOOK AFTER THEM KID FOLK, Y'HEAR?
SHUT
BLAST YOU, JOE!
BLAST YOU!
T-12
DON'T TAKE IT SO HARD, GOOD BUDDY! YOU GOT ME THIS FAR -- RECKON I CAN TRUCK THE REST!
IT'S JUST A SHORT HAUL TO NOWHERE!

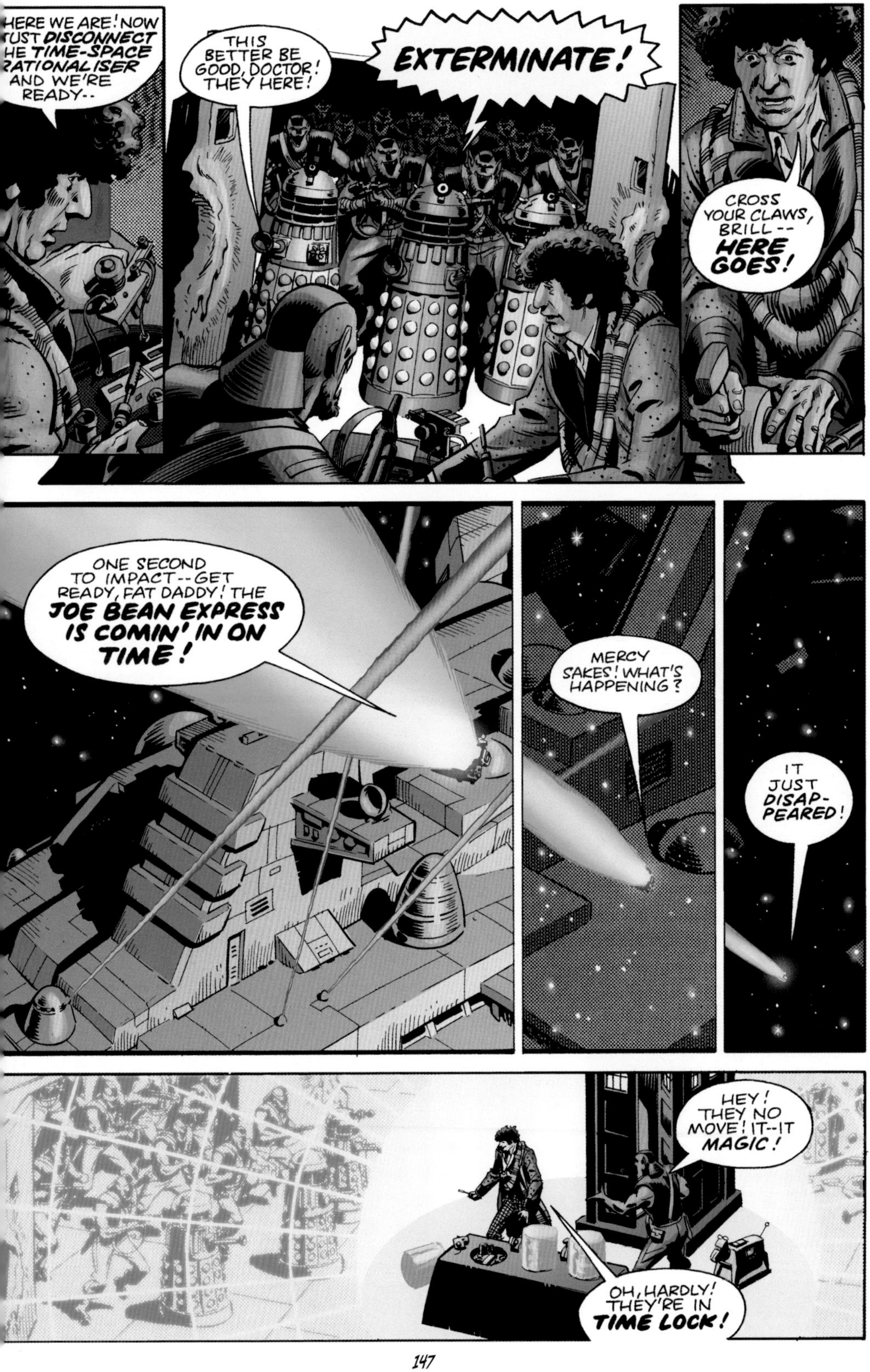
HERE WE ARE! NOW JUST DISCONNECT THE TIME-SPACE RATIONALISER AND WE'RE READY--
THIS BETTER BE GOOD, DOCTOR! THEY HERE!
EXTERMINATE!
CROSS YOUR CLAWS, BRILL -- HERE GOES!
ONE SECOND TO IMPACT--GET READY, FAT DADDY! THE JOE BEAN EXPRESS IS COMIN' IN ON TIME!
MERCY SAKES! WHAT'S HAPPENING?
IT JUST DISAP-PEARED!
HEY! THEY NO MOVE! IT--IT MAGIC!
OH, HARDLY! THEY'RE IN TIME LOCK!

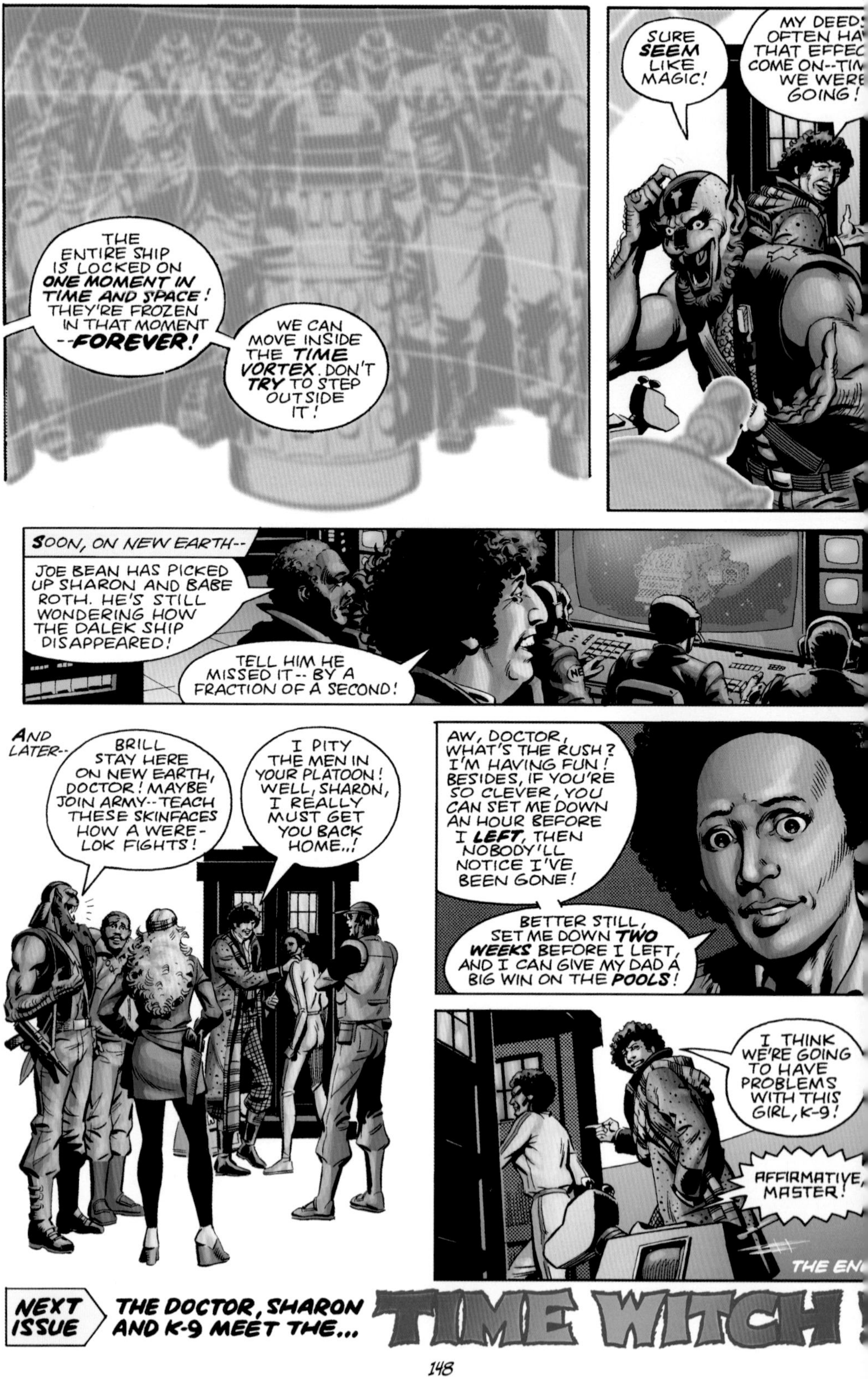
THE ENTIRE SHIP IS LOCKED ON ONE MOMENT IN TIME AND SPACE! THEY'RE FROZEN IN THAT MOMENT --FOREVER!
WE CAN MOVE INSIDE THE TIME VORTEX. DON'T TRY TO STEP OUTSIDE IT!
SURE SEEM LIKE MAGIC!
MY DEEDS OFTEN HA THAT EFFEC COME ON--TIM WE WERE GOING!
SOON, ON NEW EARTH--
JOE BEAN HAS PICKED UP SHARON AND BABE ROTH. HE'S STILL WONDERING HOW THE DALEK SHIP DISAPPEARED!
TELL HIM HE MISSED IT -- BY A FRACTION OF A SECOND!
AND LATER--
BRILL STAY HERE ON NEW EARTH, DOCTOR! MAYBE JOIN ARMY--TEACH THESE SKINFACES HOW A WERE-LOK FIGHTS!
I PITY THE MEN IN YOUR PLATOON! WELL, SHARON, I REALLY MUST GET YOU BACK HOME..!
AW, DOCTOR, WHAT'S THE RUSH? I'M HAVING FUN! BESIDES, IF YOU'RE SO CLEVER, YOU CAN SET ME DOWN AN HOUR BEFORE I LEFT, THEN NOBODY'LL NOTICE I'VE BEEN GONE!
BETTER STILL, SET ME DOWN TWO WEEKS BEFORE I LEFT, AND I CAN GIVE MY DAD A BIG WIN ON THE POOLS!
I THINK WE'RE GOING TO HAVE PROBLEMS WITH THIS GIRL, K-9!
AFFIRMATIVE, MASTER!
THE EN
NEXT ISSUE
THE DOCTOR, SHARON AND K-9 MEET THE...
TIME WITCH

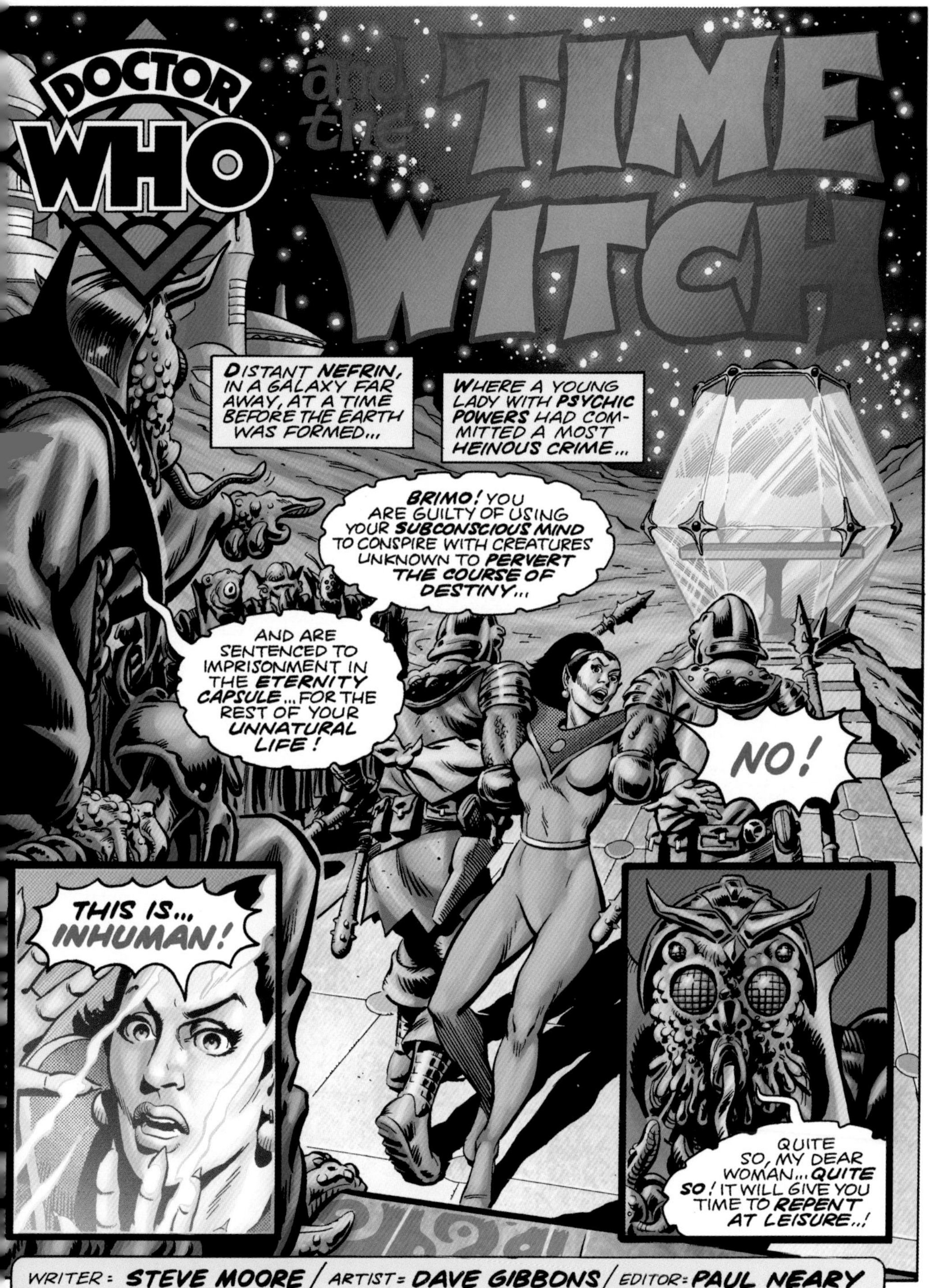
DOCTOR WHO
and the TIME WITCH
DISTANT NEFRIN, IN A GALAXY FAR AWAY, AT A TIME BEFORE THE EARTH WAS FORMED...
WHERE A YOUNG LADY WITH PSYCHIC POWERS HAD COMMITTED A MOST HEINOUS CRIME...
BRIMO! YOU ARE GUILTY OF USING YOUR SUBCONSCIOUS MIND TO CONSPIRE WITH CREATURES UNKNOWN TO PERVERT THE COURSE OF DESTINY...
AND ARE SENTENCED TO IMPRISONMENT IN THE ETERNITY CAPSULE... FOR THE REST OF YOUR UNNATURAL LIFE!
NO!
THIS IS... INHUMAN!
QUITE SO, MY DEAR WOMAN... QUITE SO! IT WILL GIVE YOU TIME TO REPENT AT LEISURE...!
WRITER: STEVE MOORE / ARTIST: DAVE GIBBONS / EDITOR: PAUL NEARY

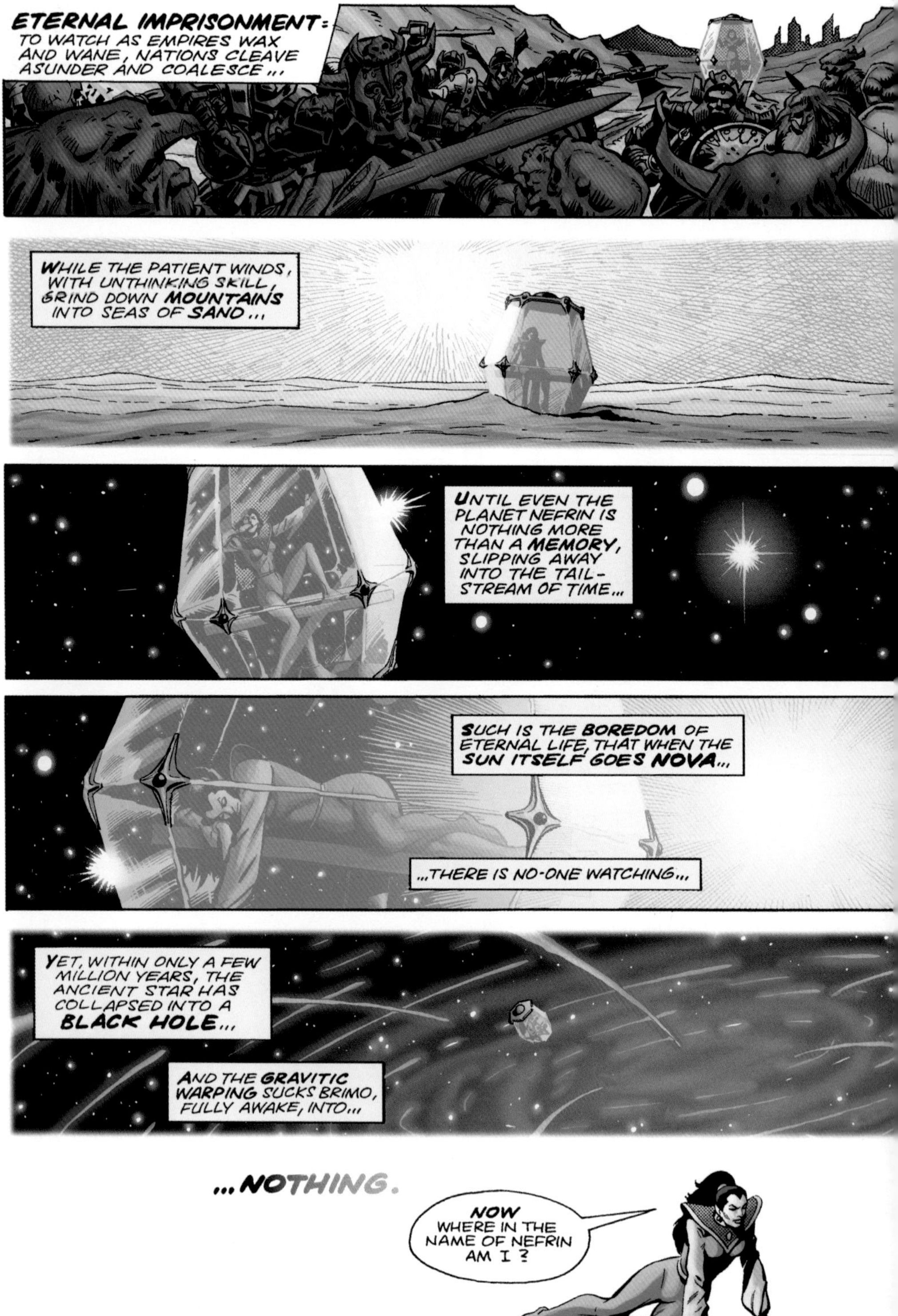
ETERNAL IMPRISONMENT: TO WATCH AS EMPIRES WAX AND WANE, NATIONS CLEAVE ASUNDER AND COALESCE...
WHILE THE PATIENT WINDS, WITH UNTHINKING SKILL, GRIND DOWN MOUNTAINS INTO SEAS OF SAND...
UNTIL EVEN THE PLANET NEFRIN IS NOTHING MORE THAN A MEMORY, SLIPPING AWAY INTO THE TAIL-STREAM OF TIME...
SUCH IS THE BOREDOM OF ETERNAL LIFE, THAT WHEN THE SUN ITSELF GOES NOVA...
...THERE IS NO-ONE WATCHING...
YET, WITHIN ONLY A FEW MILLION YEARS, THE ANCIENT STAR HAS COLLAPSED INTO A BLACK HOLE...
AND THE GRAVITIC WARPING SUCKS BRIMO, FULLY AWAKE, INTO...
...NOTHING.
NOW WHERE IN THE NAME OF NEFRIN AM I?

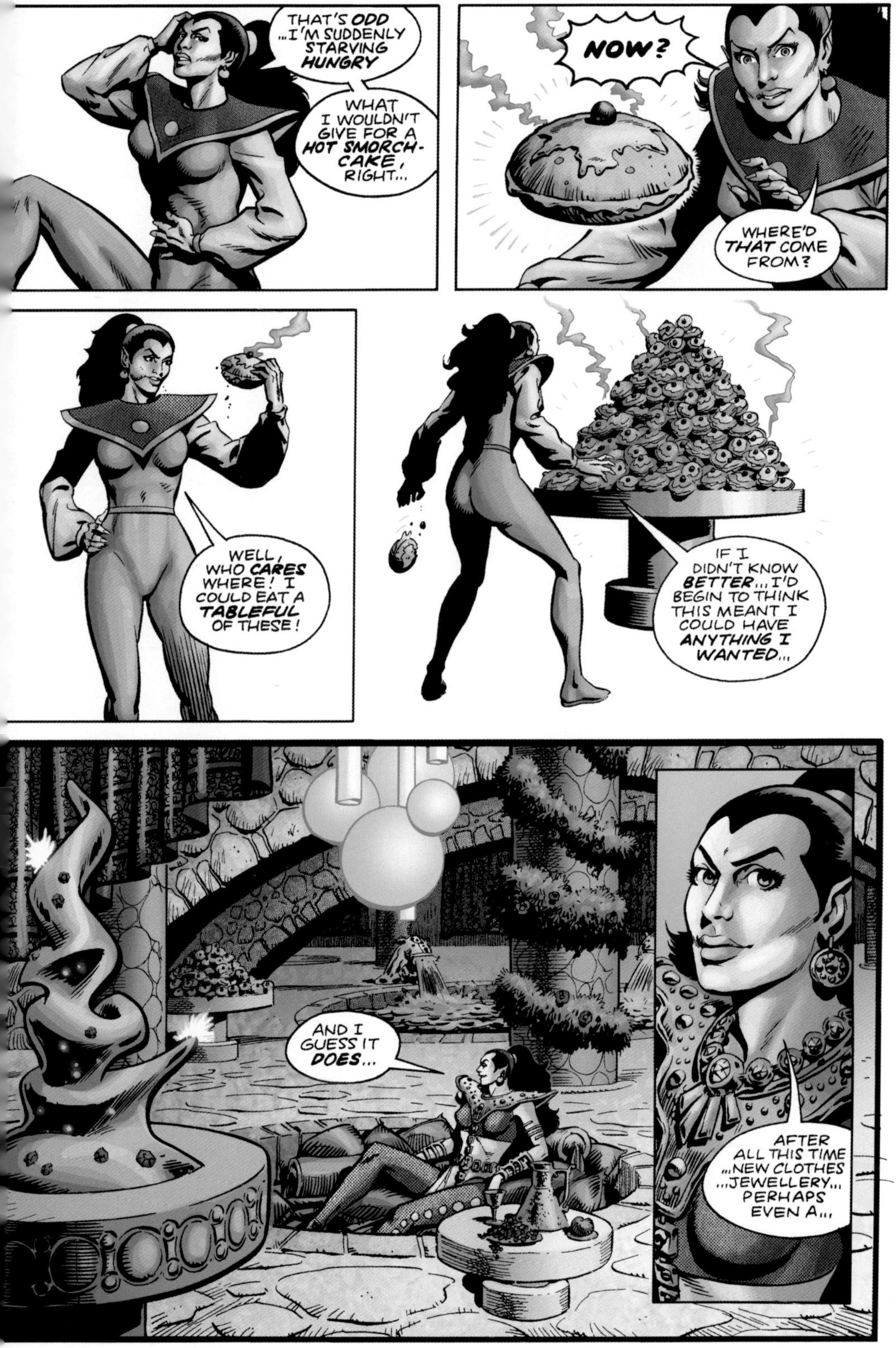
THAT'S ODD ...I'M SUDDENLY STARVING HUNGRY
WHAT I WOULDN'T GIVE FOR A HOT SMORCH-CAKE, RIGHT...
NOW?
WHERE'D THAT COME FROM?
WELL, WHO CARES WHERE! I COULD EAT A TABLEFUL OF THESE!
IF I DIDN'T KNOW BETTER... I'D BEGIN TO THINK THIS MEANT I COULD HAVE ANYTHING I WANTED...
AND I GUESS IT DOES...
AFTER ALL THIS TIME ...NEW CLOTHES ...JEWELLERY... PERHAPS EVEN A...

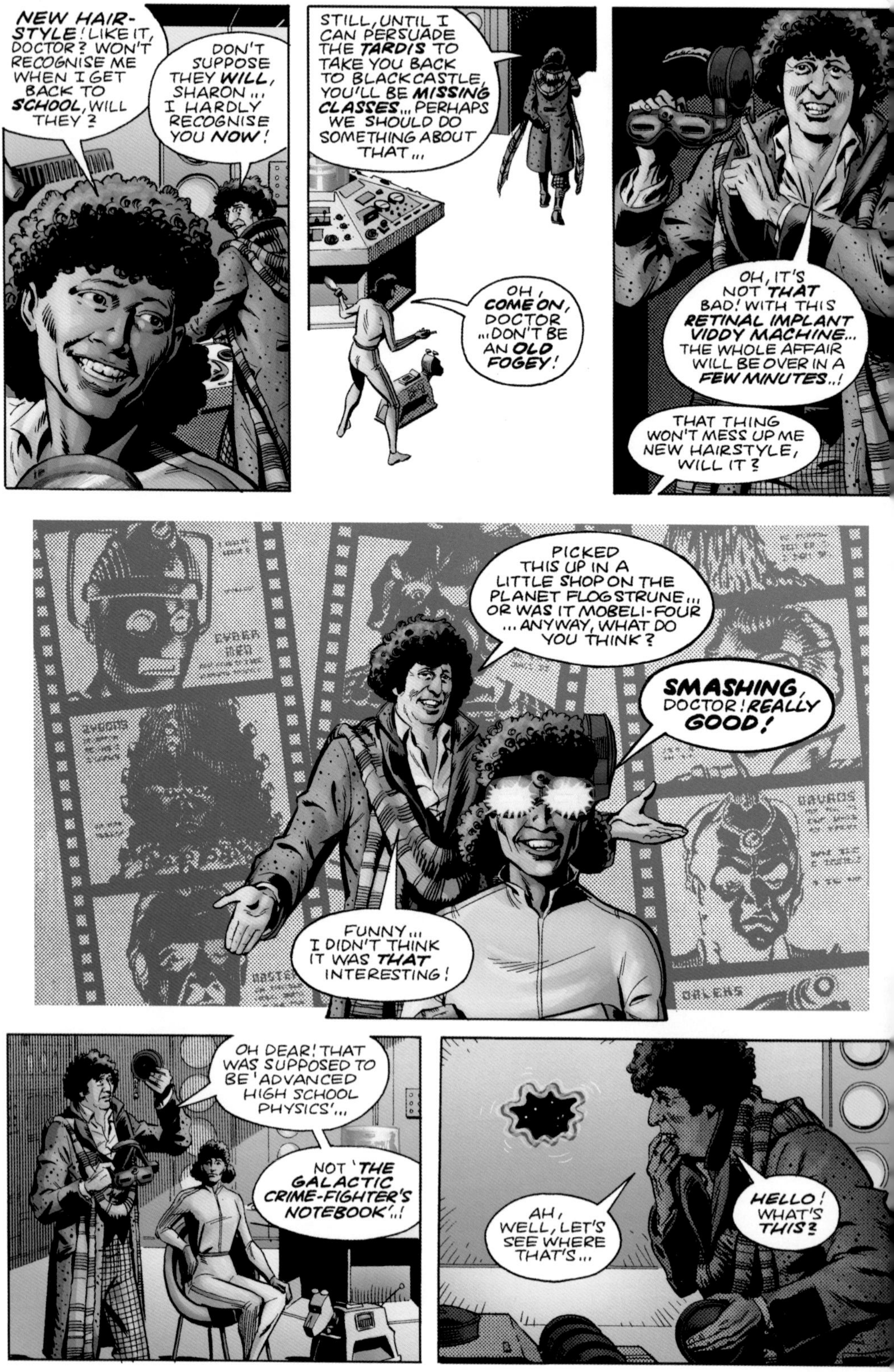
NEW HAIR-STYLE! LIKE IT, DOCTOR? WON'T RECOGNISE ME WHEN I GET BACK TO SCHOOL, WILL THEY?
DON'T SUPPOSE THEY WILL, SHARON... I HARDLY RECOGNISE YOU NOW!
STILL, UNTIL I CAN PERSUADE THE TARDIS TO TAKE YOU BACK TO BLACKCASTLE, YOU'LL BE MISSING CLASSES... PERHAPS WE SHOULD DO SOMETHING ABOUT THAT...
OH, COME ON, DOCTOR ...DON'T BE AN OLD FOGEY!
OH, IT'S NOT THAT BAD! WITH THIS RETINAL IMPLANT VIDDY MACHINE... THE WHOLE AFFAIR WILL BE OVER IN A FEW MINUTES...!
THAT THING WON'T MESS UP ME NEW HAIRSTYLE, WILL IT?
PICKED THIS UP IN A LITTLE SHOP ON THE PLANET FLOGSTRUNE... OR WAS IT MOBELI-FOUR ...ANYWAY, WHAT DO YOU THINK?
SMASHING, DOCTOR! REALLY GOOD!
FUNNY... I DIDN'T THINK IT WAS THAT INTERESTING!
CYBER MEN
DAVROS
DALEKS
OH DEAR! THAT WAS SUPPOSED TO BE 'ADVANCED HIGH SCHOOL PHYSICS'...
NOT 'THE GALACTIC CRIME-FIGHTER'S NOTEBOOK'...!
AH, WELL, LET'S SEE WHERE THAT'S...
HELLO! WHAT'S THIS?

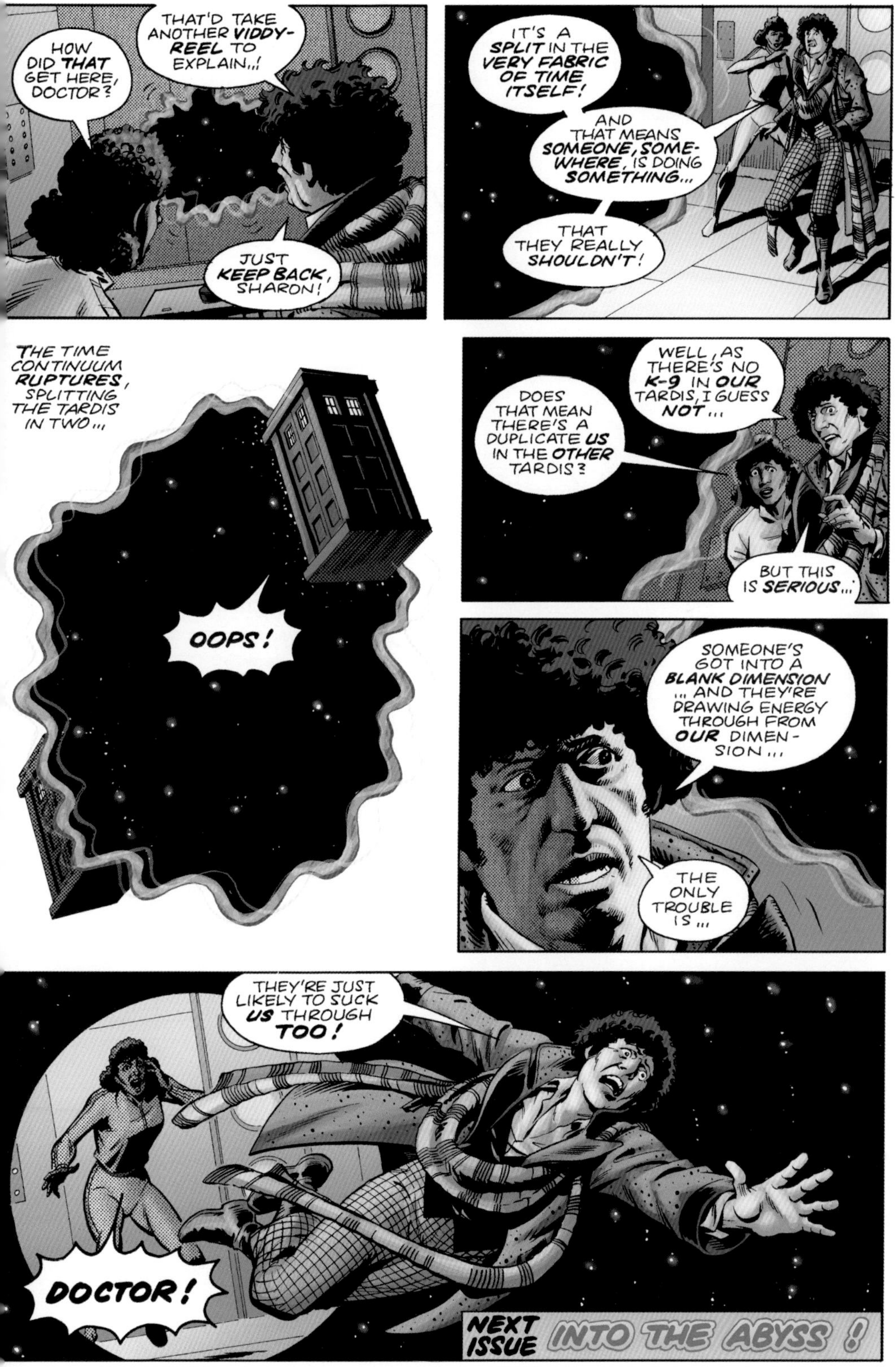

HOW DID THAT GET HERE, DOCTOR?
THAT'D TAKE ANOTHER VIDDY-REEL TO EXPLAIN...!
JUST KEEP BACK, SHARON!
IT'S A SPLIT IN THE VERY FABRIC OF TIME ITSELF!
AND THAT MEANS SOMEONE, SOME-WHERE, IS DOING SOMETHING...
THAT THEY REALLY SHOULDN'T!
THE TIME CONTINUUM RUPTURES, SPLITTING THE TARDIS IN TWO...
OOPS!
DOES THAT MEAN THERE'S A DUPLICATE US IN THE OTHER TARDIS?
WELL, AS THERE'S NO K-9 IN OUR TARDIS, I GUESS NOT...
BUT THIS IS SERIOUS...
SOMEONE'S GOT INTO A BLANK DIMENSION ... AND THEY'RE DRAWING ENERGY THROUGH FROM OUR DIMEN-SION...
THE ONLY TROUBLE IS...
THEY'RE JUST LIKELY TO SUCK US THROUGH TOO!
DOCTOR!
NEXT ISSUE INTO THE ABYSS!

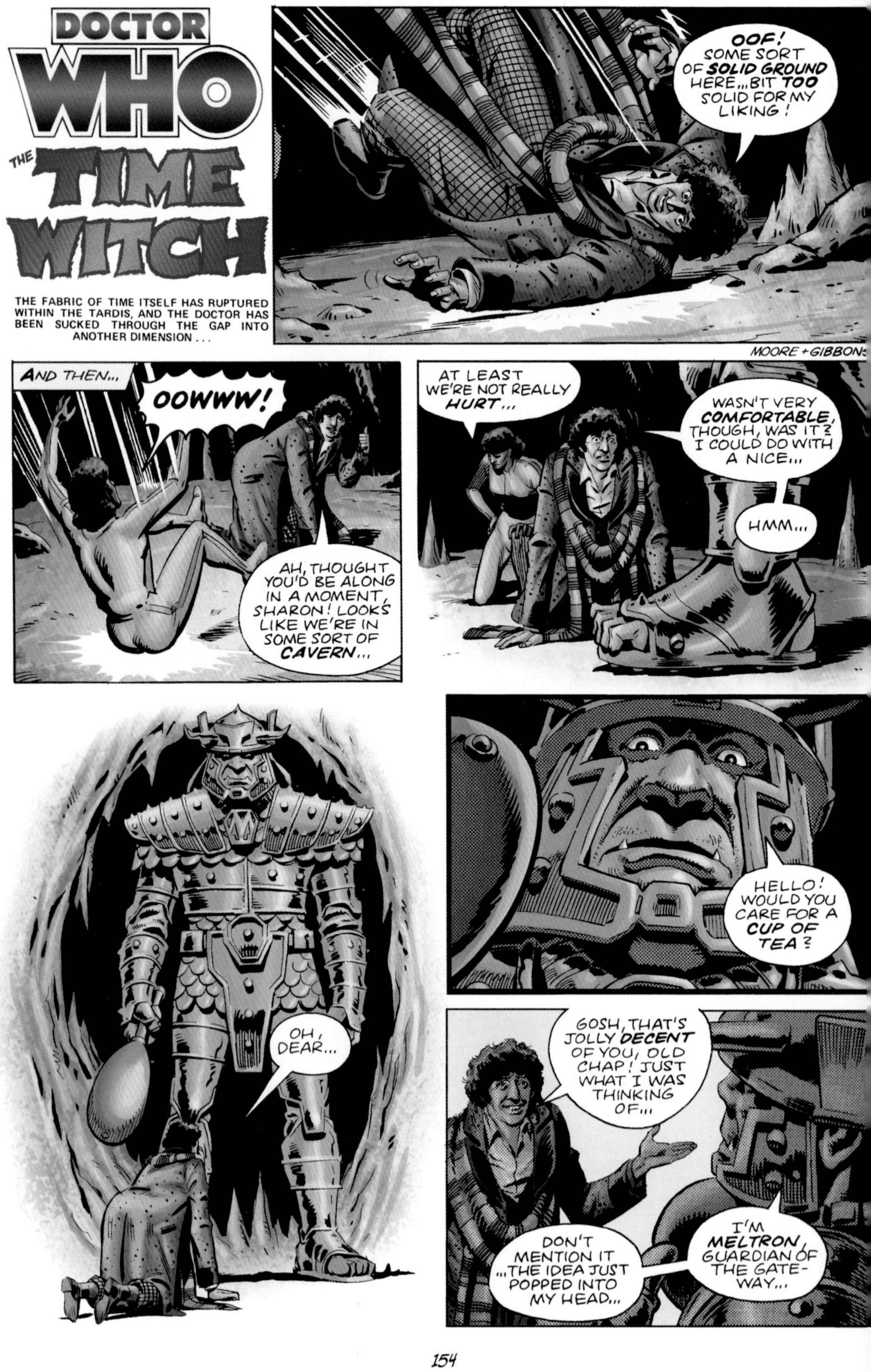
DOCTOR WHO
THE TIME WITCH
THE FABRIC OF TIME ITSELF HAS RUPTURED WITHIN THE TARDIS, AND THE DOCTOR HAS BEEN SUCKED THROUGH THE GAP INTO ANOTHER DIMENSION . . .
OOF! SOME SORT OF SOLID GROUND HERE... BIT TOO SOLID FOR MY LIKING!
MOORE + GIBBONS
AND THEN...
OOWWW!
AH, THOUGHT YOU'D BE ALONG IN A MOMENT, SHARON! LOOKS LIKE WE'RE IN SOME SORT OF CAVERN...
AT LEAST WE'RE NOT REALLY HURT...
WASN'T VERY COMFORTABLE, THOUGH, WAS IT? I COULD DO WITH A NICE...
HMM...
OH, DEAR...
HELLO! WOULD YOU CARE FOR A CUP OF TEA?
GOSH, THAT'S JOLLY DECENT OF YOU, OLD CHAP! JUST WHAT I WAS THINKING OF...
DON'T MENTION IT ...THE IDEA JUST POPPED INTO MY HEAD...
I'M MELTRON, GUARDIAN OF THE GATE-WAY...

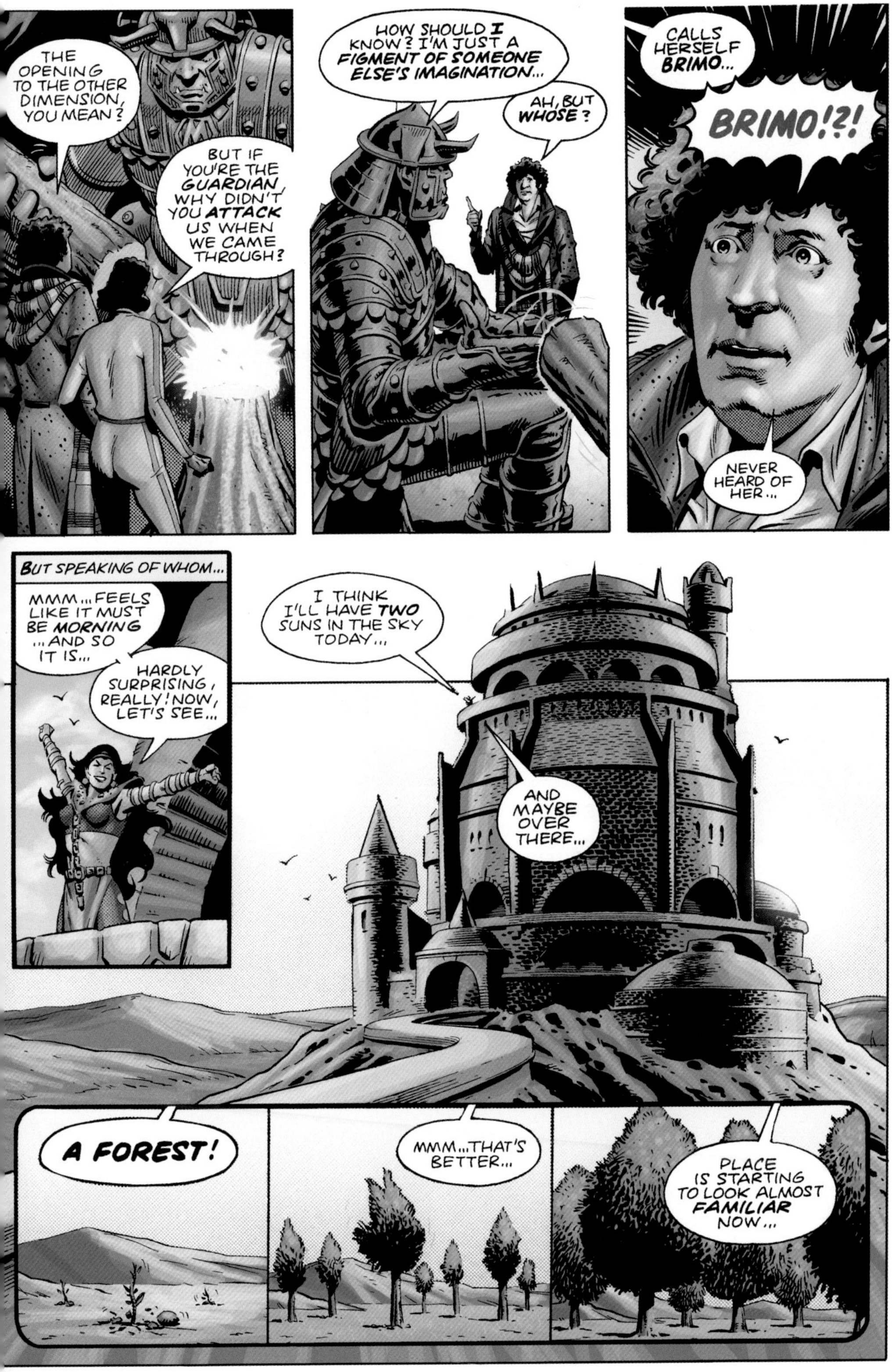
THE OPENING TO THE OTHER DIMENSION, YOU MEAN?
BUT IF YOU'RE THE GUARDIAN, WHY DIDN'T YOU ATTACK US WHEN WE CAME THROUGH?
HOW SHOULD I KNOW? I'M JUST A FIGMENT OF SOMEONE ELSE'S IMAGINATION...
AH, BUT WHOSE?
CALLS HERSELF BRIMO...
BRIMO!?!
NEVER HEARD OF HER...
BUT SPEAKING OF WHOM...
MMM... FEELS LIKE IT MUST BE MORNING ...AND SO IT IS...
HARDLY SURPRISING, REALLY! NOW, LET'S SEE...
I THINK I'LL HAVE TWO SUNS IN THE SKY TODAY...
AND MAYBE OVER THERE...
A FOREST!
MMM... THAT'S BETTER...
PLACE IS STARTING TO LOOK ALMOST FAMILIAR NOW...

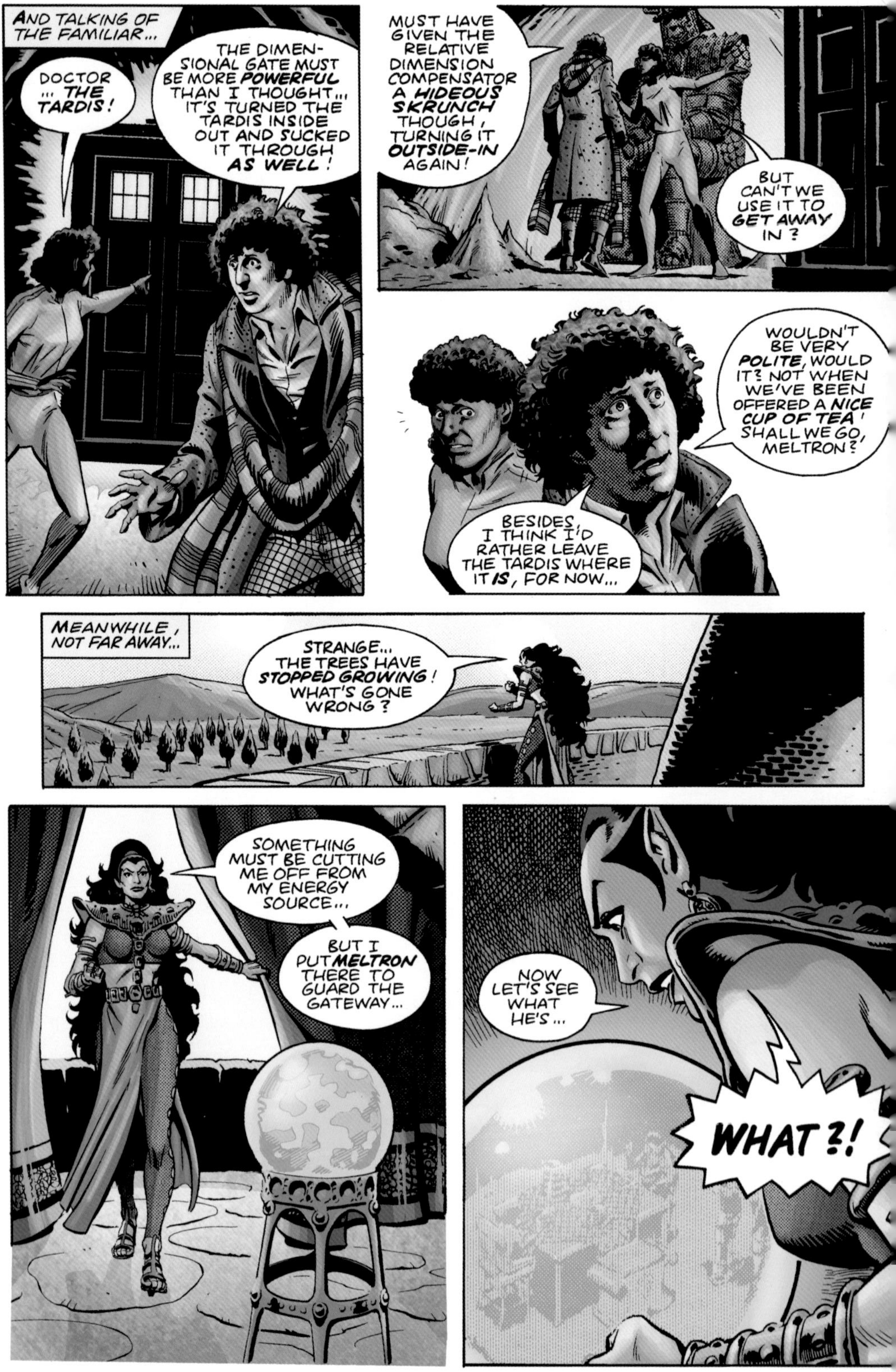
AND TALKING OF THE FAMILIAR...
DOCTOR ... THE TARDIS!
THE DIMENSIONAL GATE MUST BE MORE POWERFUL THAN I THOUGHT... IT'S TURNED THE TARDIS INSIDE OUT AND SUCKED IT THROUGH AS WELL!
MUST HAVE GIVEN THE RELATIVE DIMENSION COMPENSATOR A HIDEOUS SKRUNCH THOUGH, TURNING IT OUTSIDE-IN AGAIN!
BUT CAN'T WE USE IT TO GET AWAY IN?
WOULDN'T BE VERY POLITE, WOULD IT? NOT WHEN WE'VE BEEN OFFERED A NICE CUP OF TEA! SHALL WE GO, MELTRON?
BESIDES, I THINK I'D RATHER LEAVE THE TARDIS WHERE IT IS, FOR NOW...
MEANWHILE, NOT FAR AWAY...
STRANGE... THE TREES HAVE STOPPED GROWING! WHAT'S GONE WRONG?
SOMETHING MUST BE CUTTING ME OFF FROM MY ENERGY SOURCE...
BUT I PUT MELTRON THERE TO GUARD THE GATEWAY...
NOW LET'S SEE WHAT HE'S...
WHAT?!

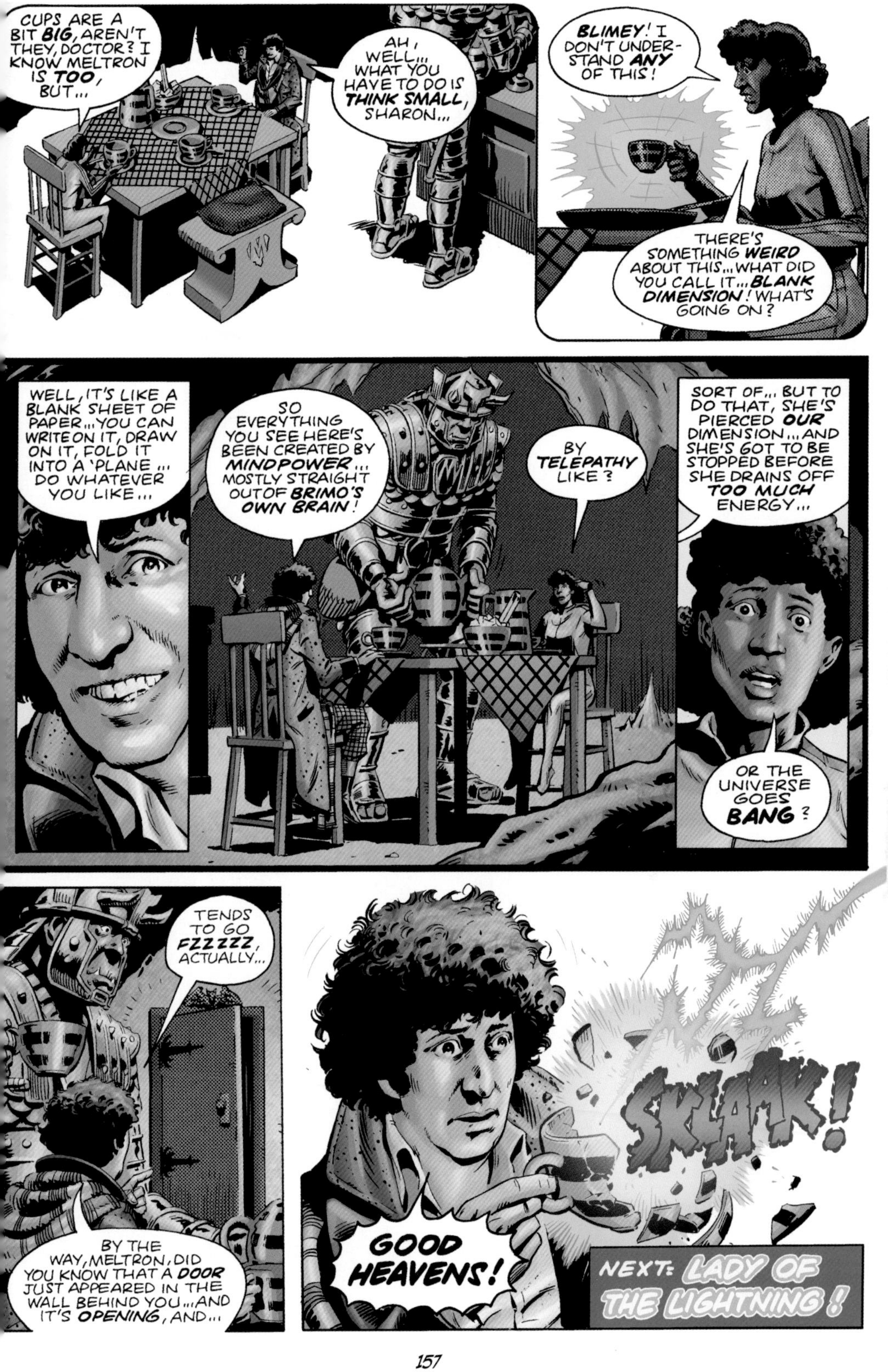
CUPS ARE A BIT BIG, AREN'T THEY, DOCTOR? I KNOW MELTRON IS TOO, BUT...
AH, WELL... WHAT YOU HAVE TO DO IS THINK SMALL, SHARON...
BLIMEY! I DON'T UNDERSTAND ANY OF THIS!
THERE'S SOMETHING WEIRD ABOUT THIS... WHAT DID YOU CALL IT... BLANK DIMENSION! WHAT'S GOING ON?
WELL, IT'S LIKE A BLANK SHEET OF PAPER... YOU CAN WRITE ON IT, DRAW ON IT, FOLD IT INTO A 'PLANE ... DO WHATEVER YOU LIKE...
SO EVERYTHING YOU SEE HERE'S BEEN CREATED BY MINDPOWER... MOSTLY STRAIGHT OUT OF BRIMO'S OWN BRAIN!
BY TELEPATHY LIKE?
SORT OF... BUT TO DO THAT, SHE'S PIERCED OUR DIMENSION... AND SHE'S GOT TO BE STOPPED BEFORE SHE DRAINS OFF TOO MUCH ENERGY...
OR THE UNIVERSE GOES BANG?
TENDS TO GO FZZZZZ, ACTUALLY...
BY THE WAY, MELTRON, DID YOU KNOW THAT A DOOR JUST APPEARED IN THE WALL BEHIND YOU... AND IT'S OPENING, AND...
SKLAAK!
GOOD HEAVENS!
NEXT: LADY OF THE LIGHTNING!

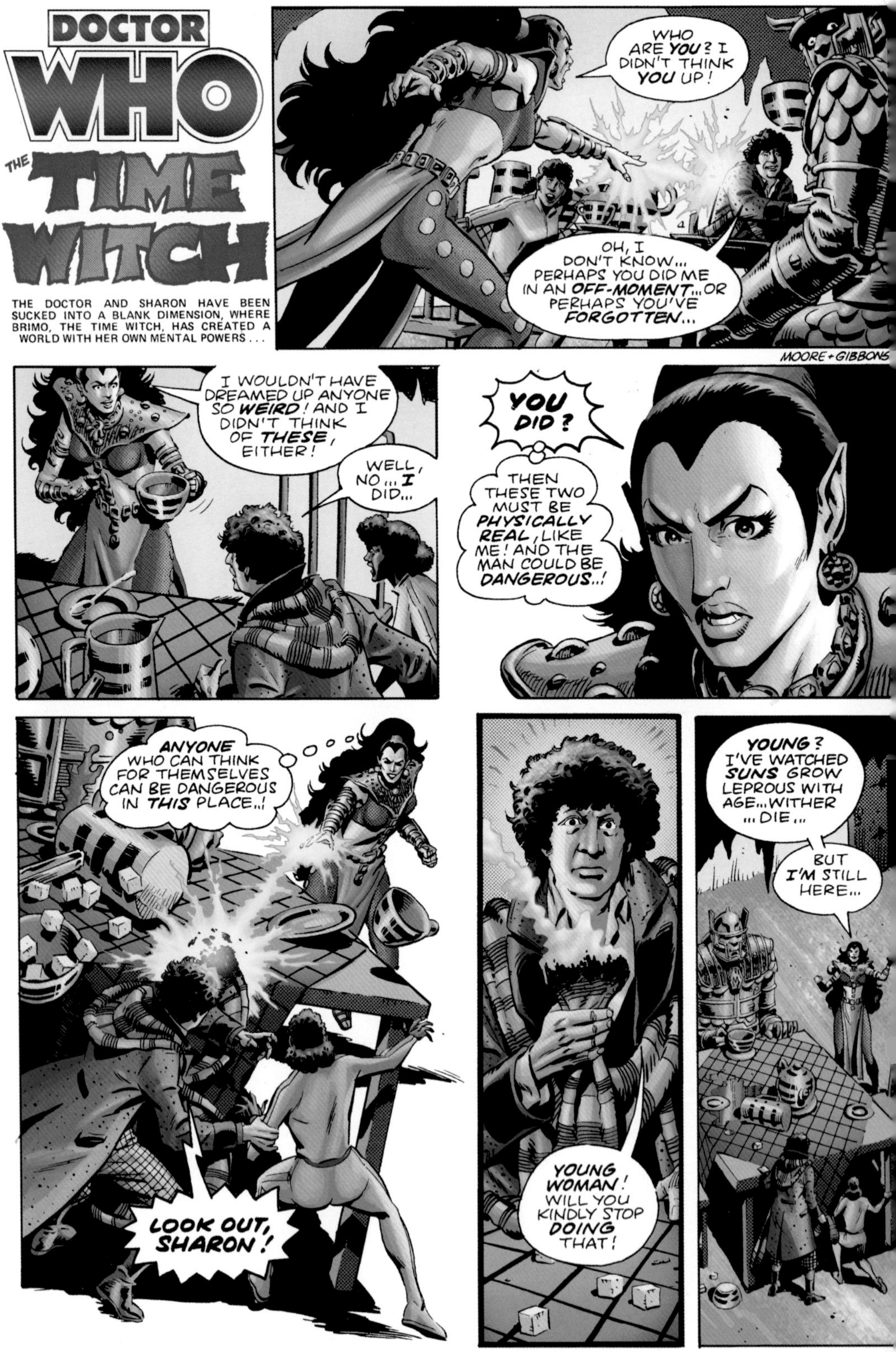
DOCTOR WHO
THE TIME WITCH
THE DOCTOR AND SHARON HAVE BEEN SUCKED INTO A BLANK DIMENSION, WHERE BRIMO, THE TIME WITCH, HAS CREATED A WORLD WITH HER OWN MENTAL POWERS . . .
WHO ARE YOU? I DIDN'T THINK YOU UP!
OH, I DON'T KNOW... PERHAPS YOU DID ME IN AN OFF-MOMENT... OR PERHAPS YOU'VE FORGOTTEN...
MOORE + GIBBONS
I WOULDN'T HAVE DREAMED UP ANYONE SO WEIRD! AND I DIDN'T THINK OF THESE, EITHER!
WELL, NO... I DID...
YOU DID?
THEN THESE TWO MUST BE PHYSICALLY REAL, LIKE ME! AND THE MAN COULD BE DANGEROUS..!
ANYONE WHO CAN THINK FOR THEMSELVES CAN BE DANGEROUS IN THIS PLACE..!
LOOK OUT, SHARON!
YOUNG WOMAN! WILL YOU KINDLY STOP DOING THAT!
YOUNG? I'VE WATCHED SUNS GROW LEPROUS WITH AGE... WITHER ... DIE...
BUT I'M STILL HERE...

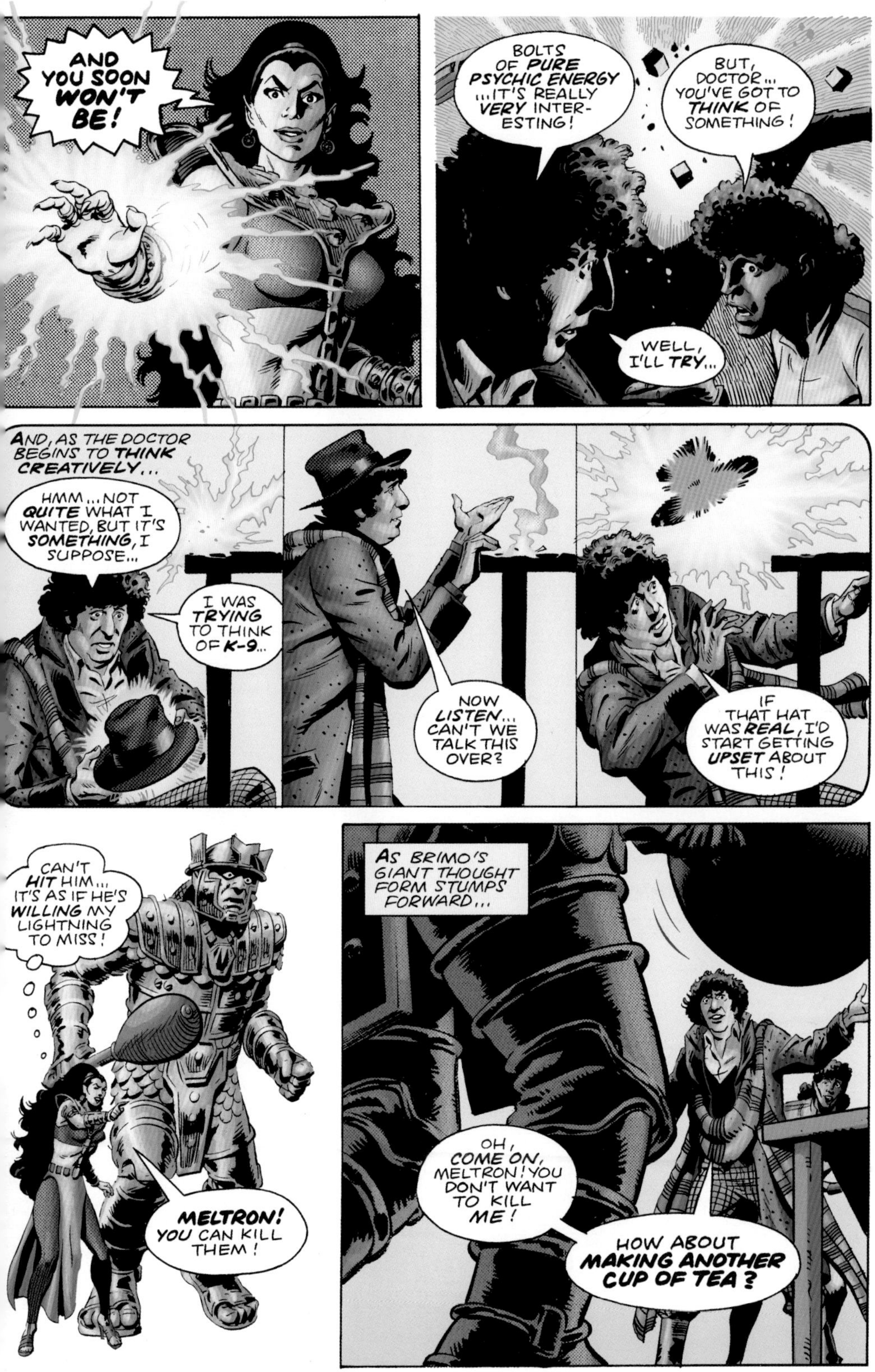
AND YOU SOON WON'T BE!
BOLTS OF PURE PSYCHIC ENERGY ...IT'S REALLY VERY INTER-ESTING!
BUT, DOCTOR... YOU'VE GOT TO THINK OF SOMETHING!
WELL, I'LL TRY...
AND, AS THE DOCTOR BEGINS TO THINK CREATIVELY...
HMM... NOT QUITE WHAT I WANTED, BUT IT'S SOMETHING, I SUPPOSE...
I WAS TRYING TO THINK OF K-9...
NOW LISTEN... CAN'T WE TALK THIS OVER?
IF THAT HAT WAS REAL, I'D START GETTING UPSET ABOUT THIS!
CAN'T HIT HIM... IT'S AS IF HE'S WILLING MY LIGHTNING TO MISS!
MELTRON! YOU CAN KILL THEM!
AS BRIMO'S GIANT THOUGHT FORM STUMPS FORWARD...
OH, COME ON, MELTRON! YOU DON'T WANT TO KILL ME!
HOW ABOUT MAKING ANOTHER CUP OF TEA?

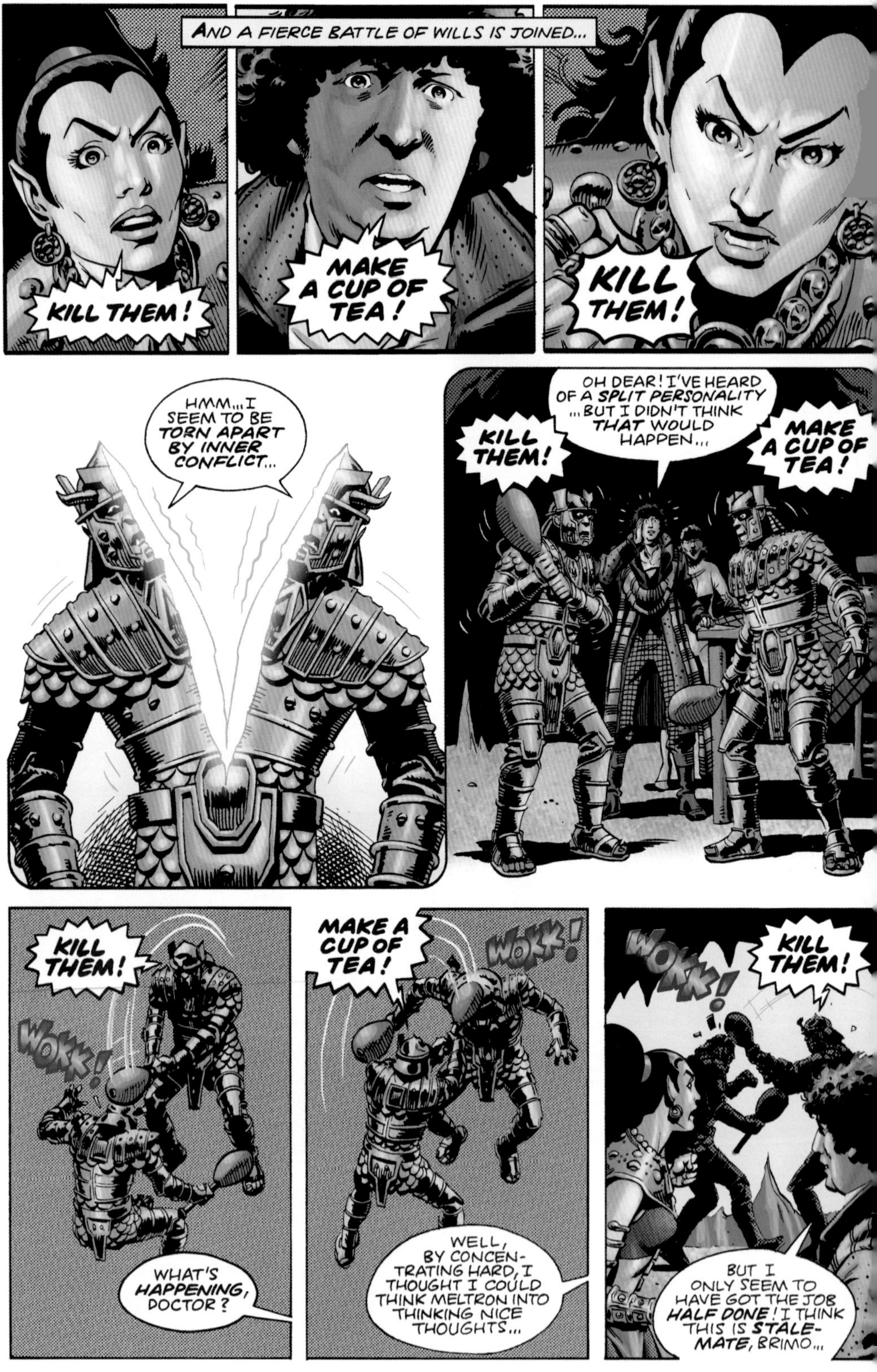
AND A FIERCE BATTLE OF WILLS IS JOINED...
KILL THEM!
MAKE A CUP OF TEA!
KILL THEM!
HMM... I SEEM TO BE TORN APART BY INNER CONFLICT...
KILL THEM!
OH DEAR! I'VE HEARD OF A SPLIT PERSONALITY ...BUT I DIDN'T THINK THAT WOULD HAPPEN...
MAKE A CUP OF TEA!
KILL THEM!
WOKK!
WHAT'S HAPPENING, DOCTOR?
MAKE A CUP OF TEA!
WOKK!
WELL, BY CONCEN-TRATING HARD, I THOUGHT I COULD THINK MELTRON INTO THINKING NICE THOUGHTS...
WOKK!
KILL THEM!
BUT I ONLY SEEM TO HAVE GOT THE JOB HALF DONE! I THINK THIS IS STALE-MATE, BRIMO...

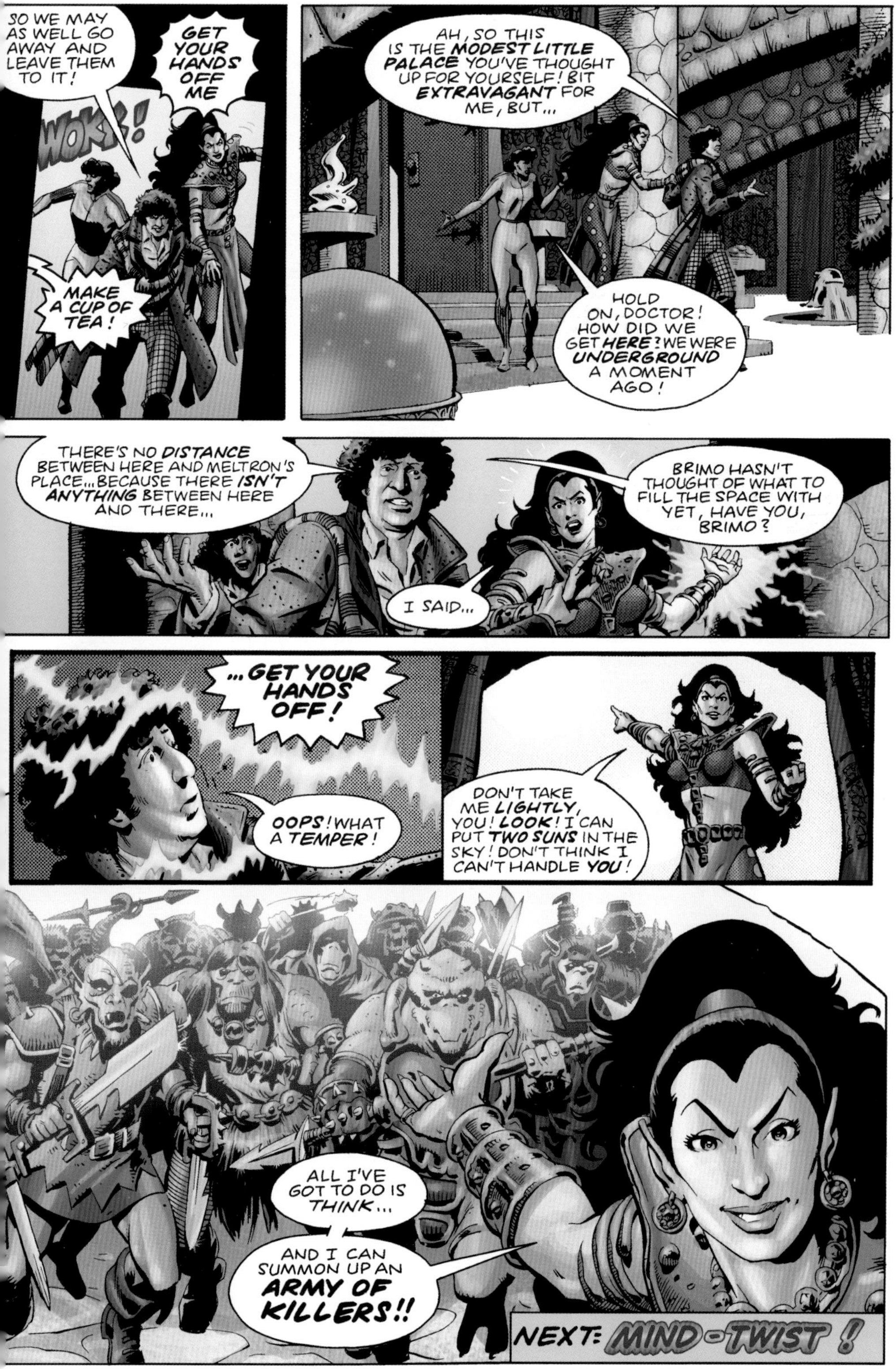
SO WE MAY AS WELL GO AWAY AND LEAVE THEM TO IT!
GET YOUR HANDS OFF ME
MAKE A CUP OF TEA!
AH, SO THIS IS THE MODEST LITTLE PALACE YOU'VE THOUGHT UP FOR YOURSELF! BIT EXTRAVAGANT FOR ME, BUT...
HOLD ON, DOCTOR! HOW DID WE GET HERE? WE WERE UNDERGROUND A MOMENT AGO!
THERE'S NO DISTANCE BETWEEN HERE AND MELTRON'S PLACE... BECAUSE THERE ISN'T ANYTHING BETWEEN HERE AND THERE...
BRIMO HASN'T THOUGHT OF WHAT TO FILL THE SPACE WITH YET, HAVE YOU, BRIMO?
I SAID...
...GET YOUR HANDS OFF!
OOPS! WHAT A TEMPER!
DON'T TAKE ME LIGHTLY, YOU! LOOK! I CAN PUT TWO SUNS IN THE SKY! DON'T THINK I CAN'T HANDLE YOU!
ALL I'VE GOT TO DO IS THINK...
AND I CAN SUMMON UP AN ARMY OF KILLERS!!
NEXT: MIND-TWIST!

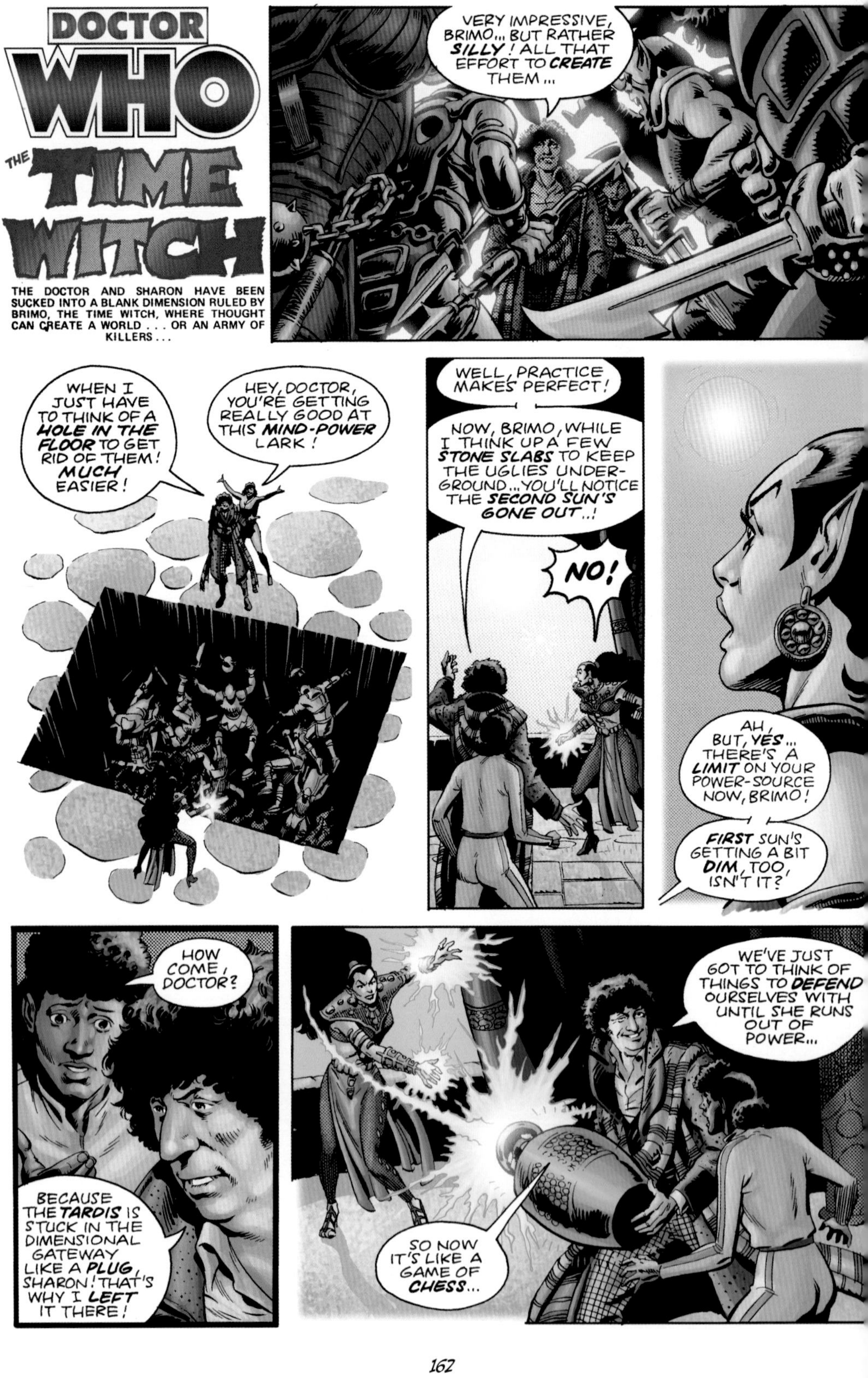
DOCTOR WHO
THE TIME WITCH
THE DOCTOR AND SHARON HAVE BEEN SUCKED INTO A BLANK DIMENSION RULED BY BRIMO, THE TIME WITCH, WHERE THOUGHT CAN CREATE A WORLD . . . OR AN ARMY OF KILLERS . . .
VERY IMPRESSIVE, BRIMO... BUT RATHER SILLY! ALL THAT EFFORT TO CREATE THEM...
WHEN I JUST HAVE TO THINK OF A HOLE IN THE FLOOR TO GET RID OF THEM! MUCH EASIER!
HEY, DOCTOR, YOU'RE GETTING REALLY GOOD AT THIS MIND-POWER LARK!
WELL, PRACTICE MAKES PERFECT!
NOW, BRIMO, WHILE I THINK UP A FEW STONE SLABS TO KEEP THE UGLIES UNDER-GROUND... YOU'LL NOTICE THE SECOND SUN'S GONE OUT..!
NO!
AH, BUT, YES... THERE'S A LIMIT ON YOUR POWER-SOURCE NOW, BRIMO!
FIRST SUN'S GETTING A BIT DIM, TOO, ISN'T IT?
HOW COME, DOCTOR?
BECAUSE THE TARDIS IS STUCK IN THE DIMENSIONAL GATEWAY LIKE A PLUG, SHARON! THAT'S WHY I LEFT IT THERE!
WE'VE JUST GOT TO THINK OF THINGS TO DEFEND OURSELVES WITH UNTIL SHE RUNS OUT OF POWER...
SO NOW IT'S LIKE A GAME OF CHESS...

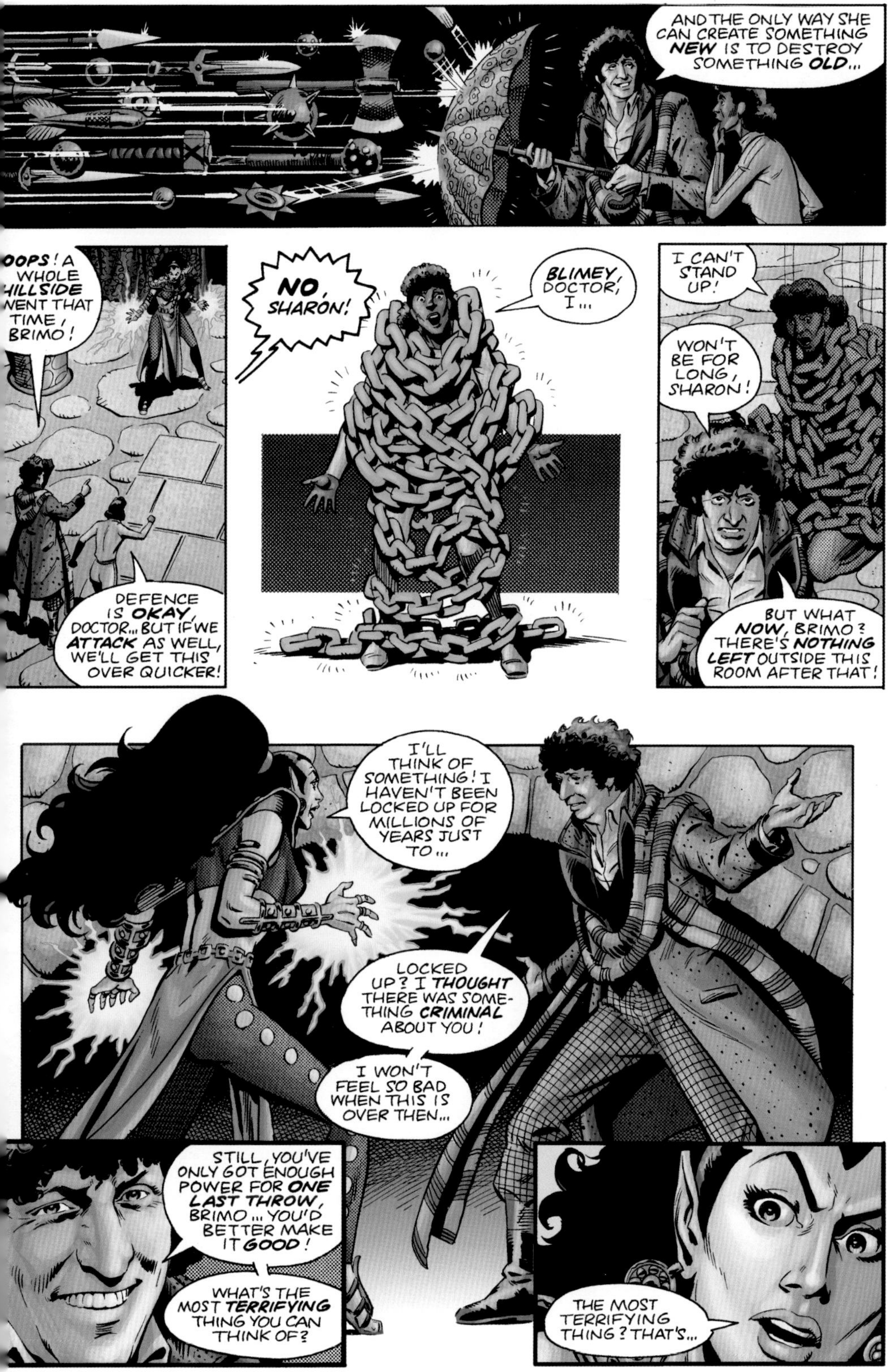
AND THE ONLY WAY SHE CAN CREATE SOMETHING **NEW** IS TO DESTROY SOMETHING **OLD**...
OOPS! A WHOLE **HILLSIDE** WENT THAT TIME, BRIMO!
DEFENCE IS **OKAY**, DOCTOR... BUT IF WE **ATTACK** AS WELL, WE'LL GET THIS OVER QUICKER!
NO, SHARON!
BLIMEY, DOCTOR, I...
I CAN'T STAND UP!
WON'T BE FOR LONG, SHARON!
BUT WHAT **NOW**, BRIMO? THERE'S **NOTHING LEFT** OUTSIDE THIS ROOM AFTER THAT!
I'LL THINK OF SOMETHING! I HAVEN'T BEEN LOCKED UP FOR MILLIONS OF YEARS JUST TO...
LOCKED UP? I **THOUGHT** THERE WAS SOME-THING **CRIMINAL** ABOUT YOU!
I WON'T FEEL SO BAD WHEN THIS IS OVER THEN...
STILL, YOU'VE ONLY GOT ENOUGH POWER FOR **ONE LAST THROW**, BRIMO... YOU'D BETTER MAKE IT **GOOD**!
WHAT'S THE MOST **TERRIFYING** THING YOU CAN THINK OF?
THE MOST TERRIFYING THING? THAT'S...

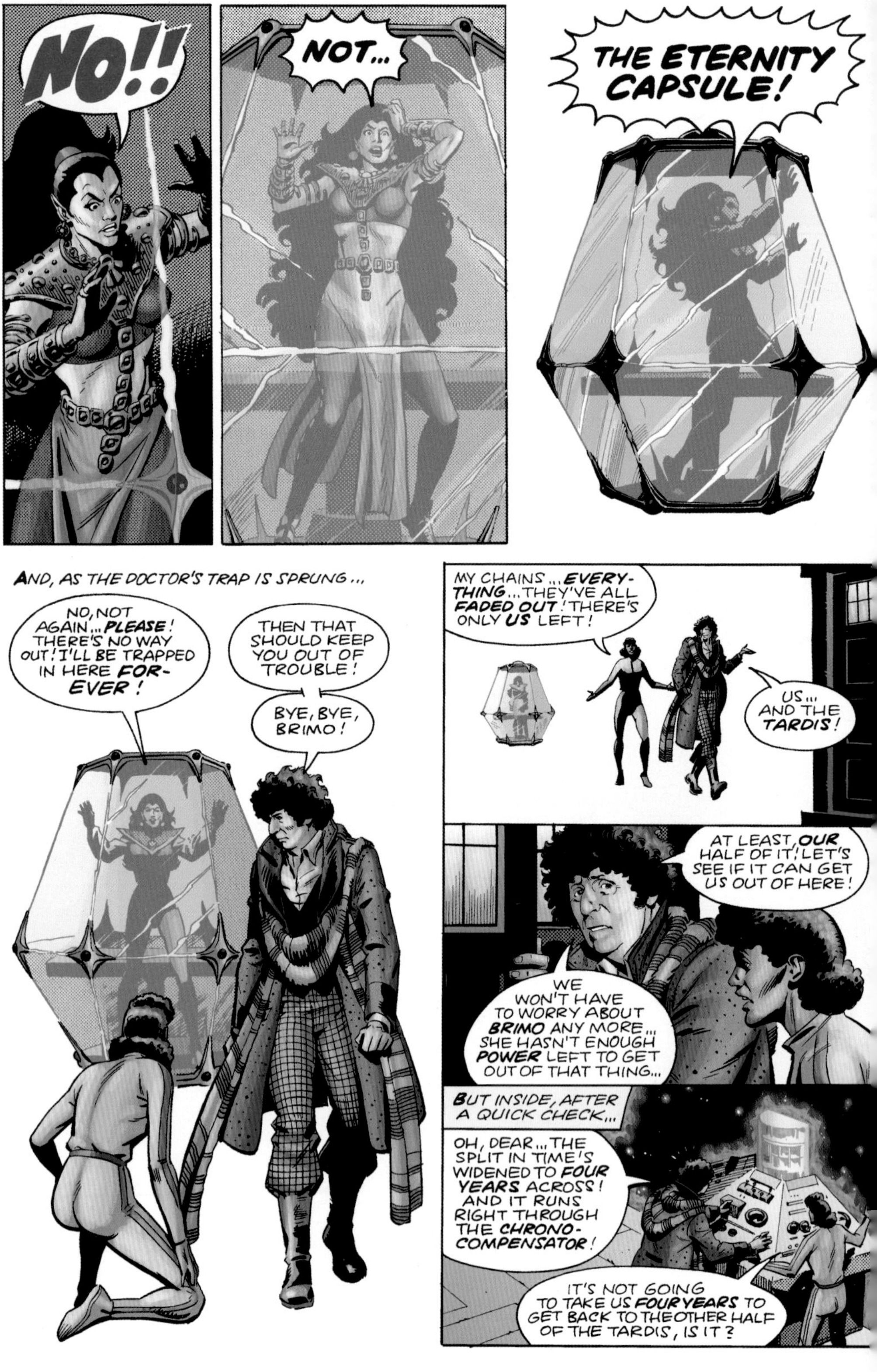

NO!!
NOT...
THE ETERNITY CAPSULE!
AND, AS THE DOCTOR'S TRAP IS SPRUNG...
NO, NOT AGAIN... PLEASE! THERE'S NO WAY OUT! I'LL BE TRAPPED IN HERE FOR-EVER!
THEN THAT SHOULD KEEP YOU OUT OF TROUBLE!
BYE, BYE, BRIMO!
MY CHAINS... EVERY-THING... THEY'VE ALL FADED OUT! THERE'S ONLY US LEFT!
US... AND THE TARDIS!
AT LEAST, OUR HALF OF IT! LET'S SEE IF IT CAN GET US OUT OF HERE!
WE WON'T HAVE TO WORRY ABOUT BRIMO ANY MORE... SHE HASN'T ENOUGH POWER LEFT TO GET OUT OF THAT THING...
BUT INSIDE, AFTER A QUICK CHECK...
OH, DEAR... THE SPLIT IN TIME'S WIDENED TO FOUR YEARS ACROSS! AND IT RUNS RIGHT THROUGH THE CHRONO-COMPENSATOR!
IT'S NOT GOING TO TAKE US FOUR YEARS TO GET BACK TO THE OTHER HALF OF THE TARDIS, IS IT?

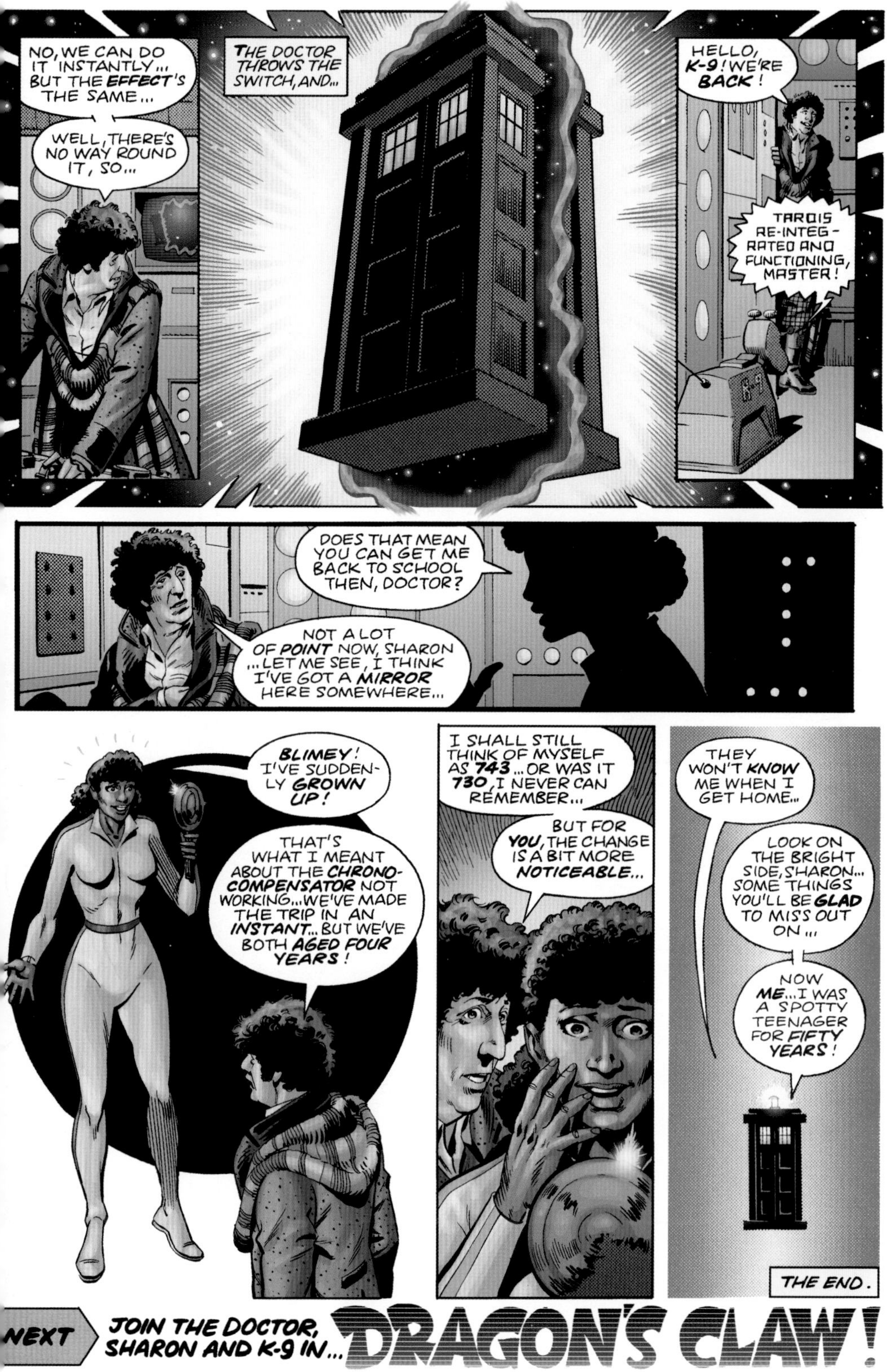
NO, WE CAN DO IT INSTANTLY... BUT THE EFFECT'S THE SAME...
WELL, THERE'S NO WAY ROUND IT, SO...
THE DOCTOR THROWS THE SWITCH, AND...
HELLO, K-9! WE'RE BACK!
TARDIS RE-INTEGRATED AND FUNCTIONING, MASTER!
DOES THAT MEAN YOU CAN GET ME BACK TO SCHOOL THEN, DOCTOR?
NOT A LOT OF POINT NOW, SHARON ...LET ME SEE, I THINK I'VE GOT A MIRROR HERE SOMEWHERE...
BLIMEY! I'VE SUDDENLY GROWN UP!
THAT'S WHAT I MEANT ABOUT THE CHRONO-COMPENSATOR NOT WORKING... WE'VE MADE THE TRIP IN AN INSTANT... BUT WE'VE BOTH AGED FOUR YEARS!
I SHALL STILL THINK OF MYSELF AS 743... OR WAS IT 730, I NEVER CAN REMEMBER...
BUT FOR YOU, THE CHANGE IS A BIT MORE NOTICEABLE...
THEY WON'T KNOW ME WHEN I GET HOME...
LOOK ON THE BRIGHT SIDE, SHARON... SOME THINGS YOU'LL BE GLAD TO MISS OUT ON...
NOW ME... I WAS A SPOTTY TEENAGER FOR FIFTY YEARS!
THE END.
NEXT
JOIN THE DOCTOR, SHARON AND K-9 IN... DRAGON'S CLAW!

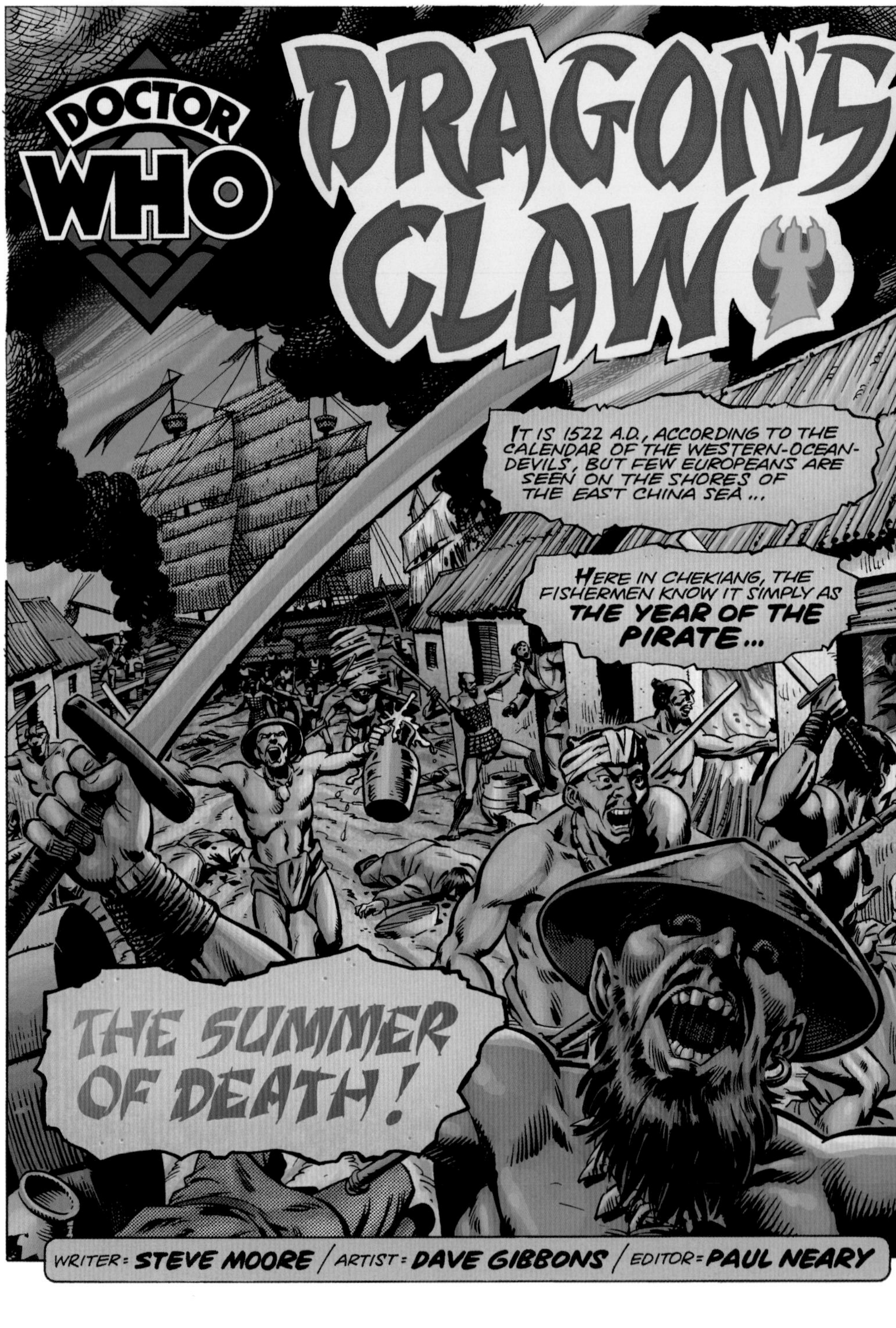

DOCTOR WHO
DRAGON'S CLAW
IT IS 1522 A.D., ACCORDING TO THE CALENDAR OF THE WESTERN-OCEAN-DEVILS, BUT FEW EUROPEANS ARE SEEN ON THE SHORES OF THE EAST CHINA SEA...
HERE IN CHEKIANG, THE FISHERMEN KNOW IT SIMPLY AS THE YEAR OF THE PIRATE...
THE SUMMER OF DEATH!
WRITER = STEVE MOORE / ARTIST = DAVE GIBBONS / EDITOR = PAUL NEARY

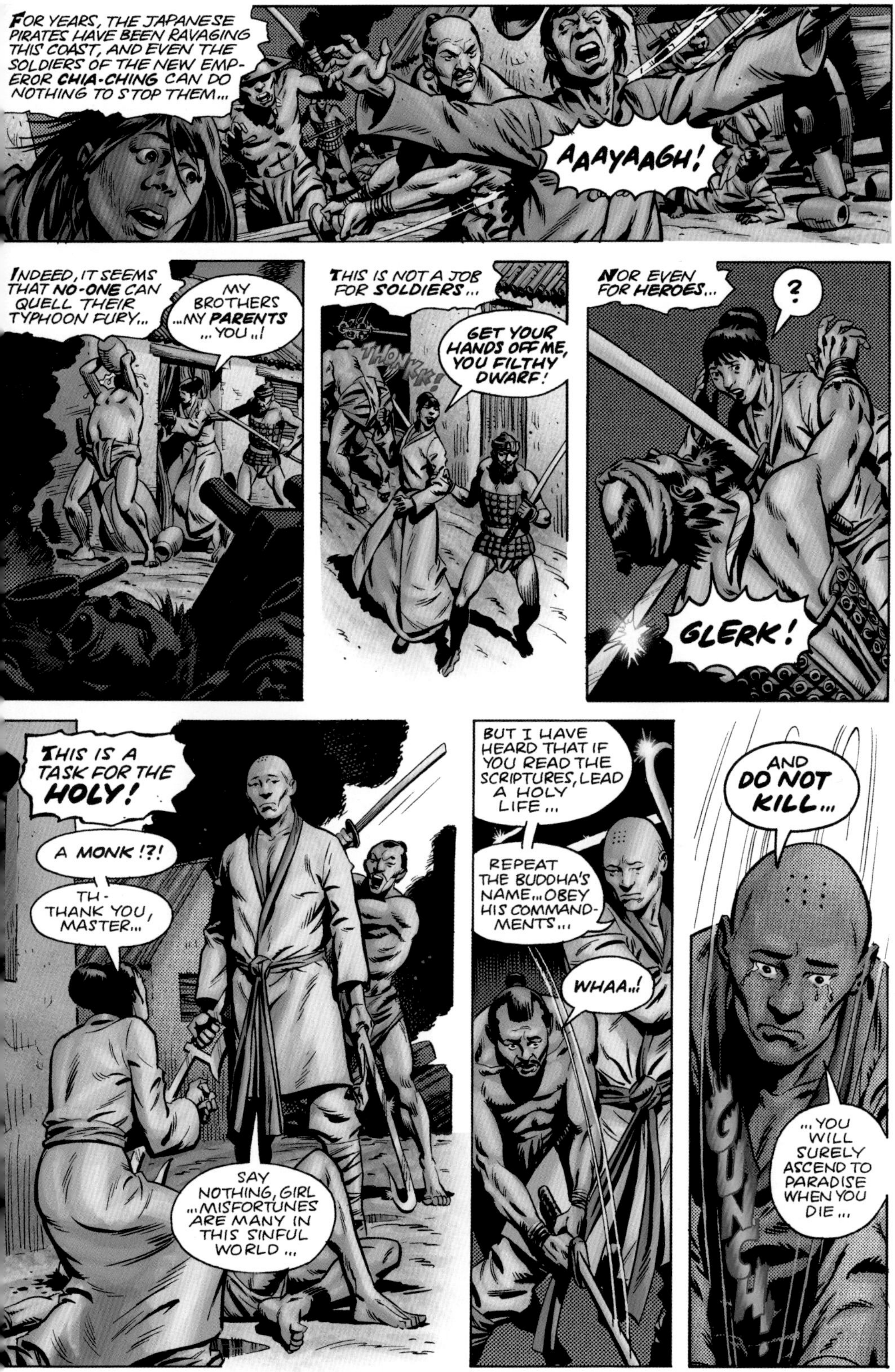

FOR YEARS, THE JAPANESE PIRATES HAVE BEEN RAVAGING THIS COAST, AND EVEN THE SOLDIERS OF THE NEW EMPEROR CHIA-CHING CAN DO NOTHING TO STOP THEM...
AAAYAAGH!
INDEED, IT SEEMS THAT NO-ONE CAN QUELL THEIR TYPHOON FURY...
MY BROTHERS ...MY PARENTS ...YOU...!
THIS IS NOT A JOB FOR SOLDIERS...
THONK!
GET YOUR HANDS OFF ME, YOU FILTHY DWARF!
NOR EVEN FOR HEROES...
?
GLERK!
THIS IS A TASK FOR THE HOLY!
A MONK!?!
TH-THANK YOU, MASTER...
SAY NOTHING, GIRL ...MISFORTUNES ARE MANY IN THIS SINFUL WORLD...
BUT I HAVE HEARD THAT IF YOU READ THE SCRIPTURES, LEAD A HOLY LIFE...
REPEAT THE BUDDHA'S NAME...OBEY HIS COMMANDMENTS...
WHAA..!
AND DO NOT KILL...
...YOU WILL SURELY ASCEND TO PARADISE WHEN YOU DIE...

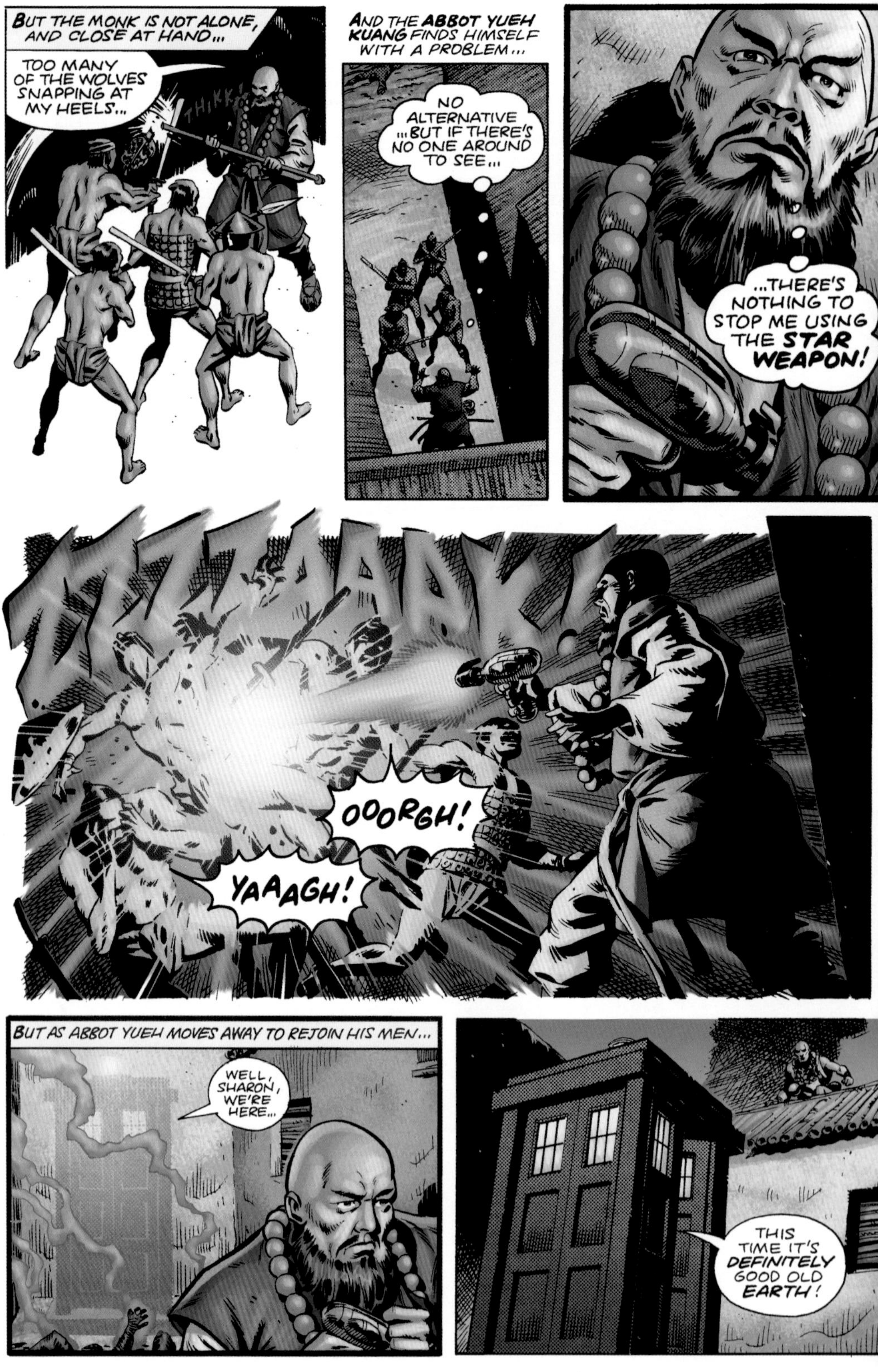
But the monk is not alone, and close at hand...
Too many of the wolves snapping at my heels...
THIKK!
And the Abbot Yueh Kuang finds himself with a problem...
No alternative ...but if there's no one around to see...
...there's nothing to stop me using the star weapon!
ZZZAAAK!
OOORGH!
YAAAGH!
But as Abbot Yueh moves away to rejoin his men...
Well, Sharon, we're here...
This time it's definitely good old Earth!

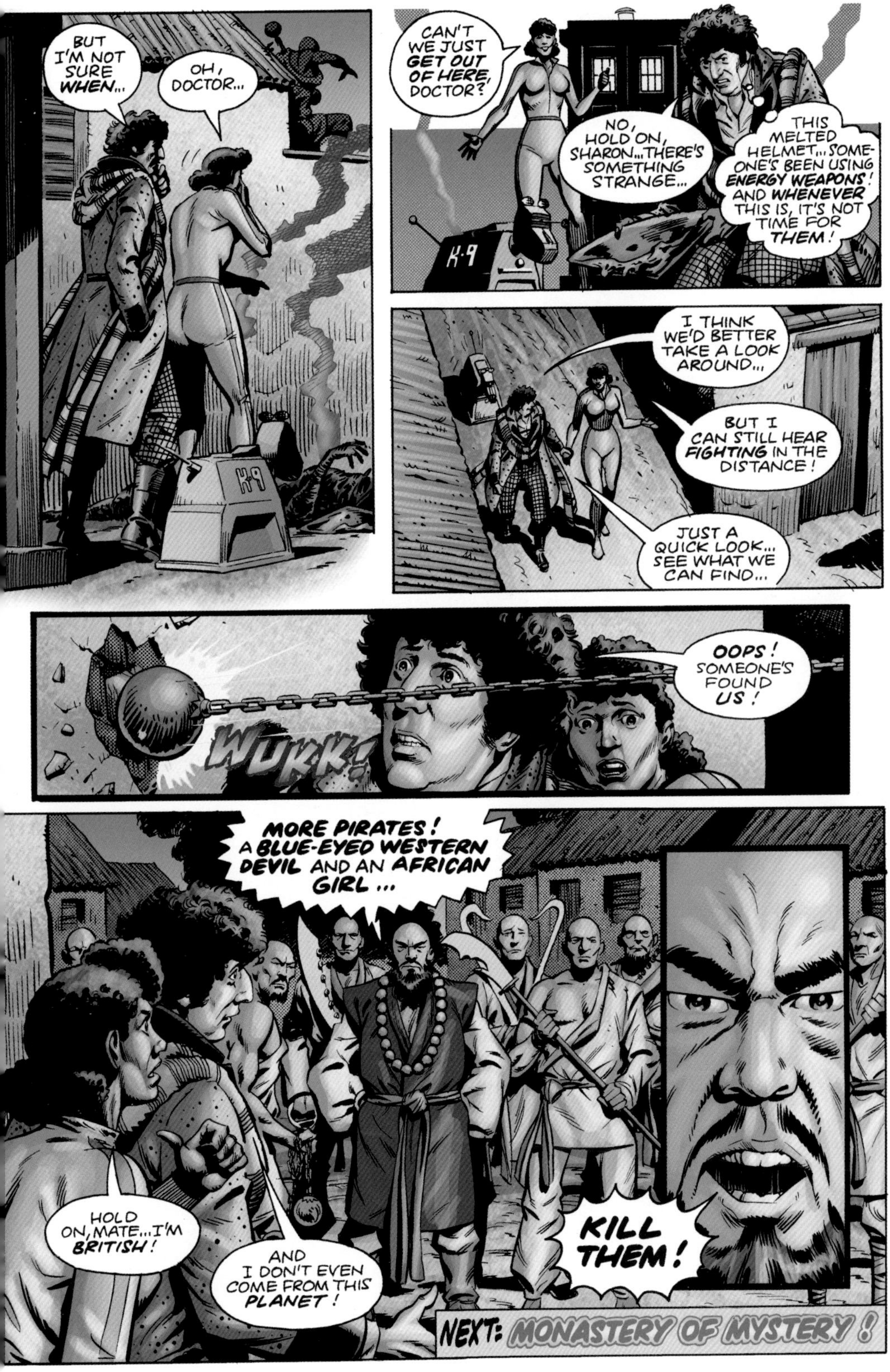
BUT I'M NOT SURE WHEN...
OH, DOCTOR...
CAN'T WE JUST GET OUT OF HERE, DOCTOR?
NO, HOLD ON, SHARON... THERE'S SOMETHING STRANGE...
THIS MELTED HELMET... SOMEONE'S BEEN USING ENERGY WEAPONS! AND WHENEVER THIS IS, IT'S NOT TIME FOR THEM!
K-9
K-9
I THINK WE'D BETTER TAKE A LOOK AROUND...
BUT I CAN STILL HEAR FIGHTING IN THE DISTANCE!
JUST A QUICK LOOK... SEE WHAT WE CAN FIND...
WUKK!
OOPS! SOMEONE'S FOUND US!
MORE PIRATES! A BLUE-EYED WESTERN DEVIL AND AN AFRICAN GIRL...
HOLD ON, MATE... I'M BRITISH!
AND I DON'T EVEN COME FROM THIS PLANET!
KILL THEM!
NEXT: MONASTERY OF MYSTERY!

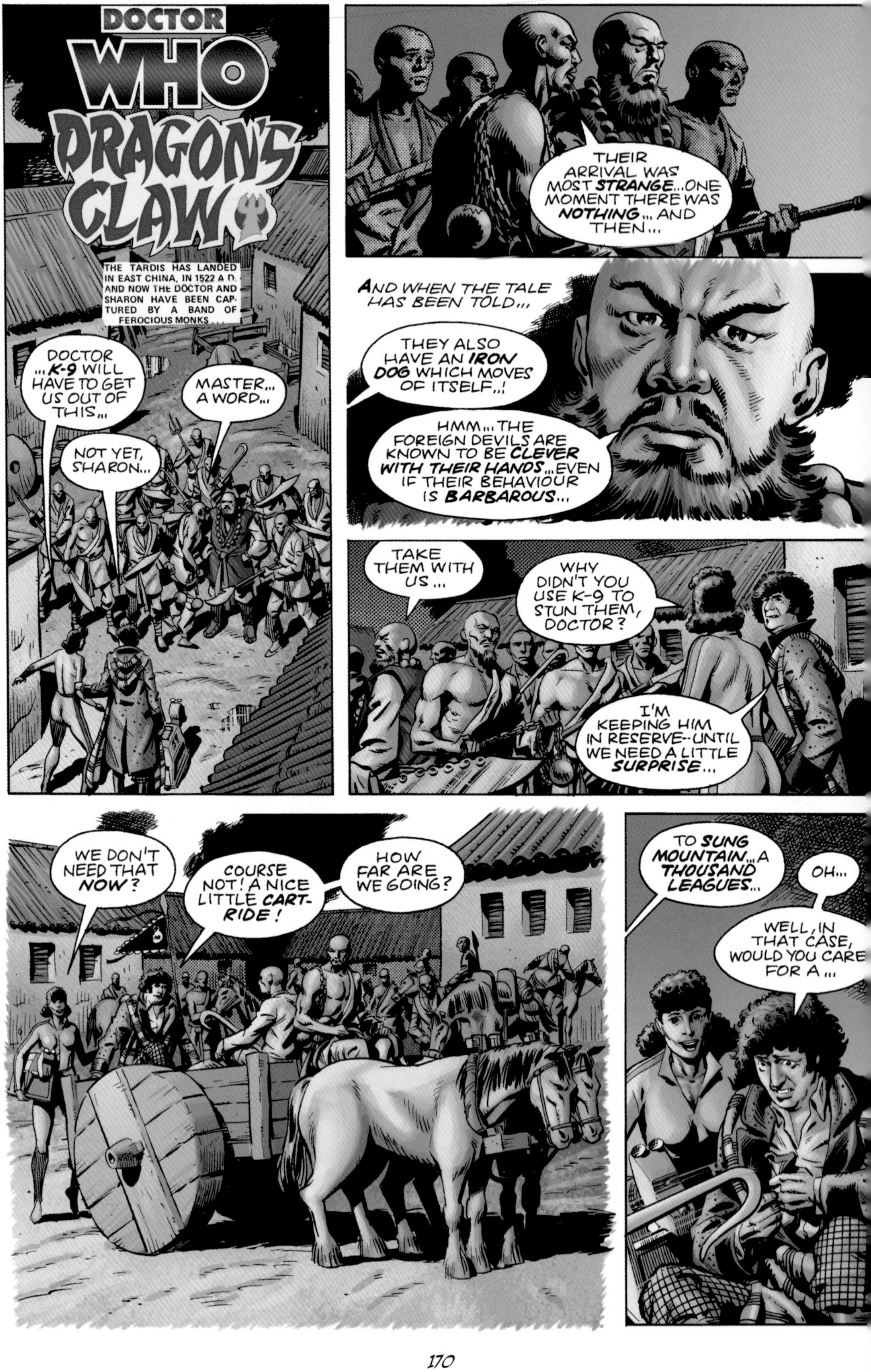

DOCTOR WHO
DRAGON'S CLAW
THE TARDIS HAS LANDED IN EAST CHINA, IN 1522 A.D. AND NOW THE DOCTOR AND SHARON HAVE BEEN CAPTURED BY A BAND OF FEROCIOUS MONKS . . .
DOCTOR ...K-9 WILL HAVE TO GET US OUT OF THIS...
MASTER... A WORD...
NOT YET, SHARON...
THEIR ARRIVAL WAS MOST STRANGE...ONE MOMENT THERE WAS NOTHING... AND THEN...
AND WHEN THE TALE HAS BEEN TOLD...
THEY ALSO HAVE AN IRON DOG WHICH MOVES OF ITSELF..!
HMM... THE FOREIGN DEVILS ARE KNOWN TO BE CLEVER WITH THEIR HANDS...EVEN IF THEIR BEHAVIOUR IS BARBAROUS...
TAKE THEM WITH US...
WHY DIDN'T YOU USE K-9 TO STUN THEM, DOCTOR?
I'M KEEPING HIM IN RESERVE--UNTIL WE NEED A LITTLE SURPRISE...
WE DON'T NEED THAT NOW?
COURSE NOT! A NICE LITTLE CART-RIDE!
HOW FAR ARE WE GOING?
TO SUNG MOUNTAIN...A THOUSAND LEAGUES...
OH...
WELL, IN THAT CASE, WOULD YOU CARE FOR A...

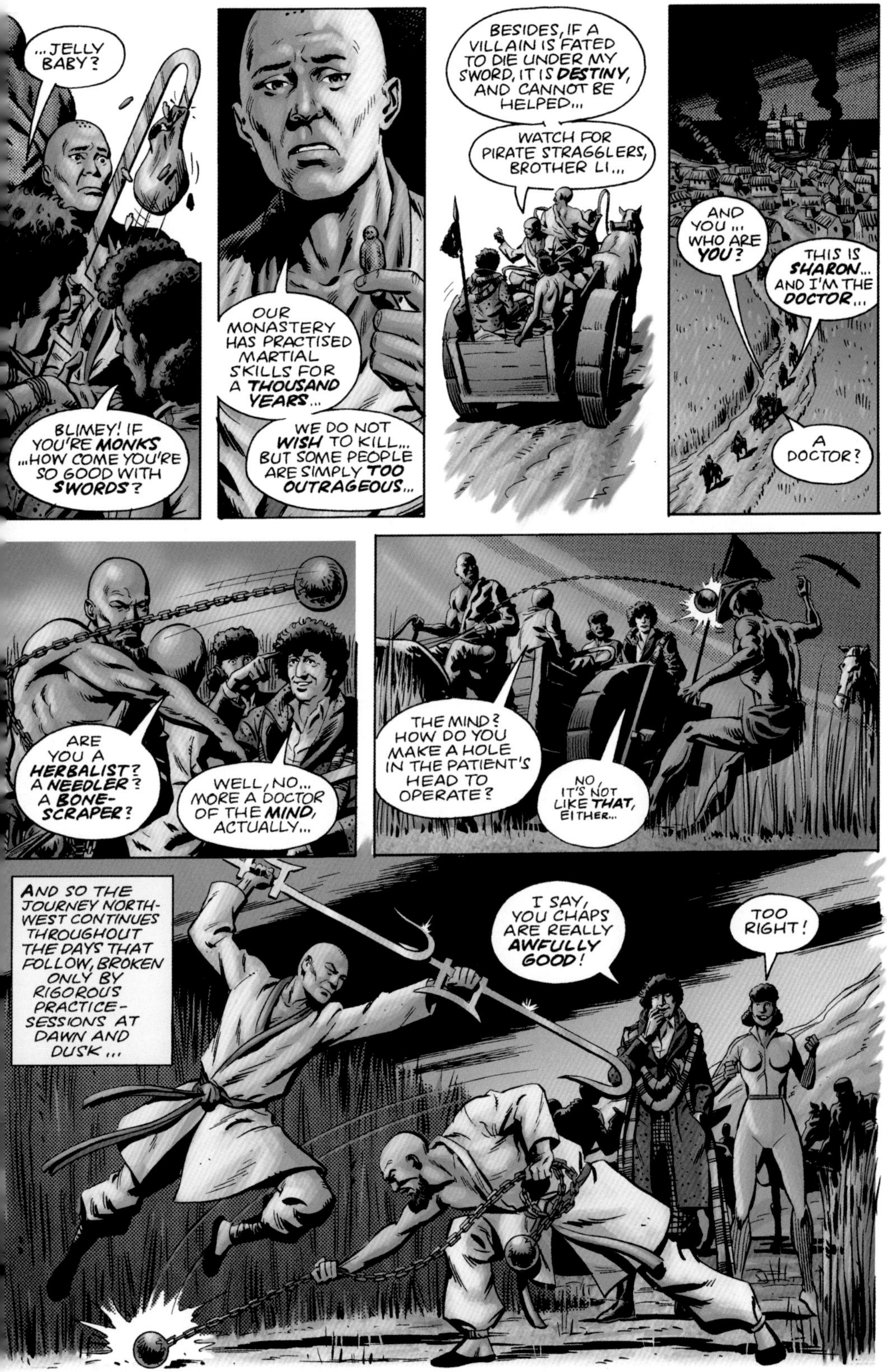
...JELLY BABY?
OUR MONASTERY HAS PRACTISED MARTIAL SKILLS FOR A **THOUSAND YEARS**...
BLIMEY! IF YOU'RE **MONKS** ...HOW COME YOU'RE SO GOOD WITH **SWORDS**?
WE DO NOT **WISH** TO KILL... BUT SOME PEOPLE ARE SIMPLY **TOO OUTRAGEOUS**...
BESIDES, IF A VILLAIN IS FATED TO DIE UNDER MY SWORD, IT IS **DESTINY**, AND CANNOT BE HELPED...
WATCH FOR PIRATE STRAGGLERS, BROTHER LI...
AND YOU... WHO ARE **YOU**?
THIS IS **SHARON**... AND I'M THE **DOCTOR**...
A DOCTOR?
ARE YOU A **HERBALIST**? A **NEEDLER**? A **BONE-SCRAPER**?
WELL, NO... MORE A DOCTOR OF THE **MIND**, ACTUALLY...
THE MIND? HOW DO YOU MAKE A HOLE IN THE PATIENT'S HEAD TO OPERATE?
NO, IT'S NOT LIKE **THAT**, EITHER...
AND SO THE JOURNEY NORTH-WEST CONTINUES THROUGHOUT THE DAYS THAT FOLLOW, BROKEN ONLY BY RIGOROUS PRACTICE-SESSIONS AT DAWN AND DUSK...
I SAY, YOU CHAPS ARE REALLY **AWFULLY GOOD**!
TOO RIGHT!

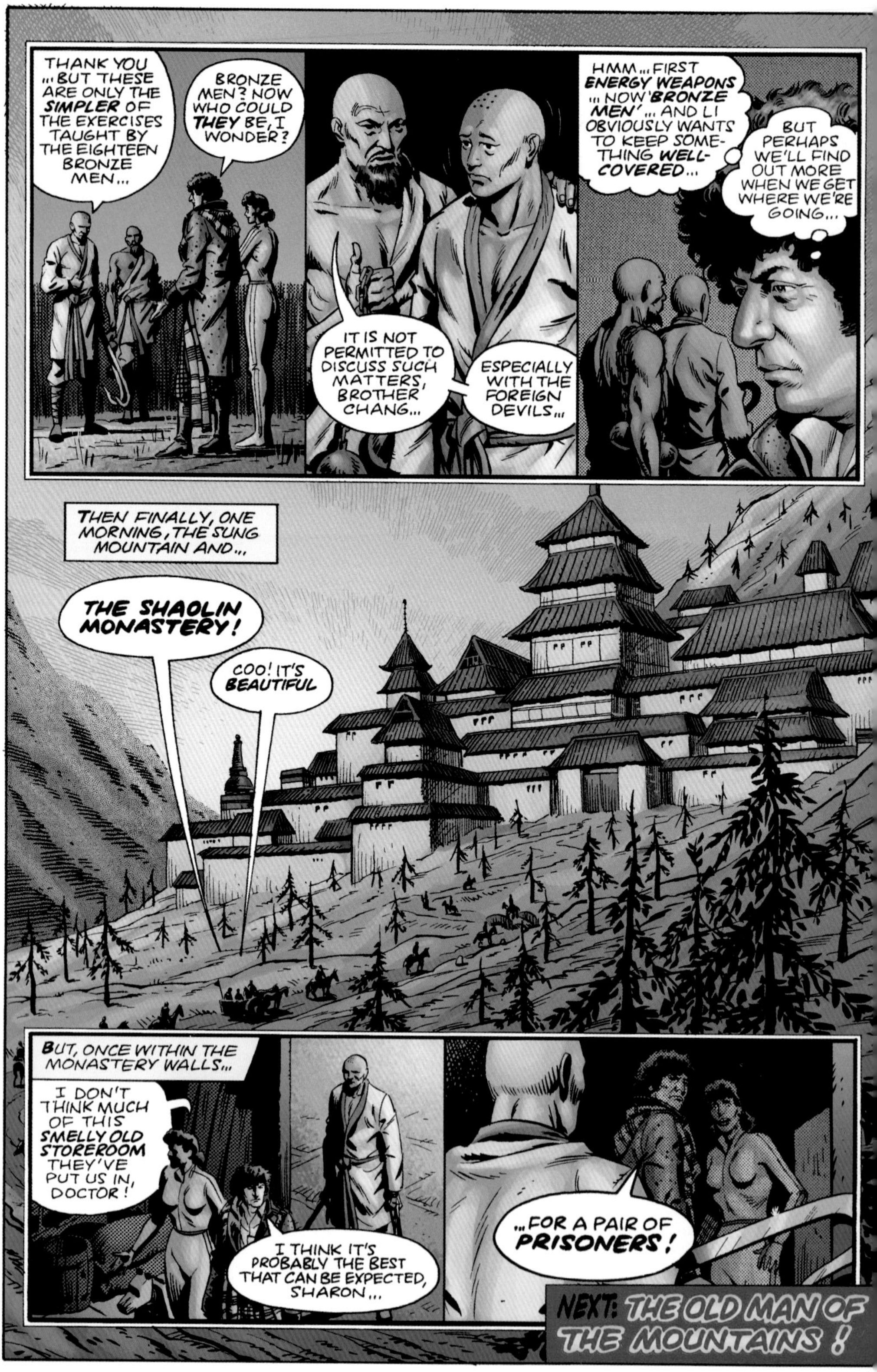
THANK YOU ...BUT THESE ARE ONLY THE SIMPLER OF THE EXERCISES TAUGHT BY THE EIGHTEEN BRONZE MEN...
BRONZE MEN? NOW WHO COULD THEY BE, I WONDER?
IT IS NOT PERMITTED TO DISCUSS SUCH MATTERS, BROTHER CHANG...
ESPECIALLY WITH THE FOREIGN DEVILS...
HMM... FIRST ENERGY WEAPONS ... NOW 'BRONZE MEN' ... AND LI OBVIOUSLY WANTS TO KEEP SOMETHING WELL-COVERED...
BUT PERHAPS WE'LL FIND OUT MORE WHEN WE GET WHERE WE'RE GOING...
THEN FINALLY, ONE MORNING, THE SUNG MOUNTAIN AND...
THE SHAOLIN MONASTERY!
COO! IT'S BEAUTIFUL
BUT, ONCE WITHIN THE MONASTERY WALLS...
I DON'T THINK MUCH OF THIS SMELLY OLD STOREROOM THEY'VE PUT US IN, DOCTOR!
I THINK IT'S PROBABLY THE BEST THAT CAN BE EXPECTED, SHARON...
...FOR A PAIR OF PRISONERS!
NEXT: THE OLD MAN OF THE MOUNTAINS!

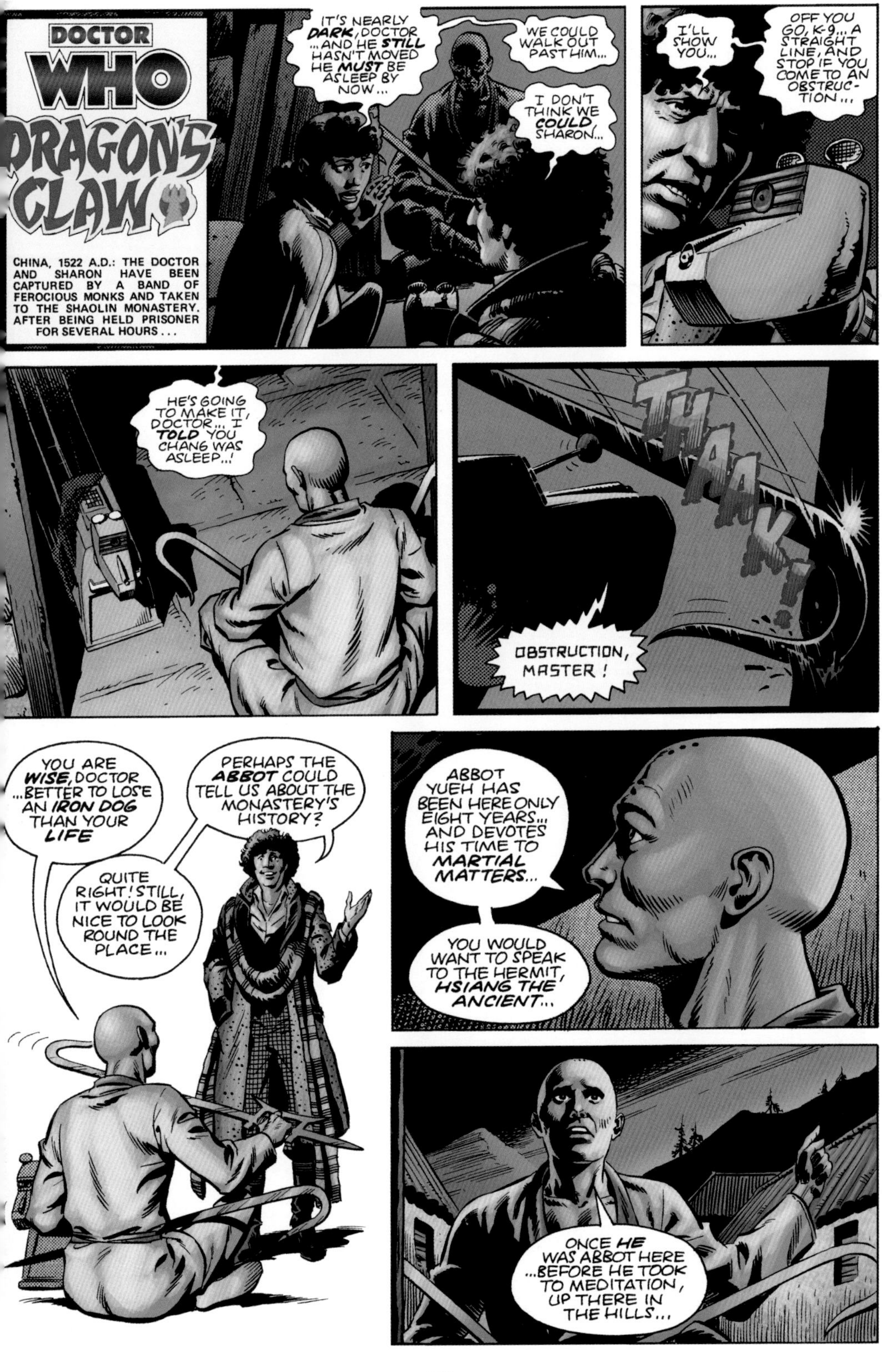
DOCTOR WHO
DRAGON'S CLAW
CHINA, 1522 A.D.: THE DOCTOR AND SHARON HAVE BEEN CAPTURED BY A BAND OF FEROCIOUS MONKS AND TAKEN TO THE SHAOLIN MONASTERY. AFTER BEING HELD PRISONER FOR SEVERAL HOURS . . .
IT'S NEARLY DARK, DOCTOR ...AND HE STILL HASN'T MOVED HE MUST BE ASLEEP BY NOW...
WE COULD WALK OUT PAST HIM...
I DON'T THINK WE COULD SHARON...
I'LL SHOW YOU...
OFF YOU GO, K-9... A STRAIGHT LINE, AND STOP IF YOU COME TO AN OBSTRUCTION...
HE'S GOING TO MAKE IT, DOCTOR... I TOLD YOU CHANG WAS ASLEEP...!
THAAK!
OBSTRUCTION, MASTER!
YOU ARE WISE, DOCTOR ...BETTER TO LOSE AN IRON DOG THAN YOUR LIFE
QUITE RIGHT! STILL, IT WOULD BE NICE TO LOOK ROUND THE PLACE...
PERHAPS THE ABBOT COULD TELL US ABOUT THE MONASTERY'S HISTORY?
ABBOT YUEH HAS BEEN HERE ONLY EIGHT YEARS... AND DEVOTES HIS TIME TO MARTIAL MATTERS...
YOU WOULD WANT TO SPEAK TO THE HERMIT, HSIANG THE ANCIENT...
ONCE HE WAS ABBOT HERE ...BEFORE HE TOOK TO MEDITATION, UP THERE IN THE HILLS...

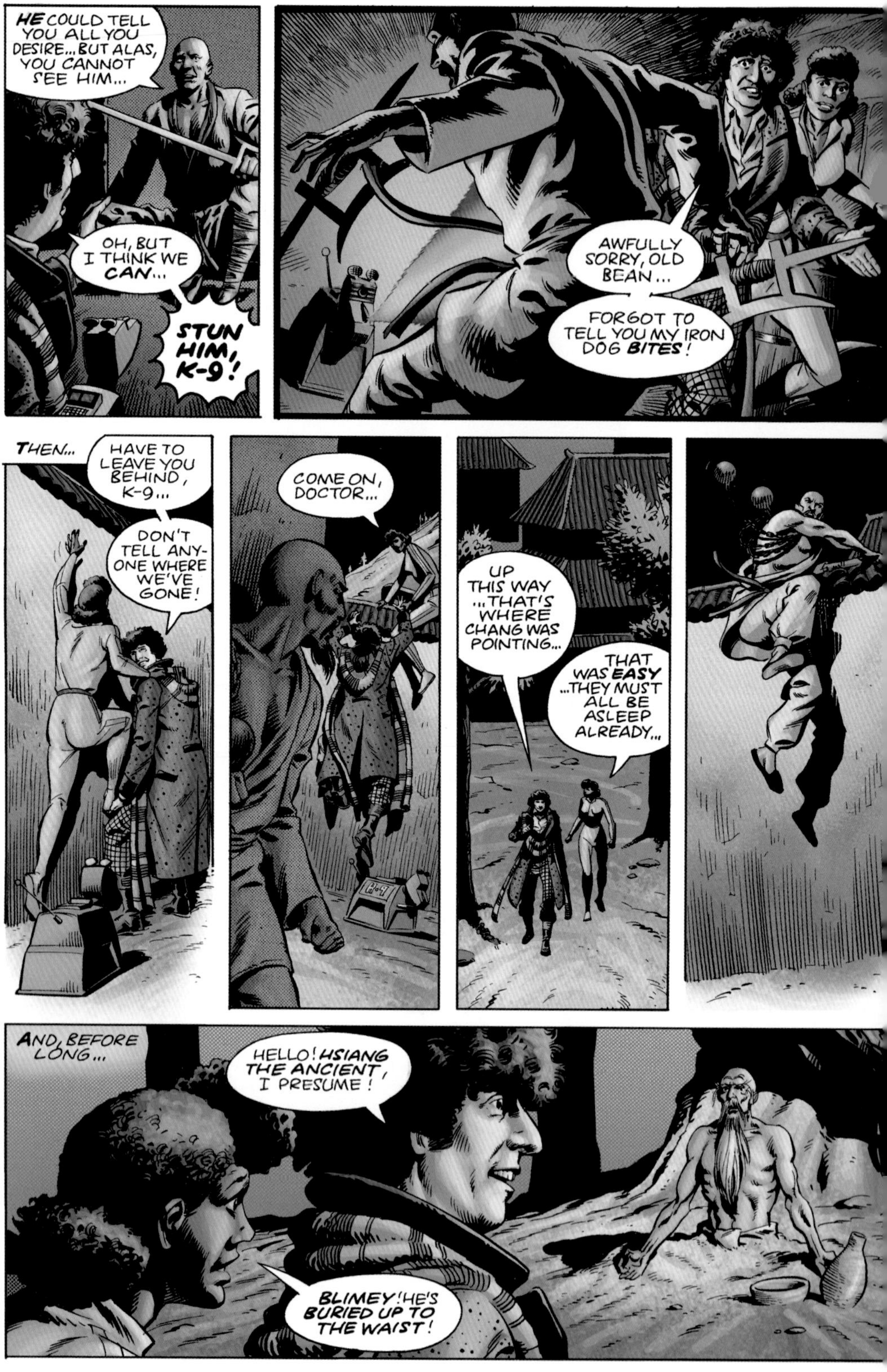

HE COULD TELL YOU ALL YOU DESIRE... BUT ALAS, YOU CANNOT SEE HIM...
OH, BUT I THINK WE CAN...
STUN HIM, K-9!
AWFULLY SORRY, OLD BEAN...
FORGOT TO TELL YOU MY IRON DOG BITES!
THEN...
HAVE TO LEAVE YOU BEHIND, K-9...
DON'T TELL ANYONE WHERE WE'VE GONE!
COME ON, DOCTOR...
UP THIS WAY ...THAT'S WHERE CHANG WAS POINTING...
THAT WAS EASY ...THEY MUST ALL BE ASLEEP ALREADY...
AND, BEFORE LONG...
HELLO! HSIANG THE ANCIENT, I PRESUME!
BLIMEY! HE'S BURIED UP TO THE WAIST!

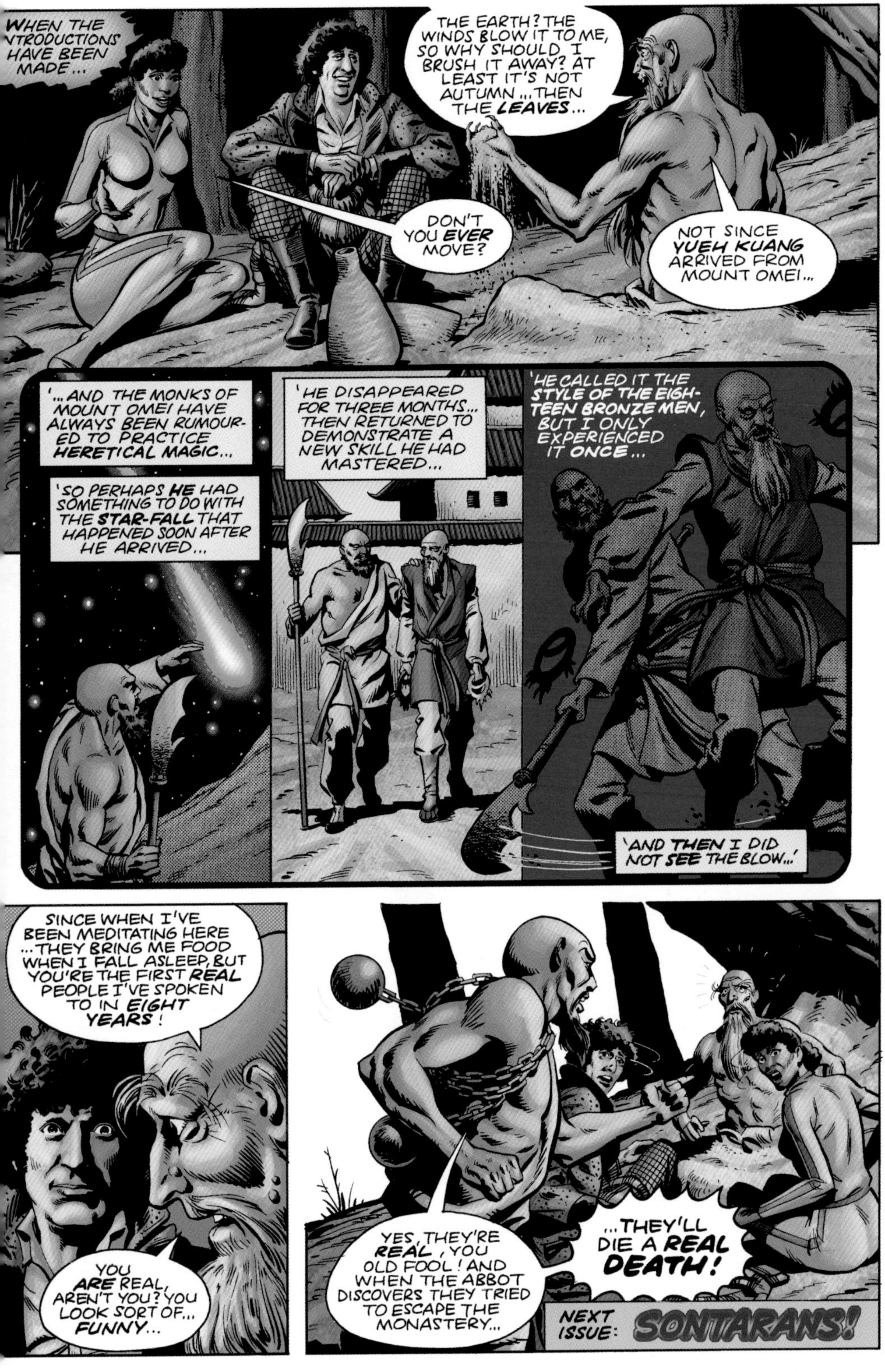

WHEN THE INTRODUCTIONS HAVE BEEN MADE...
THE EARTH? THE WINDS BLOW IT TO ME, SO WHY SHOULD I BRUSH IT AWAY? AT LEAST IT'S NOT AUTUMN... THEN THE LEAVES...
DON'T YOU EVER MOVE?
NOT SINCE YUEH KUANG ARRIVED FROM MOUNT OMEI...
'...AND THE MONKS OF MOUNT OMEI HAVE ALWAYS BEEN RUMOURED TO PRACTICE HERETICAL MAGIC...
'SO PERHAPS HE HAD SOMETHING TO DO WITH THE STAR-FALL THAT HAPPENED SOON AFTER HE ARRIVED...
'HE DISAPPEARED FOR THREE MONTHS... THEN RETURNED TO DEMONSTRATE A NEW SKILL HE HAD MASTERED...
'HE CALLED IT THE STYLE OF THE EIGHTEEN BRONZE MEN, BUT I ONLY EXPERIENCED IT ONCE...
'AND THEN I DID NOT SEE THE BLOW...'
SINCE WHEN I'VE BEEN MEDITATING HERE ...THEY BRING ME FOOD WHEN I FALL ASLEEP, BUT YOU'RE THE FIRST REAL PEOPLE I'VE SPOKEN TO IN EIGHT YEARS!
YOU ARE REAL, AREN'T YOU? YOU LOOK SORT OF... FUNNY...
YES, THEY'RE REAL, YOU OLD FOOL! AND WHEN THE ABBOT DISCOVERS THEY TRIED TO ESCAPE THE MONASTERY...
...THEY'LL DIE A REAL DEATH!
NEXT ISSUE: SONTARANS!

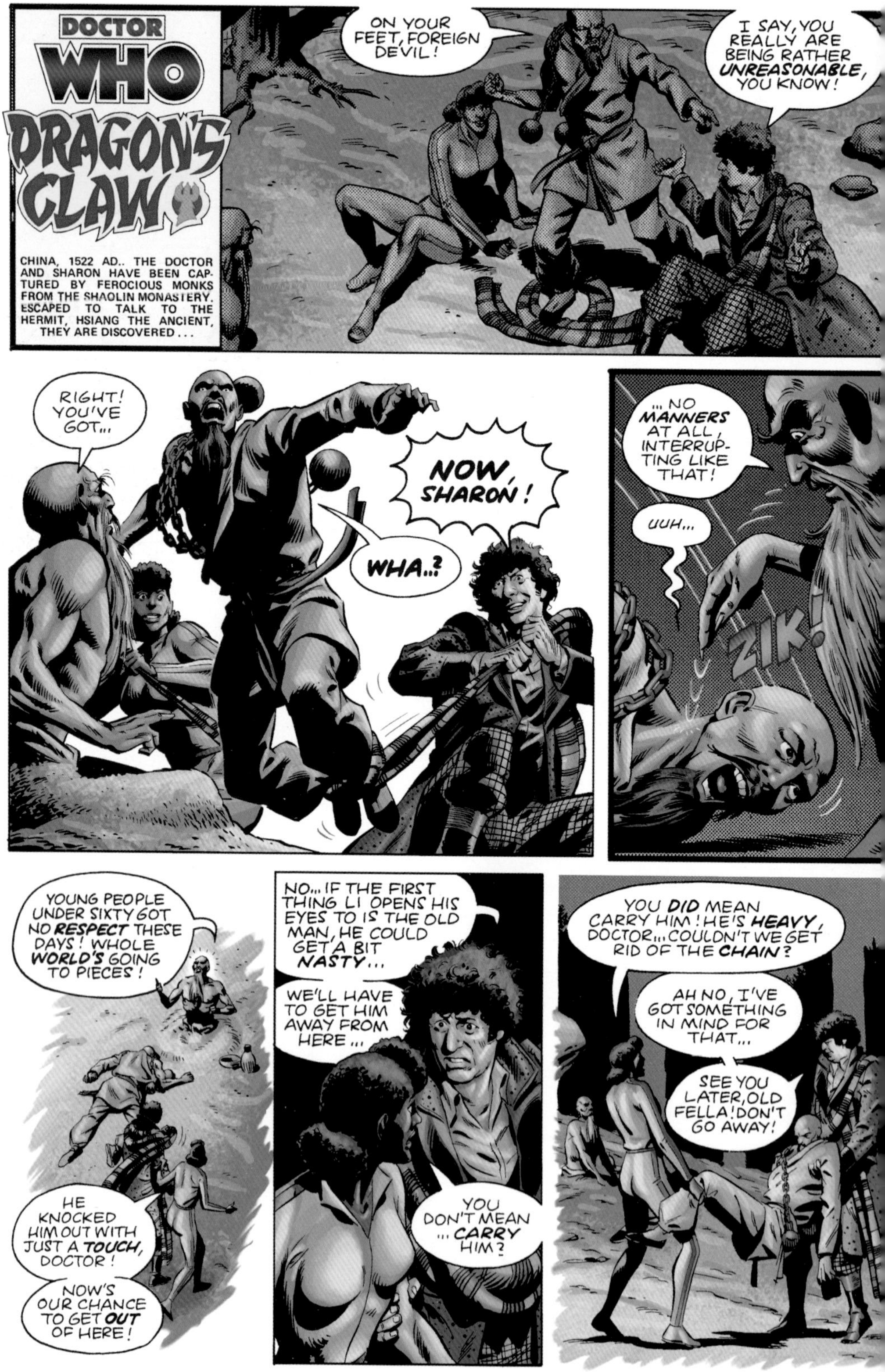
DOCTOR WHO
DRAGON'S CLAW
CHINA, 1522 AD.. THE DOCTOR AND SHARON HAVE BEEN CAPTURED BY FEROCIOUS MONKS FROM THE SHAOLIN MONASTERY. ESCAPED TO TALK TO THE HERMIT, HSIANG THE ANCIENT, THEY ARE DISCOVERED . . .
ON YOUR FEET, FOREIGN DEVIL!
I SAY, YOU REALLY ARE BEING RATHER UNREASONABLE, YOU KNOW!
RIGHT! YOU'VE GOT...
NOW, SHARON!
WHA..?
... NO MANNERS AT ALL, INTERRUPTING LIKE THAT!
UUH...
ZIK!
YOUNG PEOPLE UNDER SIXTY GOT NO RESPECT THESE DAYS! WHOLE WORLD'S GOING TO PIECES!
HE KNOCKED HIM OUT WITH JUST A TOUCH, DOCTOR!
NOW'S OUR CHANCE TO GET OUT OF HERE!
NO... IF THE FIRST THING LI OPENS HIS EYES TO IS THE OLD MAN, HE COULD GET A BIT NASTY...
WE'LL HAVE TO GET HIM AWAY FROM HERE...
YOU DON'T MEAN ...CARRY HIM?
YOU DID MEAN CARRY HIM! HE'S HEAVY, DOCTOR... COULDN'T WE GET RID OF THE CHAIN?
AH NO, I'VE GOT SOMETHING IN MIND FOR THAT...
SEE YOU LATER, OLD FELLA! DON'T GO AWAY!

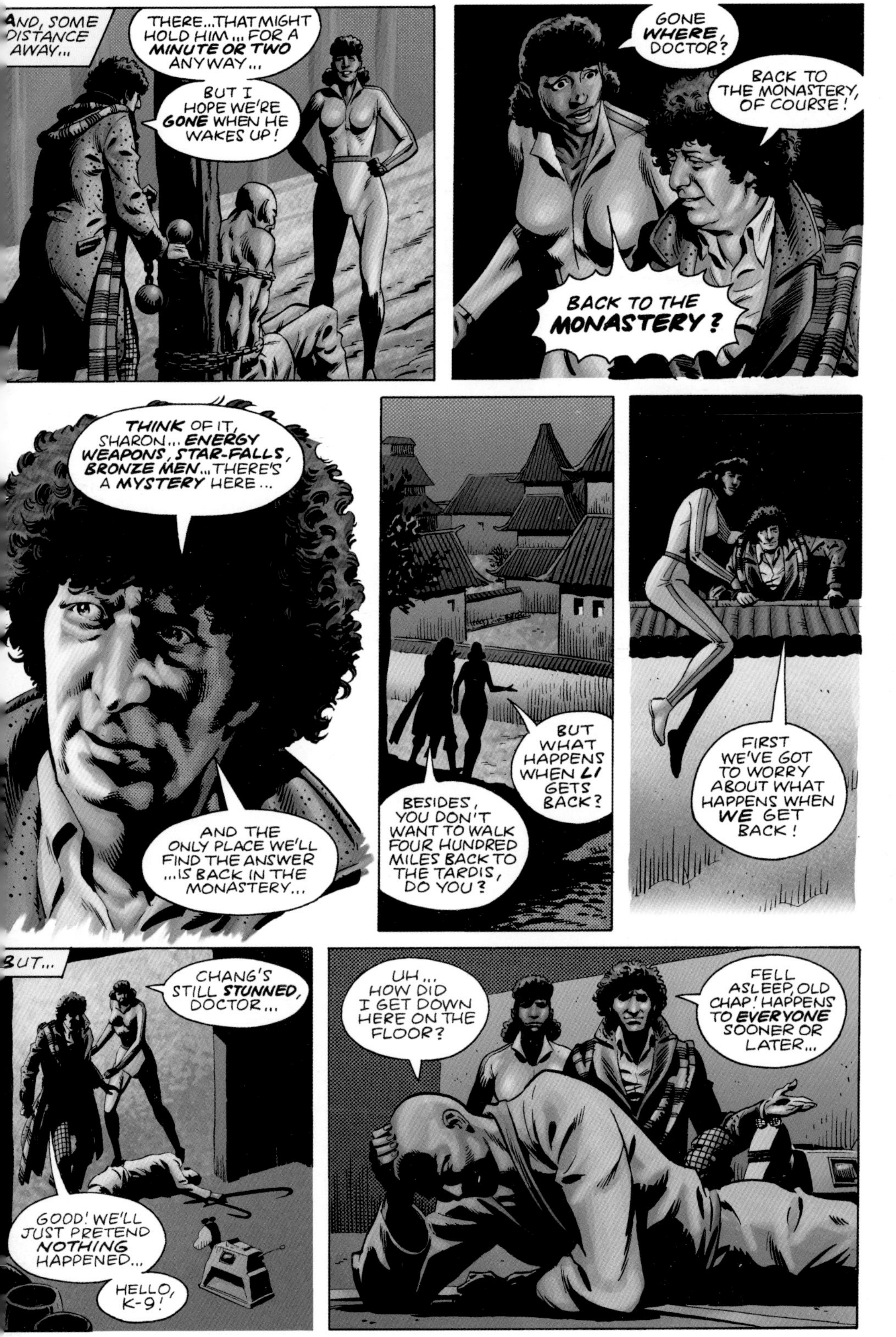

AND, SOME DISTANCE AWAY...
THERE...THAT MIGHT HOLD HIM... FOR A MINUTE OR TWO ANYWAY...
BUT I HOPE WE'RE GONE WHEN HE WAKES UP!
GONE WHERE, DOCTOR?
BACK TO THE MONASTERY, OF COURSE!
BACK TO THE MONASTERY?
THINK OF IT, SHARON... ENERGY WEAPONS, STAR-FALLS, BRONZE MEN... THERE'S A MYSTERY HERE...
AND THE ONLY PLACE WE'LL FIND THE ANSWER ...IS BACK IN THE MONASTERY...
BUT WHAT HAPPENS WHEN LI GETS BACK?
BESIDES, YOU DON'T WANT TO WALK FOUR HUNDRED MILES BACK TO THE TARDIS, DO YOU?
FIRST WE'VE GOT TO WORRY ABOUT WHAT HAPPENS WHEN WE GET BACK!
BUT...
CHANG'S STILL STUNNED, DOCTOR...
GOOD! WE'LL JUST PRETEND NOTHING HAPPENED...
HELLO, K-9!
UH... HOW DID I GET DOWN HERE ON THE FLOOR?
FELL ASLEEP, OLD CHAP! HAPPENS TO EVERYONE SOONER OR LATER...

ASLEEP? **MOST** STRANGE!

BUT I AM SURPRISED YOU DID NOT **ESCAPE**!

WHO... US? DIDN'T **TRY**!

WE **SUCCEEDED** ...BUT THE LESS YOU KNOW ABOUT THAT, THE BETTER!

BUT WHEN DAWN CASTS A ROSY GLOW OVER THE SUNG MOUNTAIN

ABBOT YUEH WANTS TO TALK TO THE FOREIGN DEVIL YOU TAKE HIM...I'M TO STAY HERE AND GUARD THE GIRL AND DOG...

SPLENDID! I'VE BEEN WAITING TO HAVE A CHAT!

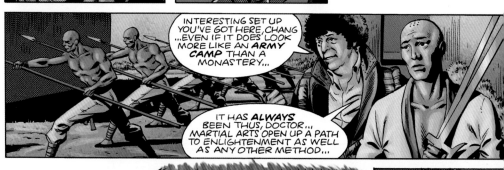

INTERESTING SET UP YOU'VE GOT HERE, CHANG ...EVEN IF IT DOES LOOK MORE LIKE AN **ARMY CAMP** THAN A MONASTERY...

IT HAS **ALWAYS** BEEN THUS, DOCTOR... MARTIAL ARTS OPEN UP A PATH TO ENLIGHTENMENT AS WELL AS ANY OTHER METHOD...

AND WHAT'S **THIS** PLACE WITH THE MASSIVE DOORS?

THAT? THE HALL OF THE **EIGHTEEN BRONZE MEN**...

WHERE OUR FIGHTING SKILLS ARE GIVEN THEIR **FINAL TESTING**...

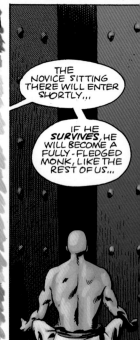

THE NOVICE SITTING THERE WILL ENTER SHORTLY...

IF HE **SURVIVES**, HE WILL BECOME A FULLY-FLEDGED MONK, LIKE THE REST OF US...

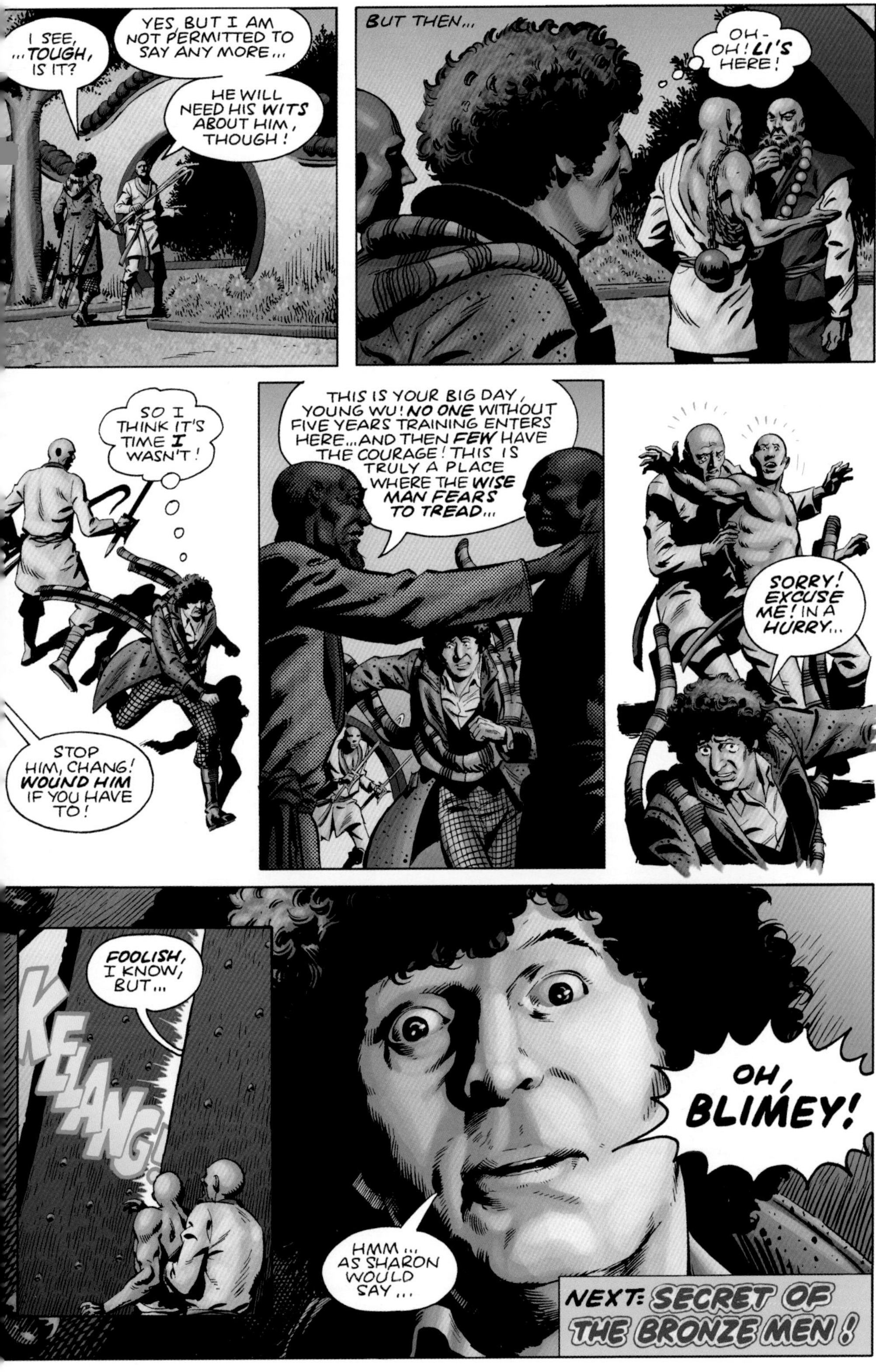
I SEE, ...TOUGH, IS IT?
YES, BUT I AM NOT PERMITTED TO SAY ANY MORE...
HE WILL NEED HIS WITS ABOUT HIM, THOUGH!
BUT THEN...
OH-OH! LI'S HERE!
SO I THINK IT'S TIME I WASN'T!
STOP HIM, CHANG! WOUND HIM IF YOU HAVE TO!
THIS IS YOUR BIG DAY, YOUNG WU! NO ONE WITHOUT FIVE YEARS TRAINING ENTERS HERE...AND THEN FEW HAVE THE COURAGE! THIS IS TRULY A PLACE WHERE THE WISE MAN FEARS TO TREAD...
SORRY! EXCUSE ME! IN A HURRY...
FOOLISH, I KNOW, BUT...
KELANG!
HMM... AS SHARON WOULD SAY...
OH, BLIMEY!
NEXT: SECRET OF THE BRONZE MEN!

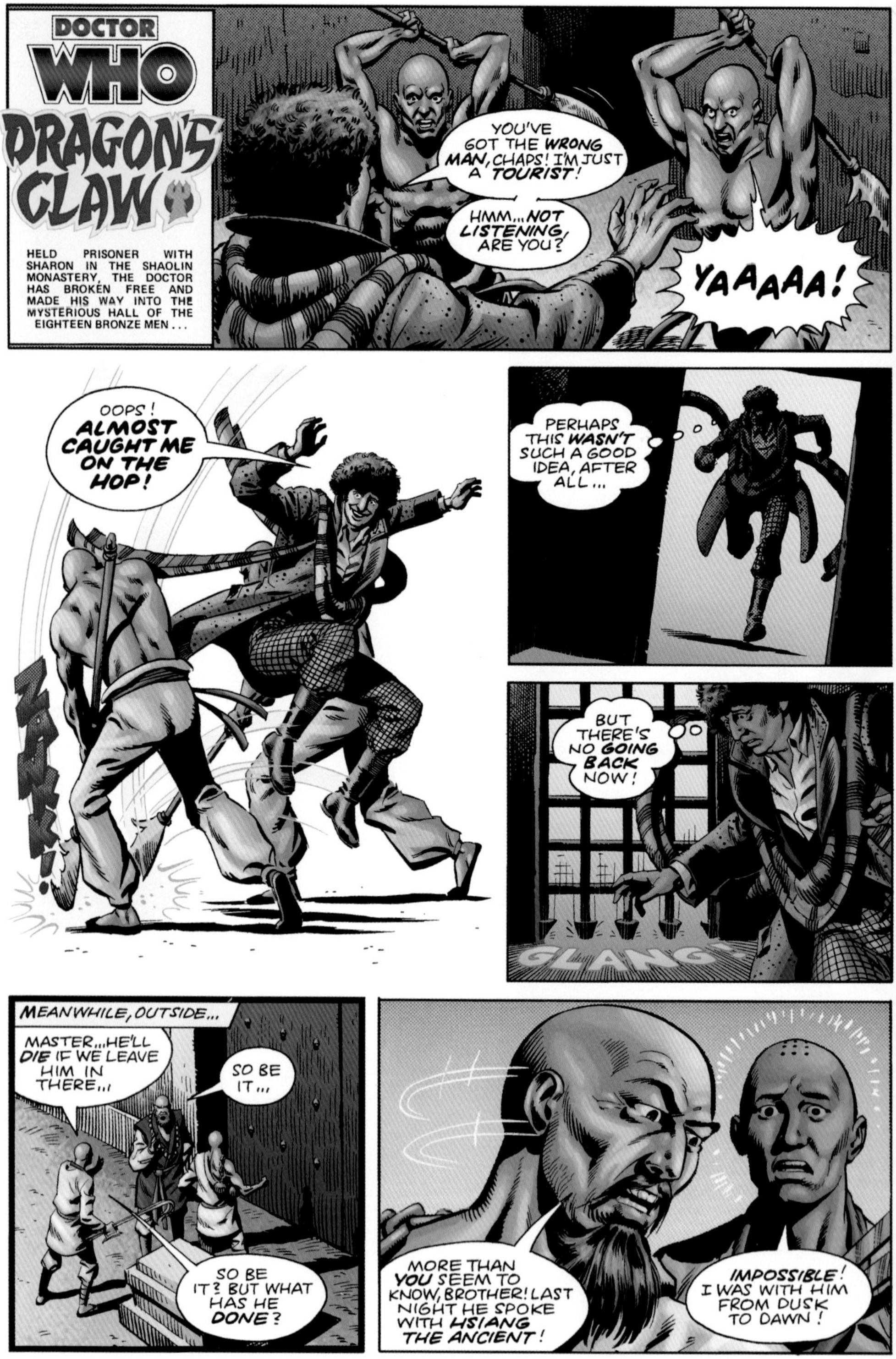
DOCTOR WHO
DRAGON'S CLAW
HELD PRISONER WITH SHARON IN THE SHAOLIN MONASTERY, THE DOCTOR HAS BROKEN FREE AND MADE HIS WAY INTO THE MYSTERIOUS HALL OF THE EIGHTEEN BRONZE MEN . . .
YOU'VE GOT THE WRONG MAN, CHAPS! I'M JUST A TOURIST!
HMM... NOT LISTENING, ARE YOU?
YAAAAAA!
OOPS! ALMOST CAUGHT ME ON THE HOP!
ZANK!
PERHAPS THIS WASN'T SUCH A GOOD IDEA, AFTER ALL...
BUT THERE'S NO GOING BACK NOW!
GLANG!
MEANWHILE, OUTSIDE...
MASTER... HE'LL DIE IF WE LEAVE HIM IN THERE...
SO BE IT...
SO BE IT? BUT WHAT HAS HE DONE?
MORE THAN YOU SEEM TO KNOW, BROTHER! LAST NIGHT HE SPOKE WITH HSIANG THE ANCIENT!
IMPOSSIBLE! I WAS WITH HIM FROM DUSK TO DAWN!

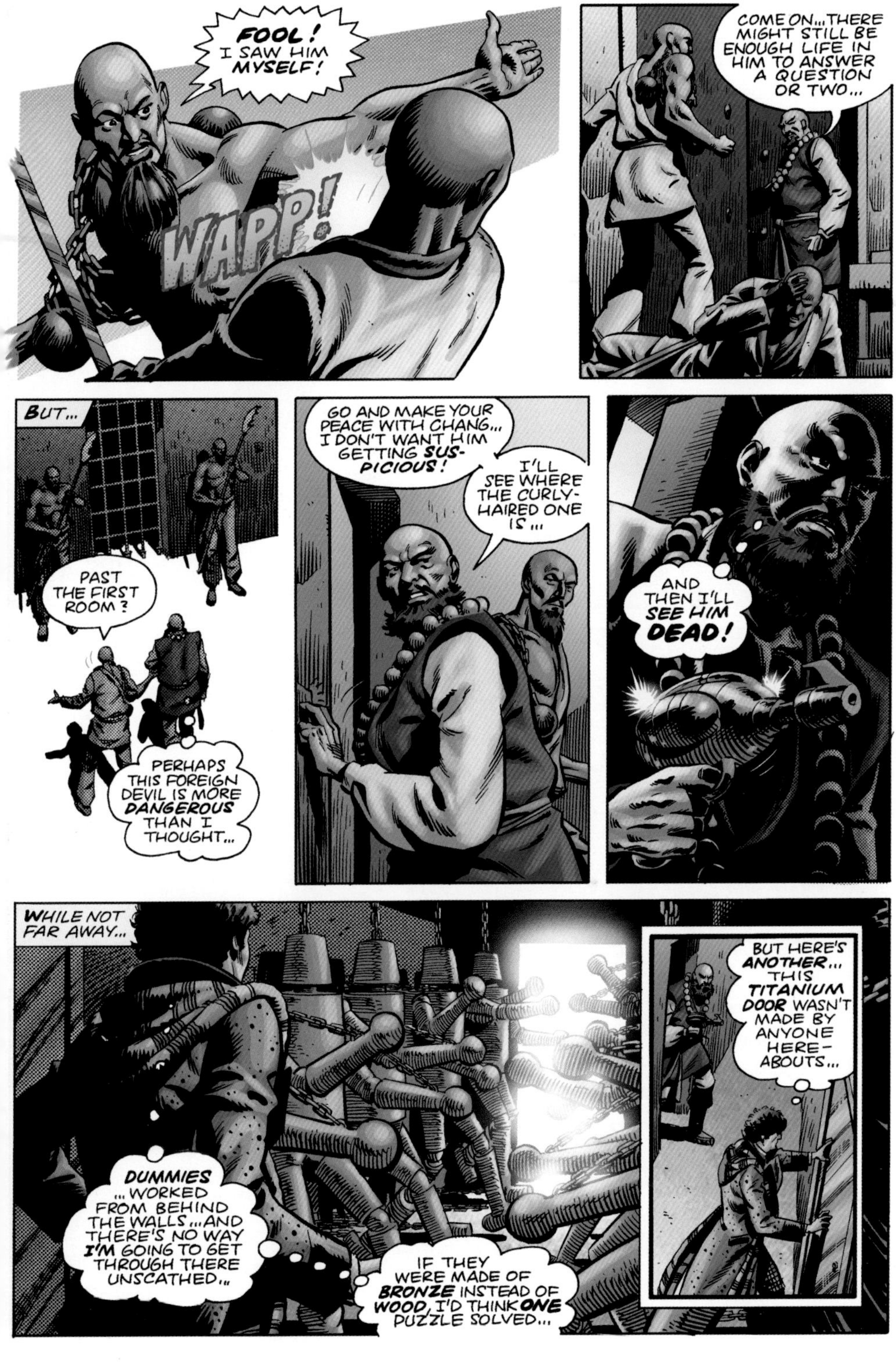
FOOL! I SAW HIM MYSELF!
WAPP!
COME ON... THERE MIGHT STILL BE ENOUGH LIFE IN HIM TO ANSWER A QUESTION OR TWO...
BUT...
PAST THE FIRST ROOM?
PERHAPS THIS FOREIGN DEVIL IS MORE DANGEROUS THAN I THOUGHT...
GO AND MAKE YOUR PEACE WITH CHANG... I DON'T WANT HIM GETTING SUSPICIOUS!
I'LL SEE WHERE THE CURLY-HAIRED ONE IS...
AND THEN I'LL SEE HIM DEAD!
WHILE NOT FAR AWAY...
DUMMIES ... WORKED FROM BEHIND THE WALLS... AND THERE'S NO WAY I'M GOING TO GET THROUGH THERE UNSCATHED...
IF THEY WERE MADE OF BRONZE INSTEAD OF WOOD, I'D THINK ONE PUZZLE SOLVED...
BUT HERE'S ANOTHER... THIS TITANIUM DOOR WASN'T MADE BY ANYONE HERE-ABOUTS...

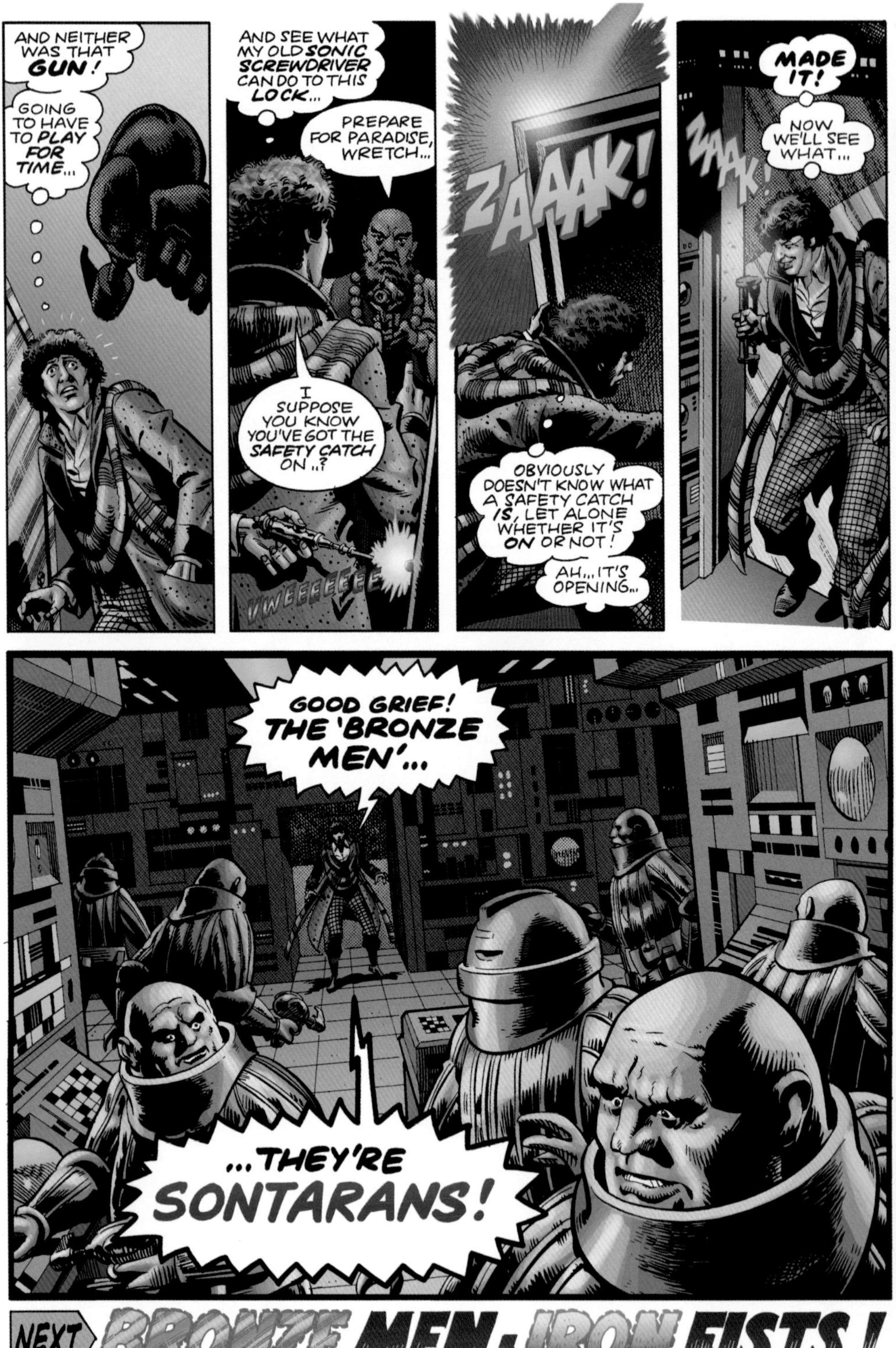
AND NEITHER WAS THAT GUN!
GOING TO HAVE TO PLAY FOR TIME...
AND SEE WHAT MY OLD SONIC SCREWDRIVER CAN DO TO THIS LOCK...
PREPARE FOR PARADISE, WRETCH...
I SUPPOSE YOU KNOW YOU'VE GOT THE SAFETY CATCH ON..?
VWEEEEEEE
ZAAAK!
OBVIOUSLY DOESN'T KNOW WHAT A SAFETY CATCH IS, LET ALONE WHETHER IT'S ON OR NOT!
AH... IT'S OPENING...
MADE IT!
NOW WE'LL SEE WHAT...
ZAAAK!
GOOD GRIEF! THE 'BRONZE MEN'...
...THEY'RE SONTARANS!
NEXT BRONZE MEN - IRON FISTS!

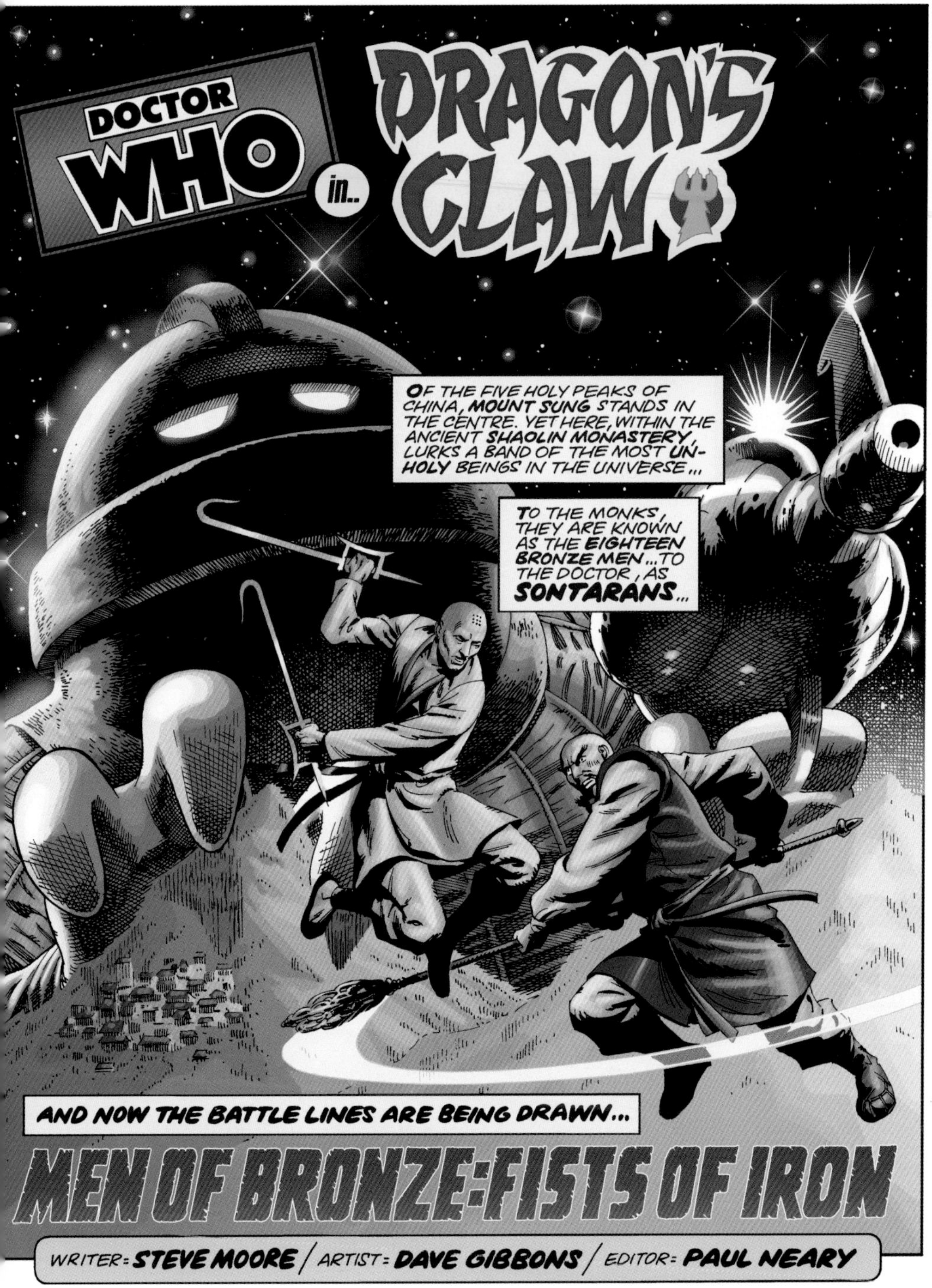
DOCTOR WHO in.. DRAGON'S CLAW
OF THE FIVE HOLY PEAKS OF CHINA, MOUNT SUNG STANDS IN THE CENTRE. YET HERE, WITHIN THE ANCIENT SHAOLIN MONASTERY, LURKS A BAND OF THE MOST UNHOLY BEINGS IN THE UNIVERSE...
TO THE MONKS, THEY ARE KNOWN AS THE EIGHTEEN BRONZE MEN...TO THE DOCTOR, AS SONTARANS...
AND NOW THE BATTLE LINES ARE BEING DRAWN...
MEN OF BRONZE: FISTS OF IRON
WRITER= STEVE MOORE / ARTIST= DAVE GIBBONS / EDITOR= PAUL NEARY

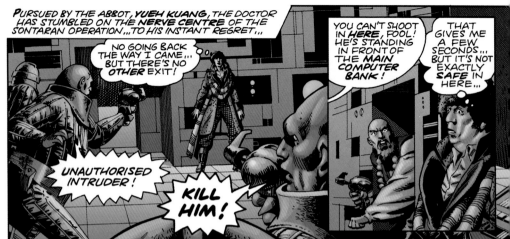

PURSUED BY THE ABBOT, *YUEH KUANG*, THE DOCTOR HAS STUMBLED ON THE *NERVE CENTRE* OF THE SONTARAN OPERATION... TO HIS INSTANT REGRET...

NO GOING BACK THE WAY I CAME... BUT THERE'S NO *OTHER* EXIT!

UNAUTHORISED INTRUDER!

KILL HIM!

YOU CAN'T SHOOT IN *HERE*, FOOL! HE'S STANDING IN FRONT OF THE *MAIN COMPUTER BANK!*

THAT GIVES ME A FEW SECONDS... BUT IT'S NOT EXACTLY *SAFE* IN HERE...

NOR, ALAS, OUTSIDE...

YOU MUST FORGIVE THE BLOW I STRUCK, BROTHER CHANG...

BUT THIS FOREIGN DEVIL *DOCTOR* IS SO GREAT A *THREAT*...

BUT ALL HE DID WAS CLIMB OVER THE WALL...

AND, TALKING OF 'WALLS'...

NOW YOU CAN SHOOT HIM ...THERE'S NO EQUIP-MENT...

SOMETIMES I THINK I SHOULD CHANGE MY NAME FROM *DOCTOR* TO *DONALD!*

ZZAKK!

ALL I EVER SEEM TO DO IS *DUCK!*

UUNNNHH!

BROTHER LI! WHA..?

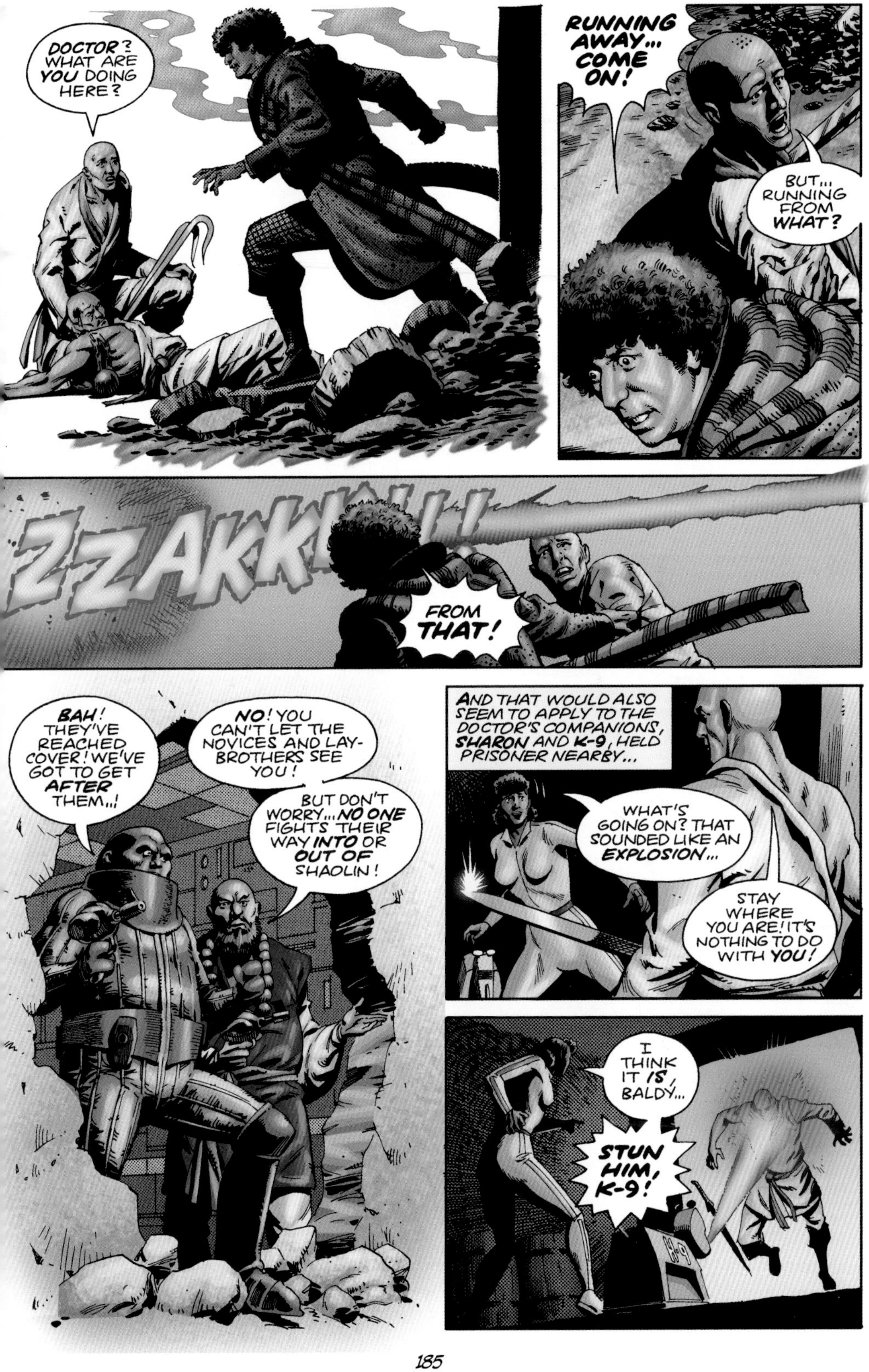
DOCTOR? WHAT ARE YOU DOING HERE?
RUNNING AWAY... COME ON!
BUT... RUNNING FROM WHAT?
ZZAKK!!!
FROM THAT!
BAH! THEY'VE REACHED COVER! WE'VE GOT TO GET AFTER THEM...!
NO! YOU CAN'T LET THE NOVICES AND LAY-BROTHERS SEE YOU!
BUT DON'T WORRY... NO ONE FIGHTS THEIR WAY INTO OR OUT OF SHAOLIN!
AND THAT WOULD ALSO SEEM TO APPLY TO THE DOCTOR'S COMPANIONS, SHARON AND K-9, HELD PRISONER NEARBY...
WHAT'S GOING ON? THAT SOUNDED LIKE AN EXPLOSION...
STAY WHERE YOU ARE! IT'S NOTHING TO DO WITH YOU!
I THINK IT IS, BALDY...
STUN HIM, K-9!

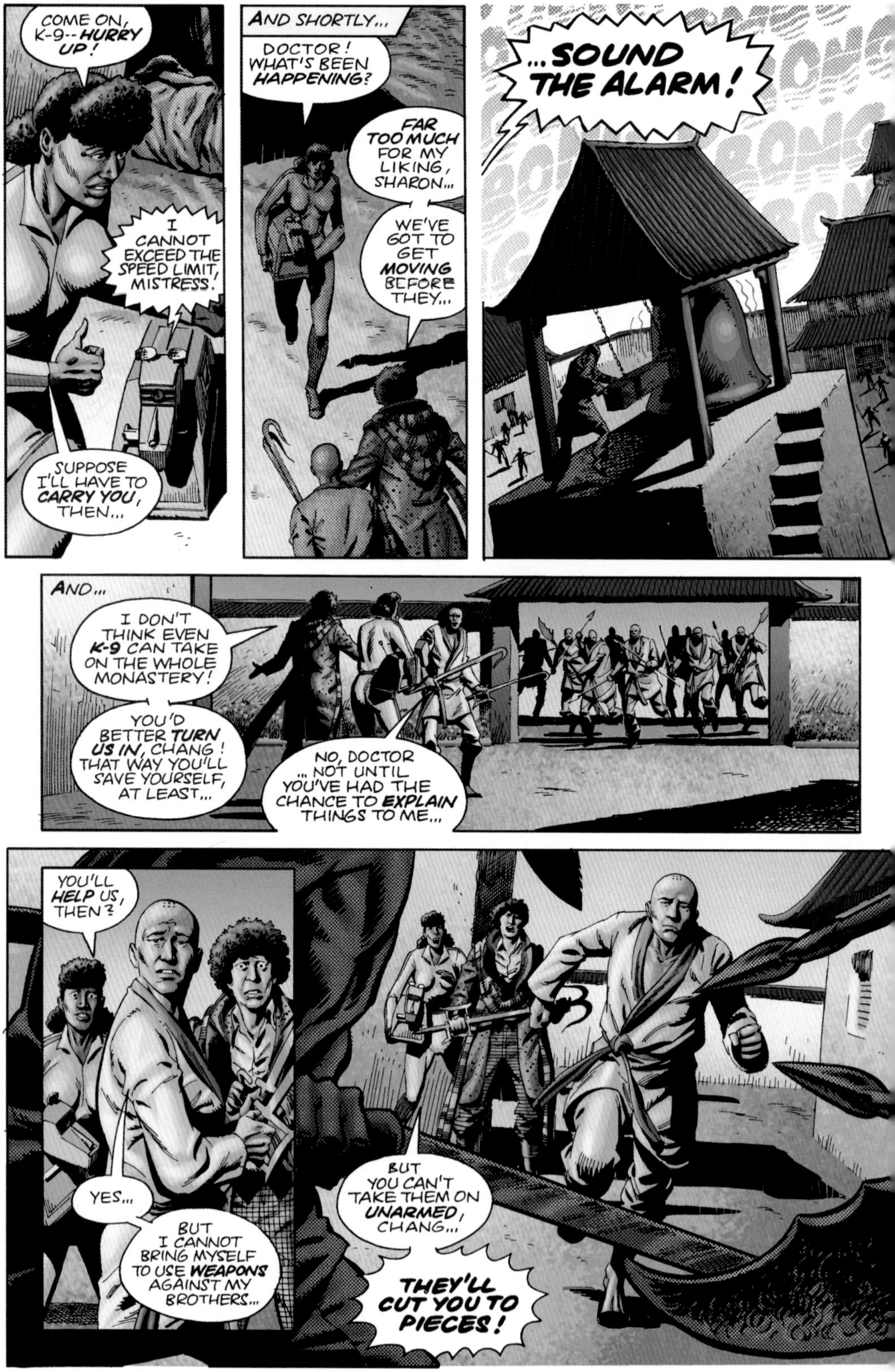
COME ON, K-9-- HURRY UP!
I CANNOT EXCEED THE SPEED LIMIT, MISTRESS!
SUPPOSE I'LL HAVE TO CARRY YOU, THEN...
AND SHORTLY...
DOCTOR! WHAT'S BEEN HAPPENING?
FAR TOO MUCH FOR MY LIKING, SHARON...
WE'VE GOT TO GET MOVING BEFORE THEY...
...SOUND THE ALARM!
AND...
I DON'T THINK EVEN K-9 CAN TAKE ON THE WHOLE MONASTERY!
YOU'D BETTER TURN US IN, CHANG! THAT WAY YOU'LL SAVE YOURSELF, AT LEAST...
NO, DOCTOR ... NOT UNTIL YOU'VE HAD THE CHANCE TO EXPLAIN THINGS TO ME...
YOU'LL HELP US, THEN?
YES...
BUT I CANNOT BRING MYSELF TO USE WEAPONS AGAINST MY BROTHERS...
BUT YOU CAN'T TAKE THEM ON UNARMED, CHANG...
THEY'LL CUT YOU TO PIECES!

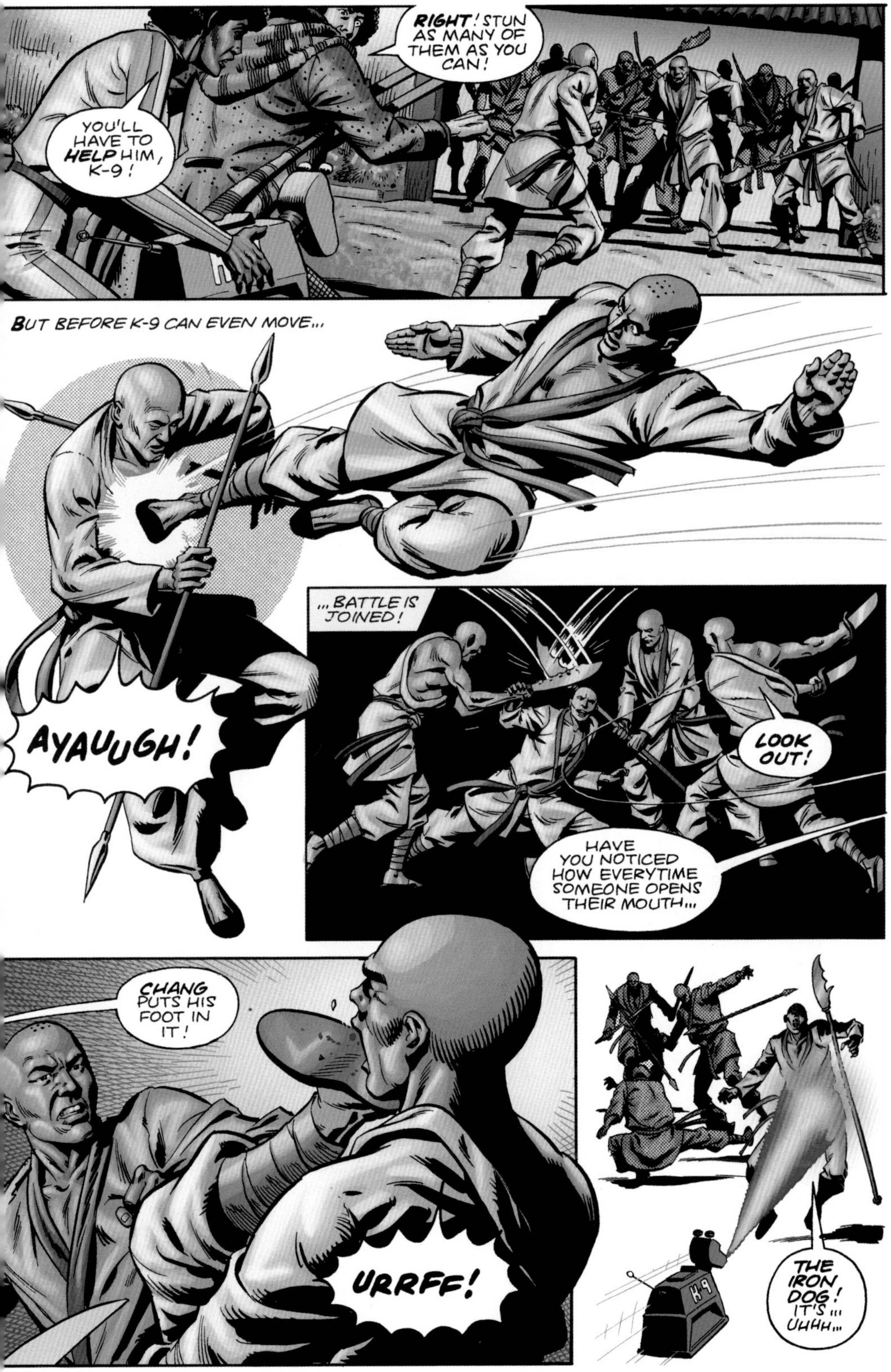
RIGHT! STUN AS MANY OF THEM AS YOU CAN!
YOU'LL HAVE TO HELP HIM, K-9!
BUT BEFORE K-9 CAN EVEN MOVE...
AYAUUGH!
...BATTLE IS JOINED!
LOOK OUT!
HAVE YOU NOTICED HOW EVERYTIME SOMEONE OPENS THEIR MOUTH...
CHANG PUTS HIS FOOT IN IT!
URRFF!
K-9
THE IRON DOG! IT'S... UHHH...

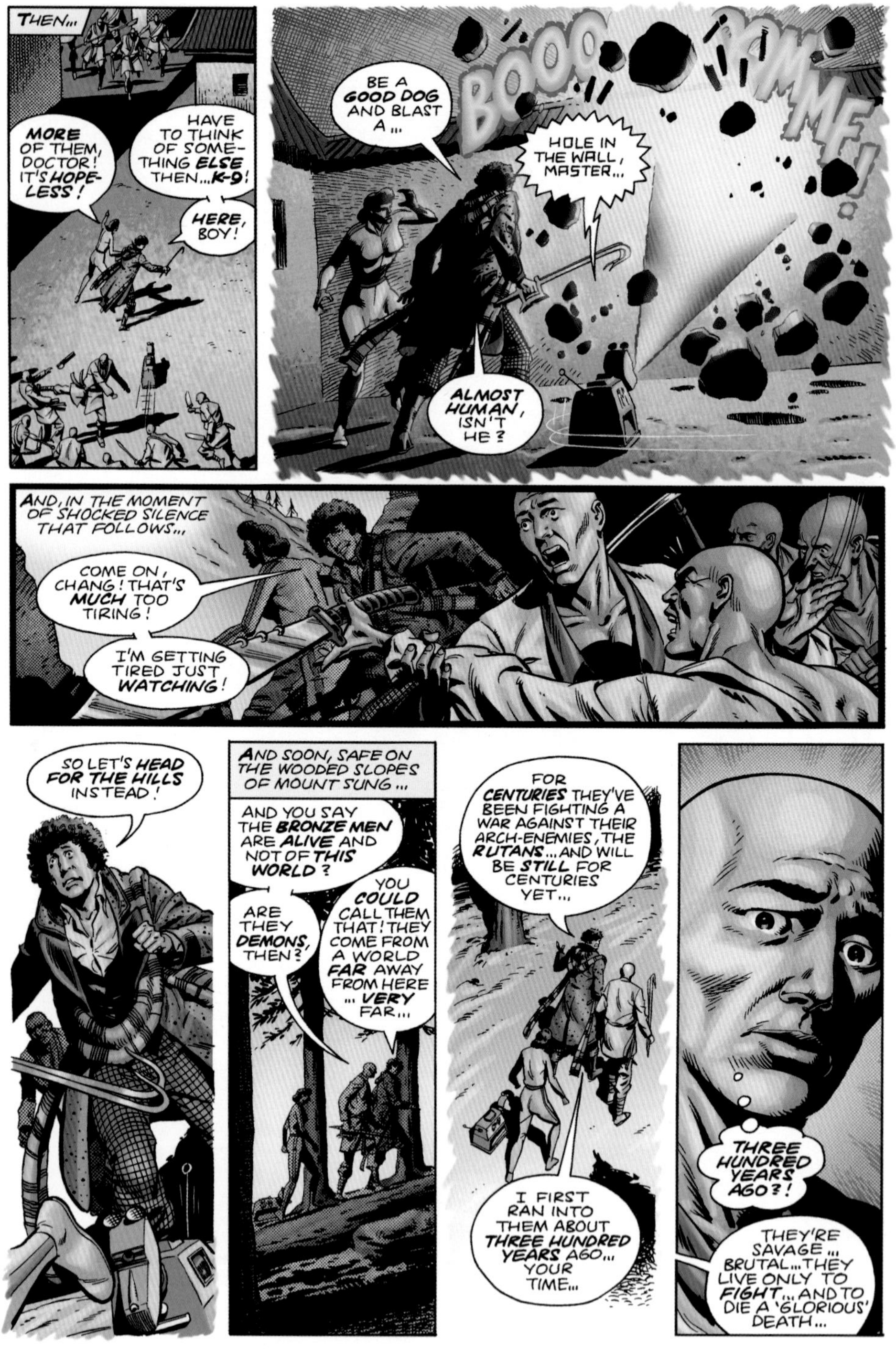
THEN...
MORE OF THEM, DOCTOR! IT'S HOPELESS!
HAVE TO THINK OF SOMETHING ELSE THEN... K-9!
HERE, BOY!
BE A GOOD DOG AND BLAST A...
HOLE IN THE WALL, MASTER...
BOOOOMMF!
ALMOST HUMAN, ISN'T HE?
AND, IN THE MOMENT OF SHOCKED SILENCE THAT FOLLOWS...
COME ON, CHANG! THAT'S MUCH TOO TIRING!
I'M GETTING TIRED JUST WATCHING!
SO LET'S HEAD FOR THE HILLS INSTEAD!
AND SOON, SAFE ON THE WOODED SLOPES OF MOUNT SUNG...
AND YOU SAY THE BRONZE MEN ARE ALIVE AND NOT OF THIS WORLD?
ARE THEY DEMONS, THEN?
YOU COULD CALL THEM THAT! THEY COME FROM A WORLD FAR AWAY FROM HERE ... VERY FAR...
FOR CENTURIES THEY'VE BEEN FIGHTING A WAR AGAINST THEIR ARCH-ENEMIES, THE RUTANS... AND WILL BE STILL FOR CENTURIES YET...
I FIRST RAN INTO THEM ABOUT THREE HUNDRED YEARS AGO... YOUR TIME...
THREE HUNDRED YEARS AGO?!
THEY'RE SAVAGE... BRUTAL... THEY LIVE ONLY TO FIGHT... AND TO DIE A 'GLORIOUS' DEATH...

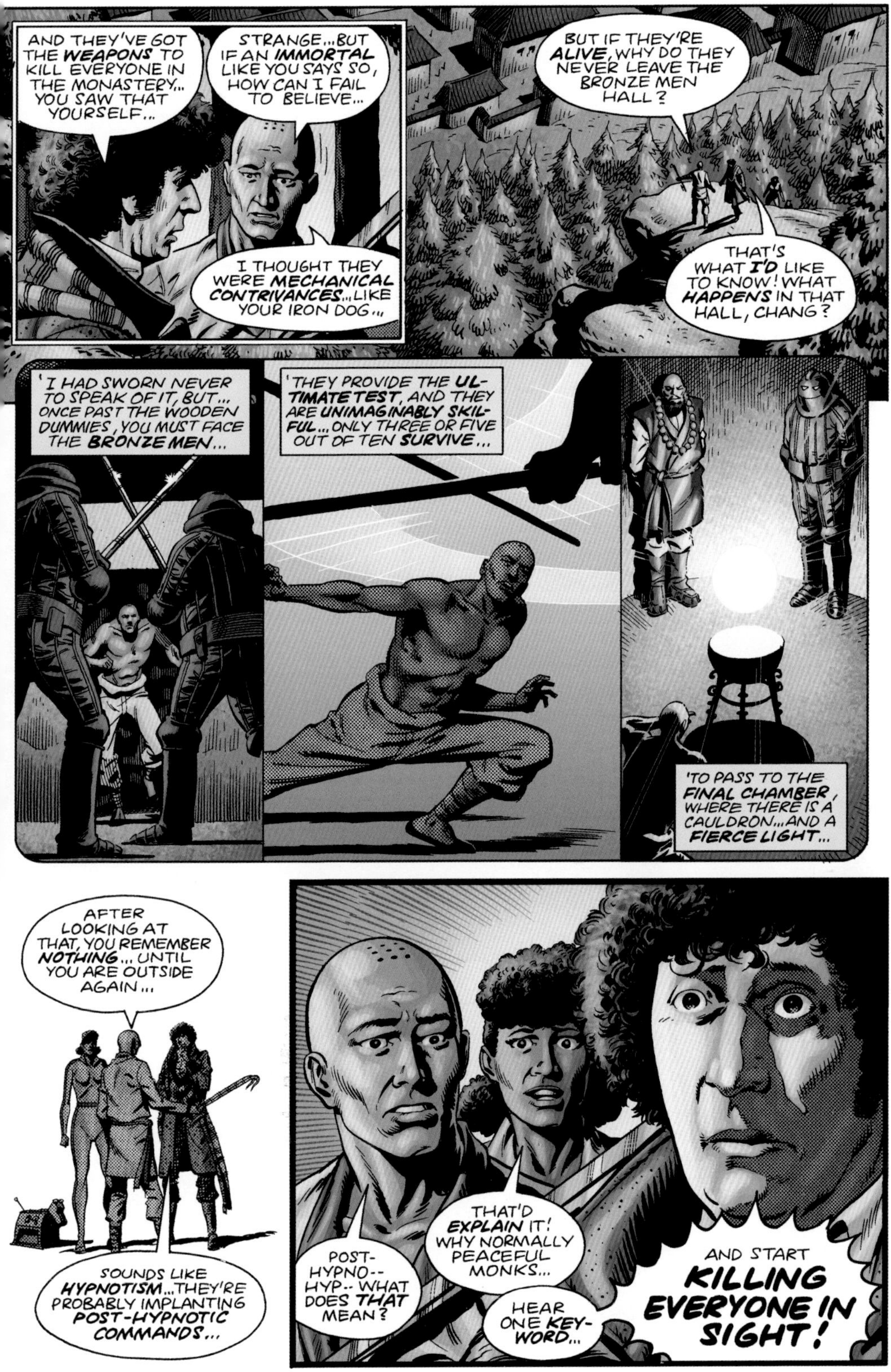
AND THEY'VE GOT THE WEAPONS TO KILL EVERYONE IN THE MONASTERY... YOU SAW THAT YOURSELF...
STRANGE...BUT IF AN IMMORTAL LIKE YOU SAYS SO, HOW CAN I FAIL TO BELIEVE...
I THOUGHT THEY WERE MECHANICAL CONTRIVANCES...LIKE YOUR IRON DOG...
BUT IF THEY'RE ALIVE, WHY DO THEY NEVER LEAVE THE BRONZE MEN HALL?
THAT'S WHAT I'D LIKE TO KNOW! WHAT HAPPENS IN THAT HALL, CHANG?
'I HAD SWORN NEVER TO SPEAK OF IT, BUT... ONCE PAST THE WOODEN DUMMIES, YOU MUST FACE THE BRONZE MEN...
'THEY PROVIDE THE ULTIMATE TEST, AND THEY ARE UNIMAGINABLY SKILFUL... ONLY THREE OR FIVE OUT OF TEN SURVIVE...
'TO PASS TO THE FINAL CHAMBER, WHERE THERE IS A CAULDRON...AND A FIERCE LIGHT...
AFTER LOOKING AT THAT, YOU REMEMBER NOTHING... UNTIL YOU ARE OUTSIDE AGAIN...
SOUNDS LIKE HYPNOTISM...THEY'RE PROBABLY IMPLANTING POST-HYPNOTIC COMMANDS...
POST-HYPNO--HYP-- WHAT DOES THAT MEAN?
THAT'D EXPLAIN IT! WHY NORMALLY PEACEFUL MONKS...
HEAR ONE KEY-WORD...
AND START KILLING EVERYONE IN SIGHT!

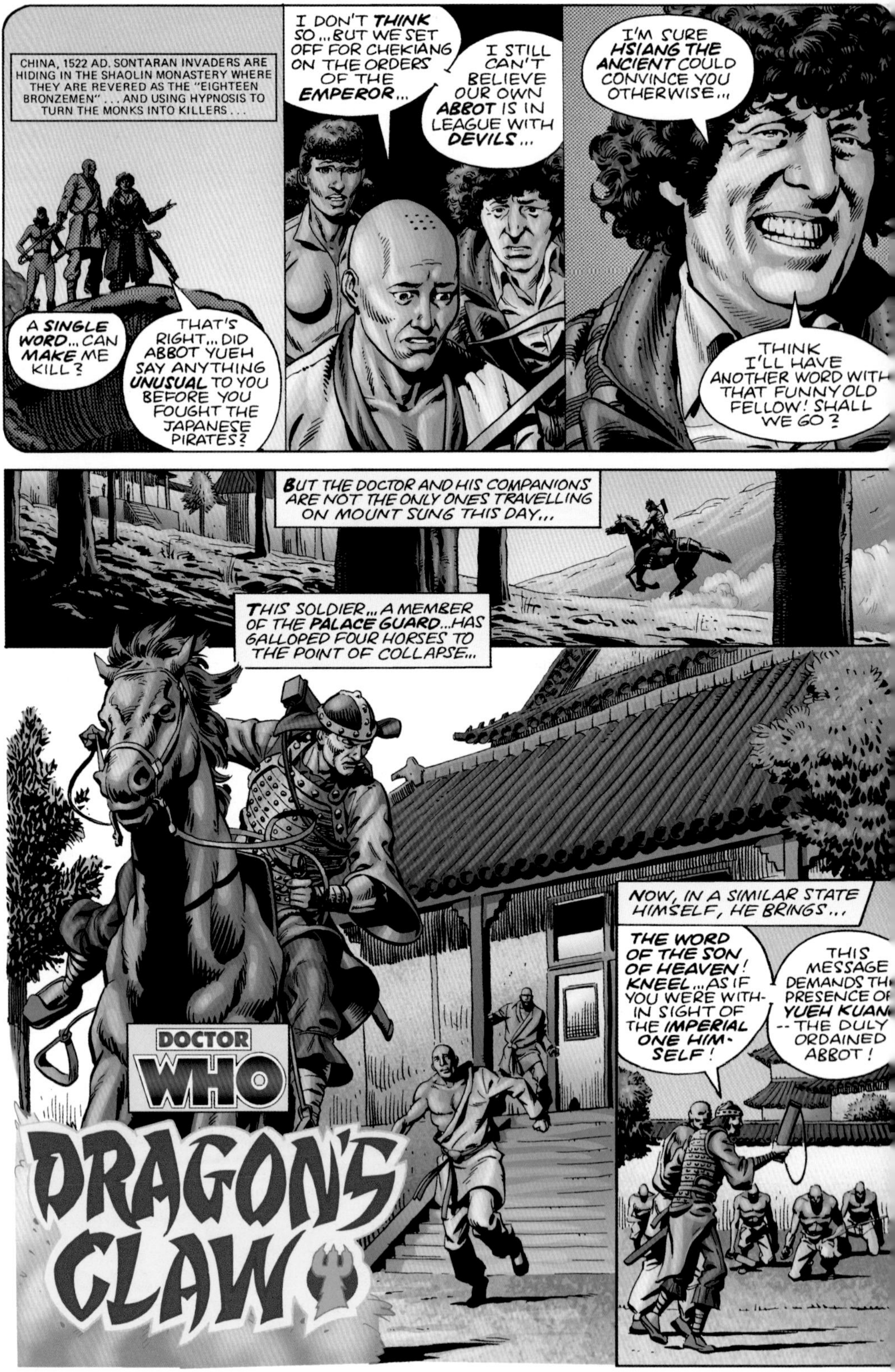

CHINA, 1522 AD. SONTARAN INVADERS ARE HIDING IN THE SHAOLIN MONASTERY WHERE THEY ARE REVERED AS THE "EIGHTEEN BRONZEMEN" . . . AND USING HYPNOSIS TO TURN THE MONKS INTO KILLERS . . .
A SINGLE WORD... CAN MAKE ME KILL?
THAT'S RIGHT... DID ABBOT YUEH SAY ANYTHING UNUSUAL TO YOU BEFORE YOU FOUGHT THE JAPANESE PIRATES?
I DON'T THINK SO... BUT WE SET OFF FOR CHEKIANG ON THE ORDERS OF THE EMPEROR...
I STILL CAN'T BELIEVE OUR OWN ABBOT IS IN LEAGUE WITH DEVILS...
I'M SURE HSIANG THE ANCIENT COULD CONVINCE YOU OTHERWISE...
THINK I'LL HAVE ANOTHER WORD WITH THAT FUNNY OLD FELLOW! SHALL WE GO?
BUT THE DOCTOR AND HIS COMPANIONS ARE NOT THE ONLY ONES TRAVELLING ON MOUNT SUNG THIS DAY...
THIS SOLDIER... A MEMBER OF THE PALACE GUARD... HAS GALLOPED FOUR HORSES TO THE POINT OF COLLAPSE...
DOCTOR WHO
DRAGON'S CLAW
NOW, IN A SIMILAR STATE HIMSELF, HE BRINGS...
THE WORD OF THE SON OF HEAVEN! KNEEL... AS IF YOU WERE WITH-IN SIGHT OF THE IMPERIAL ONE HIM-SELF!
THIS MESSAGE DEMANDS THE PRESENCE OF YUEH KUAN -- THE DULY ORDAINED ABBOT!

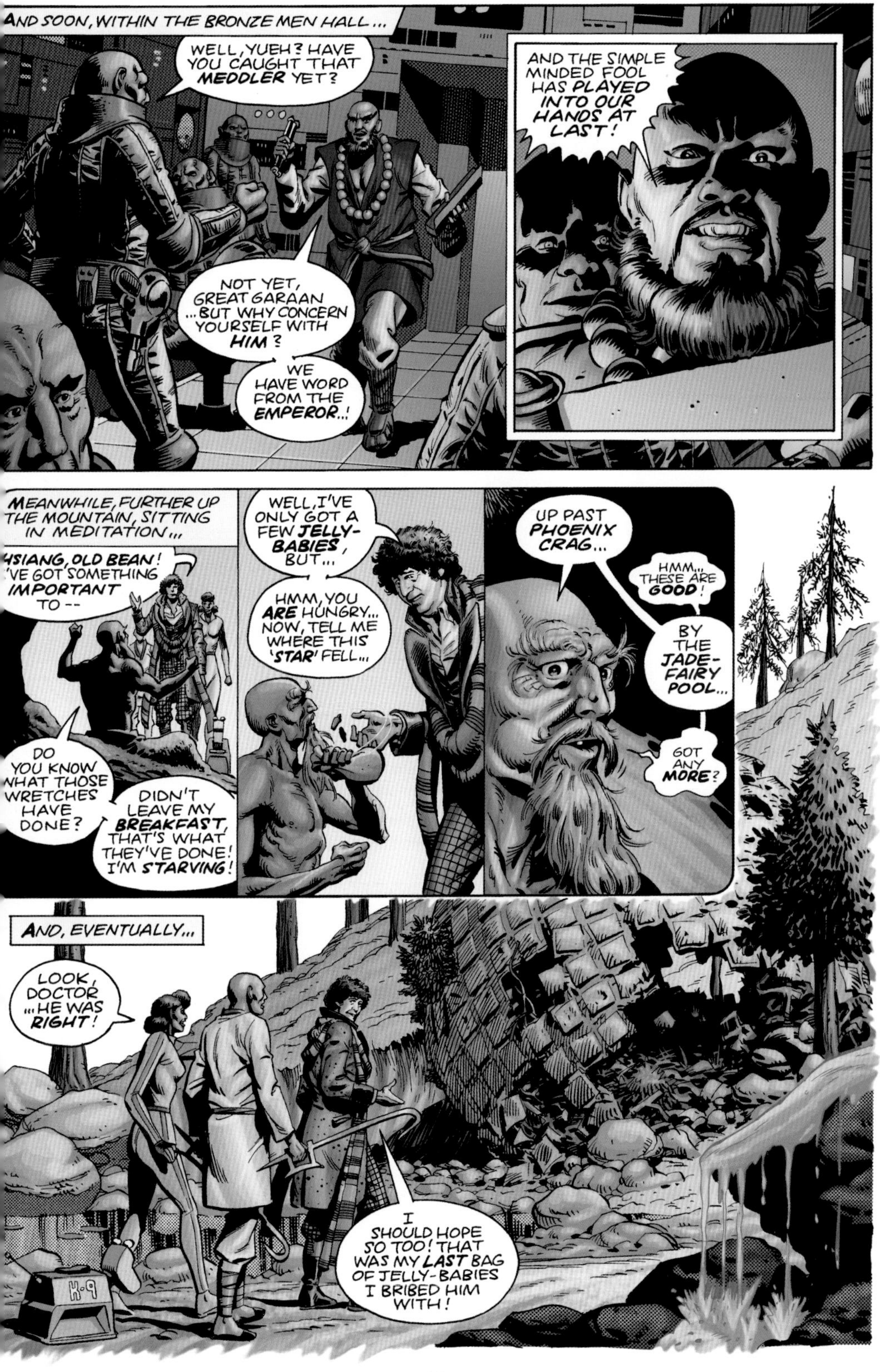
AND SOON, WITHIN THE BRONZE MEN HALL...
WELL, YUEH? HAVE YOU CAUGHT THAT MEDDLER YET?
NOT YET, GREAT GARAAN ...BUT WHY CONCERN YOURSELF WITH HIM?
WE HAVE WORD FROM THE EMPEROR..!
AND THE SIMPLE MINDED FOOL HAS PLAYED INTO OUR HANDS AT LAST!
MEANWHILE, FURTHER UP THE MOUNTAIN, SITTING IN MEDITATION...
HSIANG, OLD BEAN! I'VE GOT SOMETHING IMPORTANT TO --
DO YOU KNOW WHAT THOSE WRETCHES HAVE DONE?
DIDN'T LEAVE MY BREAKFAST, THAT'S WHAT THEY'VE DONE! I'M STARVING!
WELL, I'VE ONLY GOT A FEW JELLY-BABIES, BUT...
HMM, YOU ARE HUNGRY... NOW, TELL ME WHERE THIS 'STAR' FELL...
UP PAST PHOENIX CRAG...
HMM... THESE ARE GOOD!
BY THE JADE-FAIRY POOL...
GOT ANY MORE?
AND, EVENTUALLY...
LOOK, DOCTOR ...HE WAS RIGHT!
I SHOULD HOPE SO TOO! THAT WAS MY LAST BAG OF JELLY-BABIES I BRIBED HIM WITH!
K-9

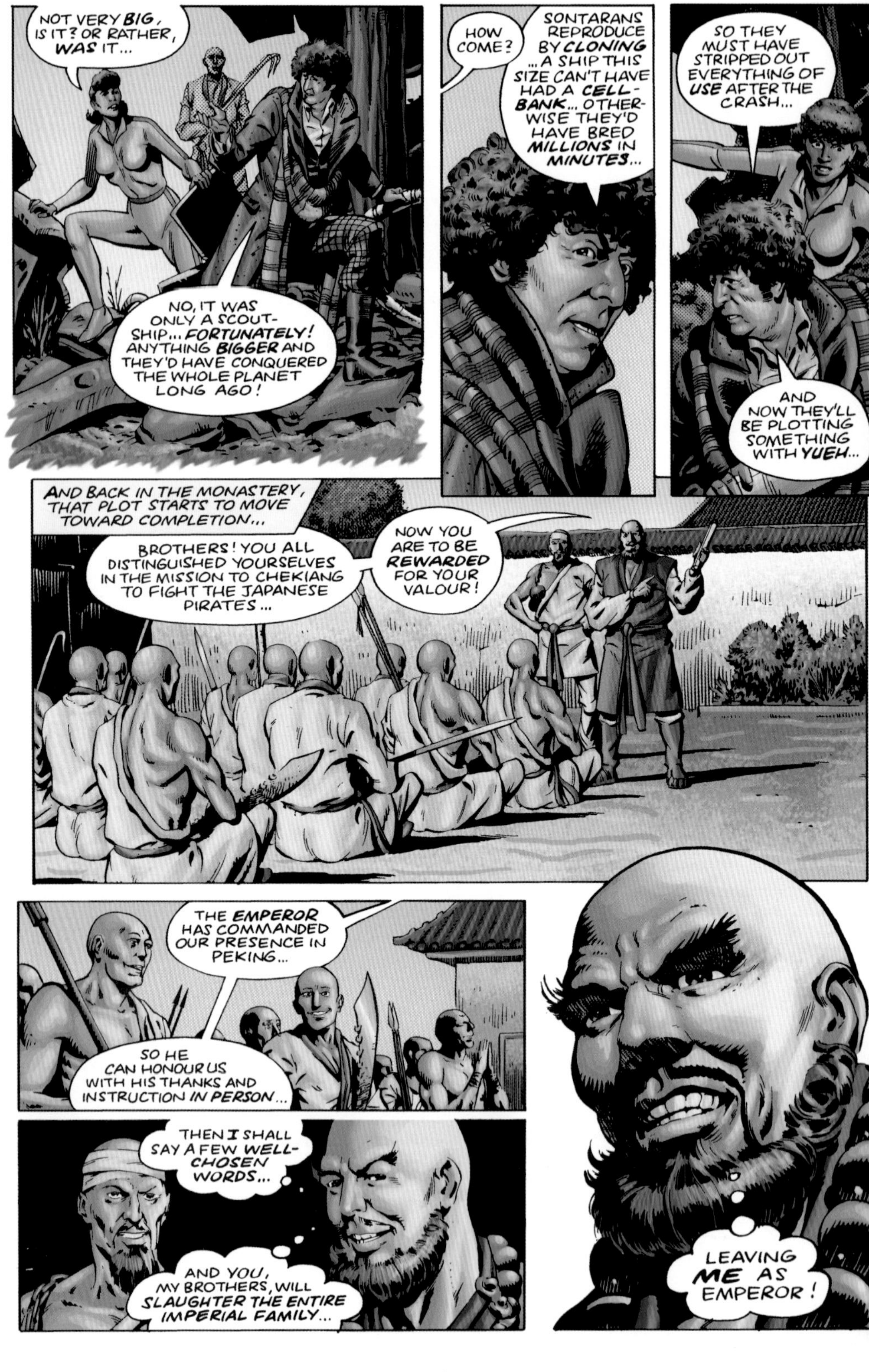

NOT VERY BIG, IS IT? OR RATHER, WAS IT...
NO, IT WAS ONLY A SCOUT-SHIP... FORTUNATELY! ANYTHING BIGGER AND THEY'D HAVE CONQUERED THE WHOLE PLANET LONG AGO!
HOW COME?
SONTARANS REPRODUCE BY CLONING ... A SHIP THIS SIZE CAN'T HAVE HAD A CELL-BANK... OTHERWISE THEY'D HAVE BRED MILLIONS IN MINUTES...
SO THEY MUST HAVE STRIPPED OUT EVERYTHING OF USE AFTER THE CRASH...
AND NOW THEY'LL BE PLOTTING SOMETHING WITH YUEH...
AND BACK IN THE MONASTERY, THAT PLOT STARTS TO MOVE TOWARD COMPLETION...
BROTHERS! YOU ALL DISTINGUISHED YOURSELVES IN THE MISSION TO CHEKIANG TO FIGHT THE JAPANESE PIRATES...
NOW YOU ARE TO BE REWARDED FOR YOUR VALOUR!
THE EMPEROR HAS COMMANDED OUR PRESENCE IN PEKING...
SO HE CAN HONOUR US WITH HIS THANKS AND INSTRUCTION IN PERSON...
THEN I SHALL SAY A FEW WELL-CHOSEN WORDS...
AND YOU, MY BROTHERS, WILL SLAUGHTER THE ENTIRE IMPERIAL FAMILY...
LEAVING ME AS EMPEROR!

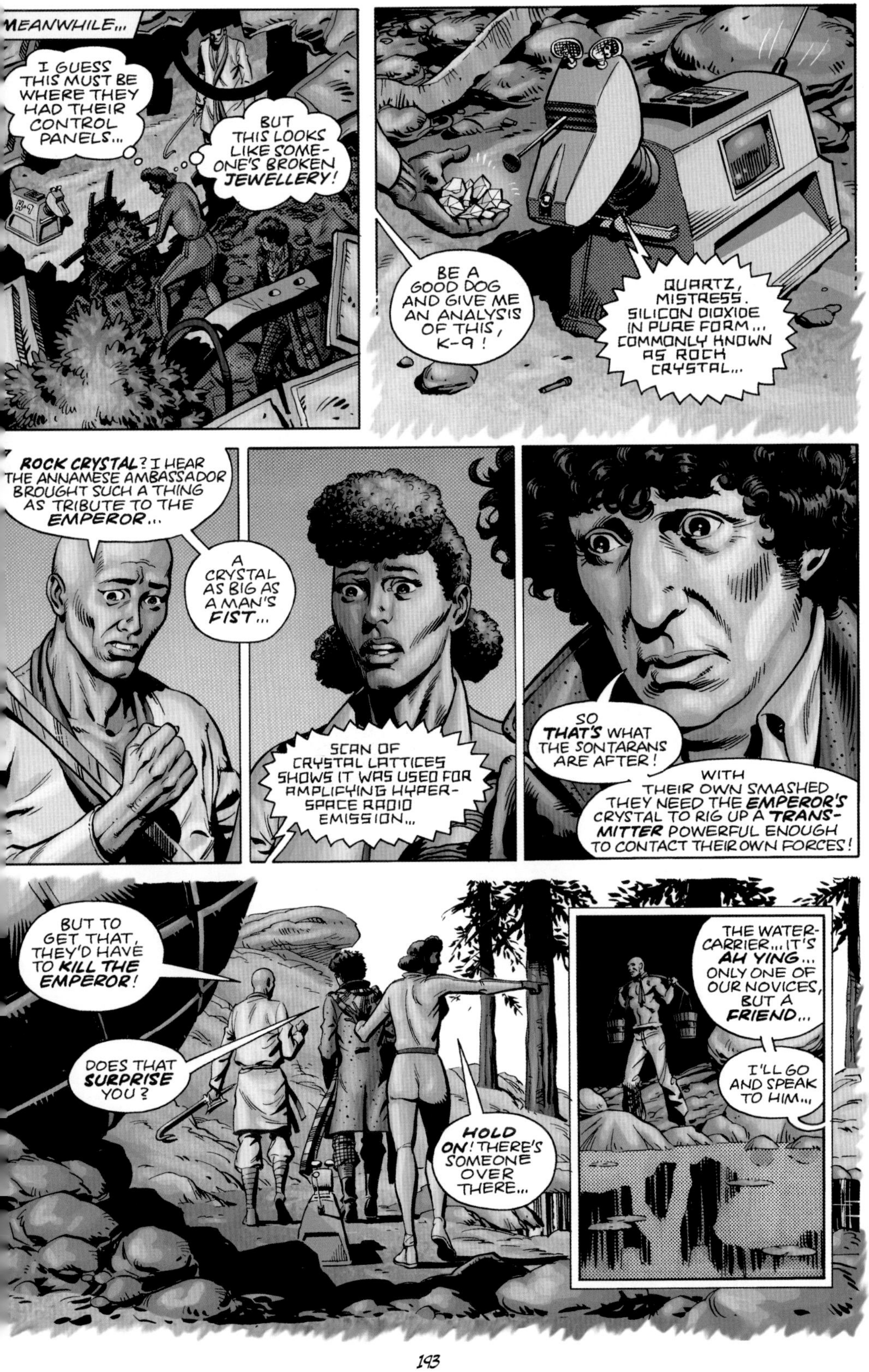
MEANWHILE...
I GUESS THIS MUST BE WHERE THEY HAD THEIR CONTROL PANELS...
BUT THIS LOOKS LIKE SOME-ONE'S BROKEN JEWELLERY!
BE A GOOD DOG AND GIVE ME AN ANALYSIS OF THIS, K-9!
QUARTZ, MISTRESS. SILICON DIOXIDE IN PURE FORM... COMMONLY KNOWN AS ROCK CRYSTAL...
ROCK CRYSTAL? I HEAR THE ANNAMESE AMBASSADOR BROUGHT SUCH A THING AS TRIBUTE TO THE EMPEROR...
A CRYSTAL AS BIG AS A MAN'S FIST...
SCAN OF CRYSTAL LATTICES SHOWS IT WAS USED FOR AMPLIFYING HYPER-SPACE RADIO EMISSION...
SO THAT'S WHAT THE SONTARANS ARE AFTER!
WITH THEIR OWN SMASHED THEY NEED THE EMPEROR'S CRYSTAL TO RIG UP A TRANS-MITTER POWERFUL ENOUGH TO CONTACT THEIR OWN FORCES!
BUT TO GET THAT, THEY'D HAVE TO KILL THE EMPEROR!
DOES THAT SURPRISE YOU?
HOLD ON! THERE'S SOMEONE OVER THERE...
THE WATER-CARRIER... IT'S AH YING... ONLY ONE OF OUR NOVICES, BUT A FRIEND...
I'LL GO AND SPEAK TO HIM...

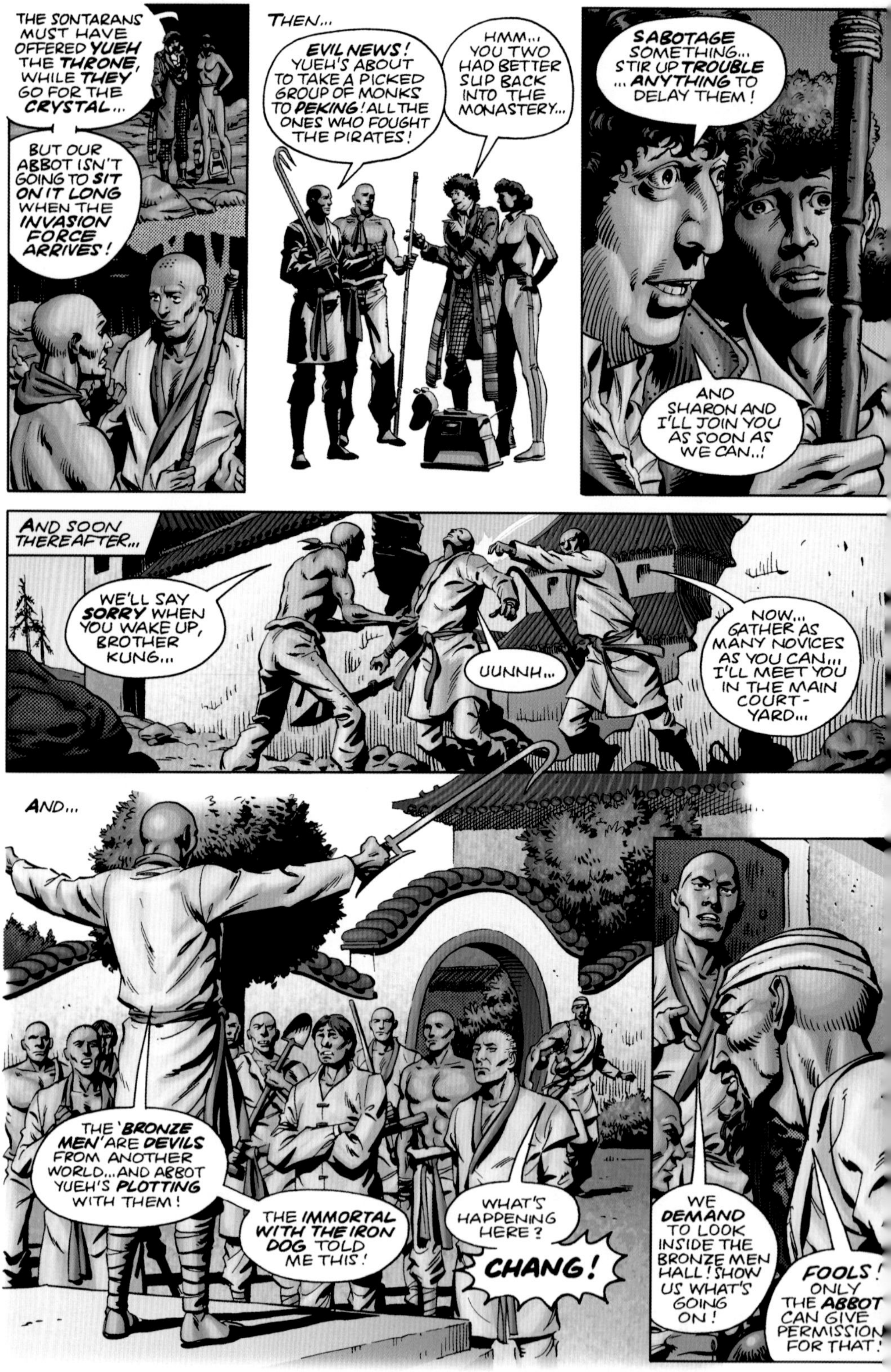
THE SONTARANS MUST HAVE OFFERED YUEH THE THRONE, WHILE THEY GO FOR THE CRYSTAL...
BUT OUR ABBOT ISN'T GOING TO SIT ON IT LONG WHEN THE INVASION FORCE ARRIVES!
THEN...
EVIL NEWS! YUEH'S ABOUT TO TAKE A PICKED GROUP OF MONKS TO PEKING! ALL THE ONES WHO FOUGHT THE PIRATES!
HMM... YOU TWO HAD BETTER SLIP BACK INTO THE MONASTERY...
SABOTAGE SOMETHING... STIR UP TROUBLE ...ANYTHING TO DELAY THEM!
AND SHARON AND I'LL JOIN YOU AS SOON AS WE CAN..!
AND SOON THEREAFTER...
WE'LL SAY SORRY WHEN YOU WAKE UP, BROTHER KUNG...
UUNNH...
NOW... GATHER AS MANY NOVICES AS YOU CAN... I'LL MEET YOU IN THE MAIN COURT-YARD...
AND...
THE 'BRONZE MEN' ARE DEVILS FROM ANOTHER WORLD... AND ABBOT YUEH'S PLOTTING WITH THEM!
THE IMMORTAL WITH THE IRON DOG TOLD ME THIS!
WHAT'S HAPPENING HERE?
CHANG!
WE DEMAND TO LOOK INSIDE THE BRONZE MEN HALL! SHOW US WHAT'S GOING ON!
FOOLS! ONLY THE ABBOT CAN GIVE PERMISSION FOR THAT!

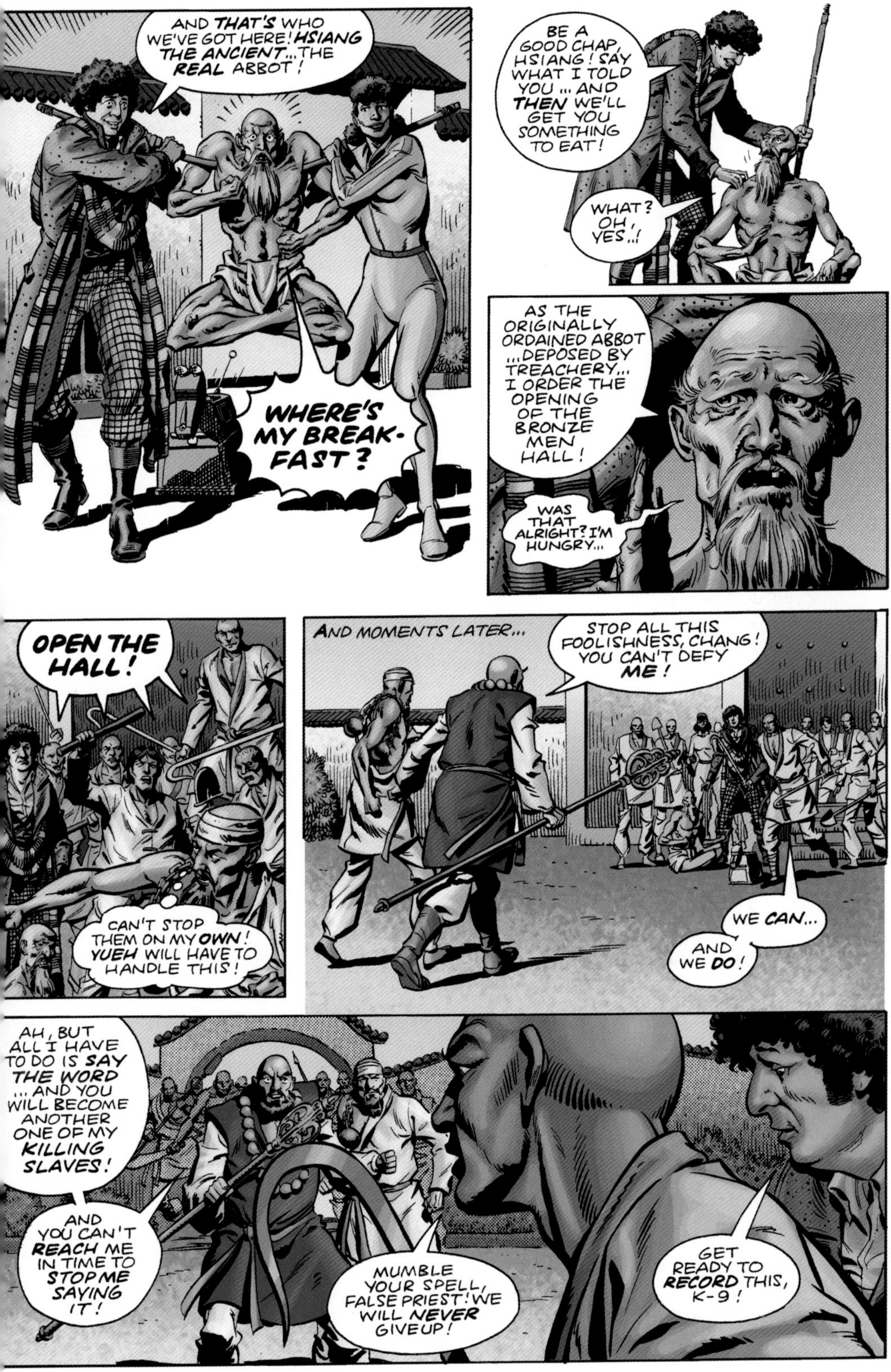

AND THAT'S WHO WE'VE GOT HERE! HSIANG THE ANCIENT... THE REAL ABBOT!
WHERE'S MY BREAK-FAST?
BE A GOOD CHAP, HSIANG! SAY WHAT I TOLD YOU ... AND THEN WE'LL GET YOU SOMETHING TO EAT!
WHAT? OH, YES...!
AS THE ORIGINALLY ORDAINED ABBOT ...DEPOSED BY TREACHERY... I ORDER THE OPENING OF THE BRONZE MEN HALL!
WAS THAT ALRIGHT? I'M HUNGRY...
OPEN THE HALL!
CAN'T STOP THEM ON MY OWN! YUEH WILL HAVE TO HANDLE THIS!
AND MOMENTS LATER...
STOP ALL THIS FOOLISHNESS, CHANG! YOU CAN'T DEFY ME!
WE CAN...
AND WE DO!
AH, BUT ALL I HAVE TO DO IS SAY THE WORD ... AND YOU WILL BECOME ANOTHER ONE OF MY KILLING SLAVES!
AND YOU CAN'T REACH ME IN TIME TO STOP ME SAYING IT!
MUMBLE YOUR SPELL, FALSE PRIEST! WE WILL NEVER GIVE UP!
GET READY TO RECORD THIS, K-9!

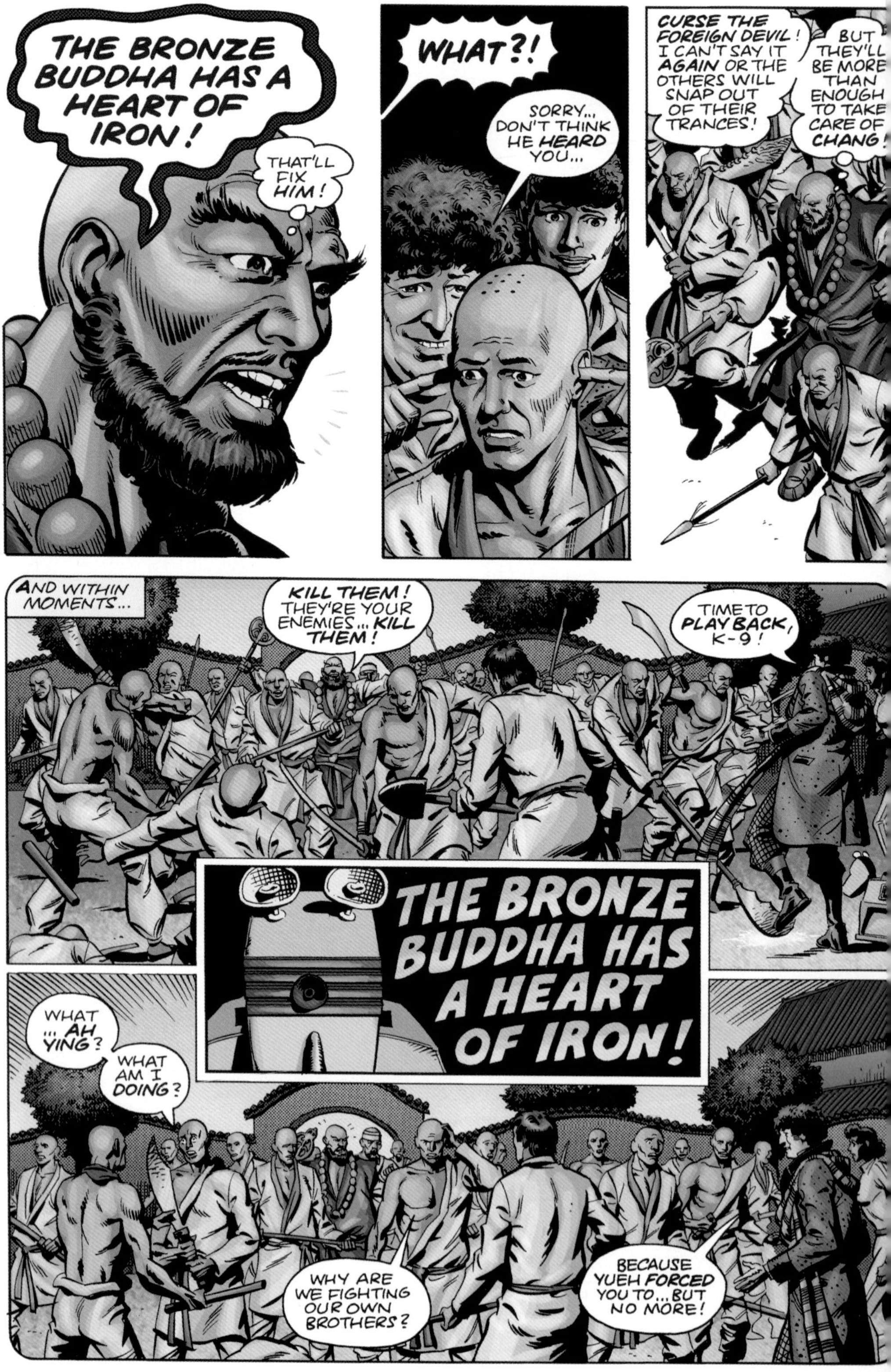
THE BRONZE BUDDHA HAS A HEART OF IRON!
THAT'LL FIX HIM!
WHAT?!
SORRY... DON'T THINK HE HEARD YOU...
CURSE THE FOREIGN DEVIL! I CAN'T SAY IT AGAIN OR THE OTHERS WILL SNAP OUT OF THEIR TRANCES!
BUT THEY'LL BE MORE THAN ENOUGH TO TAKE CARE OF CHANG!
AND WITHIN MOMENTS...
KILL THEM! THEY'RE YOUR ENEMIES... KILL THEM!
TIME TO PLAY BACK, K-9!
THE BRONZE BUDDHA HAS A HEART OF IRON!
WHAT ...AH YING?
WHAT AM I DOING?
WHY ARE WE FIGHTING OUR OWN BROTHERS?
BECAUSE YUEH FORCED YOU TO... BUT NO MORE!

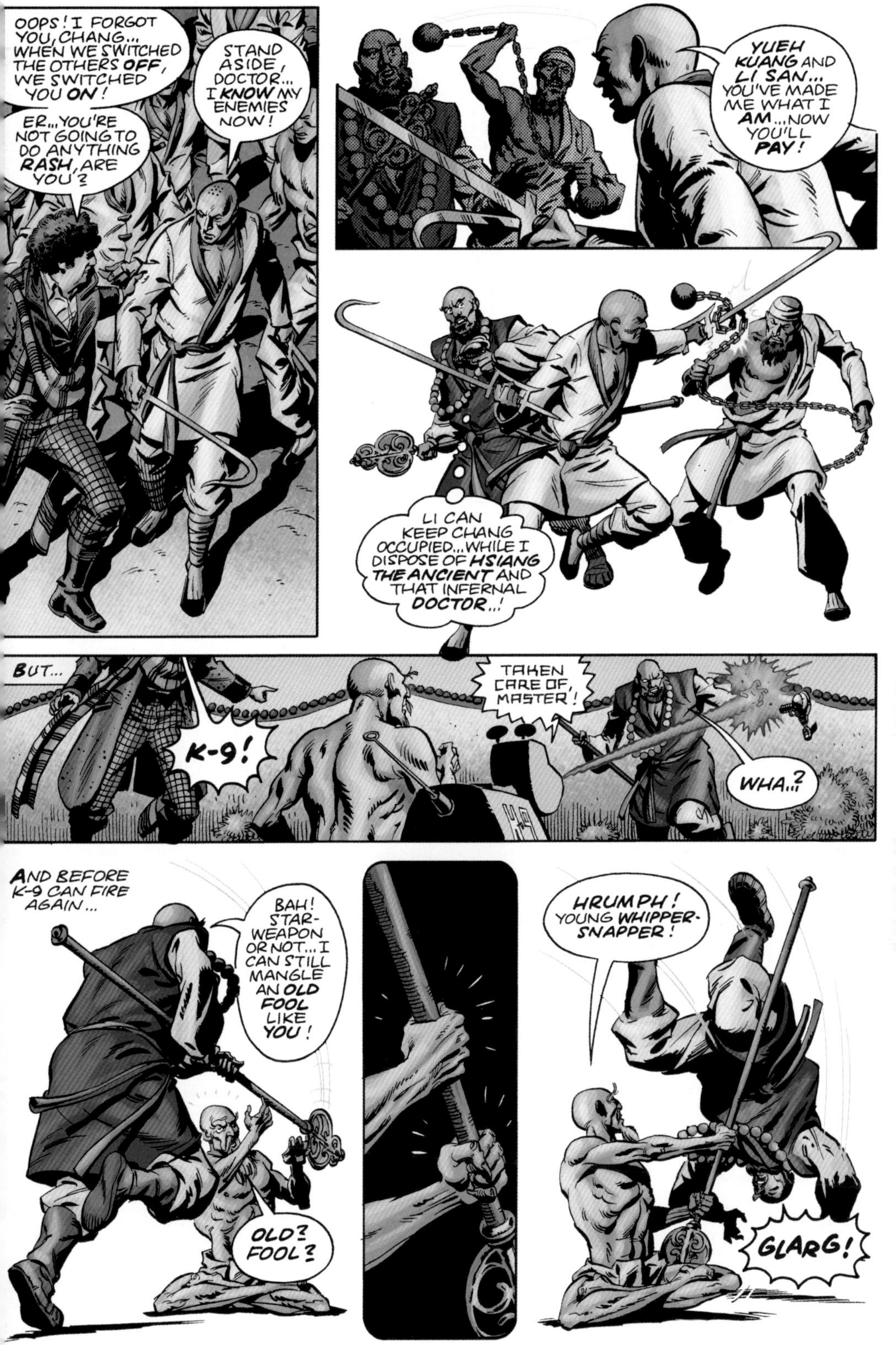
OOPS! I FORGOT YOU, CHANG... WHEN WE SWITCHED THE OTHERS OFF, WE SWITCHED YOU ON!
ER... YOU'RE NOT GOING TO DO ANYTHING RASH, ARE YOU?
STAND ASIDE, DOCTOR... I KNOW MY ENEMIES NOW!
YUEH KUANG AND LI SAN... YOU'VE MADE ME WHAT I AM... NOW YOU'LL PAY!
LI CAN KEEP CHANG OCCUPIED... WHILE I DISPOSE OF HSIANG THE ANCIENT AND THAT INFERNAL DOCTOR...!
BUT...
K-9!
TAKEN CARE OF, MASTER!
WHA..?
AND BEFORE K-9 CAN FIRE AGAIN...
BAH! STAR-WEAPON OR NOT... I CAN STILL MANGLE AN OLD FOOL LIKE YOU!
OLD? FOOL?
HRUMPH! YOUNG WHIPPER-SNAPPER!
GLARG!

DOCTOR! HERE COMES CHANG!

ARE YOU ALRIGHT, CHANG? WHAT ABOUT LI?

LI FOUGHT WELL...

I'LL HAVE TO GET HIM AWAY WHERE NO ONE ELSE CAN HEAR AND PLAY BACK K-9'S TAPE...OTHERWISE HE'LL CREATE HAVOC!

BUT THERE'S NO TIME FOR THAT NOW! WE'VE GOT TO GET INTO THE BRONZE MEN HALL!

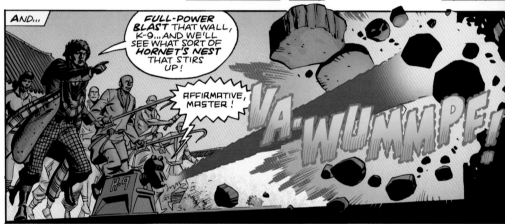

AND...

FULL-POWER BLAST THAT WALL, K-9...AND WE'LL SEE WHAT SORT OF HORNET'S NEST THAT STIRS UP!

AFFIRMATIVE, MASTER!

WA-WUMMPF!

NOW, AS SOON AS ANY SONTARANS APPEAR, I WANT YOU TO STOP THEM, K-9...

MASTER...!

ZZZAKK!

YAUUGH!

NO NEED FOR YOUR IRON DOG, DOCTOR...

THEY WILL NOT BE COMING OUT!

NO, CHANG! YOU CAN'T...!

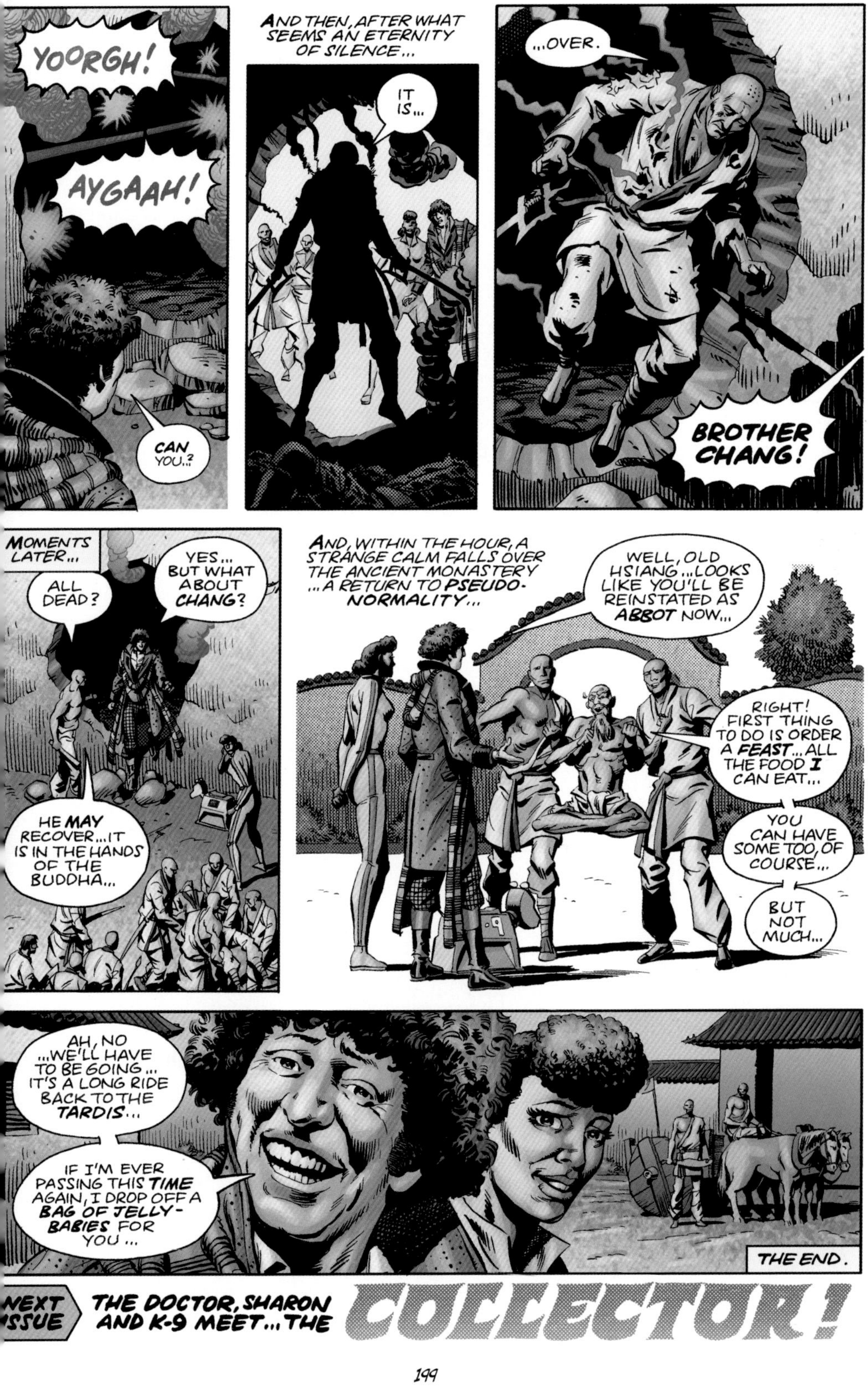

YOORGH!
AYGAAH!
CAN YOU..?
AND THEN, AFTER WHAT SEEMS AN ETERNITY OF SILENCE...
IT IS...
...OVER.
BROTHER CHANG!
MOMENTS LATER...
ALL DEAD?
YES... BUT WHAT ABOUT CHANG?
HE MAY RECOVER...IT IS IN THE HANDS OF THE BUDDHA...
AND, WITHIN THE HOUR, A STRANGE CALM FALLS OVER THE ANCIENT MONASTERY ...A RETURN TO PSEUDO-NORMALITY...
WELL, OLD HSIANG...LOOKS LIKE YOU'LL BE REINSTATED AS ABBOT NOW...
RIGHT! FIRST THING TO DO IS ORDER A FEAST...ALL THE FOOD I CAN EAT...
YOU CAN HAVE SOME TOO, OF COURSE...
BUT NOT MUCH...
AH, NO ...WE'LL HAVE TO BE GOING... IT'S A LONG RIDE BACK TO THE TARDIS...
IF I'M EVER PASSING THIS TIME AGAIN, I DROP OFF A BAG OF JELLY-BABIES FOR YOU...
THE END.
NEXT ISSUE
THE DOCTOR, SHARON AND K-9 MEET... THE COLLECTOR!

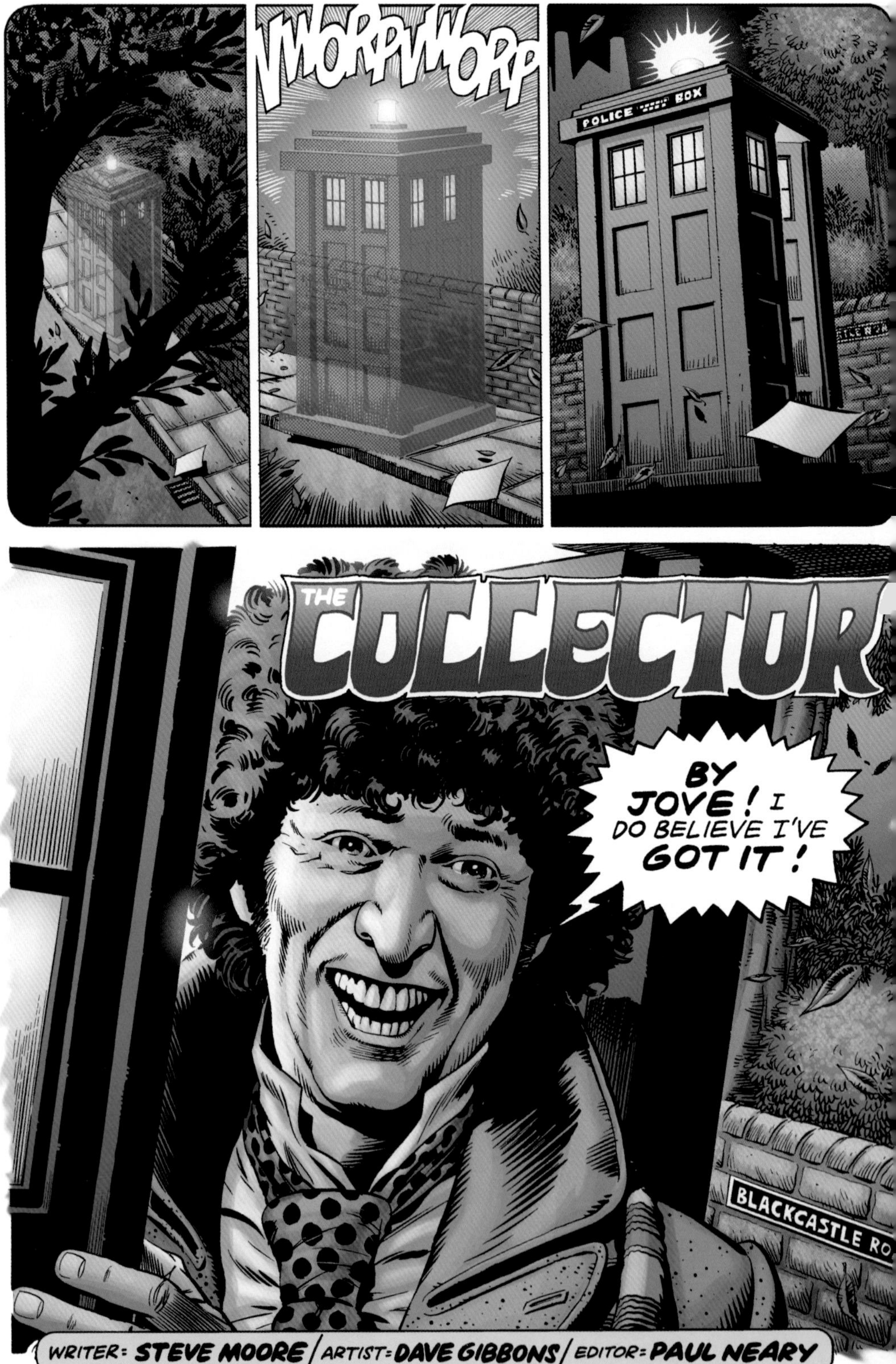
VWORP VWORP
POLICE
BOX
THE COLLECTOR
BY JOVE! I DO BELIEVE I'VE GOT IT!
BLACKCASTLE RO
WRITER: STEVE MOORE / ARTIST: DAVE GIBBONS / EDITOR: PAUL NEARY

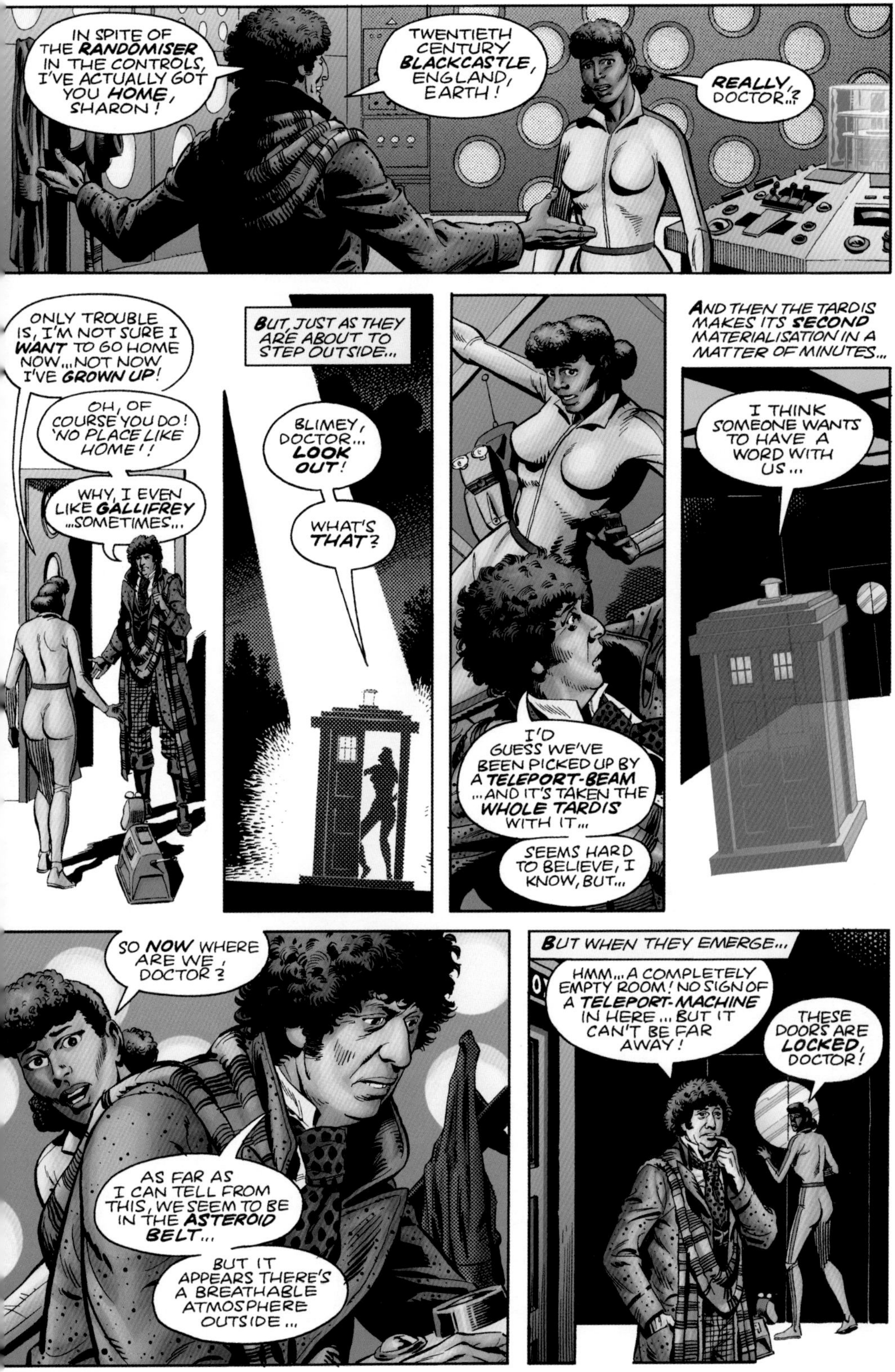
IN SPITE OF THE RANDOMISER IN THE CONTROLS, I'VE ACTUALLY GOT YOU HOME, SHARON!
TWENTIETH CENTURY BLACKCASTLE, ENGLAND, EARTH!
REALLY, DOCTOR..?
ONLY TROUBLE IS, I'M NOT SURE I WANT TO GO HOME NOW... NOT NOW I'VE GROWN UP!
OH, OF COURSE YOU DO! 'NO PLACE LIKE HOME'!
WHY, I EVEN LIKE GALLIFREY ...SOMETIMES...
BUT, JUST AS THEY ARE ABOUT TO STEP OUTSIDE...
BLIMEY, DOCTOR... LOOK OUT!
WHAT'S THAT?
I'D GUESS WE'VE BEEN PICKED UP BY A TELEPORT-BEAM ...AND IT'S TAKEN THE WHOLE TARDIS WITH IT...
SEEMS HARD TO BELIEVE, I KNOW, BUT...
AND THEN THE TARDIS MAKES ITS SECOND MATERIALISATION IN A MATTER OF MINUTES...
I THINK SOMEONE WANTS TO HAVE A WORD WITH US...
SO NOW WHERE ARE WE, DOCTOR?
AS FAR AS I CAN TELL FROM THIS, WE SEEM TO BE IN THE ASTEROID BELT...
BUT IT APPEARS THERE'S A BREATHABLE ATMOSPHERE OUTSIDE...
BUT WHEN THEY EMERGE...
HMM... A COMPLETELY EMPTY ROOM! NO SIGN OF A TELEPORT-MACHINE IN HERE... BUT IT CAN'T BE FAR AWAY!
THESE DOORS ARE LOCKED, DOCTOR!

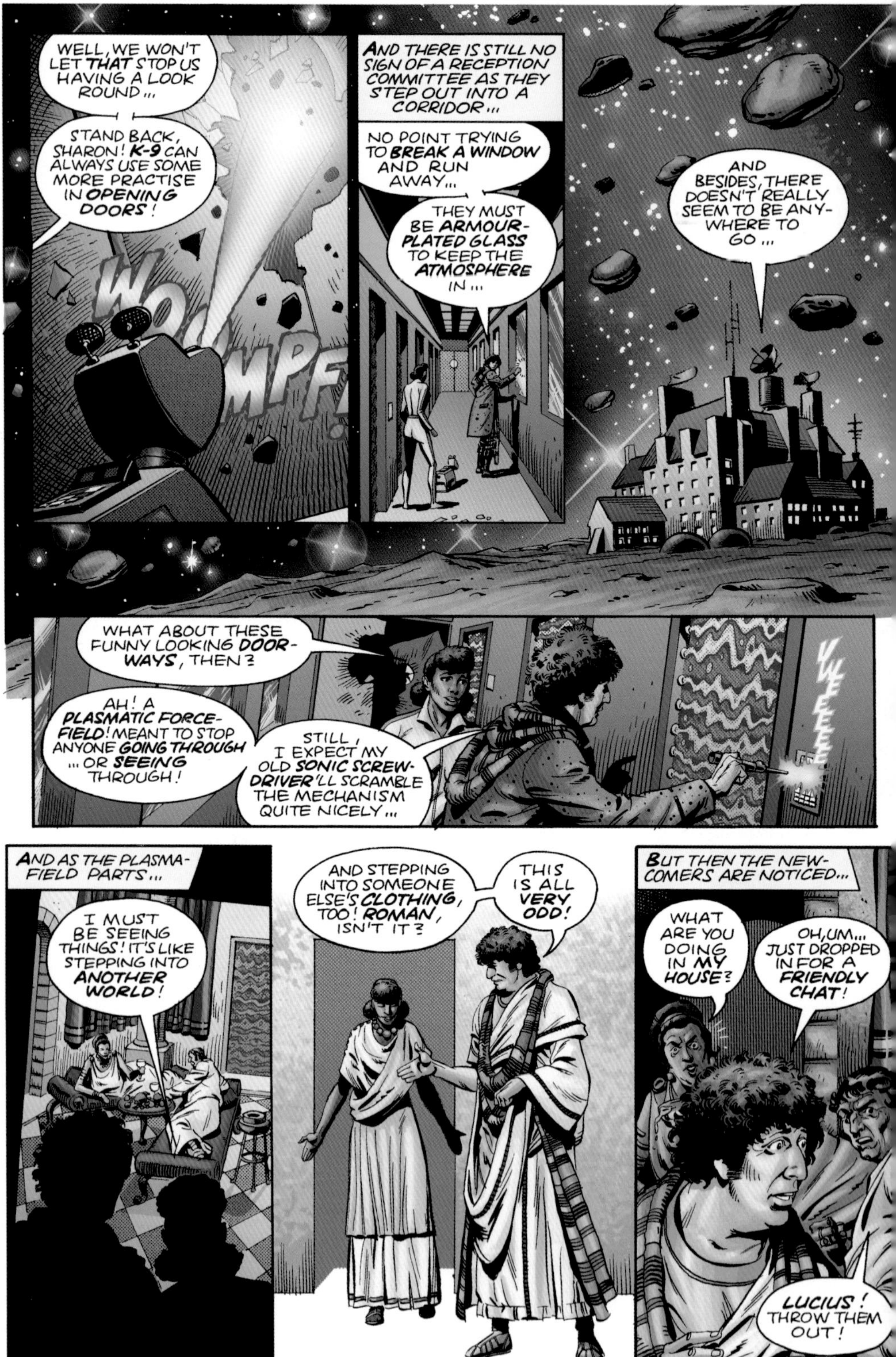

WELL, WE WON'T LET THAT STOP US HAVING A LOOK ROUND...
STAND BACK, SHARON! K-9 CAN ALWAYS USE SOME MORE PRACTISE IN OPENING DOORS!
WOOMPF!
AND THERE IS STILL NO SIGN OF A RECEPTION COMMITTEE AS THEY STEP OUT INTO A CORRIDOR...
NO POINT TRYING TO BREAK A WINDOW AND RUN AWAY...
THEY MUST BE ARMOUR-PLATED GLASS TO KEEP THE ATMOSPHERE IN...
AND BESIDES, THERE DOESN'T REALLY SEEM TO BE ANYWHERE TO GO...
WHAT ABOUT THESE FUNNY LOOKING DOORWAYS, THEN?
AH! A PLASMATIC FORCE-FIELD! MEANT TO STOP ANYONE GOING THROUGH ...OR SEEING THROUGH!
STILL, I EXPECT MY OLD SONIC SCREWDRIVER'LL SCRAMBLE THE MECHANISM QUITE NICELY...
VWEEEEE
AND AS THE PLASMA-FIELD PARTS...
I MUST BE SEEING THINGS! IT'S LIKE STEPPING INTO ANOTHER WORLD!
AND STEPPING INTO SOMEONE ELSE'S CLOTHING, TOO! ROMAN, ISN'T IT?
THIS IS ALL VERY ODD!
BUT THEN THE NEWCOMERS ARE NOTICED...
WHAT ARE YOU DOING IN MY HOUSE?
OH, UM... JUST DROPPED IN FOR A FRIENDLY CHAT!
LUCIUS! THROW THEM OUT!

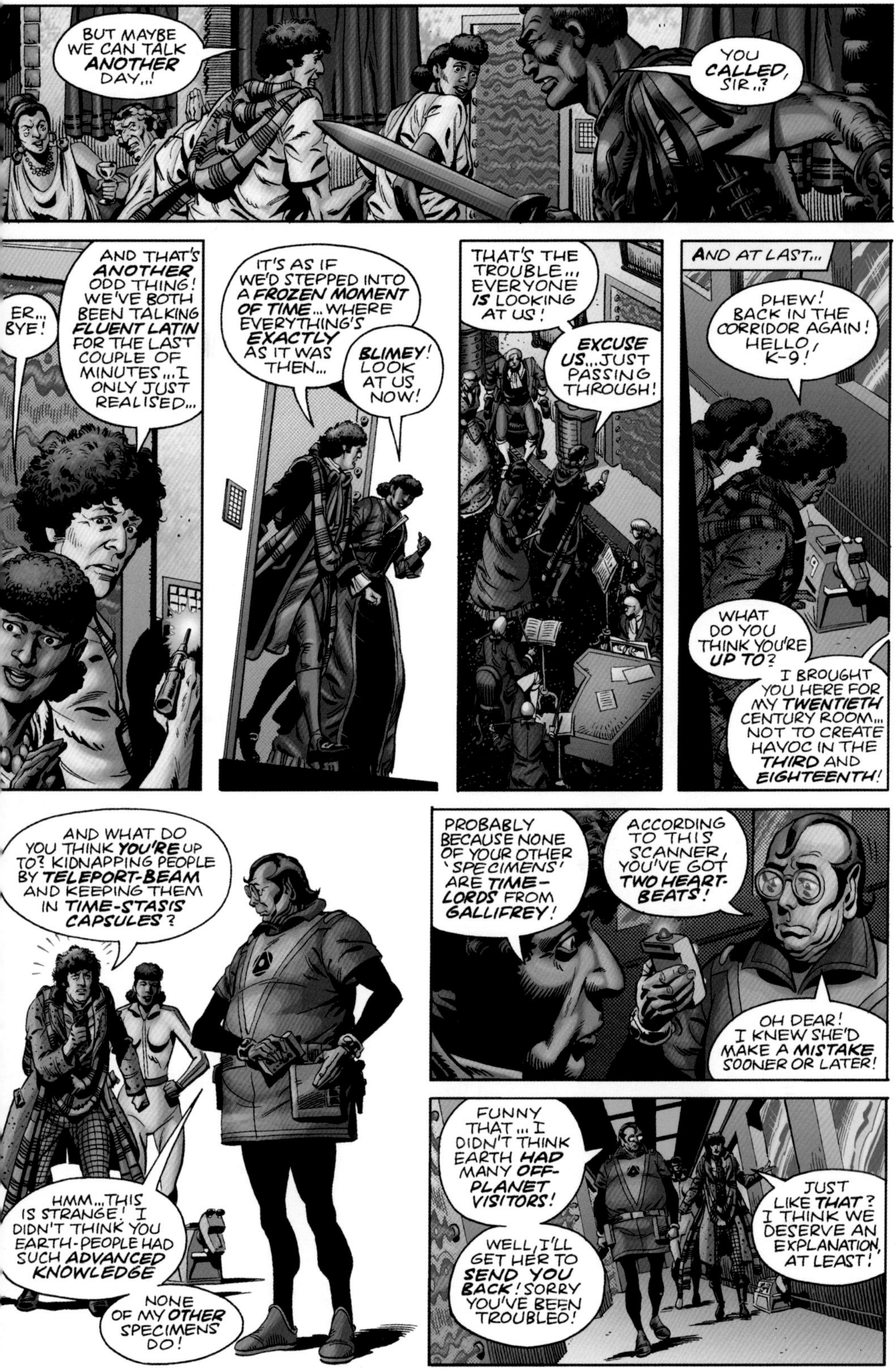
BUT MAYBE WE CAN TALK **ANOTHER** DAY..!
YOU **CALLED**, SIR..?
ER... BYE!
AND THAT'S **ANOTHER** ODD THING! WE'VE BOTH BEEN TALKING **FLUENT LATIN** FOR THE LAST COUPLE OF MINUTES... I ONLY JUST REALISED...
IT'S AS IF WE'D STEPPED INTO A **FROZEN MOMENT OF TIME**... WHERE EVERYTHING'S **EXACTLY** AS IT WAS THEN...
BLIMEY! LOOK AT US NOW!
THAT'S THE TROUBLE... EVERYONE **IS** LOOKING AT US!
EXCUSE US... JUST PASSING THROUGH!
AND AT LAST...
PHEW! BACK IN THE CORRIDOR AGAIN! HELLO, K-9!
WHAT DO YOU THINK YOU'RE **UP TO**?
I BROUGHT YOU HERE FOR MY **TWENTIETH** CENTURY ROOM... NOT TO CREATE HAVOC IN THE **THIRD** AND **EIGHTEENTH**!
AND WHAT DO YOU THINK **YOU'RE** UP TO? KIDNAPPING PEOPLE BY **TELEPORT-BEAM** AND KEEPING THEM IN **TIME-STASIS CAPSULES**?
HMM... THIS IS STRANGE! I DIDN'T THINK YOU EARTH-PEOPLE HAD SUCH **ADVANCED KNOWLEDGE**
NONE OF MY **OTHER** SPECIMENS DO!
PROBABLY BECAUSE NONE OF YOUR OTHER 'SPECIMENS' ARE **TIME-LORDS** FROM **GALLIFREY**!
ACCORDING TO THIS SCANNER, YOU'VE GOT **TWO HEART-BEATS**!
OH DEAR! I KNEW SHE'D MAKE A **MISTAKE** SOONER OR LATER!
FUNNY THAT... I DIDN'T THINK EARTH **HAD** MANY **OFF-PLANET VISITORS**!
WELL, I'LL GET HER TO **SEND YOU BACK**! SORRY YOU'VE BEEN TROUBLED!
JUST LIKE **THAT**? I THINK WE DESERVE AN EXPLANATION, AT LEAST!

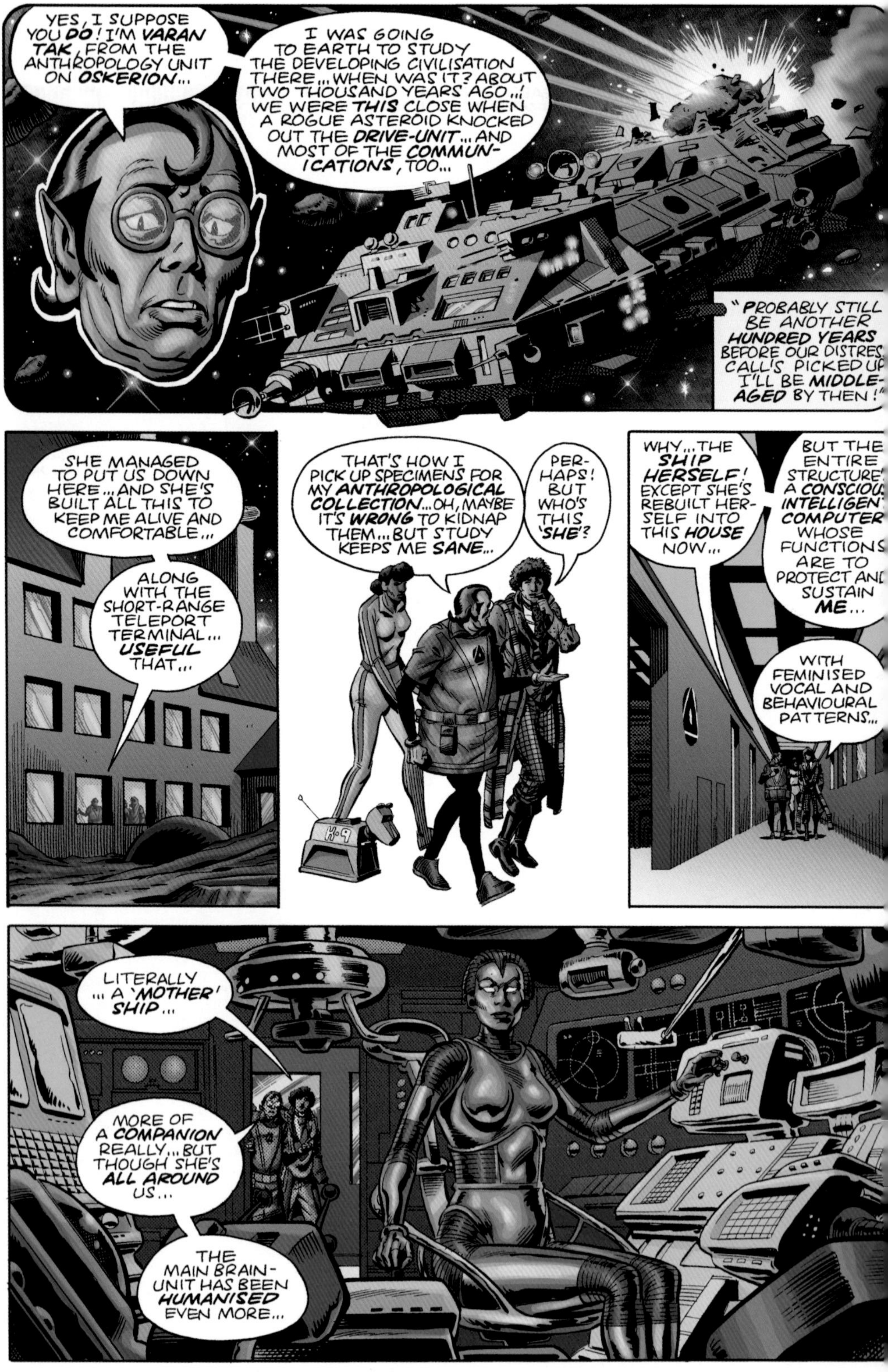
YES, I SUPPOSE YOU DO! I'M VARAN TAK, FROM THE ANTHROPOLOGY UNIT ON OSKERION...
I WAS GOING TO EARTH TO STUDY THE DEVELOPING CIVILISATION THERE... WHEN WAS IT? ABOUT TWO THOUSAND YEARS AGO...! WE WERE THIS CLOSE WHEN A ROGUE ASTEROID KNOCKED OUT THE DRIVE-UNIT... AND MOST OF THE COMMUNICATIONS, TOO...
"PROBABLY STILL BE ANOTHER HUNDRED YEARS BEFORE OUR DISTRESS CALL'S PICKED UP. I'LL BE MIDDLE-AGED BY THEN!"
SHE MANAGED TO PUT US DOWN HERE... AND SHE'S BUILT ALL THIS TO KEEP ME ALIVE AND COMFORTABLE...
ALONG WITH THE SHORT-RANGE TELEPORT TERMINAL... USEFUL THAT...
THAT'S HOW I PICK UP SPECIMENS FOR MY ANTHROPOLOGICAL COLLECTION... OH, MAYBE IT'S WRONG TO KIDNAP THEM... BUT STUDY KEEPS ME SANE...
PERHAPS! BUT WHO'S THIS 'SHE'?
K-9
WHY... THE SHIP HERSELF! EXCEPT SHE'S REBUILT HERSELF INTO THIS HOUSE NOW...
BUT THE ENTIRE STRUCTURE'S A CONSCIOUS INTELLIGENT COMPUTER WHOSE FUNCTIONS ARE TO PROTECT AND SUSTAIN ME...
WITH FEMINISED VOCAL AND BEHAVIOURAL PATTERNS...
LITERALLY... A 'MOTHER' SHIP...
MORE OF A COMPANION REALLY... BUT THOUGH SHE'S ALL AROUND US...
THE MAIN BRAIN-UNIT HAS BEEN HUMANISED EVEN MORE...

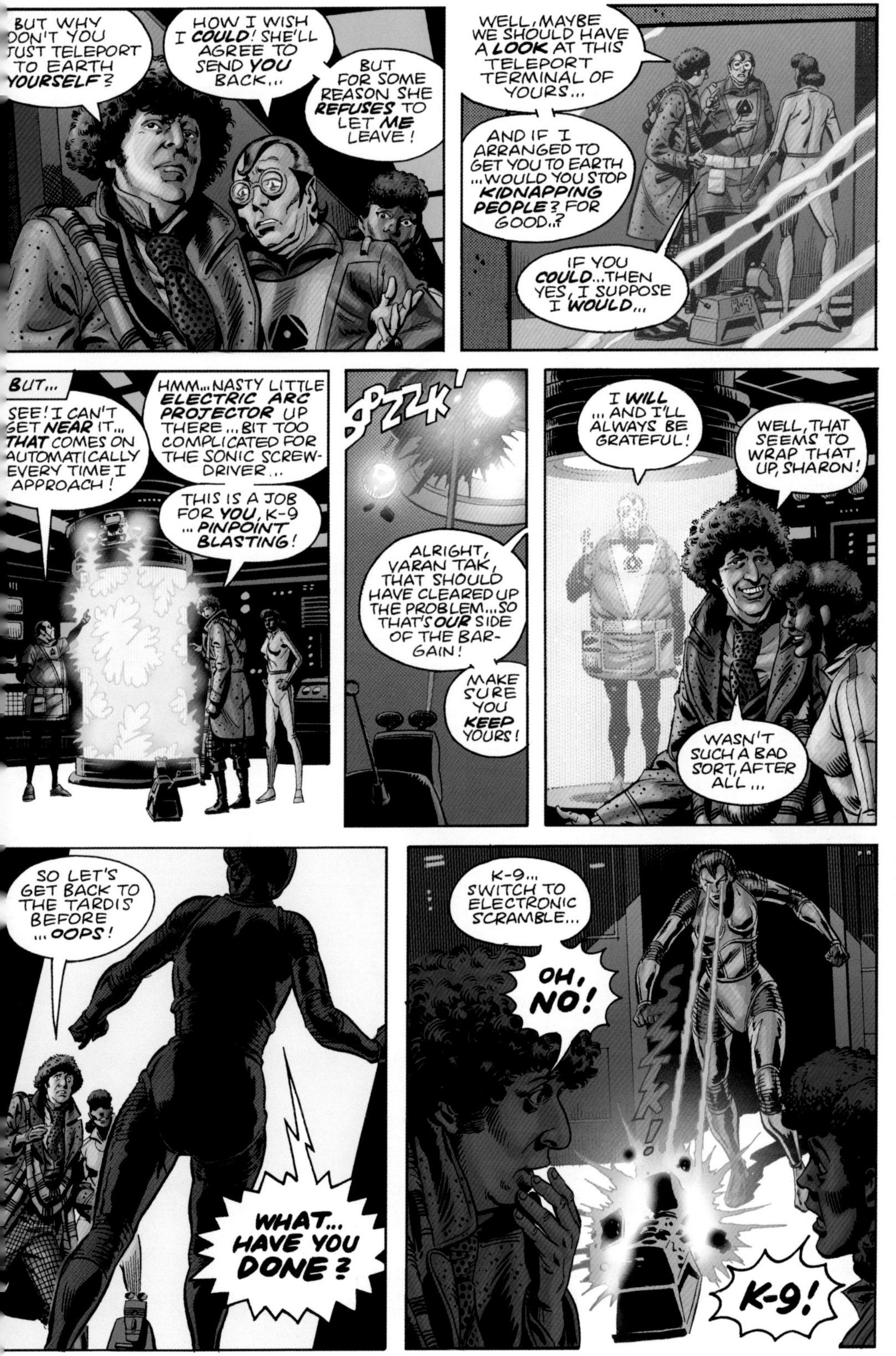
BUT WHY DON'T YOU JUST TELEPORT TO EARTH YOURSELF?
HOW I WISH I COULD! SHE'LL AGREE TO SEND YOU BACK...
BUT FOR SOME REASON SHE REFUSES TO LET ME LEAVE!
WELL, MAYBE WE SHOULD HAVE A LOOK AT THIS TELEPORT TERMINAL OF YOURS...
AND IF I ARRANGED TO GET YOU TO EARTH ...WOULD YOU STOP KIDNAPPING PEOPLE? FOR GOOD..?
IF YOU COULD...THEN YES, I SUPPOSE I WOULD...
BUT...
SEE! I CAN'T GET NEAR IT... THAT COMES ON AUTOMATICALLY EVERY TIME I APPROACH!
HMM... NASTY LITTLE ELECTRIC ARC PROJECTOR UP THERE... BIT TOO COMPLICATED FOR THE SONIC SCREW-DRIVER...
THIS IS A JOB FOR YOU, K-9 ...PINPOINT BLASTING!
SPZZK!
ALRIGHT, VARAN TAK, THAT SHOULD HAVE CLEARED UP THE PROBLEM... SO THAT'S OUR SIDE OF THE BAR-GAIN!
MAKE SURE YOU KEEP YOURS!
I WILL ...AND I'LL ALWAYS BE GRATEFUL!
WELL, THAT SEEMS TO WRAP THAT UP, SHARON!
WASN'T SUCH A BAD SORT, AFTER ALL...
SO LET'S GET BACK TO THE TARDIS BEFORE ...OOPS!
WHAT... HAVE YOU DONE?
K-9... SWITCH TO ELECTRONIC SCRAMBLE...
OH, NO!
K-9!

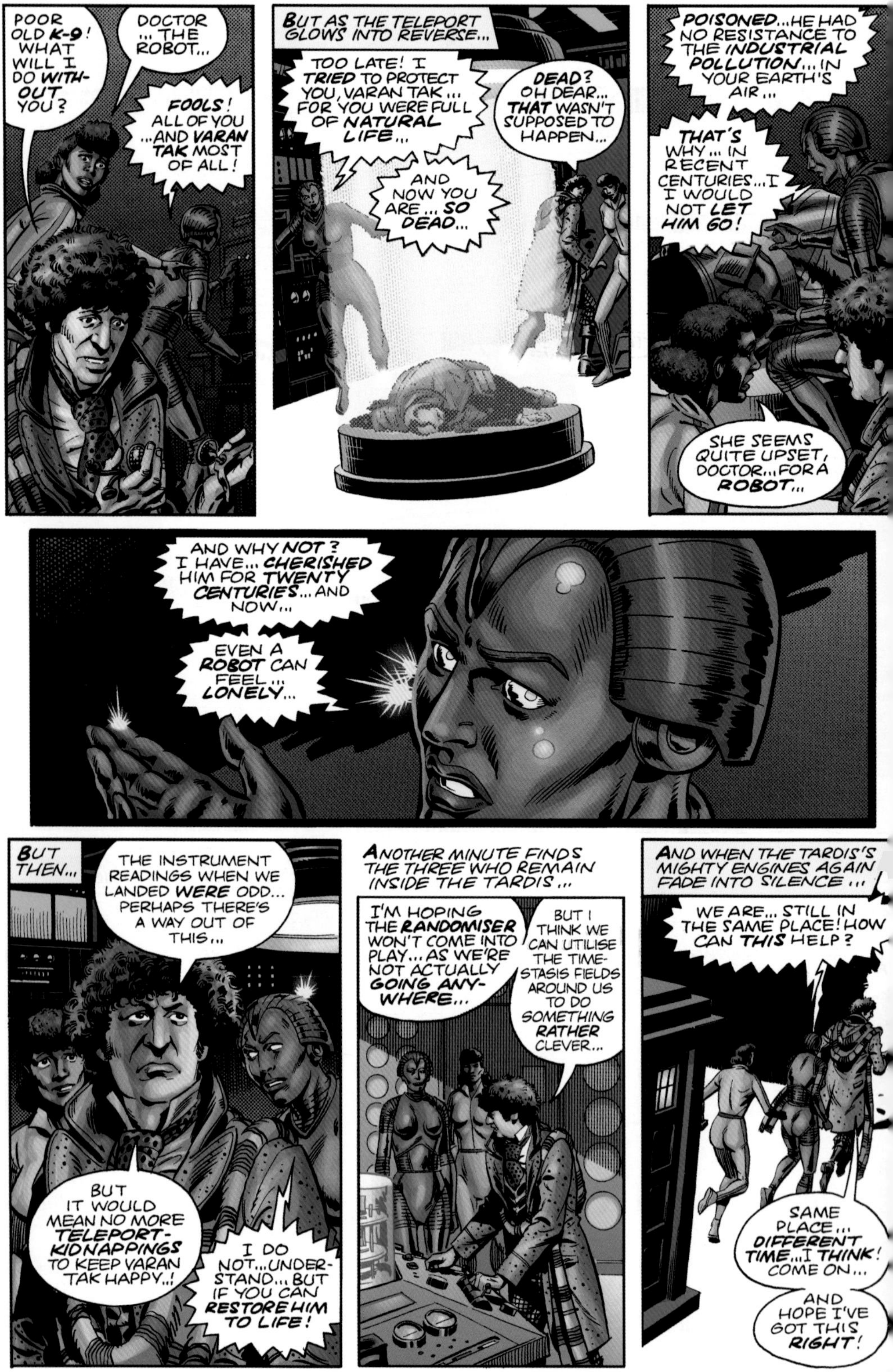
POOR OLD K-9! WHAT WILL I DO WITHOUT YOU?
DOCTOR ... THE ROBOT...
FOOLS! ALL OF YOU ...AND VARAN TAK MOST OF ALL!
BUT AS THE TELEPORT GLOWS INTO REVERSE...
TOO LATE! I TRIED TO PROTECT YOU, VARAN TAK... FOR YOU WERE FULL OF NATURAL LIFE...
DEAD? OH DEAR... THAT WASN'T SUPPOSED TO HAPPEN...
AND NOW YOU ARE... SO DEAD...
POISONED... HE HAD NO RESISTANCE TO THE INDUSTRIAL POLLUTION... IN YOUR EARTH'S AIR...
THAT'S WHY... IN RECENT CENTURIES... I WOULD NOT LET HIM GO!
SHE SEEMS QUITE UPSET, DOCTOR... FOR A ROBOT...
AND WHY NOT? I HAVE... CHERISHED HIM FOR TWENTY CENTURIES... AND NOW...
EVEN A ROBOT CAN FEEL... LONELY...
BUT THEN...
THE INSTRUMENT READINGS WHEN WE LANDED WERE ODD... PERHAPS THERE'S A WAY OUT OF THIS...
BUT IT WOULD MEAN NO MORE TELEPORT-KIDNAPPINGS TO KEEP VARAN TAK HAPPY..!
I DO NOT... UNDERSTAND... BUT IF YOU CAN RESTORE HIM TO LIFE!
ANOTHER MINUTE FINDS THE THREE WHO REMAIN INSIDE THE TARDIS...
I'M HOPING THE RANDOMISER WON'T COME INTO PLAY... AS WE'RE NOT ACTUALLY GOING ANYWHERE...
BUT I THINK WE CAN UTILISE THE TIME-STASIS FIELDS AROUND US TO DO SOMETHING RATHER CLEVER...
AND WHEN THE TARDIS'S MIGHTY ENGINES AGAIN FADE INTO SILENCE...
WE ARE... STILL IN THE SAME PLACE! HOW CAN THIS HELP?
SAME PLACE... DIFFERENT TIME... I THINK! COME ON...
AND HOPE I'VE GOT THIS RIGHT!

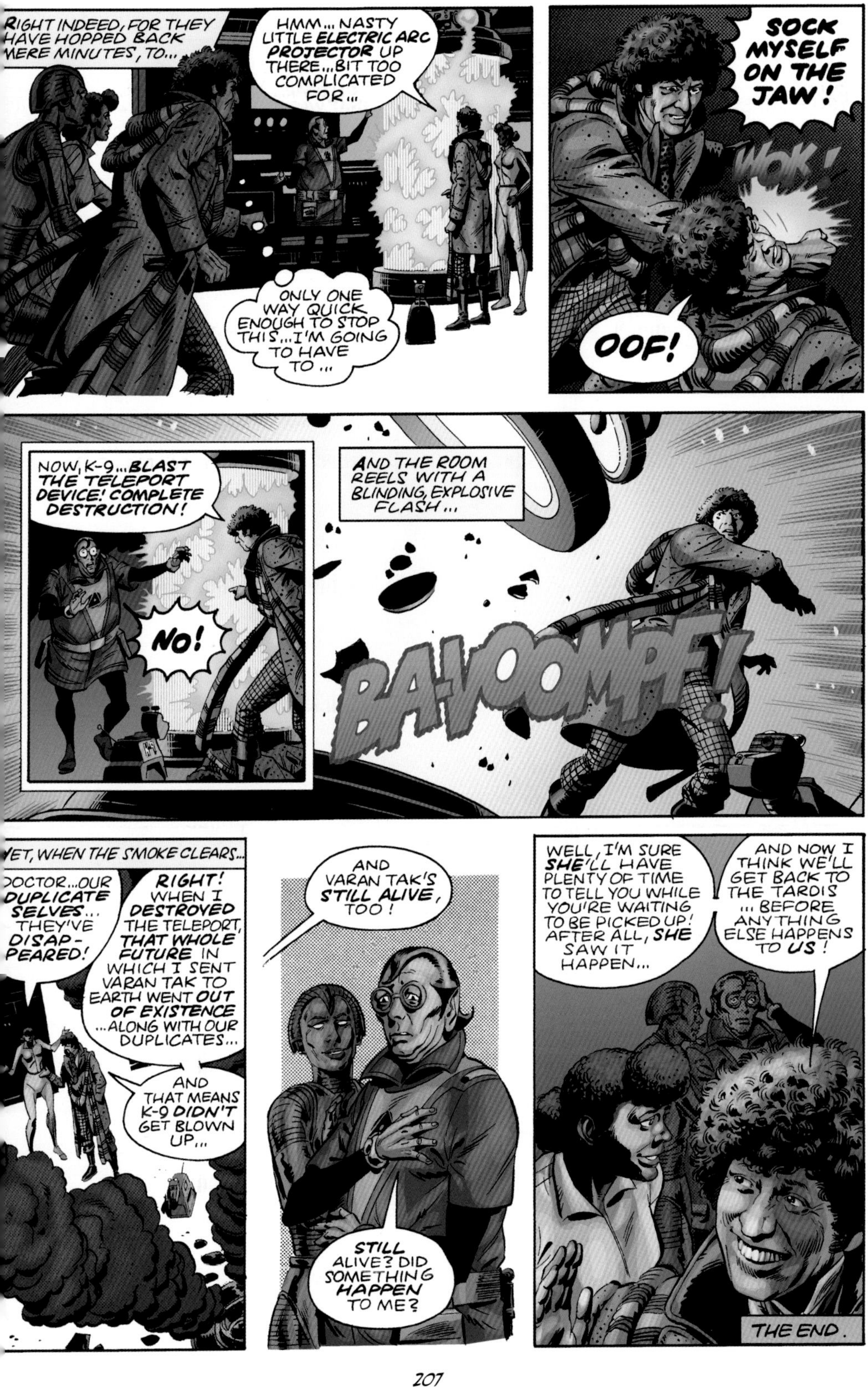
RIGHT INDEED, FOR THEY HAVE HOPPED BACK MERE MINUTES, TO...
HMM... NASTY LITTLE ELECTRIC ARC PROJECTOR UP THERE... BIT TOO COMPLICATED FOR...
ONLY ONE WAY QUICK ENOUGH TO STOP THIS... I'M GOING TO HAVE TO...
SOCK MYSELF ON THE JAW!
WOK!
OOF!
NOW, K-9... BLAST THE TELEPORT DEVICE! COMPLETE DESTRUCTION!
NO!
AND THE ROOM REELS WITH A BLINDING, EXPLOSIVE FLASH...
BA-VOOMPF!
YET, WHEN THE SMOKE CLEARS...
DOCTOR... OUR DUPLICATE SELVES... THEY'VE DISAP-PEARED!
RIGHT! WHEN I DESTROYED THE TELEPORT, THAT WHOLE FUTURE IN WHICH I SENT VARAN TAK TO EARTH WENT OUT OF EXISTENCE ...ALONG WITH OUR DUPLICATES...
AND THAT MEANS K-9 DIDN'T GET BLOWN UP...
AND VARAN TAK'S STILL ALIVE, TOO!
STILL ALIVE? DID SOMETHING HAPPEN TO ME?
WELL, I'M SURE SHE'LL HAVE PLENTY OF TIME TO TELL YOU WHILE YOU'RE WAITING TO BE PICKED UP! AFTER ALL, SHE SAW IT HAPPEN...
AND NOW I THINK WE'LL GET BACK TO THE TARDIS ... BEFORE ANYTHING ELSE HAPPENS TO US!
THE END.

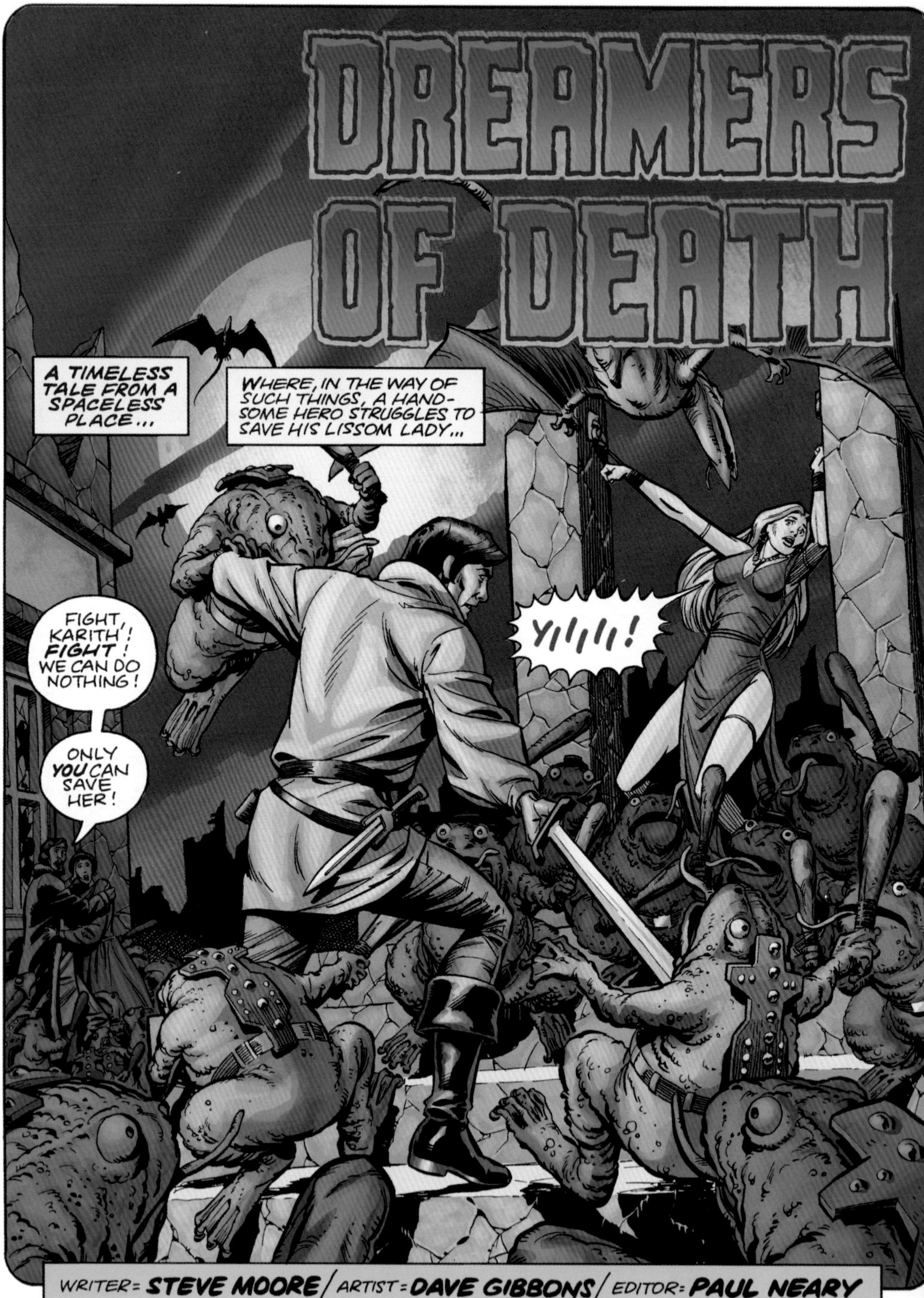
DREAMERS OF DEATH
A TIMELESS TALE FROM A SPACELESS PLACE...
WHERE, IN THE WAY OF SUCH THINGS, A HANDSOME HERO STRUGGLES TO SAVE HIS LISSOM LADY...
FIGHT, KARITH! FIGHT! WE CAN DO NOTHING!
ONLY YOU CAN SAVE HER!
YIIIII!
WRITER= STEVE MOORE / ARTIST= DAVE GIBBONS / EDITOR= PAUL NEARY

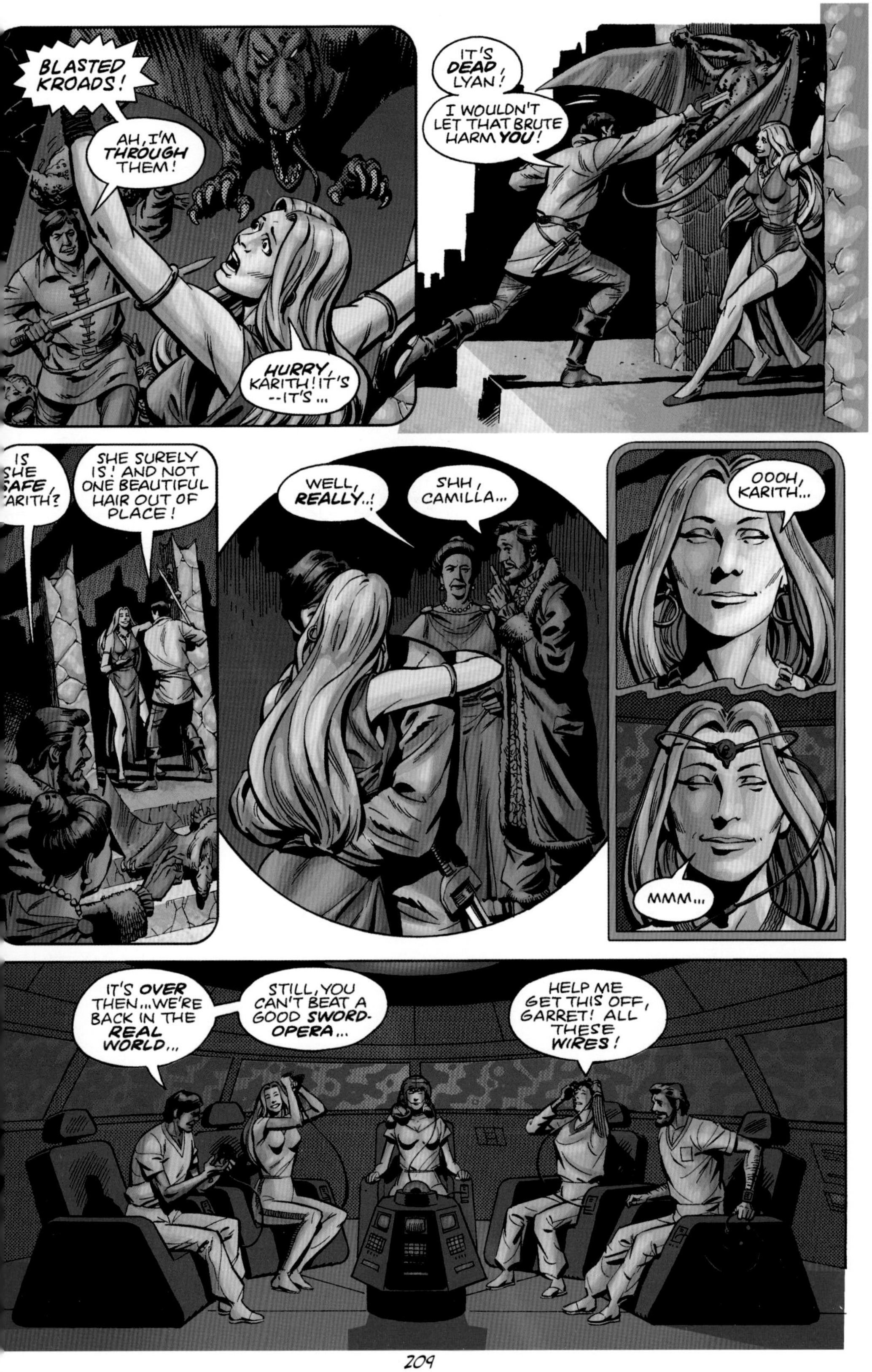

BLASTED KROADS!
AH, I'M THROUGH THEM!
HURRY, KARITH! IT'S --IT'S ...
IT'S DEAD, LYAN!
I WOULDN'T LET THAT BRUTE HARM YOU!
IS SHE SAFE, KARITH?
SHE SURELY IS! AND NOT ONE BEAUTIFUL HAIR OUT OF PLACE!
WELL, REALLY..!
SHH, CAMILLA...
OOOH, KARITH...
MMM...
IT'S OVER THEN... WE'RE BACK IN THE REAL WORLD...
STILL, YOU CAN'T BEAT A GOOD SWORD-OPERA...
HELP ME GET THIS OFF, GARRET! ALL THESE WIRES!

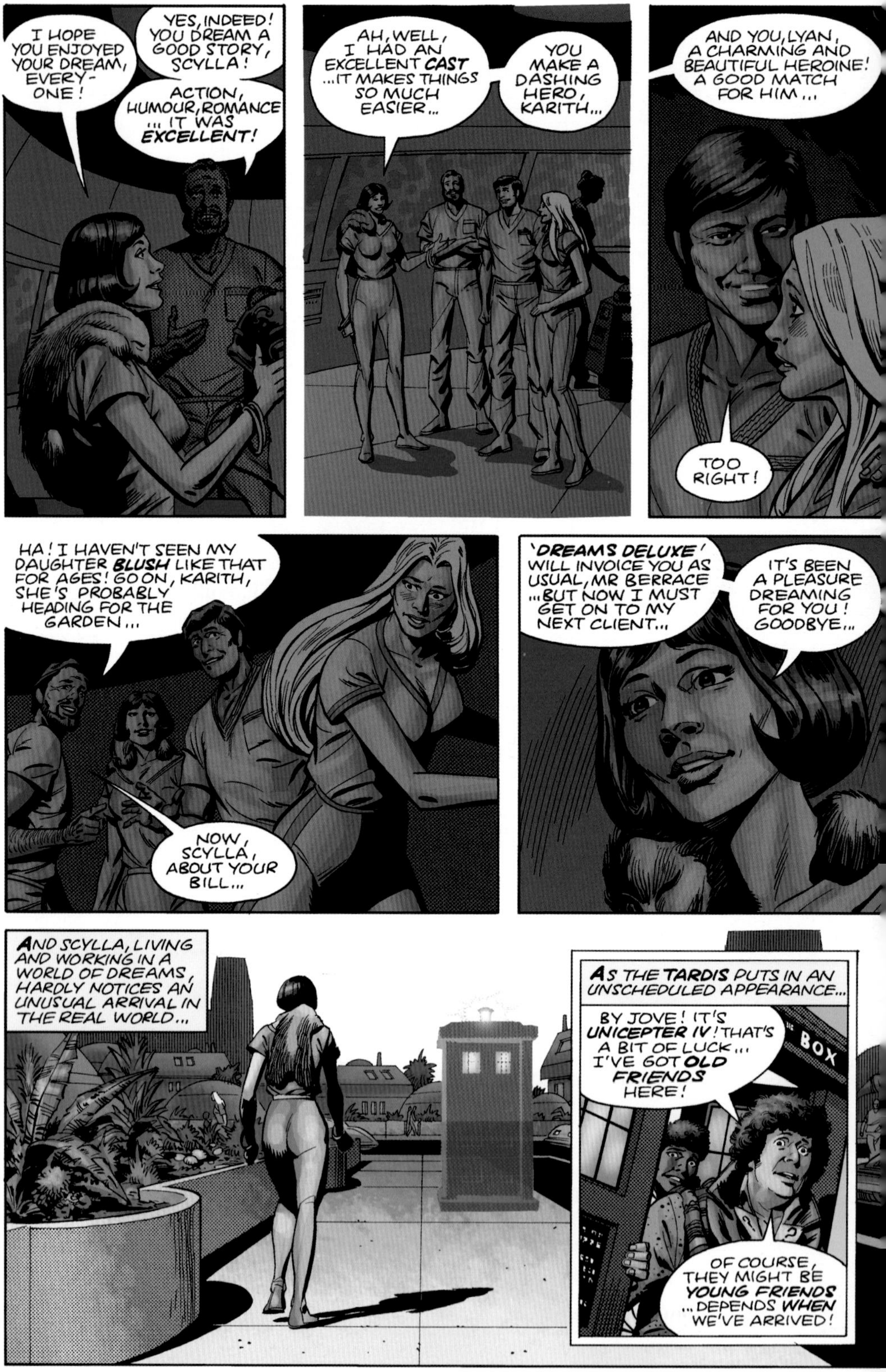
I HOPE YOU ENJOYED YOUR DREAM, EVERY-ONE!
YES, INDEED! YOU DREAM A GOOD STORY, SCYLLA!
ACTION, HUMOUR, ROMANCE ... IT WAS EXCELLENT!
AH, WELL, I HAD AN EXCELLENT CAST ...IT MAKES THINGS SO MUCH EASIER...
YOU MAKE A DASHING HERO, KARITH...
AND YOU, LYAN, A CHARMING AND BEAUTIFUL HEROINE! A GOOD MATCH FOR HIM...
TOO RIGHT!
HA! I HAVEN'T SEEN MY DAUGHTER BLUSH LIKE THAT FOR AGES! GO ON, KARITH, SHE'S PROBABLY HEADING FOR THE GARDEN...
NOW, SCYLLA, ABOUT YOUR BILL...
'DREAMS DELUXE' WILL INVOICE YOU AS USUAL, MR BERRACE ...BUT NOW I MUST GET ON TO MY NEXT CLIENT...
IT'S BEEN A PLEASURE DREAMING FOR YOU! GOODBYE...
AND SCYLLA, LIVING AND WORKING IN A WORLD OF DREAMS, HARDLY NOTICES AN UNUSUAL ARRIVAL IN THE REAL WORLD...
AS THE TARDIS PUTS IN AN UNSCHEDULED APPEARANCE...
BY JOVE! IT'S UNICEPTER IV! THAT'S A BIT OF LUCK... I'VE GOT OLD FRIENDS HERE!
BOX
OF COURSE, THEY MIGHT BE YOUNG FRIENDS ...DEPENDS WHEN WE'VE ARRIVED!

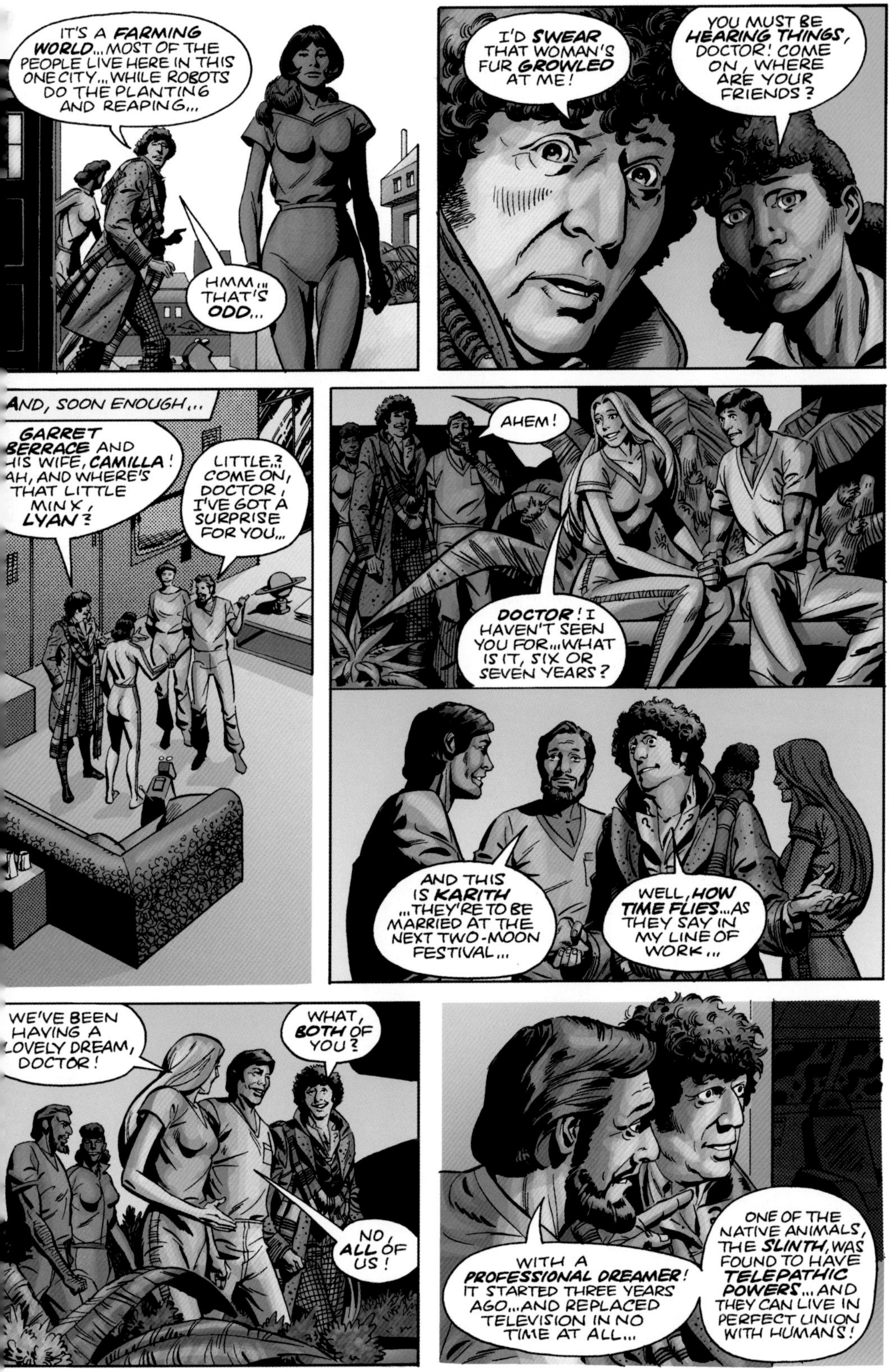
IT'S A FARMING WORLD... MOST OF THE PEOPLE LIVE HERE IN THIS ONE CITY... WHILE ROBOTS DO THE PLANTING AND REAPING...
HMM... THAT'S ODD...
I'D SWEAR THAT WOMAN'S FUR GROWLED AT ME!
YOU MUST BE HEARING THINGS, DOCTOR! COME ON, WHERE ARE YOUR FRIENDS?
AND, SOON ENOUGH...
GARRET BERRACE AND HIS WIFE, CAMILLA! AH, AND WHERE'S THAT LITTLE MINX, LYAN?
LITTLE..? COME ON, DOCTOR, I'VE GOT A SURPRISE FOR YOU...
AHEM!
DOCTOR! I HAVEN'T SEEN YOU FOR... WHAT IS IT, SIX OR SEVEN YEARS?
AND THIS IS KARITH ...THEY'RE TO BE MARRIED AT THE NEXT TWO-MOON FESTIVAL...
WELL, HOW TIME FLIES... AS THEY SAY IN MY LINE OF WORK...
WE'VE BEEN HAVING A LOVELY DREAM, DOCTOR!
WHAT, BOTH OF YOU?
NO, ALL OF US!
WITH A PROFESSIONAL DREAMER! IT STARTED THREE YEARS AGO... AND REPLACED TELEVISION IN NO TIME AT ALL...
ONE OF THE NATIVE ANIMALS, THE SLINTH, WAS FOUND TO HAVE TELEPATHIC POWERS... AND THEY CAN LIVE IN PERFECT UNION WITH HUMANS!

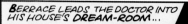

BERRACE LEADS THE DOCTOR INTO HIS HOUSE'S **DREAM-ROOM**...

THESE HEAD-PIECES CONNECT US TO THE DREAMER...AND WITH THE AID OF THE **SLINTH**...WE ALL TAKE PART IN A **FULLY-CONTROLLED DREAM-STORY**...ON WHATEVER SUBJECT WE CHOOSE...

SOME **RICH** PEOPLE, LIKE **LORD VEITH**, HAVE **PERSONAL DREAMERS** ON THEIR PERMANENT STAFF...

OH, DADDY... WE'VE **GOT** TO GET A DREAMER WHILE THE DOCTOR'S HERE! IT'S THE **COMPLETE FRENZY**, AFTER ALL!

COMPLETE FRENZY? OH...YOU MEAN IT'S **ALL THE RAGE!**

WELL, AS LONG AS IT'S NOTHING **TOO EXCITING**! YOU KNOW WHAT AN **UNADVENTUROUS SORT** I AM, GARRET...

I'LL SEE IF I CAN HIRE **VERNOR ALLEN** ...HIS **DREAMSCAPES** ARE TRULY POETIC...

AS THE DAY FADES SLOWLY INTO NIGHT...

YOU KNOW, DOCTOR, I ALWAYS THOUGHT OF YOU AS A **LONER**...IT'S A BIT **STRANGE** TO SEE YOU JUST RELAXING WITH FRIENDS...

WELL, NO ONE SPENDS **ALL** THEIR TIME FIXING UP THE UNIVERSE, SHARON...

EXCUSE ME, DOCTOR...

I DON'T WANT TO **WORRY** YOU, DOCTOR, BUT I JUST HEARD THERE'S BEEN AN ACCIDENT! LORD VEITH, HIS DREAMER, AND TWO OTHERS HAVE BEEN KILLED...

THEY THINK IT WAS AN **ELECTRICAL FAULT**, BUT THEY'RE STILL WORKING THERE...

IT'S NEVER HAPPENED BEFORE, SO IT'S PROBABLY JUST ONE OF THOSE THINGS! STILL, I'LL CHECK ALL MY APPARATUS...

RIGHT ...AND I THINK I'LL HAVE A QUICK WORD WITH K-9...

AND NOT LONG AFTER THE CHECKS HAVE BEEN MADE

GOOD EVENING, EVERYONE... I'M **VERNOR ALLEN**, YOUR DREAMER FOR TONIGHT...

AND I SEE WE'VE GOT OFF-WORLD **VISITORS**, TOO! THIS IS VERY PLEASANT...

SO THIS IS YOUR *SLINTH*, VERNOR?... ER... IS HE SAFE TO TOUCH?

OF COURSE! A SLINTH IS A DREAMER'S BEST FRIEND! HIS NAME'S *MIKI*...

HASN'T LEFT MY SHOULDER FOR NEARLY THREE YEARS...

AND ARE *YOU* GOING TO BE IN THIS DREAM, VERNOR?

I'M AFRAID NOT... THE DREAMER'S TOO BUSY CONTROLLING THINGS...

THAT'S A SHAME...

THEN, AS THEY ENTER THE DREAM-ROOM...

IF YOU'RE ALL COMFORTABLE..? WE'LL BE DREAMING '*THE FIRST LANDING ON THE BLISS-WORLD OF ANSILLAR*'... YOU'LL PLAY MEMBERS OF THE SURVEY TEAM...

AH, THERE YOU ARE, K-9... BEHAVE YOURSELF...

AND THE NEXT THING THEY KNOW...

BY JOVE! IT'S ALMOST *REAL*... THE SPACE-SHIP... THE SUIT...

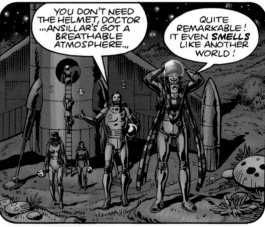

YOU DON'T NEED THE HELMET, DOCTOR ...ANSILLAR'S GOT A BREATHABLE ATMOSPHERE...

QUITE REMARKABLE! IT EVEN *SMELLS* LIKE ANOTHER WORLD!

AND LOOK AT THAT *CITY* ON THE HORIZON... SPARKLING LIKE A JEWEL!

SEVEN *MOONS*, KARITH ...THAT'S FIVE MORE THAN WE'VE GOT ON UNICEPTER...

AND THEN...

LOOK! A *PROCESSION* COMING THIS WAY...

AND THAT *MUSIC*...SO STRANGE...SO HAUNTING...

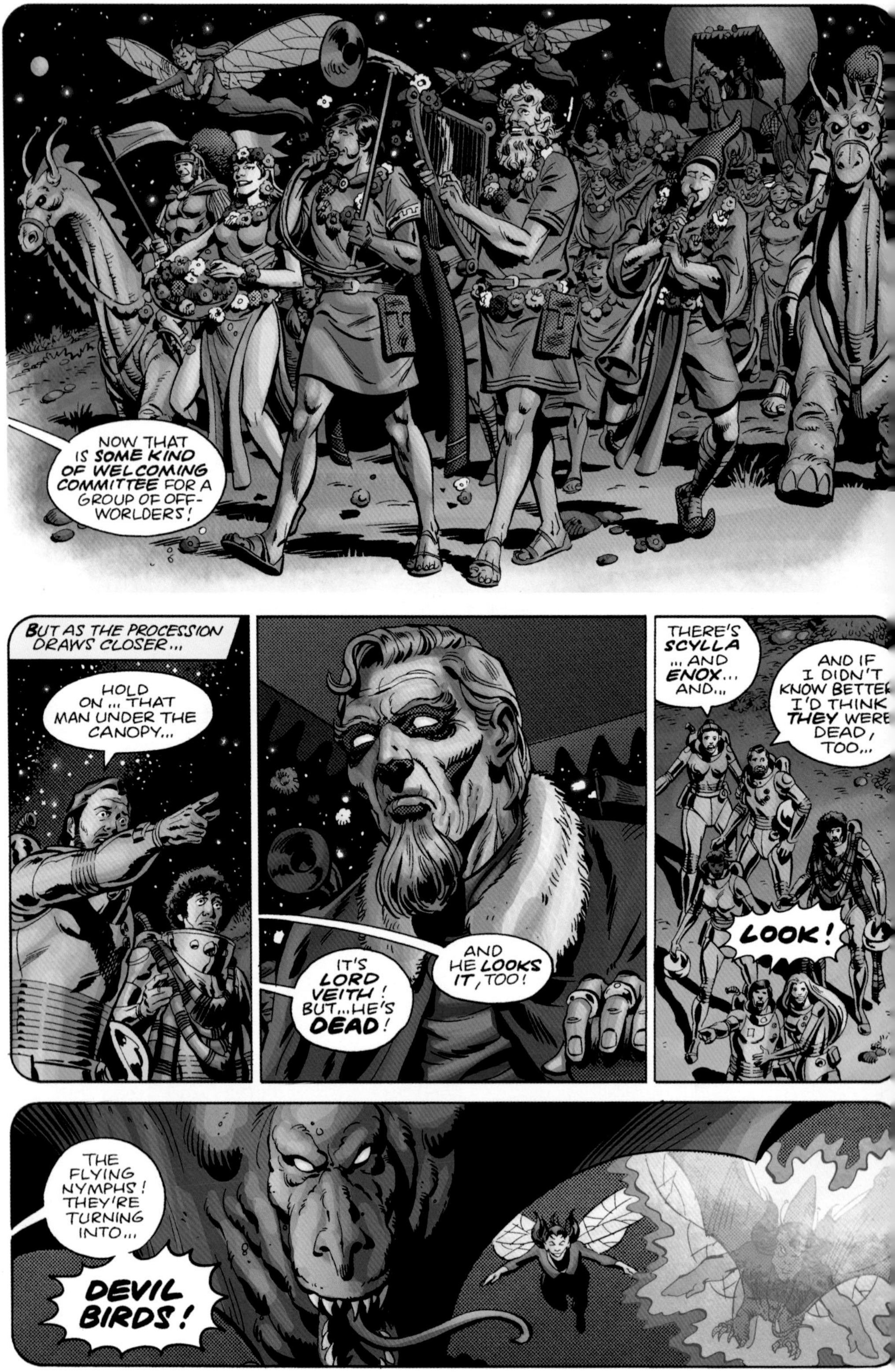

NOW THAT IS SOME KIND OF WELCOMING COMMITTEE FOR A GROUP OF OFF-WORLDERS!
BUT AS THE PROCESSION DRAWS CLOSER...
HOLD ON... THAT MAN UNDER THE CANOPY...
IT'S LORD VEITH! BUT...HE'S DEAD!
AND HE LOOKS IT, TOO!
THERE'S SCYLLA ...AND ENOX... AND...
AND IF I DIDN'T KNOW BETTER I'D THINK THEY WERE DEAD, TOO...
LOOK!
THE FLYING NYMPHS! THEY'RE TURNING INTO...
DEVIL BIRDS!

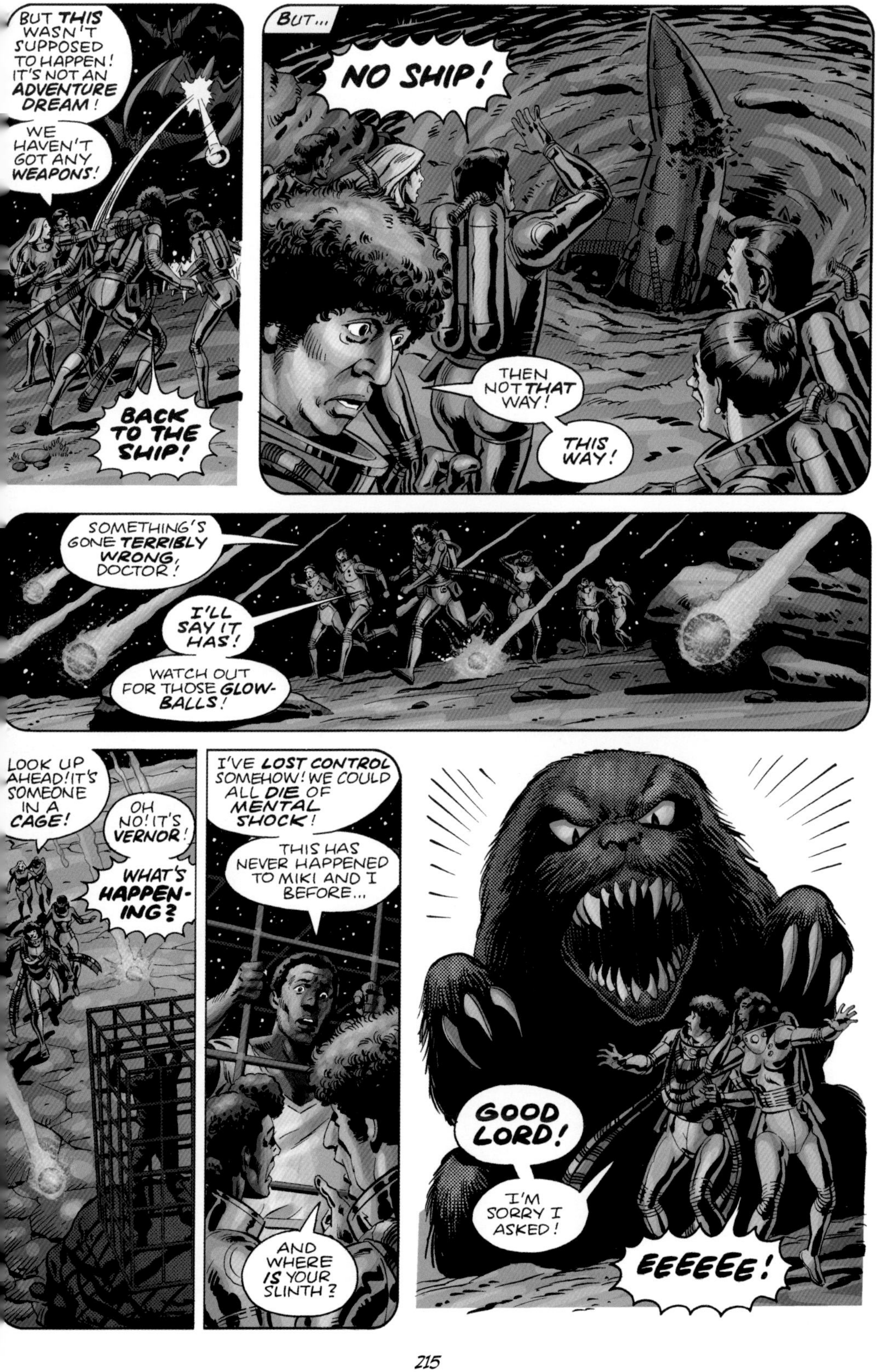

BUT THIS WASN'T SUPPOSED TO HAPPEN! IT'S NOT AN ADVENTURE DREAM!
WE HAVEN'T GOT ANY WEAPONS!
BACK TO THE SHIP!
BUT...
NO SHIP!
THEN NOT THAT WAY!
THIS WAY!
SOMETHING'S GONE TERRIBLY WRONG, DOCTOR!
I'LL SAY IT HAS!
WATCH OUT FOR THOSE GLOW-BALLS!
LOOK UP AHEAD! IT'S SOMEONE IN A CAGE!
OH NO! IT'S VERNOR!
WHAT'S HAPPEN-ING?
I'VE LOST CONTROL SOMEHOW! WE COULD ALL DIE OF MENTAL SHOCK!
THIS HAS NEVER HAPPENED TO MIKI AND I BEFORE...
AND WHERE IS YOUR SLINTH?
GOOD LORD!
I'M SORRY I ASKED!
EEEEEE!

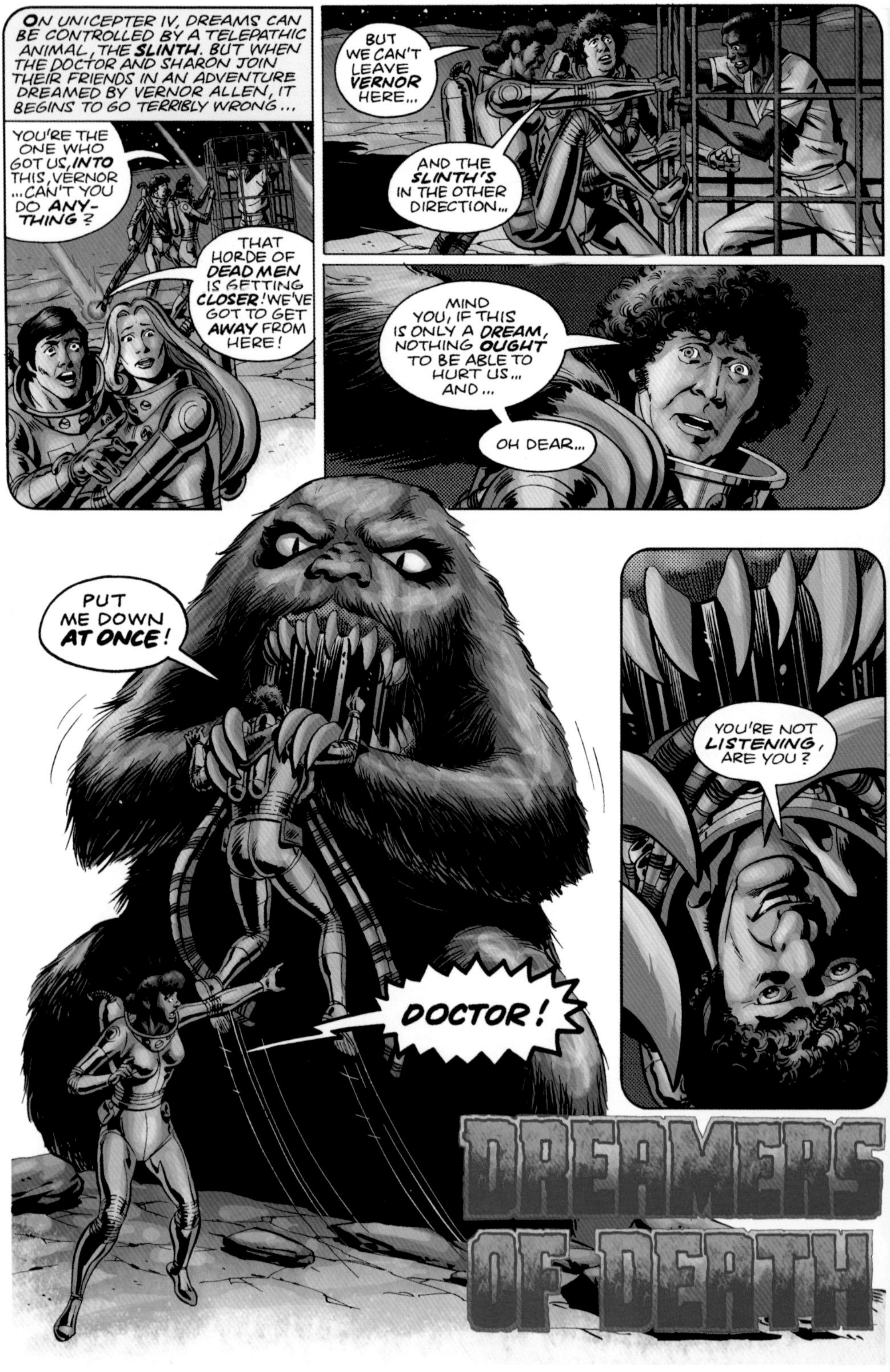

ON UNICEPTER IV, DREAMS CAN BE CONTROLLED BY A TELEPATHIC ANIMAL, THE SLINTH. BUT WHEN THE DOCTOR AND SHARON JOIN THEIR FRIENDS IN AN ADVENTURE DREAMED BY VERNOR ALLEN, IT BEGINS TO GO TERRIBLY WRONG...
YOU'RE THE ONE WHO GOT US, INTO THIS, VERNOR ...CAN'T YOU DO ANYTHING?
THAT HORDE OF DEAD MEN IS GETTING CLOSER! WE'VE GOT TO GET AWAY FROM HERE!
BUT WE CAN'T LEAVE VERNOR HERE...
AND THE SLINTH'S IN THE OTHER DIRECTION...
MIND YOU, IF THIS IS ONLY A DREAM, NOTHING OUGHT TO BE ABLE TO HURT US... AND...
OH DEAR...
PUT ME DOWN AT ONCE!
YOU'RE NOT LISTENING, ARE YOU?
DOCTOR!
DREAMERS OF DEATH

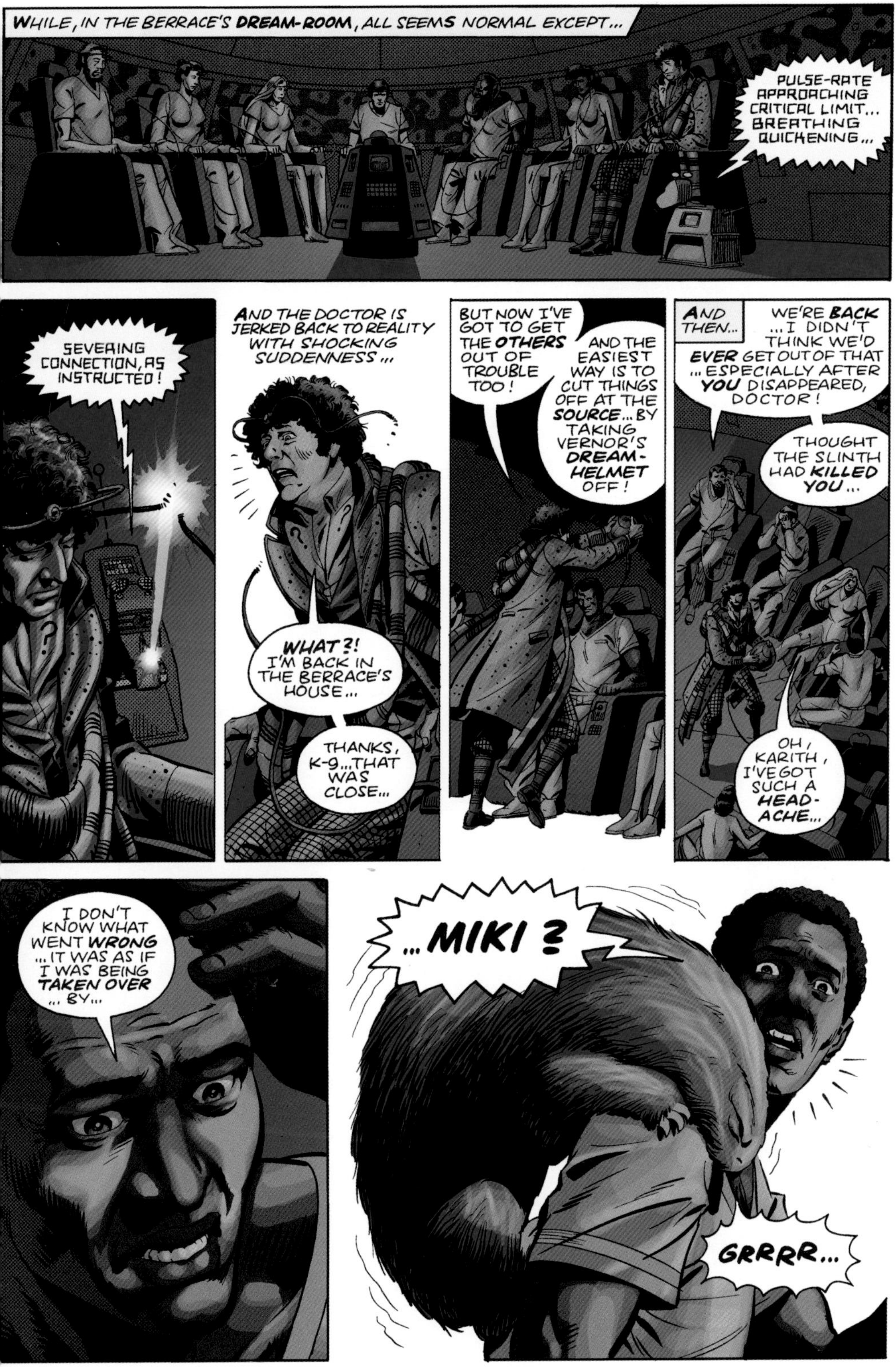

WHILE, IN THE BERRACE'S DREAM-ROOM, ALL SEEMS NORMAL EXCEPT...
PULSE-RATE APPROACHING CRITICAL LIMIT... BREATHING QUICKENING...
SEVERING CONNECTION, AS INSTRUCTED!
AND THE DOCTOR IS JERKED BACK TO REALITY WITH SHOCKING SUDDENNESS...
WHAT?! I'M BACK IN THE BERRACE'S HOUSE...
THANKS, K-9... THAT WAS CLOSE...
BUT NOW I'VE GOT TO GET THE OTHERS OUT OF TROUBLE TOO!
AND THE EASIEST WAY IS TO CUT THINGS OFF AT THE SOURCE... BY TAKING VERNOR'S DREAM-HELMET OFF!
AND THEN...
WE'RE BACK ...I DIDN'T THINK WE'D EVER GET OUT OF THAT ...ESPECIALLY AFTER YOU DISAPPEARED, DOCTOR!
THOUGHT THE SLINTH HAD KILLED YOU...
OH, KARITH, I'VE GOT SUCH A HEAD-ACHE...
I DON'T KNOW WHAT WENT WRONG ...IT WAS AS IF I WAS BEING TAKEN OVER ... BY...
...MIKI?
GRRRR...

YOU'RE PROBABLY *RIGHT*, VERNOR... THIS THING'S *DANGEROUS*...

SNARRR!

IT LOOKS ALMOST... *BLOATED!*

MIKI! COME BACK!

NO, LET IT GO! NOW, IS EVERYONE ALRIGHT?

I THINK SO ... BUT HOW DID YOU SAVE US, DOCTOR?

I WAS *SUSPICIOUS* WHEN I HEARD ABOUT LORD VEITH BEING KILLED... AND AS THIS WAS SUPPOSED TO BE A PEACE- FUL, POETIC DREAM ...

I TOLD *K-9* TO MONITOR MY REACTIONS... SO IF I GOT TOO *EXCITED*, HE'D BREAK THE CONNECTION...

BUT I STILL DON'T UNDERSTAND ...WE'VE NEVER HAD TROUBLE WITH SLINTHS *BEFORE*...

HOLD ON ...THAT'S THE *GENERAL ALARM SIREN* ...I'D BETTER SWITCH ON THE *VIS- NEWS!*

VWEEEHVWEEETH

REPORTS ARE COMING IN OF A NUMBER OF *FATAL ACCIDENTS* INVOLVING DREAMERS AND THEIR CLIENTS ...

THE *SLINTHS* ARE BELIEVED TO BE RESPONSIBLE, AND IT IS FEARED THAT THE DEATH-TOLL MAY RUN INTO HUNDREDS ...

YOU ARE THEREFORE ADVISED *NOT TO DREAM* UNDER ANY CIRCUMSTANCES...

SLINTHS ARE TO BE REGARDED AS *VERMIN* AND *DESTROYED!*

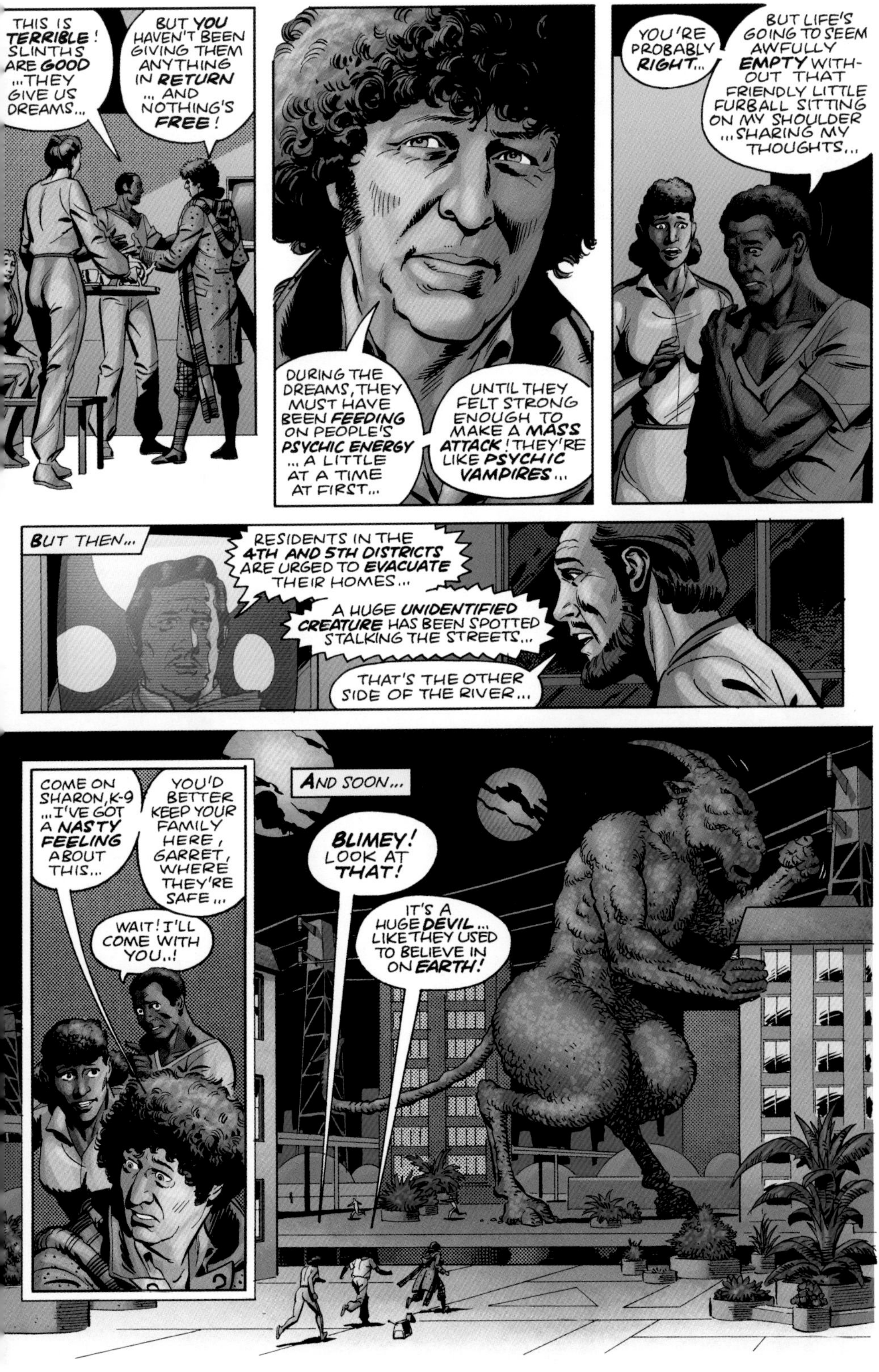
THIS IS TERRIBLE! SLINTHS ARE GOOD ...THEY GIVE US DREAMS...
BUT YOU HAVEN'T BEEN GIVING THEM ANYTHING IN RETURN ... AND NOTHING'S FREE!
DURING THE DREAMS, THEY MUST HAVE BEEN FEEDING ON PEOPLE'S PSYCHIC ENERGY ... A LITTLE AT A TIME AT FIRST...
UNTIL THEY FELT STRONG ENOUGH TO MAKE A MASS ATTACK! THEY'RE LIKE PSYCHIC VAMPIRES...
YOU'RE PROBABLY RIGHT...
BUT LIFE'S GOING TO SEEM AWFULLY EMPTY WITH-OUT THAT FRIENDLY LITTLE FURBALL SITTING ON MY SHOULDER ...SHARING MY THOUGHTS...
BUT THEN...
RESIDENTS IN THE 4TH AND 5TH DISTRICTS ARE URGED TO EVACUATE THEIR HOMES...
A HUGE UNIDENTIFIED CREATURE HAS BEEN SPOTTED STALKING THE STREETS...
THAT'S THE OTHER SIDE OF THE RIVER...
COME ON SHARON, K-9 ...I'VE GOT A NASTY FEELING ABOUT THIS...
YOU'D BETTER KEEP YOUR FAMILY HERE, GARRET, WHERE THEY'RE SAFE...
WAIT! I'LL COME WITH YOU..!
AND SOON...
BLIMEY! LOOK AT THAT!
IT'S A HUGE DEVIL... LIKE THEY USED TO BELIEVE IN ON EARTH!

BECAUSE *FEAR* AND *TERROR* GENERATE MOST *PSYCHIC ENERGY* FOR THEM TO *FEED ON*...

HERE COMES THE *MILITARY*...

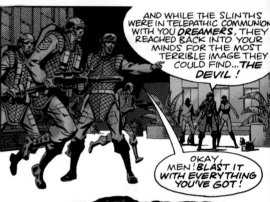

AND WHILE THE SLINTHS WERE IN TELEPATHIC COMMUNION WITH YOU *DREAMERS*, THEY REACHED BACK INTO YOUR MINDS FOR THE MOST TERRIBLE IMAGE THEY COULD FIND...*THE DEVIL!*

BUT ITS BODY'S MADE UP OF *HUNDREDS OF SLINTHS*... ACTING TOGETHER AS A *GROUP MIND* ...WITH A *SINGLE BODY*

BUT WHY MAKE A DEVIL?

OKAY, MEN! *BLAST IT* WITH EVERYTHING YOU'VE GOT!

BUT...

IT'S NOT *WORKING!* WE'RE HITTING IT WITH *THORSEN-303'S*... AND IT'S JUST *SOAKING THEM UP!*

IN FACT... IT'S GETTING *BIGGER!*

TELL YOUR MEN TO *CEASE FIRE*, CAPTAIN! THE SLINTHS ARE JUST *ABSORBING THE ENERGY!*

OLD-FASHIONED *PROJECTILE WEAPONS* MIGHT WORK, BUT...

COME ON, SHARON... WE'LL BE BACK, DOCTOR...

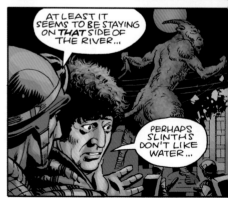

AT LEAST IT SEEMS TO BE STAYING ON *THAT* SIDE OF THE RIVER...

PERHAPS SLINTHS DON'T LIKE WATER...

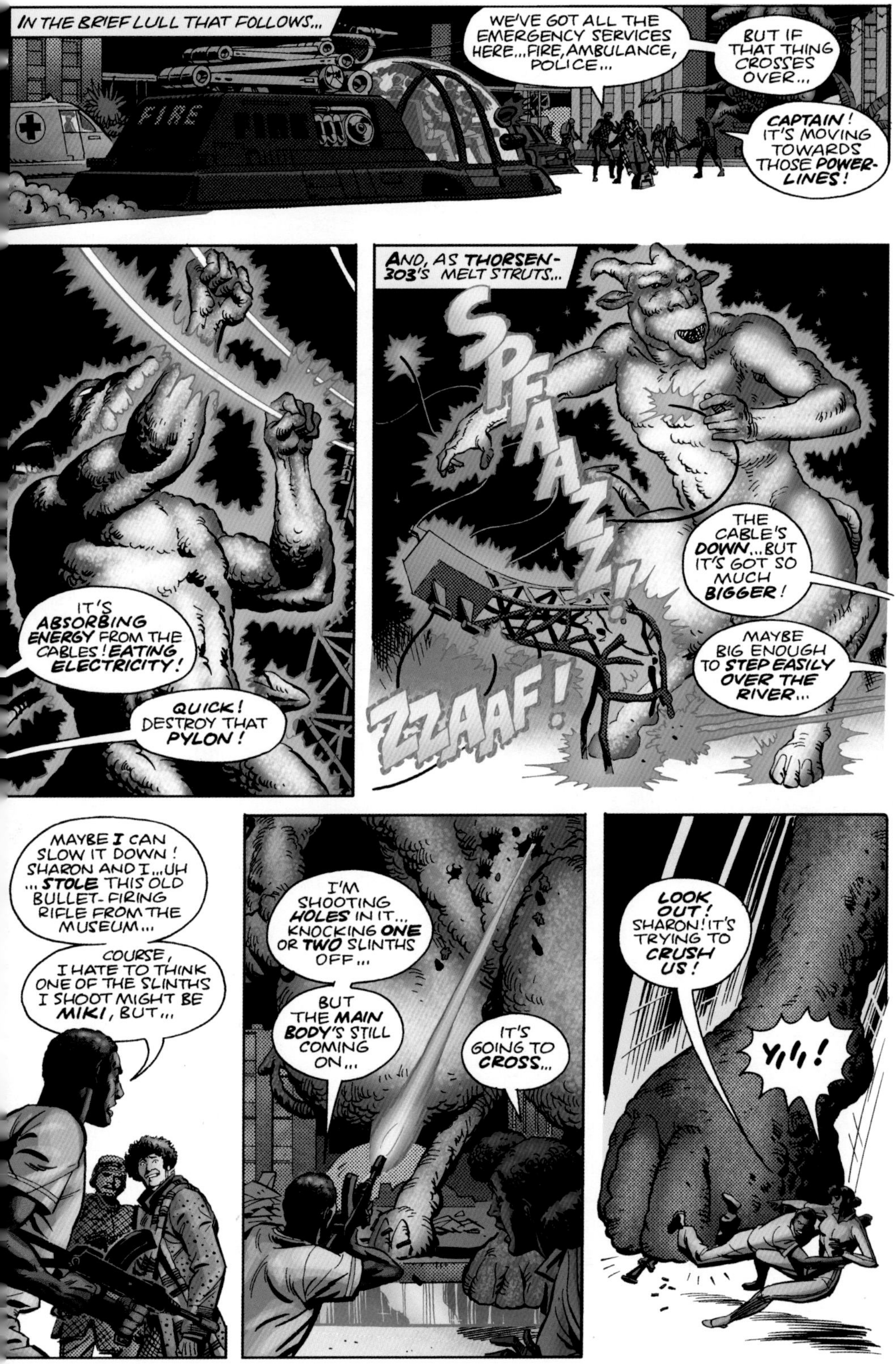
IN THE BRIEF LULL THAT FOLLOWS...
FIRE
FIRE
WE'VE GOT ALL THE EMERGENCY SERVICES HERE...FIRE, AMBULANCE, POLICE...
BUT IF THAT THING CROSSES OVER...
CAPTAIN! IT'S MOVING TOWARDS THOSE POWER-LINES!
IT'S ABSORBING ENERGY FROM THE CABLES! EATING ELECTRICITY!
QUICK! DESTROY THAT PYLON!
AND, AS THORSEN-303'S MELT STRUTS...
SPFAAZZZ!
ZZAAF!
THE CABLE'S DOWN...BUT IT'S GOT SO MUCH BIGGER!
MAYBE BIG ENOUGH TO STEP EASILY OVER THE RIVER...
MAYBE I CAN SLOW IT DOWN! SHARON AND I...UH ...STOLE THIS OLD BULLET-FIRING RIFLE FROM THE MUSEUM...
COURSE, I HATE TO THINK ONE OF THE SLINTHS I SHOOT MIGHT BE MIKI, BUT...
I'M SHOOTING HOLES IN IT... KNOCKING ONE OR TWO SLINTHS OFF...
BUT THE MAIN BODY'S STILL COMING ON...
IT'S GOING TO CROSS...
LOOK OUT! SHARON! IT'S TRYING TO CRUSH US!
YI!!

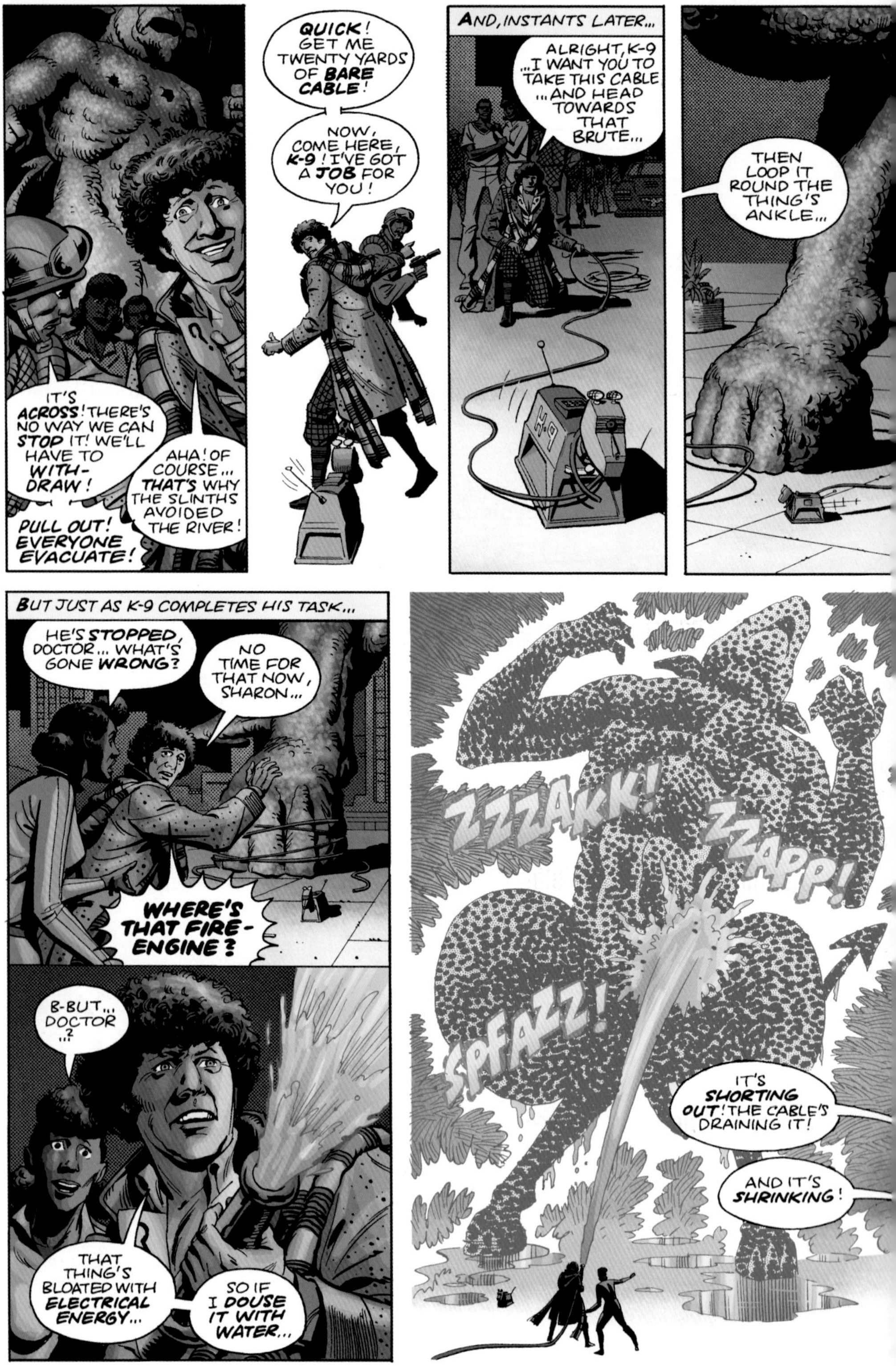

QUICK! GET ME TWENTY YARDS OF BARE CABLE!
NOW, COME HERE, K-9! I'VE GOT A JOB FOR YOU!
IT'S ACROSS! THERE'S NO WAY WE CAN STOP IT! WE'LL HAVE TO WITH-DRAW!
AHA! OF COURSE... THAT'S WHY THE SLINTHS AVOIDED THE RIVER!
PULL OUT! EVERYONE EVACUATE!
AND, INSTANTS LATER...
ALRIGHT, K-9 ...I WANT YOU TO TAKE THIS CABLE ...AND HEAD TOWARDS THAT BRUTE...
THEN LOOP IT ROUND THE THING'S ANKLE...
BUT JUST AS K-9 COMPLETES HIS TASK...
HE'S STOPPED, DOCTOR... WHAT'S GONE WRONG?
NO TIME FOR THAT NOW, SHARON...
WHERE'S THAT FIRE-ENGINE?
B-BUT... DOCTOR ...?
THAT THING'S BLOATED WITH ELECTRICAL ENERGY...
SO IF I DOUSE IT WITH WATER...
ZZZAKK!
ZZAPP!
SPFAZZ!
IT'S SHORTING OUT! THE CABLE'S DRAINING IT!
AND IT'S SHRINKING!

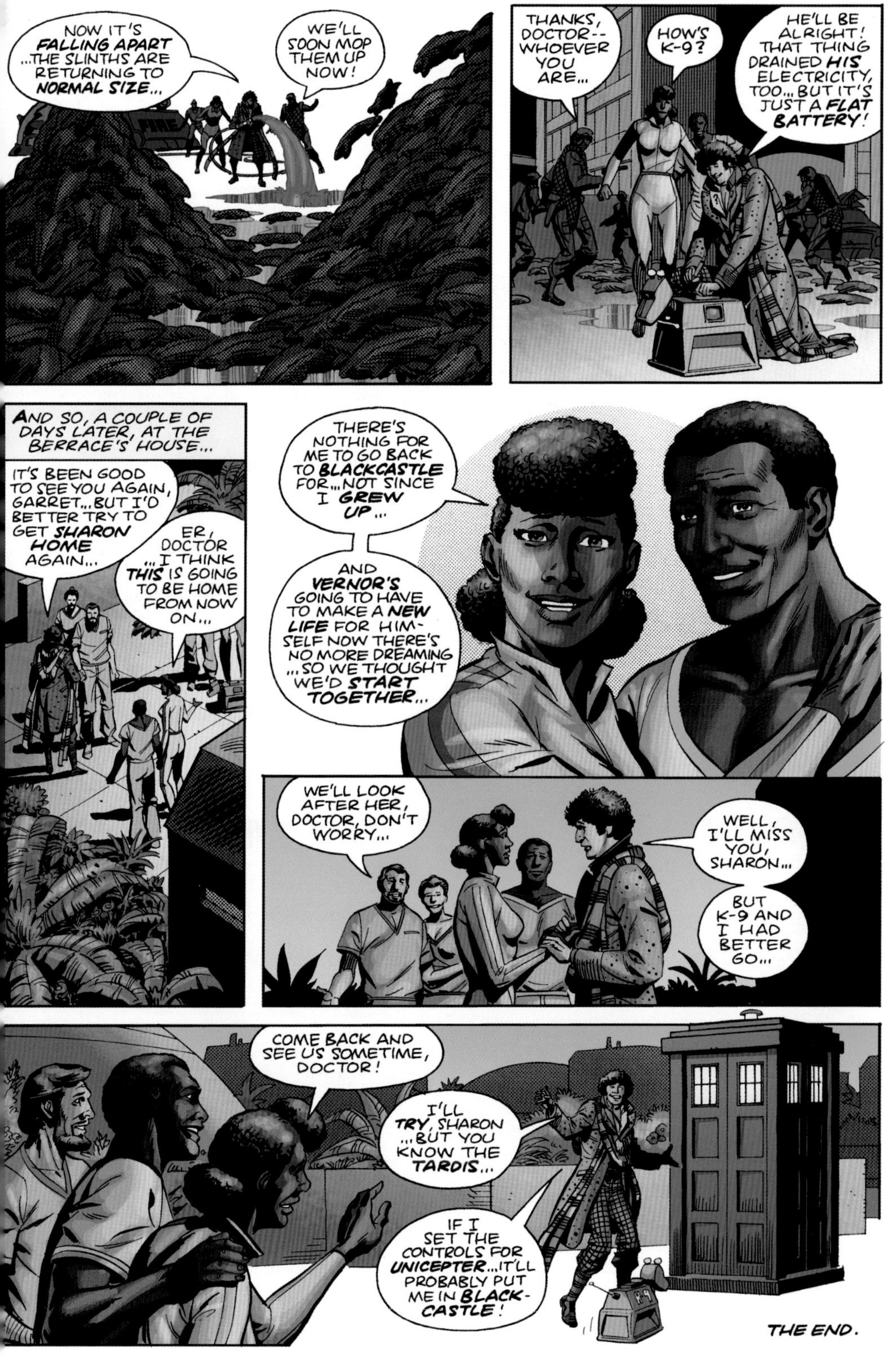
NOW IT'S FALLING APART ...THE SLINTHS ARE RETURNING TO NORMAL SIZE...
WE'LL SOON MOP THEM UP NOW!
FIRE
THANKS, DOCTOR-- WHOEVER YOU ARE...
HOW'S K-9?
HE'LL BE ALRIGHT! THAT THING DRAINED HIS ELECTRICITY, TOO... BUT IT'S JUST A FLAT BATTERY!
AND SO, A COUPLE OF DAYS LATER, AT THE BERRACE'S HOUSE...
IT'S BEEN GOOD TO SEE YOU AGAIN, GARRET... BUT I'D BETTER TRY TO GET SHARON HOME AGAIN...
ER, DOCTOR ...I THINK THIS IS GOING TO BE HOME FROM NOW ON...
THERE'S NOTHING FOR ME TO GO BACK TO BLACKCASTLE FOR... NOT SINCE I GREW UP...
AND VERNOR'S GOING TO HAVE TO MAKE A NEW LIFE FOR HIMSELF NOW THERE'S NO MORE DREAMING ...SO WE THOUGHT WE'D START TOGETHER...
WE'LL LOOK AFTER HER, DOCTOR, DON'T WORRY...
WELL, I'LL MISS YOU, SHARON...
BUT K-9 AND I HAD BETTER GO...
COME BACK AND SEE US SOMETIME, DOCTOR!
I'LL TRY, SHARON ...BUT YOU KNOW THE TARDIS...
IF I SET THE CONTROLS FOR UNICEPTER...IT'LL PROBABLY PUT ME IN BLACKCASTLE!
THE END.

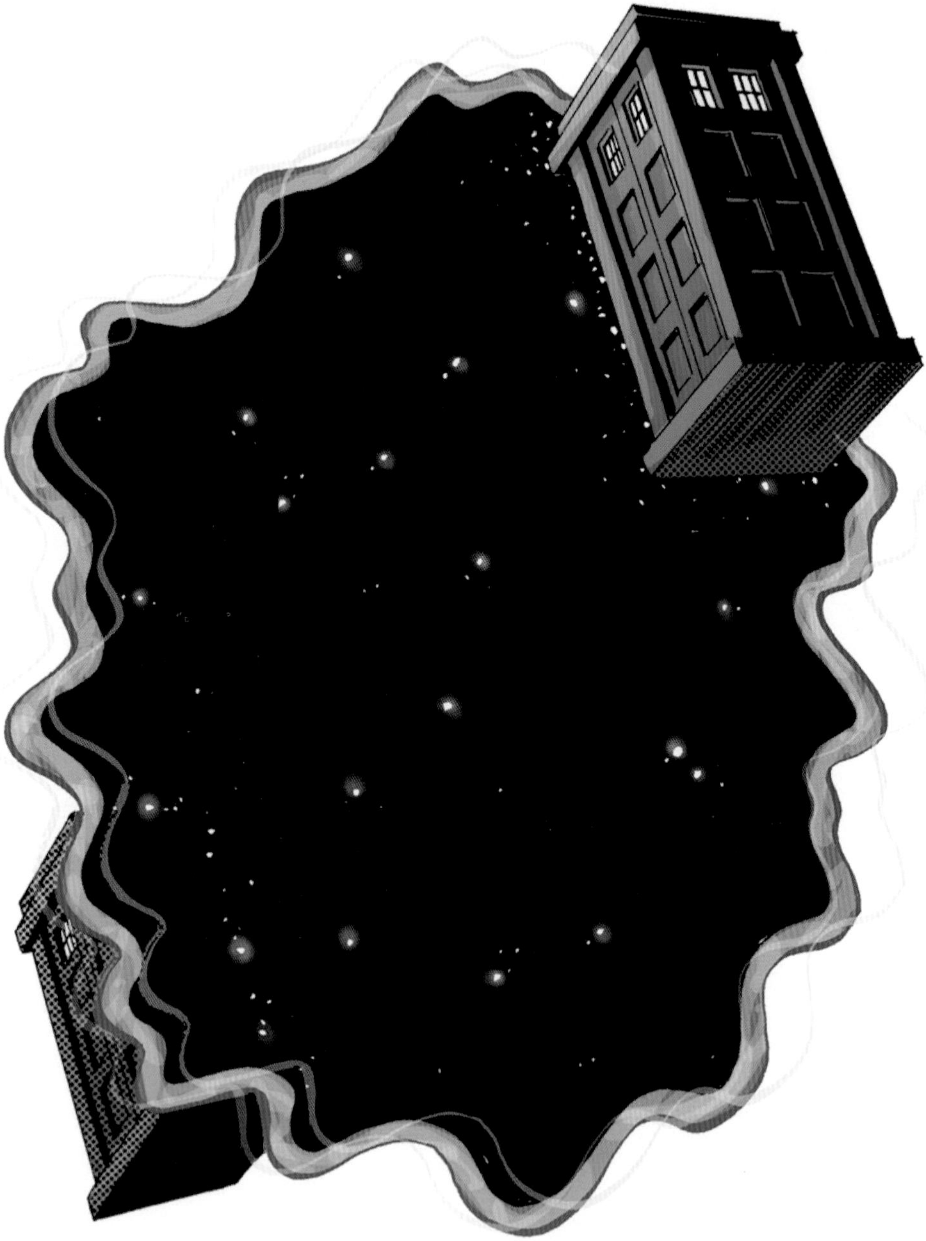

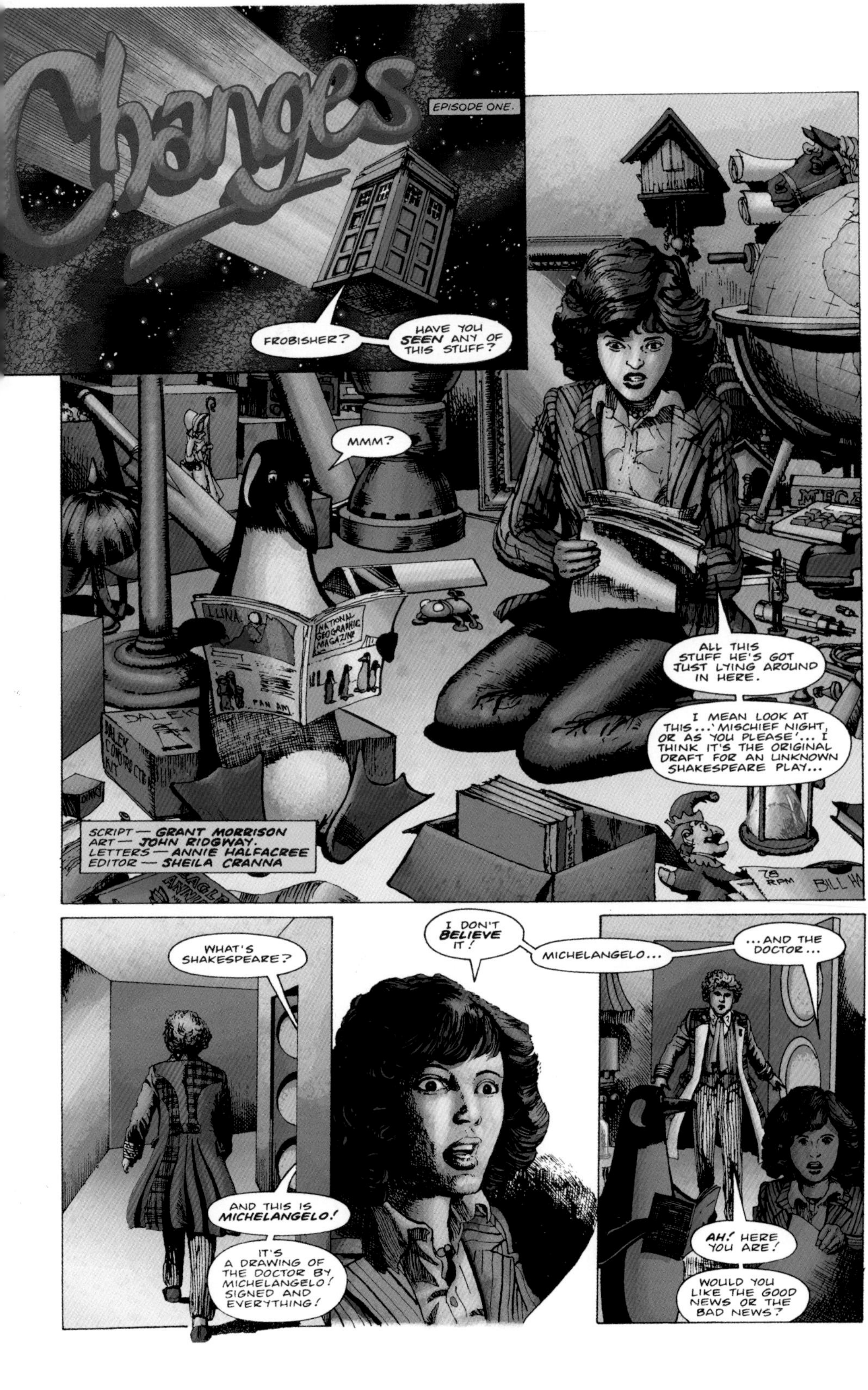
Changes
EPISODE ONE.
FROBISHER?
HAVE YOU SEEN ANY OF THIS STUFF?
MMM?
ALL THIS STUFF HE'S GOT JUST LYING AROUND IN HERE.
I MEAN LOOK AT THIS... 'MISCHIEF NIGHT, OR AS YOU PLEASE'... I THINK IT'S THE ORIGINAL DRAFT FOR AN UNKNOWN SHAKESPEARE PLAY...
SCRIPT — GRANT MORRISON
ART — JOHN RIDGWAY.
LETTERS — ANNIE HALFACREE
EDITOR — SHEILA CRANNA
WHAT'S SHAKESPEARE?
AND THIS IS MICHELANGELO!
IT'S A DRAWING OF THE DOCTOR BY MICHELANGELO! SIGNED AND EVERYTHING!
I DON'T BELIEVE IT!
MICHELANGELO...
...AND THE DOCTOR...
AH! HERE YOU ARE!
WOULD YOU LIKE THE GOOD NEWS OR THE BAD NEWS?

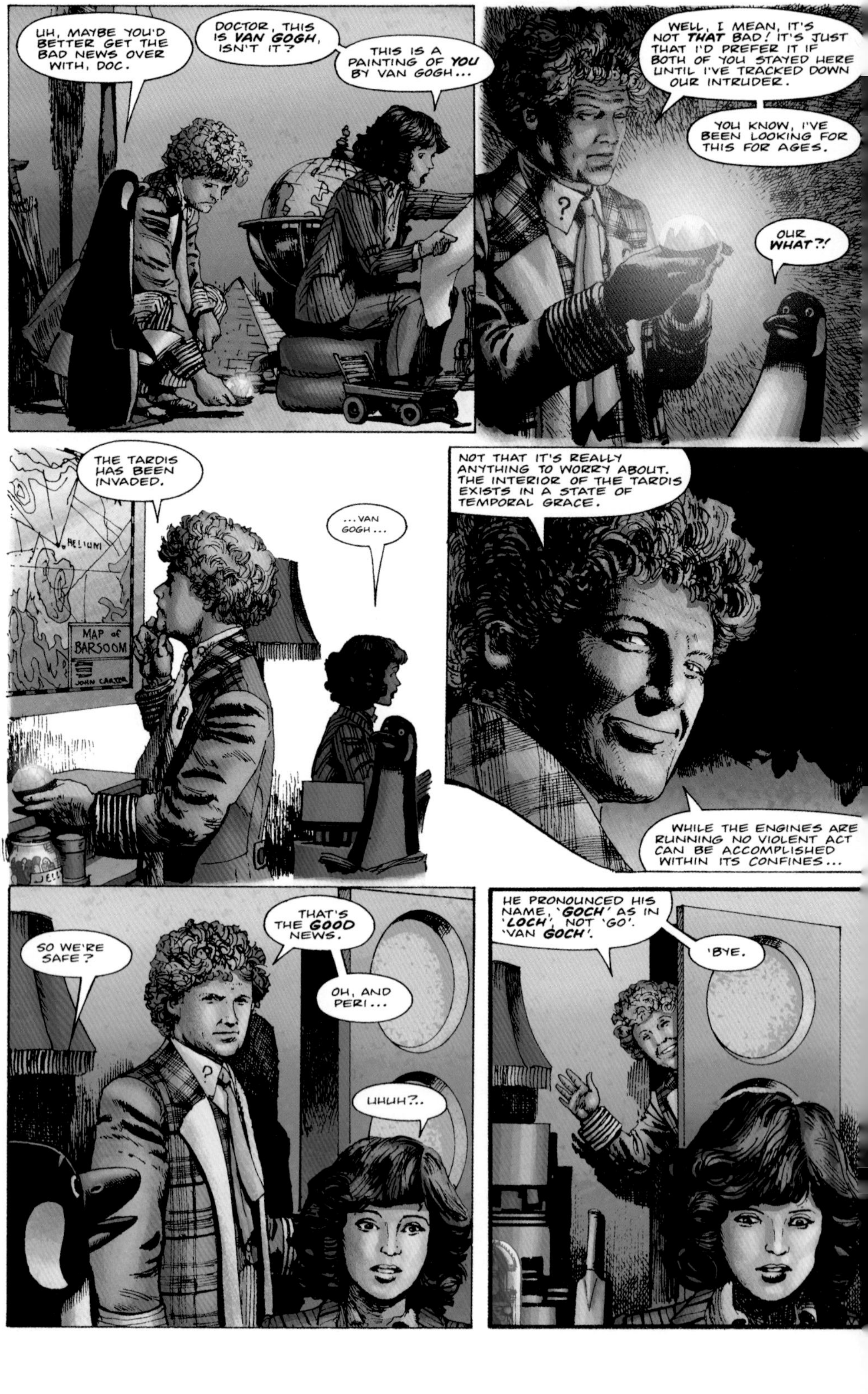
UH, MAYBE YOU'D BETTER GET THE BAD NEWS OVER WITH, DOC.
DOCTOR, THIS IS VAN GOGH, ISN'T IT?
THIS IS A PAINTING OF YOU BY VAN GOGH...
WELL, I MEAN, IT'S NOT THAT BAD! IT'S JUST THAT I'D PREFER IT IF BOTH OF YOU STAYED HERE UNTIL I'VE TRACKED DOWN OUR INTRUDER.
YOU KNOW, I'VE BEEN LOOKING FOR THIS FOR AGES.
OUR WHAT?!
THE TARDIS HAS BEEN INVADED.
MAP of BARSOOM
JOHN CARTER
HELIUM
...VAN GOGH...
NOT THAT IT'S REALLY ANYTHING TO WORRY ABOUT. THE INTERIOR OF THE TARDIS EXISTS IN A STATE OF TEMPORAL GRACE.
WHILE THE ENGINES ARE RUNNING NO VIOLENT ACT CAN BE ACCOMPLISHED WITHIN ITS CONFINES...
SO WE'RE SAFE?
THAT'S THE GOOD NEWS.
OH, AND PERI...
UHUH?..
HE PRONOUNCED HIS NAME, 'GOCH' AS IN 'LOCH', NOT 'GO'. 'VAN GOCH'.
'BYE.

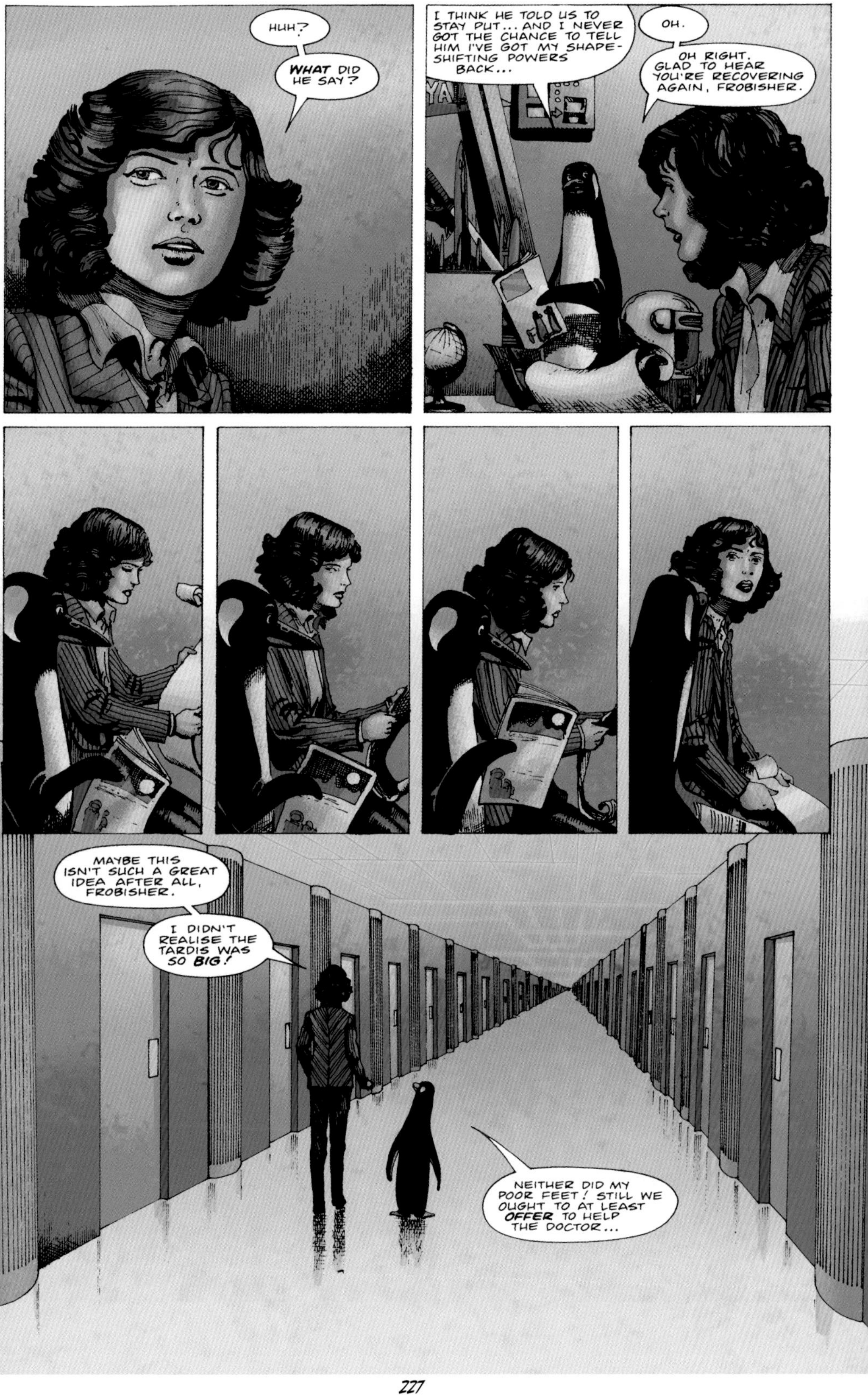
HUH?
WHAT DID HE SAY?
I THINK HE TOLD US TO STAY PUT... AND I NEVER GOT THE CHANCE TO TELL HIM I'VE GOT MY SHAPE-SHIFTING POWERS BACK...
OH.
OH RIGHT. GLAD TO HEAR YOU'RE RECOVERING AGAIN, FROBISHER.
MAYBE THIS ISN'T SUCH A GREAT IDEA AFTER ALL, FROBISHER.
I DIDN'T REALISE THE TARDIS WAS SO BIG!
NEITHER DID MY POOR FEET! STILL WE OUGHT TO AT LEAST OFFER TO HELP THE DOCTOR...

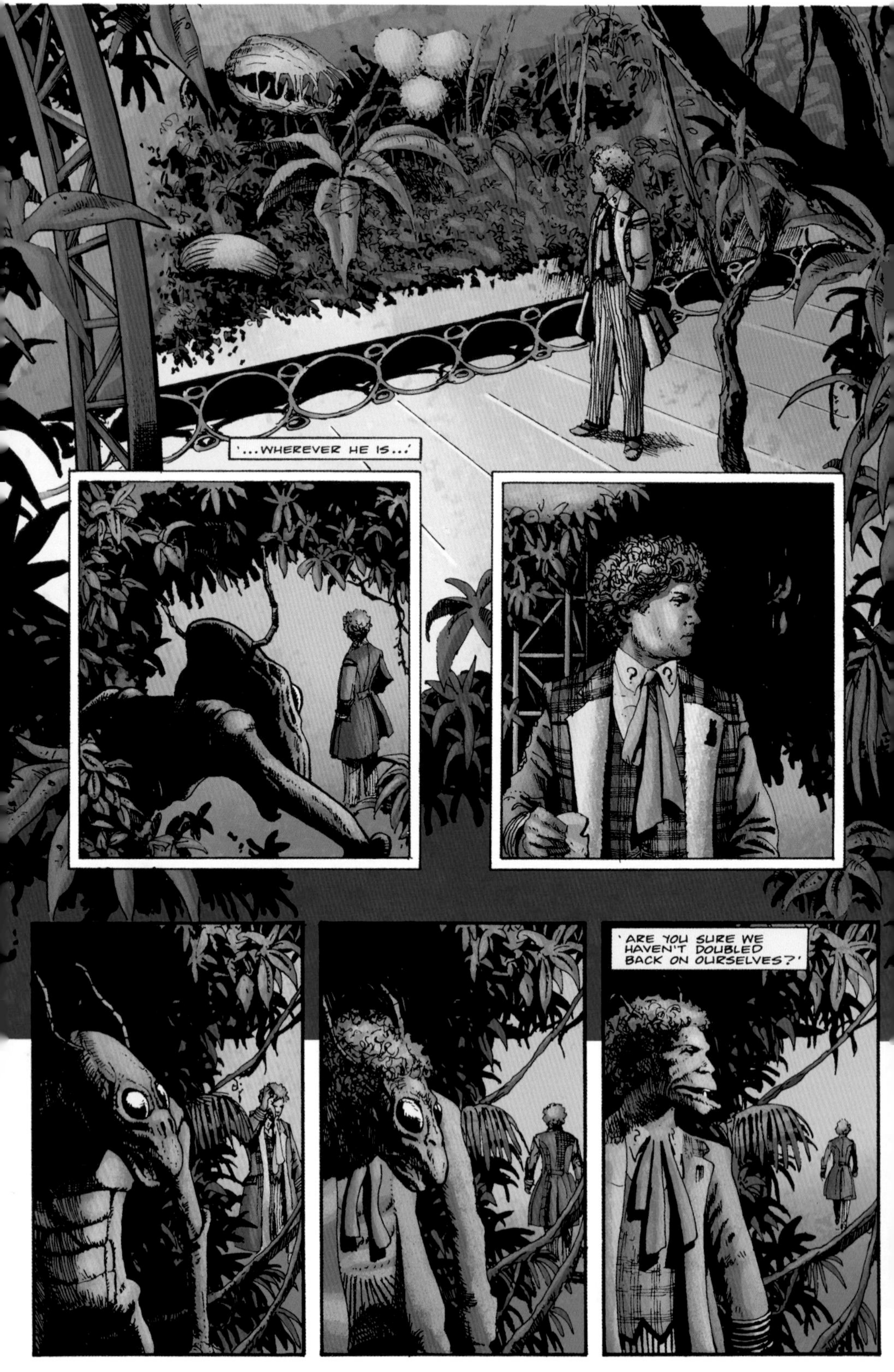
'...WHEREVER HE IS...'
'ARE YOU SURE WE HAVEN'T DOUBLED BACK ON OURSELVES?'

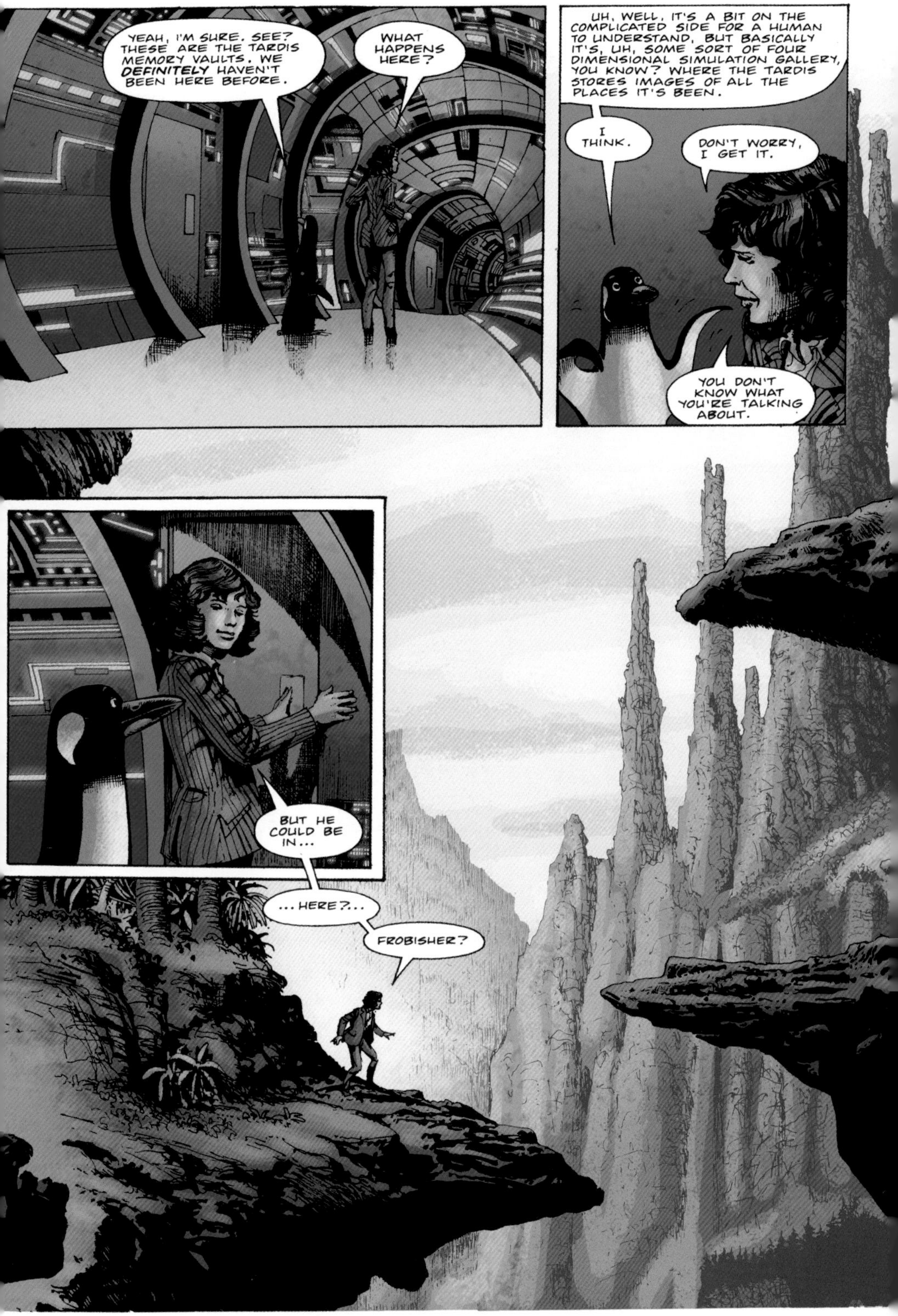
YEAH, I'M SURE. SEE? THESE ARE THE TARDIS MEMORY VAULTS. WE DEFINITELY HAVEN'T BEEN HERE BEFORE.
WHAT HAPPENS HERE?
UH, WELL, IT'S A BIT ON THE COMPLICATED SIDE FOR A HUMAN TO UNDERSTAND, BUT BASICALLY IT'S, UH, SOME SORT OF FOUR DIMENSIONAL SIMULATION GALLERY, YOU KNOW? WHERE THE TARDIS STORES IMAGES OF ALL THE PLACES IT'S BEEN.
I THINK.
DON'T WORRY, I GET IT.
YOU DON'T KNOW WHAT YOU'RE TALKING ABOUT.
BUT HE COULD BE IN...
...HERE?...
FROBISHER?

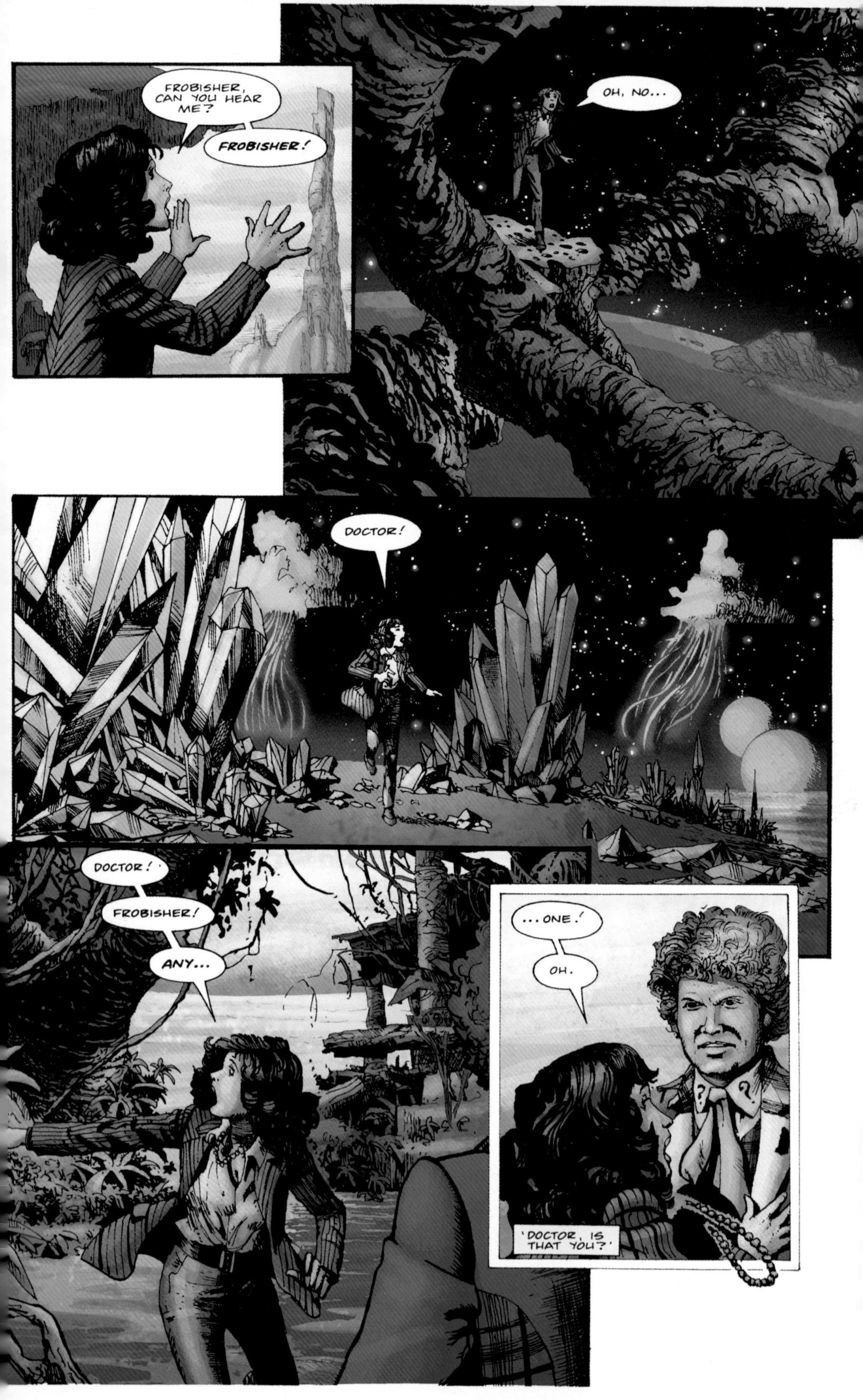
FROBISHER, CAN YOU HEAR ME?
FROBISHER!
OH, NO...
DOCTOR!
DOCTOR!
FROBISHER!
ANY...
...ONE!
OH.
'DOCTOR, IS THAT YOU?'

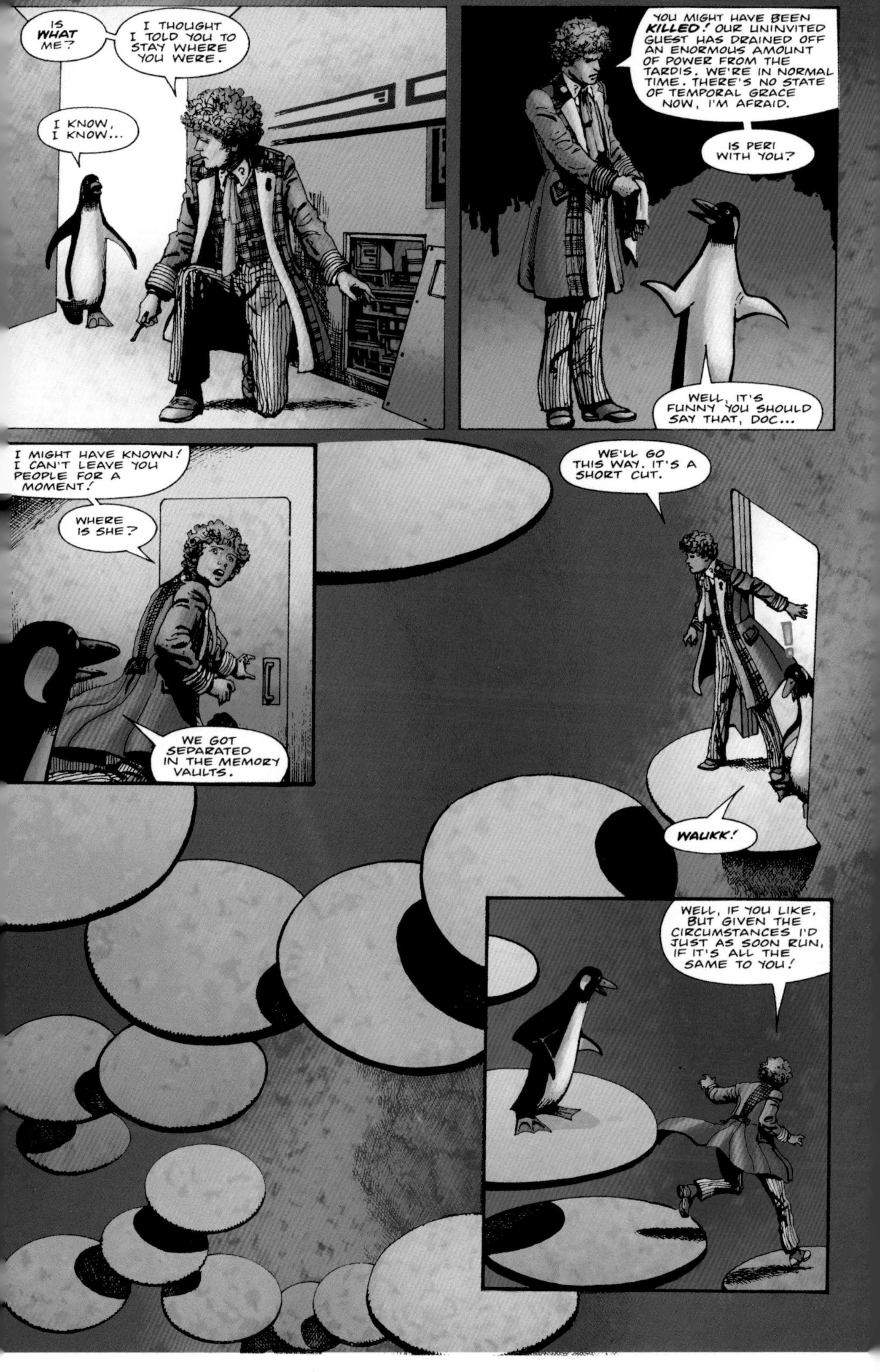

IS WHAT ME?
I THOUGHT I TOLD YOU TO STAY WHERE YOU WERE.
I KNOW, I KNOW...
YOU MIGHT HAVE BEEN KILLED! OUR UNINVITED GUEST HAS DRAINED OFF AN ENORMOUS AMOUNT OF POWER FROM THE TARDIS. WE'RE IN NORMAL TIME. THERE'S NO STATE OF TEMPORAL GRACE NOW, I'M AFRAID.
IS PERI WITH YOU?
WELL, IT'S FUNNY YOU SHOULD SAY THAT, DOC...
I MIGHT HAVE KNOWN! I CAN'T LEAVE YOU PEOPLE FOR A MOMENT!
WHERE IS SHE?
WE GOT SEPARATED IN THE MEMORY VAULTS.
WE'LL GO THIS WAY. IT'S A SHORT CUT.
WAUKK!
WELL, IF YOU LIKE, BUT GIVEN THE CIRCUMSTANCES I'D JUST AS SOON RUN, IF IT'S ALL THE SAME TO YOU!

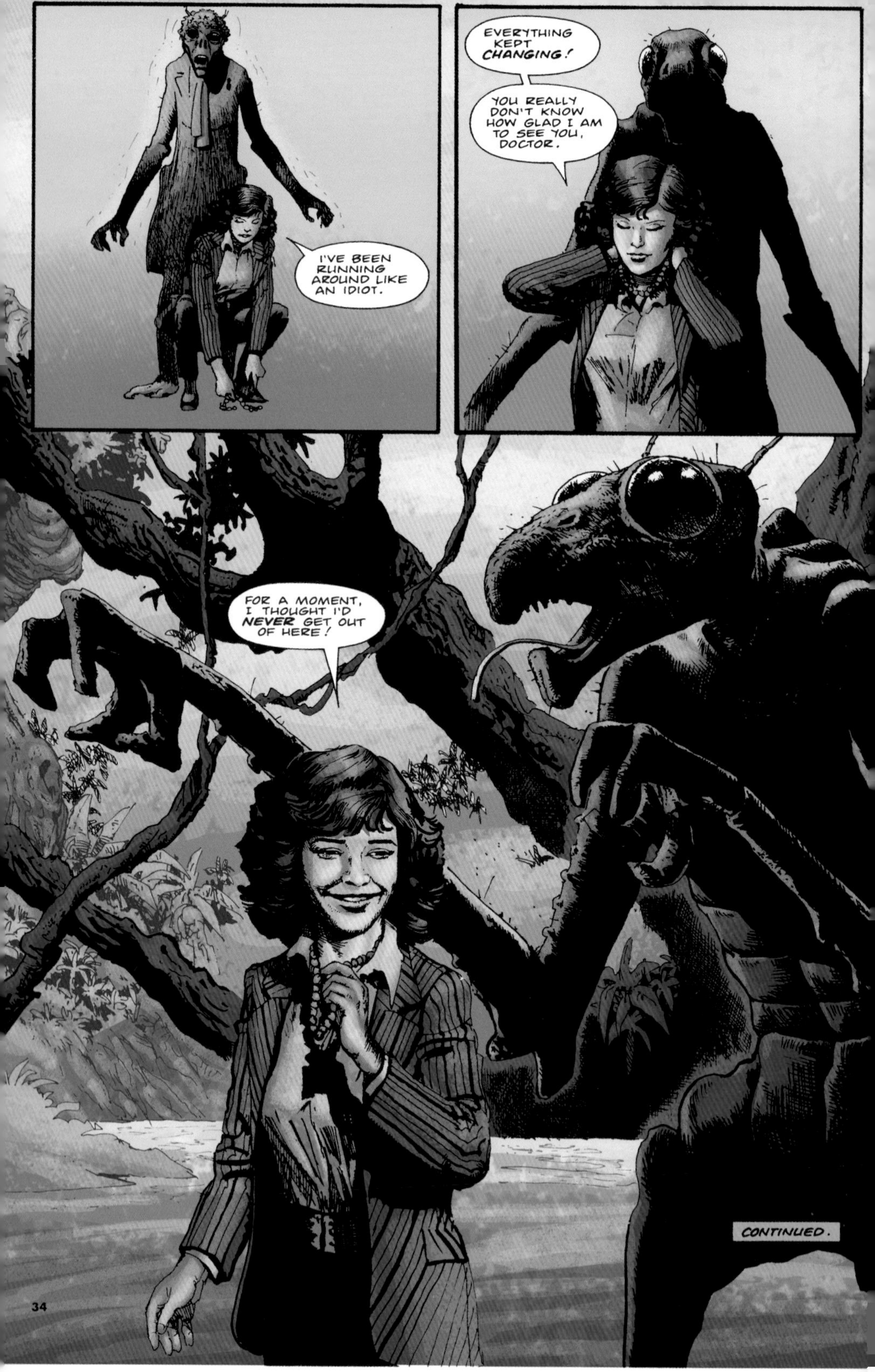
I'VE BEEN RUNNING AROUND LIKE AN IDIOT.
EVERYTHING KEPT CHANGING!
YOU REALLY DON'T KNOW HOW GLAD I AM TO SEE YOU, DOCTOR.
FOR A MOMENT, I THOUGHT I'D NEVER GET OUT OF HERE!
CONTINUED.
34

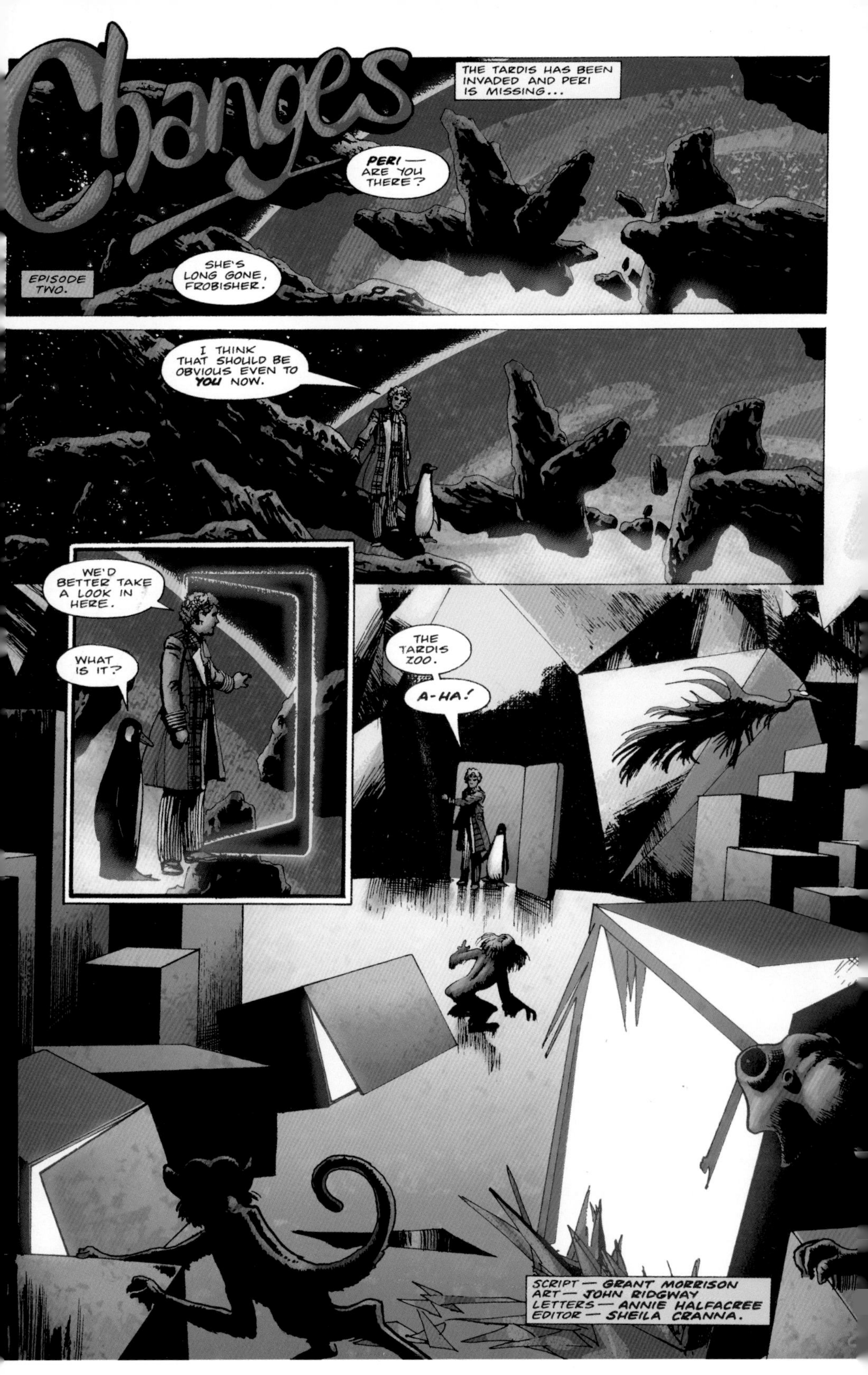
Changes
THE TARDIS HAS BEEN INVADED AND PERI IS MISSING...
PERI — ARE YOU THERE?
EPISODE TWO.
SHE'S LONG GONE, FROBISHER.
I THINK THAT SHOULD BE OBVIOUS EVEN TO YOU NOW.
WE'D BETTER TAKE A LOOK IN HERE.
WHAT IS IT?
THE TARDIS ZOO.
A-HA!
SCRIPT — GRANT MORRISON
ART — JOHN RIDGWAY
LETTERS — ANNIE HALFACREE
EDITOR — SHEILA CRANNA.

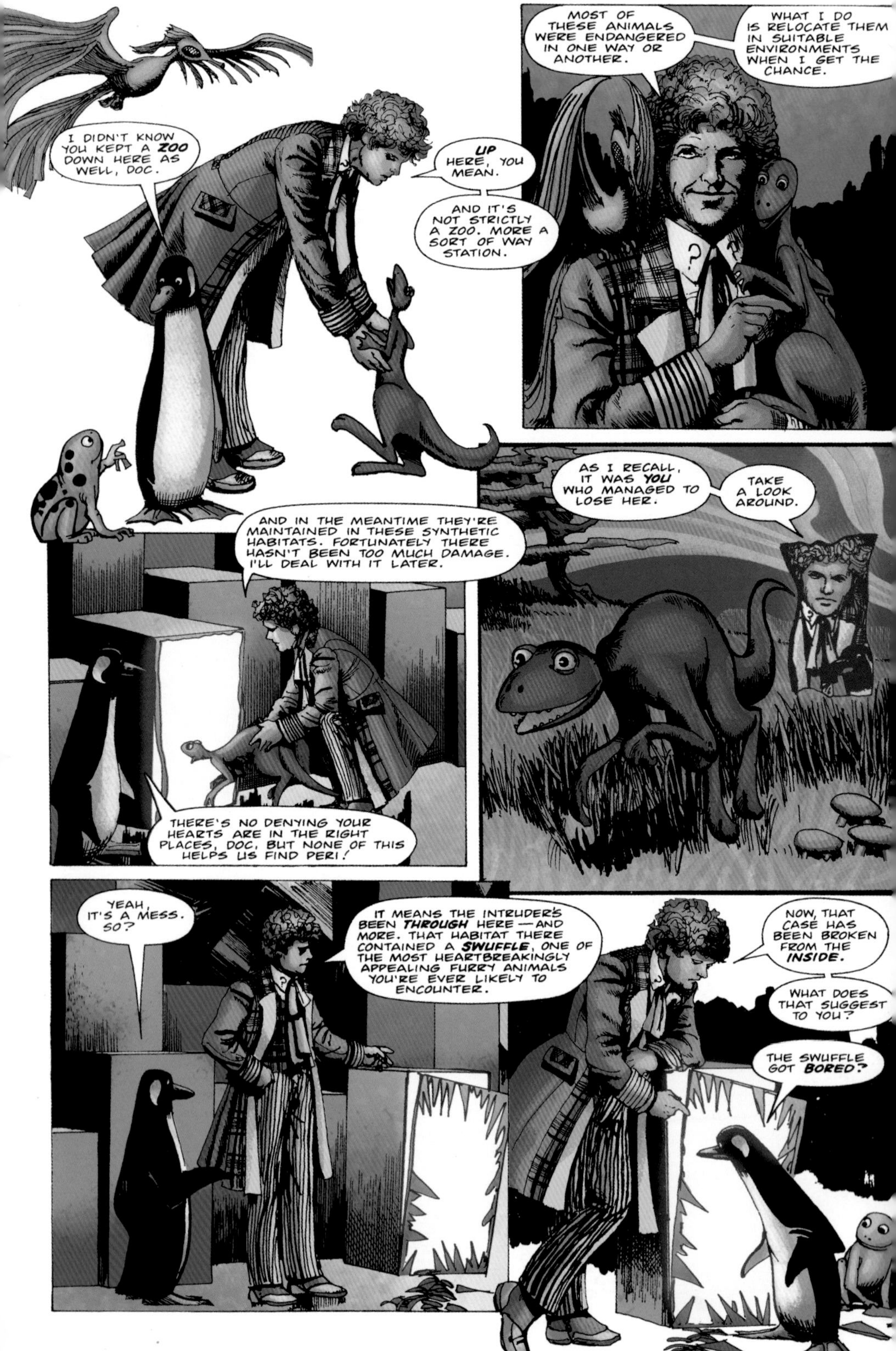
I DIDN'T KNOW YOU KEPT A ZOO DOWN HERE AS WELL, DOC.
UP HERE, YOU MEAN.
AND IT'S NOT STRICTLY A ZOO. MORE A SORT OF WAY STATION.
MOST OF THESE ANIMALS WERE ENDANGERED IN ONE WAY OR ANOTHER.
WHAT I DO IS RELOCATE THEM IN SUITABLE ENVIRONMENTS WHEN I GET THE CHANCE.
AND IN THE MEANTIME THEY'RE MAINTAINED IN THESE SYNTHETIC HABITATS. FORTUNATELY THERE HASN'T BEEN TOO MUCH DAMAGE. I'LL DEAL WITH IT LATER.
THERE'S NO DENYING YOUR HEARTS ARE IN THE RIGHT PLACES, DOC, BUT NONE OF THIS HELPS US FIND PERI!
AS I RECALL, IT WAS YOU WHO MANAGED TO LOSE HER.
TAKE A LOOK AROUND.
YEAH, IT'S A MESS. SO?
IT MEANS THE INTRUDER'S BEEN THROUGH HERE — AND MORE. THAT HABITAT THERE CONTAINED A SWUFFLE, ONE OF THE MOST HEARTBREAKINGLY APPEALING FURRY ANIMALS YOU'RE EVER LIKELY TO ENCOUNTER.
NOW, THAT CASE HAS BEEN BROKEN FROM THE INSIDE.
WHAT DOES THAT SUGGEST TO YOU?
THE SWUFFLE GOT BORED?

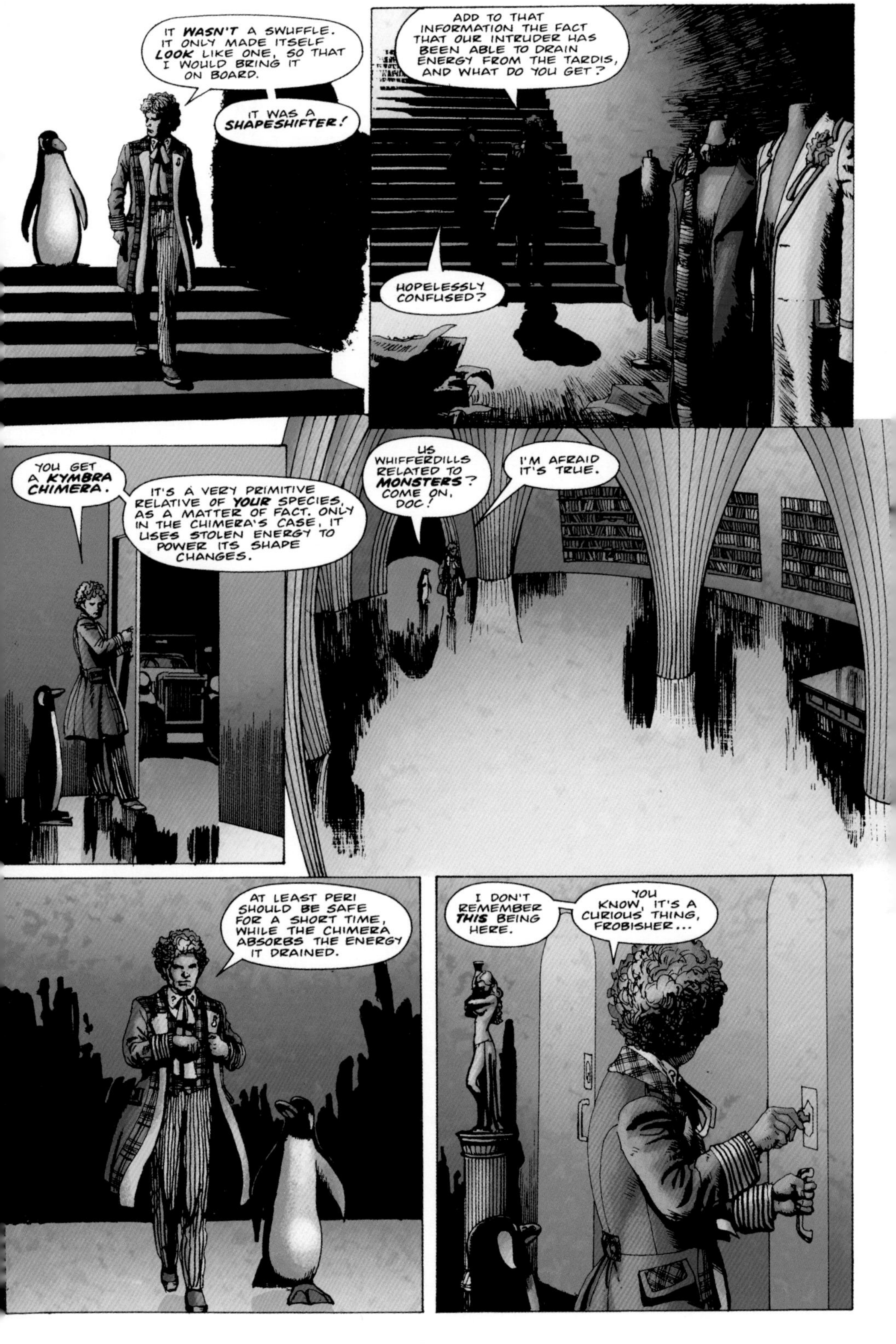

IT WASN'T A SWUFFLE. IT ONLY MADE ITSELF LOOK LIKE ONE, SO THAT I WOULD BRING IT ON BOARD.
IT WAS A SHAPESHIFTER!
ADD TO THAT INFORMATION THE FACT THAT OUR INTRUDER HAS BEEN ABLE TO DRAIN ENERGY FROM THE TARDIS, AND WHAT DO YOU GET?
HOPELESSLY CONFUSED?
YOU GET A KYMBRA CHIMERA.
IT'S A VERY PRIMITIVE RELATIVE OF YOUR SPECIES, AS A MATTER OF FACT. ONLY IN THE CHIMERA'S CASE, IT USES STOLEN ENERGY TO POWER ITS SHAPE CHANGES.
US WHIFFERDILLS RELATED TO MONSTERS? COME ON, DOC!
I'M AFRAID IT'S TRUE.
AT LEAST PERI SHOULD BE SAFE FOR A SHORT TIME, WHILE THE CHIMERA ABSORBS THE ENERGY IT DRAINED.
I DON'T REMEMBER THIS BEING HERE.
YOU KNOW, IT'S A CURIOUS THING, FROBISHER...

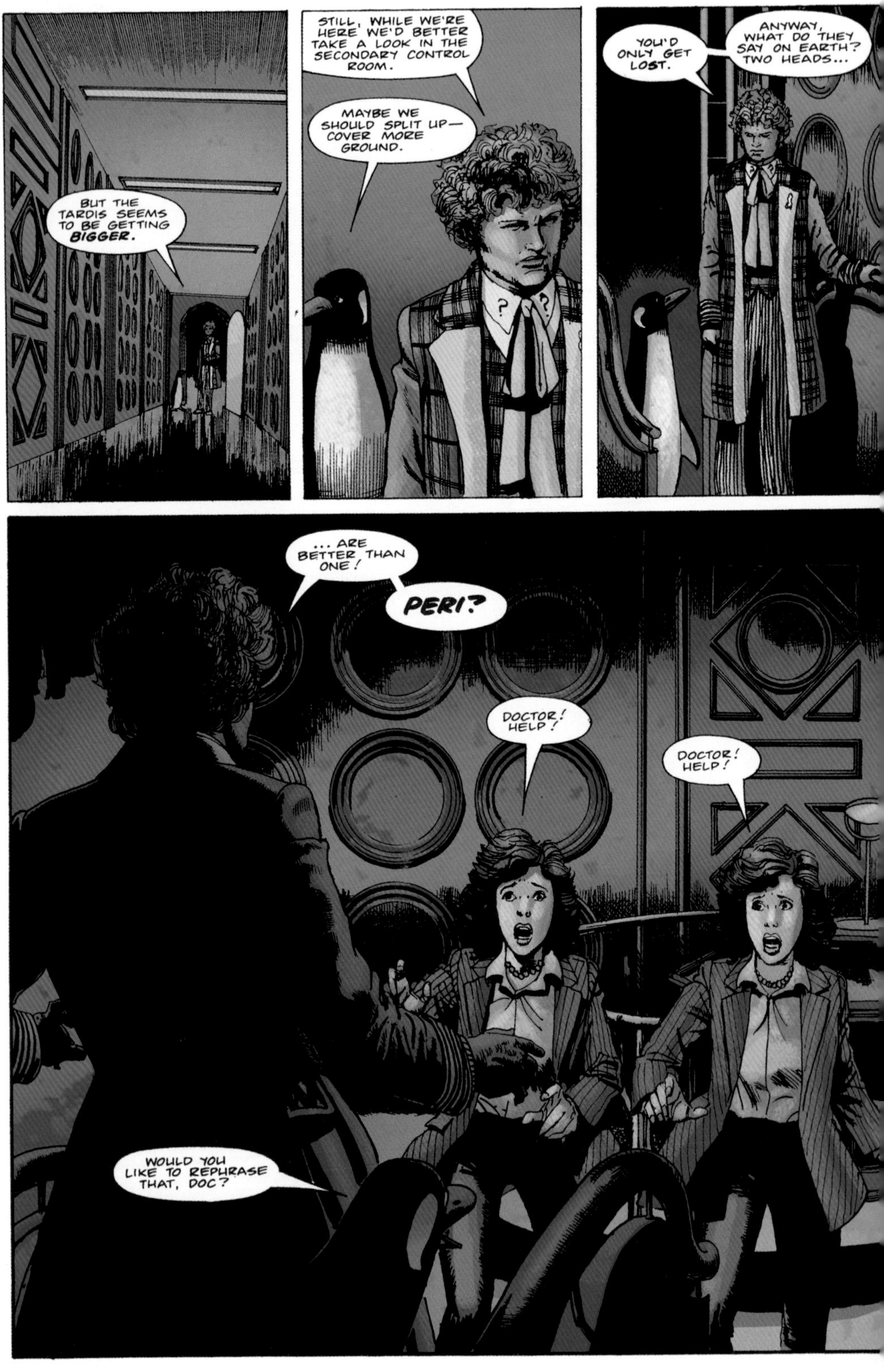
BUT THE TARDIS SEEMS TO BE GETTING BIGGER.
STILL, WHILE WE'RE HERE WE'D BETTER TAKE A LOOK IN THE SECONDARY CONTROL ROOM.
MAYBE WE SHOULD SPLIT UP—COVER MORE GROUND.
YOU'D ONLY GET LOST.
ANYWAY, WHAT DO THEY SAY ON EARTH? TWO HEADS...
... ARE BETTER THAN ONE!
PERI?
DOCTOR! HELP!
DOCTOR! HELP!
WOULD YOU LIKE TO REPHRASE THAT, DOC?

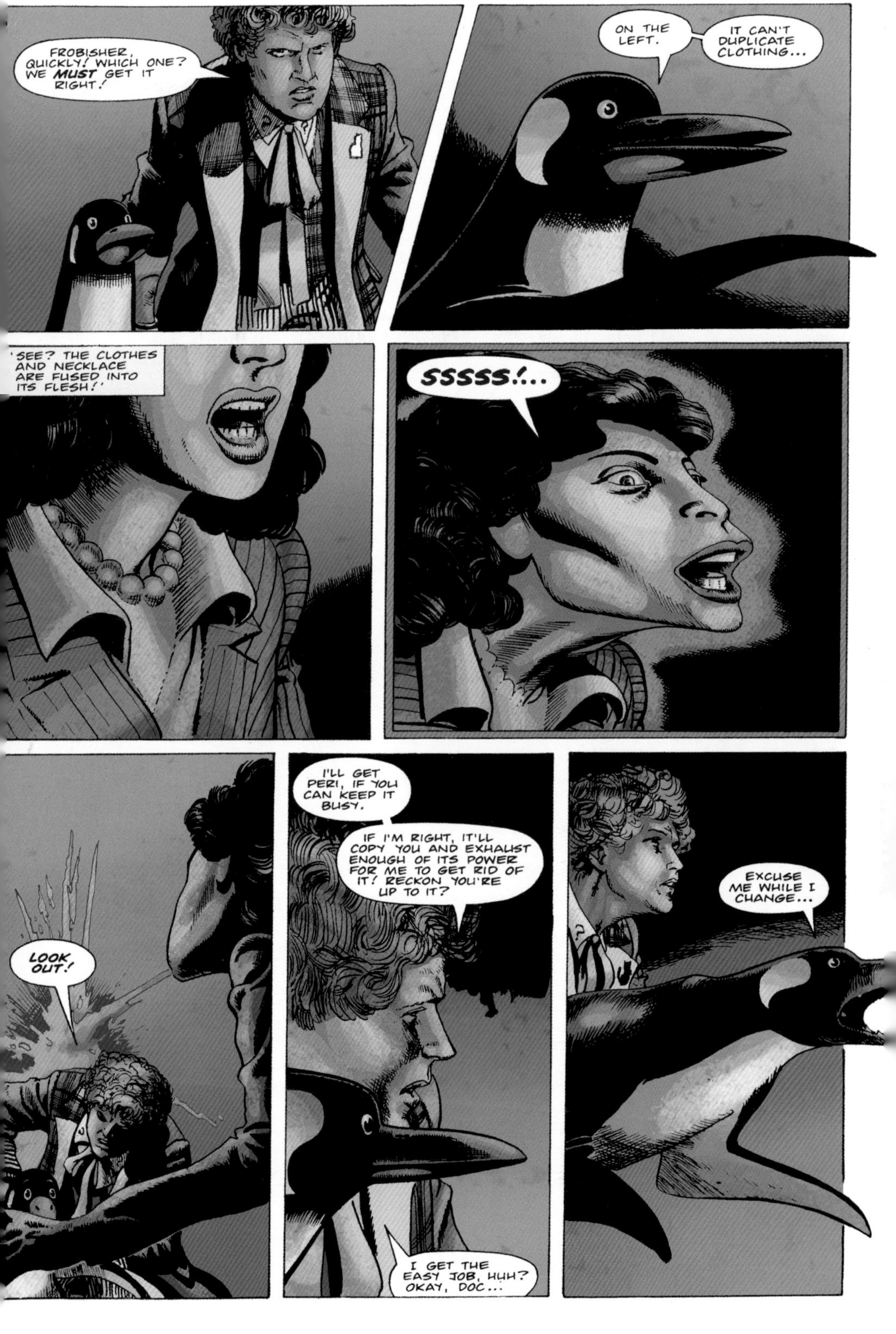
FROBISHER, QUICKLY! WHICH ONE? WE **MUST** GET IT RIGHT!
ON THE LEFT.
IT CAN'T DUPLICATE CLOTHING...
'SEE? THE CLOTHES AND NECKLACE ARE FUSED INTO ITS FLESH!'
SSSSS!...
LOOK OUT!
I'LL GET PERI, IF YOU CAN KEEP IT BUSY.
IF I'M RIGHT, IT'LL COPY YOU AND EXHAUST ENOUGH OF ITS POWER FOR ME TO GET RID OF IT! RECKON YOU'RE UP TO IT?
I GET THE EASY JOB, HUH? OKAY, DOC...
EXCUSE ME WHILE I CHANGE...

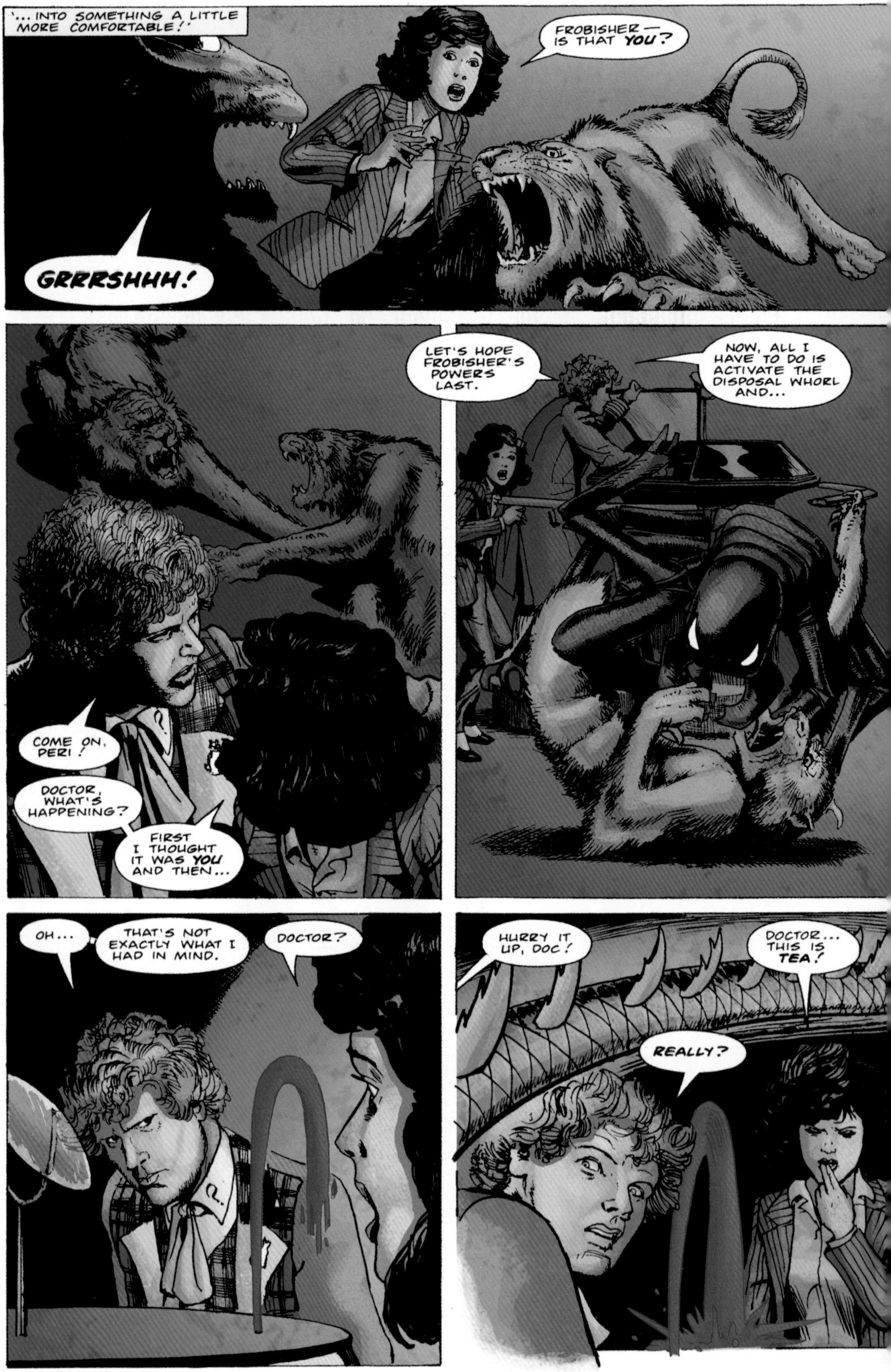
'... INTO SOMETHING A LITTLE MORE COMFORTABLE!'
FROBISHER — IS THAT YOU?
GRRRSHHH!
COME ON, PERI!
DOCTOR, WHAT'S HAPPENING?
FIRST I THOUGHT IT WAS YOU AND THEN...
LET'S HOPE FROBISHER'S POWERS LAST.
NOW, ALL I HAVE TO DO IS ACTIVATE THE DISPOSAL WHORL AND...
OH...
THAT'S NOT EXACTLY WHAT I HAD IN MIND.
DOCTOR?
HURRY IT UP, DOC!
DOCTOR... THIS IS TEA!
REALLY?

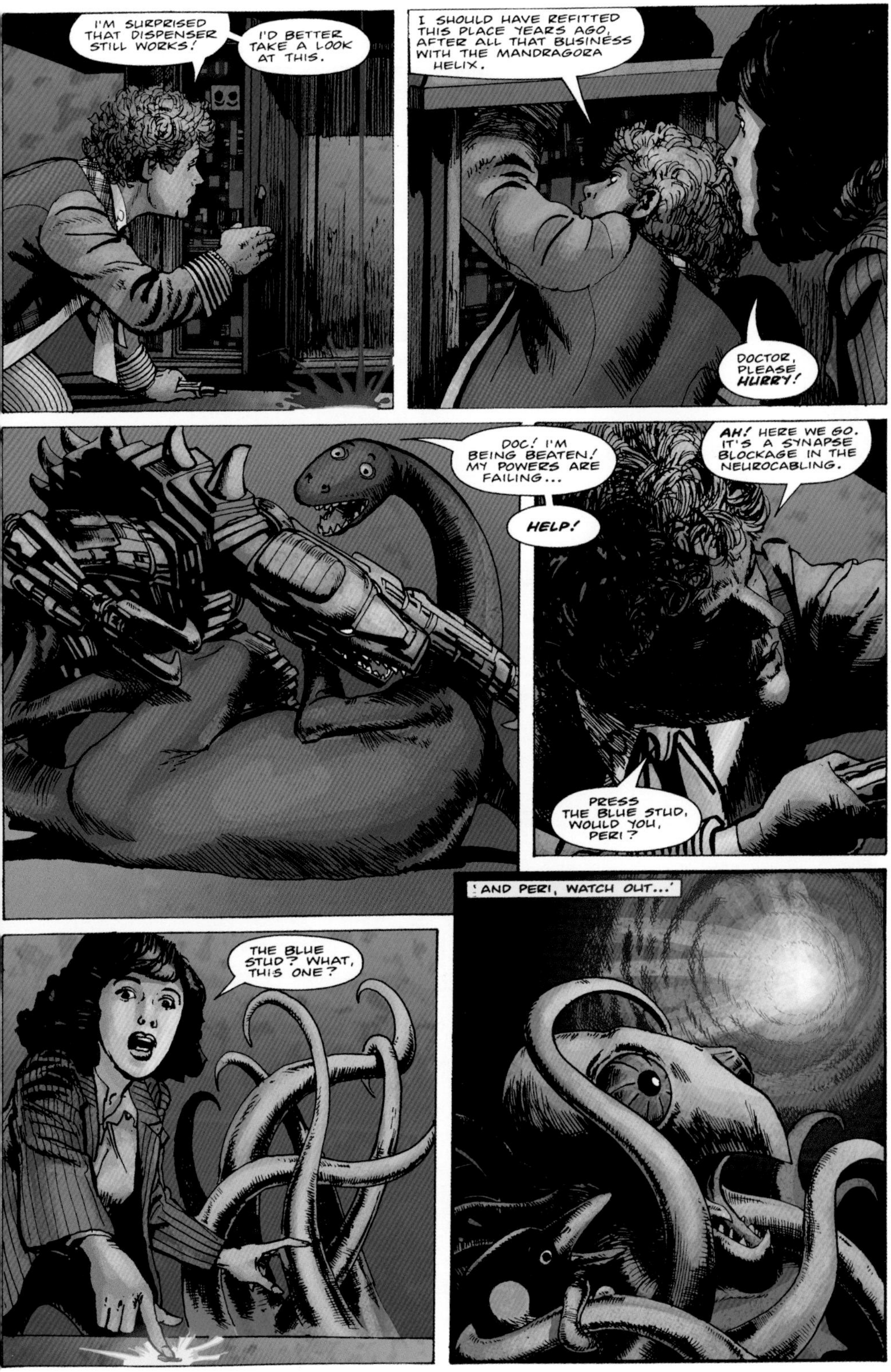
I'M SURPRISED THAT DISPENSER STILL WORKS!
I'D BETTER TAKE A LOOK AT THIS.
I SHOULD HAVE REFITTED THIS PLACE YEARS AGO, AFTER ALL THAT BUSINESS WITH THE MANDRAGORA HELIX.
DOCTOR, PLEASE HURRY!
DOC! I'M BEING BEATEN! MY POWERS ARE FAILING...
HELP!
AH! HERE WE GO. IT'S A SYNAPSE BLOCKAGE IN THE NEUROCABLING.
PRESS THE BLUE STUD, WOULD YOU, PERI?
THE BLUE STUD? WHAT, THIS ONE?
'AND PERI, WATCH OUT...'

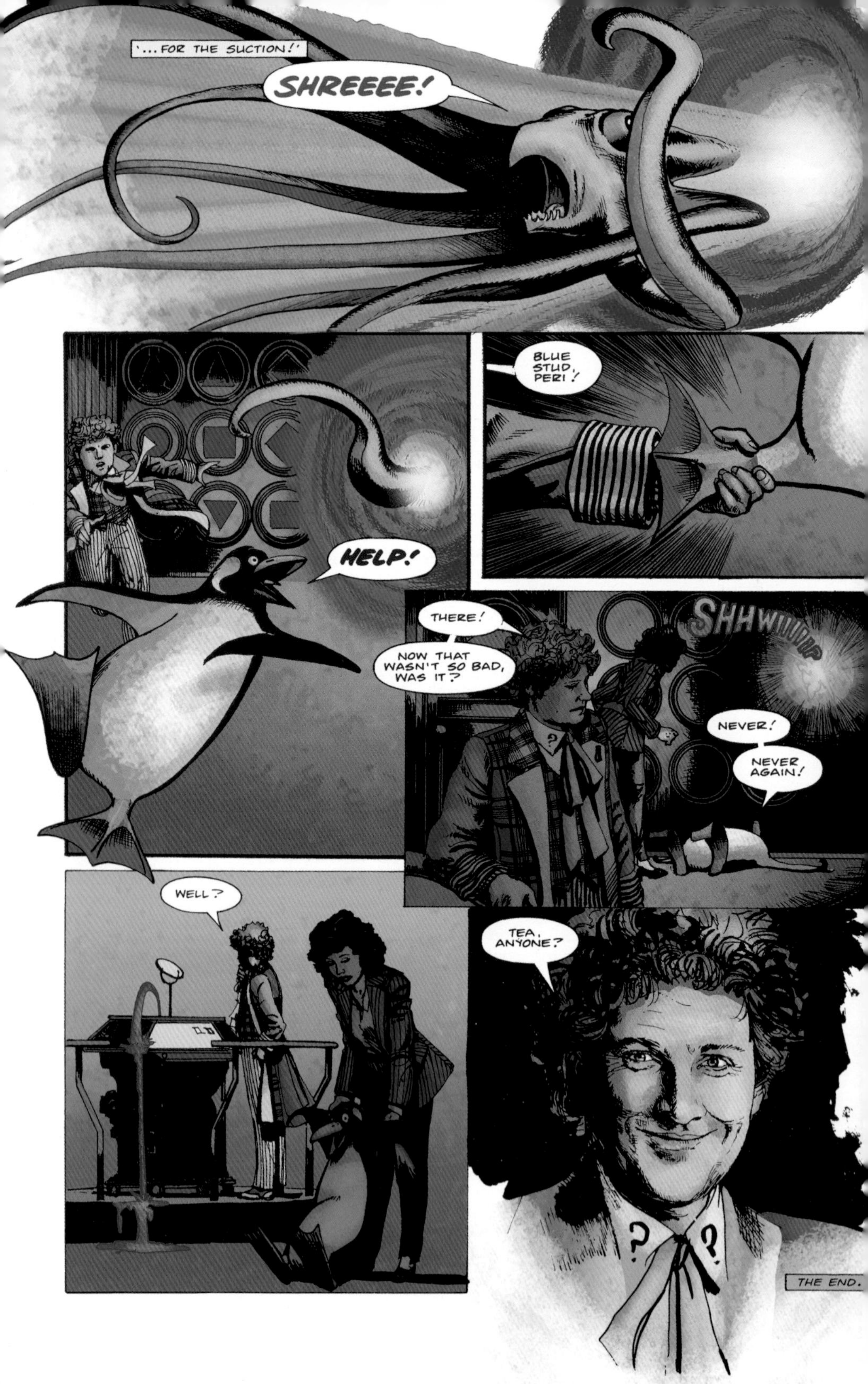
'...FOR THE SUCTION!'
SHREEEE!
HELP!
BLUE STUD, PERI!
THERE!
NOW THAT WASN'T SO BAD, WAS IT?
NEVER!
NEVER AGAIN!
WELL?
TEA, ANYONE?
THE END.

WE ARE LOST.
ALL IS LOST
THE ELECTRIC FOG OF OUR SYNTELLIGENCE IS ALIVE WITH THE RAW MATHEMATICS OF FEAR.
THE END HAS COME. THE CULTURE FACES EXTINCTION.
THE INVADERS FROM OUTER SPACE HAVE BROUGHT ANNIHILATION AND MADNESS TO OUR CALM TUNNEL OCEANS. THEY STRIKE SILENTLY.
AND WITH NO WARNING.
SUNDERSELF! WHY DO YOU SLOW?!
IS SOMETHING WRONG?
...WE...
...INSIDE...
THEY ARE INSIDE WE!
CULTURE SHOCK!
EVERYWHERE. THE INVADERS ARE EVERYWHERE.
THERE IS NO DEFENCE. NO SALVATION.
WE ARE LOST.

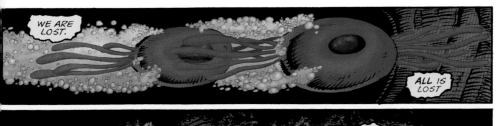

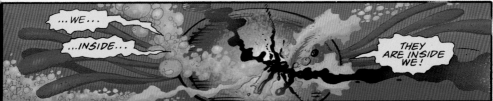

Script **GRANT MORRISON** Art **BRYAN HITCH** Lettering **ZED** Editor **RICHARD STARKINGS**

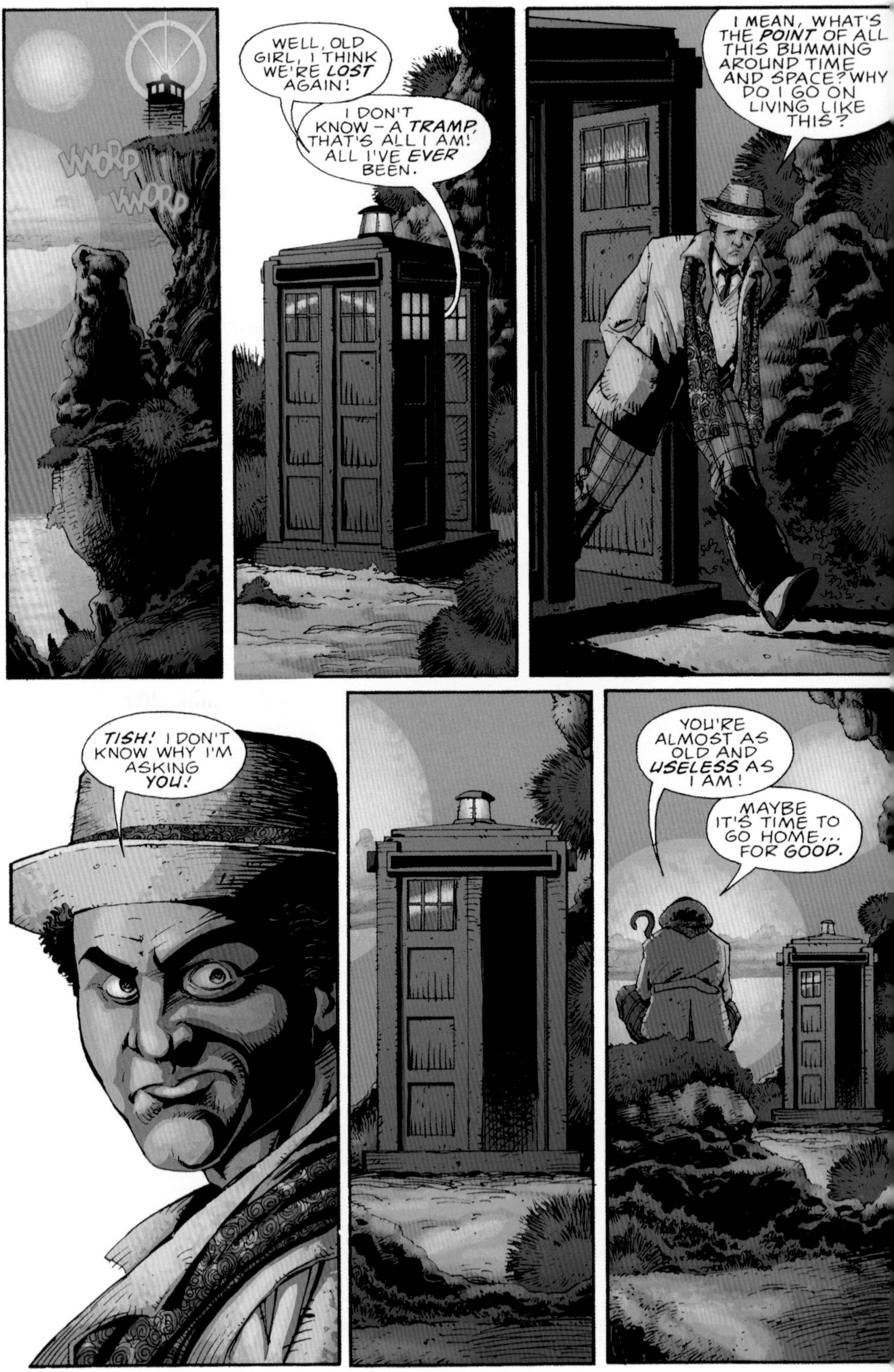
VWORP
VWORP
WELL, OLD GIRL, I THINK WE'RE LOST AGAIN!
I DON'T KNOW – A TRAMP, THAT'S ALL I AM! ALL I'VE EVER BEEN.
I MEAN, WHAT'S THE POINT OF ALL THIS BUMMING AROUND TIME AND SPACE? WHY DO I GO ON LIVING LIKE THIS?
TISH! I DON'T KNOW WHY I'M ASKING YOU!
YOU'RE ALMOST AS OLD AND USELESS AS I AM!
MAYBE IT'S TIME TO GO HOME... FOR GOOD.

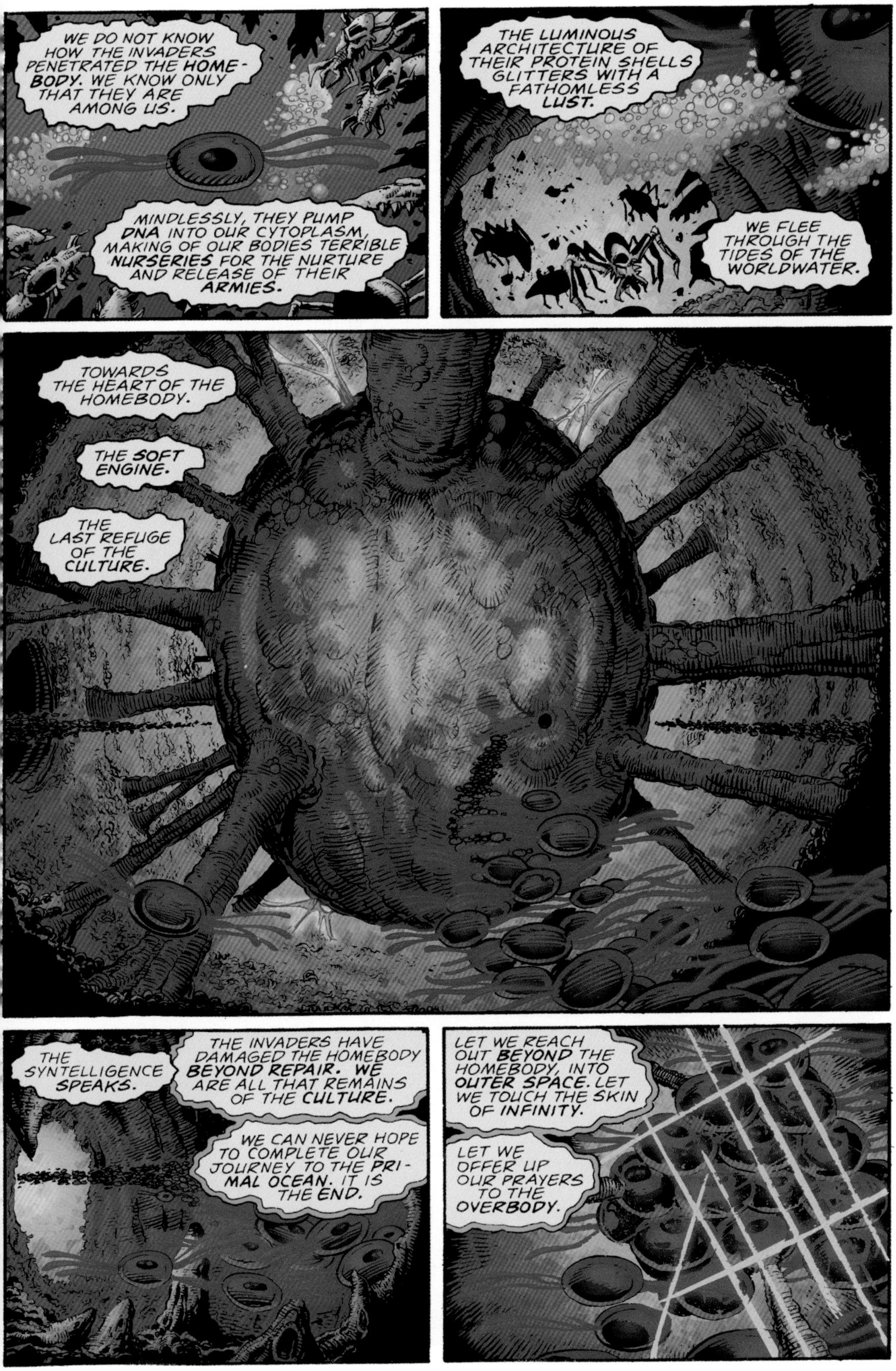
WE DO NOT KNOW HOW THE INVADERS PENETRATED THE HOME-BODY. WE KNOW ONLY THAT THEY ARE AMONG US.
MINDLESSLY, THEY PUMP DNA INTO OUR CYTOPLASM, MAKING OF OUR BODIES TERRIBLE NURSERIES FOR THE NURTURE AND RELEASE OF THEIR ARMIES.
THE LUMINOUS ARCHITECTURE OF THEIR PROTEIN SHELLS GLITTERS WITH A FATHOMLESS LUST.
WE FLEE THROUGH THE TIDES OF THE WORLDWATER.
TOWARDS THE HEART OF THE HOMEBODY.
THE SOFT ENGINE.
THE LAST REFUGE OF THE CULTURE.
THE SYNTELLIGENCE SPEAKS.
THE INVADERS HAVE DAMAGED THE HOMEBODY BEYOND REPAIR. WE ARE ALL THAT REMAINS OF THE CULTURE.
WE CAN NEVER HOPE TO COMPLETE OUR JOURNEY TO THE PRI-MAL OCEAN. IT IS THE END.
LET WE REACH OUT BEYOND THE HOMEBODY, INTO OUTER SPACE. LET WE TOUCH THE SKIN OF INFINITY.
LET WE OFFER UP OUR PRAYERS TO THE OVERBODY.

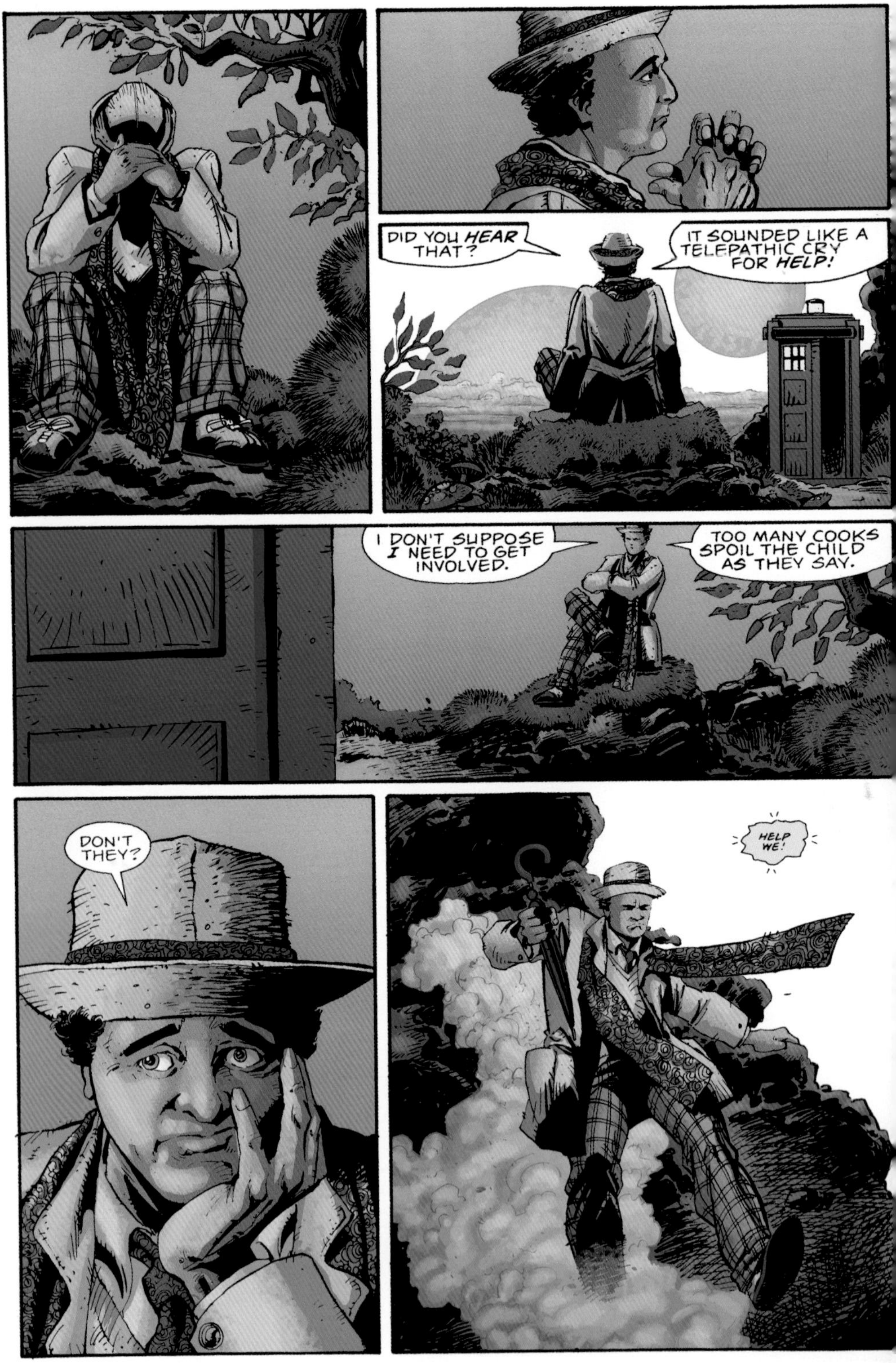
DID YOU HEAR THAT?
IT SOUNDED LIKE A TELEPATHIC CRY FOR HELP!
I DON'T SUPPOSE I NEED TO GET INVOLVED.
TOO MANY COOKS SPOIL THE CHILD AS THEY SAY.
DON'T THEY?
HELP WE!

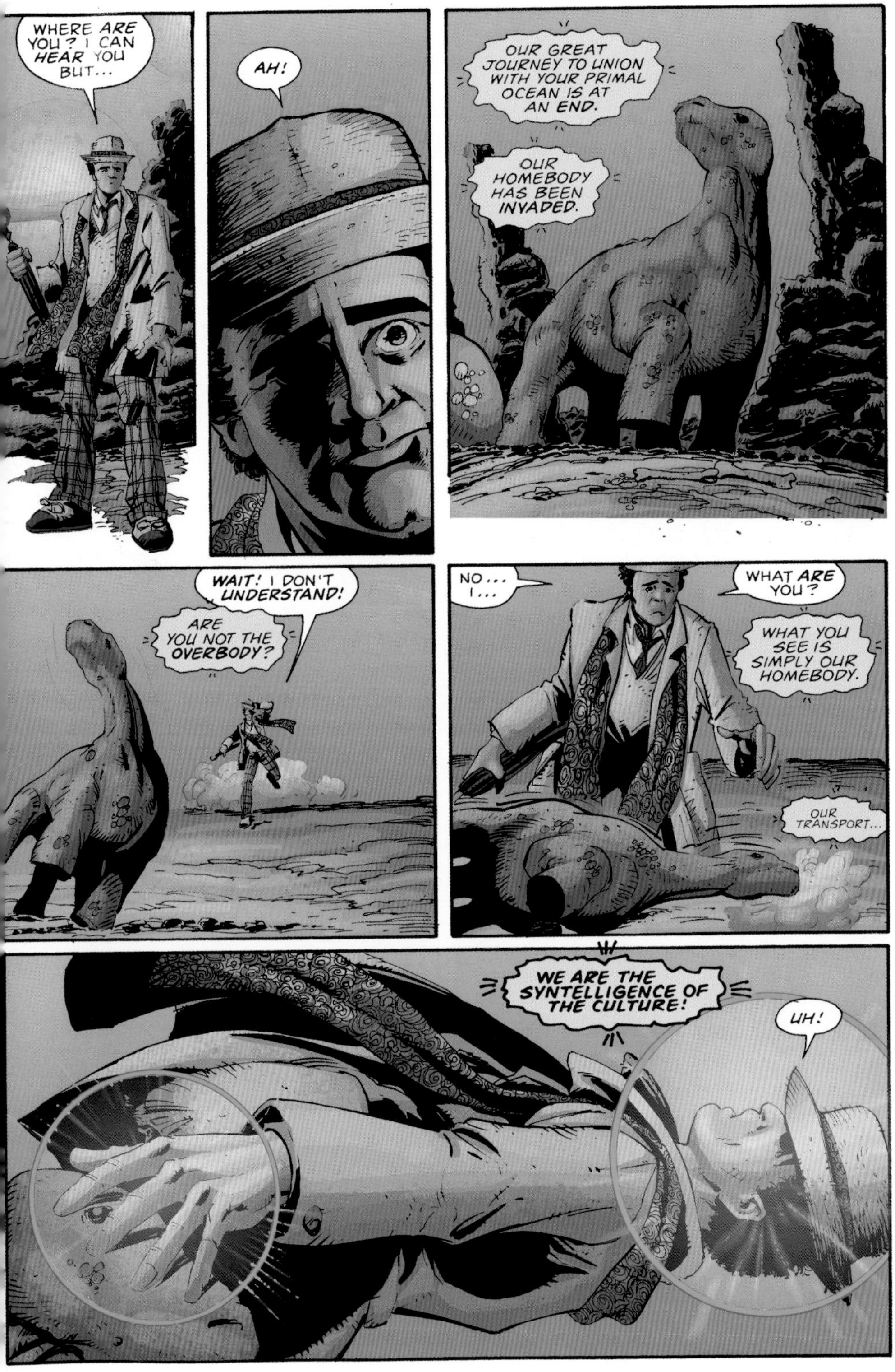
WHERE *ARE* YOU? I CAN *HEAR* YOU BUT...
AH!
OUR GREAT JOURNEY TO UNION WITH YOUR PRIMAL OCEAN IS AT AN *END*.
OUR HOMEBODY HAS BEEN *INVADED*.
WAIT! I DON'T *UNDERSTAND!*
ARE YOU NOT THE *OVERBODY?*
NO... I...
WHAT *ARE* YOU?
WHAT YOU SEE IS SIMPLY OUR HOMEBODY.
OUR TRANSPORT...
WE ARE THE SYNTELLIGENCE OF THE CULTURE!
UH!

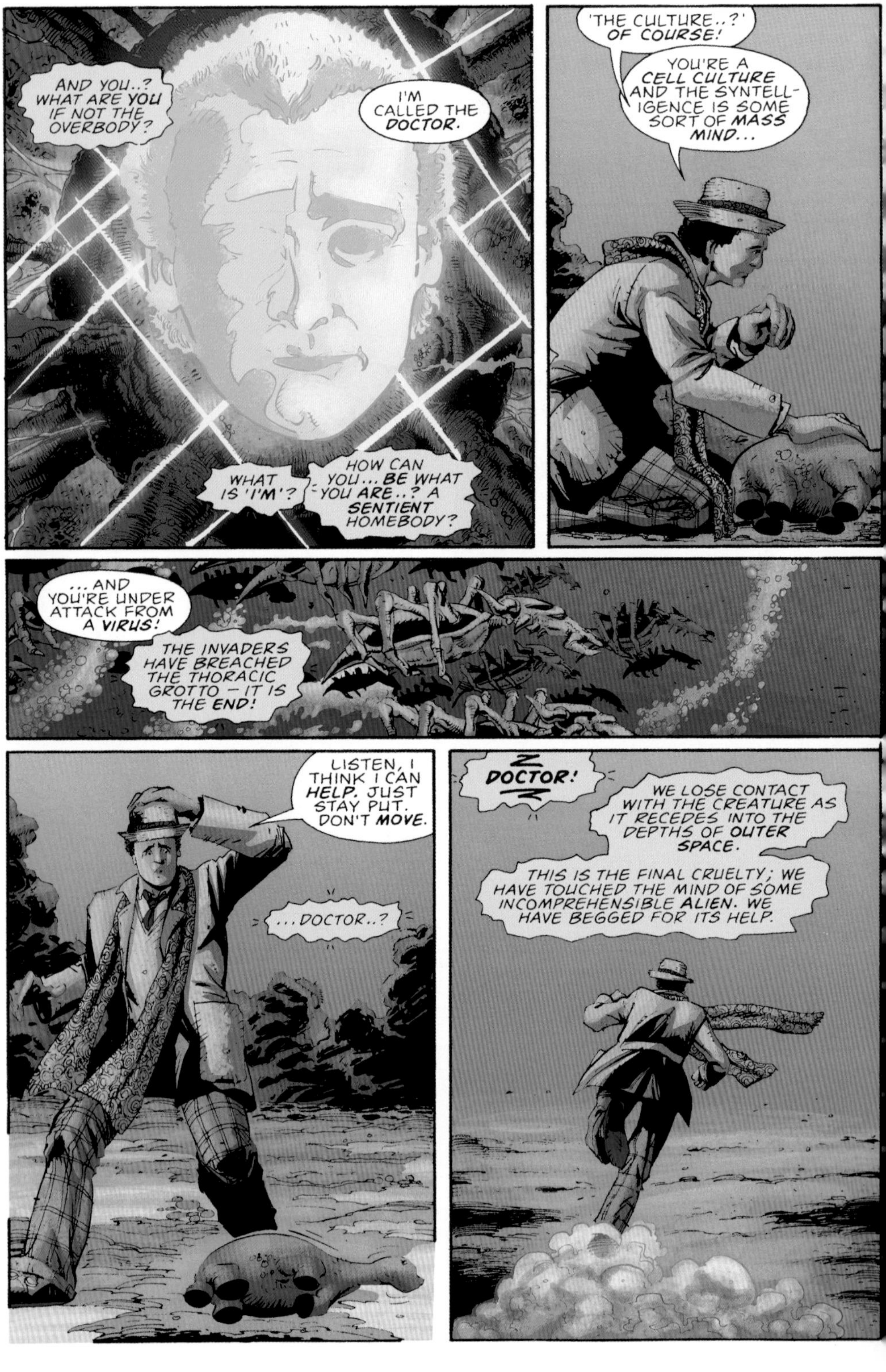
AND YOU..? WHAT ARE YOU IF NOT THE OVERBODY?
I'M CALLED THE DOCTOR.
WHAT IS 'I'M'?
HOW CAN YOU... BE WHAT YOU ARE..? A SENTIENT HOMEBODY?
'THE CULTURE..?' OF COURSE!
YOU'RE A CELL CULTURE AND THE SYNTELL-IGENCE IS SOME SORT OF MASS MIND...
...AND YOU'RE UNDER ATTACK FROM A VIRUS!
THE INVADERS HAVE BREACHED THE THORACIC GROTTO — IT IS THE END!
LISTEN, I THINK I CAN HELP. JUST STAY PUT. DON'T MOVE.
...DOCTOR..?
DOCTOR!
WE LOSE CONTACT WITH THE CREATURE AS IT RECEDES INTO THE DEPTHS OF OUTER SPACE.
THIS IS THE FINAL CRUELTY; WE HAVE TOUCHED THE MIND OF SOME INCOMPREHENSIBLE ALIEN. WE HAVE BEGGED FOR ITS HELP.

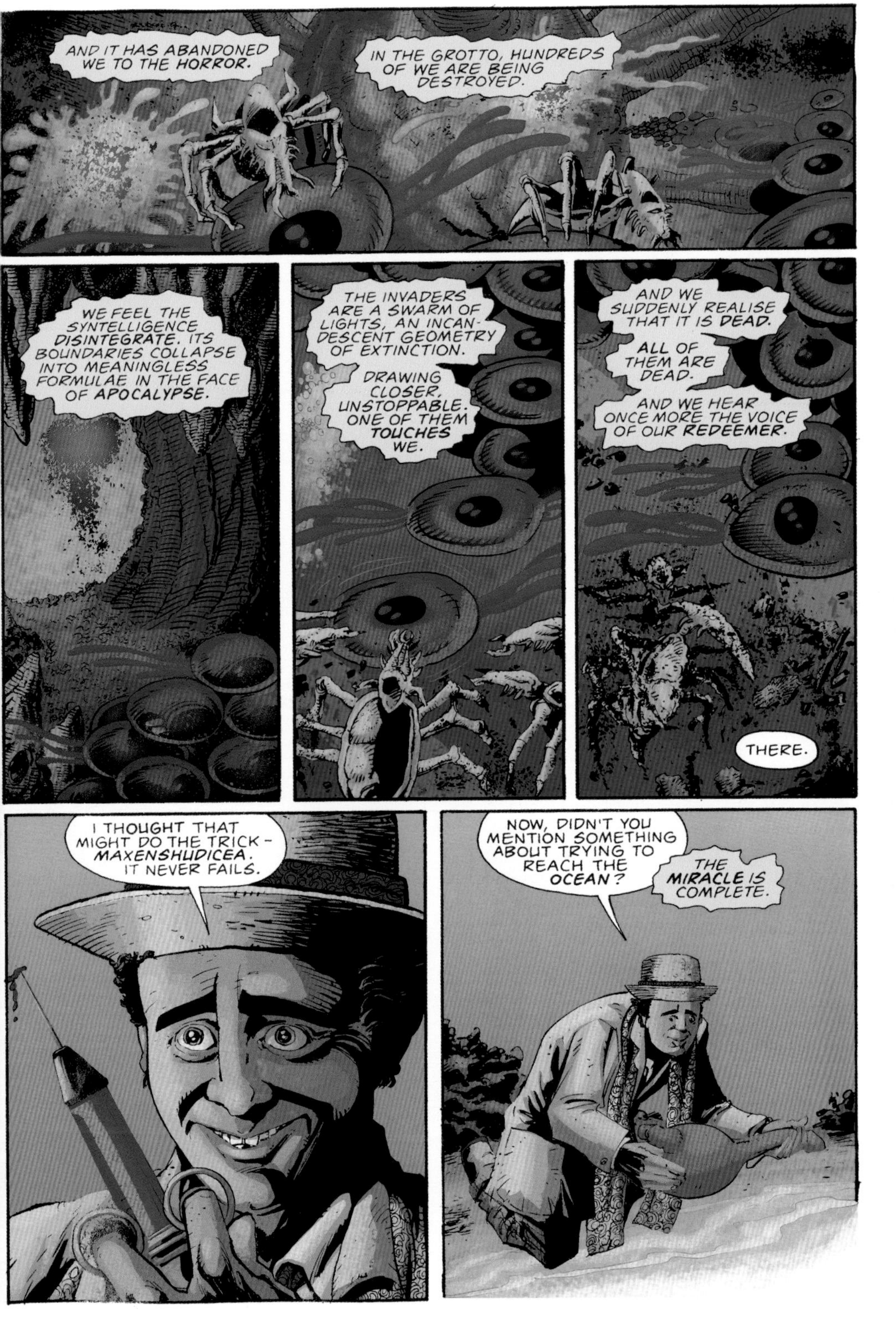
AND IT HAS ABANDONED WE TO THE HORROR.
IN THE GROTTO, HUNDREDS OF WE ARE BEING DESTROYED.
WE FEEL THE SYNTELLIGENCE DISINTEGRATE. ITS BOUNDARIES COLLAPSE INTO MEANINGLESS FORMULAE IN THE FACE OF APOCALYPSE.
THE INVADERS ARE A SWARM OF LIGHTS, AN INCANDESCENT GEOMETRY OF EXTINCTION.
DRAWING CLOSER, UNSTOPPABLE. ONE OF THEM TOUCHES WE.
AND WE SUDDENLY REALISE THAT IT IS DEAD.
ALL OF THEM ARE DEAD.
AND WE HEAR ONCE MORE THE VOICE OF OUR REDEEMER.
THERE.
I THOUGHT THAT MIGHT DO THE TRICK - MAXENSHUDICEA. IT NEVER FAILS.
NOW, DIDN'T YOU MENTION SOMETHING ABOUT TRYING TO REACH THE OCEAN?
THE MIRACLE IS COMPLETE.

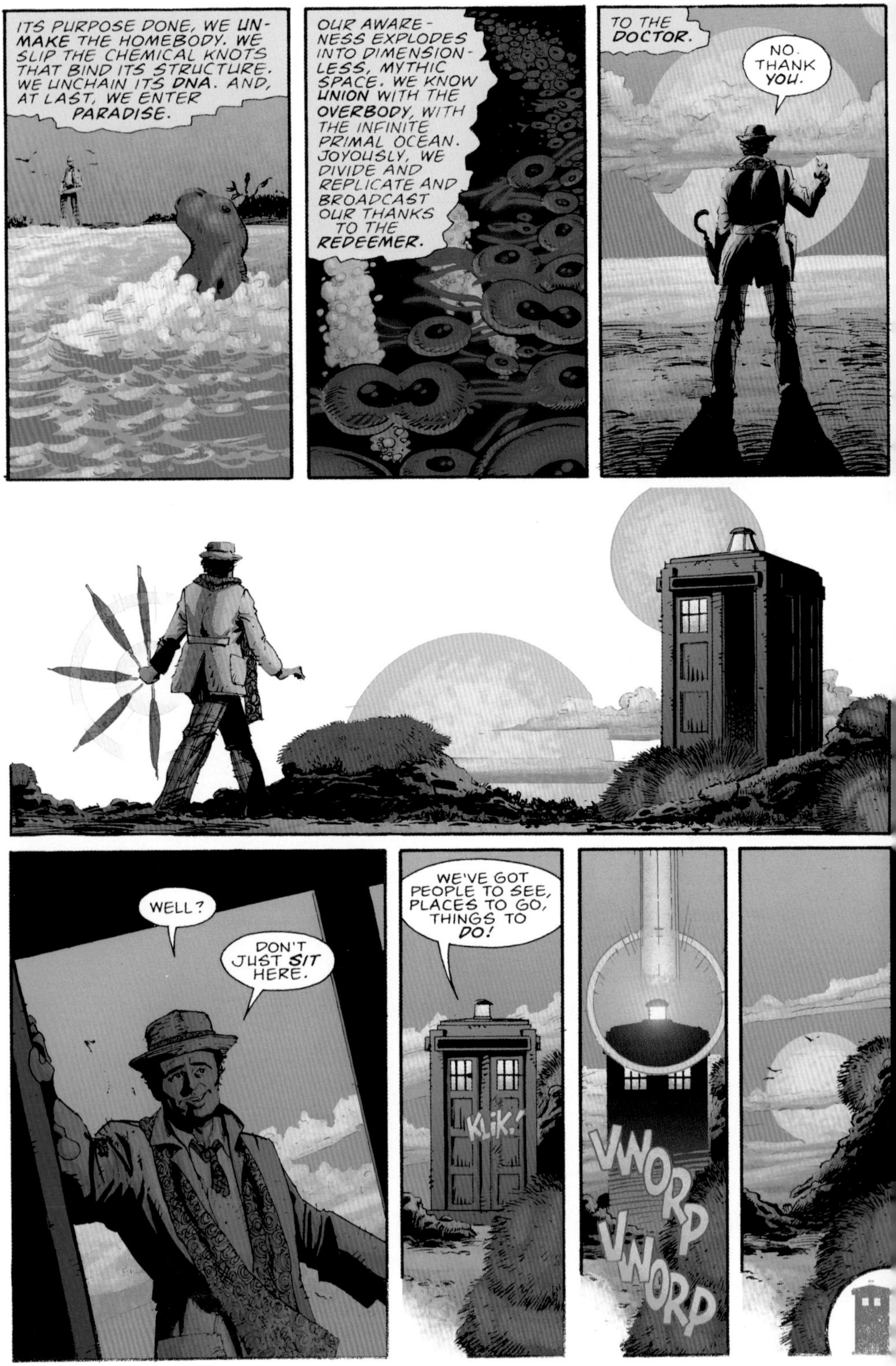
ITS PURPOSE DONE, WE UNMAKE THE HOMEBODY. WE SLIP THE CHEMICAL KNOTS THAT BIND ITS STRUCTURE. WE UNCHAIN ITS DNA. AND, AT LAST, WE ENTER PARADISE.
OUR AWARENESS EXPLODES INTO DIMENSIONLESS, MYTHIC SPACE. WE KNOW UNION WITH THE OVERBODY, WITH THE INFINITE PRIMAL OCEAN. JOYOUSLY, WE DIVIDE AND REPLICATE AND BROADCAST OUR THANKS TO THE REDEEMER.
TO THE DOCTOR.
NO. THANK YOU.
WELL?
DON'T JUST SIT HERE.
WE'VE GOT PEOPLE TO SEE, PLACES TO GO, THINGS TO DO!
KLIK!
VWORP
VWORP
VWORP

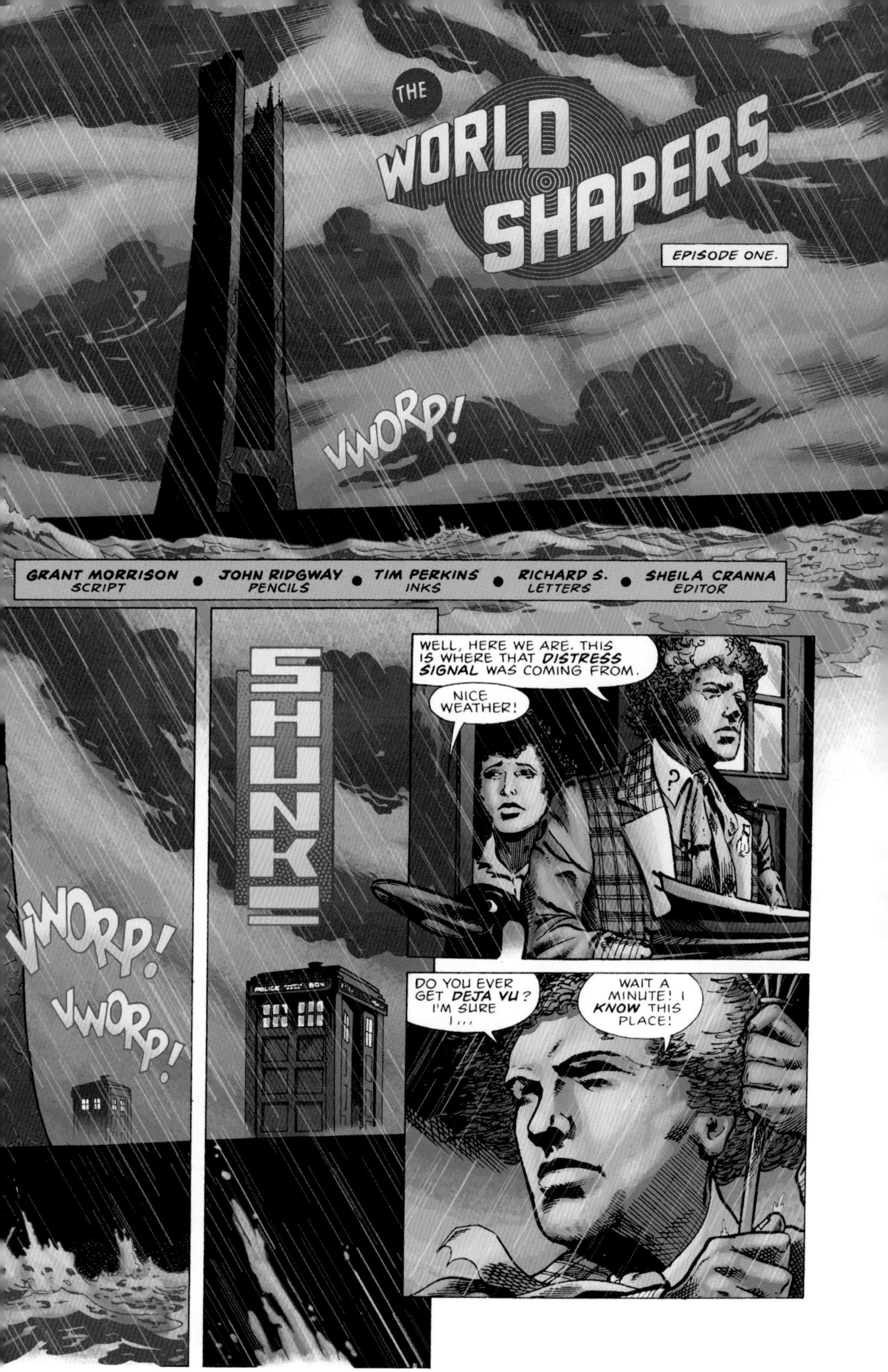
THE WORLD SHAPERS
EPISODE ONE.
VWORP!
GRANT MORRISON SCRIPT • JOHN RIDGWAY PENCILS • TIM PERKINS INKS • RICHARD S. LETTERS • SHEILA CRANNA EDITOR
VWORP! VWORP!
SHUNK!
WELL, HERE WE ARE. THIS IS WHERE THAT DISTRESS SIGNAL WAS COMING FROM.
NICE WEATHER!
DO YOU EVER GET DEJA VU? I'M SURE I...
WAIT A MINUTE! I KNOW THIS PLACE!

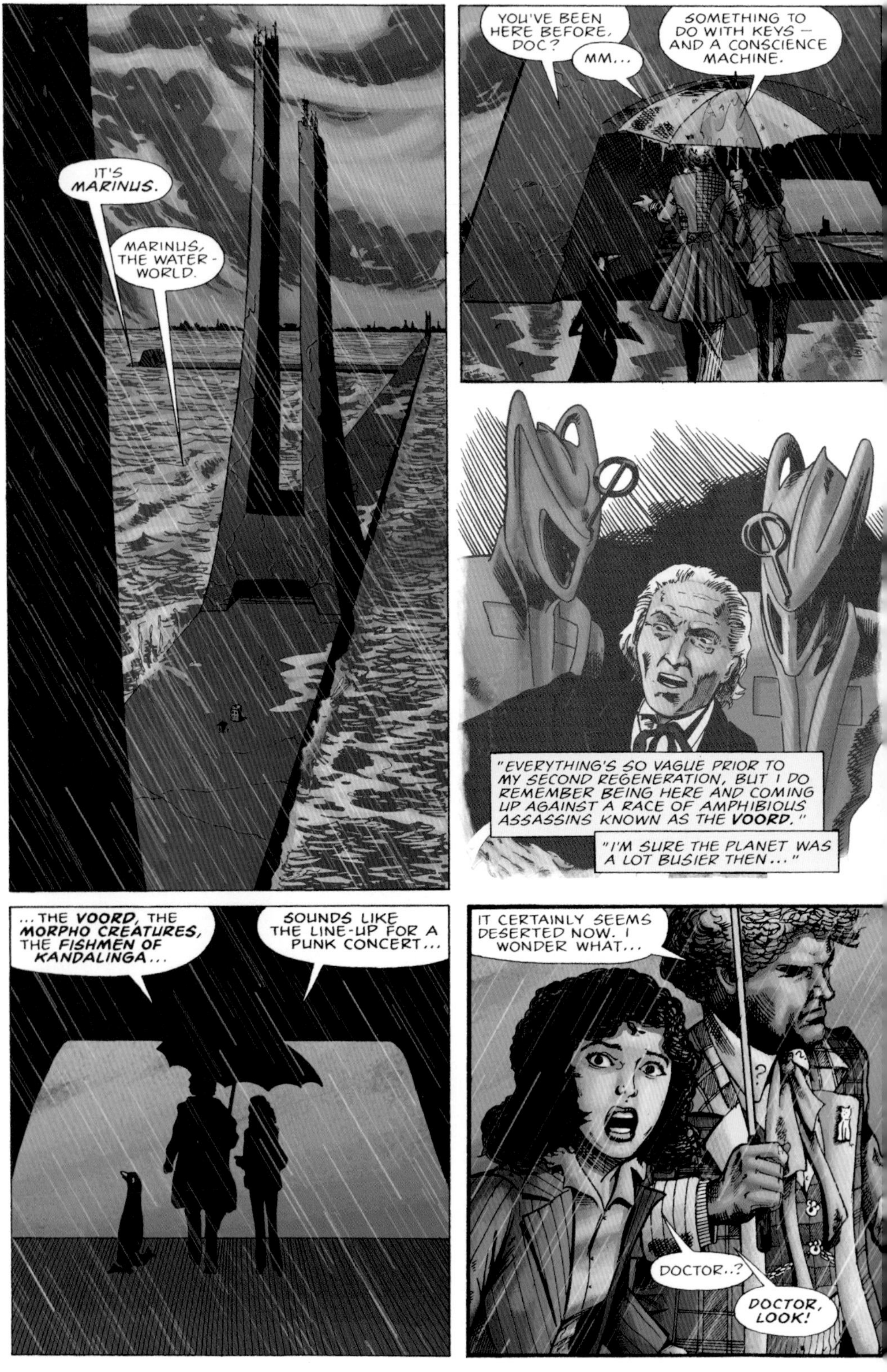

IT'S MARINUS.
MARINUS, THE WATER-WORLD.
YOU'VE BEEN HERE BEFORE, DOC?
MM...
SOMETHING TO DO WITH KEYS — AND A CONSCIENCE MACHINE.
"EVERYTHING'S SO VAGUE PRIOR TO MY SECOND REGENERATION, BUT I DO REMEMBER BEING HERE AND COMING UP AGAINST A RACE OF AMPHIBIOUS ASSASSINS KNOWN AS THE VOORD."
"I'M SURE THE PLANET WAS A LOT BUSIER THEN..."
...THE VOORD, THE MORPHO CREATURES, THE FISHMEN OF KANDALINGA...
SOUNDS LIKE THE LINE-UP FOR A PUNK CONCERT...
IT CERTAINLY SEEMS DESERTED NOW. I WONDER WHAT...
DOCTOR..?
DOCTOR, LOOK!

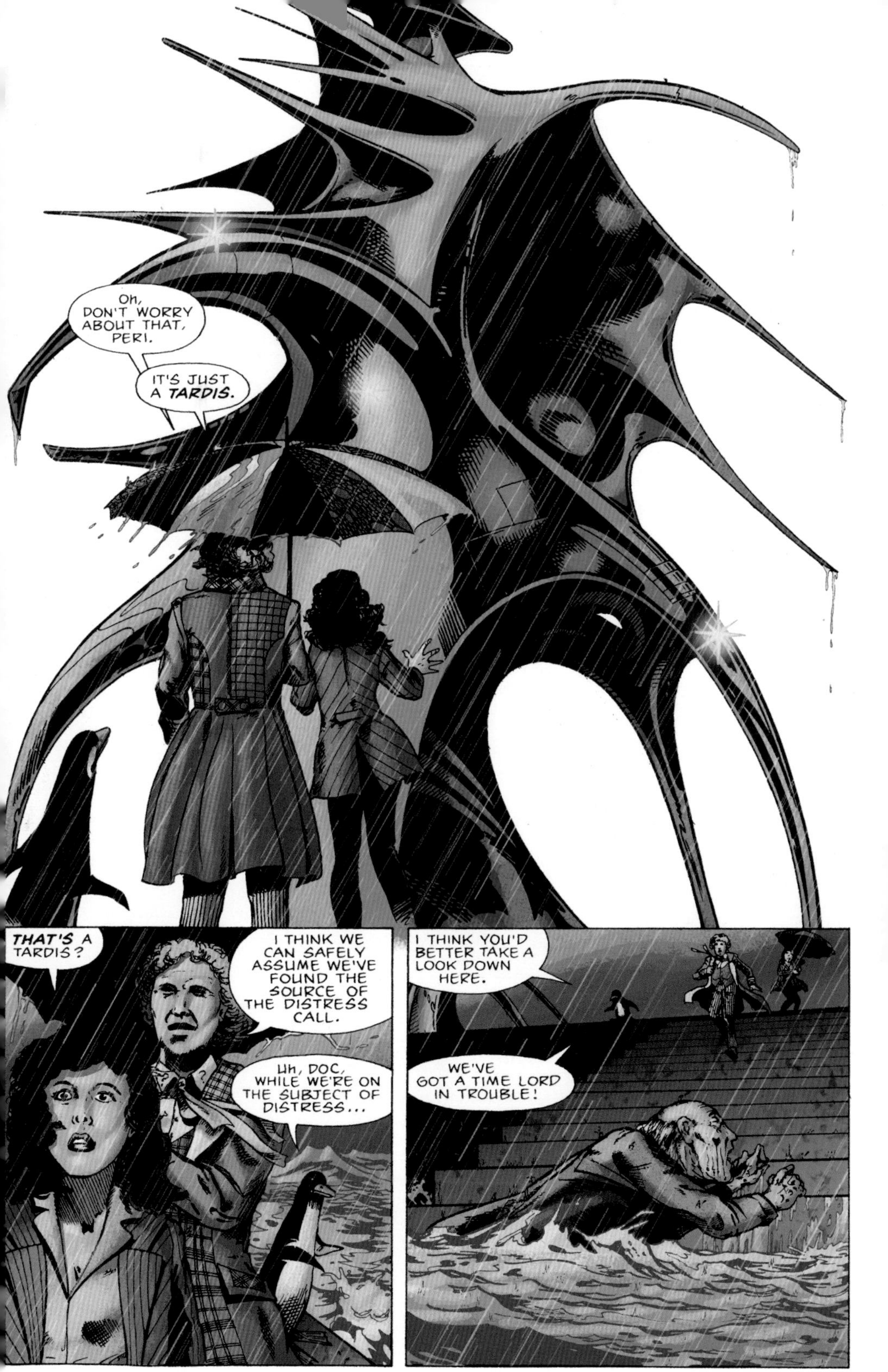
Oh, DON'T WORRY ABOUT THAT, PERI.
IT'S JUST A TARDIS.
THAT'S A TARDIS?
I THINK WE CAN SAFELY ASSUME WE'VE FOUND THE SOURCE OF THE DISTRESS CALL.
Uh, DOC, WHILE WE'RE ON THE SUBJECT OF DISTRESS...
I THINK YOU'D BETTER TAKE A LOOK DOWN HERE.
WE'VE GOT A TIME LORD IN TROUBLE!

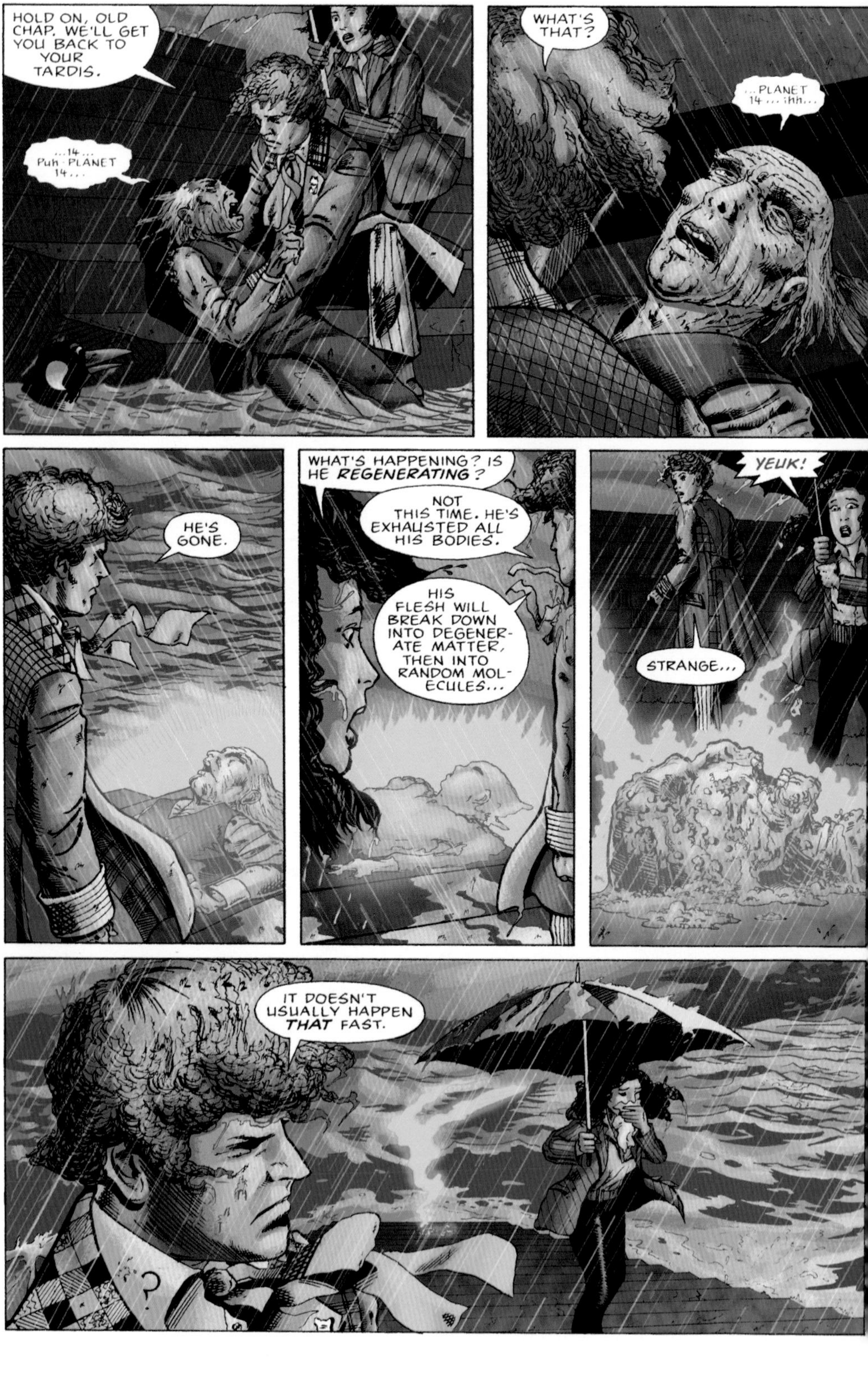
HOLD ON, OLD CHAP. WE'LL GET YOU BACK TO YOUR TARDIS.
...14... Puh-PLANET 14...
WHAT'S THAT?
...PLANET 14...ihh...
HE'S GONE.
WHAT'S HAPPENING? IS HE REGENERATING?
NOT THIS TIME. HE'S EXHAUSTED ALL HIS BODIES.
HIS FLESH WILL BREAK DOWN INTO DEGENERATE MATTER, THEN INTO RANDOM MOLECULES...
YEUK!
STRANGE...
IT DOESN'T USUALLY HAPPEN THAT FAST.

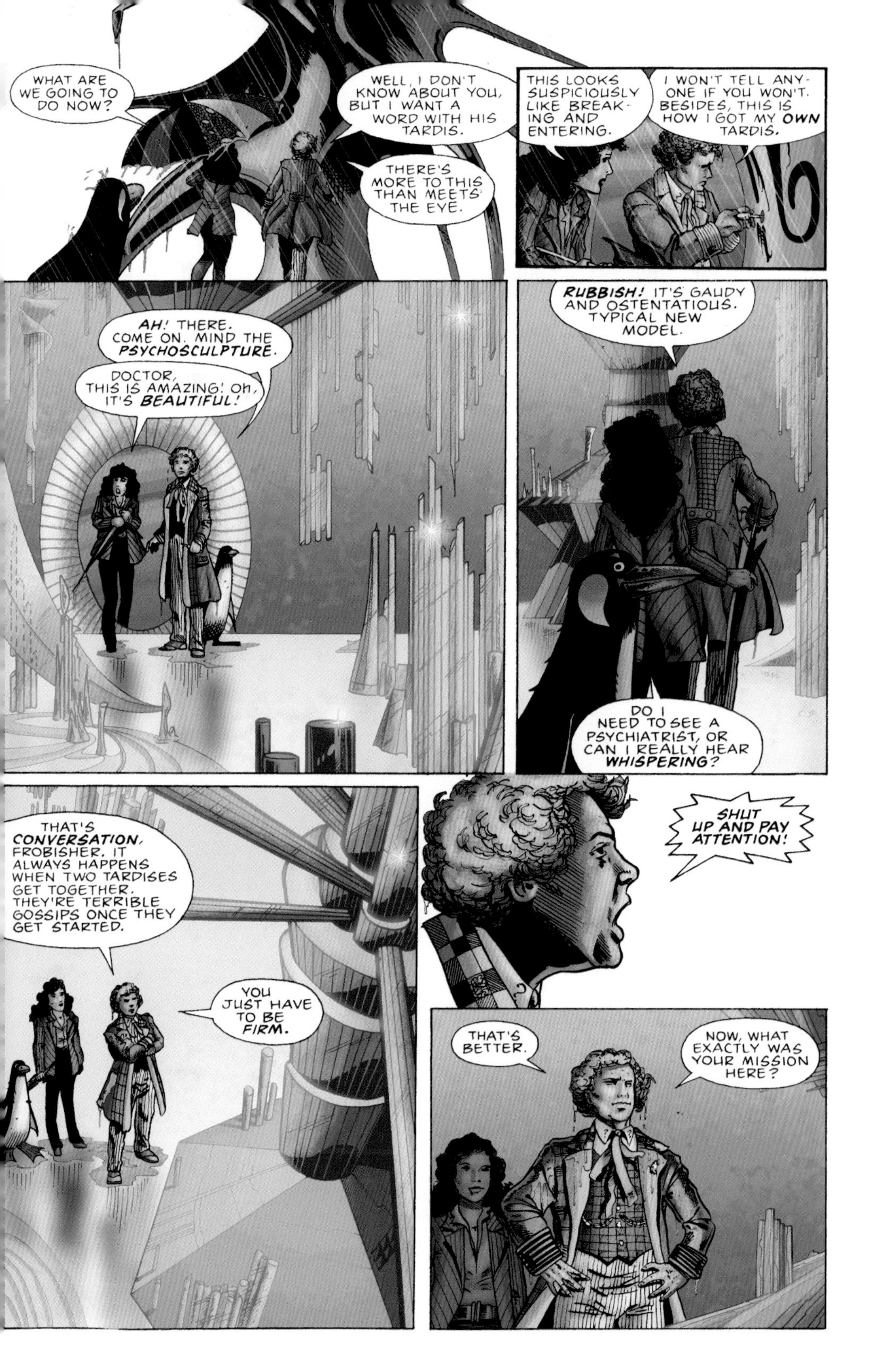
WHAT ARE WE GOING TO DO NOW?
WELL, I DON'T KNOW ABOUT YOU, BUT I WANT A WORD WITH HIS TARDIS.
THERE'S MORE TO THIS THAN MEETS THE EYE.
THIS LOOKS SUSPICIOUSLY LIKE BREAKING AND ENTERING.
I WON'T TELL ANYONE IF YOU WON'T. BESIDES, THIS IS HOW I GOT MY OWN TARDIS.
AH! THERE. COME ON. MIND THE PSYCHOSCULPTURE.
DOCTOR, THIS IS AMAZING! Oh, IT'S BEAUTIFUL!
RUBBISH! IT'S GAUDY AND OSTENTATIOUS. TYPICAL NEW MODEL.
DO I NEED TO SEE A PSYCHIATRIST, OR CAN I REALLY HEAR WHISPERING?
THAT'S CONVERSATION, FROBISHER. IT ALWAYS HAPPENS WHEN TWO TARDISES GET TOGETHER. THEY'RE TERRIBLE GOSSIPS ONCE THEY GET STARTED.
YOU JUST HAVE TO BE FIRM.
SHUT UP AND PAY ATTENTION!
THAT'S BETTER.
NOW, WHAT EXACTLY WAS YOUR MISSION HERE?

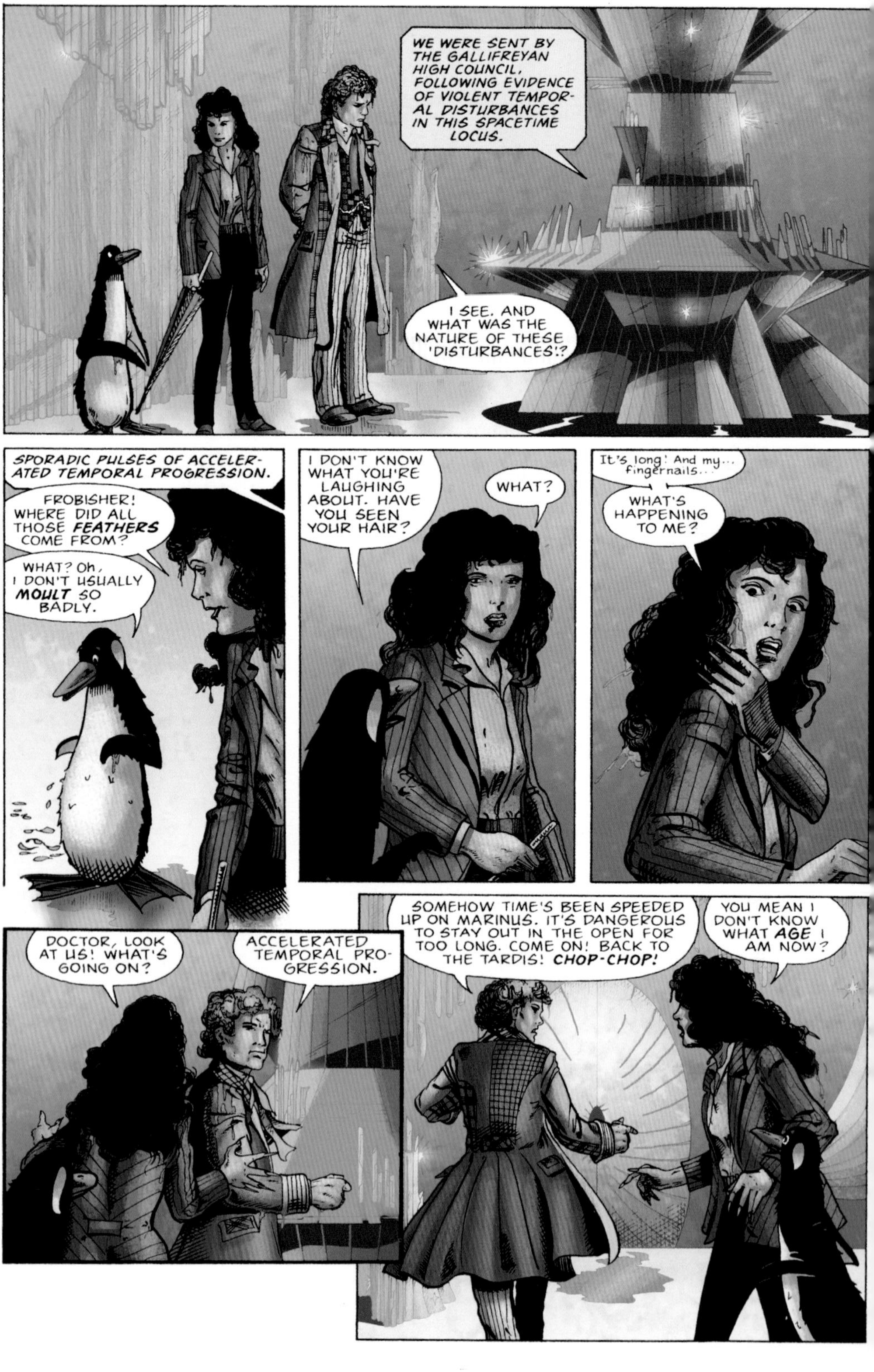
WE WERE SENT BY THE GALLIFREYAN HIGH COUNCIL, FOLLOWING EVIDENCE OF VIOLENT TEMPORAL DISTURBANCES IN THIS SPACETIME LOCUS.
I SEE. AND WHAT WAS THE NATURE OF THESE 'DISTURBANCES'?
SPORADIC PULSES OF ACCELERATED TEMPORAL PROGRESSION.
FROBISHER! WHERE DID ALL THOSE FEATHERS COME FROM?
WHAT? Oh, I DON'T USUALLY MOULT SO BADLY.
I DON'T KNOW WHAT YOU'RE LAUGHING ABOUT. HAVE YOU SEEN YOUR HAIR?
WHAT?
It's long! And my... fingernails...
WHAT'S HAPPENING TO ME?
DOCTOR, LOOK AT US! WHAT'S GOING ON?
ACCELERATED TEMPORAL PROGRESSION.
SOMEHOW TIME'S BEEN SPEEDED UP ON MARINUS. IT'S DANGEROUS TO STAY OUT IN THE OPEN FOR TOO LONG. COME ON! BACK TO THE TARDIS! CHOP-CHOP!
YOU MEAN I DON'T KNOW WHAT AGE I AM NOW?

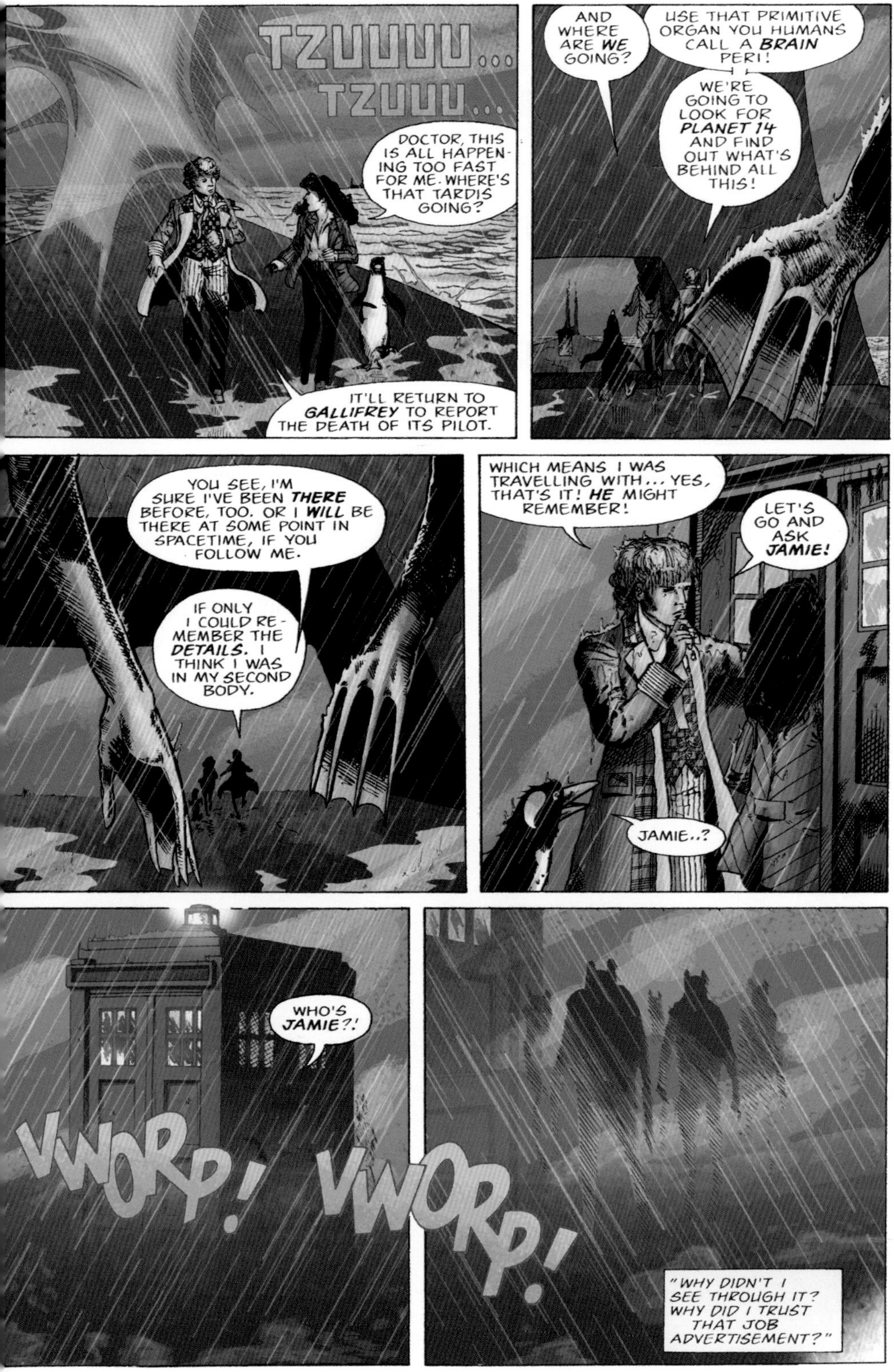
TZUUUU...
TZUUU...
DOCTOR, THIS IS ALL HAPPENING TOO FAST FOR ME. WHERE'S THAT TARDIS GOING?
IT'LL RETURN TO GALLIFREY TO REPORT THE DEATH OF ITS PILOT.
AND WHERE ARE WE GOING?
USE THAT PRIMITIVE ORGAN YOU HUMANS CALL A BRAIN PERI!
WE'RE GOING TO LOOK FOR PLANET 14 AND FIND OUT WHAT'S BEHIND ALL THIS!
YOU SEE, I'M SURE I'VE BEEN THERE BEFORE, TOO. OR I WILL BE THERE AT SOME POINT IN SPACETIME, IF YOU FOLLOW ME.
IF ONLY I COULD REMEMBER THE DETAILS. I THINK I WAS IN MY SECOND BODY.
WHICH MEANS I WAS TRAVELLING WITH... YES, THAT'S IT! HE MIGHT REMEMBER!
LET'S GO AND ASK JAMIE!
JAMIE..?
WHO'S JAMIE?!
VWORP! VWORP!
"WHY DIDN'T I SEE THROUGH IT? WHY DID I TRUST THAT JOB ADVERTISEMENT?"

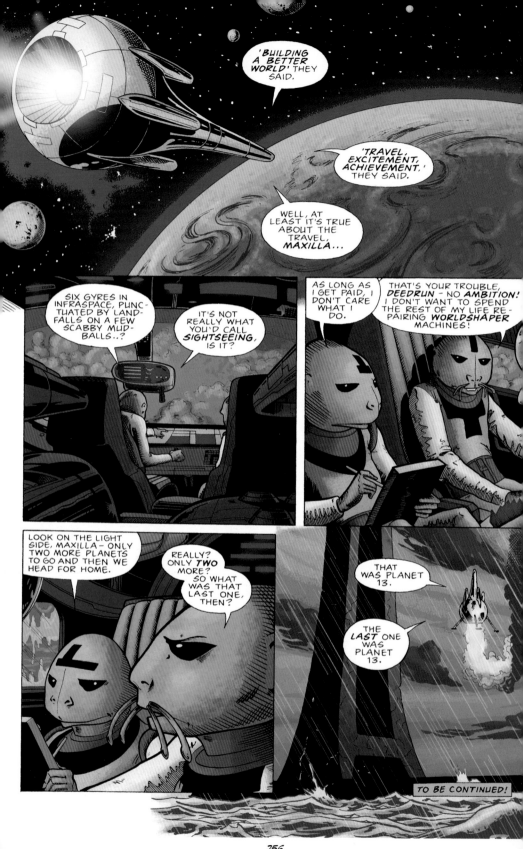

'BUILDING A BETTER WORLD' THEY SAID.

'TRAVEL, EXCITEMENT, ACHIEVEMENT,' THEY SAID.

WELL, AT LEAST IT'S TRUE ABOUT THE TRAVEL, MAXILLA...

SIX GYRES IN INFRASPACE, PUNCTUATED BY LANDFALLS ON A FEW SCABBY MUDBALLS..?

IT'S NOT REALLY WHAT YOU'D CALL SIGHTSEEING, IS IT?

AS LONG AS I GET PAID, I DON'T CARE WHAT I DO.

THAT'S YOUR TROUBLE, DEEDRUN – NO AMBITION! I DON'T WANT TO SPEND THE REST OF MY LIFE REPAIRING WORLDSHAPER MACHINES!

LOOK ON THE LIGHT SIDE, MAXILLA – ONLY TWO MORE PLANETS TO GO AND THEN WE HEAD FOR HOME.

REALLY? ONLY TWO MORE? SO WHAT WAS THAT LAST ONE, THEN?

THAT WAS PLANET 13.

THE LAST ONE WAS PLANET 13.

TO BE CONTINUED!

256

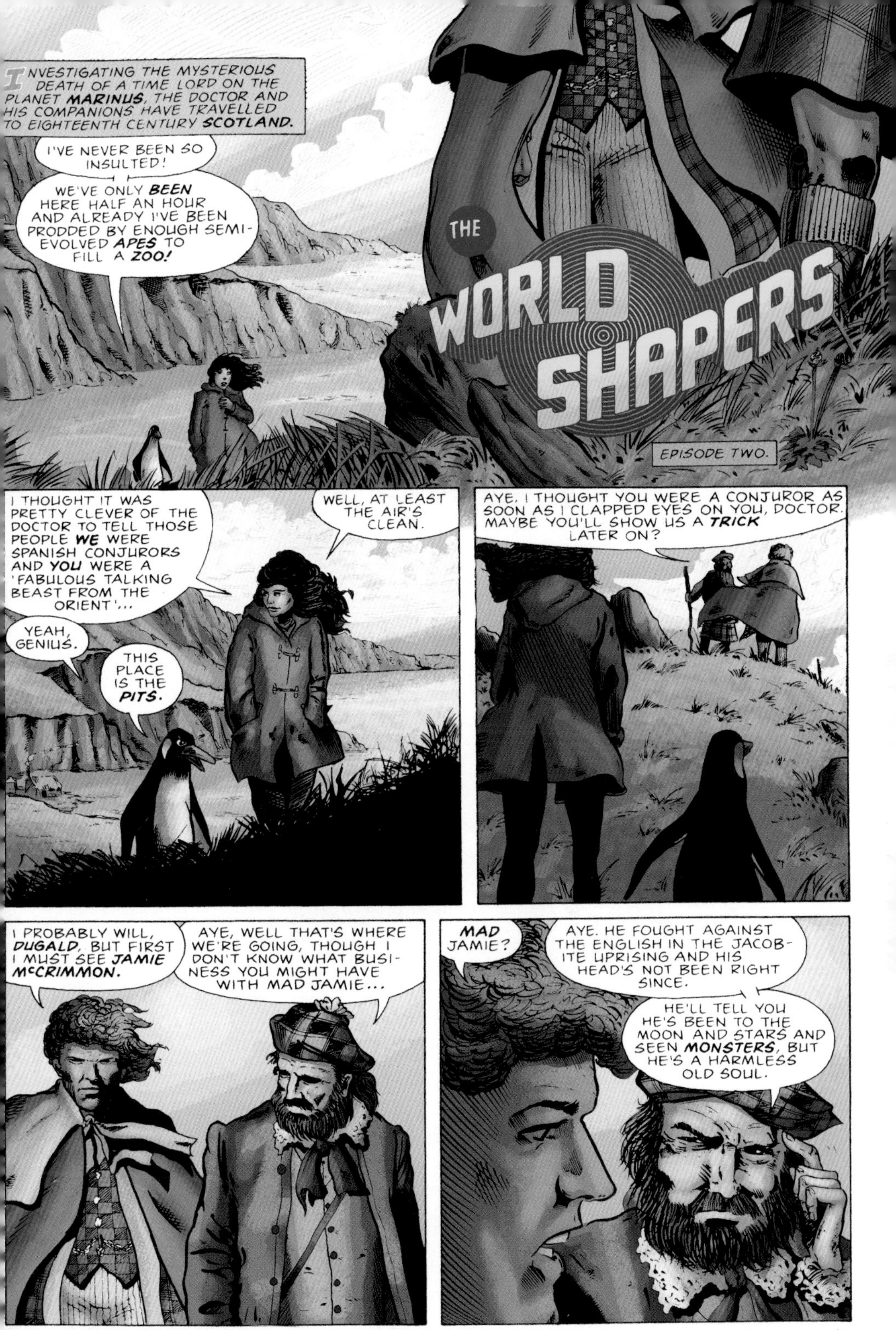
INVESTIGATING THE MYSTERIOUS DEATH OF A TIME LORD ON THE PLANET MARINUS, THE DOCTOR AND HIS COMPANIONS HAVE TRAVELLED TO EIGHTEENTH CENTURY SCOTLAND.
I'VE NEVER BEEN SO INSULTED!
WE'VE ONLY BEEN HERE HALF AN HOUR AND ALREADY I'VE BEEN PRODDED BY ENOUGH SEMI-EVOLVED APES TO FILL A ZOO!
THE WORLD SHAPERS
EPISODE TWO.
I THOUGHT IT WAS PRETTY CLEVER OF THE DOCTOR TO TELL THOSE PEOPLE WE WERE SPANISH CONJURORS AND YOU WERE A 'FABULOUS TALKING BEAST FROM THE ORIENT'...
WELL, AT LEAST THE AIR'S CLEAN.
YEAH, GENIUS.
THIS PLACE IS THE PITS.
AYE. I THOUGHT YOU WERE A CONJUROR AS SOON AS I CLAPPED EYES ON YOU, DOCTOR. MAYBE YOU'LL SHOW US A TRICK LATER ON?
I PROBABLY WILL, DUGALD, BUT FIRST I MUST SEE JAMIE McCRIMMON.
AYE, WELL THAT'S WHERE WE'RE GOING, THOUGH I DON'T KNOW WHAT BUSINESS YOU MIGHT HAVE WITH MAD JAMIE...
MAD JAMIE?
AYE. HE FOUGHT AGAINST THE ENGLISH IN THE JACOBITE UPRISING AND HIS HEAD'S NOT BEEN RIGHT SINCE.
HE'LL TELL YOU HE'S BEEN TO THE MOON AND STARS AND SEEN MONSTERS, BUT HE'S A HARMLESS OLD SOUL.

GRANT MORRISON SCRIPT • JOHN RIDGWAY BREAKDOWNS • TIM PERKINS FINISHED ART • RICHARD STARKINGS LETTERS • SHEILA CRANNA EDITOR

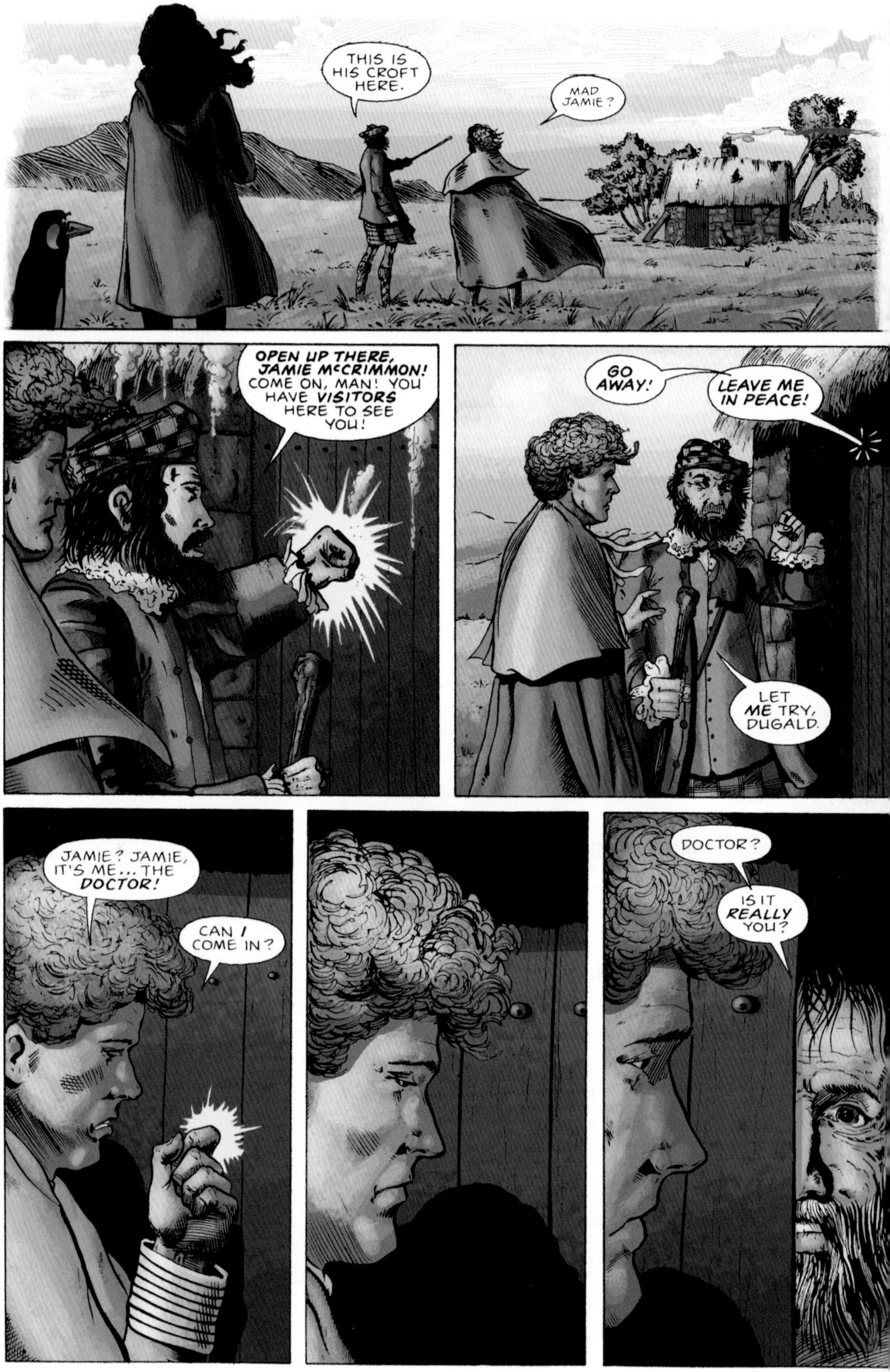
THIS IS HIS CROFT HERE.
MAD JAMIE?
OPEN UP THERE, JAMIE McCRIMMON! COME ON, MAN! YOU HAVE VISITORS HERE TO SEE YOU!
GO AWAY!
LEAVE ME IN PEACE!
LET ME TRY, DUGALD.
JAMIE? JAMIE, IT'S ME... THE DOCTOR!
CAN I COME IN?
DOCTOR?
IS IT REALLY YOU?

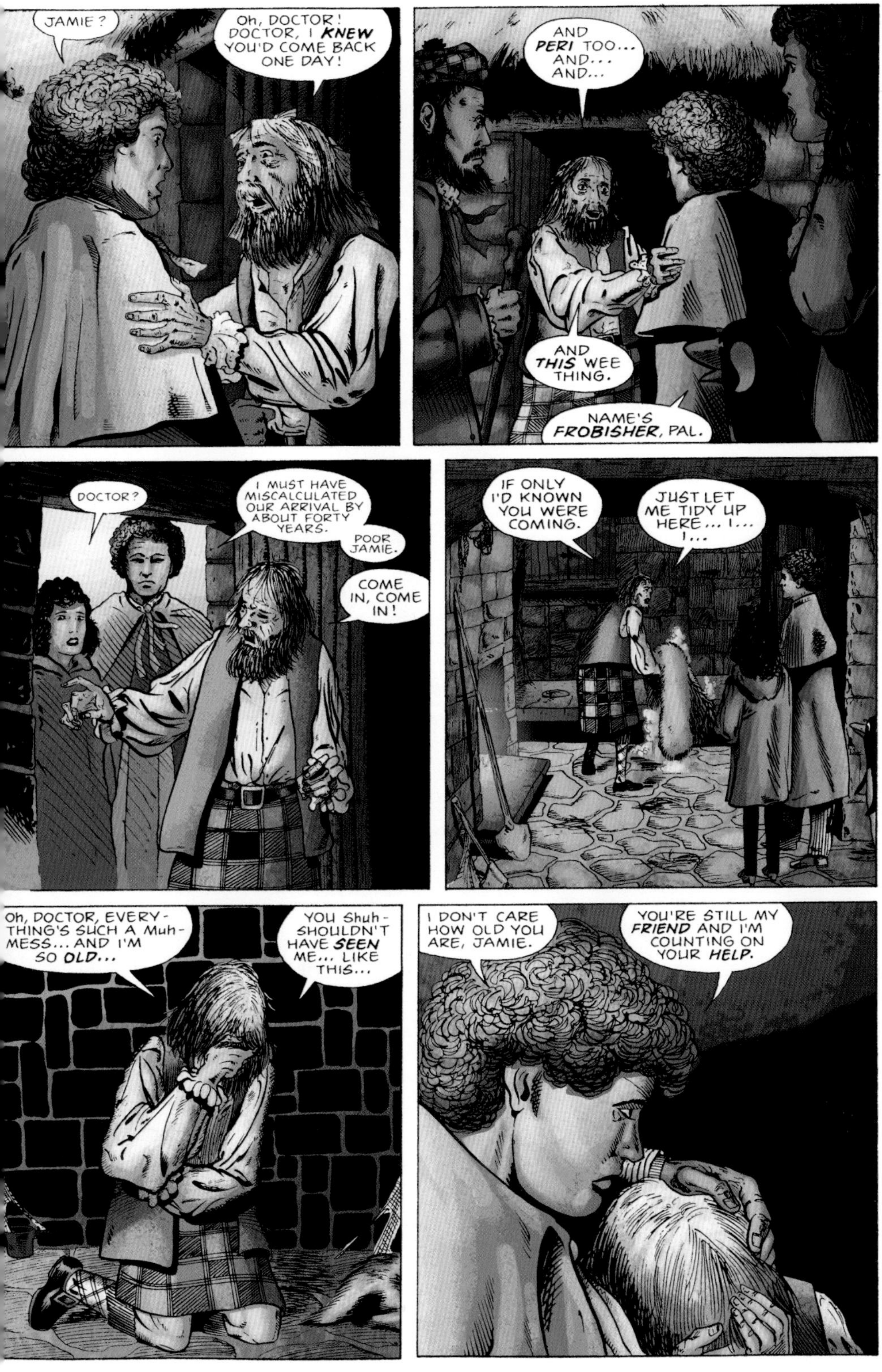
JAMIE?
Oh, DOCTOR! DOCTOR, I KNEW YOU'D COME BACK ONE DAY!
AND PERI TOO... AND... AND...
AND THIS WEE THING.
NAME'S FROBISHER, PAL.
DOCTOR?
I MUST HAVE MISCALCULATED OUR ARRIVAL BY ABOUT FORTY YEARS.
POOR JAMIE.
COME IN, COME IN!
IF ONLY I'D KNOWN YOU WERE COMING.
JUST LET ME TIDY UP HERE... I... I...
Oh, DOCTOR, EVERY-THING'S SUCH A Muh-MESS... AND I'M SO OLD...
YOU Shuh-SHOULDN'T HAVE SEEN ME... LIKE THIS...
I DON'T CARE HOW OLD YOU ARE, JAMIE.
YOU'RE STILL MY FRIEND AND I'M COUNTING ON YOUR HELP.

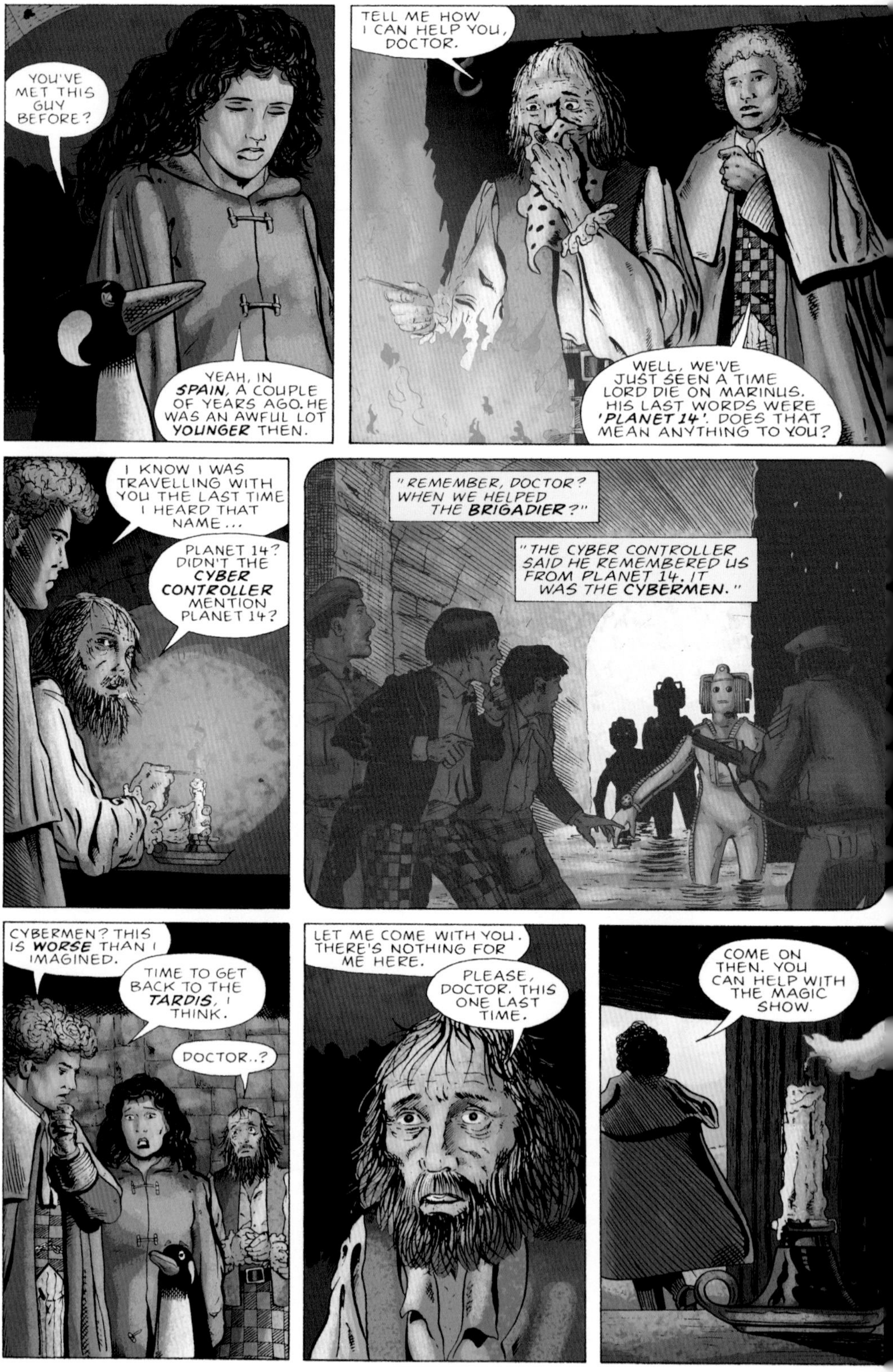
YOU'VE MET THIS GUY BEFORE?
YEAH, IN SPAIN, A COUPLE OF YEARS AGO. HE WAS AN AWFUL LOT YOUNGER THEN.
TELL ME HOW I CAN HELP YOU, DOCTOR.
WELL, WE'VE JUST SEEN A TIME LORD DIE ON MARINUS. HIS LAST WORDS WERE 'PLANET 14'. DOES THAT MEAN ANYTHING TO YOU?
I KNOW I WAS TRAVELLING WITH YOU THE LAST TIME I HEARD THAT NAME...
PLANET 14? DIDN'T THE CYBER CONTROLLER MENTION PLANET 14?
"REMEMBER, DOCTOR? WHEN WE HELPED THE BRIGADIER?"
"THE CYBER CONTROLLER SAID HE REMEMBERED US FROM PLANET 14. IT WAS THE CYBERMEN."
CYBERMEN? THIS IS WORSE THAN I IMAGINED.
TIME TO GET BACK TO THE TARDIS, I THINK.
DOCTOR..?
LET ME COME WITH YOU. THERE'S NOTHING FOR ME HERE.
PLEASE, DOCTOR. THIS ONE LAST TIME.
COME ON THEN. YOU CAN HELP WITH THE MAGIC SHOW.

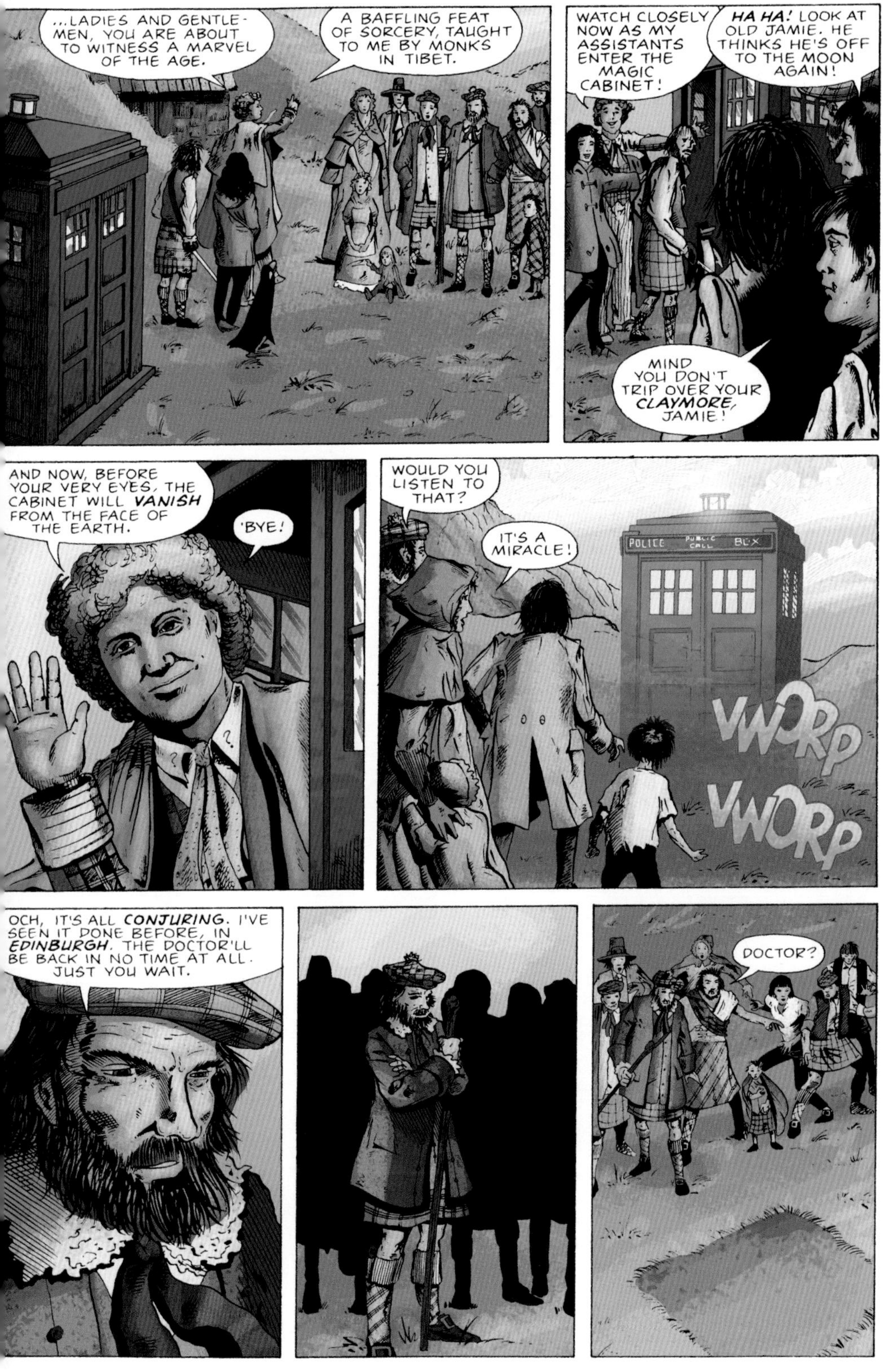
...LADIES AND GENTLE-MEN, YOU ARE ABOUT TO WITNESS A MARVEL OF THE AGE.
A BAFFLING FEAT OF SORCERY, TAUGHT TO ME BY MONKS IN TIBET.
WATCH CLOSELY NOW AS MY ASSISTANTS ENTER THE MAGIC CABINET!
HA HA! LOOK AT OLD JAMIE. HE THINKS HE'S OFF TO THE MOON AGAIN!
MIND YOU DON'T TRIP OVER YOUR CLAYMORE, JAMIE!
AND NOW, BEFORE YOUR VERY EYES, THE CABINET WILL VANISH FROM THE FACE OF THE EARTH.
'BYE!
WOULD YOU LISTEN TO THAT?
IT'S A MIRACLE!
VWORP
VWORP
OCH, IT'S ALL CONJURING. I'VE SEEN IT DONE BEFORE, IN EDINBURGH. THE DOCTOR'LL BE BACK IN NO TIME AT ALL. JUST YOU WAIT.
DOCTOR?

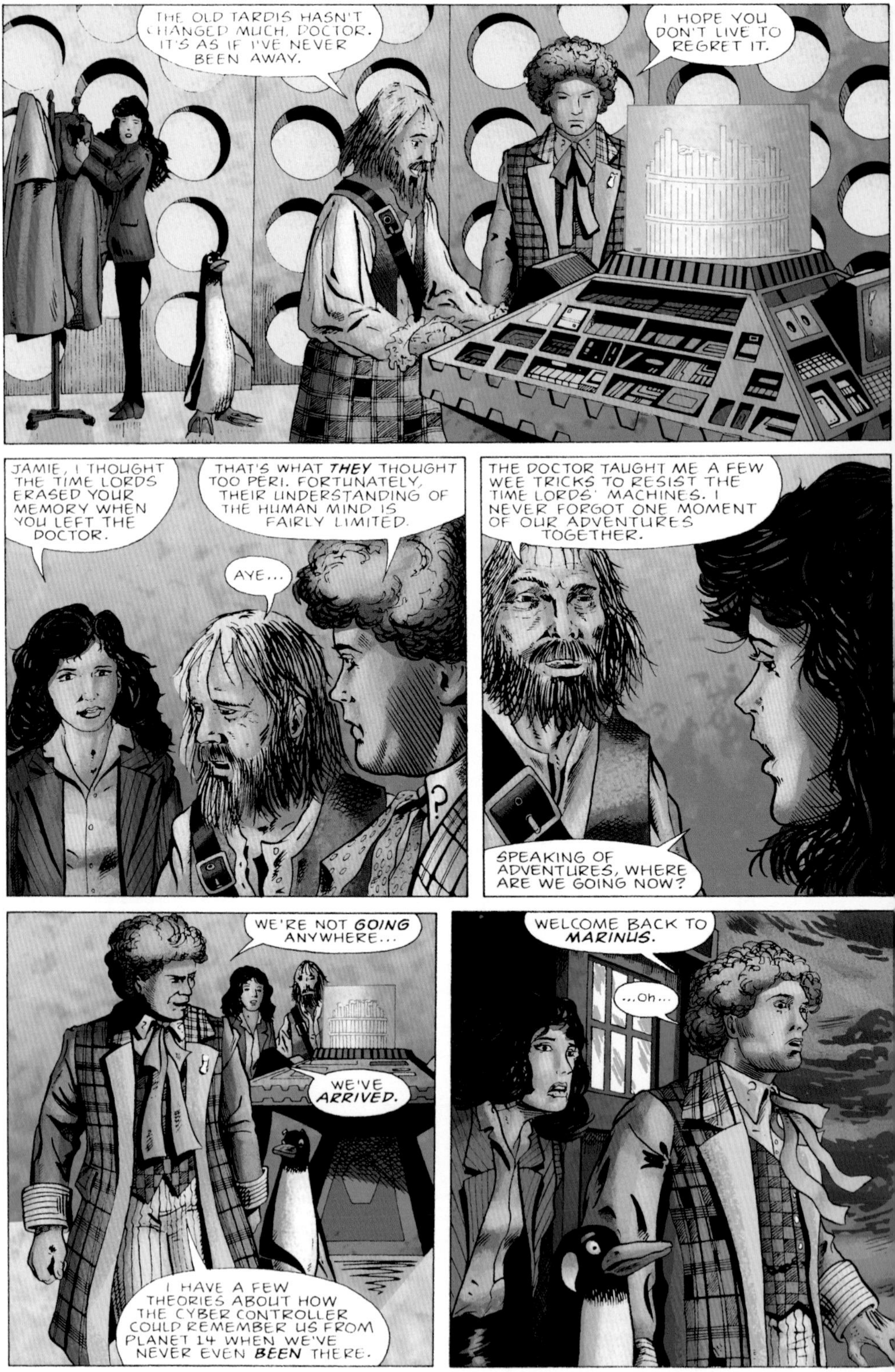
THE OLD TARDIS HASN'T CHANGED MUCH, DOCTOR. IT'S AS IF I'VE NEVER BEEN AWAY.
I HOPE YOU DON'T LIVE TO REGRET IT.
JAMIE, I THOUGHT THE TIME LORDS ERASED YOUR MEMORY WHEN YOU LEFT THE DOCTOR.
THAT'S WHAT THEY THOUGHT TOO PERI. FORTUNATELY, THEIR UNDERSTANDING OF THE HUMAN MIND IS FAIRLY LIMITED.
AYE...
THE DOCTOR TAUGHT ME A FEW WEE TRICKS TO RESIST THE TIME LORDS' MACHINES. I NEVER FORGOT ONE MOMENT OF OUR ADVENTURES TOGETHER.
SPEAKING OF ADVENTURES, WHERE ARE WE GOING NOW?
WE'RE NOT GOING ANYWHERE...
WE'VE ARRIVED.
I HAVE A FEW THEORIES ABOUT HOW THE CYBER CONTROLLER COULD REMEMBER US FROM PLANET 14 WHEN WE'VE NEVER EVEN BEEN THERE.
WELCOME BACK TO MARINUS.
...Oh...

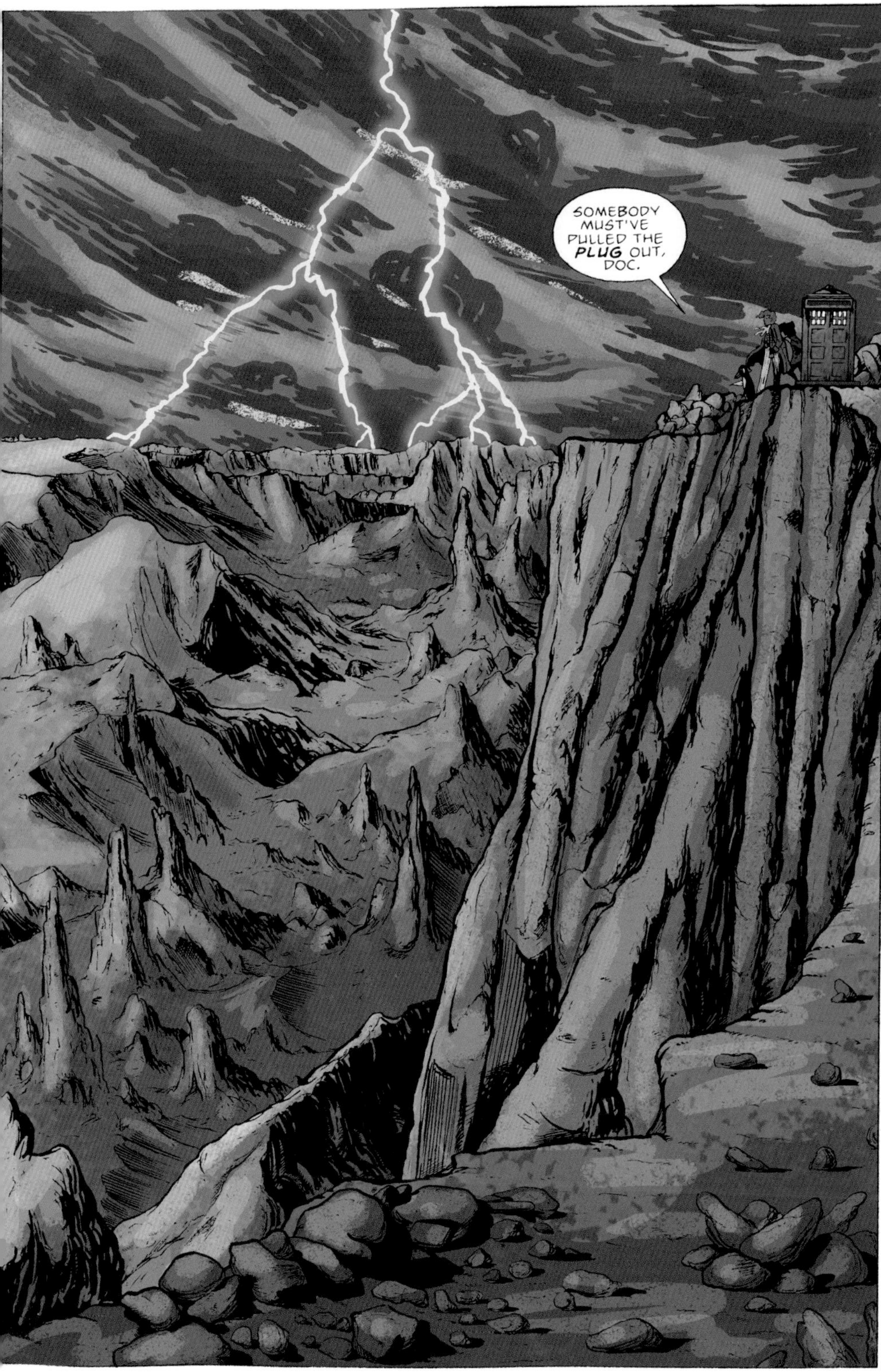
SOMEBODY MUST'VE PULLED THE **PLUG** OUT, DOC.

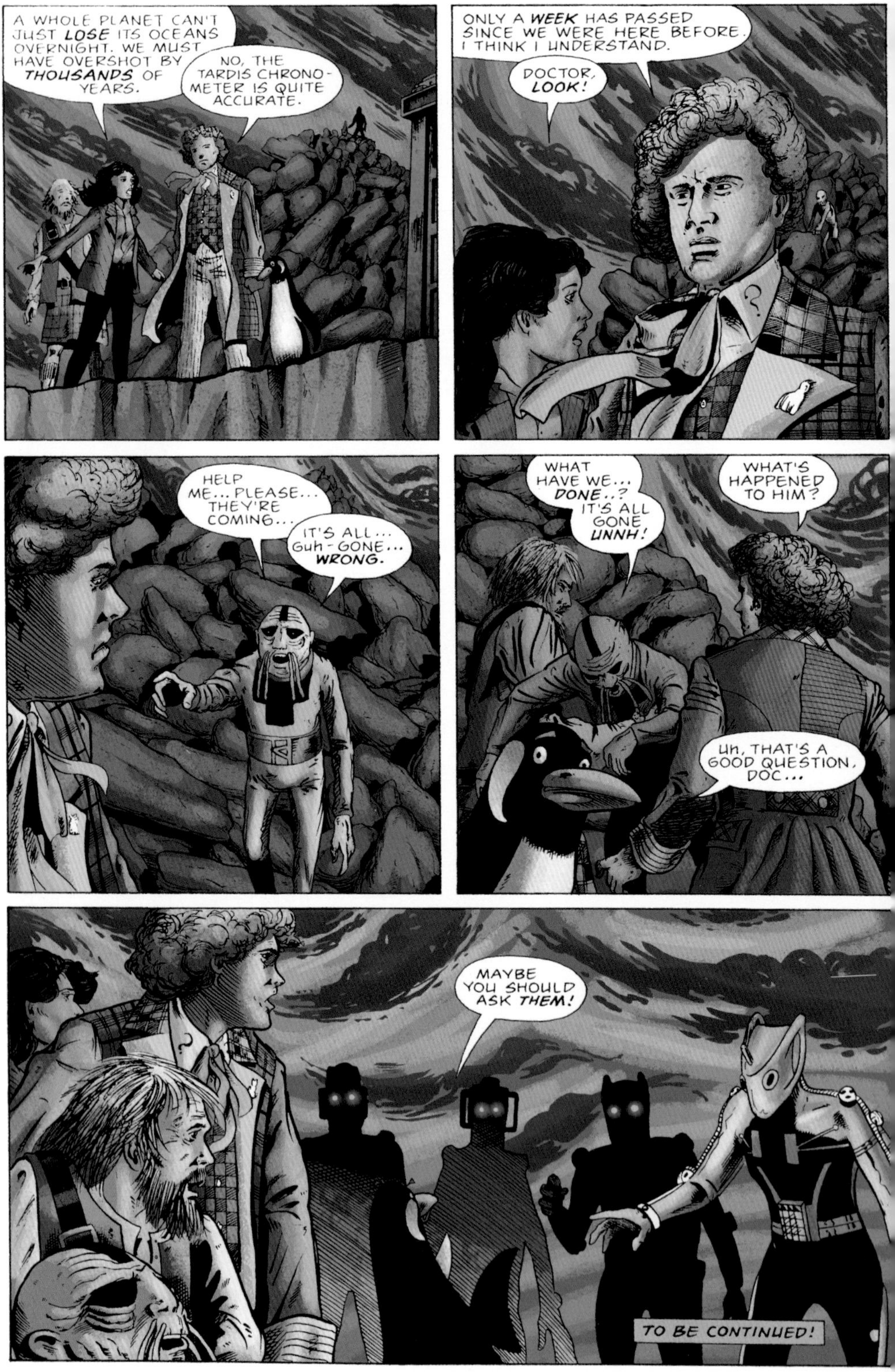
A WHOLE PLANET CAN'T JUST LOSE ITS OCEANS OVERNIGHT. WE MUST HAVE OVERSHOT BY THOUSANDS OF YEARS.
NO, THE TARDIS CHRONOMETER IS QUITE ACCURATE.
ONLY A WEEK HAS PASSED SINCE WE WERE HERE BEFORE. I THINK I UNDERSTAND.
DOCTOR, LOOK!
HELP ME... PLEASE... THEY'RE COMING...
IT'S ALL... Guh-GONE... WRONG.
WHAT HAVE WE... DONE..? IT'S ALL GONE UNNH!
WHAT'S HAPPENED TO HIM?
Uh, THAT'S A GOOD QUESTION, DOC...
MAYBE YOU SHOULD ASK THEM!
TO BE CONTINUED!

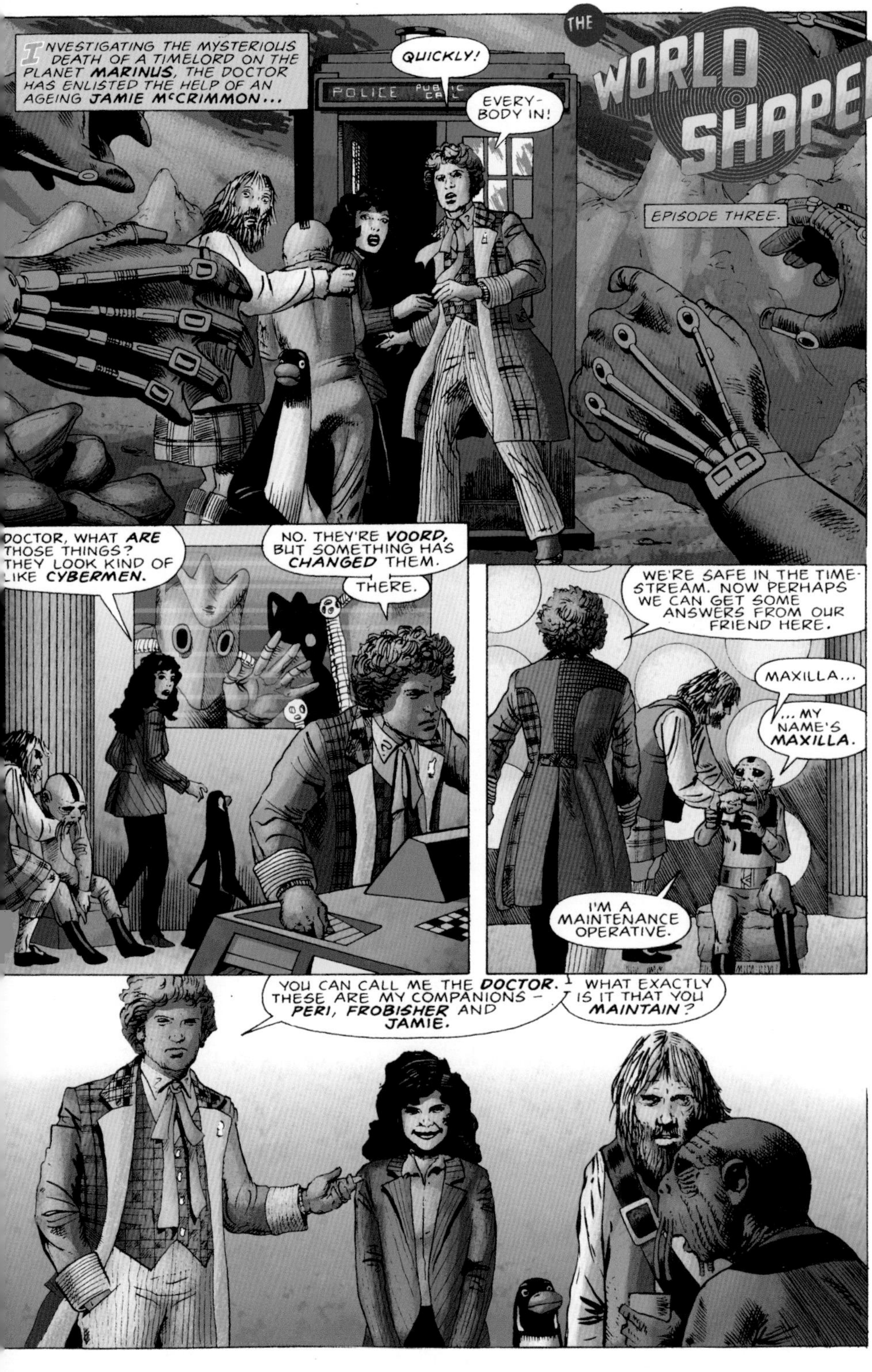
THE WORLD SHAPERS
INVESTIGATING THE MYSTERIOUS DEATH OF A TIMELORD ON THE PLANET MARINUS, THE DOCTOR HAS ENLISTED THE HELP OF AN AGEING JAMIE McCRIMMON...
QUICKLY!
POLICE PUBLIC CALL
EVERY-BODY IN!
EPISODE THREE.
DOCTOR, WHAT ARE THOSE THINGS? THEY LOOK KIND OF LIKE CYBERMEN.
NO. THEY'RE VOORD, BUT SOMETHING HAS CHANGED THEM.
THERE.
WE'RE SAFE IN THE TIME-STREAM. NOW PERHAPS WE CAN GET SOME ANSWERS FROM OUR FRIEND HERE.
MAXILLA...
... MY NAME'S MAXILLA.
I'M A MAINTENANCE OPERATIVE.
YOU CAN CALL ME THE DOCTOR. THESE ARE MY COMPANIONS - PERI, FROBISHER AND JAMIE.
WHAT EXACTLY IS IT THAT YOU MAINTAIN?

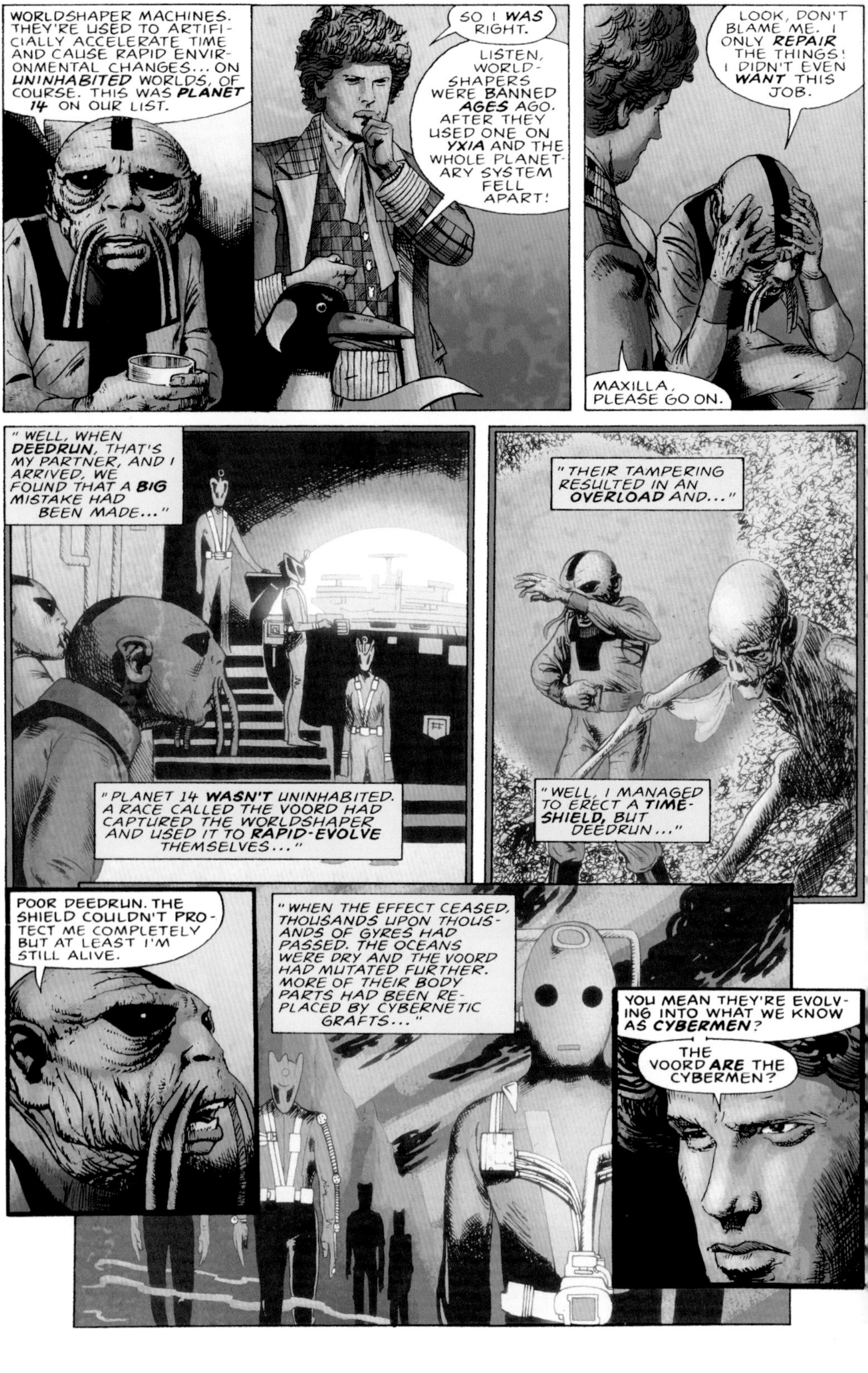
WORLDSHAPER MACHINES. THEY'RE USED TO ARTIFICIALLY ACCELERATE TIME AND CAUSE RAPID ENVIRONMENTAL CHANGES... ON UNINHABITED WORLDS, OF COURSE. THIS WAS PLANET 14 ON OUR LIST.
SO I WAS RIGHT.
LISTEN, WORLD-SHAPERS WERE BANNED AGES AGO. AFTER THEY USED ONE ON YXIA AND THE WHOLE PLANETARY SYSTEM FELL APART!
LOOK, DON'T BLAME ME. I ONLY REPAIR THE THINGS! I DIDN'T EVEN WANT THIS JOB.
MAXILLA, PLEASE GO ON.
"WELL, WHEN DEEDRUN, THAT'S MY PARTNER, AND I ARRIVED, WE FOUND THAT A BIG MISTAKE HAD BEEN MADE..."
"PLANET 14 WASN'T UNINHABITED. A RACE CALLED THE VOORD HAD CAPTURED THE WORLDSHAPER AND USED IT TO RAPID-EVOLVE THEMSELVES..."
"THEIR TAMPERING RESULTED IN AN OVERLOAD AND..."
"WELL, I MANAGED TO ERECT A TIME-SHIELD, BUT DEEDRUN..."
POOR DEEDRUN. THE SHIELD COULDN'T PROTECT ME COMPLETELY BUT AT LEAST I'M STILL ALIVE.
"WHEN THE EFFECT CEASED, THOUSANDS UPON THOUSANDS OF GYRES HAD PASSED. THE OCEANS WERE DRY AND THE VOORD HAD MUTATED FURTHER. MORE OF THEIR BODY PARTS HAD BEEN REPLACED BY CYBERNETIC GRAFTS..."
YOU MEAN THEY'RE EVOLVING INTO WHAT WE KNOW AS CYBERMEN?
THE VOORD ARE THE CYBERMEN?

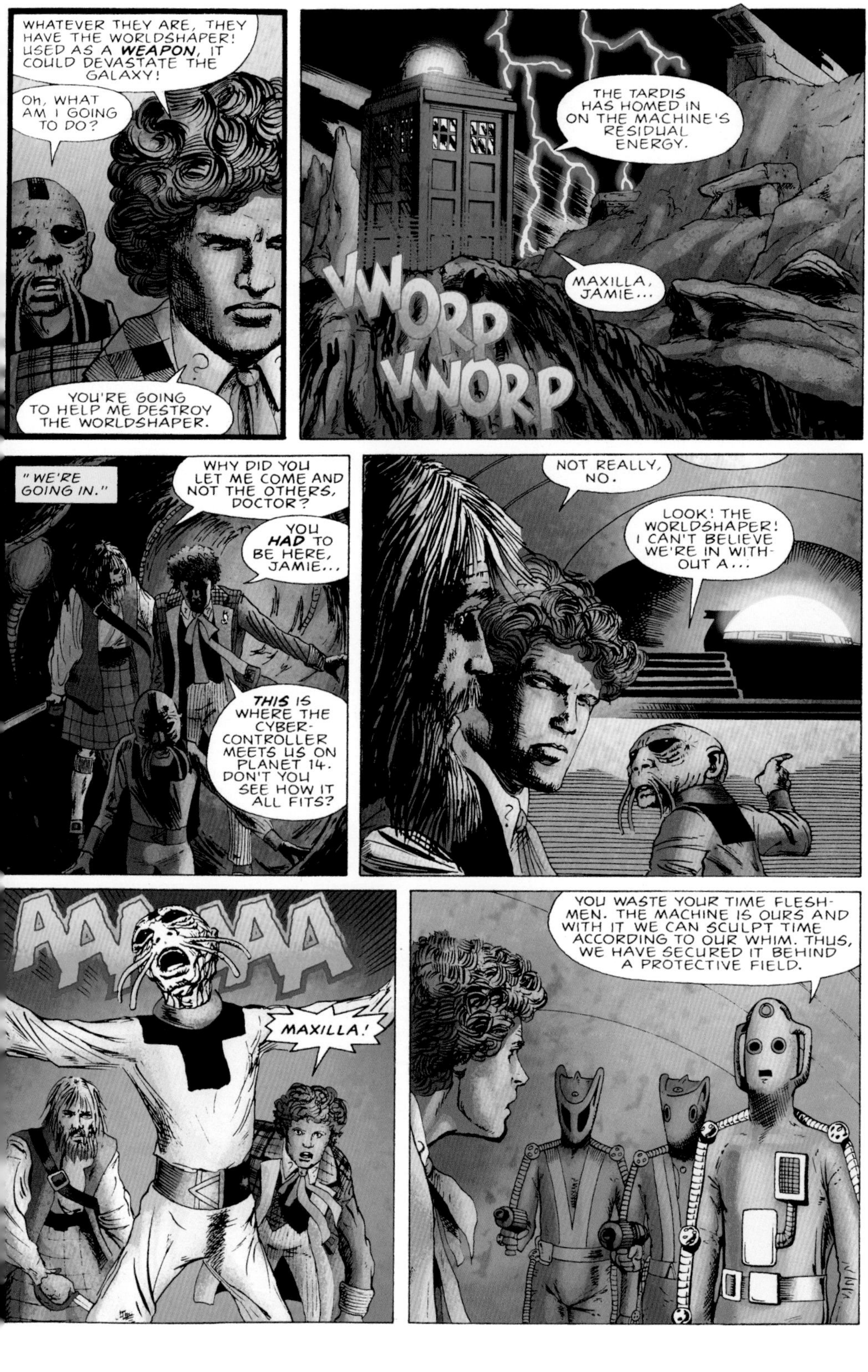
WHATEVER THEY ARE, THEY HAVE THE WORLDSHAPER! USED AS A **WEAPON**, IT COULD DEVASTATE THE GALAXY!
Oh, WHAT AM I GOING TO DO?
YOU'RE GOING TO HELP ME DESTROY THE WORLDSHAPER.
THE TARDIS HAS HOMED IN ON THE MACHINE'S RESIDUAL ENERGY.
VWORP VWORP
MAXILLA, JAMIE...
"WE'RE GOING IN."
WHY DID YOU LET ME COME AND NOT THE OTHERS, DOCTOR?
YOU **HAD** TO BE HERE, JAMIE...
THIS IS WHERE THE CYBER-CONTROLLER MEETS US ON PLANET 14. DON'T YOU SEE HOW IT ALL FITS?
NOT REALLY, NO.
LOOK! THE WORLDSHAPER! I CAN'T BELIEVE WE'RE IN WITH-OUT A...
AAAAAA
MAXILLA!
YOU WASTE YOUR TIME FLESH-MEN. THE MACHINE IS OURS AND WITH IT WE CAN SCULPT TIME ACCORDING TO OUR WHIM. THUS, WE HAVE SECURED IT BEHIND A PROTECTIVE FIELD.

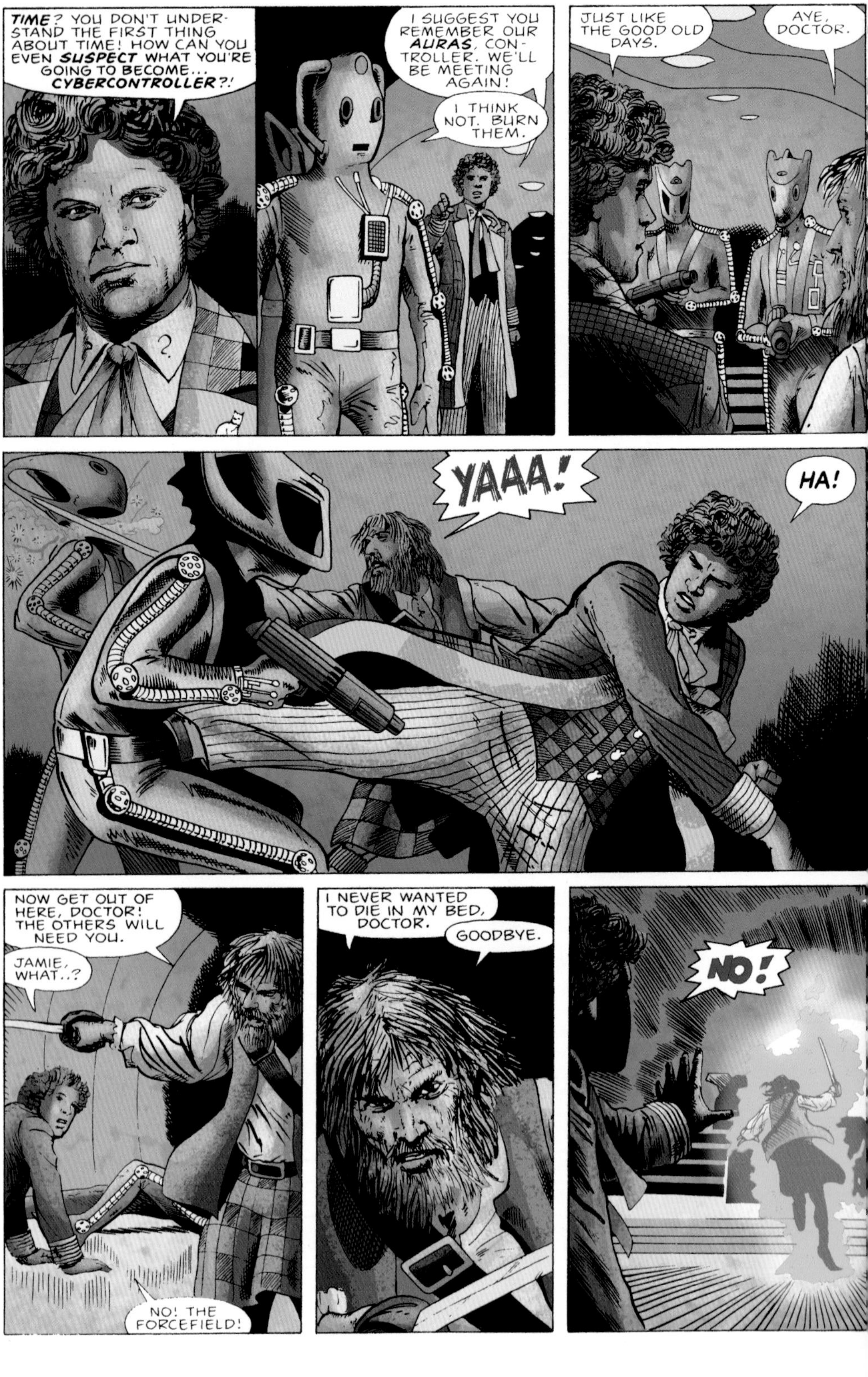
TIME? YOU DON'T UNDERSTAND THE FIRST THING ABOUT TIME! HOW CAN YOU EVEN SUSPECT WHAT YOU'RE GOING TO BECOME... CYBERCONTROLLER?!
I SUGGEST YOU REMEMBER OUR AURAS, CONTROLLER. WE'LL BE MEETING AGAIN!
I THINK NOT. BURN THEM.
JUST LIKE THE GOOD OLD DAYS.
AYE, DOCTOR.
YAAA!
HA!
NOW GET OUT OF HERE, DOCTOR! THE OTHERS WILL NEED YOU.
JAMIE, WHAT..?
NO! THE FORCEFIELD!
I NEVER WANTED TO DIE IN MY BED, DOCTOR.
GOODBYE.
NO!

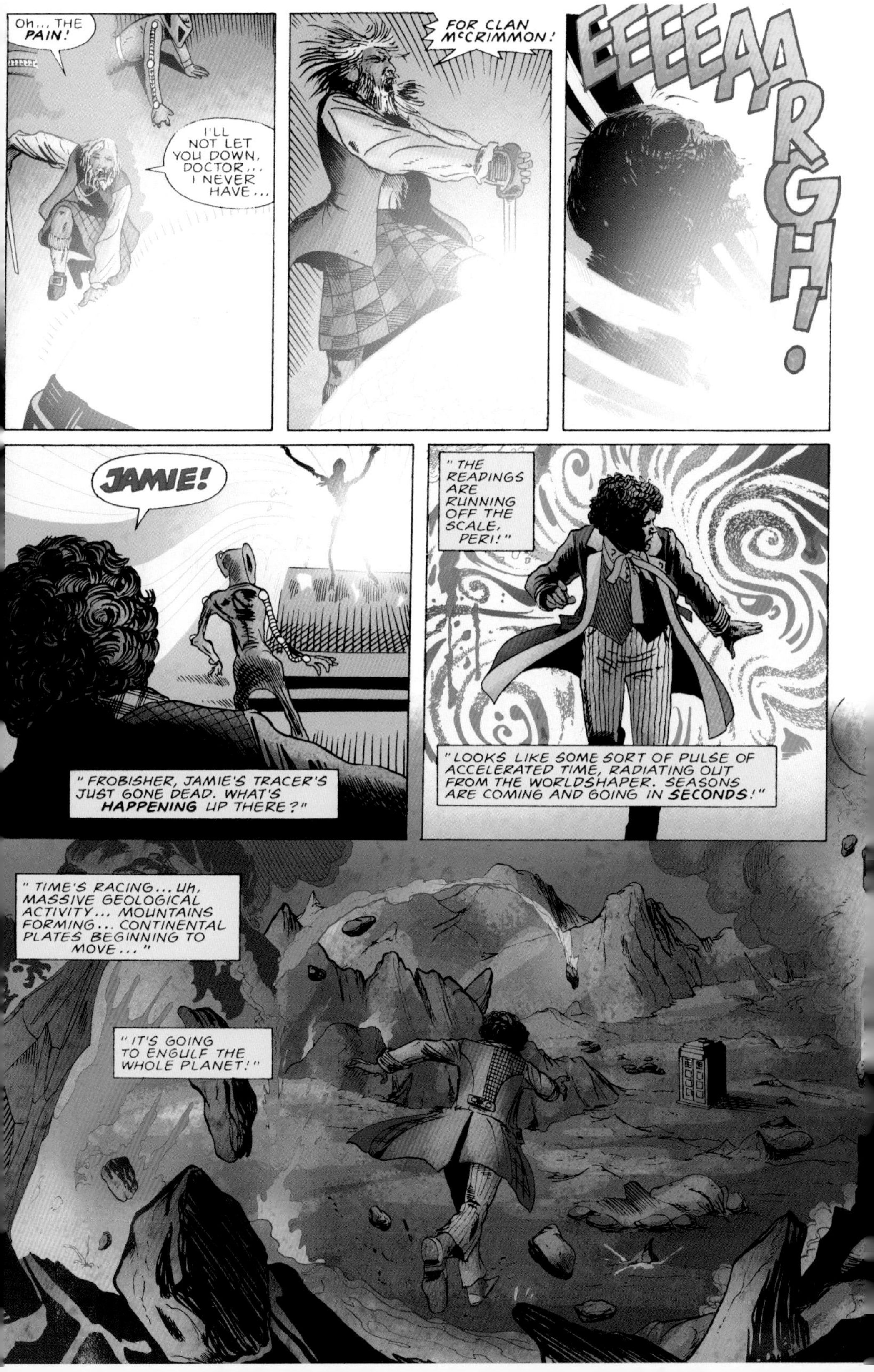
Oh... THE PAIN!
I'LL NOT LET YOU DOWN, DOCTOR... I NEVER HAVE...
FOR CLAN McCRIMMON!
EEEEAARGH!
JAMIE!
"FROBISHER, JAMIE'S TRACER'S JUST GONE DEAD. WHAT'S HAPPENING UP THERE?"
"THE READINGS ARE RUNNING OFF THE SCALE, PERI!"
"LOOKS LIKE SOME SORT OF PULSE OF ACCELERATED TIME, RADIATING OUT FROM THE WORLDSHAPER. SEASONS ARE COMING AND GOING IN SECONDS!"
"TIME'S RACING... uh, MASSIVE GEOLOGICAL ACTIVITY... MOUNTAINS FORMING... CONTINENTAL PLATES BEGINNING TO MOVE..."
"IT'S GOING TO ENGULF THE WHOLE PLANET!"

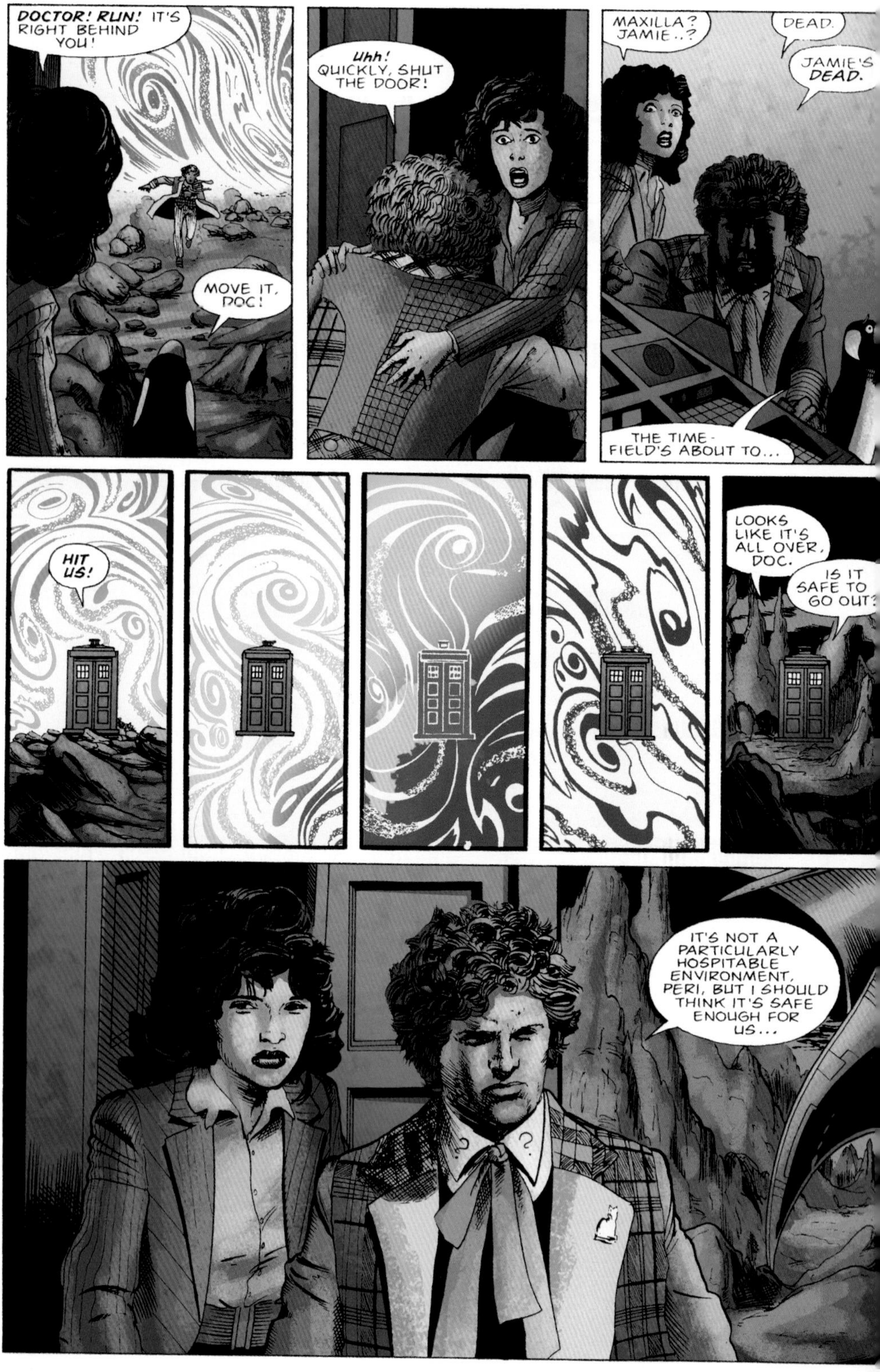
DOCTOR! RUN! IT'S RIGHT BEHIND YOU!
MOVE IT, DOC!
Uhh! QUICKLY, SHUT THE DOOR!
MAXILLA? JAMIE..?
DEAD.
JAMIE'S DEAD.
THE TIME-FIELD'S ABOUT TO...
HIT US!
LOOKS LIKE IT'S ALL OVER, DOC.
IS IT SAFE TO GO OUT?
IT'S NOT A PARTICULARLY HOSPITABLE ENVIRONMENT, PERI, BUT I SHOULD THINK IT'S SAFE ENOUGH FOR US...

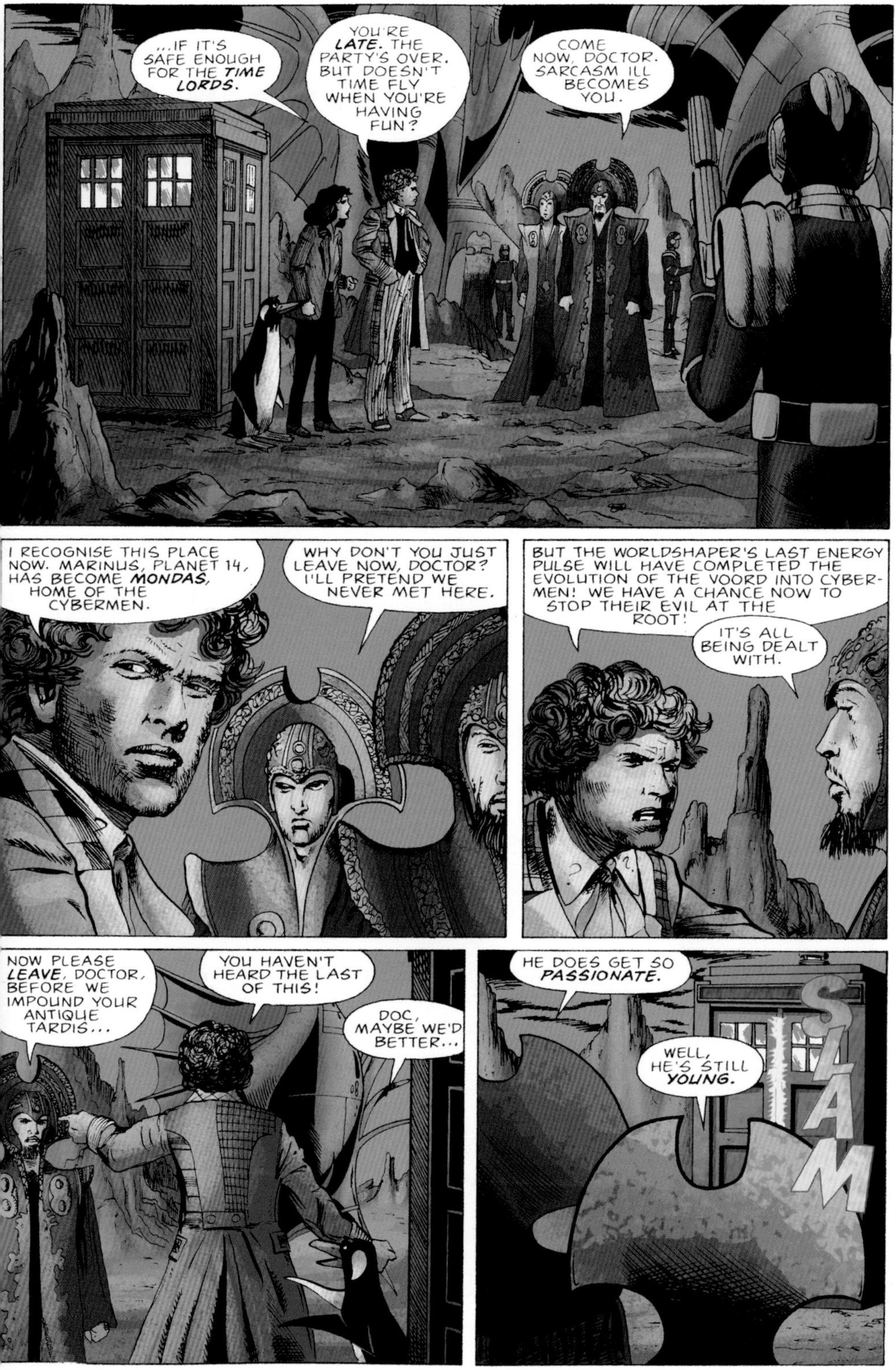
...IF IT'S SAFE ENOUGH FOR THE TIME LORDS.
YOU'RE LATE. THE PARTY'S OVER. BUT DOESN'T TIME FLY WHEN YOU'RE HAVING FUN?
COME NOW, DOCTOR. SARCASM ILL BECOMES YOU.
I RECOGNISE THIS PLACE NOW. MARINUS, PLANET 14, HAS BECOME MONDAS, HOME OF THE CYBERMEN.
WHY DON'T YOU JUST LEAVE NOW, DOCTOR? I'LL PRETEND WE NEVER MET HERE.
BUT THE WORLDSHAPER'S LAST ENERGY PULSE WILL HAVE COMPLETED THE EVOLUTION OF THE VOORD INTO CYBERMEN! WE HAVE A CHANCE NOW TO STOP THEIR EVIL AT THE ROOT!
IT'S ALL BEING DEALT WITH.
NOW PLEASE LEAVE, DOCTOR, BEFORE WE IMPOUND YOUR ANTIQUE TARDIS...
YOU HAVEN'T HEARD THE LAST OF THIS!
DOC, MAYBE WE'D BETTER...
HE DOES GET SO PASSIONATE.
WELL, HE'S STILL YOUNG.
SLAM

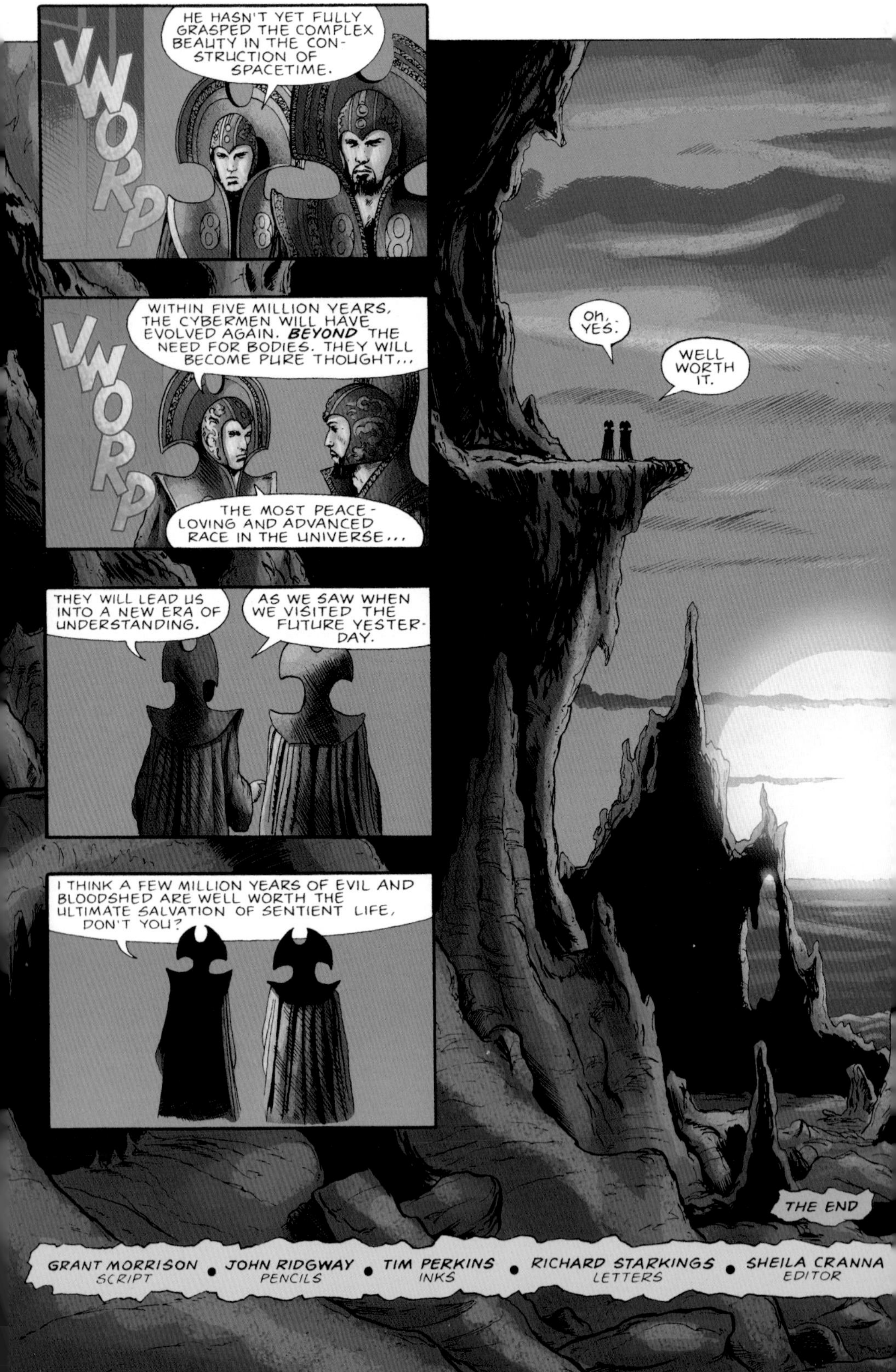

HE HASN'T YET FULLY GRASPED THE COMPLEX BEAUTY IN THE CON-STRUCTION OF SPACETIME.
VWORP
WITHIN FIVE MILLION YEARS, THE CYBERMEN WILL HAVE EVOLVED AGAIN. BEYOND THE NEED FOR BODIES. THEY WILL BECOME PURE THOUGHT...
THE MOST PEACE-LOVING AND ADVANCED RACE IN THE UNIVERSE...
VWORP
THEY WILL LEAD US INTO A NEW ERA OF UNDERSTANDING.
AS WE SAW WHEN WE VISITED THE FUTURE YESTER-DAY.
I THINK A FEW MILLION YEARS OF EVIL AND BLOODSHED ARE WELL WORTH THE ULTIMATE SALVATION OF SENTIENT LIFE, DON'T YOU?
Oh, YES.
WELL WORTH IT.
THE END
GRANT MORRISON SCRIPT • JOHN RIDGWAY PENCILS • TIM PERKINS INKS • RICHARD STARKINGS LETTERS • SHEILA CRANNA EDITOR

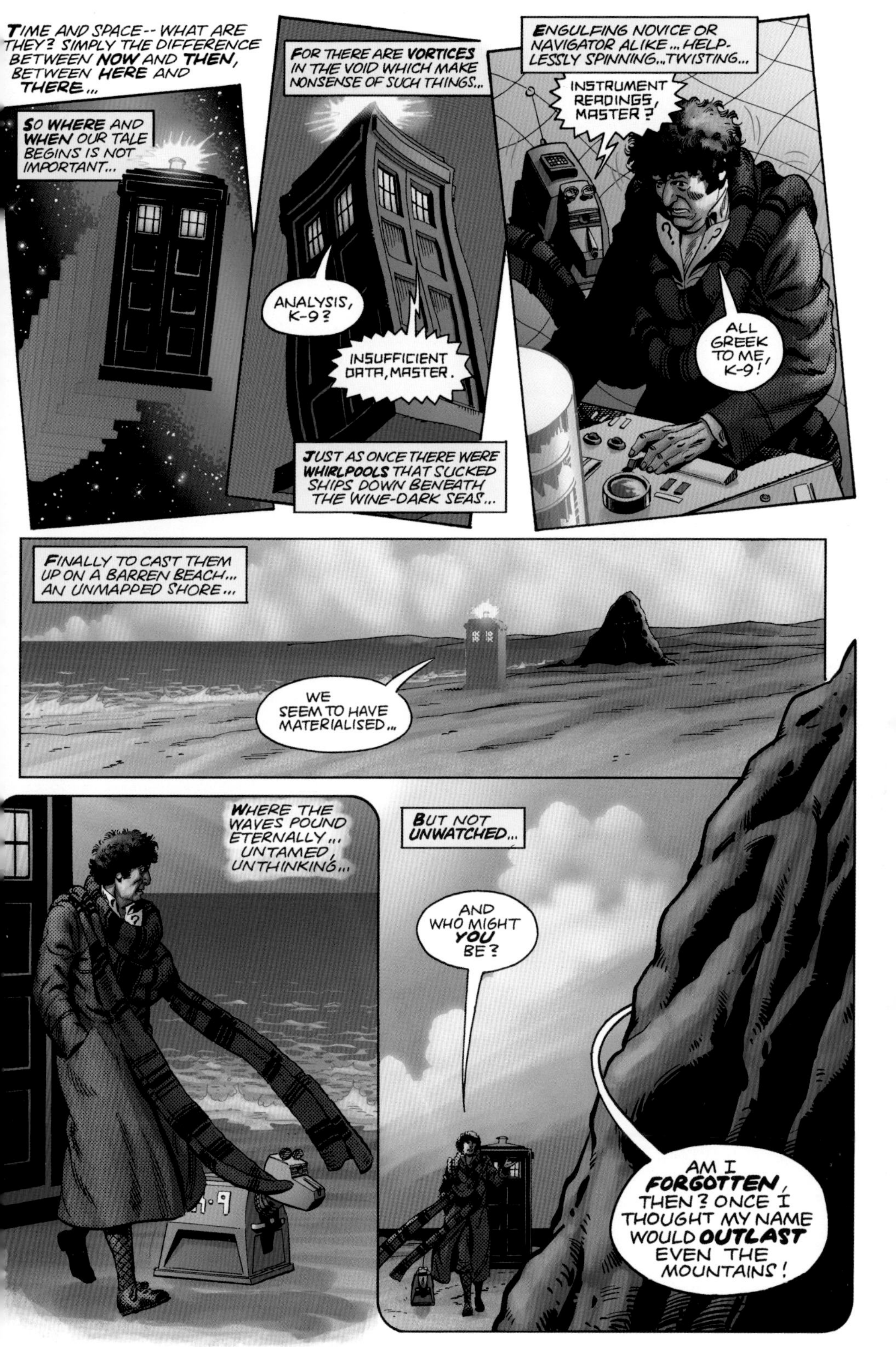
TIME AND SPACE-- WHAT ARE THEY? SIMPLY THE DIFFERENCE BETWEEN NOW AND THEN, BETWEEN HERE AND THERE...
SO WHERE AND WHEN OUR TALE BEGINS IS NOT IMPORTANT...
FOR THERE ARE VORTICES IN THE VOID WHICH MAKE NONSENSE OF SUCH THINGS...
ANALYSIS, K-9?
INSUFFICIENT DATA, MASTER.
JUST AS ONCE THERE WERE WHIRLPOOLS THAT SUCKED SHIPS DOWN BENEATH THE WINE-DARK SEAS...
ENGULFING NOVICE OR NAVIGATOR ALIKE... HELPLESSLY SPINNING... TWISTING...
INSTRUMENT READINGS, MASTER?
ALL GREEK TO ME, K-9!
FINALLY TO CAST THEM UP ON A BARREN BEACH... AN UNMAPPED SHORE...
WE SEEM TO HAVE MATERIALISED...
WHERE THE WAVES POUND ETERNALLY... UNTAMED, UNTHINKING...
BUT NOT UNWATCHED...
AND WHO MIGHT YOU BE?
AM I FORGOTTEN, THEN? ONCE I THOUGHT MY NAME WOULD OUTLAST EVEN THE MOUNTAINS!

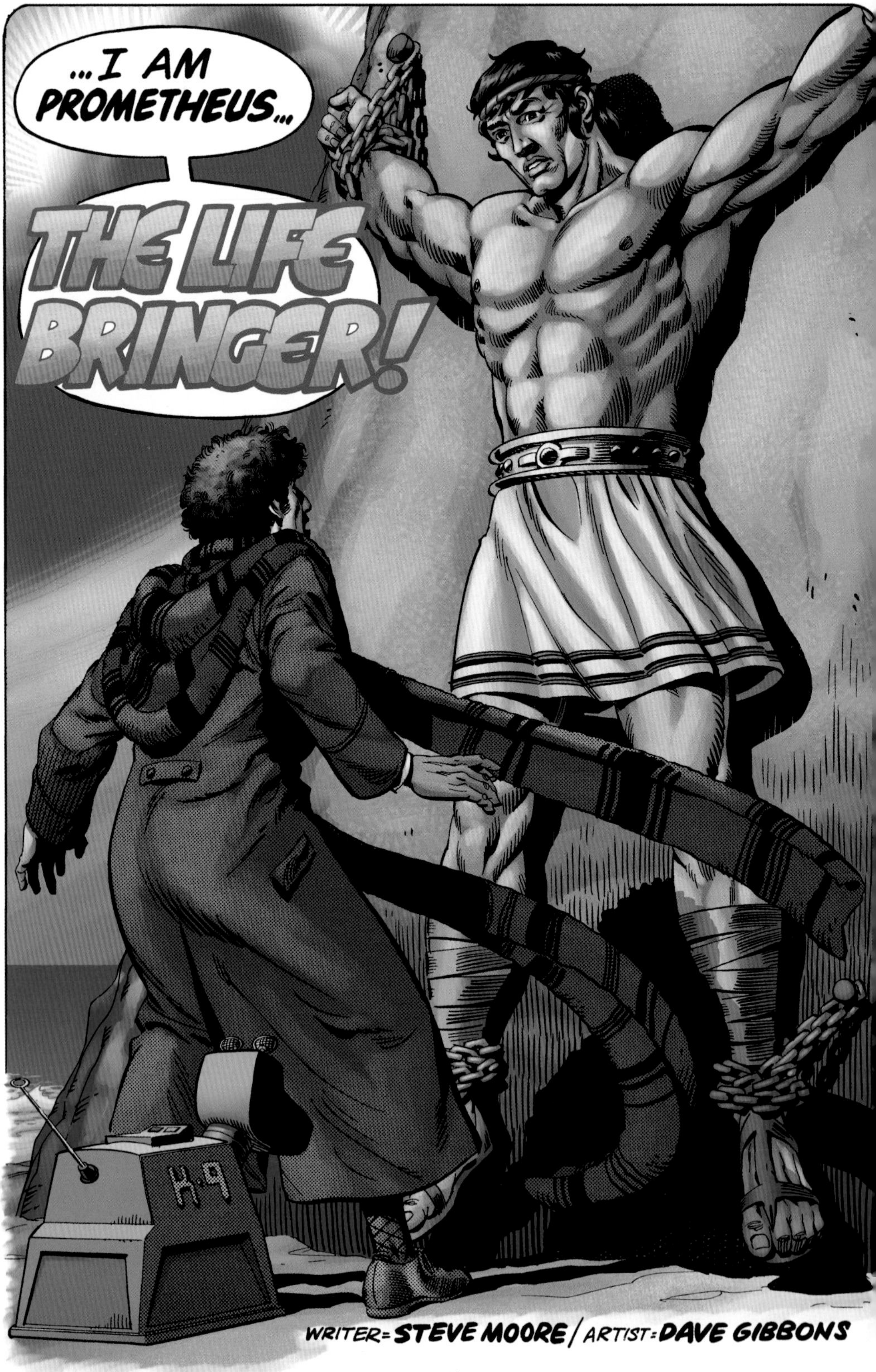
...I AM PROMETHEUS...
THE LIFE BRINGER!
K-9
WRITER=STEVE MOORE / ARTIST=DAVE GIBBONS

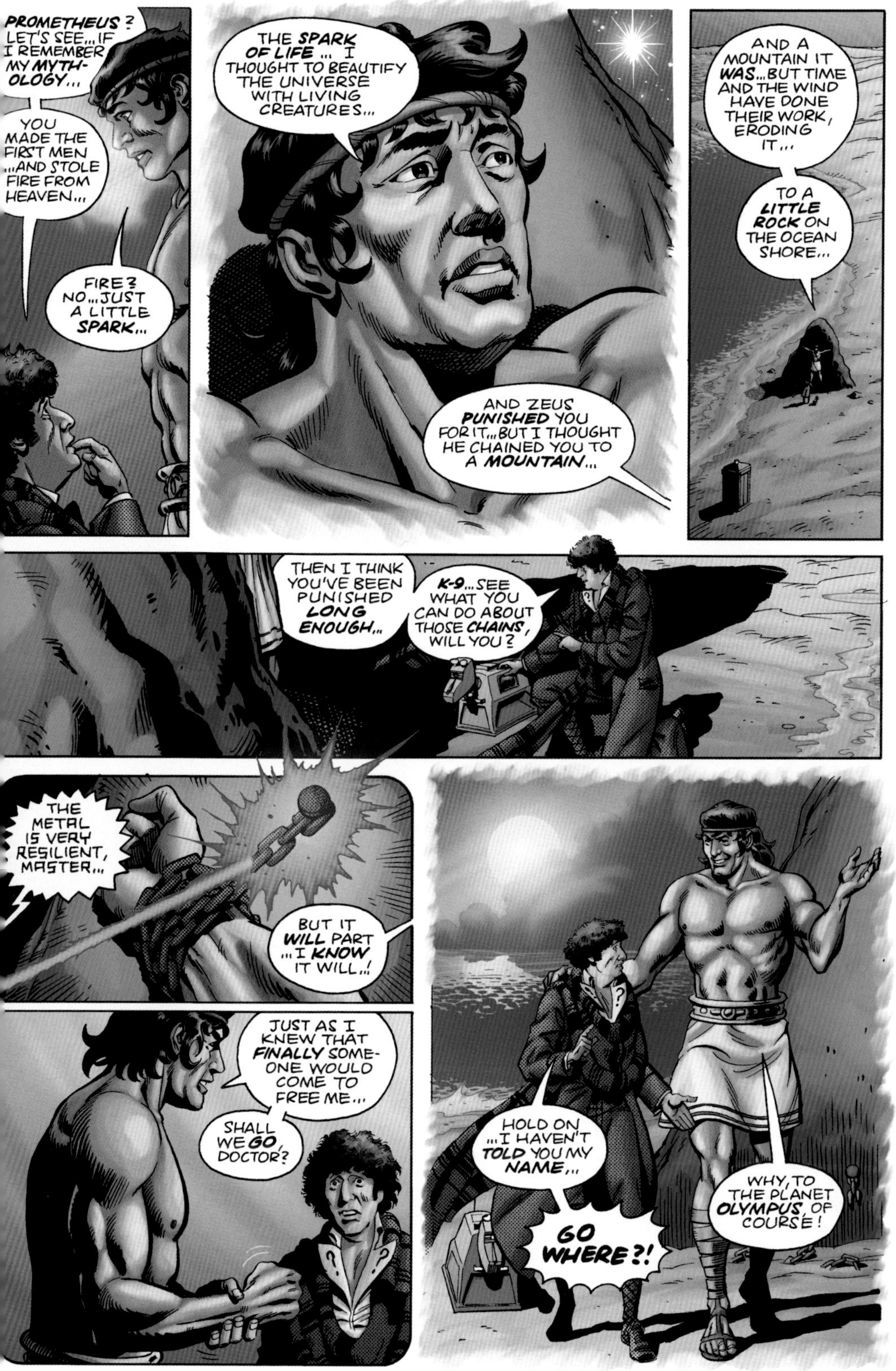
PROMETHEUS? LET'S SEE... IF I REMEMBER MY MYTHOLOGY...
YOU MADE THE FIRST MEN ...AND STOLE FIRE FROM HEAVEN...
FIRE? NO... JUST A LITTLE SPARK...
THE SPARK OF LIFE... I THOUGHT TO BEAUTIFY THE UNIVERSE WITH LIVING CREATURES...
AND ZEUS PUNISHED YOU FOR IT... BUT I THOUGHT HE CHAINED YOU TO A MOUNTAIN...
AND A MOUNTAIN IT WAS... BUT TIME AND THE WIND HAVE DONE THEIR WORK, ERODING IT...
TO A LITTLE ROCK ON THE OCEAN SHORE...
THEN I THINK YOU'VE BEEN PUNISHED LONG ENOUGH...
K-9... SEE WHAT YOU CAN DO ABOUT THOSE CHAINS, WILL YOU?
THE METAL IS VERY RESILIENT, MASTER...
BUT IT WILL PART ...I KNOW IT WILL..!
JUST AS I KNEW THAT FINALLY SOMEONE WOULD COME TO FREE ME...
SHALL WE GO, DOCTOR?
GO WHERE?!
HOLD ON ...I HAVEN'T TOLD YOU MY NAME...
WHY, TO THE PLANET OLYMPUS, OF COURSE!

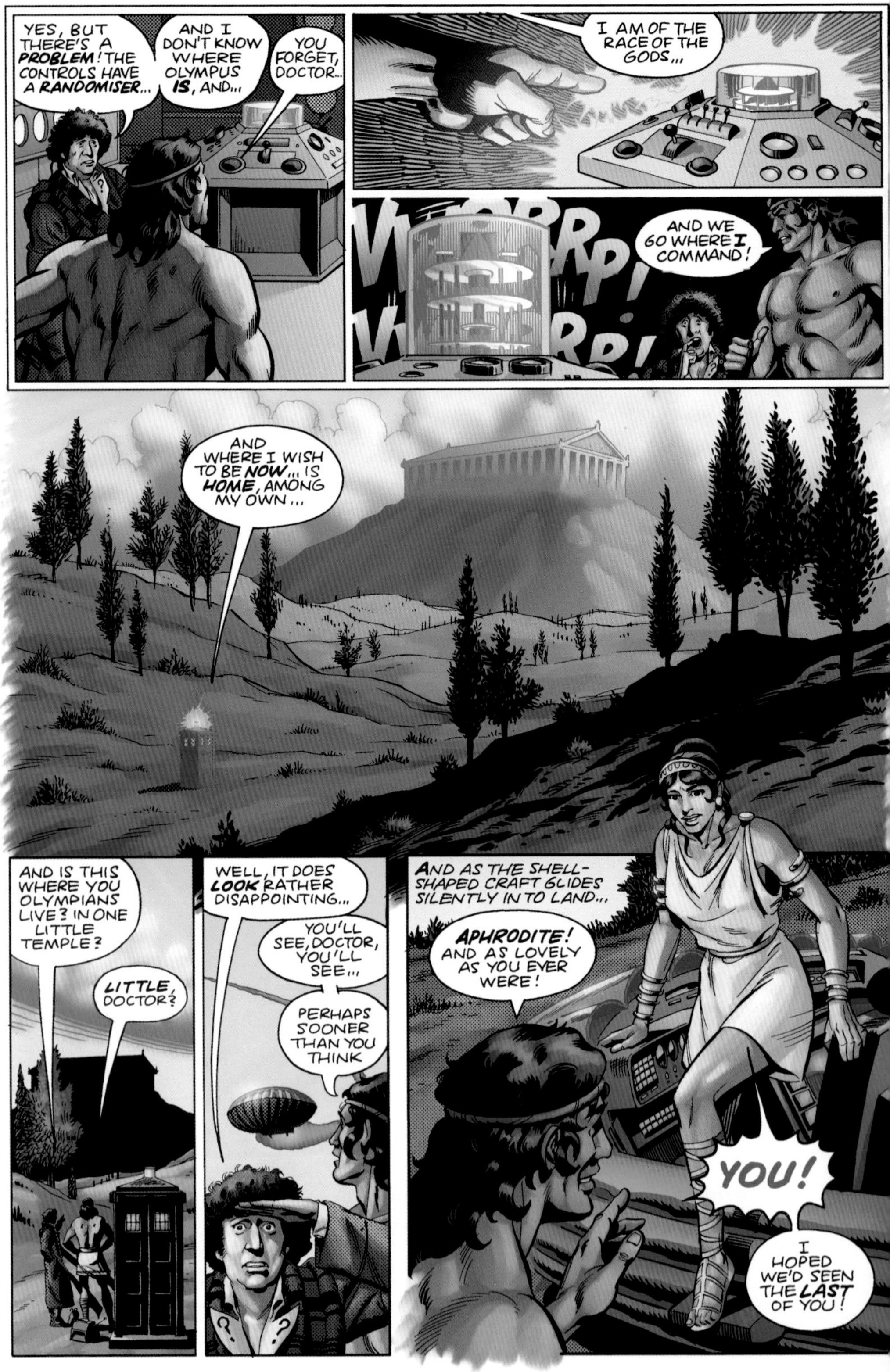
YES, BUT THERE'S A PROBLEM! THE CONTROLS HAVE A RANDOMISER...
AND I DON'T KNOW WHERE OLYMPUS IS, AND...
YOU FORGET, DOCTOR...
I AM OF THE RACE OF THE GODS...
AND WE GO WHERE I COMMAND!
AND WHERE I WISH TO BE NOW... IS HOME, AMONG MY OWN...
AND IS THIS WHERE YOU OLYMPIANS LIVE? IN ONE LITTLE TEMPLE?
LITTLE, DOCTOR?
WELL, IT DOES LOOK RATHER DISAPPOINTING...
YOU'LL SEE, DOCTOR, YOU'LL SEE...
PERHAPS SOONER THAN YOU THINK
AND AS THE SHELL-SHAPED CRAFT GLIDES SILENTLY IN TO LAND...
APHRODITE! AND AS LOVELY AS YOU EVER WERE!
YOU!
I HOPED WE'D SEEN THE LAST OF YOU!

WHAT KIND OF WELCOME IS *THAT* BEAUTEOUS ONE?

I COULD THINK OF BETTER...

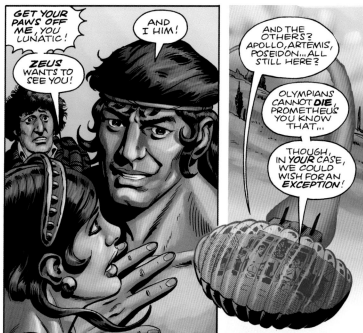

GET YOUR *PAWS OFF* ME, YOU LUNATIC!

ZEUS WANTS TO SEE YOU!

AND I *HIM!*

AND THE *OTHERS?* APOLLO, ARTEMIS, POSEIDON... ALL STILL HERE?

OLYMPIANS CANNOT *DIE* PROMETHEUS YOU KNOW THAT...

THOUGH, IN *YOUR* CASE, WE COULD WISH FOR AN *EXCEPTION!*

THEN, AS THE SHELL-CRAFT APPROACHES ITS DESTINATION...

NOW, DOCTOR... ARE YOU *STILL* DISAPPOINTED?

NO, I'M *IMPRESSED...* I DIDN'T REALISE WE'D LANDED *THIRTY MILES* AWAY...

AND THAT THE 'TEMPLE' IS ACTUALLY A *CITY*...

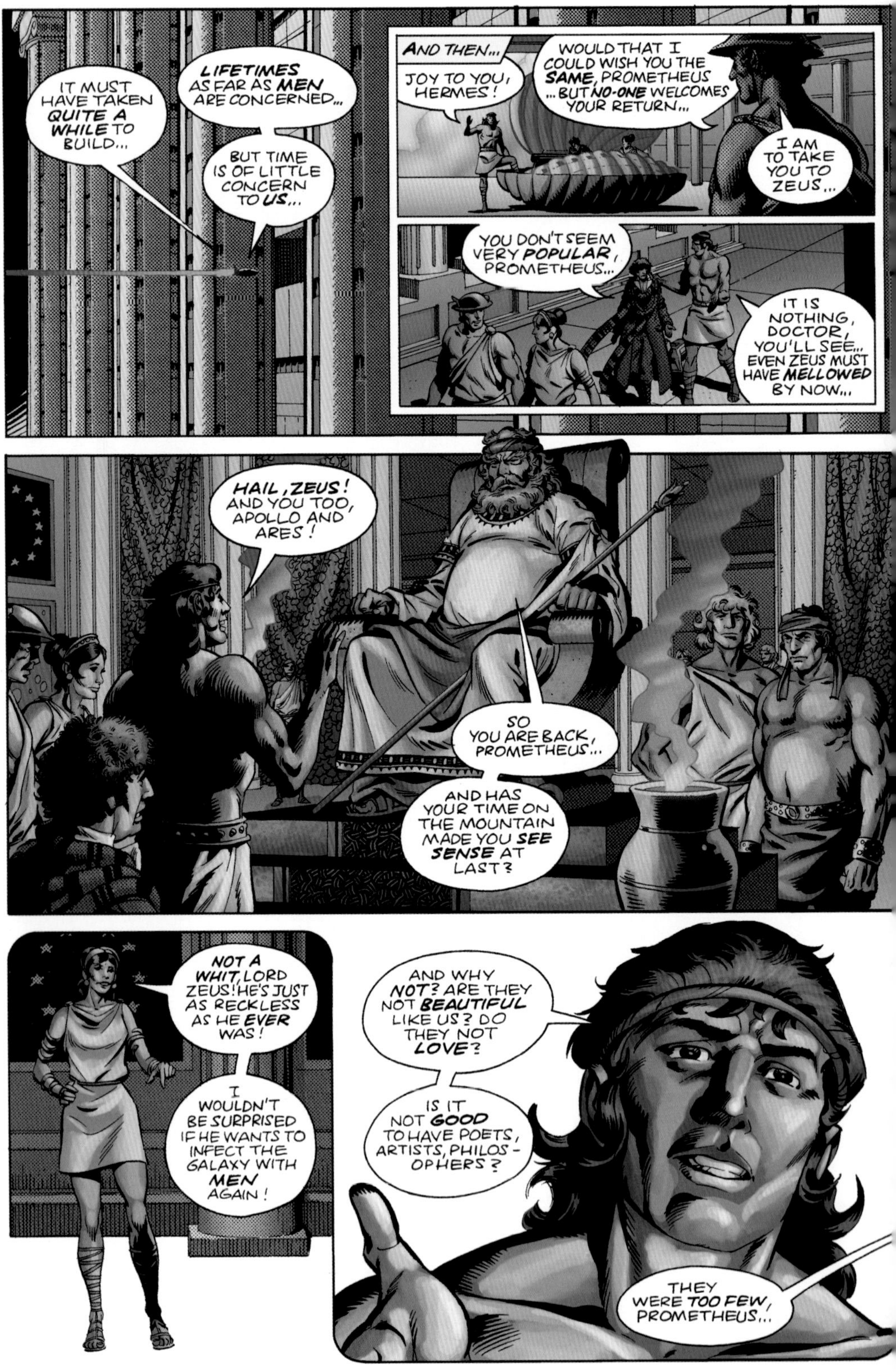
IT MUST HAVE TAKEN QUITE A WHILE TO BUILD...
LIFETIMES AS FAR AS MEN ARE CONCERNED...
BUT TIME IS OF LITTLE CONCERN TO US...
AND THEN...
JOY TO YOU, HERMES!
WOULD THAT I COULD WISH YOU THE SAME, PROMETHEUS ...BUT NO-ONE WELCOMES YOUR RETURN...
I AM TO TAKE YOU TO ZEUS...
YOU DON'T SEEM VERY POPULAR, PROMETHEUS...
IT IS NOTHING, DOCTOR, YOU'LL SEE... EVEN ZEUS MUST HAVE MELLOWED BY NOW...
HAIL, ZEUS! AND YOU TOO, APOLLO AND ARES!
SO YOU ARE BACK, PROMETHEUS...
AND HAS YOUR TIME ON THE MOUNTAIN MADE YOU SEE SENSE AT LAST?
NOT A WHIT, LORD ZEUS! HE'S JUST AS RECKLESS AS HE EVER WAS!
I WOULDN'T BE SURPRISED IF HE WANTS TO INFECT THE GALAXY WITH MEN AGAIN!
AND WHY NOT? ARE THEY NOT BEAUTIFUL LIKE US? DO THEY NOT LOVE?
IS IT NOT GOOD TO HAVE POETS, ARTISTS, PHILOS-OPHERS?
THEY WERE TOO FEW, PROMETHEUS...

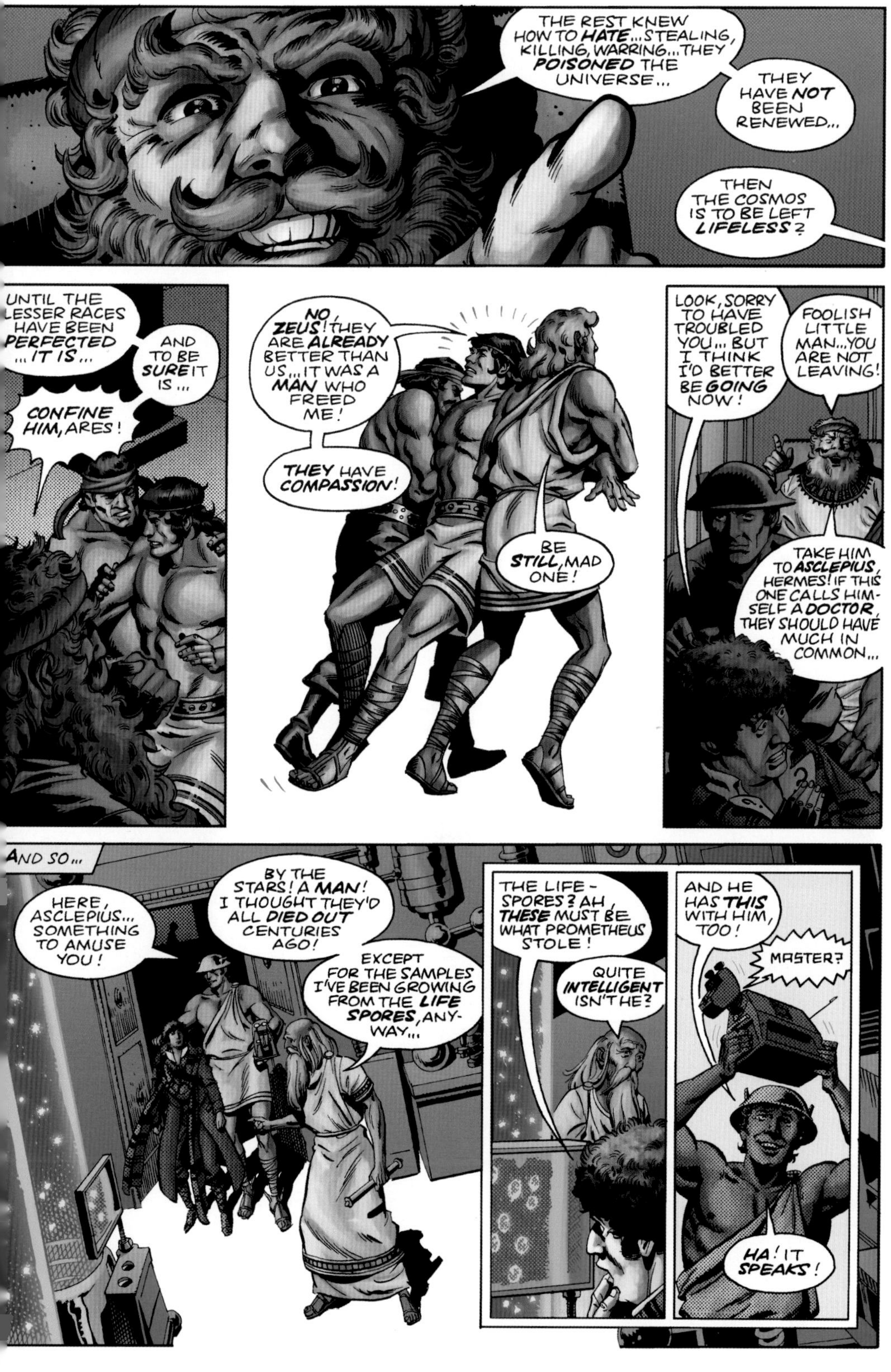
THE REST KNEW HOW TO HATE... STEALING, KILLING, WARRING... THEY POISONED THE UNIVERSE...
THEY HAVE NOT BEEN RENEWED...
THEN THE COSMOS IS TO BE LEFT LIFELESS?
UNTIL THE LESSER RACES HAVE BEEN PERFECTED ...IT IS...
AND TO BE SURE IT IS...
CONFINE HIM, ARES!
NO, ZEUS! THEY ARE ALREADY BETTER THAN US... IT WAS A MAN WHO FREED ME!
THEY HAVE COMPASSION!
BE STILL, MAD ONE!
LOOK, SORRY TO HAVE TROUBLED YOU... BUT I THINK I'D BETTER BE GOING NOW!
FOOLISH LITTLE MAN... YOU ARE NOT LEAVING!
TAKE HIM TO ASCLEPIUS, HERMES! IF THIS ONE CALLS HIMSELF A DOCTOR, THEY SHOULD HAVE MUCH IN COMMON...
AND SO...
HERE, ASCLEPIUS... SOMETHING TO AMUSE YOU!
BY THE STARS! A MAN! I THOUGHT THEY'D ALL DIED OUT CENTURIES AGO!
EXCEPT FOR THE SAMPLES I'VE BEEN GROWING FROM THE LIFE SPORES, ANYWAY...
THE LIFE-SPORES? AH, THESE MUST BE WHAT PROMETHEUS STOLE!
QUITE INTELLIGENT ISN'T HE?
AND HE HAS THIS WITH HIM, TOO!
MASTER?
HA! IT SPEAKS!

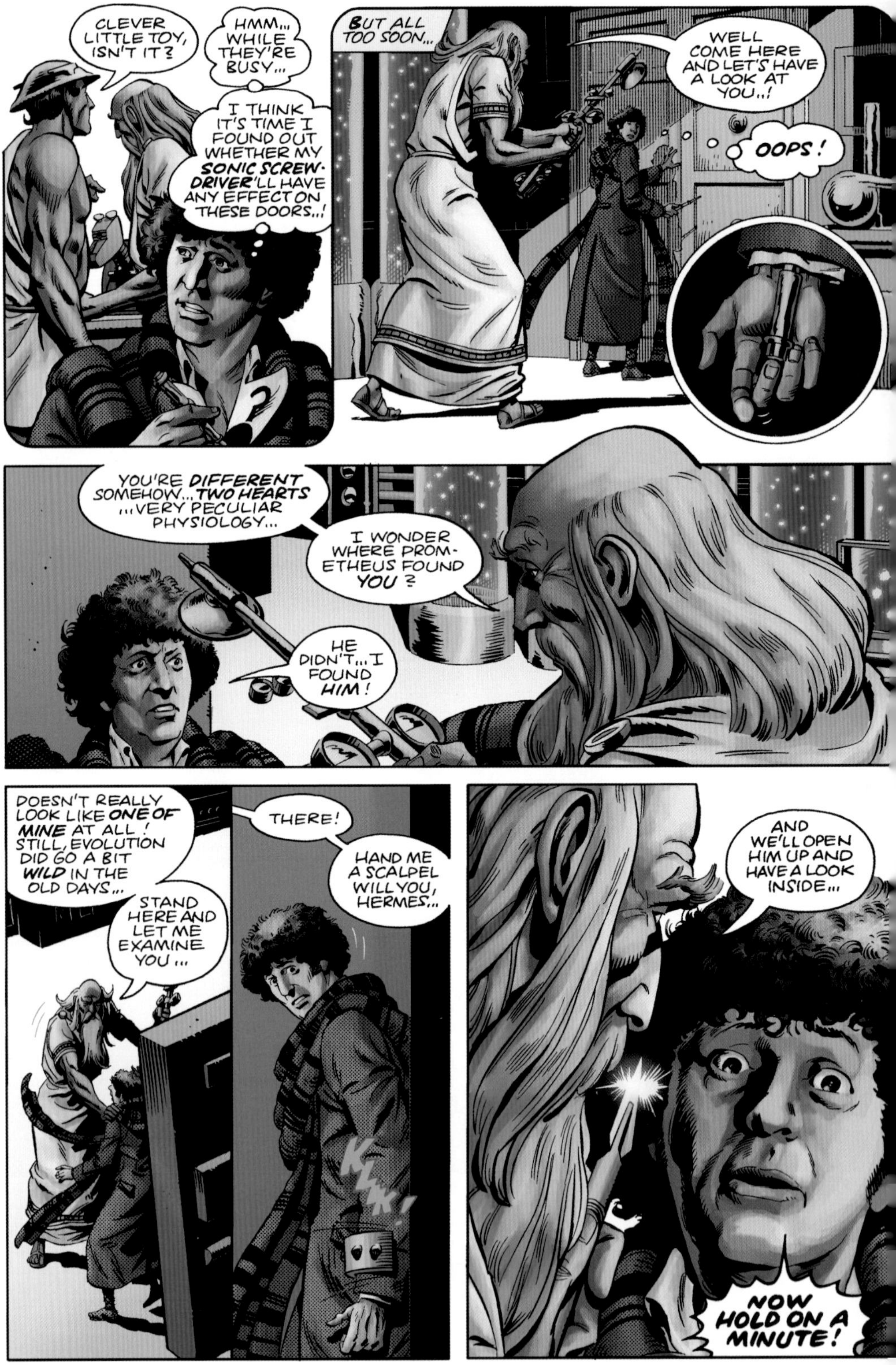
CLEVER LITTLE TOY, ISN'T IT?
HMM... WHILE THEY'RE BUSY...
I THINK IT'S TIME I FOUND OUT WHETHER MY SONIC SCREW-DRIVER'LL HAVE ANY EFFECT ON THESE DOORS...!
BUT ALL TOO SOON...
WELL COME HERE AND LET'S HAVE A LOOK AT YOU...!
OOPS!
YOU'RE DIFFERENT SOMEHOW... TWO HEARTS ...VERY PECULIAR PHYSIOLOGY...
I WONDER WHERE PROM-ETHEUS FOUND YOU?
HE DIDN'T... I FOUND HIM!
DOESN'T REALLY LOOK LIKE ONE OF MINE AT ALL! STILL, EVOLUTION DID GO A BIT WILD IN THE OLD DAYS...
STAND HERE AND LET ME EXAMINE YOU...
THERE!
HAND ME A SCALPEL WILL YOU, HERMES...
KLIK!
AND WE'LL OPEN HIM UP AND HAVE A LOOK INSIDE...
NOW HOLD ON A MINUTE!

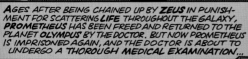

AGES AFTER BEING CHAINED UP BY **ZEUS** IN PUNISH-MENT FOR SCATTERING **LIFE** THROUGHOUT THE GALAXY, **PROMETHEUS** HAS BEEN FREED AND RETURNED TO THE PLANET **OLYMPUS** BY THE DOCTOR, BUT NOW PROMETHEUS IS IMPRISONED AGAIN, AND THE DOCTOR IS ABOUT TO UNDERGO A THOROUGH *MEDICAL* EXAMINATION...

GOODBYE, DOCTOR! THIS WILL ONLY HURT FOR A *LITTLE* WHILE!

I'D RATHER IT DIDN'T HURT *AT ALL*

STUN THEM, K-9!

WHAT IN...?

IT'S THE DOG, ASCLEPIUS!

VWEEE!

A PHOTON-BEAM BLASTER! ISN'T THAT *QUAINT*, HERMES?

I CAN HARDLY FEEL A THING... CAN YOU?

INEFFECTIVE, MASTER!

KEEP FIRING, K-9!

IT MIGHT NOT DO ANY GOOD, BUT IF IT KEEPS THEM DISTRACTED...

STORY: STEVE MOORE

ART: DAVE GIBBONS

'LIFE-BRINGER'

I SHOULD THINK IT'S QUITE EFFECTIVE AGAINST *LESS-DEVELOPED* CREATURES...!

DID *YOU* MAKE THIS, DOCTOR?

DOCTOR?

GOOD OLD SONIC SCREW-DRIVER!

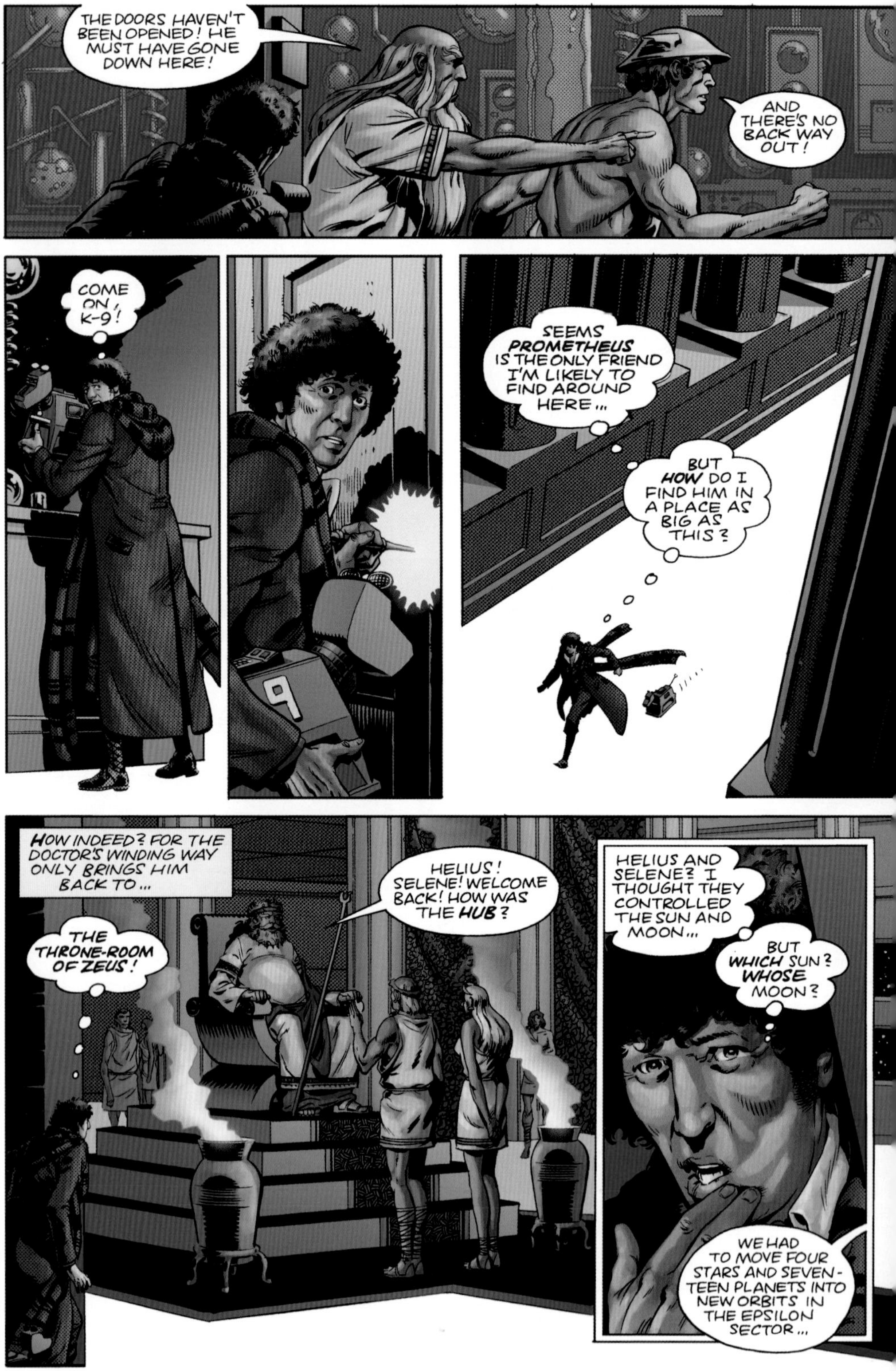

THE DOORS HAVEN'T BEEN OPENED! HE MUST HAVE GONE DOWN HERE!
AND THERE'S NO BACK WAY OUT!
COME ON, K-9!
SEEMS PROMETHEUS IS THE ONLY FRIEND I'M LIKELY TO FIND AROUND HERE...
BUT HOW DO I FIND HIM IN A PLACE AS BIG AS THIS?
HOW INDEED? FOR THE DOCTOR'S WINDING WAY ONLY BRINGS HIM BACK TO...
THE THRONE-ROOM OF ZEUS!
HELIUS! SELENE! WELCOME BACK! HOW WAS THE HUB?
HELIUS AND SELENE? I THOUGHT THEY CONTROLLED THE SUN AND MOON...
BUT WHICH SUN? WHOSE MOON?
WE HAD TO MOVE FOUR STARS AND SEVENTEEN PLANETS INTO NEW ORBITS IN THE EPSILON SECTOR...

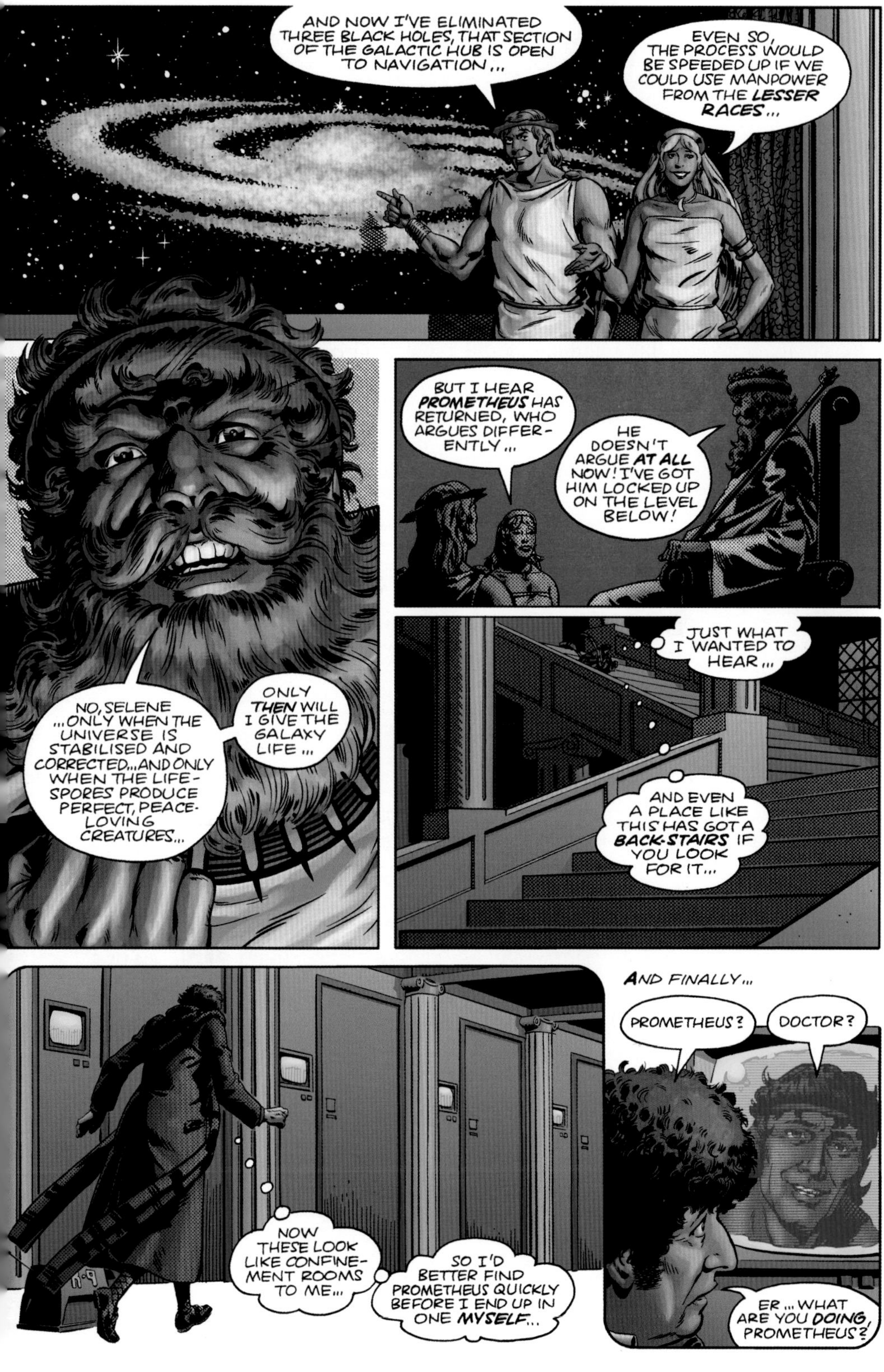
AND NOW I'VE ELIMINATED THREE BLACK HOLES, THAT SECTION OF THE GALACTIC HUB IS OPEN TO NAVIGATION...
EVEN SO, THE PROCESS WOULD BE SPEEDED UP IF WE COULD USE MANPOWER FROM THE **LESSER RACES**...
BUT I HEAR **PROMETHEUS** HAS RETURNED, WHO ARGUES DIFFER-ENTLY...
HE DOESN'T ARGUE **AT ALL** NOW! I'VE GOT HIM LOCKED UP ON THE LEVEL BELOW!
NO, SELENE ...ONLY WHEN THE UNIVERSE IS STABILISED AND CORRECTED...AND ONLY WHEN THE LIFE-SPORES PRODUCE PERFECT, PEACE-LOVING CREATURES...
ONLY **THEN** WILL I GIVE THE GALAXY LIFE...
JUST WHAT I WANTED TO HEAR...
AND EVEN A PLACE LIKE THIS HAS GOT A **BACK-STAIRS** IF YOU LOOK FOR IT...
NOW THESE LOOK LIKE CONFINE-MENT ROOMS TO ME...
SO I'D BETTER FIND PROMETHEUS QUICKLY BEFORE I END UP IN ONE **MYSELF**...
AND FINALLY...
PROMETHEUS?
DOCTOR?
ER... WHAT ARE YOU **DOING**, PROMETHEUS?

I HAVE SENSED THE WEAKEST SPOT IN THE WALL ...BY POUNDING IT FOR A THOUSAND YEARS, I WILL EVENTUALLY ESCAPE!

THAT COULD MAKE YOU AWFULLY *TIRED*, YOU KNOW!

I DO NOT TIRE EASILY, DOCTOR...

PERHAPS NOT ...BUT I'LL GET *BORED TO DEATH* WAITING FOR YOU TO ESCAPE!

SO LET ME DO YOU A LITTLE FAVOUR, INSTEAD...

AND OPEN THE DOOR ...SHALL WE GO?

WITH SOME *HASTE*, I THINK...

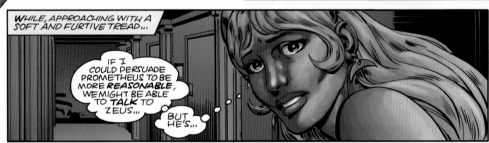

WHILE, APPROACHING WITH A SOFT AND FURTIVE TREAD...

IF I COULD PERSUADE PROMETHEUS TO BE MORE *REASONABLE*, WE MIGHT BE ABLE TO *TALK* TO ZEUS...

BUT HE'S...

GONE?!

SO MUCH FOR THAT IDEA! I'LL *HAVE* TO RAISE THE ALARM...

MEANWHILE, IN ASCLEPIUS'S LABORATORY...

WHAT CAN YOU POSSIBLY WANT HERE, PROMETHEUS?

THE *LIFE-SPORES*, DOCTOR ...I CAN'T KILL ZEUS ANY MORE THAN HE CAN KILL ME ...

BUT I'LL HAVE MY *REVENGE* FOR THOSE AGES IN CHAINS...

BY ONCE MORE SCATTERING RANDOM LIFE ACROSS HIS CLEAN, STERILE GALAXY...

RIGHT ...I'M READY TO GO!

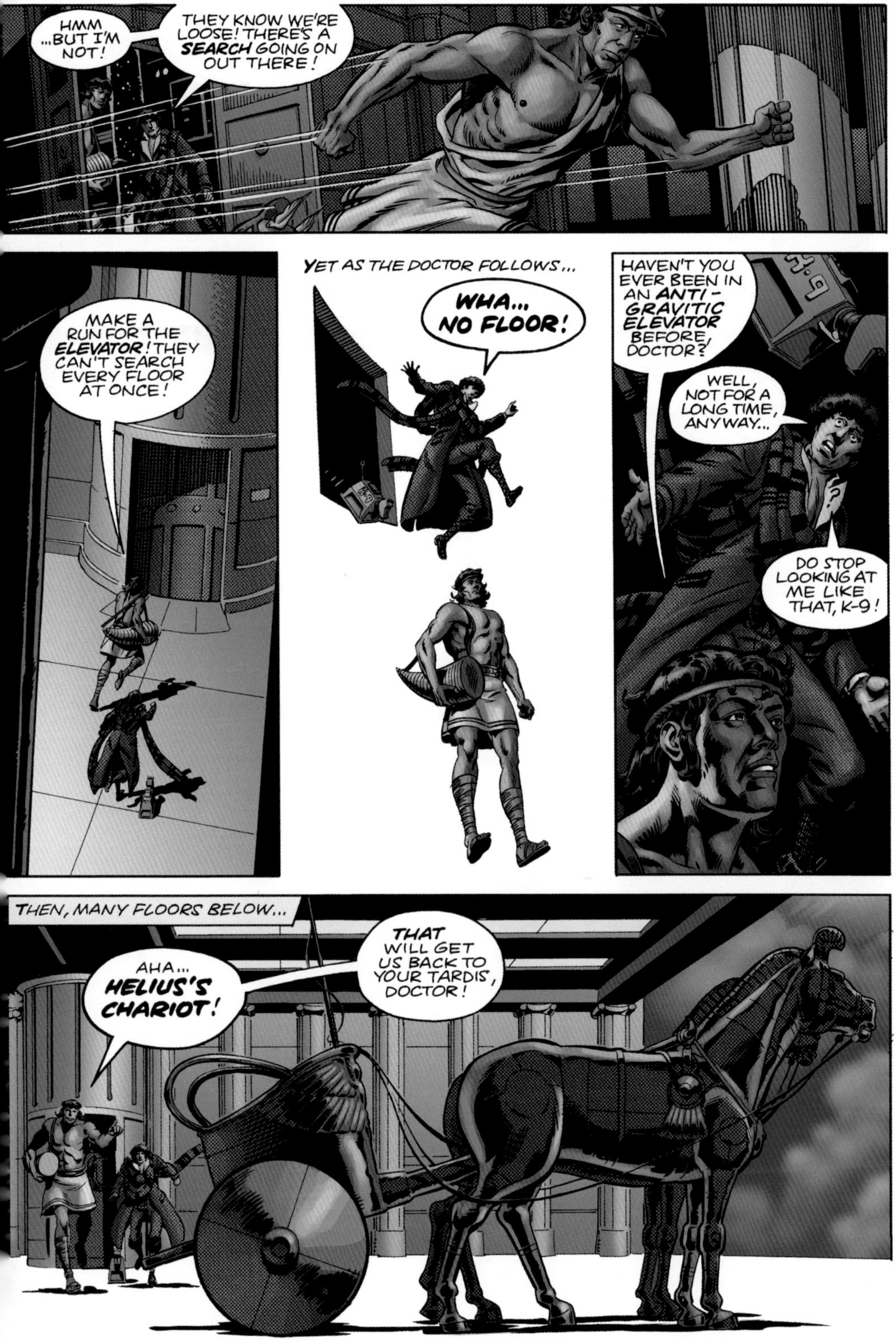
HMM ...BUT I'M NOT!
THEY KNOW WE'RE LOOSE! THERE'S A SEARCH GOING ON OUT THERE!
MAKE A RUN FOR THE ELEVATOR! THEY CAN'T SEARCH EVERY FLOOR AT ONCE!
YET AS THE DOCTOR FOLLOWS...
WHA... NO FLOOR!
HAVEN'T YOU EVER BEEN IN AN ANTI-GRAVITIC ELEVATOR BEFORE, DOCTOR?
WELL, NOT FOR A LONG TIME, ANYWAY...
DO STOP LOOKING AT ME LIKE THAT, K-9!
THEN, MANY FLOORS BELOW...
AHA... HELIUS'S CHARIOT!
THAT WILL GET US BACK TO YOUR TARDIS, DOCTOR!

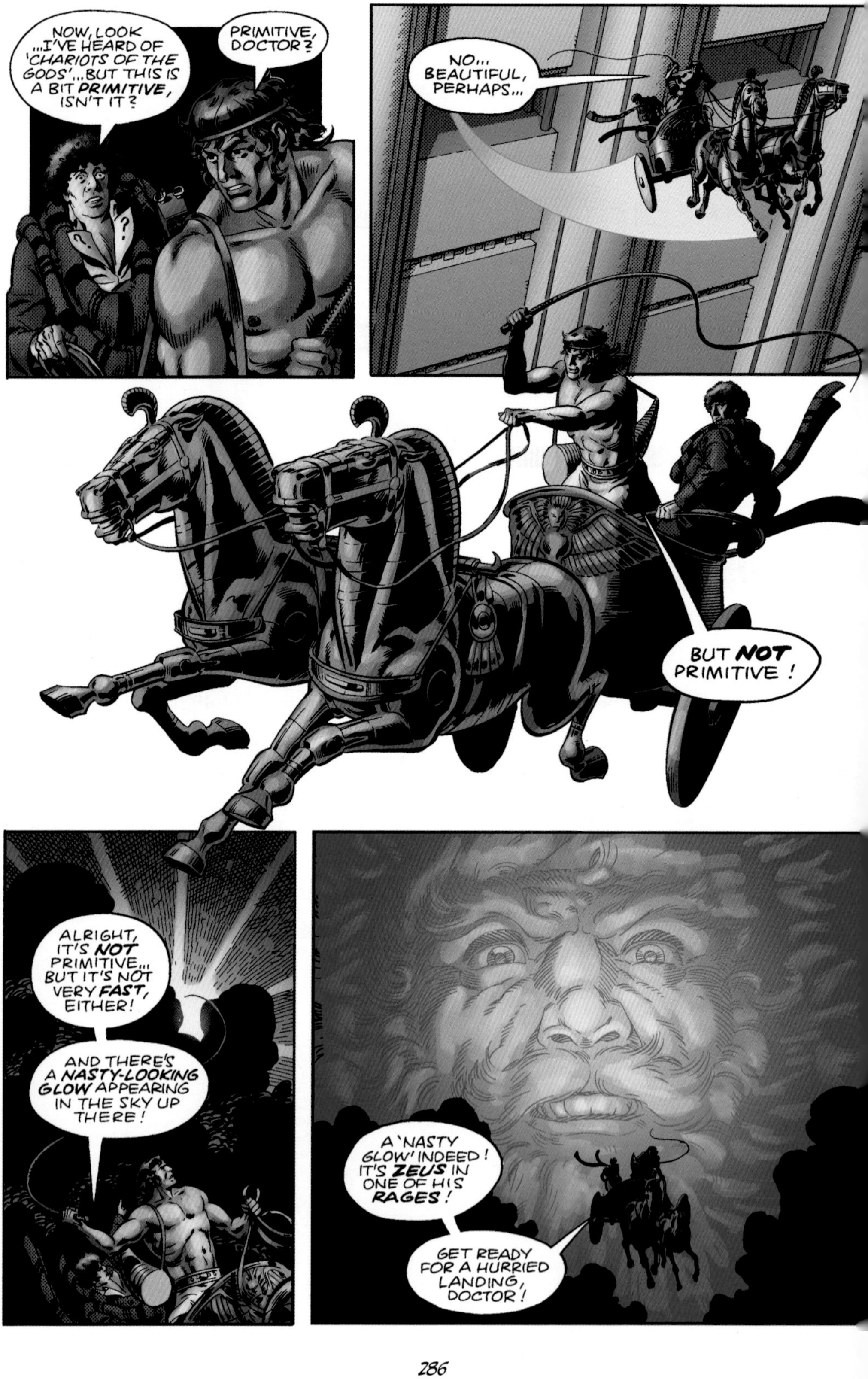
NOW, LOOK ...I'VE HEARD OF 'CHARIOTS OF THE GODS'...BUT THIS IS A BIT PRIMITIVE, ISN'T IT?
PRIMITIVE, DOCTOR?
NO... BEAUTIFUL, PERHAPS...
BUT NOT PRIMITIVE!
ALRIGHT, IT'S NOT PRIMITIVE... BUT IT'S NOT VERY FAST, EITHER!
AND THERE'S A NASTY-LOOKING GLOW APPEARING IN THE SKY UP THERE!
A 'NASTY GLOW' INDEED! IT'S ZEUS IN ONE OF HIS RAGES!
GET READY FOR A HURRIED LANDING, DOCTOR!

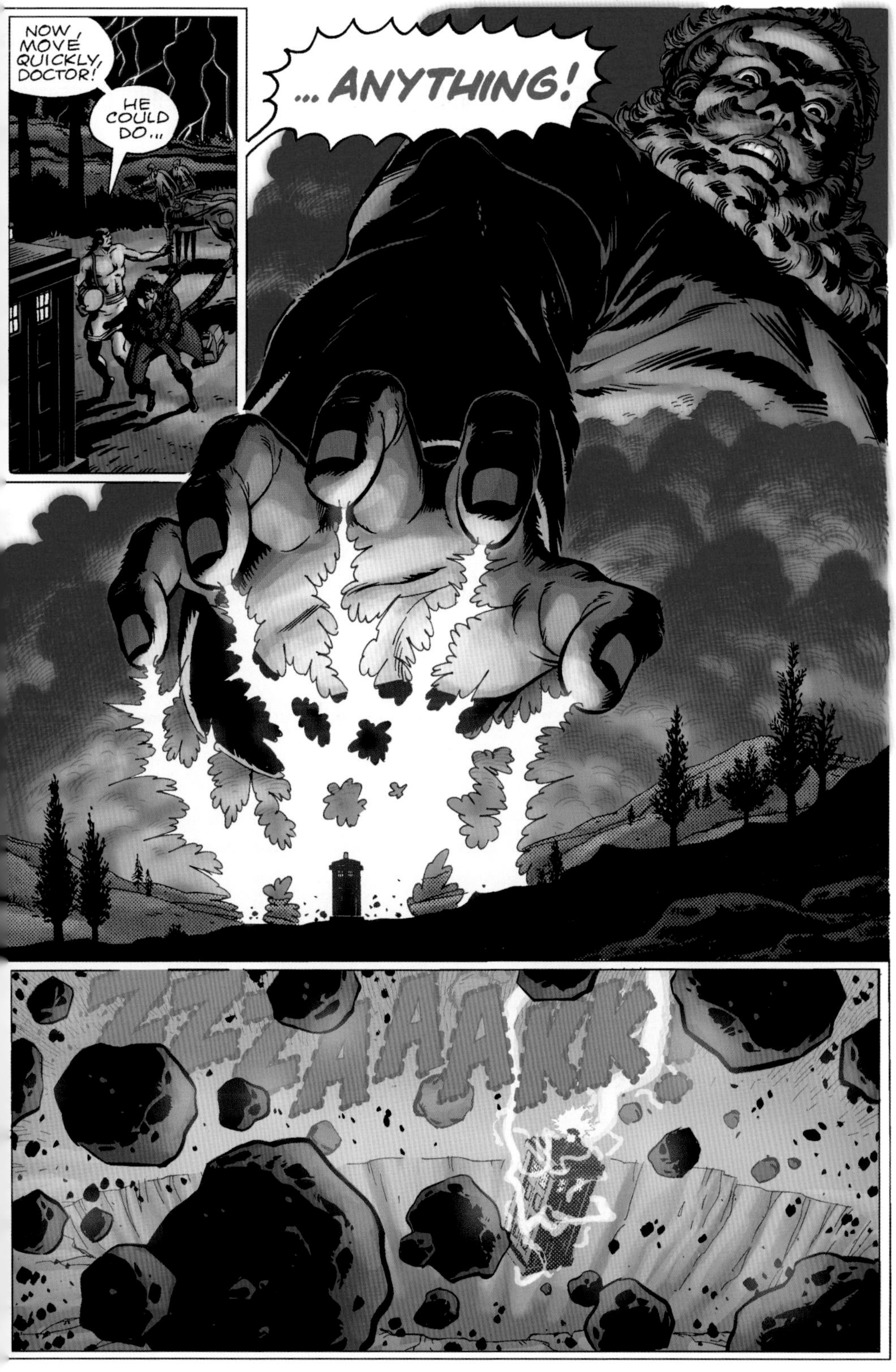
NOW, MOVE QUICKLY, DOCTOR!
HE COULD DO...
...ANYTHING!
ZZZAAAKK!

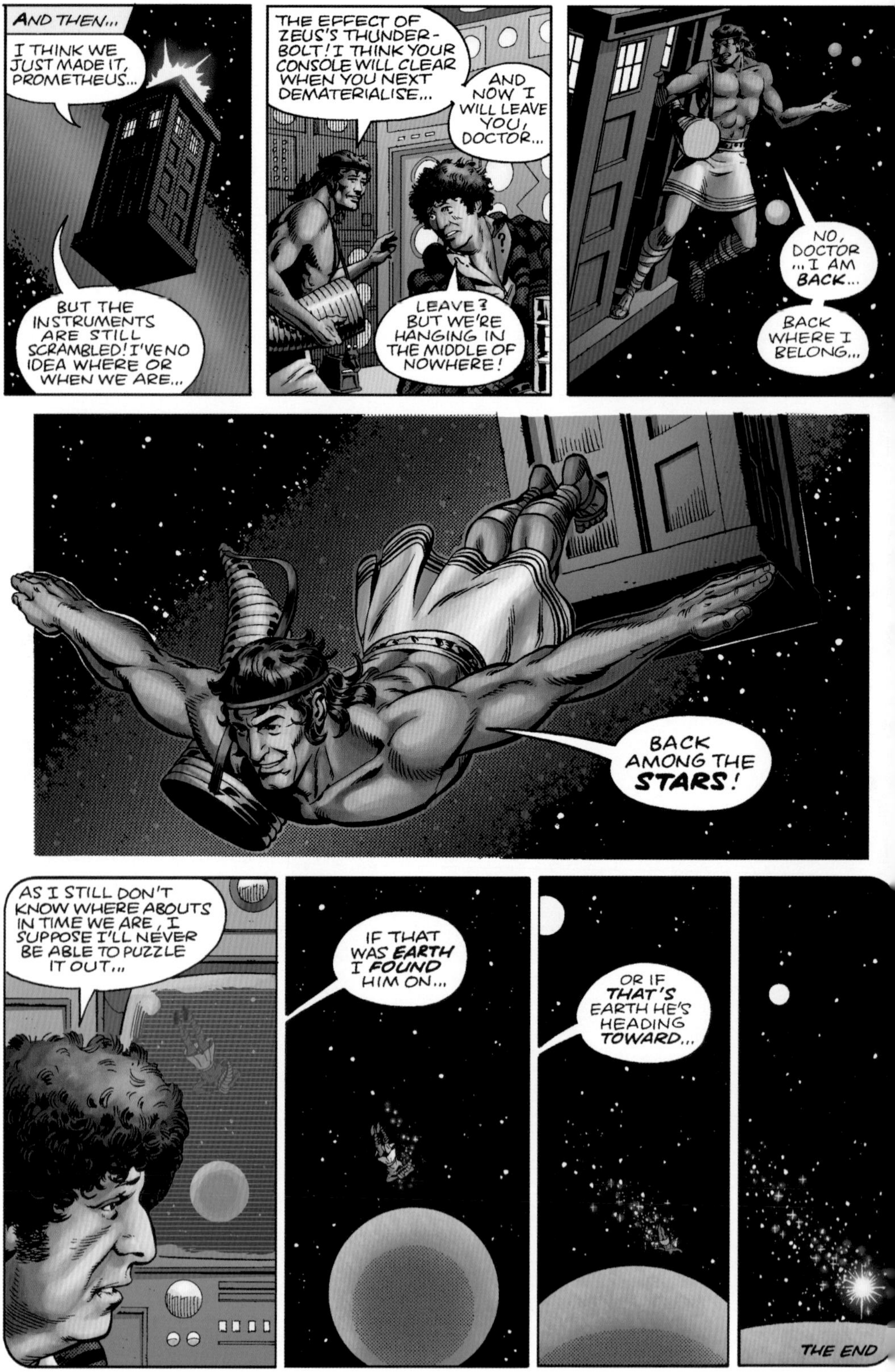
AND THEN...
I THINK WE JUST MADE IT, PROMETHEUS...
BUT THE INSTRUMENTS ARE STILL SCRAMBLED! I'VE NO IDEA WHERE OR WHEN WE ARE...
THE EFFECT OF ZEUS'S THUNDER-BOLT! I THINK YOUR CONSOLE WILL CLEAR WHEN YOU NEXT DEMATERIALISE...
AND NOW I WILL LEAVE YOU, DOCTOR...
LEAVE? BUT WE'RE HANGING IN THE MIDDLE OF NOWHERE!
NO, DOCTOR ...I AM BACK...
BACK WHERE I BELONG...
BACK AMONG THE STARS!
AS I STILL DON'T KNOW WHEREABOUTS IN TIME WE ARE, I SUPPOSE I'LL NEVER BE ABLE TO PUZZLE IT OUT...
IF THAT WAS EARTH I FOUND HIM ON...
OR IF THAT'S EARTH HE'S HEADING TOWARD...
THE END

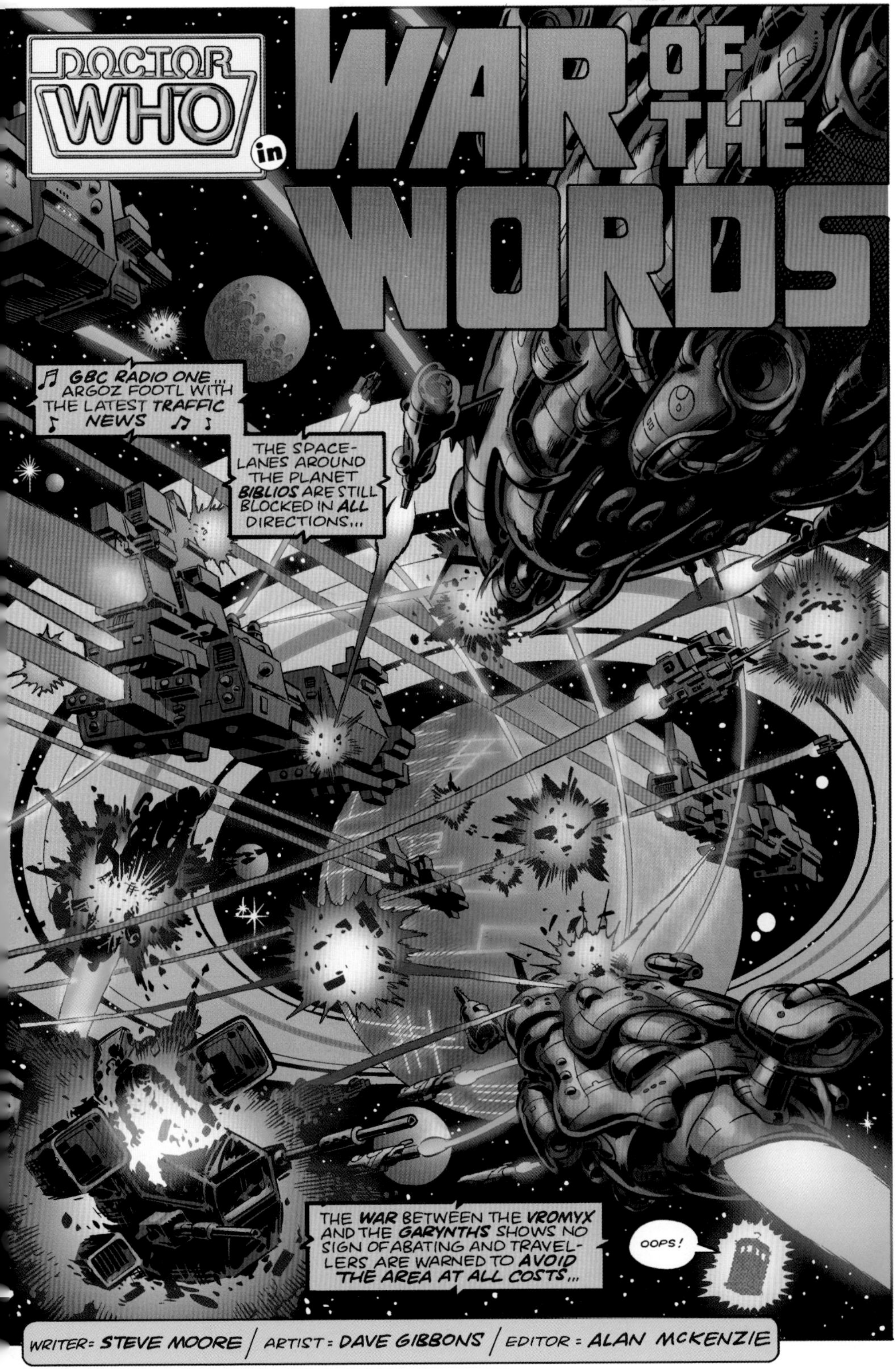
DOCTOR WHO
in
WAR OF THE WORDS
GBC RADIO ONE... ARGOZ FOOTL WITH THE LATEST TRAFFIC NEWS
THE SPACE-LANES AROUND THE PLANET BIBLIOS ARE STILL BLOCKED IN ALL DIRECTIONS...
THE WAR BETWEEN THE VROMYX AND THE GARYNTHS SHOWS NO SIGN OF ABATING AND TRAVEL-LERS ARE WARNED TO AVOID THE AREA AT ALL COSTS...
OOPS!
WRITER= STEVE MOORE / ARTIST= DAVE GIBBONS / EDITOR= ALAN McKENZIE

UNLESS, HA, HA, THEY'RE MOVING IN *ANOTHER DIMENSION!* NOW FOR SOME MORE MUSIC... ♪♫

THE TARDIS SEEMS TO HAVE GOT A BIT OF A *RATTLE,* K-9...

EITHER THAT, OR WE'VE RUN INTO SOMETHING SO UNPLEASANTLY *ENERGETIC...*

THAT IT'S RIPPING THE WHOLE SPACE-TIME CONTINUUM APART...

I THINK WE'D BETTER MAKE FOR THE NEAREST PLANET...

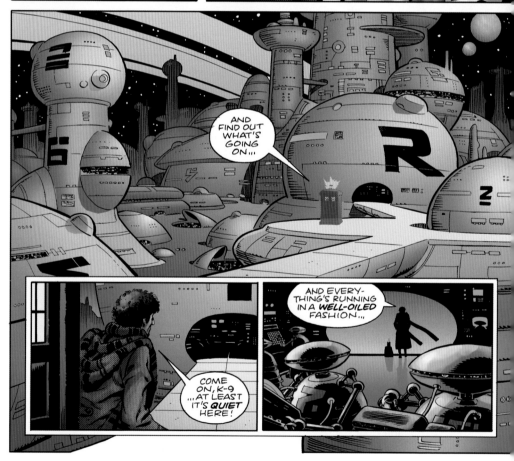

AND FIND OUT WHAT'S GOING ON...

COME ON, K-9 ...AT LEAST IT'S *QUIET* HERE!

AND EVERY-THING'S RUNNING IN A *WELL-OILED* FASHION...

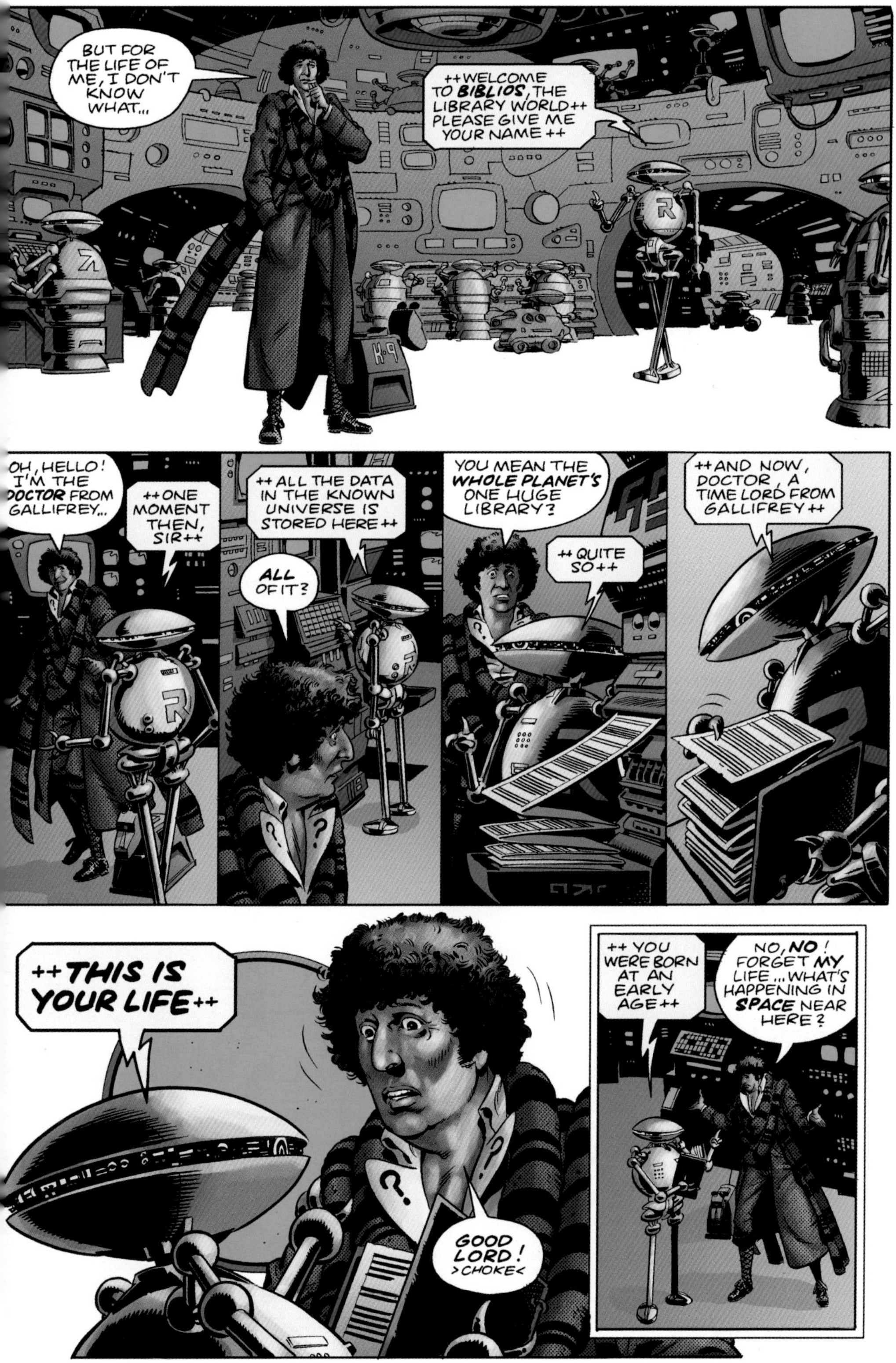
BUT FOR THE LIFE OF ME, I DON'T KNOW WHAT...
++WELCOME TO BIBLIOS, THE LIBRARY WORLD++ PLEASE GIVE ME YOUR NAME ++
OH, HELLO! I'M THE DOCTOR FROM GALLIFREY...
++ONE MOMENT THEN, SIR++
++ALL THE DATA IN THE KNOWN UNIVERSE IS STORED HERE++
ALL OF IT?
YOU MEAN THE WHOLE PLANET'S ONE HUGE LIBRARY?
++QUITE SO++
++AND NOW, DOCTOR, A TIME LORD FROM GALLIFREY++
++THIS IS YOUR LIFE++
GOOD LORD! >CHOKE<
++YOU WERE BORN AT AN EARLY AGE++
NO, NO! FORGET MY LIFE... WHAT'S HAPPENING IN SPACE NEAR HERE?

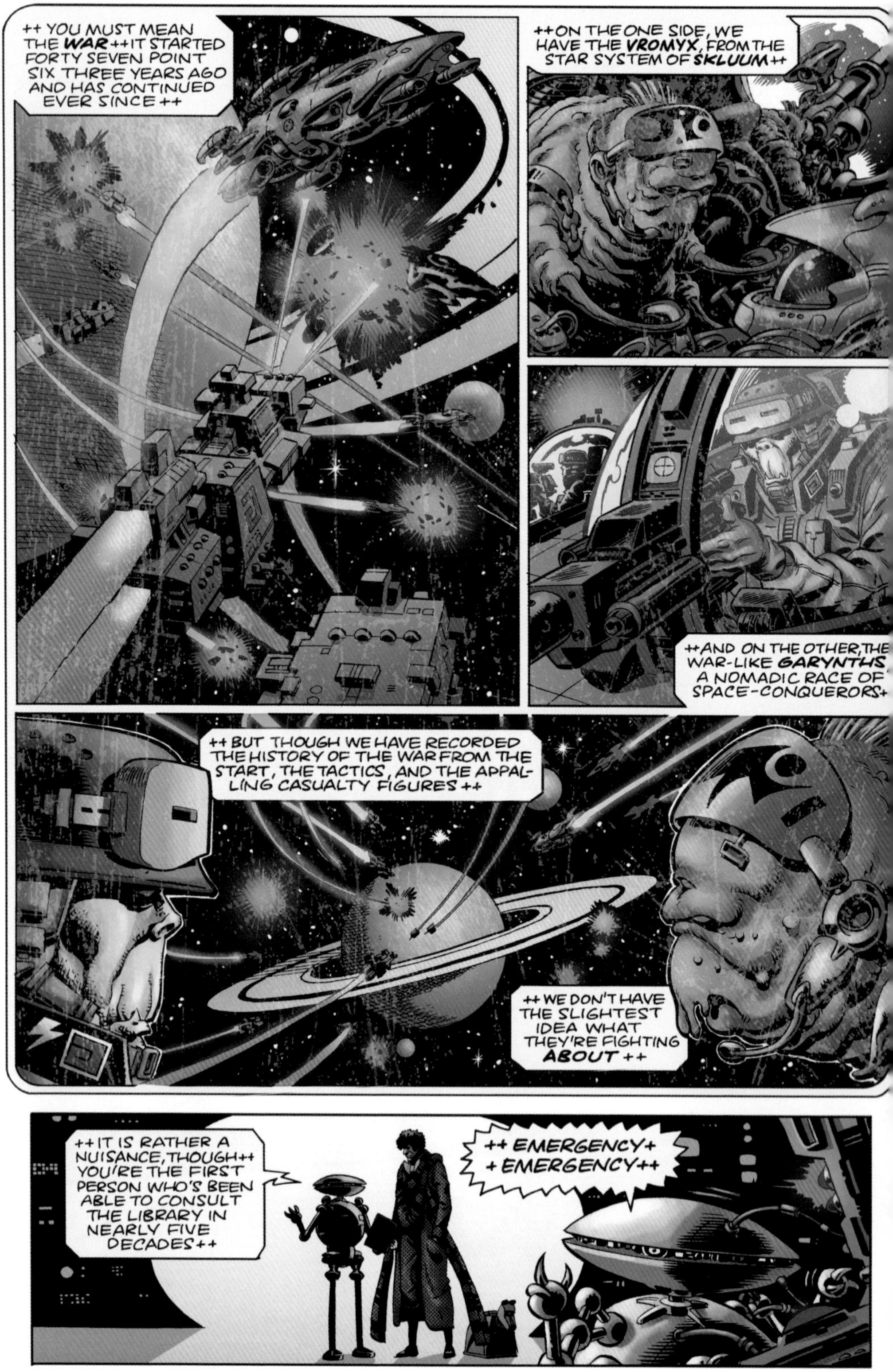
++ YOU MUST MEAN THE WAR ++ IT STARTED FORTY SEVEN POINT SIX THREE YEARS AGO AND HAS CONTINUED EVER SINCE ++
++ ON THE ONE SIDE, WE HAVE THE VROMYX, FROM THE STAR SYSTEM OF SKLUUM ++
++ AND ON THE OTHER, THE WAR-LIKE GARYNTHS, A NOMADIC RACE OF SPACE-CONQUERORS+
++ BUT THOUGH WE HAVE RECORDED THE HISTORY OF THE WAR FROM THE START, THE TACTICS, AND THE APPALLING CASUALTY FIGURES ++
++ WE DON'T HAVE THE SLIGHTEST IDEA WHAT THEY'RE FIGHTING ABOUT ++
++ IT IS RATHER A NUISANCE, THOUGH ++ YOU'RE THE FIRST PERSON WHO'S BEEN ABLE TO CONSULT THE LIBRARY IN NEARLY FIVE DECADES ++
++ EMERGENCY +
+ EMERGENCY ++

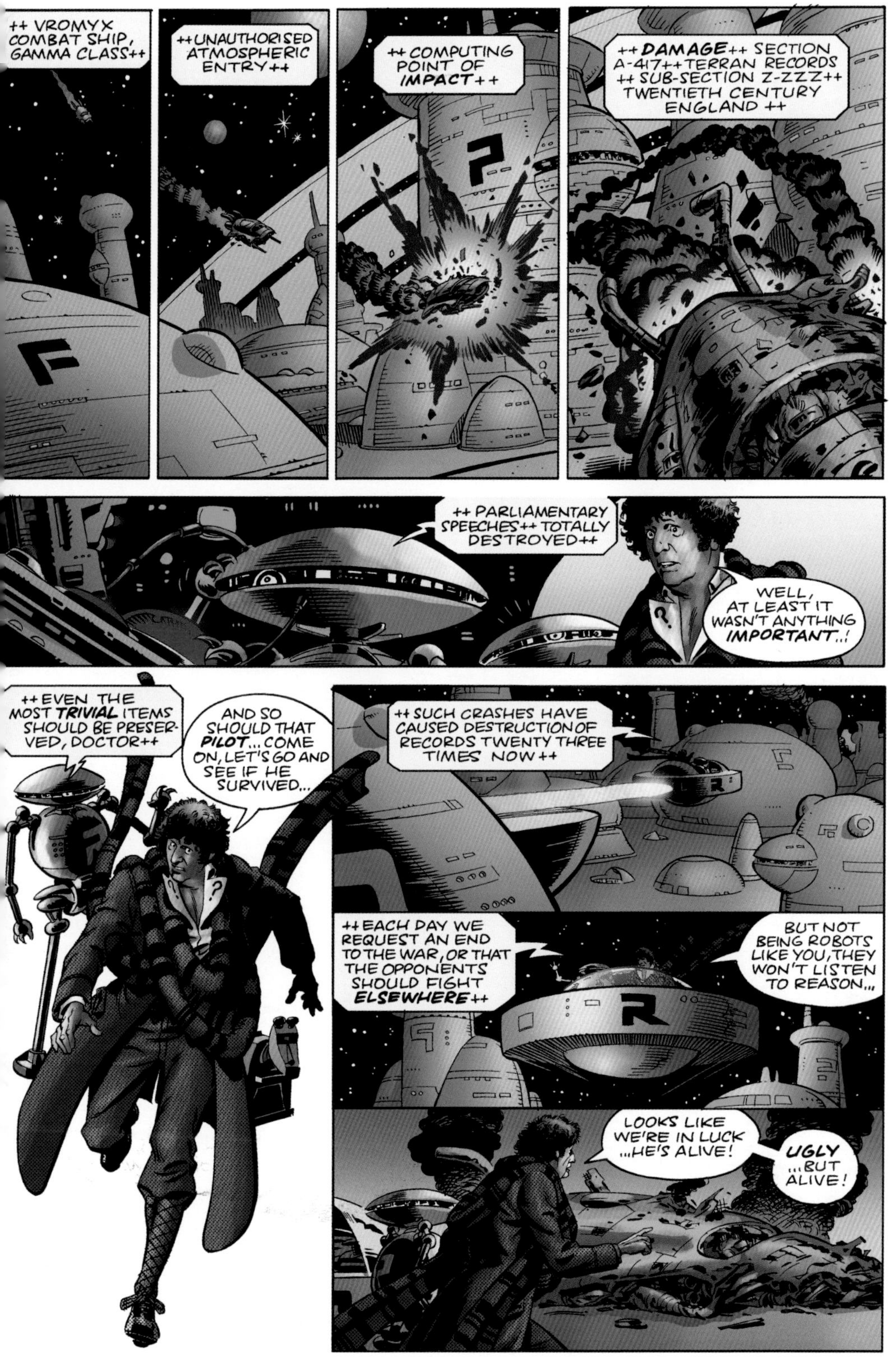
++ VROMYX COMBAT SHIP, GAMMA CLASS++
++UNAUTHORISED ATMOSPHERIC ENTRY++
++ COMPUTING POINT OF IMPACT++
++ DAMAGE++ SECTION A-417++TERRAN RECORDS ++ SUB-SECTION Z-ZZZ++ TWENTIETH CENTURY ENGLAND ++
++ PARLIAMENTARY SPEECHES++ TOTALLY DESTROYED++
WELL, AT LEAST IT WASN'T ANYTHING IMPORTANT...!
++EVEN THE MOST TRIVIAL ITEMS SHOULD BE PRESER-VED, DOCTOR++
AND SO SHOULD THAT PILOT... COME ON, LET'S GO AND SEE IF HE SURVIVED...
++ SUCH CRASHES HAVE CAUSED DESTRUCTION OF RECORDS TWENTY THREE TIMES NOW ++
++EACH DAY WE REQUEST AN END TO THE WAR, OR THAT THE OPPONENTS SHOULD FIGHT ELSEWHERE++
BUT NOT BEING ROBOTS LIKE YOU, THEY WON'T LISTEN TO REASON...
LOOKS LIKE WE'RE IN LUCK ...HE'S ALIVE!
UGLY ...BUT ALIVE!

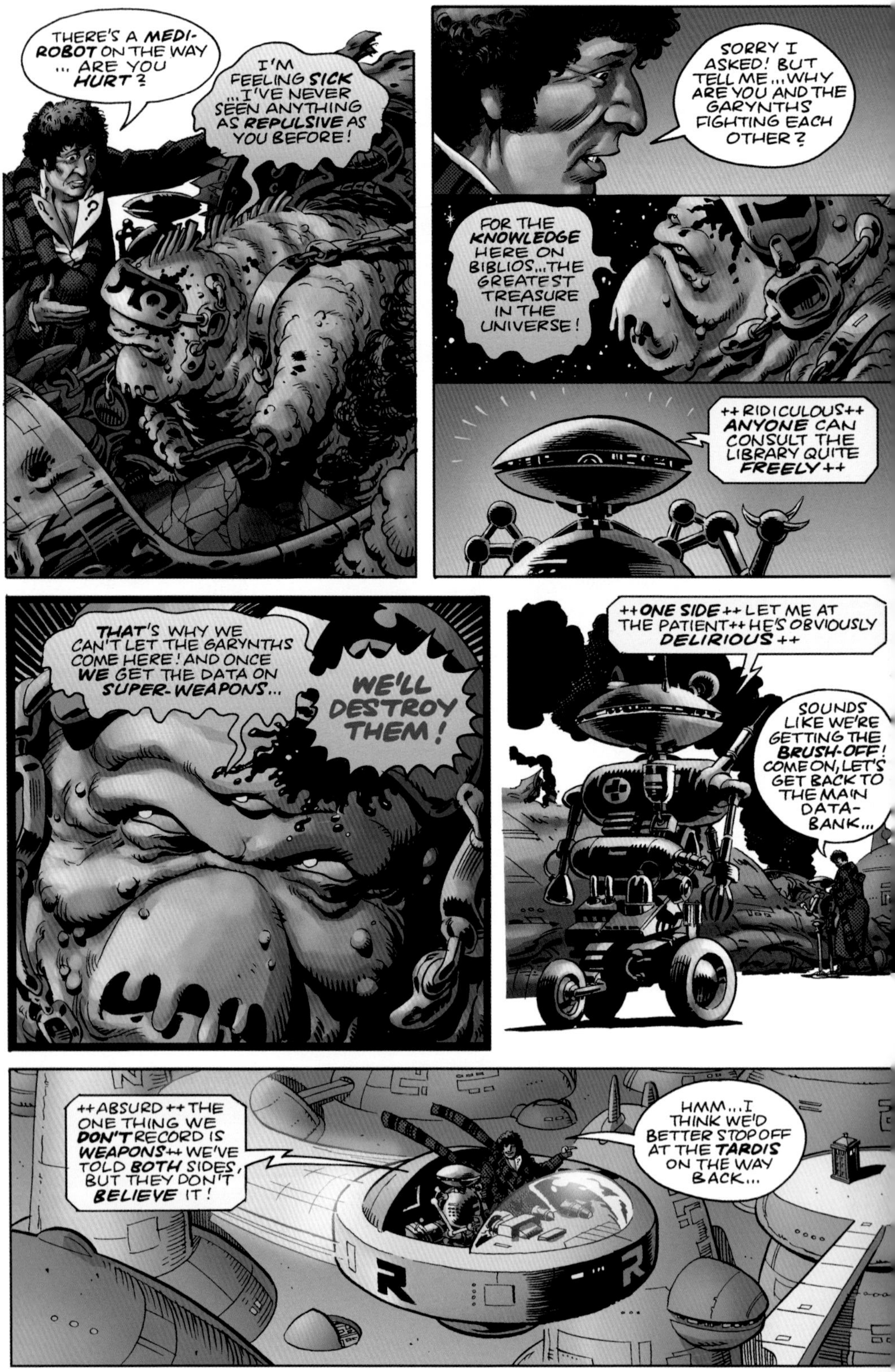

THERE'S A MEDI-ROBOT ON THE WAY ... ARE YOU HURT?
I'M FEELING SICK ... I'VE NEVER SEEN ANYTHING AS REPULSIVE AS YOU BEFORE!
SORRY I ASKED! BUT TELL ME ... WHY ARE YOU AND THE GARYNTHS FIGHTING EACH OTHER?
FOR THE KNOWLEDGE HERE ON BIBLIOS ... THE GREATEST TREASURE IN THE UNIVERSE!
++RIDICULOUS++ ANYONE CAN CONSULT THE LIBRARY QUITE FREELY++
THAT'S WHY WE CAN'T LET THE GARYNTHS COME HERE! AND ONCE WE GET THE DATA ON SUPER-WEAPONS...
WE'LL DESTROY THEM!
++ONE SIDE++ LET ME AT THE PATIENT++ HE'S OBVIOUSLY DELIRIOUS++
SOUNDS LIKE WE'RE GETTING THE BRUSH-OFF! COME ON, LET'S GET BACK TO THE MAIN DATA-BANK...
++ABSURD++ THE ONE THING WE DON'T RECORD IS WEAPONS++ WE'VE TOLD BOTH SIDES, BUT THEY DON'T BELIEVE IT!
HMM... I THINK WE'D BETTER STOP OFF AT THE TARDIS ON THE WAY BACK...

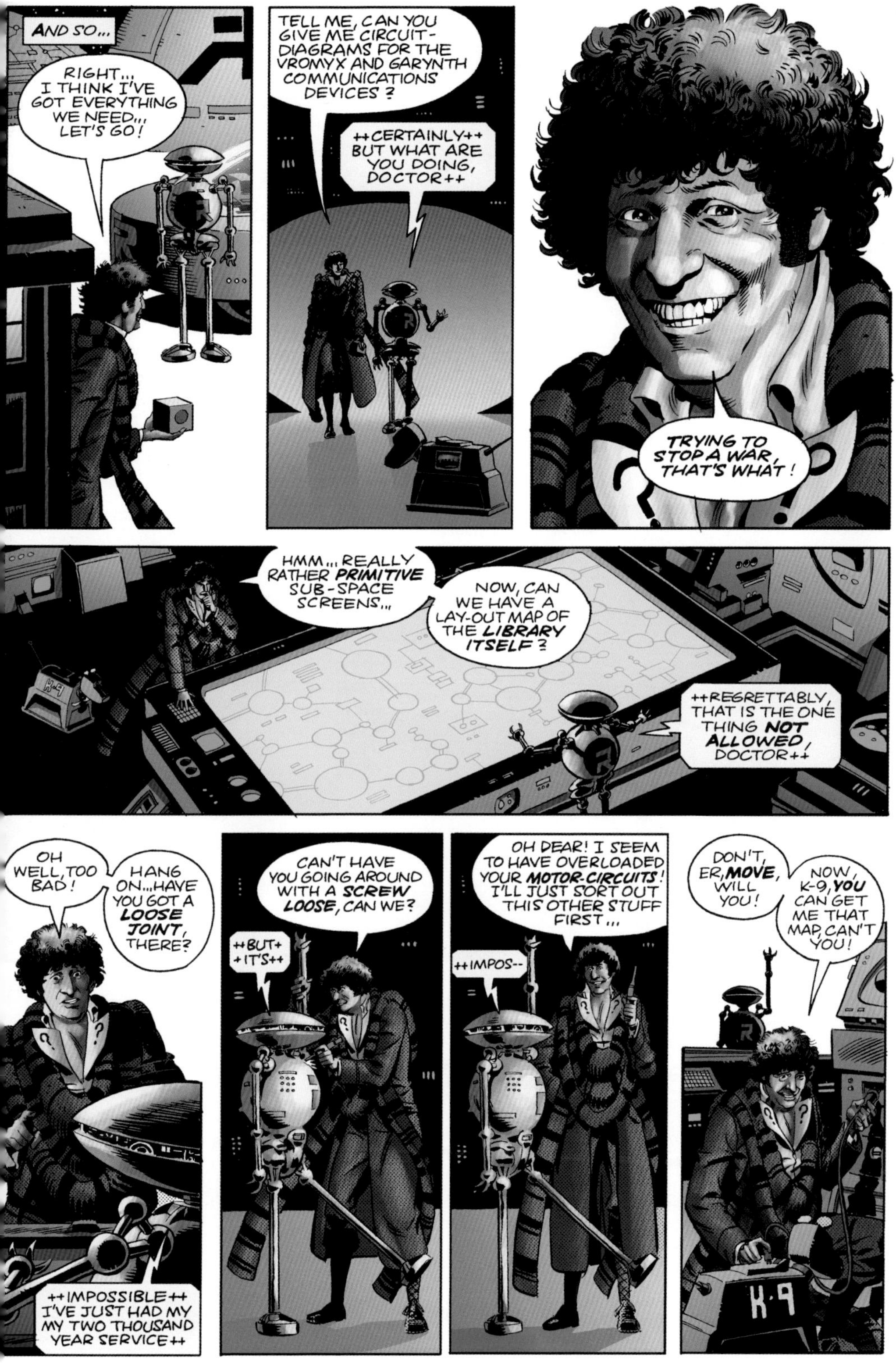
AND SO...
RIGHT... I THINK I'VE GOT EVERYTHING WE NEED... LET'S GO!
TELL ME, CAN YOU GIVE ME CIRCUIT-DIAGRAMS FOR THE VROMYX AND GARYNTH COMMUNICATIONS DEVICES?
++CERTAINLY++ BUT WHAT ARE YOU DOING, DOCTOR++
TRYING TO STOP A WAR, THAT'S WHAT!
HMM... REALLY RATHER PRIMITIVE SUB-SPACE SCREENS...
NOW, CAN WE HAVE A LAY-OUT MAP OF THE LIBRARY ITSELF?
++REGRETTABLY, THAT IS THE ONE THING NOT ALLOWED, DOCTOR++
OH WELL, TOO BAD!
HANG ON...HAVE YOU GOT A LOOSE JOINT, THERE?
++IMPOSSIBLE++ I'VE JUST HAD MY MY TWO THOUSAND YEAR SERVICE++
CAN'T HAVE YOU GOING AROUND WITH A SCREW LOOSE, CAN WE?
++BUT+ +IT'S++
OH DEAR! I SEEM TO HAVE OVERLOADED YOUR MOTOR-CIRCUITS! I'LL JUST SORT OUT THIS OTHER STUFF FIRST...
++IMPOS--
DON'T, ER, MOVE, WILL YOU!
NOW, K-9, YOU CAN GET ME THAT MAP, CAN'T YOU!
K-9

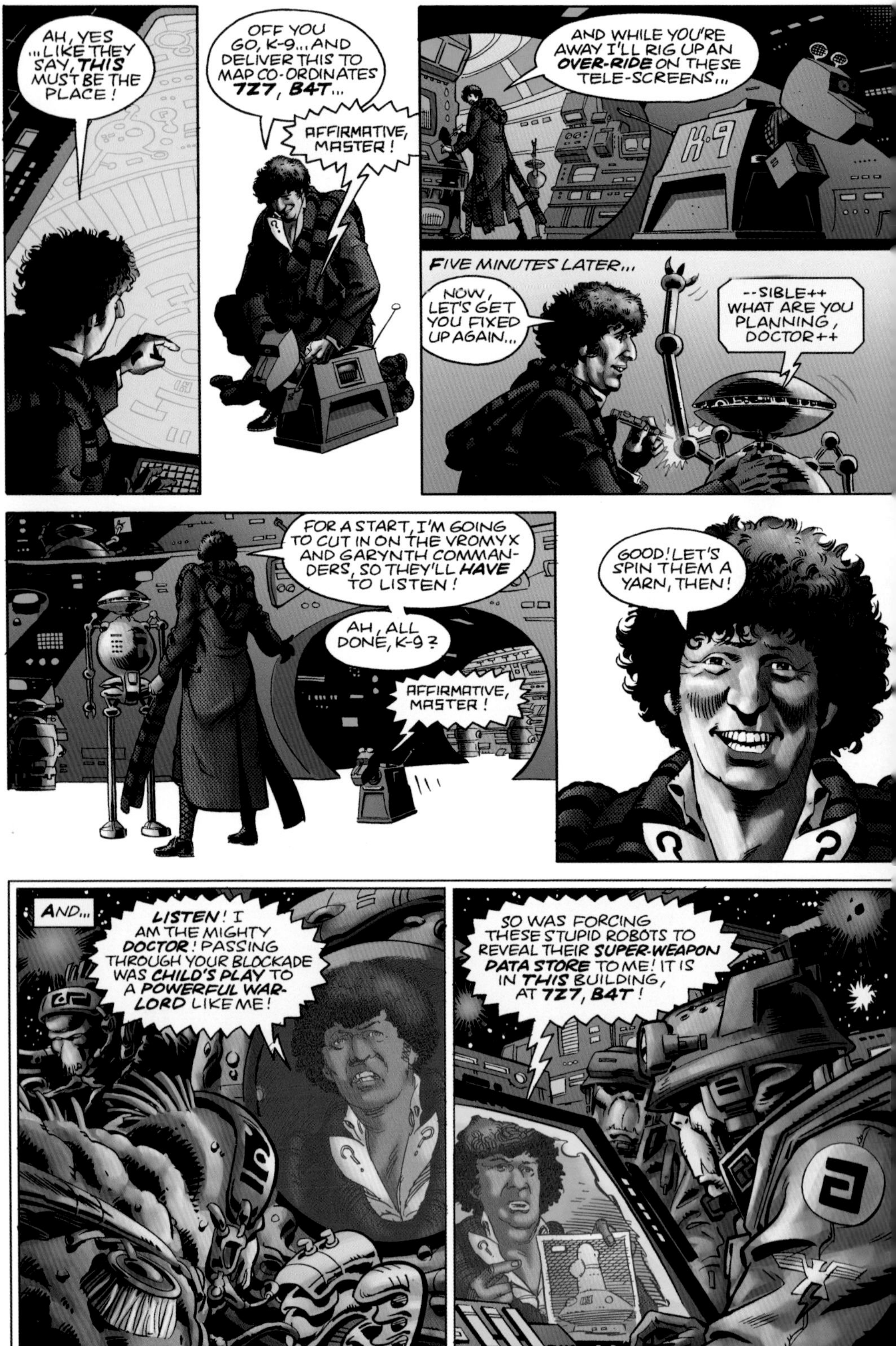
AH, YES ...LIKE THEY SAY, THIS MUST BE THE PLACE!
OFF YOU GO, K-9... AND DELIVER THIS TO MAP CO-ORDINATES 7Z7, B4T...
AFFIRMATIVE, MASTER!
AND WHILE YOU'RE AWAY I'LL RIG UP AN OVER-RIDE ON THESE TELE-SCREENS...
K-9
FIVE MINUTES LATER...
NOW, LET'S GET YOU FIXED UP AGAIN...
--SIBLE++ WHAT ARE YOU PLANNING, DOCTOR++
FOR A START, I'M GOING TO CUT IN ON THE VROMYX AND GARYNTH COMMANDERS, SO THEY'LL HAVE TO LISTEN!
AH, ALL DONE, K-9?
AFFIRMATIVE, MASTER!
GOOD! LET'S SPIN THEM A YARN, THEN!
AND...
LISTEN! I AM THE MIGHTY DOCTOR! PASSING THROUGH YOUR BLOCKADE WAS CHILD'S PLAY TO A POWERFUL WAR-LORD LIKE ME!
SO WAS FORCING THESE STUPID ROBOTS TO REVEAL THEIR SUPER-WEAPON DATA STORE TO ME! IT IS IN THIS BUILDING, AT 7Z7, B4T!

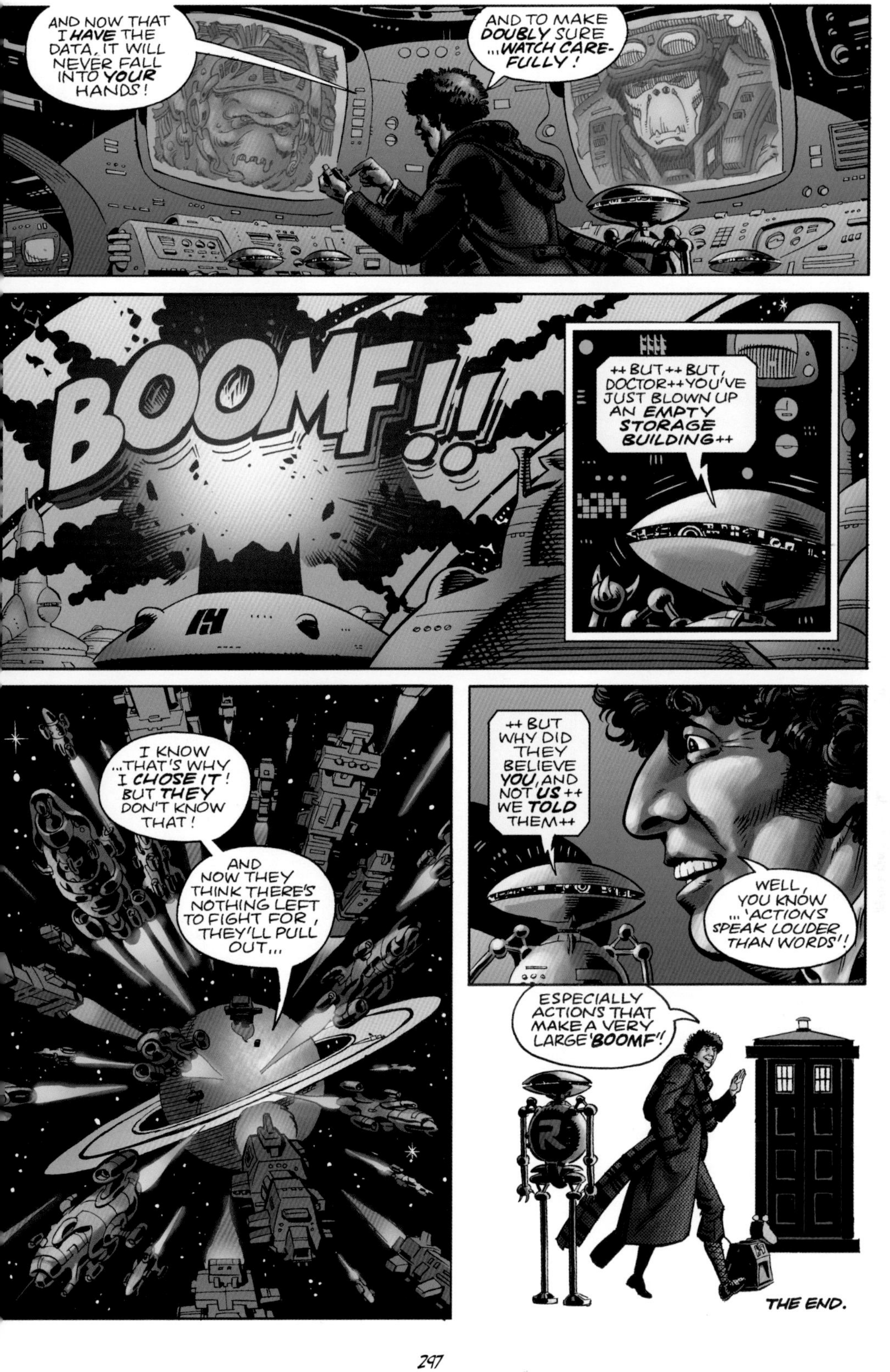
AND NOW THAT I HAVE THE DATA, IT WILL NEVER FALL INTO YOUR HANDS!
AND TO MAKE DOUBLY SURE ...WATCH CAREFULLY!
BOOMF!!
++BUT++BUT, DOCTOR++YOU'VE JUST BLOWN UP AN EMPTY STORAGE BUILDING++
I KNOW ...THAT'S WHY I CHOSE IT! BUT THEY DON'T KNOW THAT!
AND NOW THEY THINK THERE'S NOTHING LEFT TO FIGHT FOR, THEY'LL PULL OUT...
++BUT WHY DID THEY BELIEVE YOU, AND NOT US++ WE TOLD THEM++
WELL, YOU KNOW ...'ACTIONS SPEAK LOUDER THAN WORDS'!
ESPECIALLY ACTIONS THAT MAKE A VERY LARGE 'BOOMF'!
THE END.

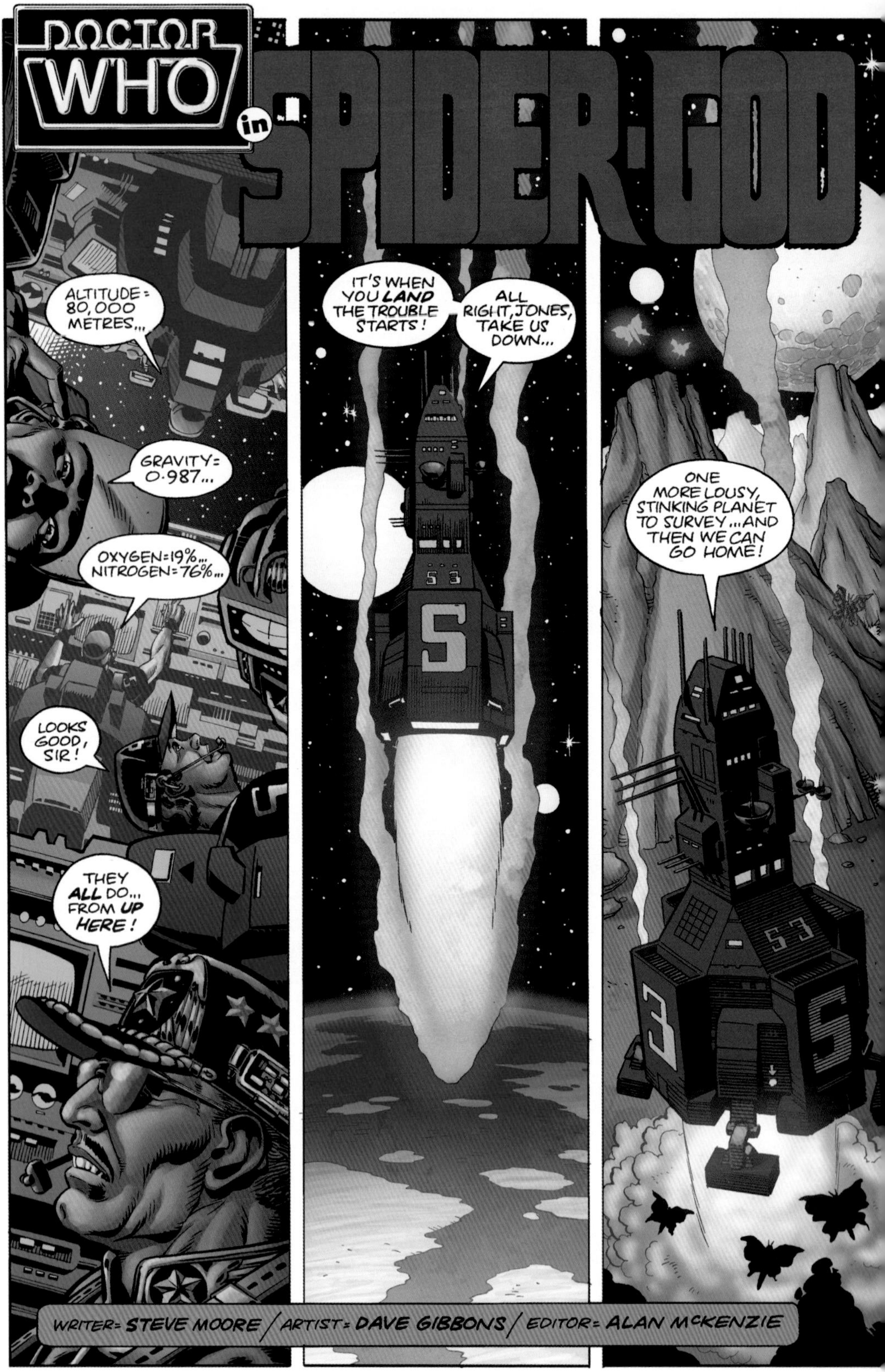
DOCTOR WHO
in
SPIDER-GOD
ALTITUDE= 80,000 METRES...
GRAVITY= 0·987...
OXYGEN=19%... NITROGEN=76%...
LOOKS GOOD, SIR!
THEY ALL DO... FROM UP HERE!
IT'S WHEN YOU LAND THE TROUBLE STARTS!
ALL RIGHT, JONES, TAKE US DOWN...
ONE MORE LOUSY, STINKING PLANET TO SURVEY... AND THEN WE CAN GO HOME!
WRITER= STEVE MOORE / ARTIST= DAVE GIBBONS / EDITOR= ALAN McKENZIE

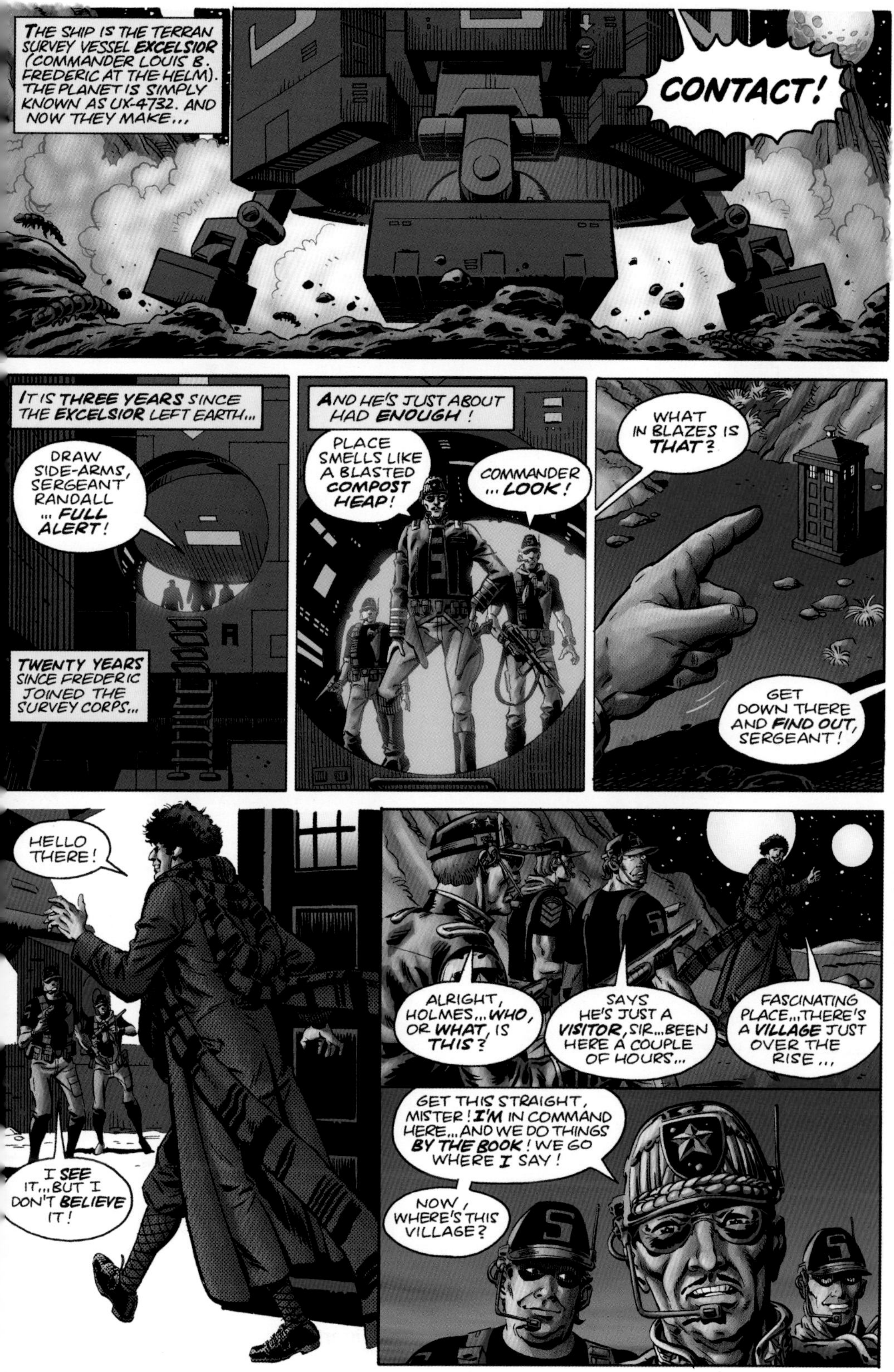
THE SHIP IS THE TERRAN SURVEY VESSEL EXCELSIOR (COMMANDER LOUIS B. FREDERIC AT THE HELM). THE PLANET IS SIMPLY KNOWN AS UX-4732. AND NOW THEY MAKE...
CONTACT!
IT IS THREE YEARS SINCE THE EXCELSIOR LEFT EARTH...
DRAW SIDE-ARMS, SERGEANT RANDALL ... FULL ALERT!
TWENTY YEARS SINCE FREDERIC JOINED THE SURVEY CORPS...
AND HE'S JUST ABOUT HAD ENOUGH!
PLACE SMELLS LIKE A BLASTED COMPOST HEAP!
COMMANDER ...LOOK!
WHAT IN BLAZES IS THAT?
GET DOWN THERE AND FIND OUT, SERGEANT!
HELLO THERE!
I SEE IT... BUT I DON'T BELIEVE IT!
ALRIGHT, HOLMES... WHO, OR WHAT, IS THIS?
SAYS HE'S JUST A VISITOR, SIR... BEEN HERE A COUPLE OF HOURS...
FASCINATING PLACE... THERE'S A VILLAGE JUST OVER THE RISE...
GET THIS STRAIGHT, MISTER! I'M IN COMMAND HERE... AND WE DO THINGS BY THE BOOK! WE GO WHERE I SAY!
NOW, WHERE'S THIS VILLAGE?

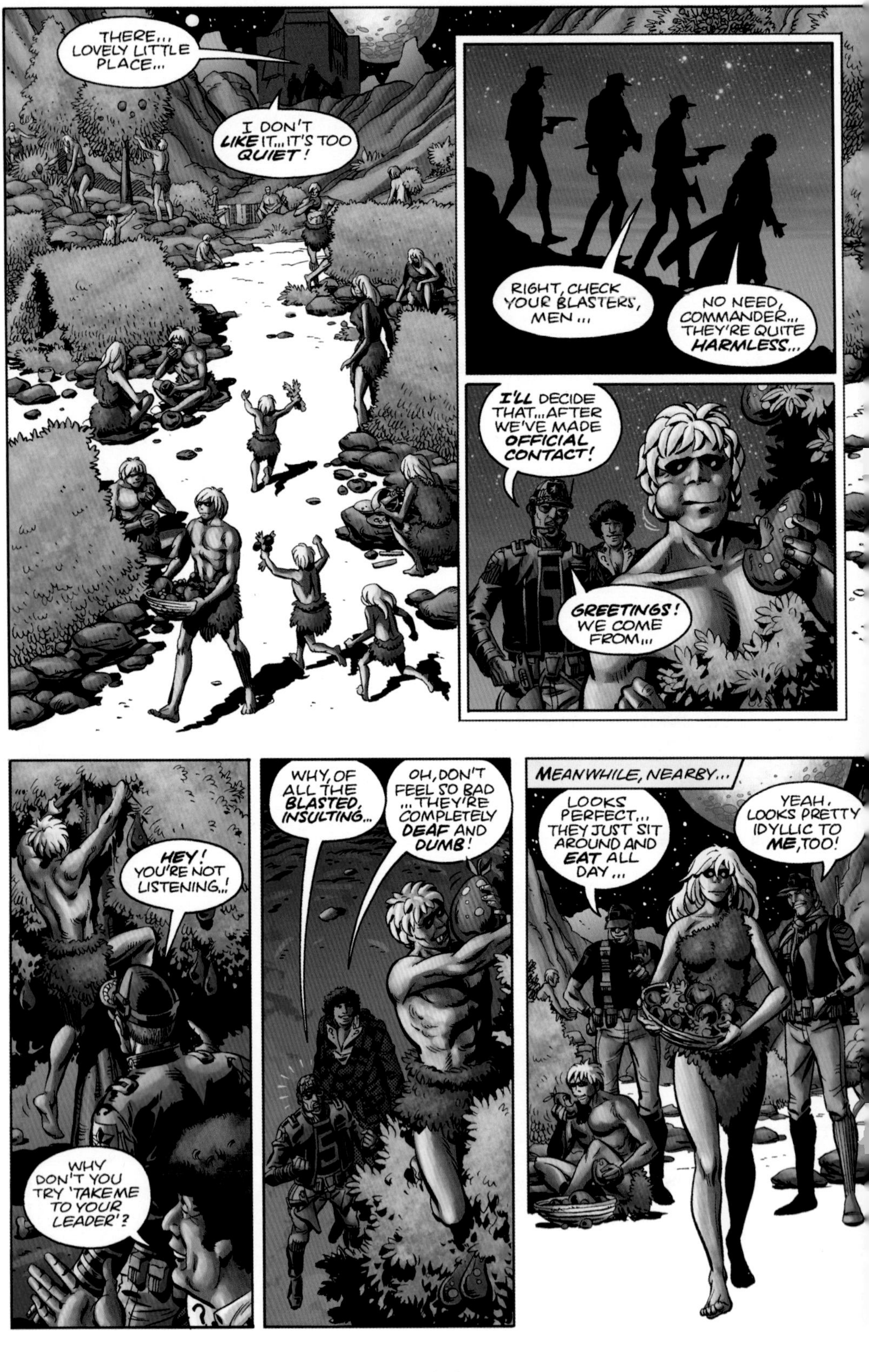

THERE... LOVELY LITTLE PLACE...
I DON'T LIKE IT... IT'S TOO QUIET!
RIGHT, CHECK YOUR BLASTERS, MEN...
NO NEED, COMMANDER... THEY'RE QUITE HARMLESS...
I'LL DECIDE THAT... AFTER WE'VE MADE OFFICIAL CONTACT!
GREETINGS! WE COME FROM...
HEY! YOU'RE NOT LISTENING..!
WHY DON'T YOU TRY 'TAKE ME TO YOUR LEADER'?
WHY, OF ALL THE BLASTED, INSULTING...
OH, DON'T FEEL SO BAD ...THEY'RE COMPLETELY DEAF AND DUMB!
MEANWHILE, NEARBY...
LOOKS PERFECT... THEY JUST SIT AROUND AND EAT ALL DAY...
YEAH, LOOKS PRETTY IDYLLIC TO ME, TOO!

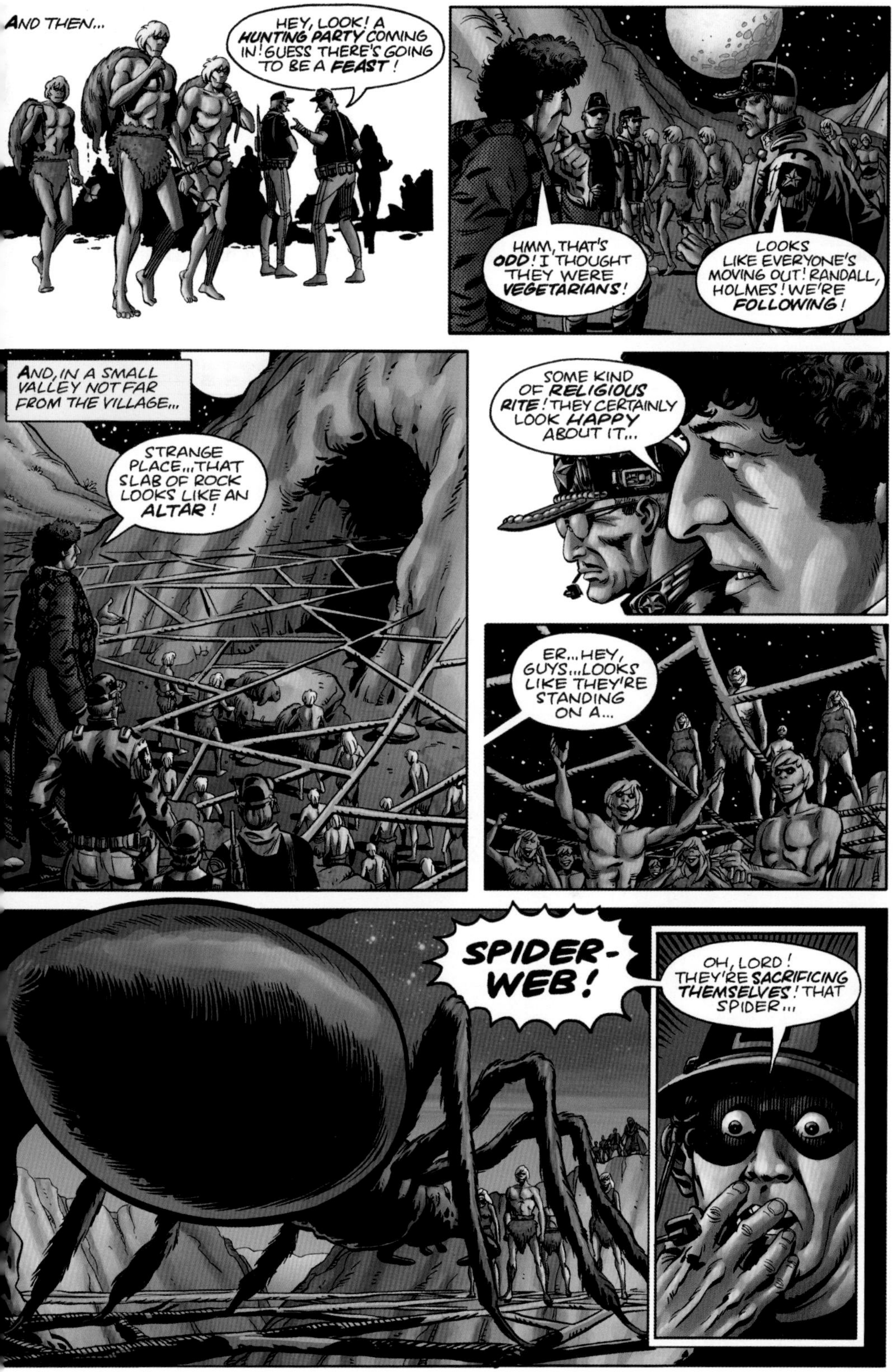
AND THEN...
HEY, LOOK! A HUNTING PARTY COMING IN! GUESS THERE'S GOING TO BE A FEAST!
HMM, THAT'S ODD! I THOUGHT THEY WERE VEGETARIANS!
LOOKS LIKE EVERYONE'S MOVING OUT! RANDALL, HOLMES! WE'RE FOLLOWING!
AND, IN A SMALL VALLEY NOT FAR FROM THE VILLAGE...
STRANGE PLACE... THAT SLAB OF ROCK LOOKS LIKE AN ALTAR!
SOME KIND OF RELIGIOUS RITE! THEY CERTAINLY LOOK HAPPY ABOUT IT...
ER... HEY, GUYS... LOOKS LIKE THEY'RE STANDING ON A...
SPIDER-WEB!
OH, LORD! THEY'RE SACRIFICING THEMSELVES! THAT SPIDER...

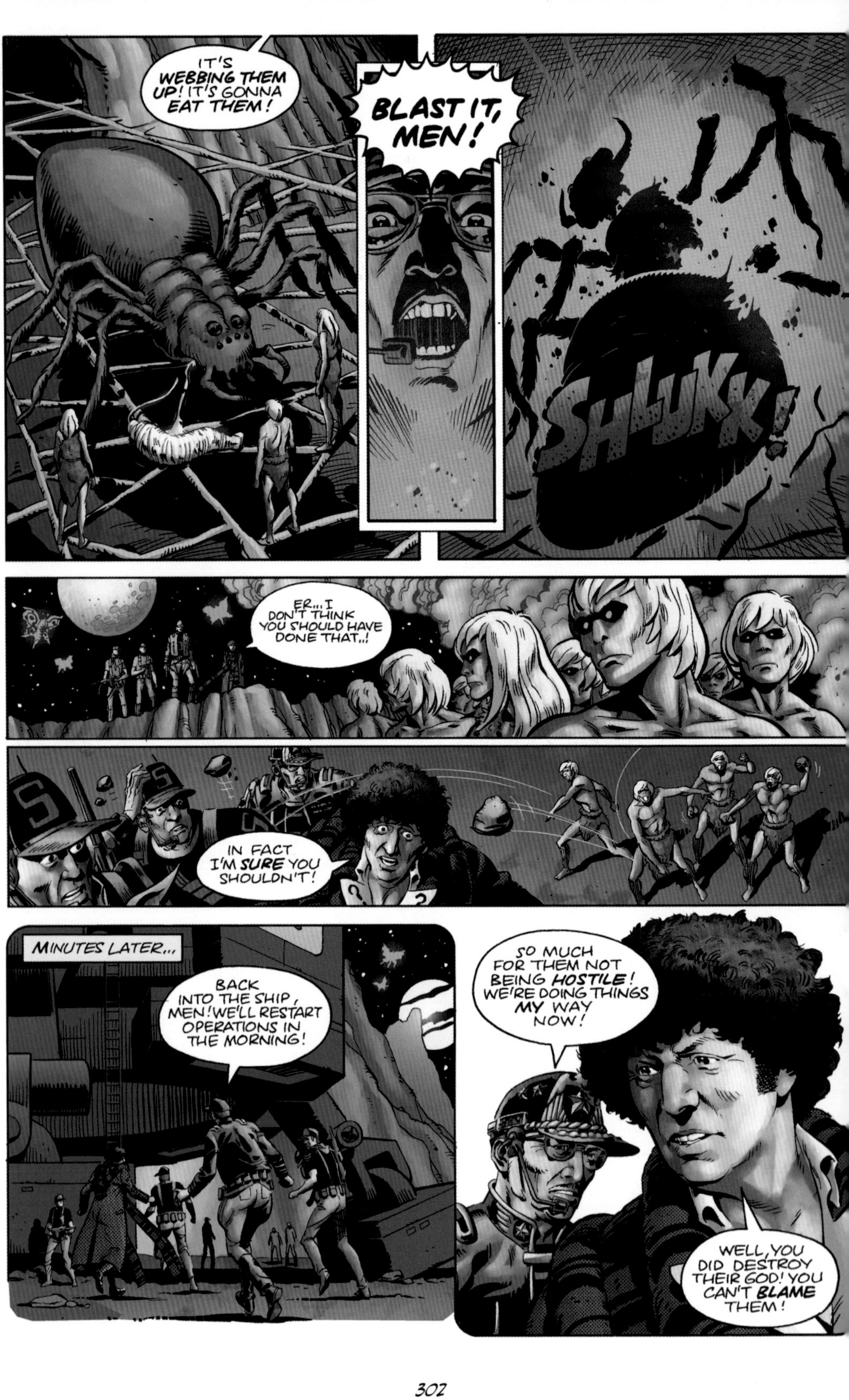
IT'S WEBBING THEM UP! IT'S GONNA EAT THEM!
BLAST IT, MEN!
SHLUKK!
ER... I DON'T THINK YOU SHOULD HAVE DONE THAT..!
IN FACT I'M SURE YOU SHOULDN'T!
MINUTES LATER...
BACK INTO THE SHIP, MEN! WE'LL RESTART OPERATIONS IN THE MORNING!
SO MUCH FOR THEM NOT BEING HOSTILE! WE'RE DOING THINGS MY WAY NOW!
WELL, YOU DID DESTROY THEIR GOD! YOU CAN'T BLAME THEM!

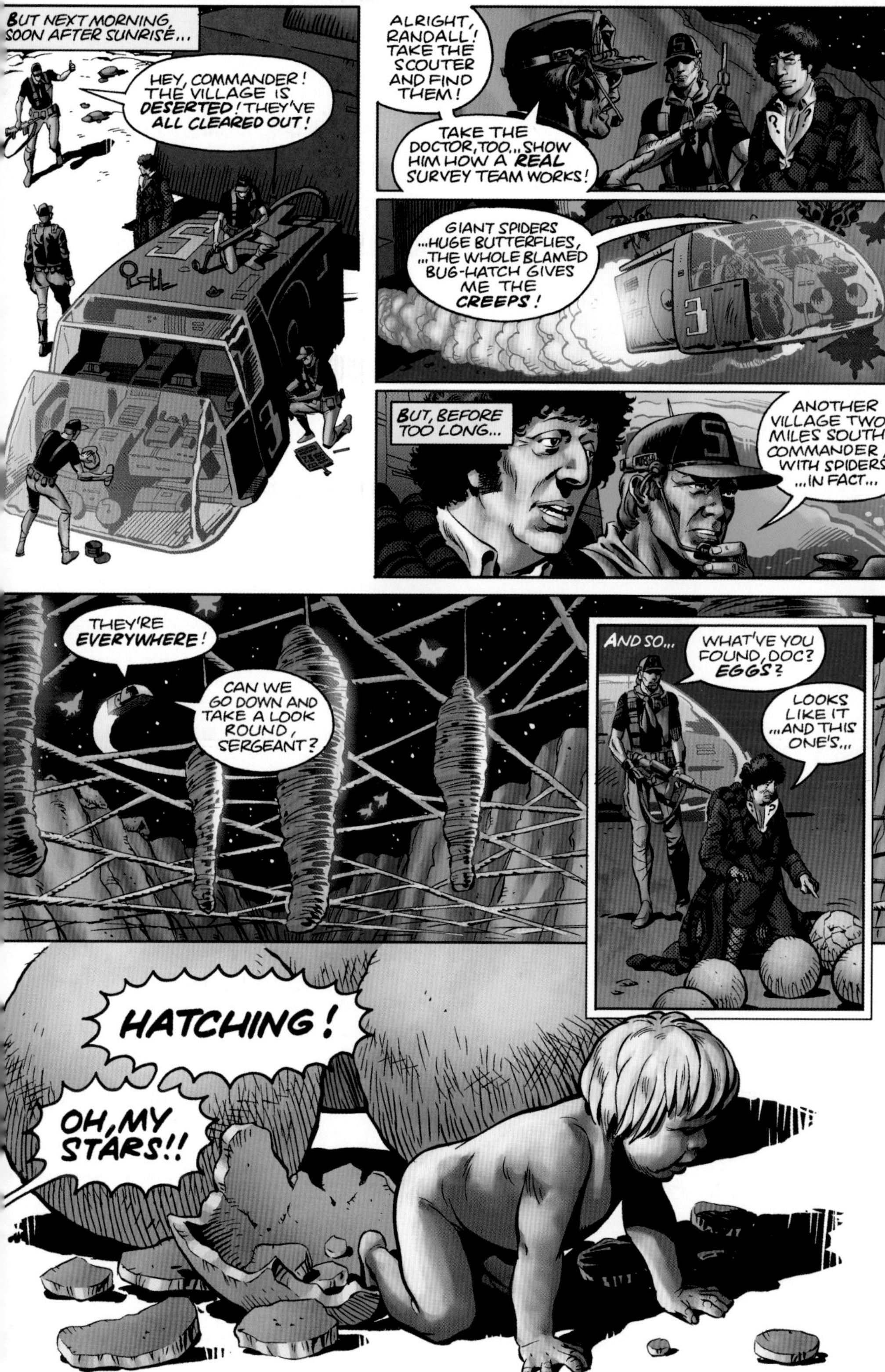

BUT NEXT MORNING, SOON AFTER SUNRISE...
HEY, COMMANDER! THE VILLAGE IS DESERTED! THEY'VE ALL CLEARED OUT!
ALRIGHT, RANDALL! TAKE THE SCOUTER AND FIND THEM!
TAKE THE DOCTOR, TOO... SHOW HIM HOW A REAL SURVEY TEAM WORKS!
GIANT SPIDERS ...HUGE BUTTERFLIES, ...THE WHOLE BLAMED BUG-HATCH GIVES ME THE CREEPS!
BUT, BEFORE TOO LONG...
ANOTHER VILLAGE TWO MILES SOUTH, COMMANDER, WITH SPIDERS ...IN FACT...
THEY'RE EVERYWHERE!
CAN WE GO DOWN AND TAKE A LOOK ROUND, SERGEANT?
AND SO...
WHAT'VE YOU FOUND, DOC? EGGS?
LOOKS LIKE IT ...AND THIS ONE'S...
HATCHING!
OH, MY STARS!!

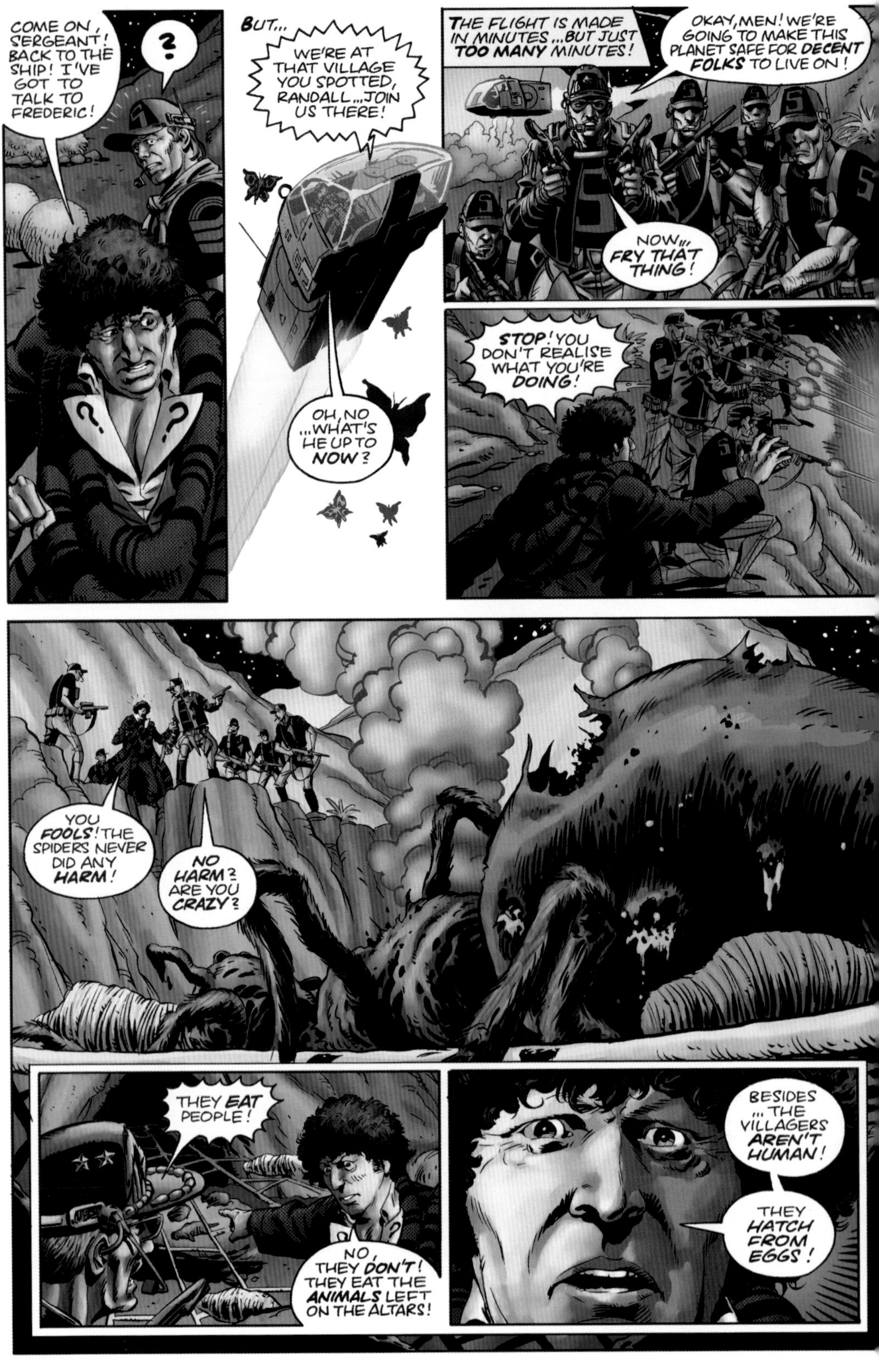
COME ON, SERGEANT! BACK TO THE SHIP! I'VE GOT TO TALK TO FREDERIC!
?
BUT...
WE'RE AT THAT VILLAGE YOU SPOTTED, RANDALL... JOIN US THERE!
OH, NO ...WHAT'S HE UP TO NOW?
THE FLIGHT IS MADE IN MINUTES ...BUT JUST TOO MANY MINUTES!
OKAY, MEN! WE'RE GOING TO MAKE THIS PLANET SAFE FOR DECENT FOLKS TO LIVE ON!
NOW... FRY THAT THING!
STOP! YOU DON'T REALISE WHAT YOU'RE DOING!
YOU FOOLS! THE SPIDERS NEVER DID ANY HARM!
NO HARM? ARE YOU CRAZY?
THEY EAT PEOPLE!
NO, THEY DON'T! THEY EAT THE ANIMALS LEFT ON THE ALTARS!
BESIDES ...THE VILLAGERS AREN'T HUMAN!
THEY HATCH FROM EGGS!

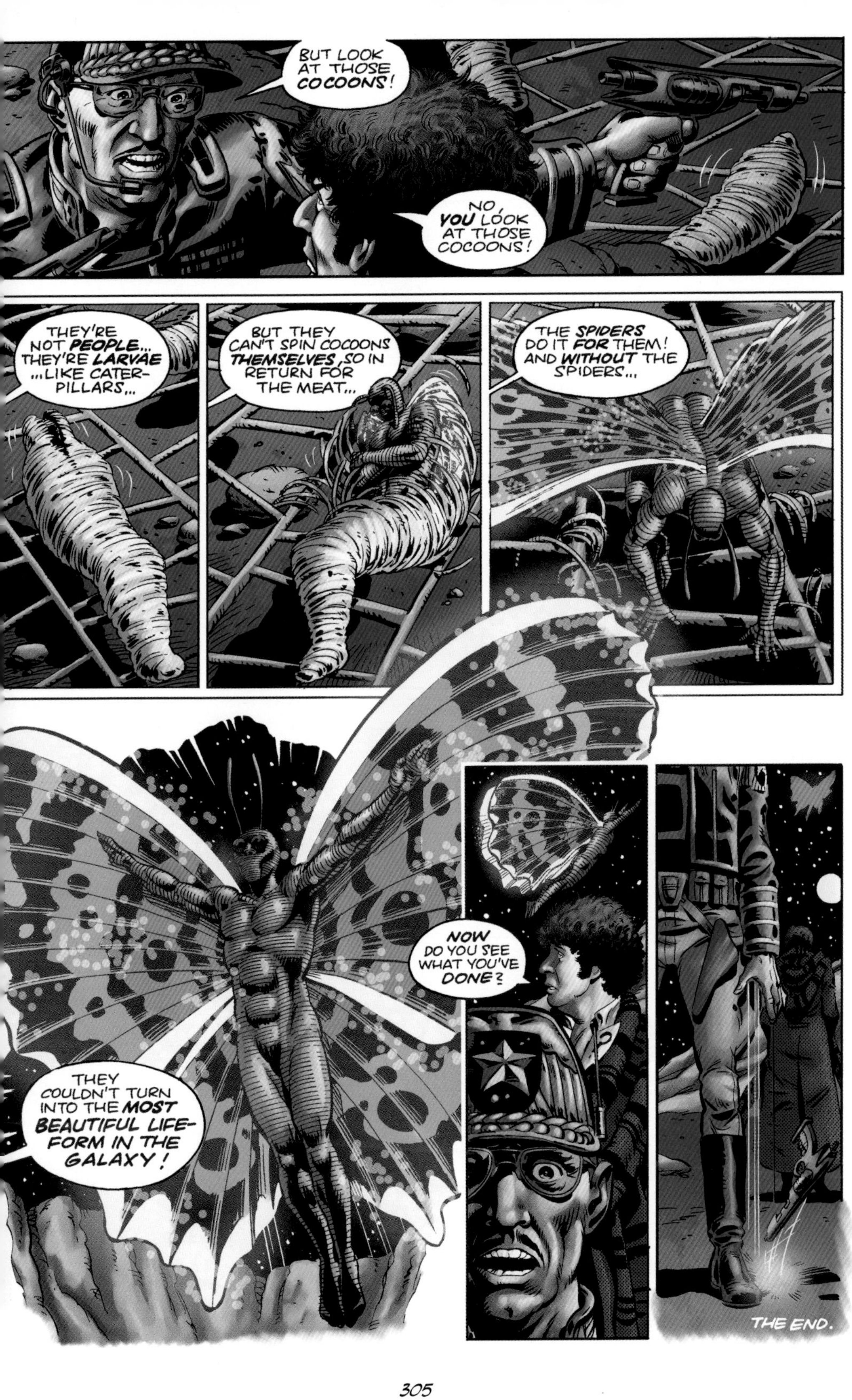
BUT LOOK AT THOSE COCOONS!
NO, YOU LOOK AT THOSE COCOONS!
THEY'RE NOT PEOPLE... THEY'RE LARVAE ...LIKE CATER-PILLARS...
BUT THEY CAN'T SPIN COCOONS THEMSELVES, SO IN RETURN FOR THE MEAT...
THE SPIDERS DO IT FOR THEM! AND WITHOUT THE SPIDERS...
THEY COULDN'T TURN INTO THE MOST BEAUTIFUL LIFE-FORM IN THE GALAXY!
NOW DO YOU SEE WHAT YOU'VE DONE?
THE END.

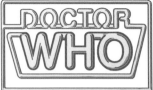

DOCTOR WHO in THE DEAL

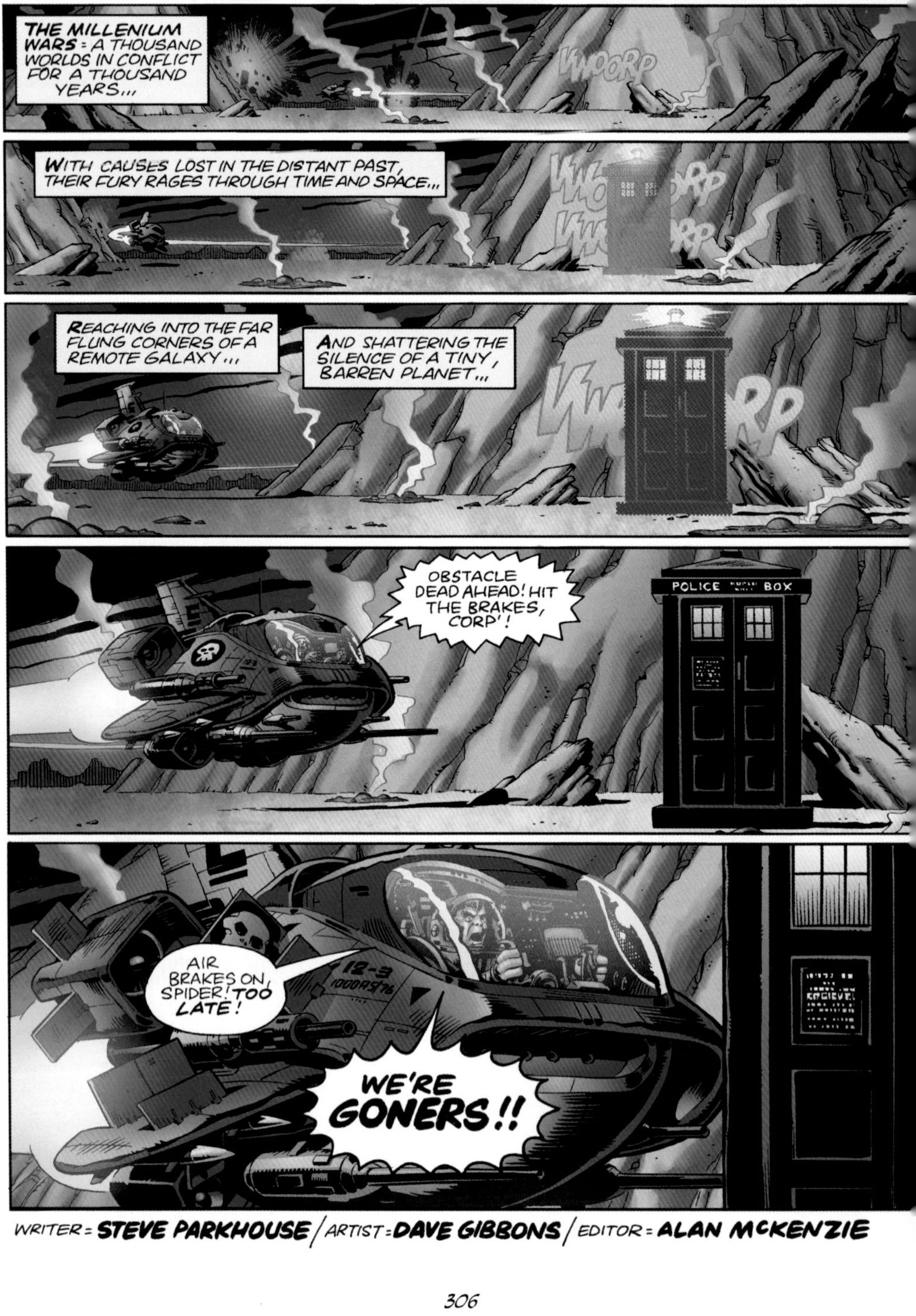

THE MILLENIUM WARS = A THOUSAND WORLDS IN CONFLICT FOR A THOUSAND YEARS...
VWOORP
WITH CAUSES LOST IN THE DISTANT PAST, THEIR FURY RAGES THROUGH TIME AND SPACE...
REACHING INTO THE FAR FLUNG CORNERS OF A REMOTE GALAXY...
AND SHATTERING THE SILENCE OF A TINY, BARREN PLANET...
OBSTACLE DEAD AHEAD! HIT THE BRAKES, CORP'!
POLICE BOX
AIR BRAKES ON, SPIDER! TOO LATE!
12-3
WE'RE GONERS!!

WRITER = **STEVE PARKHOUSE** / ARTIST = **DAVE GIBBONS** / EDITOR = **ALAN McKENZIE**

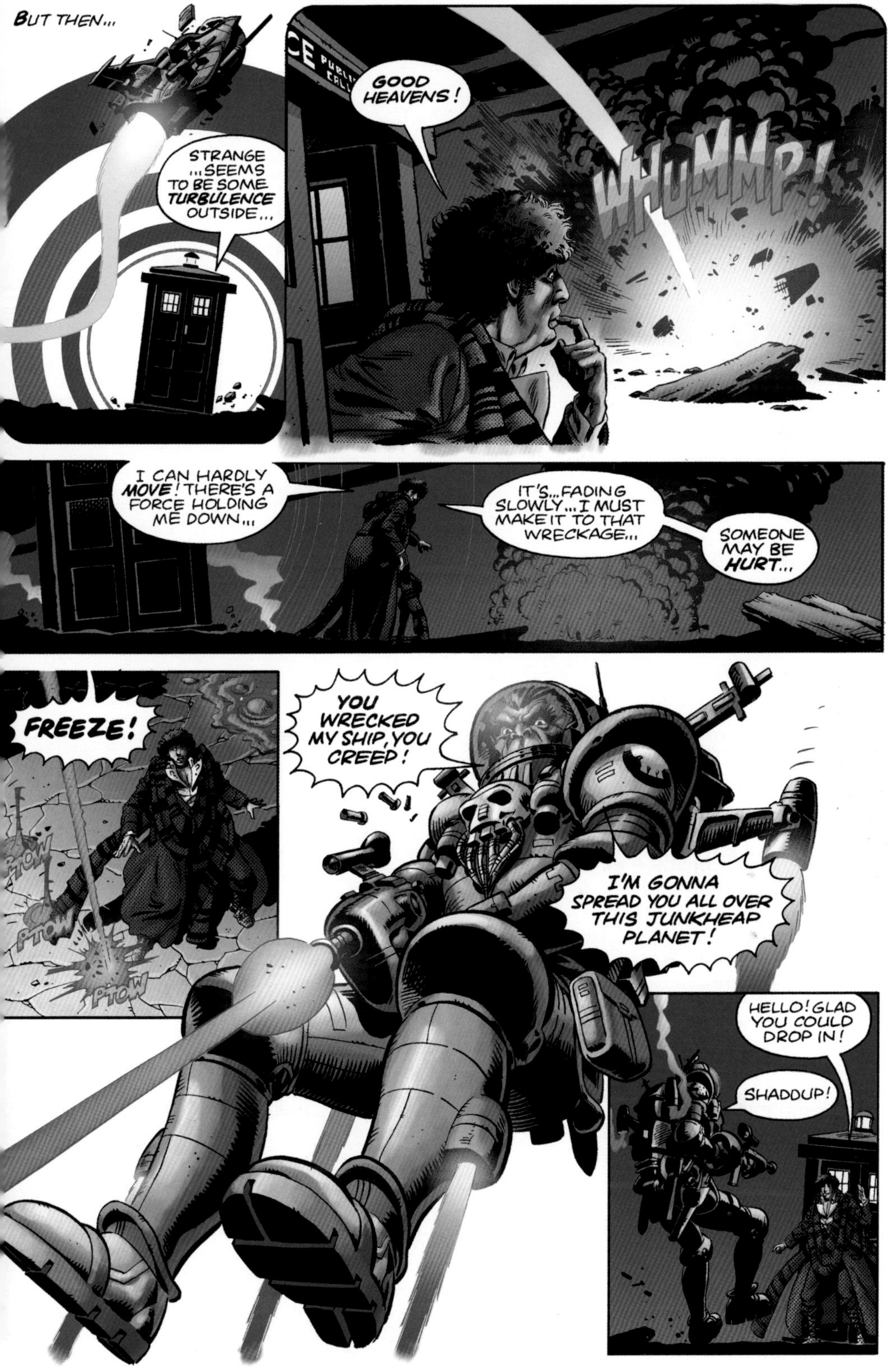

BUT THEN...
STRANGE ...SEEMS TO BE SOME TURBULENCE OUTSIDE...
GOOD HEAVENS!
WHUMMP!
I CAN HARDLY MOVE! THERE'S A FORCE HOLDING ME DOWN...
IT'S...FADING SLOWLY...I MUST MAKE IT TO THAT WRECKAGE...
SOMEONE MAY BE HURT...
FREEZE!
PTOW
PTOW
PTOW
YOU WRECKED MY SHIP, YOU CREEP!
I'M GONNA SPREAD YOU ALL OVER THIS JUNKHEAP PLANET!
HELLO! GLAD YOU COULD DROP IN!
SHADDUP!

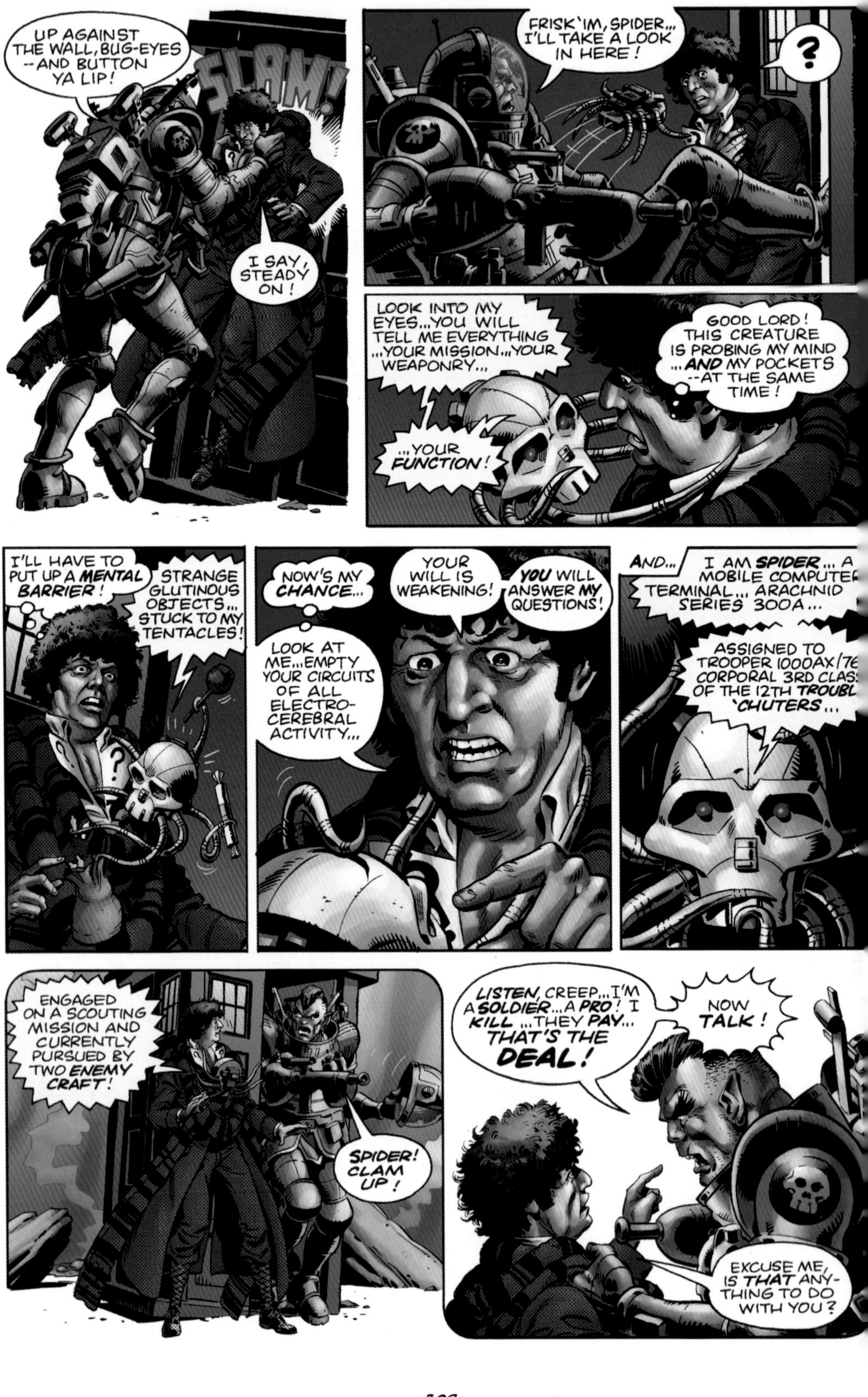
UP AGAINST THE WALL, BUG-EYES --AND BUTTON YA LIP!
SLAM!
I SAY, STEADY ON!
FRISK 'IM, SPIDER... I'LL TAKE A LOOK IN HERE!
?
LOOK INTO MY EYES... YOU WILL TELL ME EVERYTHING ...YOUR MISSION... YOUR WEAPONRY...
...YOUR FUNCTION!
GOOD LORD! THIS CREATURE IS PROBING MY MIND ...AND MY POCKETS --AT THE SAME TIME!
I'LL HAVE TO PUT UP A MENTAL BARRIER!
STRANGE GLUTINOUS OBJECTS... STUCK TO MY TENTACLES!
NOW'S MY CHANCE...
LOOK AT ME... EMPTY YOUR CIRCUITS OF ALL ELECTRO-CEREBRAL ACTIVITY...
YOUR WILL IS WEAKENING!
YOU WILL ANSWER MY QUESTIONS!
AND...
I AM SPIDER... A MOBILE COMPUTER TERMINAL... ARACHNID SERIES 300A...
ASSIGNED TO TROOPER 1000AX/76 CORPORAL 3RD CLASS OF THE 12TH TROUBL 'CHUTERS...
ENGAGED ON A SCOUTING MISSION AND CURRENTLY PURSUED BY TWO ENEMY CRAFT!
SPIDER! CLAM UP!
LISTEN, CREEP... I'M A SOLDIER... A PRO! I KILL ...THEY PAY... THAT'S THE DEAL!
NOW TALK!
EXCUSE ME, IS THAT ANY-THING TO DO WITH YOU?

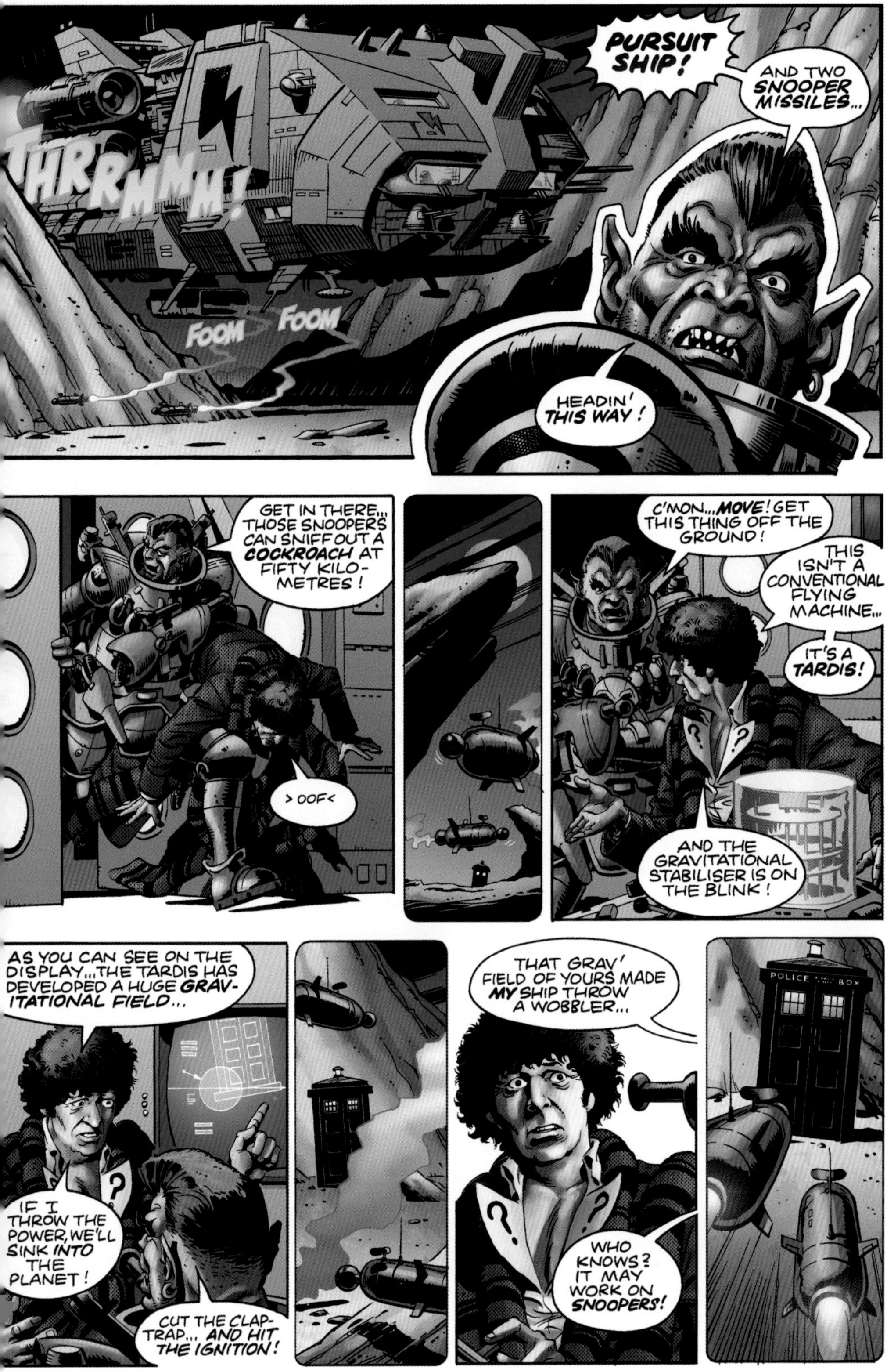
THRRMMM!
PURSUIT SHIP!
AND TWO SNOOPER MISSILES...
FOOM FOOM
HEADIN' THIS WAY!
GET IN THERE... THOSE SNOOPERS CAN SNIFF OUT A COCKROACH AT FIFTY KILO-METRES!
>OOF<
C'MON... MOVE! GET THIS THING OFF THE GROUND!
THIS ISN'T A CONVENTIONAL FLYING MACHINE...
IT'S A TARDIS!
AND THE GRAVITATIONAL STABILISER IS ON THE BLINK!
AS YOU CAN SEE ON THE DISPLAY... THE TARDIS HAS DEVELOPED A HUGE GRAV-ITATIONAL FIELD...
IF I THROW THE POWER, WE'LL SINK INTO THE PLANET!
CUT THE CLAP-TRAP... AND HIT THE IGNITION!
THAT GRAV' FIELD OF YOURS MADE MY SHIP THROW A WOBBLER...
WHO KNOWS? IT MAY WORK ON SNOOPERS!
POLICE BOX

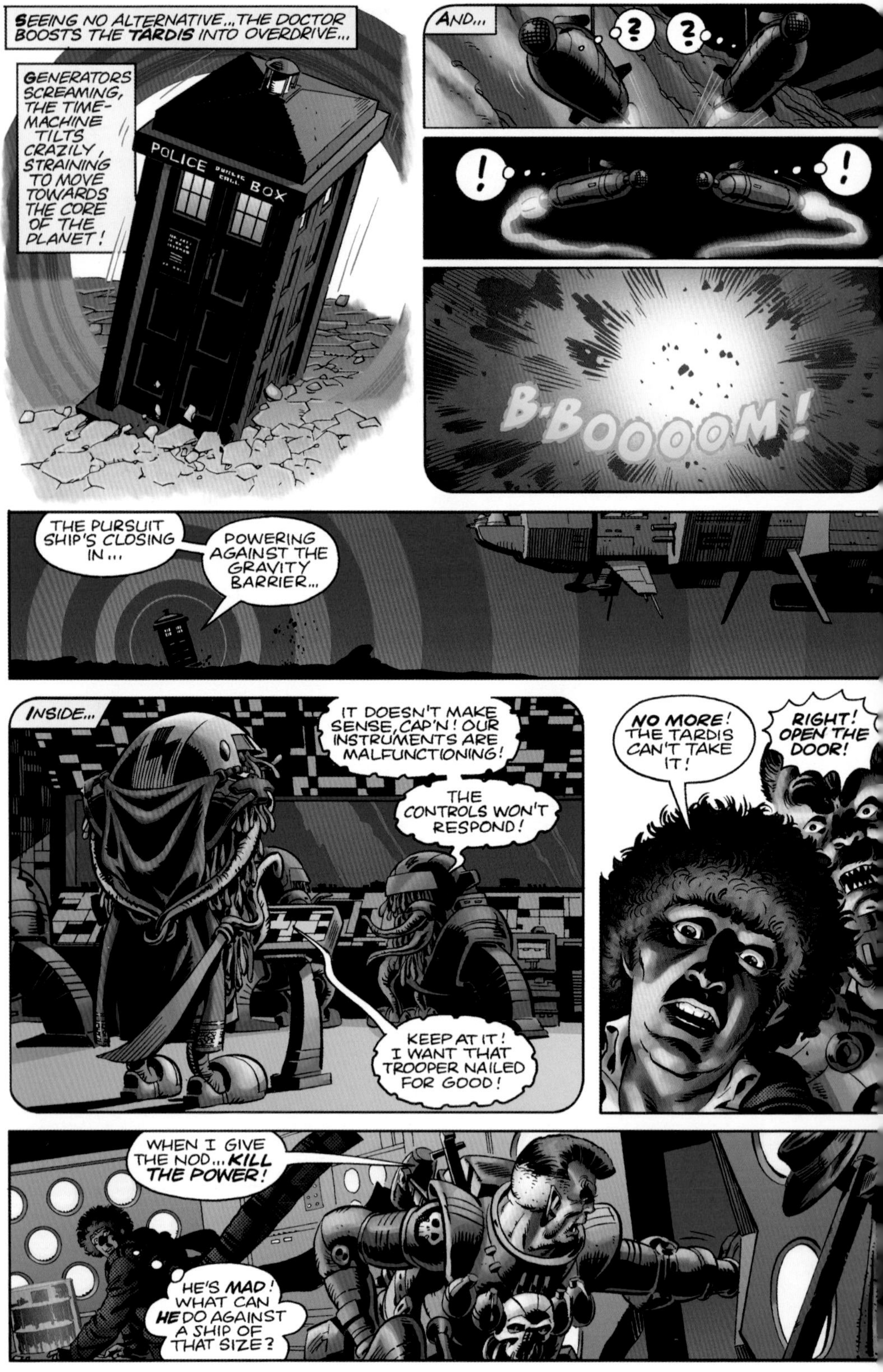
SEEING NO ALTERNATIVE... THE DOCTOR BOOSTS THE TARDIS INTO OVERDRIVE...
GENERATORS SCREAMING, THE TIME-MACHINE TILTS CRAZILY, STRAINING TO MOVE TOWARDS THE CORE OF THE PLANET!
POLICE BOX
AND...
?
?
!
!
B-BOOOOOM!
THE PURSUIT SHIP'S CLOSING IN...
POWERING AGAINST THE GRAVITY BARRIER...
INSIDE...
IT DOESN'T MAKE SENSE, CAP'N! OUR INSTRUMENTS ARE MALFUNCTIONING!
THE CONTROLS WON'T RESPOND!
KEEP AT IT! I WANT THAT TROOPER NAILED FOR GOOD!
NO MORE! THE TARDIS CAN'T TAKE IT!
RIGHT! OPEN THE DOOR!
WHEN I GIVE THE NOD... KILL THE POWER!
HE'S MAD! WHAT CAN HE DO AGAINST A SHIP OF THAT SIZE?

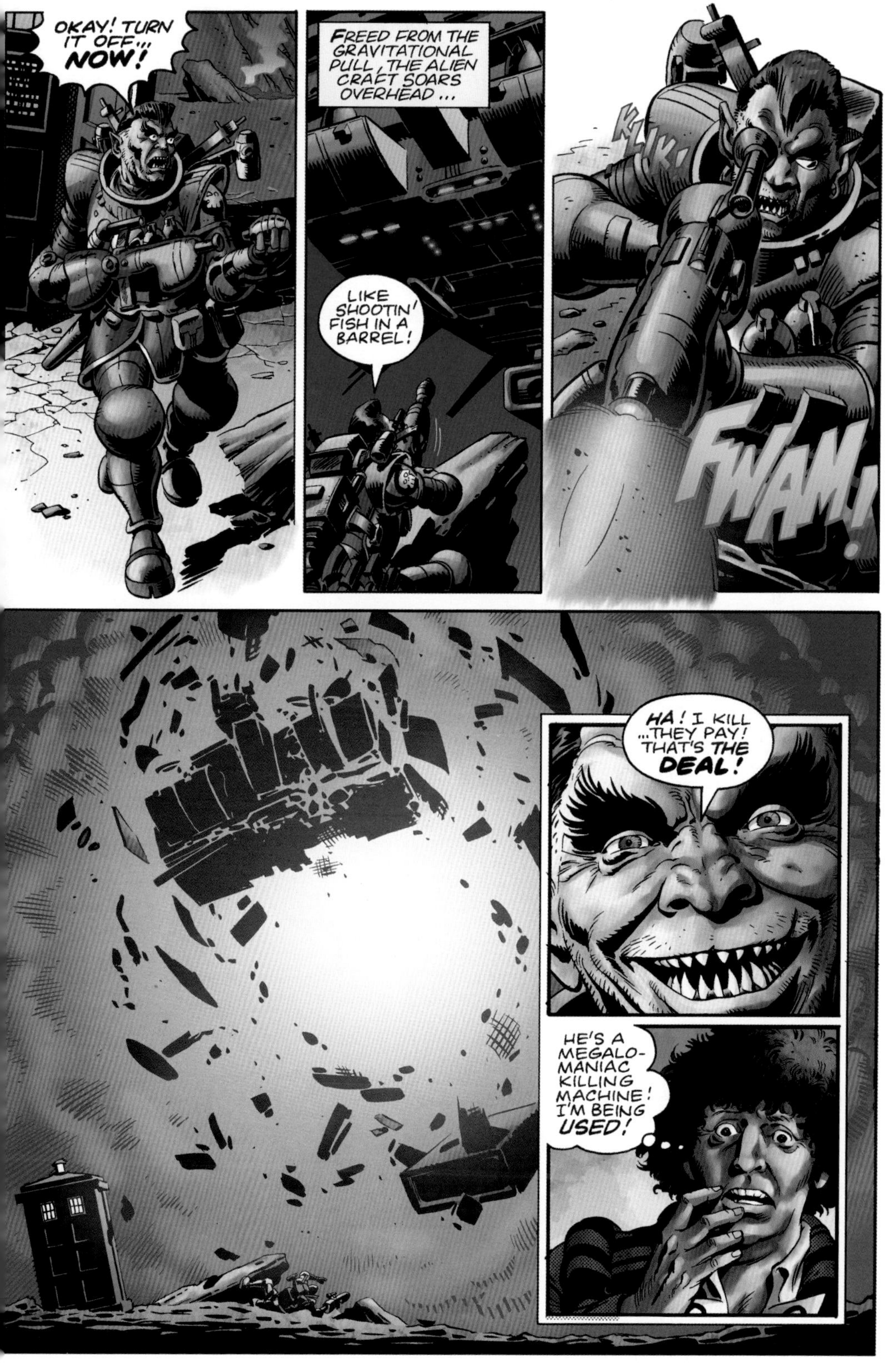
OKAY! TURN IT OFF... NOW!
FREED FROM THE GRAVITATIONAL PULL, THE ALIEN CRAFT SOARS OVERHEAD ...
LIKE SHOOTIN' FISH IN A BARREL!
KLIK!
FWAM!
HA! I KILL ...THEY PAY! THAT'S THE DEAL!
HE'S A MEGALO-MANIAC KILLING MACHINE! I'M BEING USED!

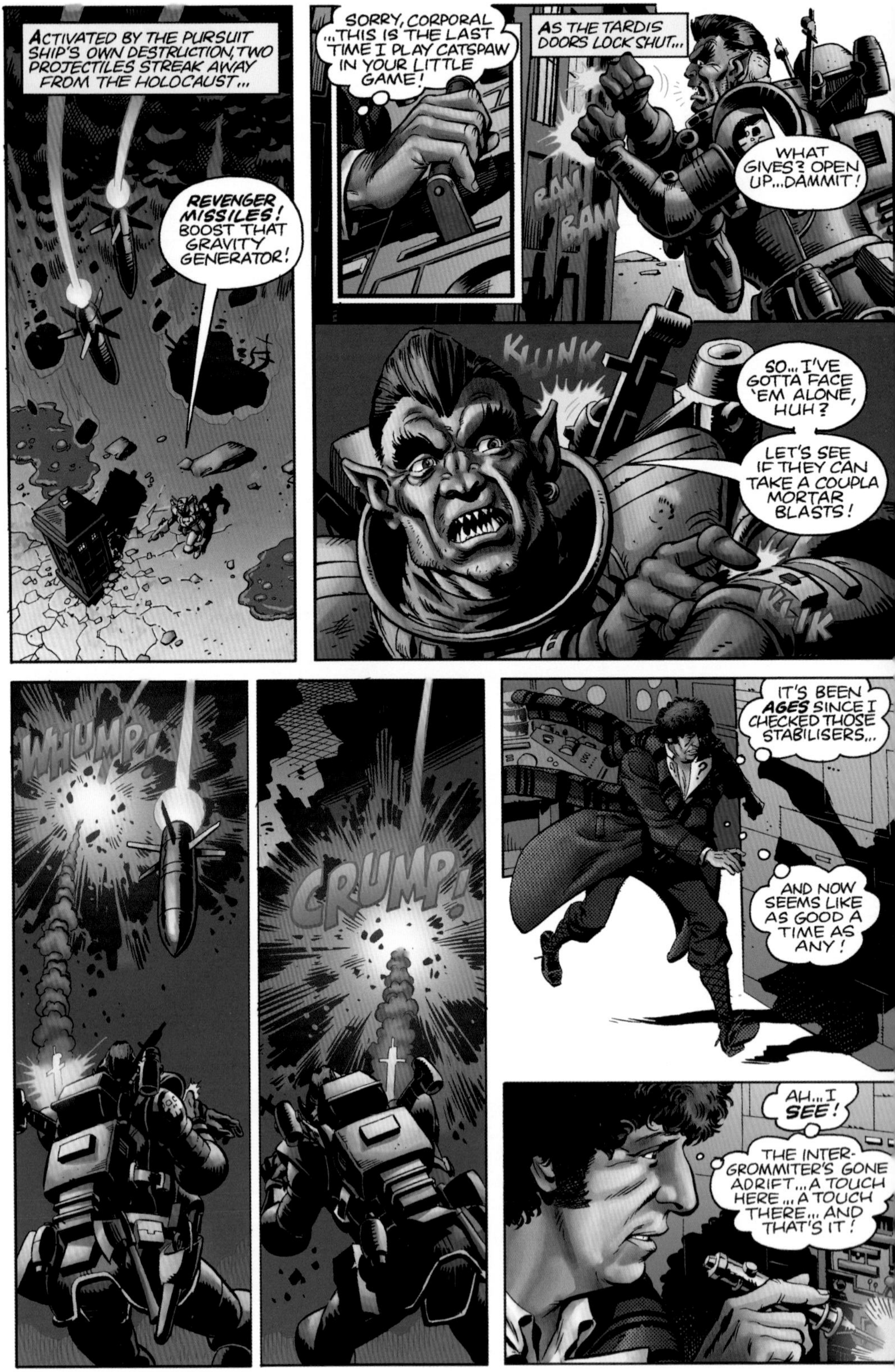
ACTIVATED BY THE PURSUIT SHIP'S OWN DESTRUCTION, TWO PROJECTILES STREAK AWAY FROM THE HOLOCAUST...
REVENGER MISSILES! BOOST THAT GRAVITY GENERATOR!
SORRY, CORPORAL ...THIS IS THE LAST TIME I PLAY CATSPAW IN YOUR LITTLE GAME!
AS THE TARDIS DOORS LOCK SHUT...
BAM
BAM
WHAT GIVES? OPEN UP...DAMMIT!
KLUNK
SO... I'VE GOTTA FACE 'EM ALONE, HUH?
LET'S SEE IF THEY CAN TAKE A COUPLA MORTAR BLASTS!
KLIK
WHUMP!
CRUMP!
IT'S BEEN AGES SINCE I CHECKED THOSE STABILISERS...
AND NOW SEEMS LIKE AS GOOD A TIME AS ANY!
AH... I SEE!
THE INTER-GROMMITER'S GONE ADRIFT... A TOUCH HERE... A TOUCH THERE... AND THAT'S IT!

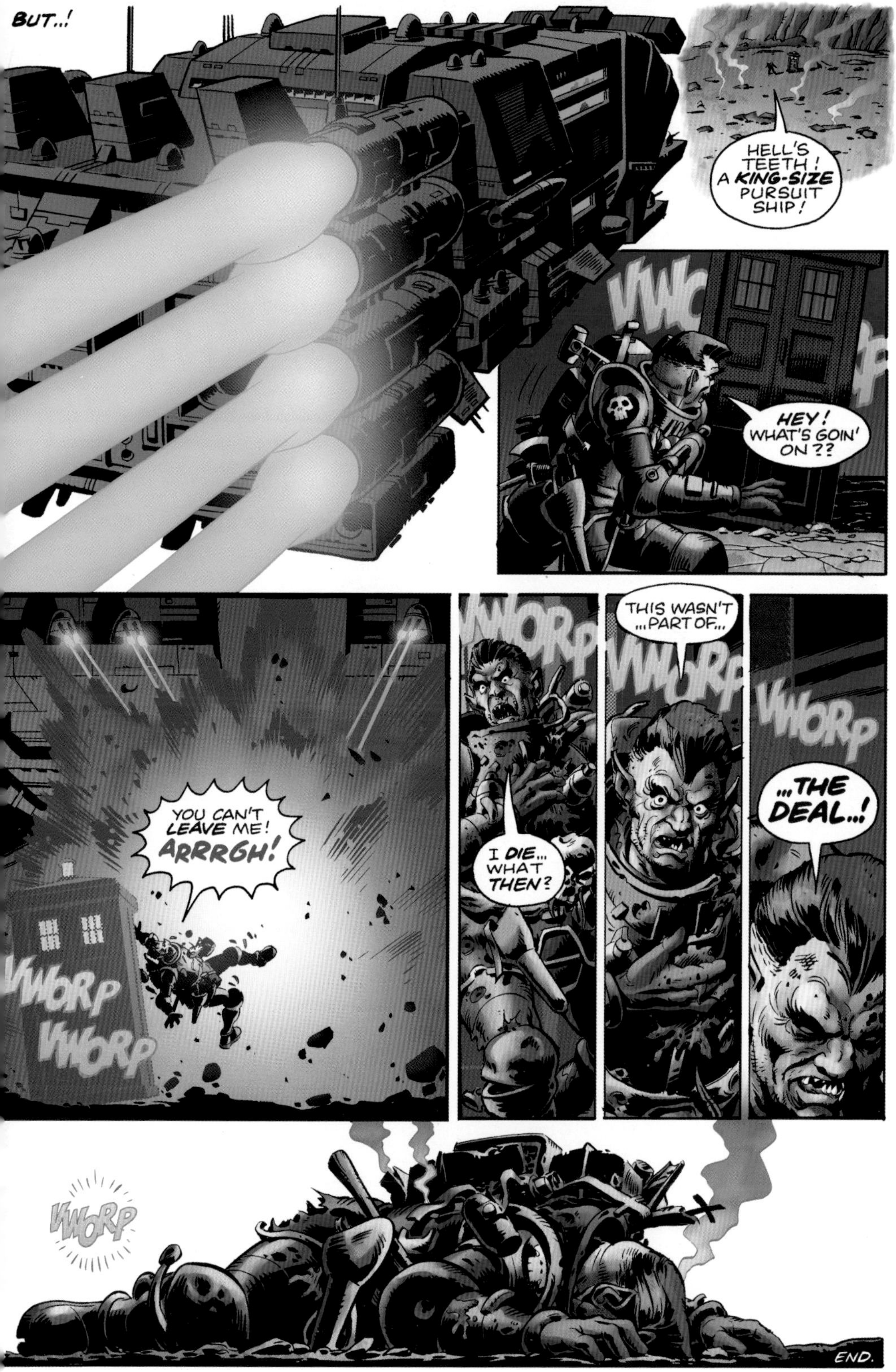
BUT..!
HELL'S TEETH! A KING-SIZE PURSUIT SHIP!
VWO
HEY! WHAT'S GOIN' ON??
YOU CAN'T LEAVE ME! ARRRGH!
VWORP
VWORP
VWORP
I DIE... WHAT THEN?
THIS WASN'T ...PART OF...
VWORP
VWORP
...THE DEAL..!
VWORP
END.

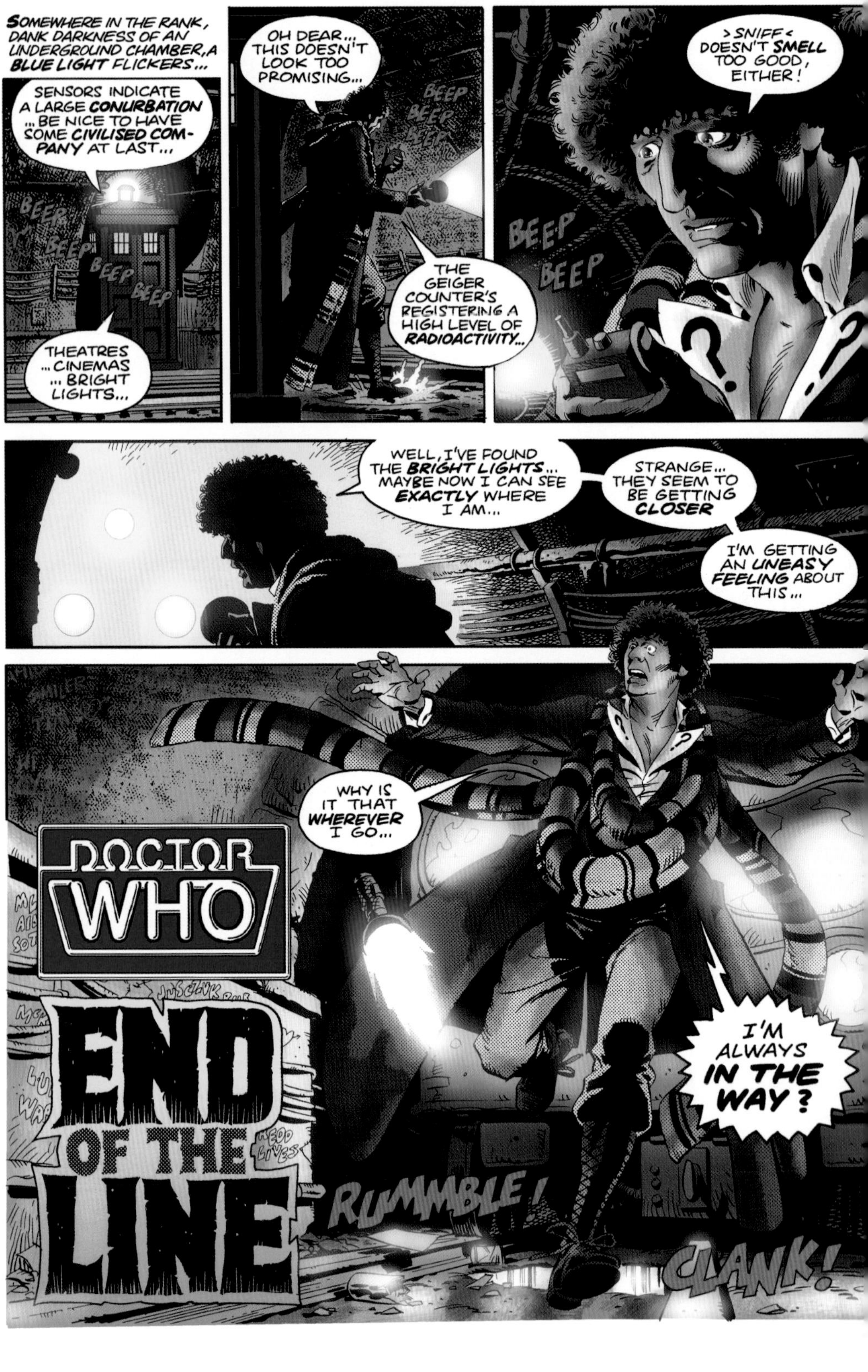
SOMEWHERE IN THE RANK, DANK DARKNESS OF AN UNDERGROUND CHAMBER, A BLUE LIGHT FLICKERS...
SENSORS INDICATE A LARGE CONURBATION ...BE NICE TO HAVE SOME CIVILISED COMPANY AT LAST...
BEEP BEEP BEEP BEEP
THEATRES ...CINEMAS ...BRIGHT LIGHTS...
OH DEAR... THIS DOESN'T LOOK TOO PROMISING...
BEEP BEEP BEEP
THE GEIGER COUNTER'S REGISTERING A HIGH LEVEL OF RADIOACTIVITY...
>SNIFF< DOESN'T SMELL TOO GOOD, EITHER!
BEEP BEEP
WELL, I'VE FOUND THE BRIGHT LIGHTS... MAYBE NOW I CAN SEE EXACTLY WHERE I AM...
STRANGE... THEY SEEM TO BE GETTING CLOSER
I'M GETTING AN UNEASY FEELING ABOUT THIS...
DOCTOR WHO
END OF THE LINE
WHY IS IT THAT WHEREVER I GO...
I'M ALWAYS IN THE WAY?
RUMMBLE!
CLANK!

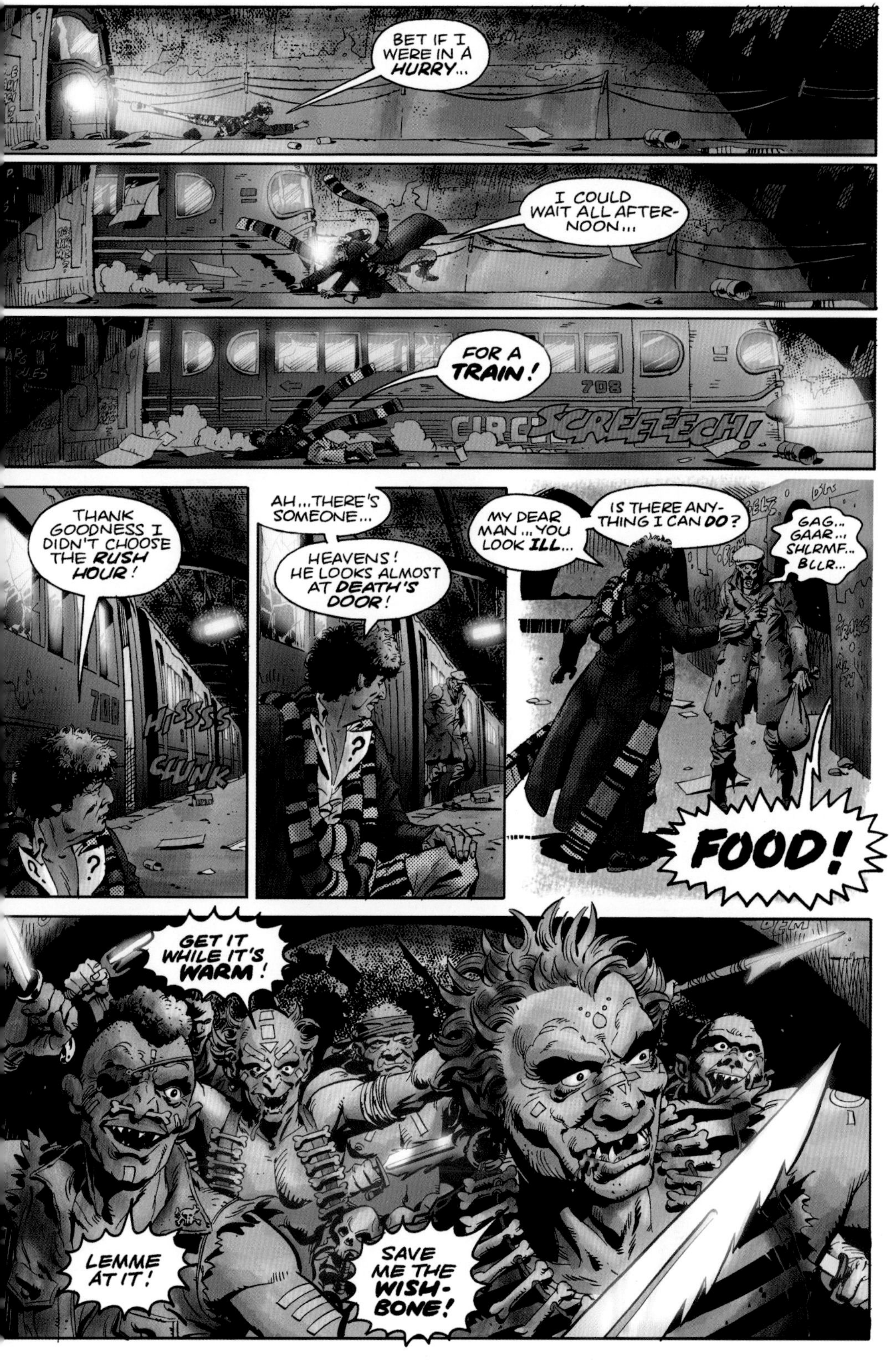
BET IF I WERE IN A HURRY...
I COULD WAIT ALL AFTER-NOON...
FOR A TRAIN!
SCREEEECH!
THANK GOODNESS I DIDN'T CHOOSE THE RUSH HOUR!
HISSSS
CHUNK
AH...THERE'S SOMEONE...
HEAVENS! HE LOOKS ALMOST AT DEATH'S DOOR!
MY DEAR MAN...YOU LOOK ILL...
IS THERE ANY-THING I CAN DO?
GAG... GAAR... SHLRMF... BLLR...
FOOD!
GET IT WHILE IT'S WARM!
LEMME AT IT!
SAVE ME THE WISH-BONE!

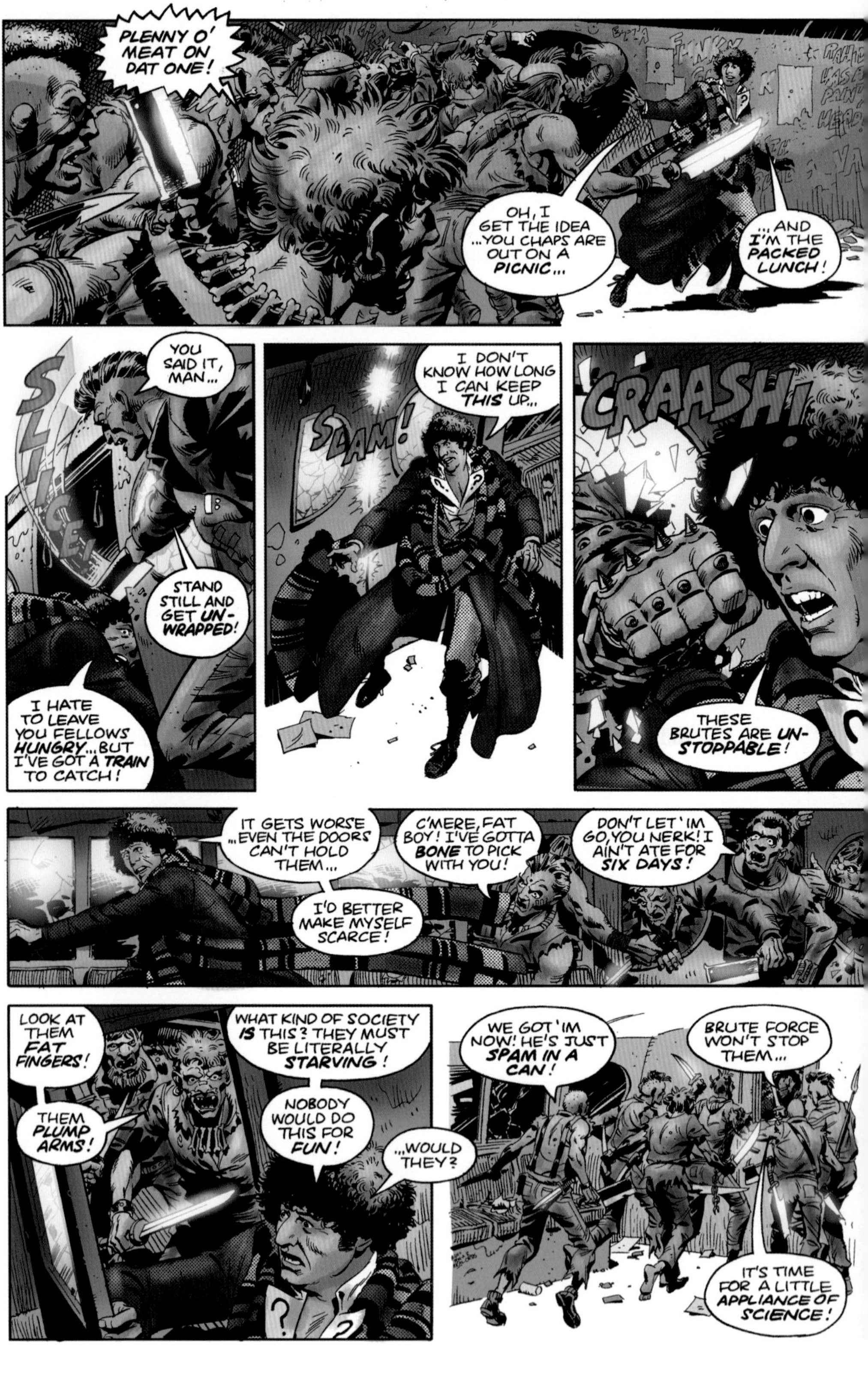
PLENNY O' MEAT ON DAT ONE!
OH, I GET THE IDEA ...YOU CHAPS ARE OUT ON A PICNIC...
...AND I'M THE PACKED LUNCH!
SLIICE!
YOU SAID IT, MAN...
STAND STILL AND GET UN-WRAPPED!
I HATE TO LEAVE YOU FELLOWS HUNGRY...BUT I'VE GOT A TRAIN TO CATCH!
SLAM!
I DON'T KNOW HOW LONG I CAN KEEP THIS UP...
CRAASH!
THESE BRUTES ARE UN-STOPPABLE!
IT GETS WORSE ...EVEN THE DOORS CAN'T HOLD THEM...
I'D BETTER MAKE MYSELF SCARCE!
C'MERE, FAT BOY! I'VE GOTTA BONE TO PICK WITH YOU!
DON'T LET 'IM GO, YOU NERK! I AIN'T ATE FOR SIX DAYS!
LOOK AT THEM FAT FINGERS!
THEM PLUMP ARMS!
WHAT KIND OF SOCIETY IS THIS? THEY MUST BE LITERALLY STARVING!
NOBODY WOULD DO THIS FOR FUN!
...WOULD THEY?
WE GOT 'IM NOW! HE'S JUST SPAM IN A CAN!
BRUTE FORCE WON'T STOP THEM...
IT'S TIME FOR A LITTLE APPLIANCE OF SCIENCE!

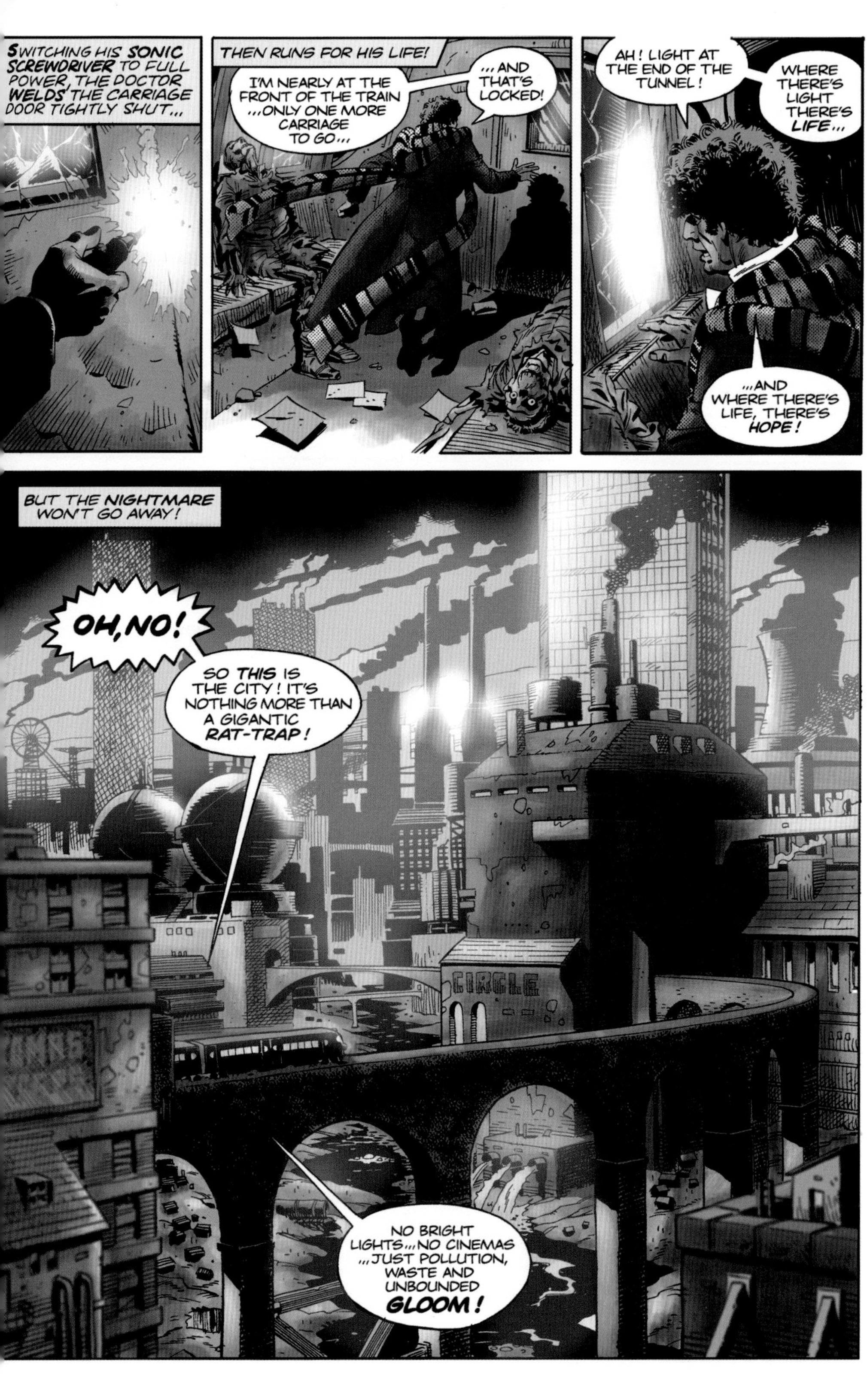
SWITCHING HIS SONIC SCREWDRIVER TO FULL POWER, THE DOCTOR WELDS THE CARRIAGE DOOR TIGHTLY SHUT...
THEN RUNS FOR HIS LIFE!
I'M NEARLY AT THE FRONT OF THE TRAIN ...ONLY ONE MORE CARRIAGE TO GO...
...AND THAT'S LOCKED!
AH! LIGHT AT THE END OF THE TUNNEL!
WHERE THERE'S LIGHT THERE'S LIFE...
...AND WHERE THERE'S LIFE, THERE'S HOPE!
BUT THE NIGHTMARE WON'T GO AWAY!
OH, NO!
SO THIS IS THE CITY! IT'S NOTHING MORE THAN A GIGANTIC RAT-TRAP!
CIRCLE
NO BRIGHT LIGHTS... NO CINEMAS ...JUST POLLUTION, WASTE AND UNBOUNDED GLOOM!

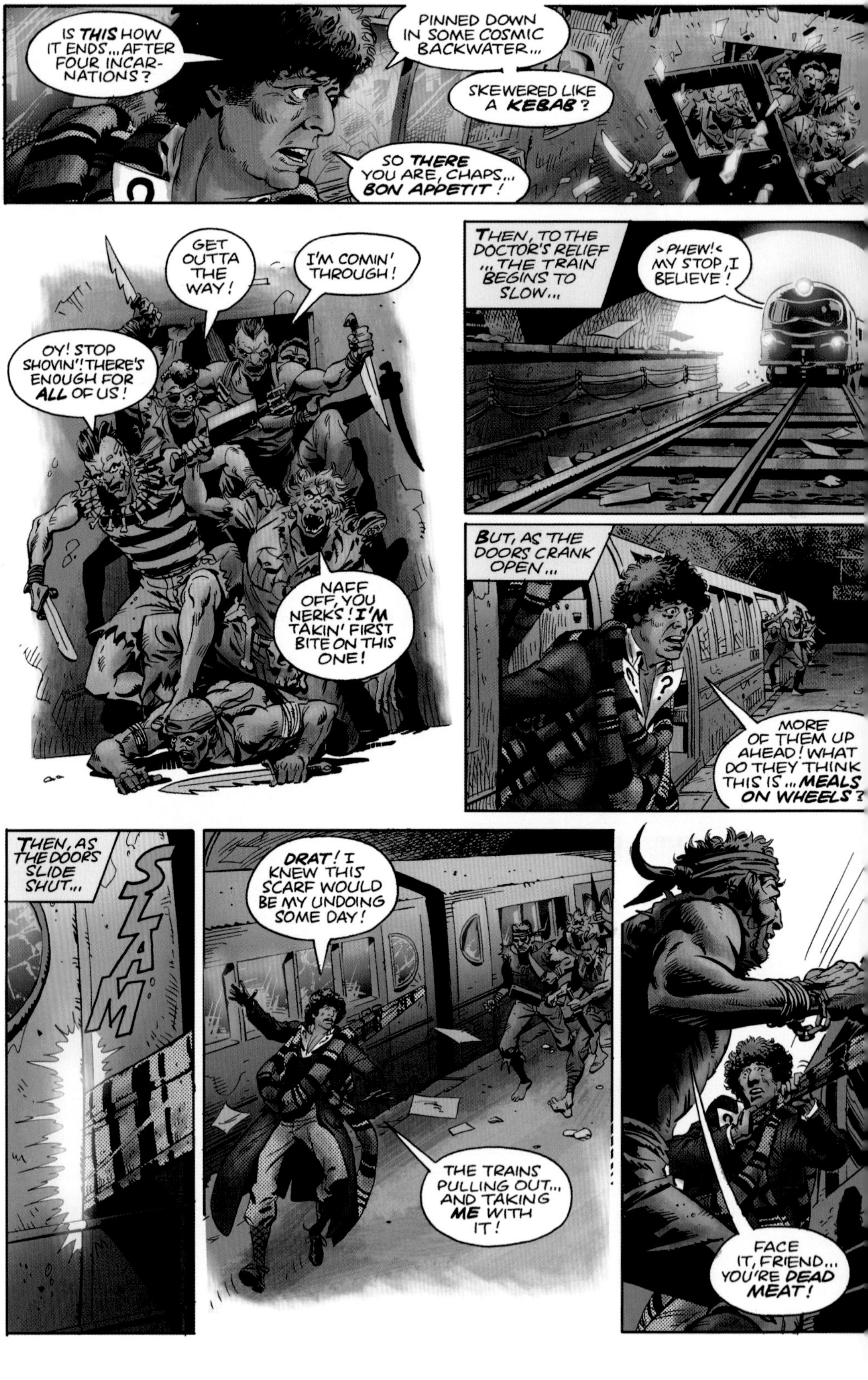
IS THIS HOW IT ENDS... AFTER FOUR INCARNATIONS?
PINNED DOWN IN SOME COSMIC BACKWATER...
SKEWERED LIKE A KEBAB?
SO THERE YOU ARE, CHAPS... BON APPETIT!
GET OUTTA THE WAY!
I'M COMIN' THROUGH!
OY! STOP SHOVIN'! THERE'S ENOUGH FOR ALL OF US!
NAFF OFF, YOU NERKS! I'M TAKIN' FIRST BITE ON THIS ONE!
THEN, TO THE DOCTOR'S RELIEF ... THE TRAIN BEGINS TO SLOW...
>PHEW!< MY STOP, I BELIEVE!
BUT, AS THE DOORS CRANK OPEN...
MORE OF THEM UP AHEAD! WHAT DO THEY THINK THIS IS... MEALS ON WHEELS?
THEN, AS THE DOORS SLIDE SHUT...
SLAM
DRAT! I KNEW THIS SCARF WOULD BE MY UNDOING SOME DAY!
THE TRAINS PULLING OUT... AND TAKING ME WITH IT!
FACE IT, FRIEND... YOU'RE DEAD MEAT!

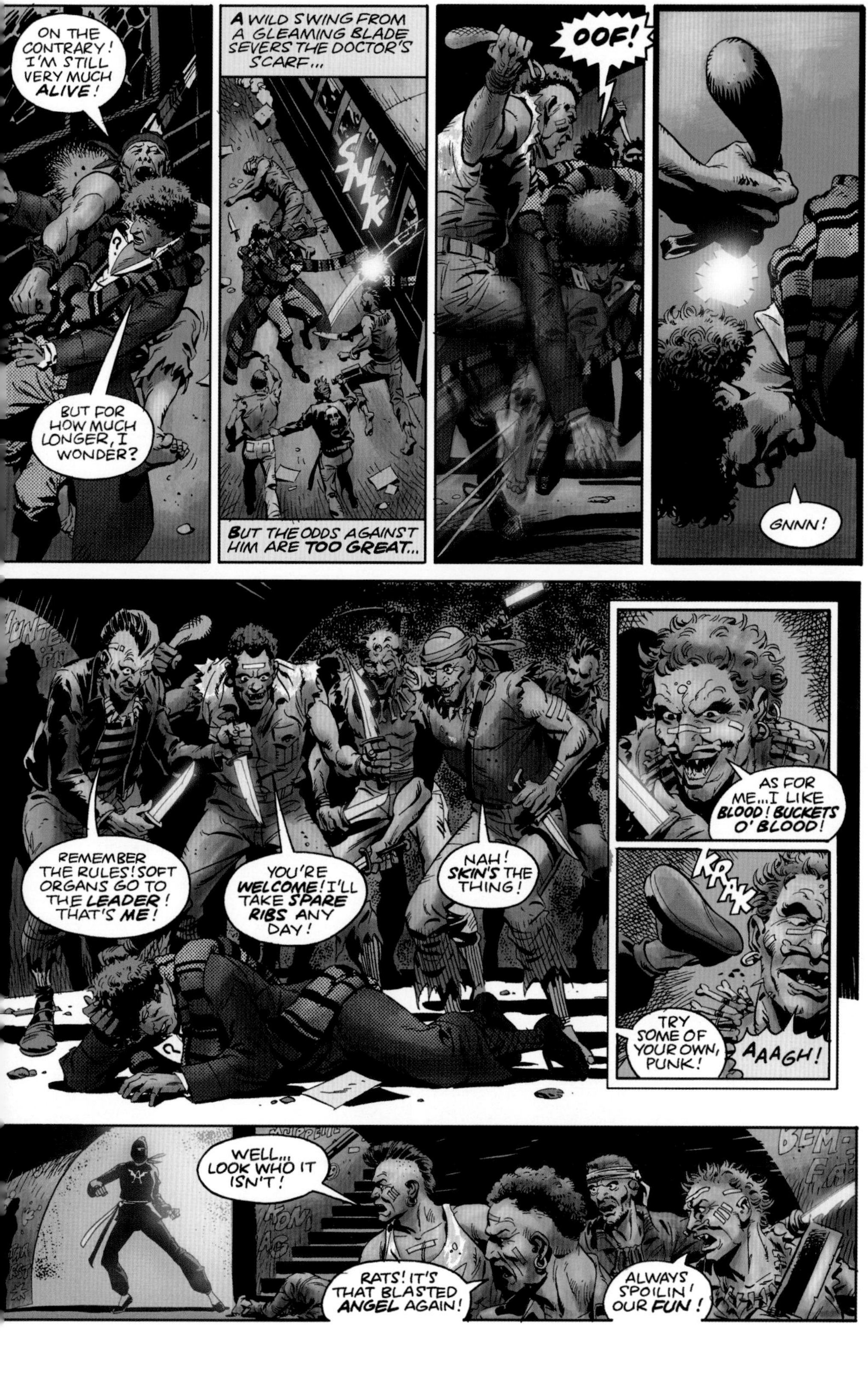
ON THE CONTRARY! I'M STILL VERY MUCH ALIVE!
BUT FOR HOW MUCH LONGER, I WONDER?
A WILD SWING FROM A GLEAMING BLADE SEVERS THE DOCTOR'S SCARF...
SNIKK
BUT THE ODDS AGAINST HIM ARE TOO GREAT...
OOF!
GNNN!
REMEMBER THE RULES! SOFT ORGANS GO TO THE LEADER! THAT'S ME!
YOU'RE WELCOME! I'LL TAKE SPARE RIBS ANY DAY!
NAH! SKIN'S THE THING!
AS FOR ME...I LIKE BLOOD! BUCKETS O' BLOOD!
KRAK
TRY SOME OF YOUR OWN, PUNK!
AAAGH!
WELL... LOOK WHO IT ISN'T!
RATS! IT'S THAT BLASTED ANGEL AGAIN!
ALWAYS SPOILIN' OUR FUN!

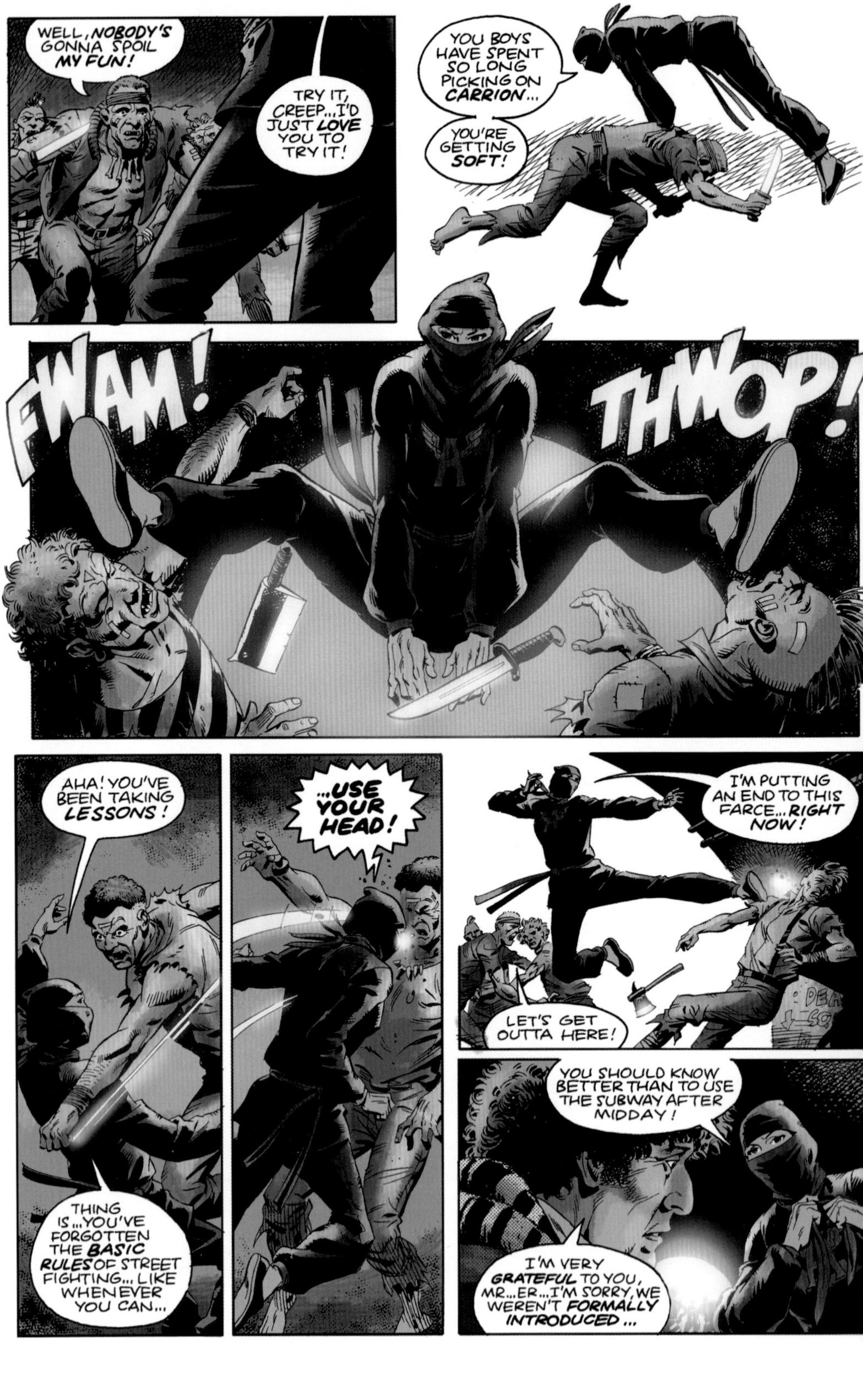
WELL, NOBODY'S GONNA SPOIL MY FUN!
TRY IT, CREEP...I'D JUST LOVE YOU TO TRY IT!
YOU BOYS HAVE SPENT SO LONG PICKING ON CARRION...
YOU'RE GETTING SOFT!
FWAM!
THWOP!
AHA! YOU'VE BEEN TAKING LESSONS!
THING IS...YOU'VE FORGOTTEN THE BASIC RULES OF STREET FIGHTING... LIKE WHENEVER YOU CAN...
...USE YOUR HEAD!
I'M PUTTING AN END TO THIS FARCE... RIGHT NOW!
LET'S GET OUTTA HERE!
YOU SHOULD KNOW BETTER THAN TO USE THE SUBWAY AFTER MIDDAY!
I'M VERY GRATEFUL TO YOU, MR...ER...I'M SORRY, WE WEREN'T FORMALLY INTRODUCED...

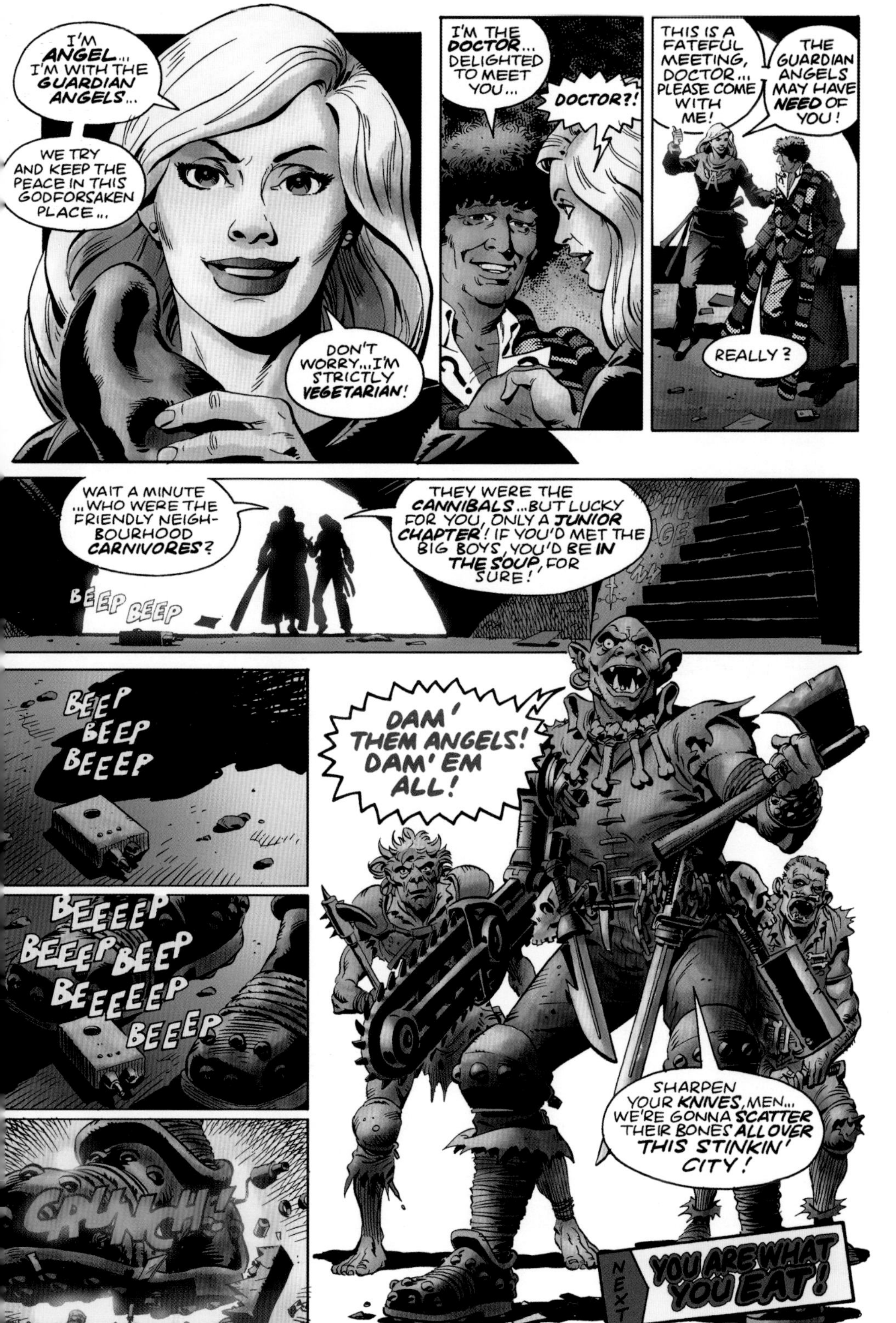
I'M ANGEL... I'M WITH THE GUARDIAN ANGELS...
WE TRY AND KEEP THE PEACE IN THIS GODFORSAKEN PLACE...
DON'T WORRY...I'M STRICTLY VEGETARIAN!
I'M THE DOCTOR... DELIGHTED TO MEET YOU...
DOCTOR?!
THIS IS A FATEFUL MEETING, DOCTOR... PLEASE COME WITH ME!
THE GUARDIAN ANGELS MAY HAVE NEED OF YOU!
REALLY?
WAIT A MINUTE ...WHO WERE THE FRIENDLY NEIGH-BOURHOOD CARNIVORES?
THEY WERE THE CANNIBALS...BUT LUCKY FOR YOU, ONLY A JUNIOR CHAPTER! IF YOU'D MET THE BIG BOYS, YOU'D BE IN THE SOUP, FOR SURE!
BEEP BEEP
BEEP BEEP BEEEP
BEEEEP BEEEP BEEP BEEEEEP BEEEP
CRUNCH!
DAM' THEM ANGELS! DAM' EM ALL!
SHARPEN YOUR KNIVES, MEN... WE'RE GONNA SCATTER THEIR BONES ALL OVER THIS STINKIN' CITY!
NEXT
YOU ARE WHAT YOU EAT!

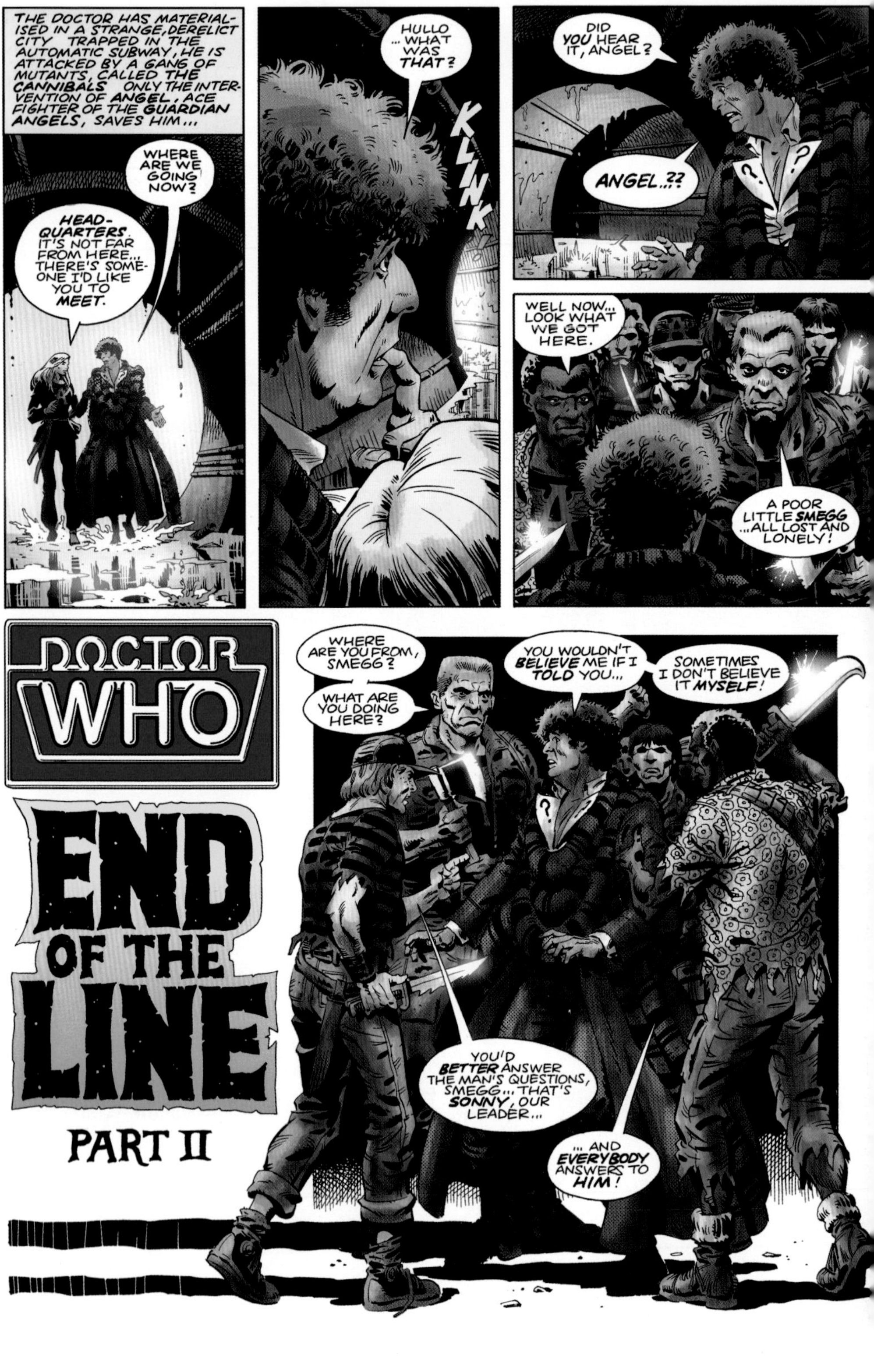
THE DOCTOR HAS MATERIALISED IN A STRANGE, DERELICT CITY. TRAPPED IN THE AUTOMATIC SUBWAY, HE IS ATTACKED BY A GANG OF MUTANTS, CALLED THE CANNIBALS. ONLY THE INTERVENTION OF ANGEL, ACE FIGHTER OF THE GUARDIAN ANGELS, SAVES HIM...
WHERE ARE WE GOING NOW?
HEAD-QUARTERS. IT'S NOT FAR FROM HERE... THERE'S SOMEONE I'D LIKE YOU TO MEET.
HULLO ...WHAT WAS THAT?
KLINK!
DID YOU HEAR IT, ANGEL?
ANGEL..??
WELL NOW... LOOK WHAT WE GOT HERE.
A POOR LITTLE SMEGG ...ALL LOST AND LONELY!
DOCTOR WHO
END OF THE LINE
PART II
WHERE ARE YOU FROM, SMEGG?
WHAT ARE YOU DOING HERE?
YOU WOULDN'T BELIEVE ME IF I TOLD YOU...
SOMETIMES I DON'T BELIEVE IT MYSELF!
YOU'D BETTER ANSWER THE MAN'S QUESTIONS, SMEGG... THAT'S SONNY, OUR LEADER...
... AND EVERYBODY ANSWERS TO HIM!

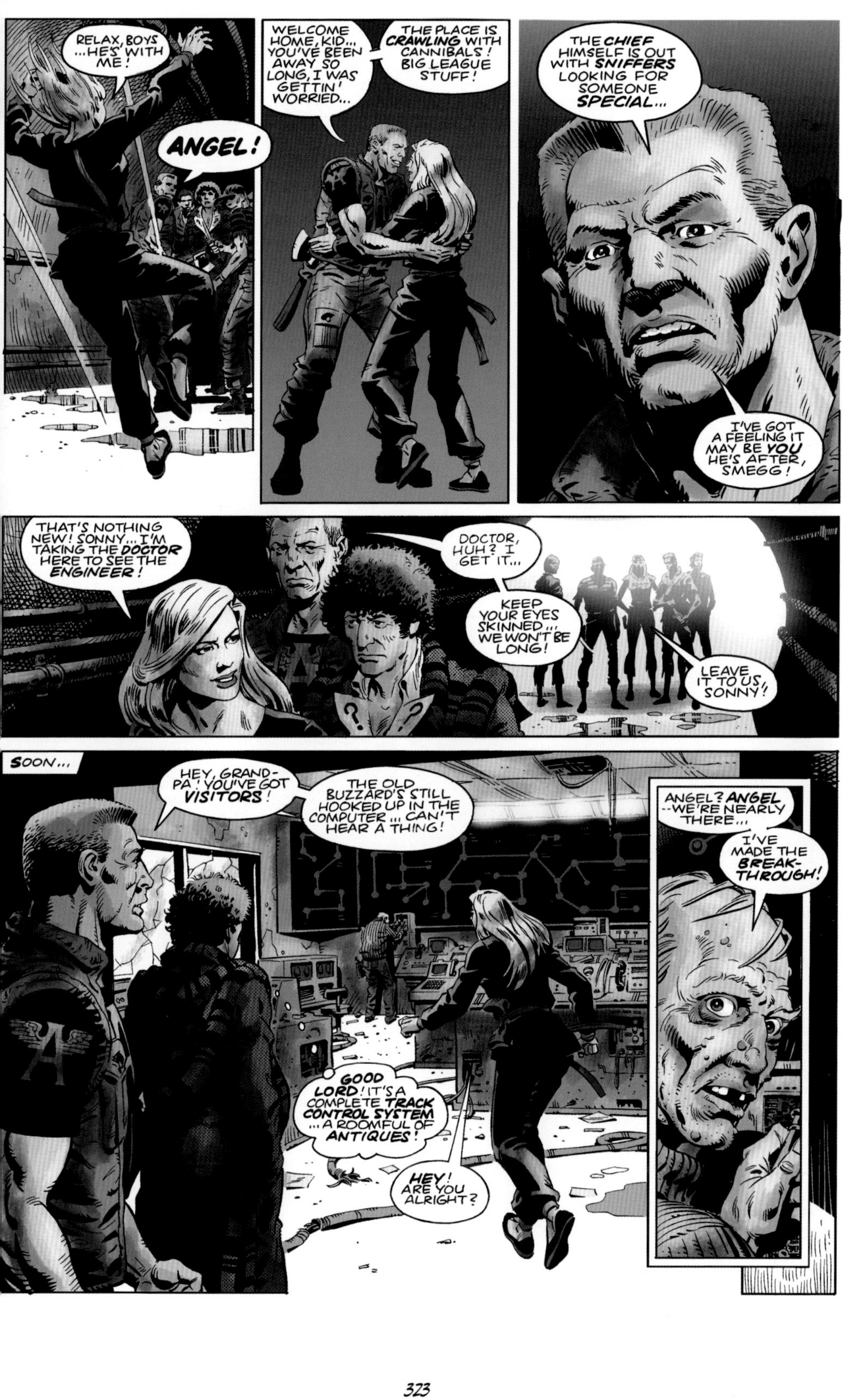
RELAX, BOYS ...HE'S WITH ME!
ANGEL!
WELCOME HOME, KID... YOU'VE BEEN AWAY SO LONG, I WAS GETTIN' WORRIED...
THE PLACE IS CRAWLING WITH CANNIBALS! BIG LEAGUE STUFF!
THE CHIEF HIMSELF IS OUT WITH SNIFFERS LOOKING FOR SOMEONE SPECIAL...
I'VE GOT A FEELING IT MAY BE YOU HE'S AFTER, SMEGG!
THAT'S NOTHING NEW! SONNY... I'M TAKING THE DOCTOR HERE TO SEE THE ENGINEER!
DOCTOR, HUH? I GET IT...
KEEP YOUR EYES SKINNED... WE WON'T BE LONG!
LEAVE IT TO US, SONNY!
SOON...
HEY, GRAND-PA! YOU'VE GOT VISITORS!
THE OLD BUZZARD'S STILL HOOKED UP IN THE COMPUTER... CAN'T HEAR A THING!
ANGEL? ANGEL --WE'RE NEARLY THERE...
I'VE MADE THE BREAK-THROUGH!
GOOD LORD! IT'S A COMPLETE TRACK CONTROL SYSTEM ...A ROOMFUL OF ANTIQUES!
HEY! ARE YOU ALRIGHT?

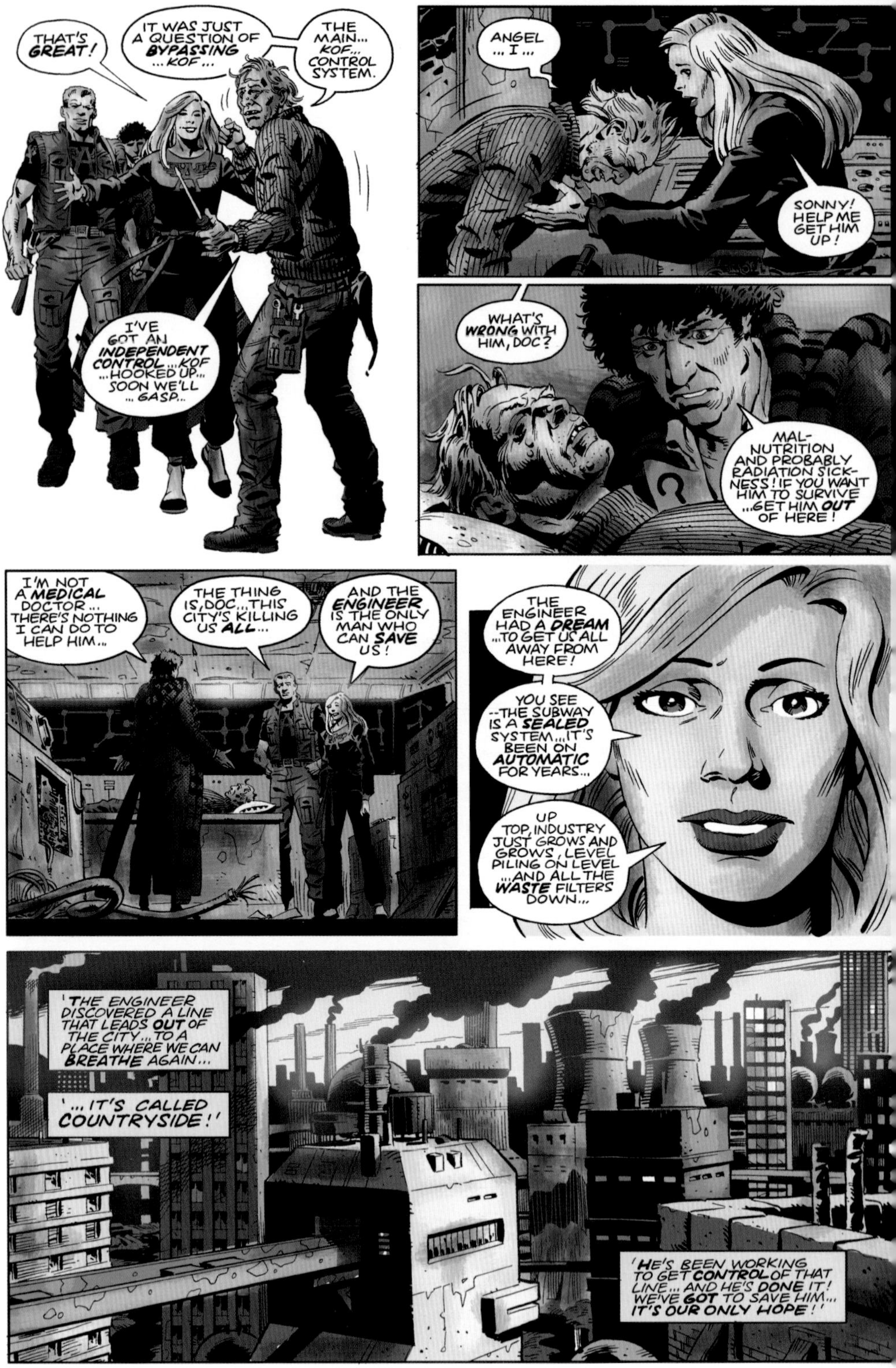
THAT'S GREAT!
IT WAS JUST A QUESTION OF BYPASSING ...KOF...
THE MAIN... KOF... CONTROL SYSTEM.
I'VE GOT AN INDEPENDENT CONTROL...KOF ...HOOKED UP... SOON WE'LL ...GASP...
ANGEL ...I...
SONNY! HELP ME GET HIM UP!
WHAT'S WRONG WITH HIM, DOC?
MAL-NUTRITION AND PROBABLY RADIATION SICKNESS! IF YOU WANT HIM TO SURVIVE ...GET HIM OUT OF HERE!
I'M NOT A MEDICAL DOCTOR... THERE'S NOTHING I CAN DO TO HELP HIM...
THE THING IS, DOC... THIS CITY'S KILLING US ALL...
AND THE ENGINEER IS THE ONLY MAN WHO CAN SAVE US!
THE ENGINEER HAD A DREAM ...TO GET US ALL AWAY FROM HERE!
YOU SEE --THE SUBWAY IS A SEALED SYSTEM... IT'S BEEN ON AUTOMATIC FOR YEARS...
UP TOP, INDUSTRY JUST GROWS AND GROWS, LEVEL PILING ON LEVEL ...AND ALL THE WASTE FILTERS DOWN...
'THE ENGINEER DISCOVERED A LINE THAT LEADS OUT OF THE CITY... TO A PLACE WHERE WE CAN BREATHE AGAIN...
'...IT'S CALLED COUNTRYSIDE!'
'HE'S BEEN WORKING TO GET CONTROL OF THAT LINE... AND HE'S DONE IT! WE'VE GOT TO SAVE HIM... IT'S OUR ONLY HOPE!'

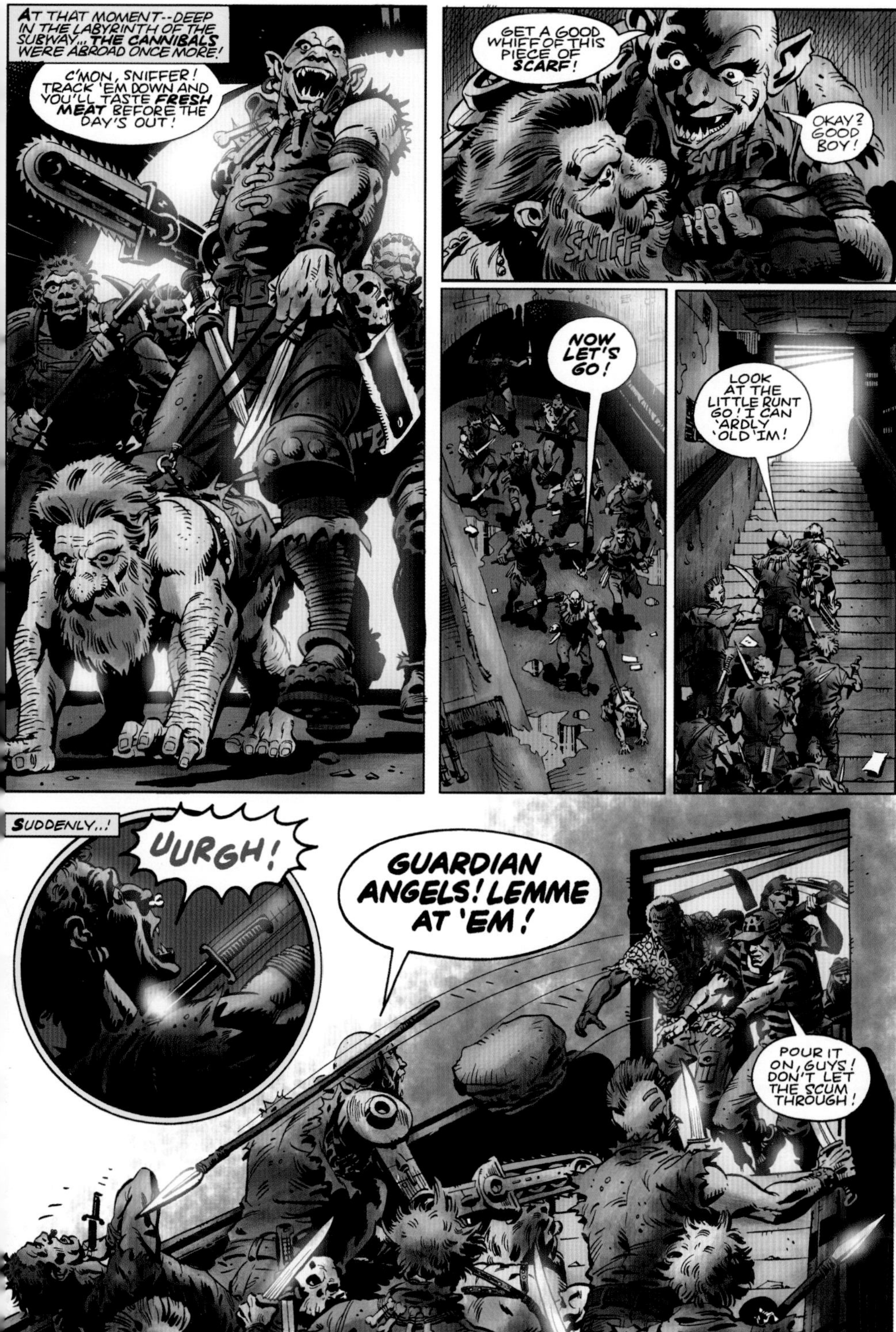
AT THAT MOMENT--DEEP IN THE LABYRINTH OF THE SUBWAY... THE CANNIBALS WERE ABROAD ONCE MORE!
C'MON, SNIFFER! TRACK 'EM DOWN AND YOU'LL TASTE FRESH MEAT BEFORE THE DAY'S OUT!
GET A GOOD WHIFF OF THIS PIECE OF SCARF!
SNIFF
SNIFF
OKAY? GOOD BOY!
NOW LET'S GO!
LOOK AT THE LITTLE RUNT GO! I CAN 'ARDLY 'OLD 'IM!
SUDDENLY..!
UURGH!
GUARDIAN ANGELS! LEMME AT 'EM!
POUR IT ON, GUYS! DON'T LET THE SCUM THROUGH!

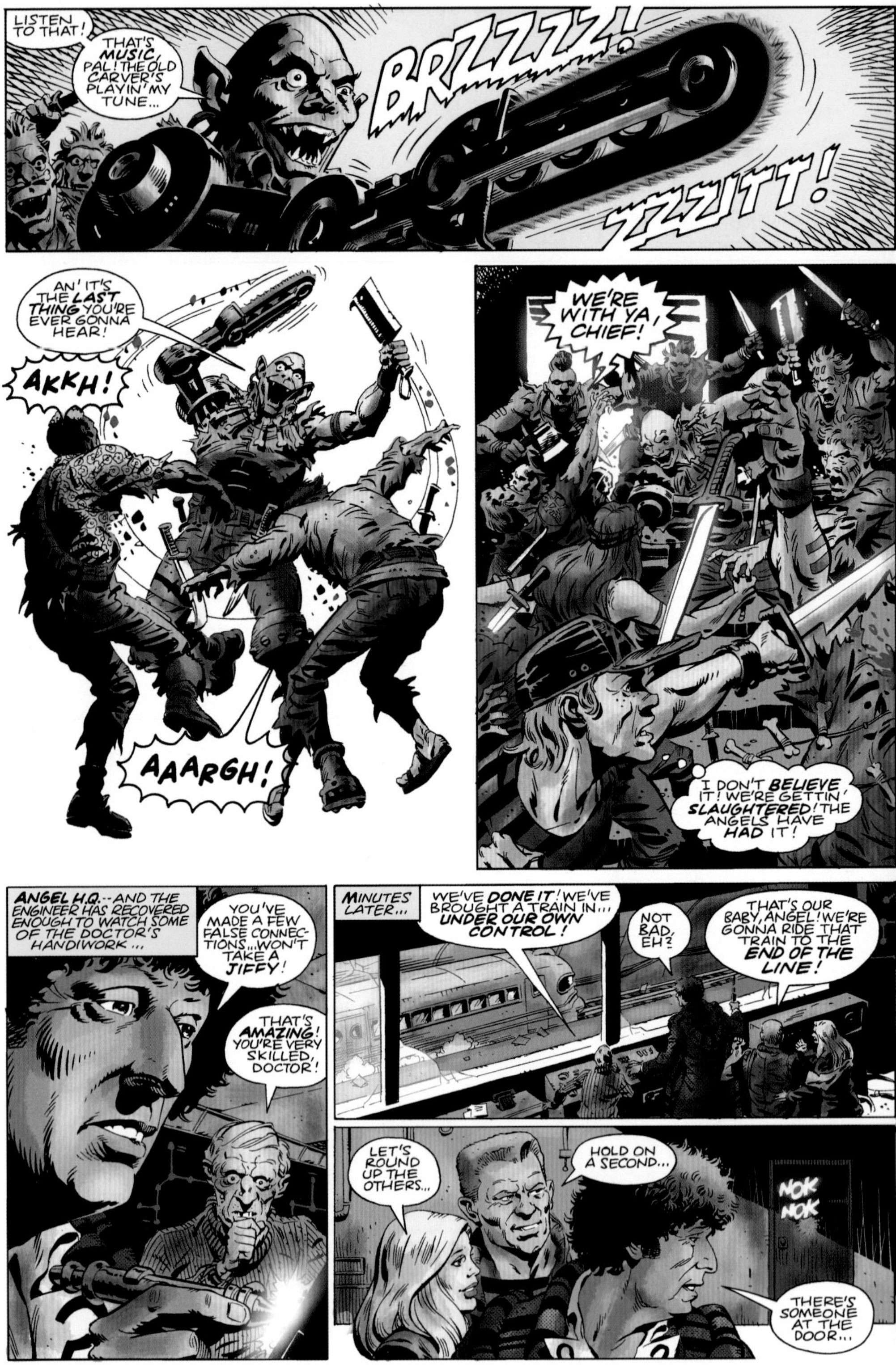
LISTEN TO THAT!
THAT'S MUSIC, PAL! THE OLD CARVER'S PLAYIN' MY TUNE...
BRZZZZZ!
ZZUTTT!
AN' IT'S THE LAST THING YOU'RE EVER GONNA HEAR!
AKKH!
AAARGH!
WE'RE WITH YA, CHIEF!
I DON'T BELIEVE IT! WE'RE GETTIN' SLAUGHTERED! THE ANGELS HAVE HAD IT!
ANGEL H.Q.--AND THE ENGINEER HAS RECOVERED ENOUGH TO WATCH SOME OF THE DOCTOR'S HANDIWORK...
YOU'VE MADE A FEW FALSE CONNECTIONS...WON'T TAKE A JIFFY!
THAT'S AMAZING! YOU'RE VERY SKILLED, DOCTOR!
MINUTES LATER...
WE'VE DONE IT! WE'VE BROUGHT A TRAIN IN... UNDER OUR OWN CONTROL!
NOT BAD, EH?
THAT'S OUR BABY, ANGEL! WE'RE GONNA RIDE THAT TRAIN TO THE END OF THE LINE!
LET'S ROUND UP THE OTHERS...
HOLD ON A SECOND...
NOK NOK
THERE'S SOMEONE AT THE DOOR...

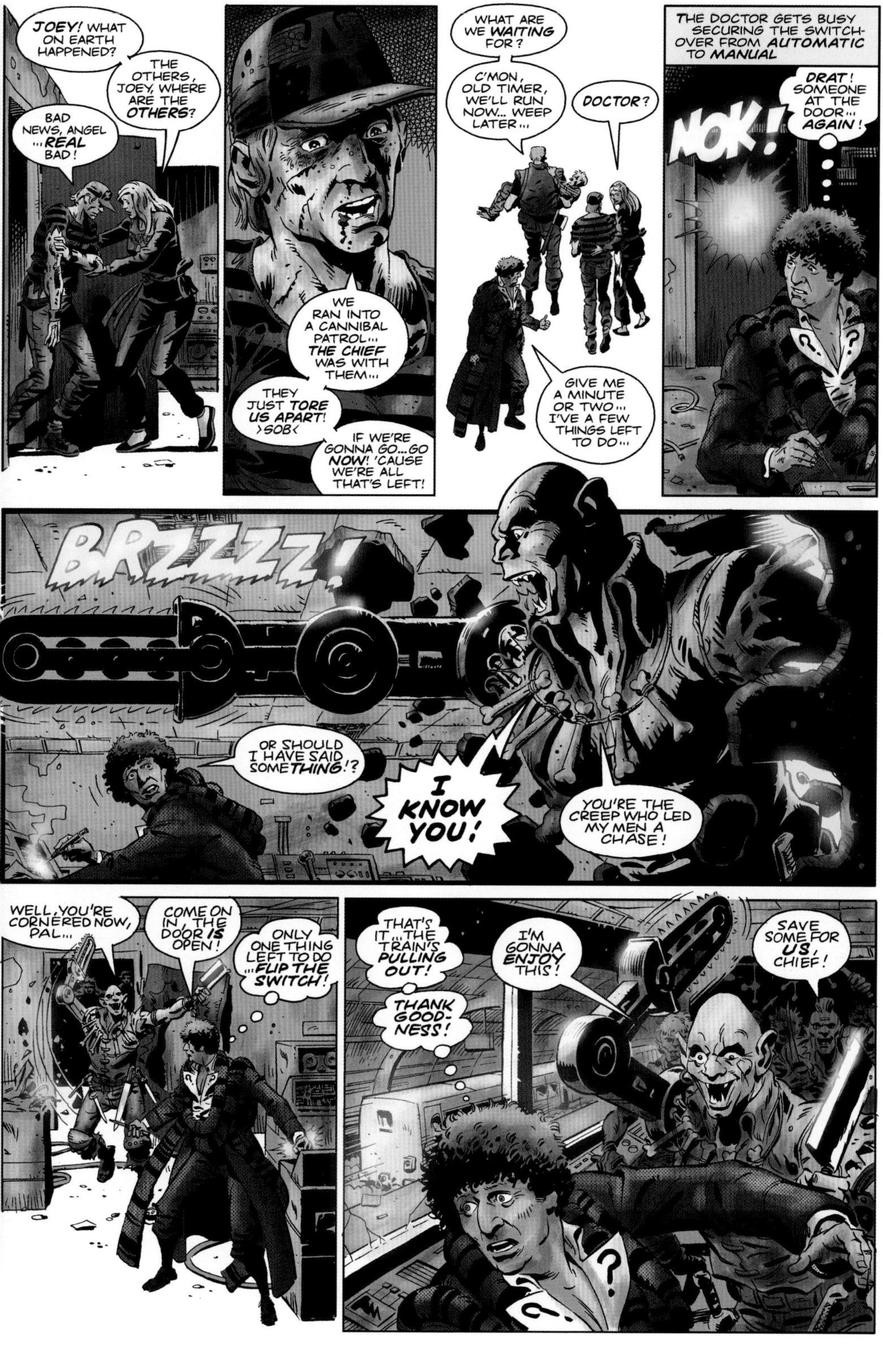
JOEY! WHAT ON EARTH HAPPENED?
THE OTHERS, JOEY, WHERE ARE THE OTHERS?
BAD NEWS, ANGEL ...REAL BAD!
WE RAN INTO A CANNIBAL PATROL... THE CHIEF WAS WITH THEM...
THEY JUST TORE US APART! >SOB<
IF WE'RE GONNA GO...GO NOW! 'CAUSE WE'RE ALL THAT'S LEFT!
WHAT ARE WE WAITING FOR?
C'MON, OLD TIMER, WE'LL RUN NOW... WEEP LATER...
DOCTOR?
GIVE ME A MINUTE OR TWO... I'VE A FEW THINGS LEFT TO DO...
THE DOCTOR GETS BUSY SECURING THE SWITCH-OVER FROM AUTOMATIC TO MANUAL
NOK!
DRAT! SOMEONE AT THE DOOR... AGAIN!
BRZZZ!
OR SHOULD I HAVE SAID SOMETHING!?
I KNOW YOU!
YOU'RE THE CREEP WHO LED MY MEN A CHASE!
WELL, YOU'RE CORNERED NOW, PAL...
COME ON IN, THE DOOR IS OPEN!
ONLY ONE THING LEFT TO DO ...FLIP THE SWITCH!
THAT'S IT...THE TRAIN'S PULLING OUT!
THANK GOOD-NESS!
I'M GONNA ENJOY THIS!
SAVE SOME FOR US, CHIEF!

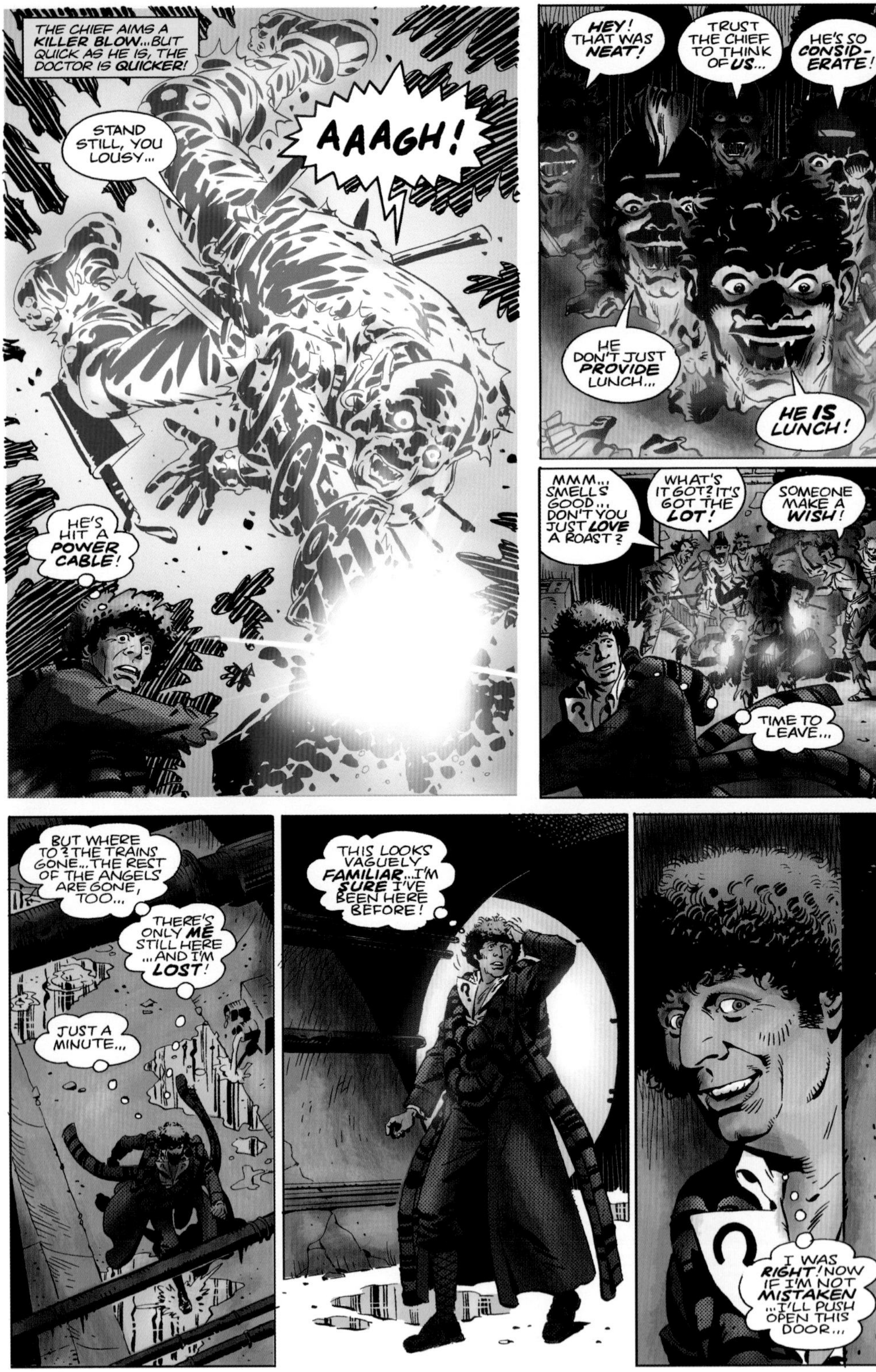
THE CHIEF AIMS A KILLER BLOW...BUT QUICK AS HE IS, THE DOCTOR IS QUICKER!
STAND STILL, YOU LOUSY...
AAAGH!
HE'S HIT A POWER CABLE!
HEY! THAT WAS NEAT!
TRUST THE CHIEF TO THINK OF US...
HE'S SO CONSID-ERATE!
HE DON'T JUST PROVIDE LUNCH...
HE IS LUNCH!
MMM... SMELLS GOOD... DON'T YOU JUST LOVE A ROAST?
WHAT'S IT GOT? IT'S GOT THE LOT!
SOMEONE MAKE A WISH!
TIME TO LEAVE...
BUT WHERE TO? THE TRAINS GONE...THE REST OF THE ANGELS ARE GONE, TOO...
THERE'S ONLY ME STILL HERE ...AND I'M LOST!
JUST A MINUTE...
THIS LOOKS VAGUELY FAMILIAR...I'M SURE I'VE BEEN HERE BEFORE!
I WAS RIGHT! NOW IF I'M NOT MISTAKEN ...I'LL PUSH OPEN THIS DOOR...

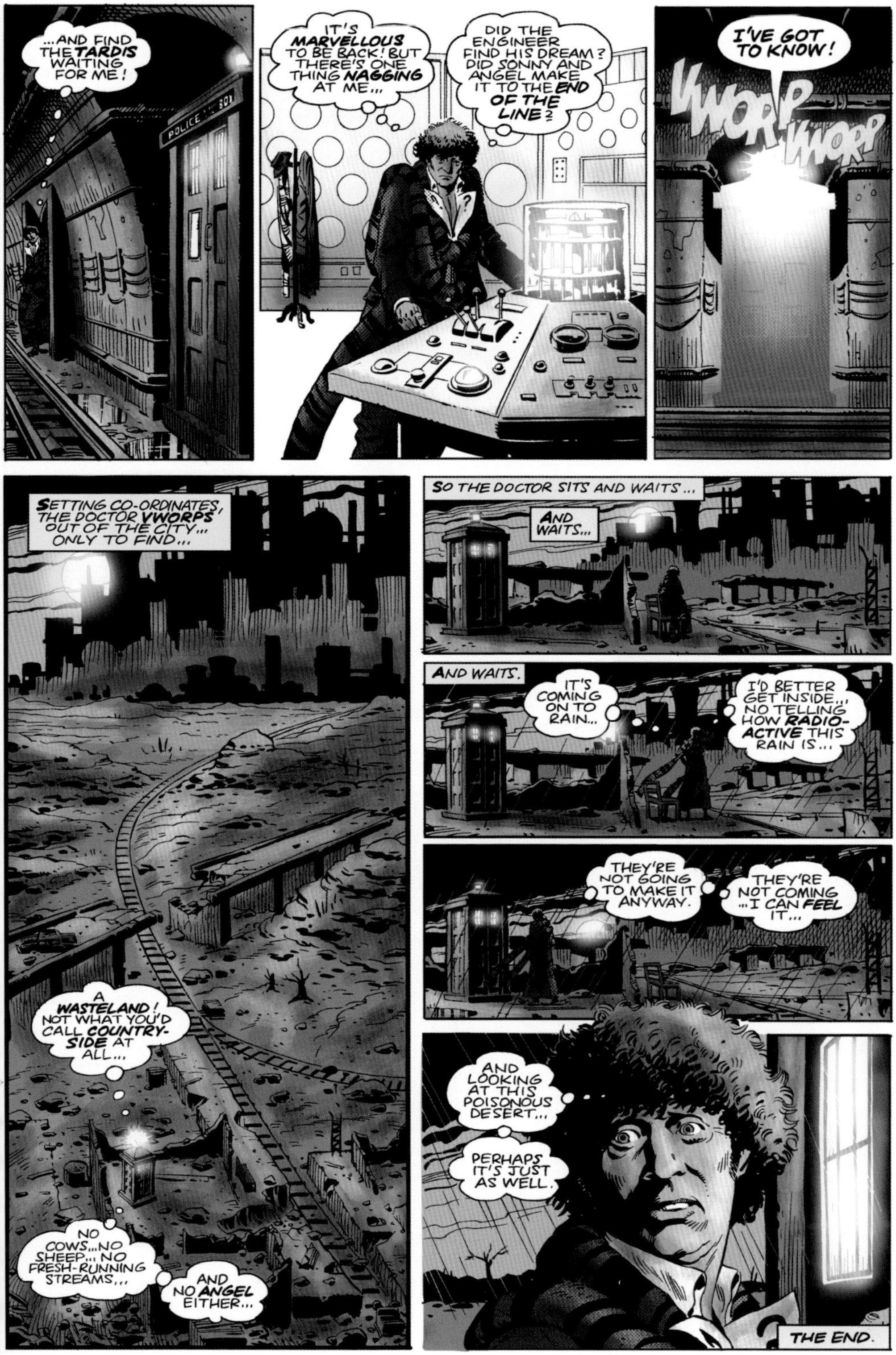
...AND FIND THE TARDIS WAITING FOR ME!
POLICE BOX
IT'S MARVELLOUS TO BE BACK! BUT THERE'S ONE THING NAGGING AT ME...
DID THE ENGINEER FIND HIS DREAM? DID SONNY AND ANGEL MAKE IT TO THE END OF THE LINE?
I'VE GOT TO KNOW!
VWORP VWORP
SETTING CO-ORDINATES, THE DOCTOR 'VWORPS' OUT OF THE CITY... ONLY TO FIND...
A WASTELAND! NOT WHAT YOU'D CALL COUNTRY-SIDE AT ALL...
NO COWS...NO SHEEP... NO FRESH-RUNNING STREAMS...
AND NO ANGEL EITHER...
SO THE DOCTOR SITS AND WAITS...
AND WAITS...
AND WAITS.
IT'S COMING ON TO RAIN...
I'D BETTER GET INSIDE... NO TELLING HOW RADIO-ACTIVE THIS RAIN IS...
THEY'RE NOT GOING TO MAKE IT ANYWAY.
THEY'RE NOT COMING ...I CAN FEEL IT...
AND LOOKING AT THIS POISONOUS DESERT...
PERHAPS IT'S JUST AS WELL.
THE END.

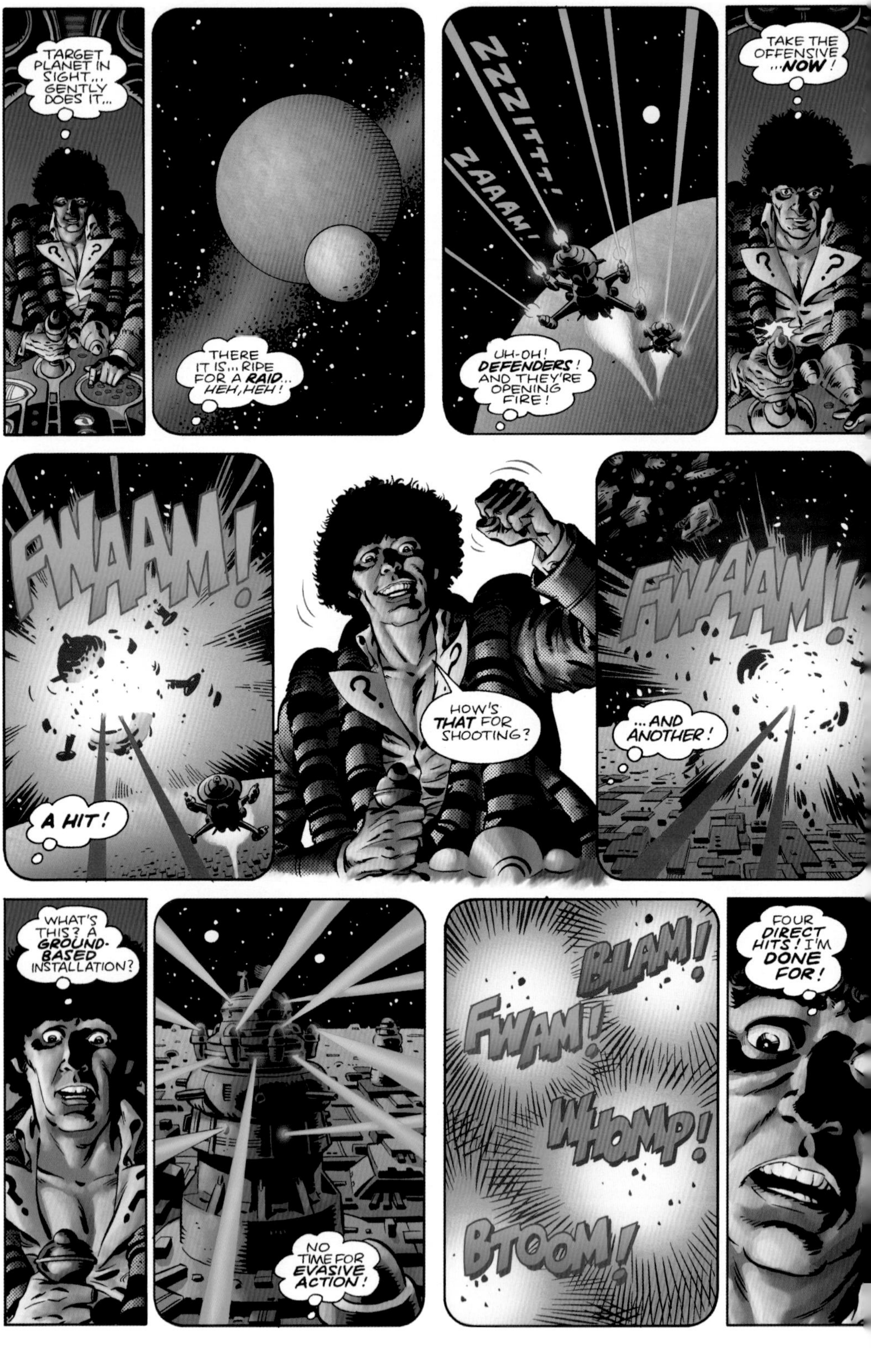
TARGET PLANET IN SIGHT... GENTLY DOES IT...
THERE IT IS... RIPE FOR A RAID... HEH, HEH!
ZZZIITTT!
ZAAAM!
UH-OH! DEFENDERS! AND THEY'RE OPENING FIRE!
TAKE THE OFFENSIVE ...NOW!
FWAAM!
A HIT!
HOW'S THAT FOR SHOOTING?
FWAAM!
...AND ANOTHER!
WHAT'S THIS? A GROUND-BASED INSTALLATION?
NO TIME FOR EVASIVE ACTION!
BLAM!
FWAM!
WHOMP!
BTOOM!
FOUR DIRECT HITS! I'M DONE FOR!

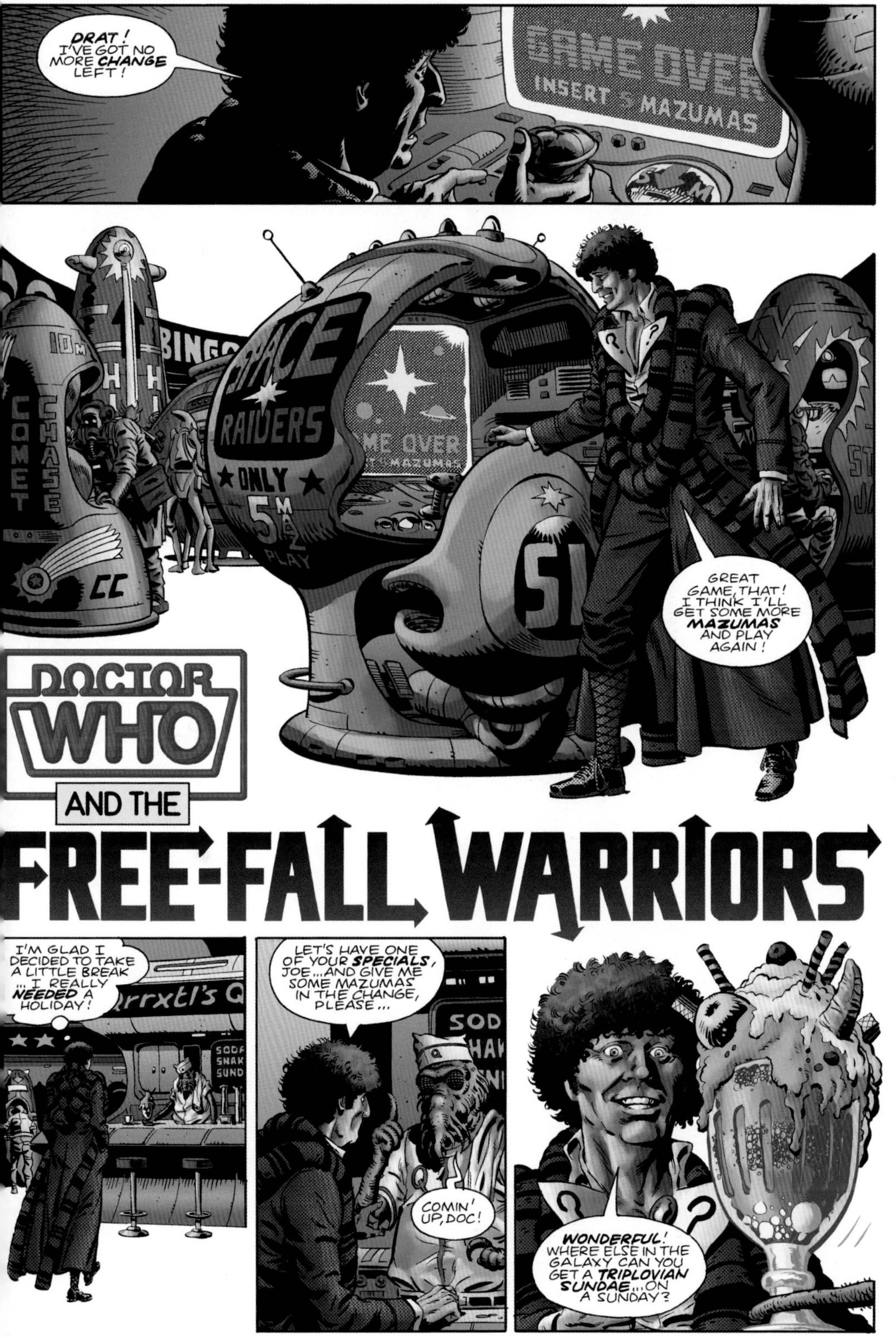
DRAT! I'VE GOT NO MORE CHANGE LEFT!
GAME OVER
INSERT 5 MAZUMAS
SPACE RAIDERS
ONLY 5 MAZ PLAY
COMET CHASE
BINGO
GREAT GAME, THAT! I THINK I'LL GET SOME MORE MAZUMAS AND PLAY AGAIN!
DOCTOR WHO
AND THE
FREE-FALL WARRIORS
I'M GLAD I DECIDED TO TAKE A LITTLE BREAK ... I REALLY NEEDED A HOLIDAY!
Rrrxtl's Q
LET'S HAVE ONE OF YOUR SPECIALS, JOE... AND GIVE ME SOME MAZUMAS IN THE CHANGE, PLEASE...
COMIN' UP, DOC!
WONDERFUL! WHERE ELSE IN THE GALAXY CAN YOU GET A TRIPLOVIAN SUNDAE... ON A SUNDAY?

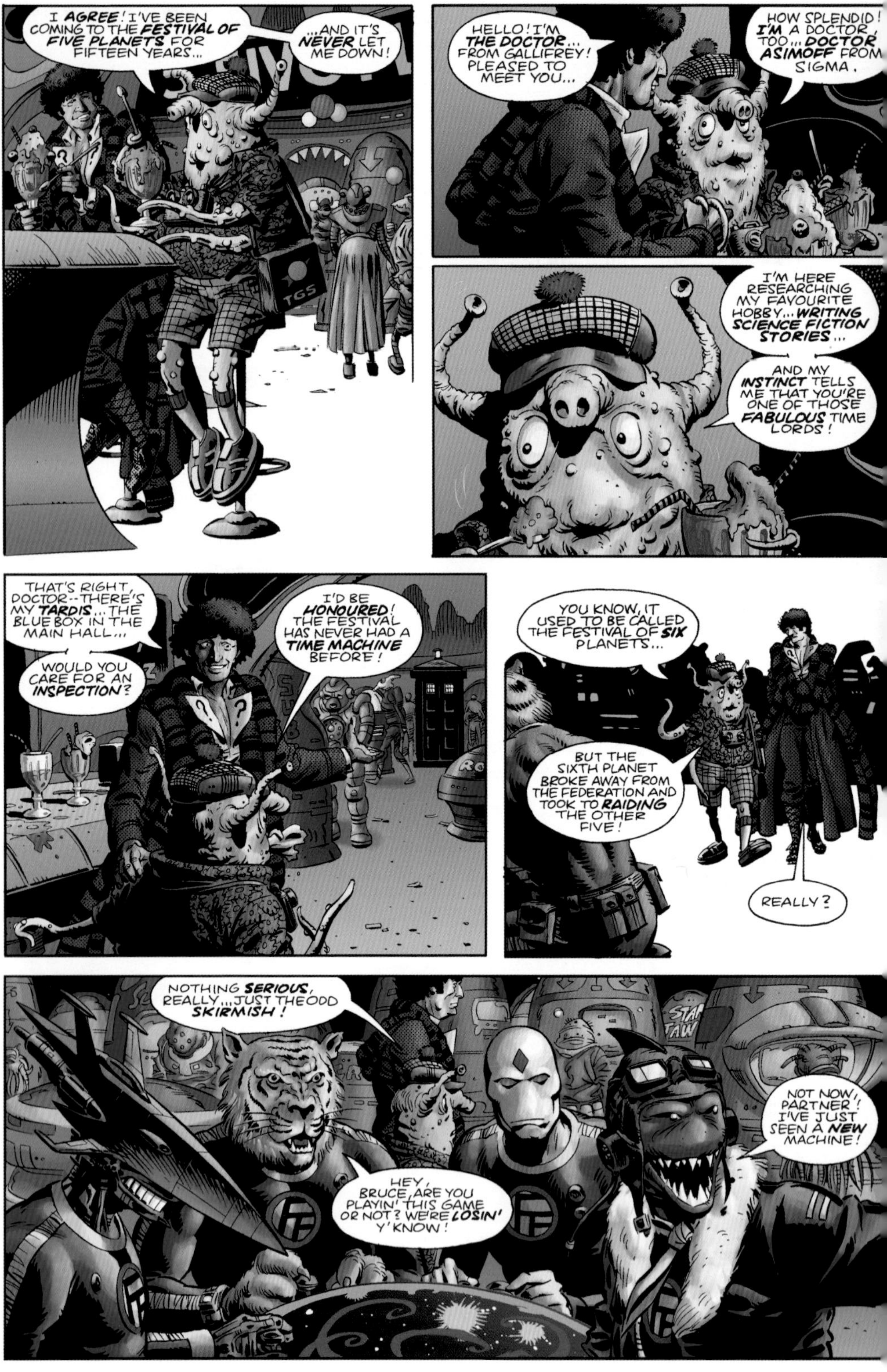
I AGREE! I'VE BEEN COMING TO THE FESTIVAL OF FIVE PLANETS FOR FIFTEEN YEARS...
...AND IT'S NEVER LET ME DOWN!
TGS
HELLO! I'M THE DOCTOR... FROM GALLIFREY! PLEASED TO MEET YOU...
HOW SPLENDID! I'M A DOCTOR, TOO... DOCTOR ASIMOFF FROM SIGMA.
I'M HERE RESEARCHING MY FAVOURITE HOBBY... WRITING SCIENCE FICTION STORIES...
AND MY INSTINCT TELLS ME THAT YOU'RE ONE OF THOSE FABULOUS TIME LORDS!
THAT'S RIGHT, DOCTOR--THERE'S MY TARDIS... THE BLUE BOX IN THE MAIN HALL...
WOULD YOU CARE FOR AN INSPECTION?
I'D BE HONOURED! THE FESTIVAL HAS NEVER HAD A TIME MACHINE BEFORE!
YOU KNOW, IT USED TO BE CALLED THE FESTIVAL OF SIX PLANETS...
BUT THE SIXTH PLANET BROKE AWAY FROM THE FEDERATION AND TOOK TO RAIDING THE OTHER FIVE!
REALLY?
NOTHING SERIOUS, REALLY... JUST THE ODD SKIRMISH!
HEY, BRUCE, ARE YOU PLAYIN' THIS GAME OR NOT? WE'RE LOSIN' Y'KNOW!
NOT NOW, PARTNER! I'VE JUST SEEN A NEW MACHINE!

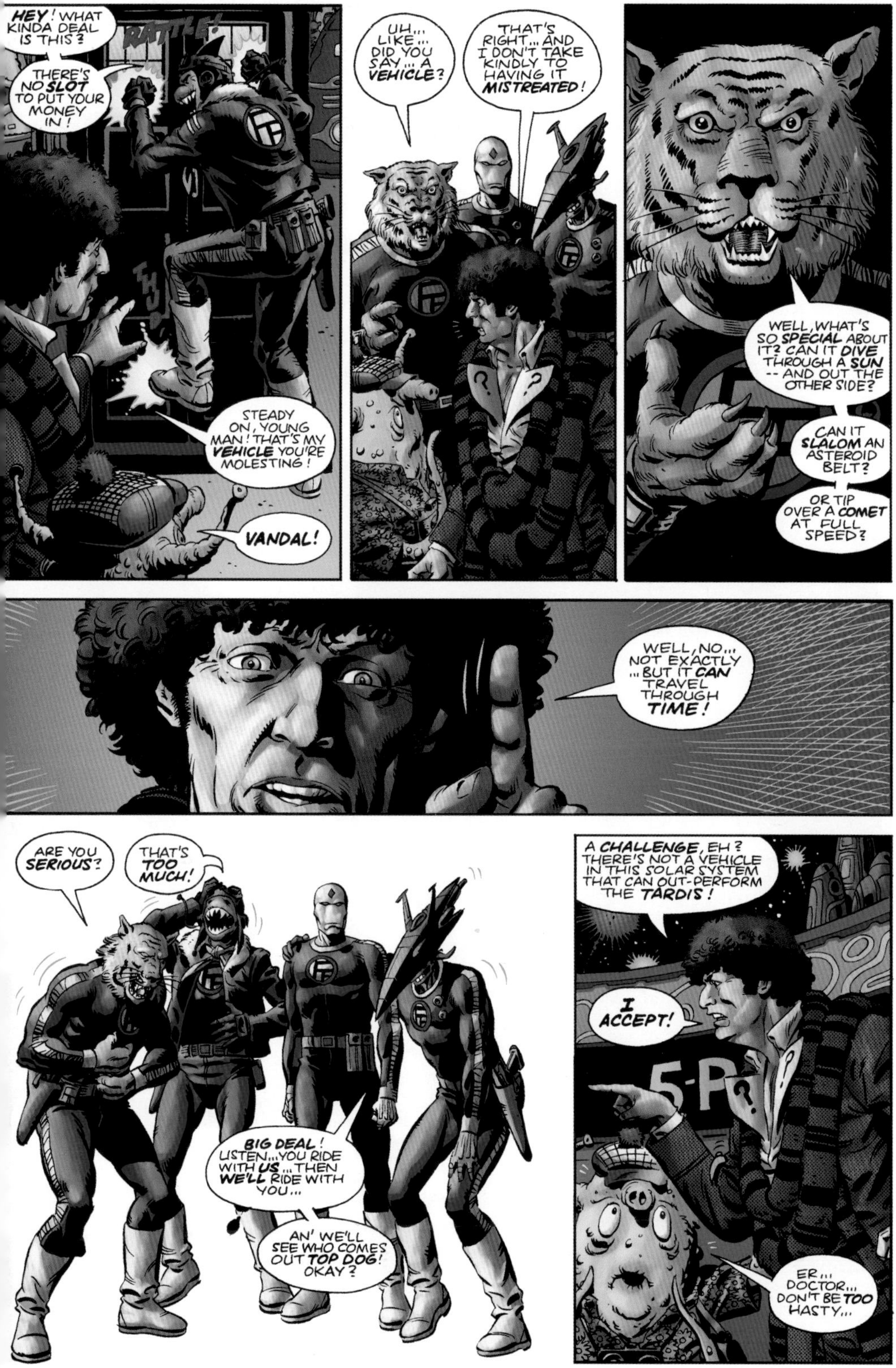
RATTLE!
HEY! WHAT KINDA DEAL IS THIS?
THERE'S NO SLOT TO PUT YOUR MONEY IN!
STEADY ON, YOUNG MAN! THAT'S MY VEHICLE YOU'RE MOLESTING!
VANDAL!
UH... LIKE... DID YOU SAY... A VEHICLE?
THAT'S RIGHT... AND I DON'T TAKE KINDLY TO HAVING IT MISTREATED!
WELL, WHAT'S SO SPECIAL ABOUT IT? CAN IT DIVE THROUGH A SUN -- AND OUT THE OTHER SIDE?
CAN IT SLALOM AN ASTEROID BELT?
OR TIP OVER A COMET AT FULL SPEED?
WELL, NO... NOT EXACTLY ...BUT IT CAN TRAVEL THROUGH TIME!
ARE YOU SERIOUS?
THAT'S TOO MUCH!
BIG DEAL! LISTEN... YOU RIDE WITH US... THEN WE'LL RIDE WITH YOU...
AN' WE'LL SEE WHO COMES OUT TOP DOG! OKAY?
A CHALLENGE, EH? THERE'S NOT A VEHICLE IN THIS SOLAR SYSTEM THAT CAN OUT-PERFORM THE TARDIS!
I ACCEPT!
5-P
ER... DOCTOR... DON'T BE TOO HASTY...

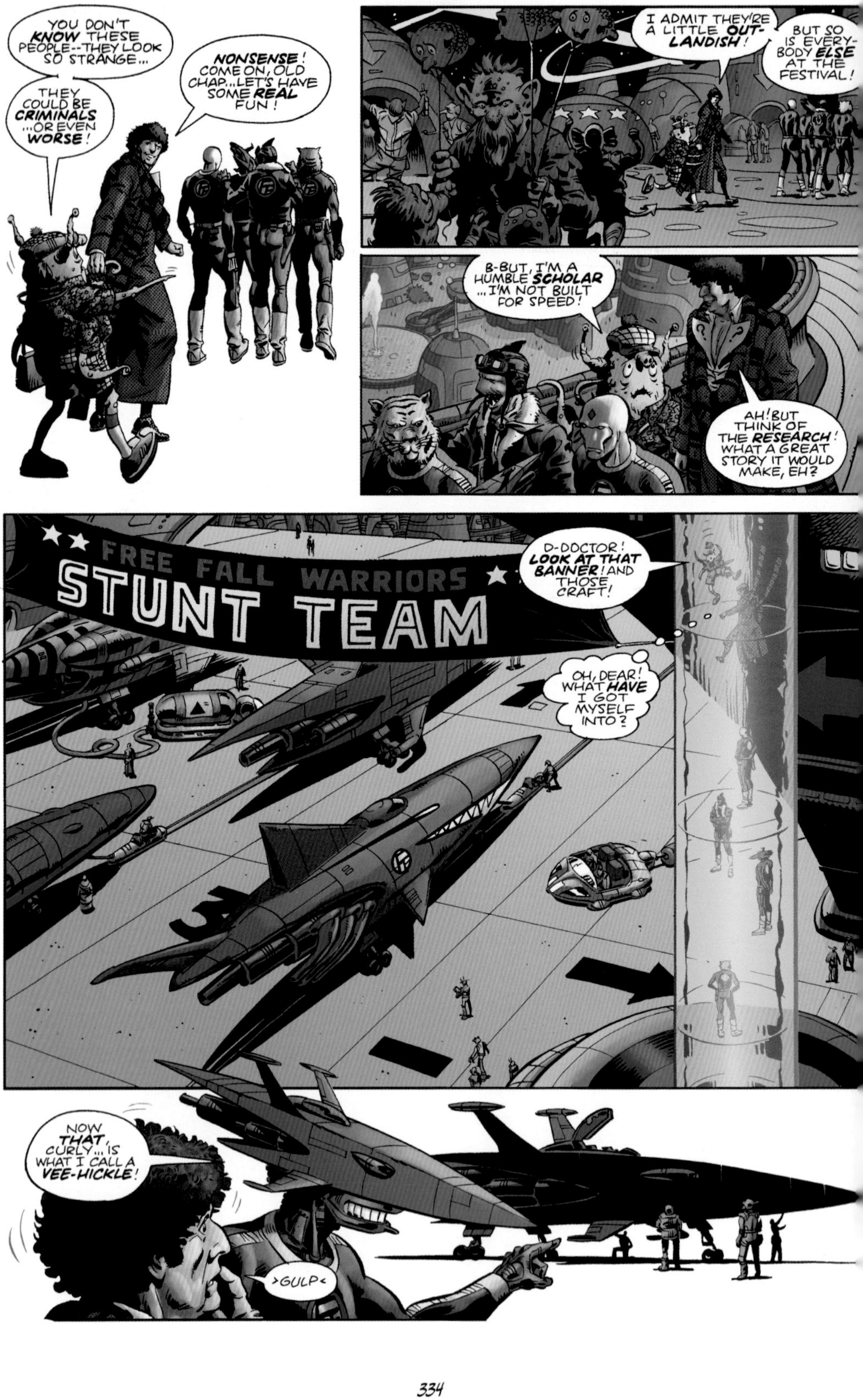

YOU DON'T KNOW THESE PEOPLE--THEY LOOK SO STRANGE...
THEY COULD BE CRIMINALS ...OR EVEN WORSE!
NONSENSE! COME ON, OLD CHAP...LET'S HAVE SOME REAL FUN!
I ADMIT THEY'RE A LITTLE OUT-LANDISH!
BUT SO IS EVERY-BODY ELSE AT THE FESTIVAL!
B-BUT, I'M A HUMBLE SCHOLAR ...I'M NOT BUILT FOR SPEED!
AH! BUT THINK OF THE RESEARCH! WHAT A GREAT STORY IT WOULD MAKE, EH?
FREE FALL WARRIORS
STUNT TEAM
D-DOCTOR! LOOK AT THAT BANNER! AND THOSE CRAFT!
OH, DEAR! WHAT HAVE I GOT MYSELF INTO?
NOW THAT, CURLY... IS WHAT I CALL A VEE-HICKLE!
>GULP<

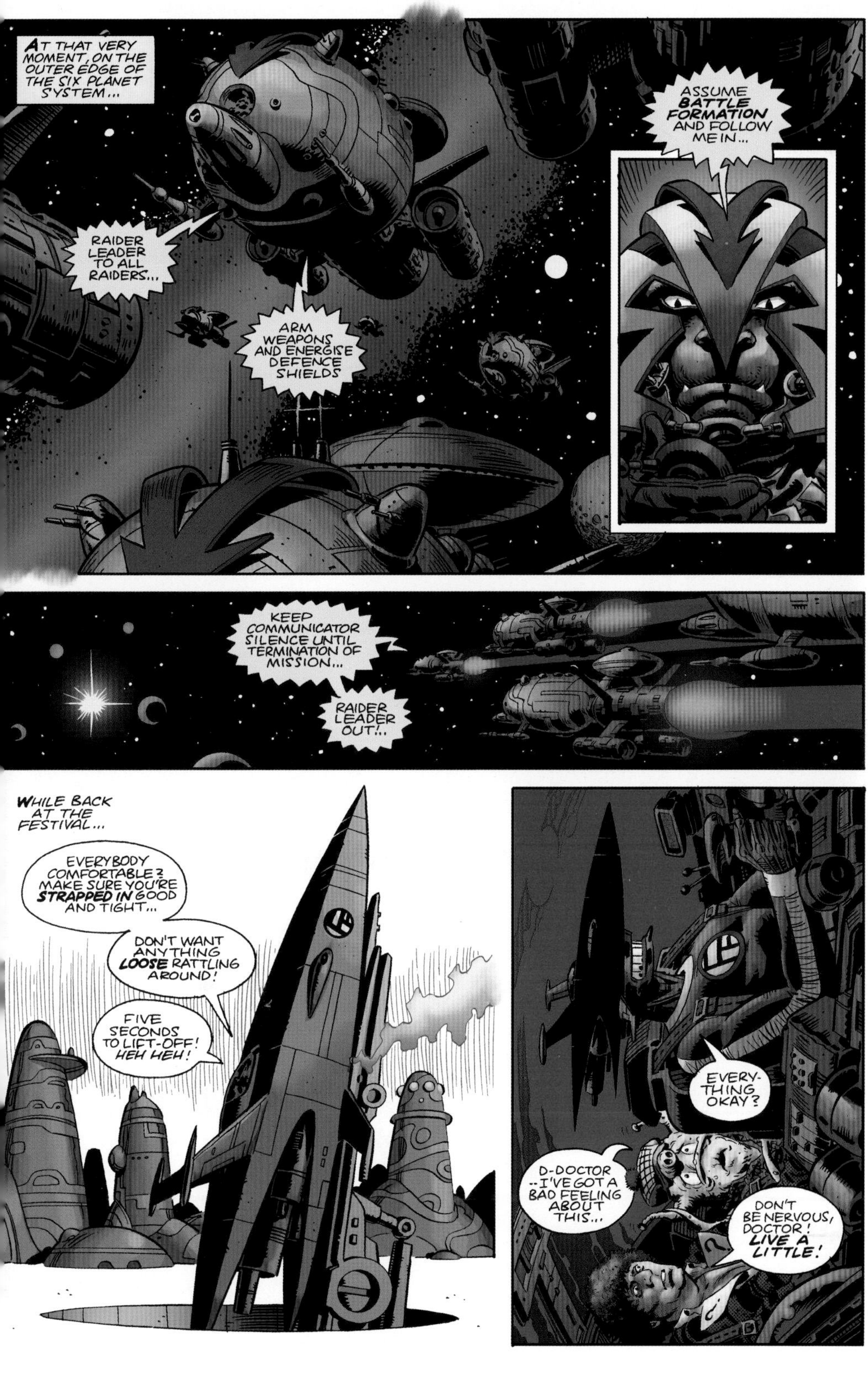
AT THAT VERY MOMENT, ON THE OUTER EDGE OF THE SIX PLANET SYSTEM...
RAIDER LEADER TO ALL RAIDERS...
ARM WEAPONS AND ENERGISE DEFENCE SHIELDS
ASSUME BATTLE FORMATION AND FOLLOW ME IN...
KEEP COMMUNICATOR SILENCE UNTIL TERMINATION OF MISSION...
RAIDER LEADER OUT!..
WHILE BACK AT THE FESTIVAL...
EVERYBODY COMFORTABLE? MAKE SURE YOU'RE STRAPPED IN GOOD AND TIGHT...
DON'T WANT ANYTHING LOOSE RATTLING AROUND!
FIVE SECONDS TO LIFT-OFF! HEH HEH!
EVERY-THING OKAY?
D-DOCTOR ..I'VE GOT A BAD FEELING ABOUT THIS...
DON'T BE NERVOUS, DOCTOR! LIVE A LITTLE!

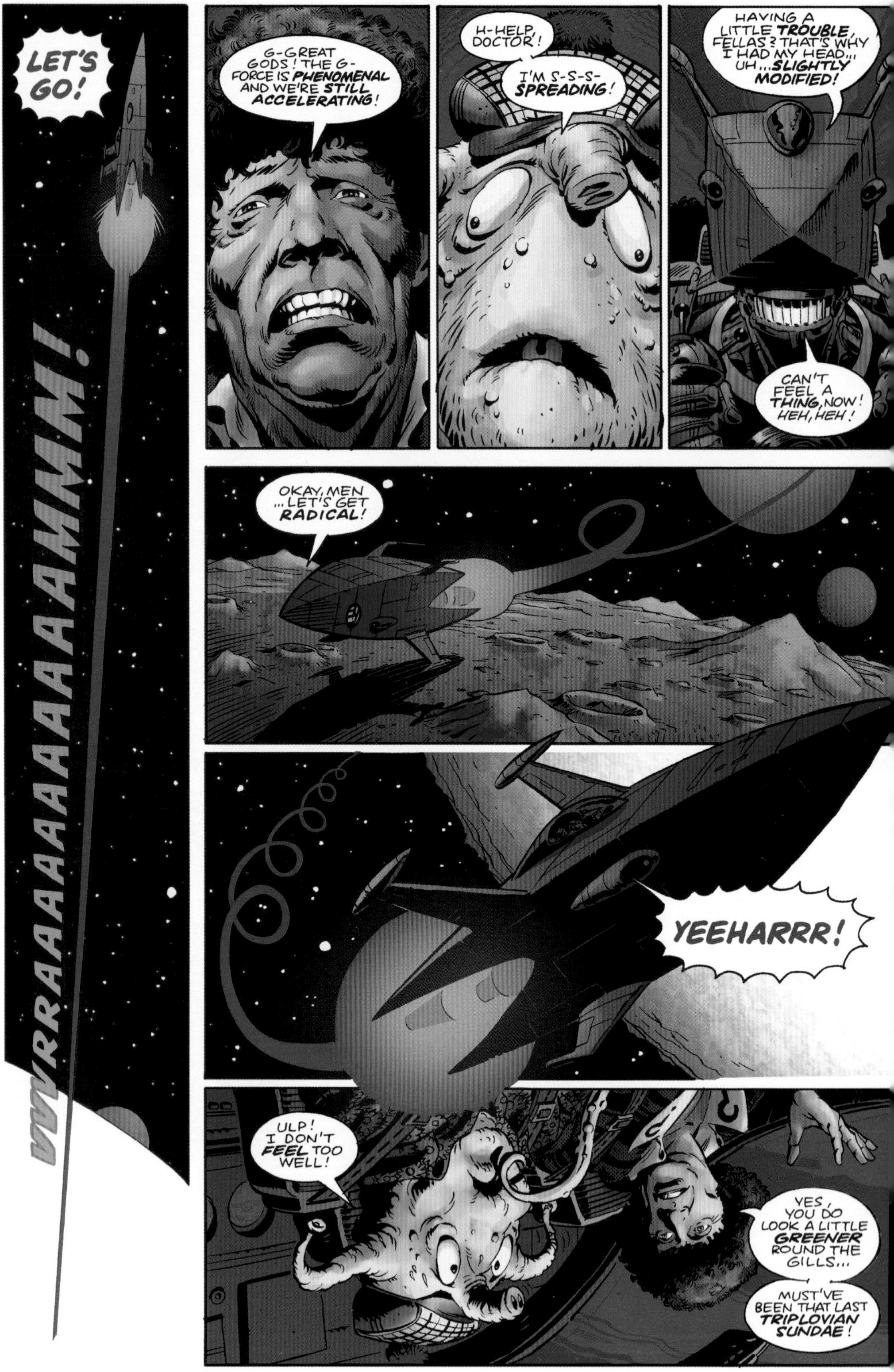

LET'S GO!
VVVRRAAAAAAAAAAAMMM!
G-GREAT GODS! THE G-FORCE IS PHENOMENAL AND WE'RE STILL ACCELERATING!
H-HELP, DOCTOR!
I'M S-S-S-SPREADING!
HAVING A LITTLE TROUBLE, FELLAS? THAT'S WHY I HAD MY HEAD... UH...SLIGHTLY MODIFIED!
CAN'T FEEL A THING, NOW! HEH, HEH!
OKAY, MEN ...LET'S GET RADICAL!
YEEHARRR!
ULP! I DON'T FEEL TOO WELL!
YES, YOU DO LOOK A LITTLE GREENER ROUND THE GILLS...
MUST'VE BEEN THAT LAST TRIPLOVIAN SUNDAE!

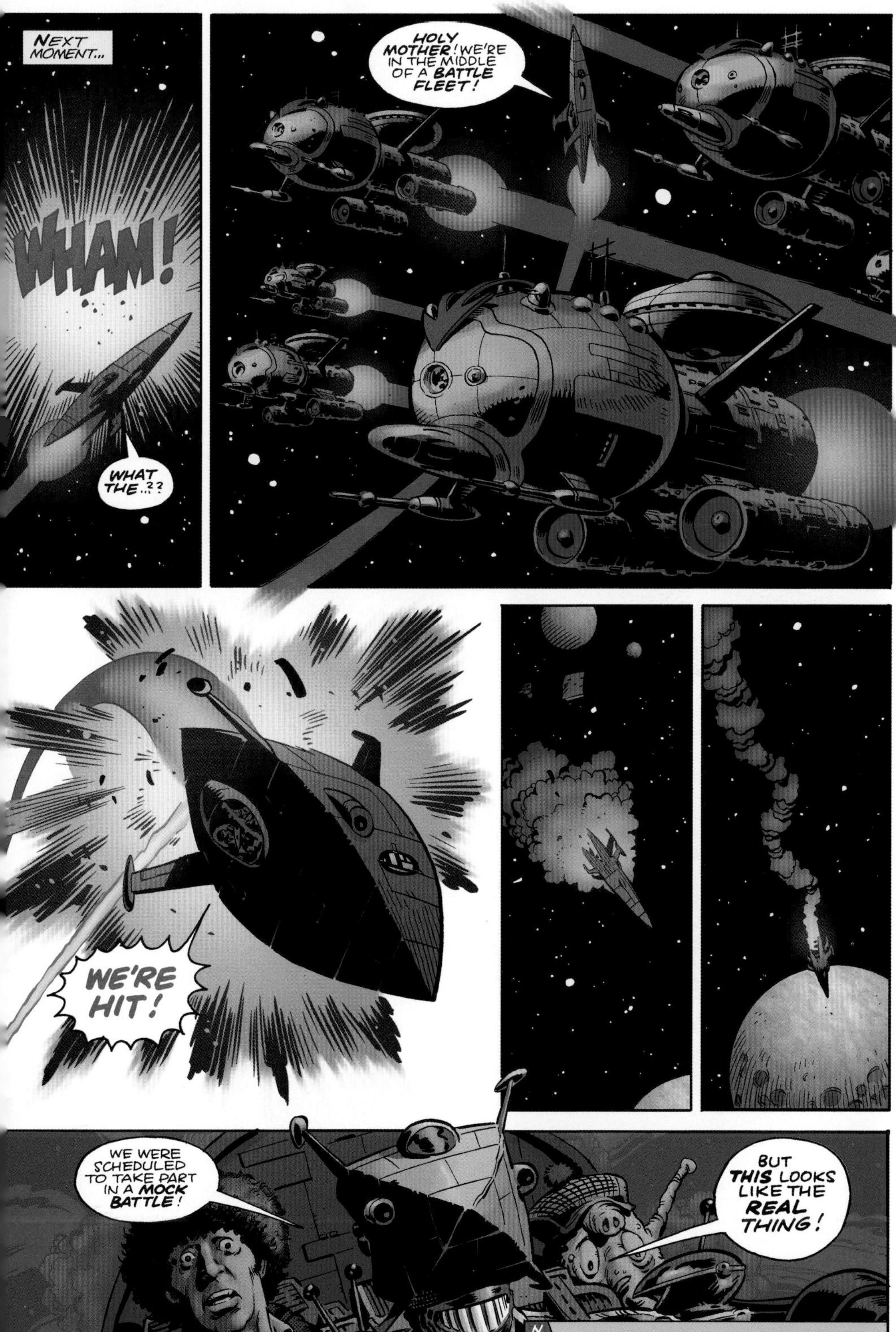
NEXT MOMENT...
WHAM!
WHAT THE...??
HOLY MOTHER! WE'RE IN THE MIDDLE OF A BATTLE FLEET!
WE'RE HIT!
WE WERE SCHEDULED TO TAKE PART IN A MOCK BATTLE!
BUT THIS LOOKS LIKE THE REAL THING!
NEXT
WARRIORS ASSEMBLE!

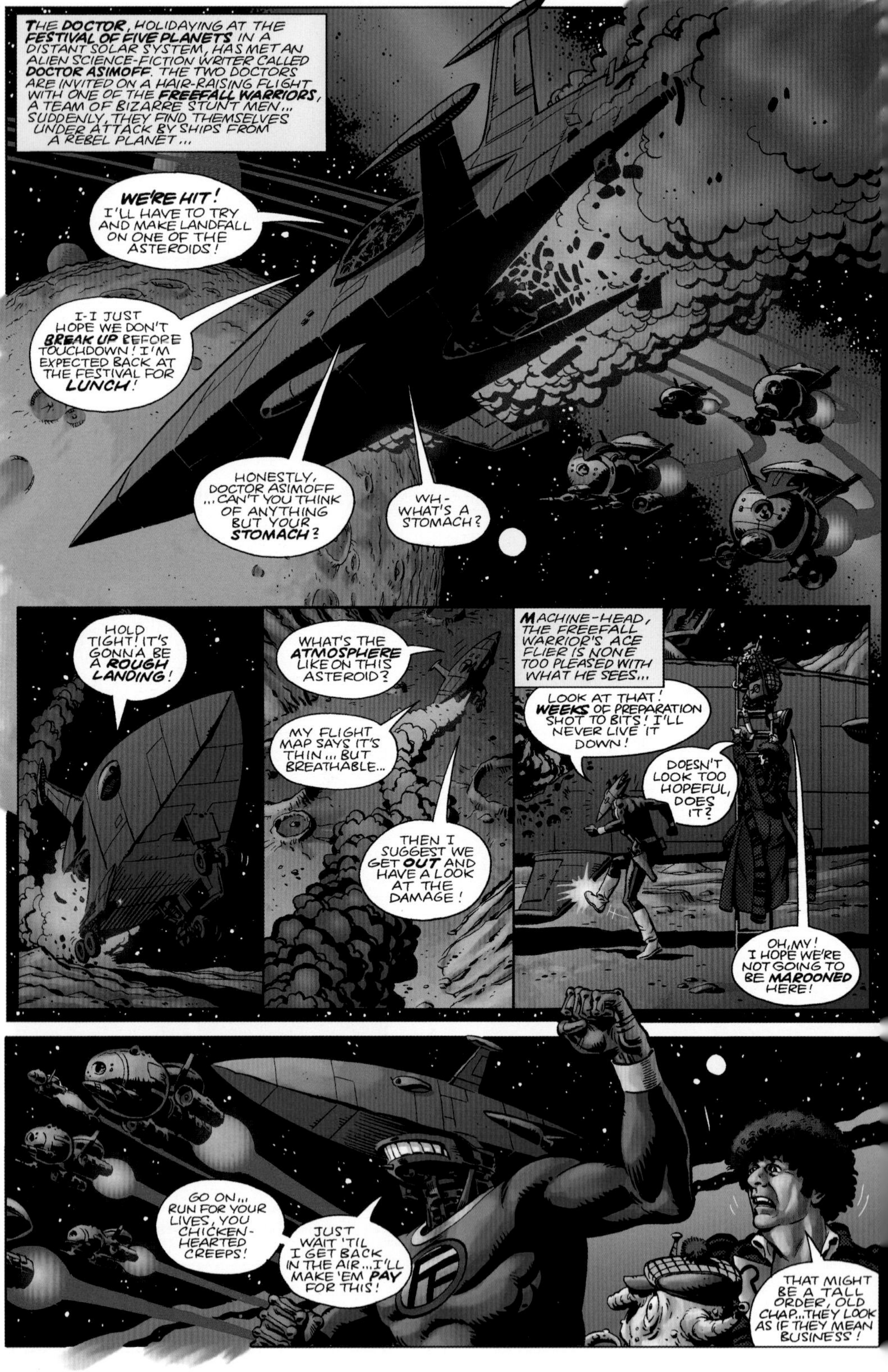
THE DOCTOR, HOLIDAYING AT THE FESTIVAL OF FIVE PLANETS IN A DISTANT SOLAR SYSTEM, HAS MET AN ALIEN SCIENCE-FICTION WRITER CALLED DOCTOR ASIMOFF. THE TWO DOCTORS ARE INVITED ON A HAIR-RAISING FLIGHT WITH ONE OF THE FREEFALL WARRIORS, A TEAM OF BIZARRE STUNT MEN... SUDDENLY, THEY FIND THEMSELVES UNDER ATTACK BY SHIPS FROM A REBEL PLANET...
WE'RE HIT! I'LL HAVE TO TRY AND MAKE LANDFALL ON ONE OF THE ASTEROIDS!
I-I JUST HOPE WE DON'T BREAK UP BEFORE TOUCHDOWN! I'M EXPECTED BACK AT THE FESTIVAL FOR LUNCH!
HONESTLY, DOCTOR ASIMOFF ...CAN'T YOU THINK OF ANYTHING BUT YOUR STOMACH?
WH- WHAT'S A STOMACH?
HOLD TIGHT! IT'S GONNA BE A ROUGH LANDING!
WHAT'S THE ATMOSPHERE LIKE ON THIS ASTEROID?
MY FLIGHT MAP SAYS IT'S THIN... BUT BREATHABLE...
THEN I SUGGEST WE GET OUT AND HAVE A LOOK AT THE DAMAGE!
MACHINE-HEAD, THE FREEFALL WARRIOR'S ACE FLIER IS NONE TOO PLEASED WITH WHAT HE SEES...
LOOK AT THAT! WEEKS OF PREPARATION SHOT TO BITS! I'LL NEVER LIVE IT DOWN!
DOESN'T LOOK TOO HOPEFUL, DOES IT?
OH, MY! I HOPE WE'RE NOT GOING TO BE MAROONED HERE!
GO ON... RUN FOR YOUR LIVES, YOU CHICKEN-HEARTED CREEPS!
JUST WAIT 'TIL I GET BACK IN THE AIR... I'LL MAKE 'EM PAY FOR THIS!
THAT MIGHT BE A TALL ORDER, OLD CHAP... THEY LOOK AS IF THEY MEAN BUSINESS!

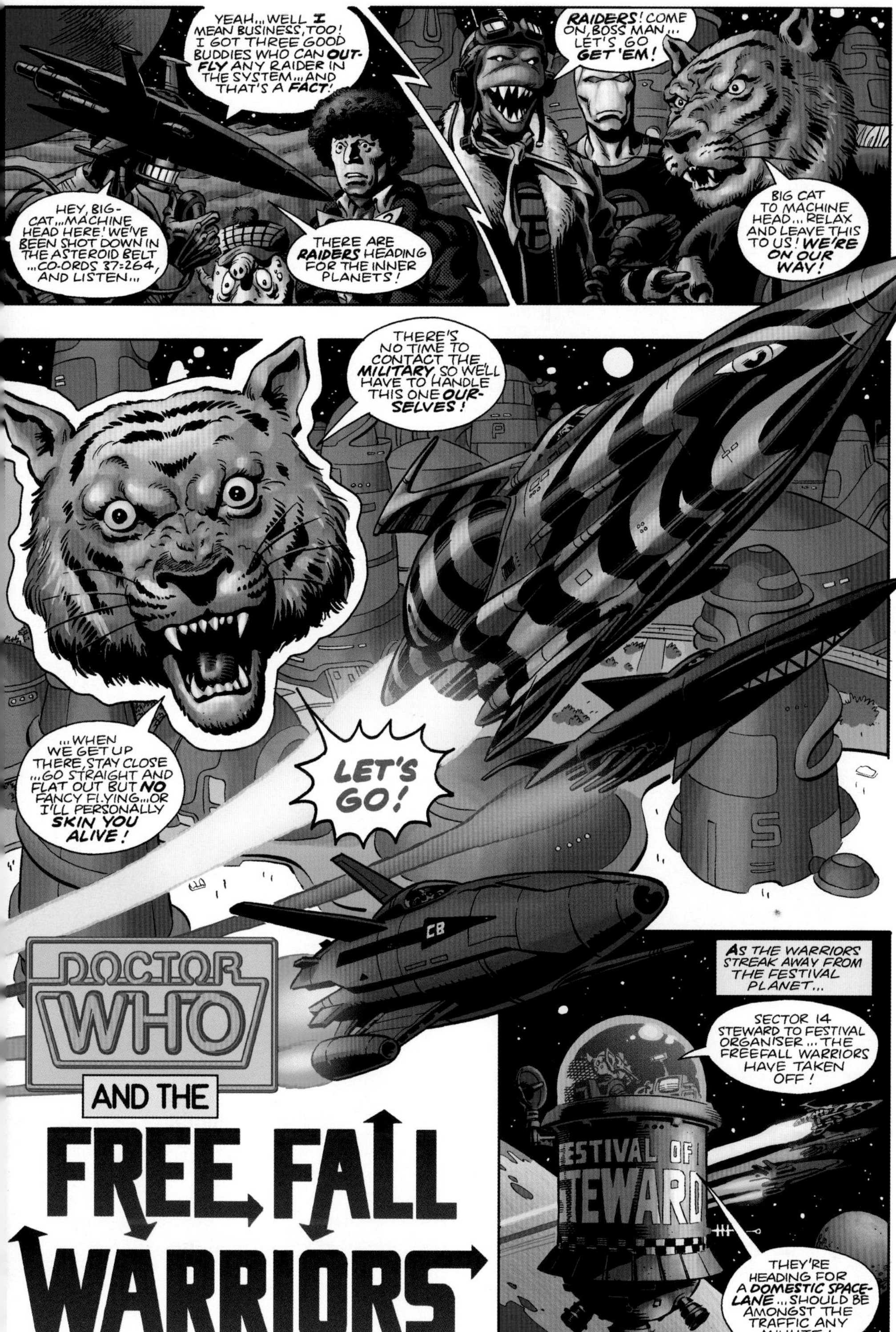
YEAH... WELL I MEAN BUSINESS, TOO! I GOT THREE GOOD BUDDIES WHO CAN OUT-FLY ANY RAIDER IN THE SYSTEM... AND THAT'S A FACT!
HEY, BIG-CAT... MACHINE HEAD HERE! WE'VE BEEN SHOT DOWN IN THE ASTEROID BELT ...CO-ORDS 37-264, AND LISTEN...
THERE ARE RAIDERS HEADING FOR THE INNER PLANETS!
RAIDERS! COME ON, BOSS MAN... LET'S GO GET 'EM!
BIG CAT TO MACHINE HEAD... RELAX AND LEAVE THIS TO US! WE'RE ON OUR WAY!
THERE'S NO TIME TO CONTACT THE MILITARY, SO WE'LL HAVE TO HANDLE THIS ONE OURSELVES!
...WHEN WE GET UP THERE, STAY CLOSE ...GO STRAIGHT AND FLAT OUT BUT NO FANCY FLYING...OR I'LL PERSONALLY SKIN YOU ALIVE!
LET'S GO!
CB
DOCTOR WHO
AND THE
FREE FALL WARRIORS
AS THE WARRIORS STREAK AWAY FROM THE FESTIVAL PLANET...
SECTOR 14 STEWARD TO FESTIVAL ORGANISER... THE FREEFALL WARRIORS HAVE TAKEN OFF!
FESTIVAL OF
STEWARD
THEY'RE HEADING FOR A DOMESTIC SPACE-LANE... SHOULD BE AMONGST THE TRAFFIC ANY MINUTE!

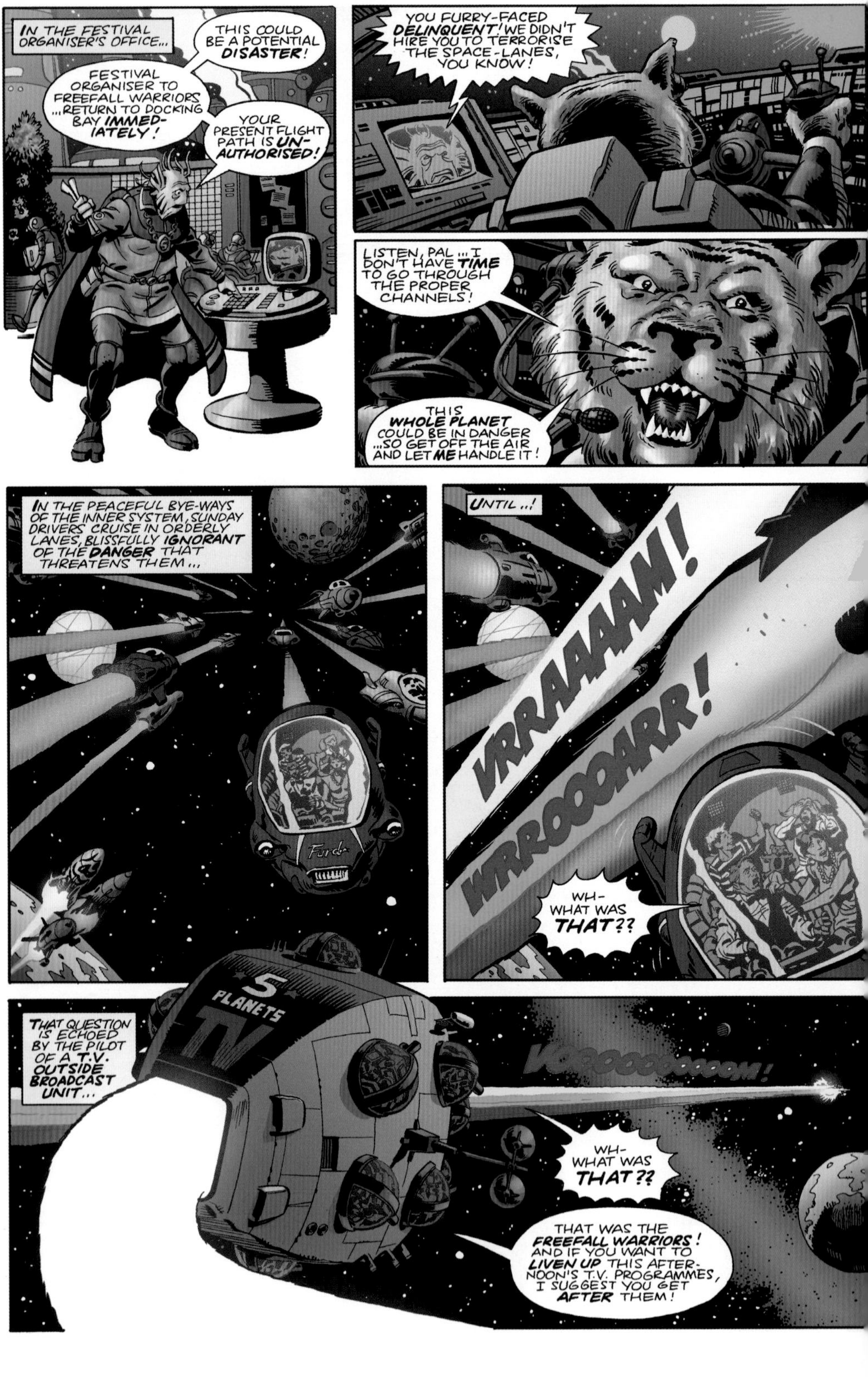
IN THE FESTIVAL ORGANISER'S OFFICE...
THIS COULD BE A POTENTIAL DISASTER!
FESTIVAL ORGANISER TO FREEFALL WARRIORS ...RETURN TO DOCKING BAY IMMED-IATELY!
YOUR PRESENT FLIGHT PATH IS UN-AUTHORISED!
YOU FURRY-FACED DELINQUENT! WE DIDN'T HIRE YOU TO TERRORISE THE SPACE-LANES, YOU KNOW!
LISTEN, PAL ... I DON'T HAVE TIME TO GO THROUGH THE PROPER CHANNELS!
THIS WHOLE PLANET COULD BE IN DANGER ...SO GET OFF THE AIR AND LET ME HANDLE IT!
IN THE PEACEFUL BYE-WAYS OF THE INNER SYSTEM, SUNDAY DRIVERS CRUISE IN ORDERLY LANES, BLISSFULLY IGNORANT OF THE DANGER THAT THREATENS THEM...
Ford
UNTIL...!
VRRAAAAM!
WRROOOARR!
WH- WHAT WAS THAT??
THAT QUESTION IS ECHOED BY THE PILOT OF A T.V. OUTSIDE BROADCAST UNIT...
5 PLANETS TV
VOOOOOOOOOOM!
WH- WHAT WAS THAT??
THAT WAS THE FREEFALL WARRIORS! AND IF YOU WANT TO LIVEN UP THIS AFTER-NOON'S T.V. PROGRAMMES, I SUGGEST YOU GET AFTER THEM!

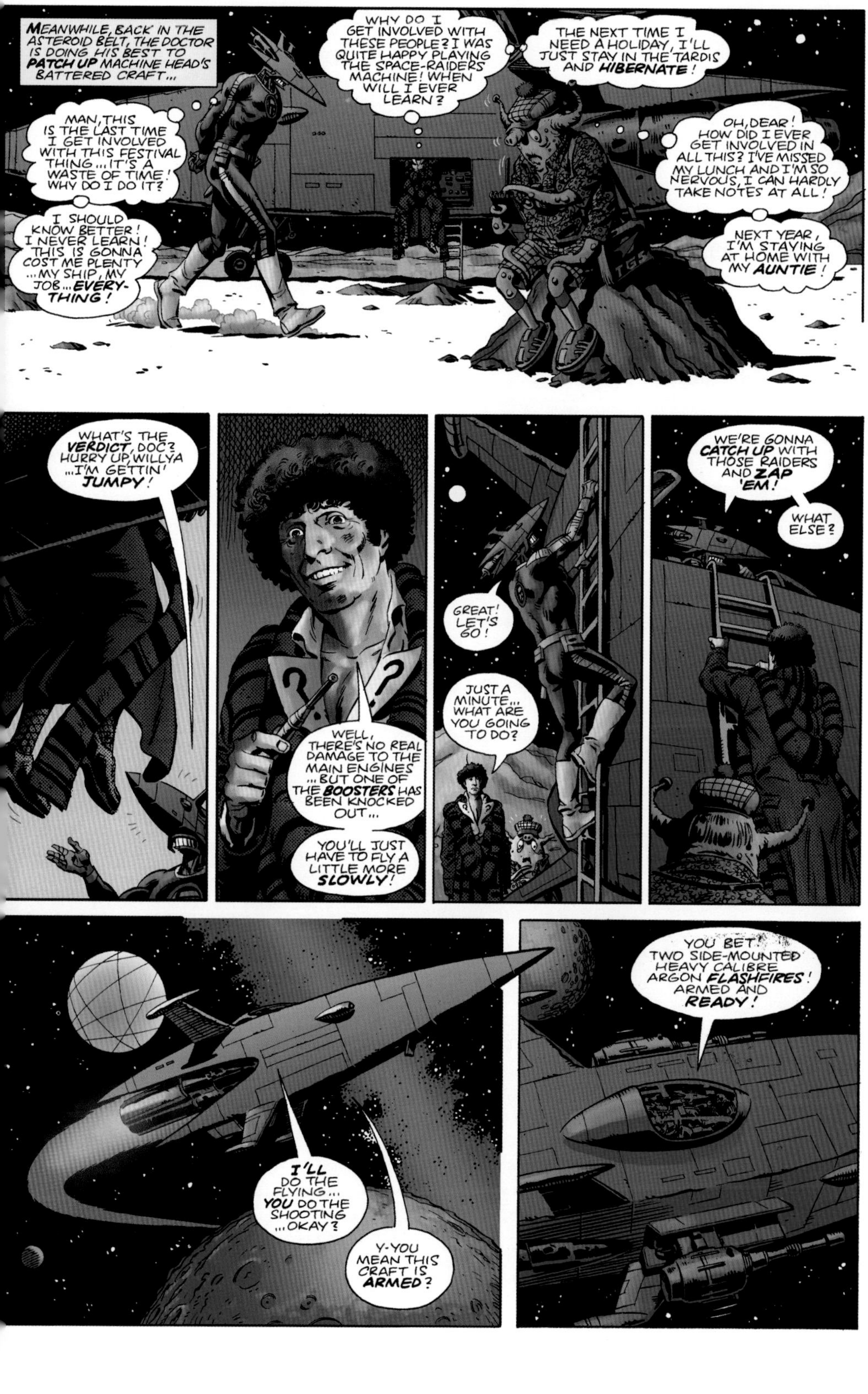
MEANWHILE, BACK IN THE ASTEROID BELT, THE DOCTOR IS DOING HIS BEST TO PATCH UP MACHINE HEAD'S BATTERED CRAFT...
WHY DO I GET INVOLVED WITH THESE PEOPLE? I WAS QUITE HAPPY PLAYING THE SPACE-RAIDERS MACHINE! WHEN WILL I EVER LEARN?
THE NEXT TIME I NEED A HOLIDAY, I'LL JUST STAY IN THE TARDIS AND HIBERNATE!
MAN, THIS IS THE LAST TIME I GET INVOLVED WITH THIS FESTIVAL THING... IT'S A WASTE OF TIME! WHY DO I DO IT?
I SHOULD KNOW BETTER! I NEVER LEARN! THIS IS GONNA COST ME PLENTY ...MY SHIP, MY JOB... EVERY-THING!
OH, DEAR! HOW DID I EVER GET INVOLVED IN ALL THIS? I'VE MISSED MY LUNCH AND I'M SO NERVOUS, I CAN HARDLY TAKE NOTES AT ALL!
NEXT YEAR, I'M STAYING AT HOME WITH MY AUNTIE!
WHAT'S THE VERDICT, DOC? HURRY UP, WILLYA ...I'M GETTIN' JUMPY!
WELL, THERE'S NO REAL DAMAGE TO THE MAIN ENGINES ...BUT ONE OF THE BOOSTERS HAS BEEN KNOCKED OUT...
YOU'LL JUST HAVE TO FLY A LITTLE MORE SLOWLY!
GREAT! LET'S GO!
JUST A MINUTE... WHAT ARE YOU GOING TO DO?
WE'RE GONNA CATCH UP WITH THOSE RAIDERS AND ZAP 'EM!
WHAT ELSE?
I'LL DO THE FLYING... YOU DO THE SHOOTING ...OKAY?
Y-YOU MEAN THIS CRAFT IS ARMED?
YOU BET! TWO SIDE-MOUNTED HEAVY CALIBRE ARGON FLASHFIRES! ARMED AND READY!

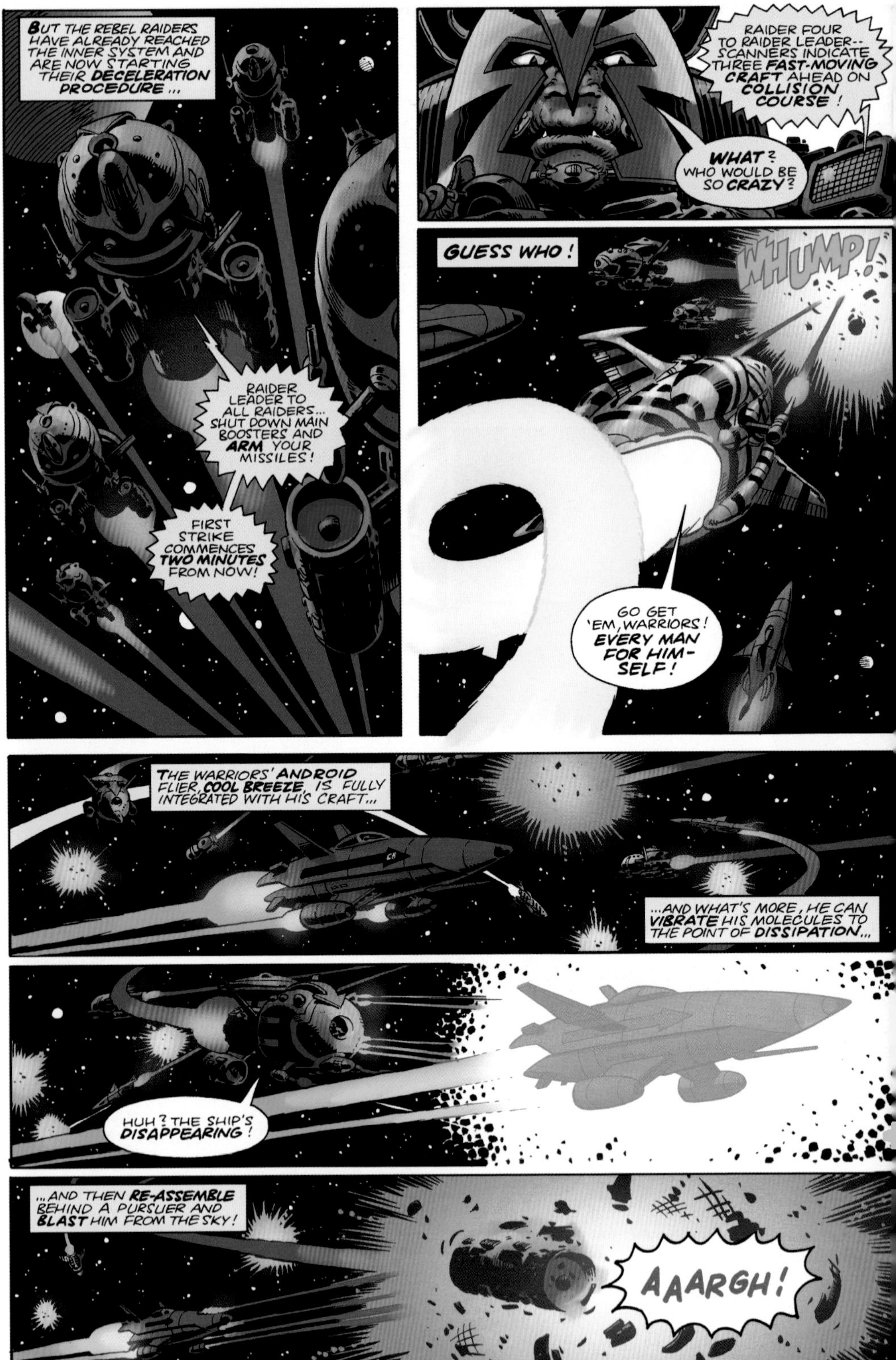
BUT THE REBEL RAIDERS HAVE ALREADY REACHED THE INNER SYSTEM AND ARE NOW STARTING THEIR DECELERATION PROCEDURE ...
RAIDER LEADER TO ALL RAIDERS... SHUT DOWN MAIN BOOSTERS AND ARM YOUR MISSILES!
FIRST STRIKE COMMENCES TWO MINUTES FROM NOW!
RAIDER FOUR TO RAIDER LEADER-- SCANNERS INDICATE THREE FAST-MOVING CRAFT AHEAD ON COLLISION COURSE!
WHAT? WHO WOULD BE SO CRAZY?
GUESS WHO!
WHUMP!
GO GET 'EM, WARRIORS! EVERY MAN FOR HIM-SELF!
THE WARRIORS' ANDROID FLIER, COOL BREEZE, IS FULLY INTEGRATED WITH HIS CRAFT...
...AND WHAT'S MORE, HE CAN VIBRATE HIS MOLECULES TO THE POINT OF DISSIPATION...
HUH? THE SHIP'S DISAPPEARING!
...AND THEN RE-ASSEMBLE BEHIND A PURSUER AND BLAST HIM FROM THE SKY!
AAARGH!

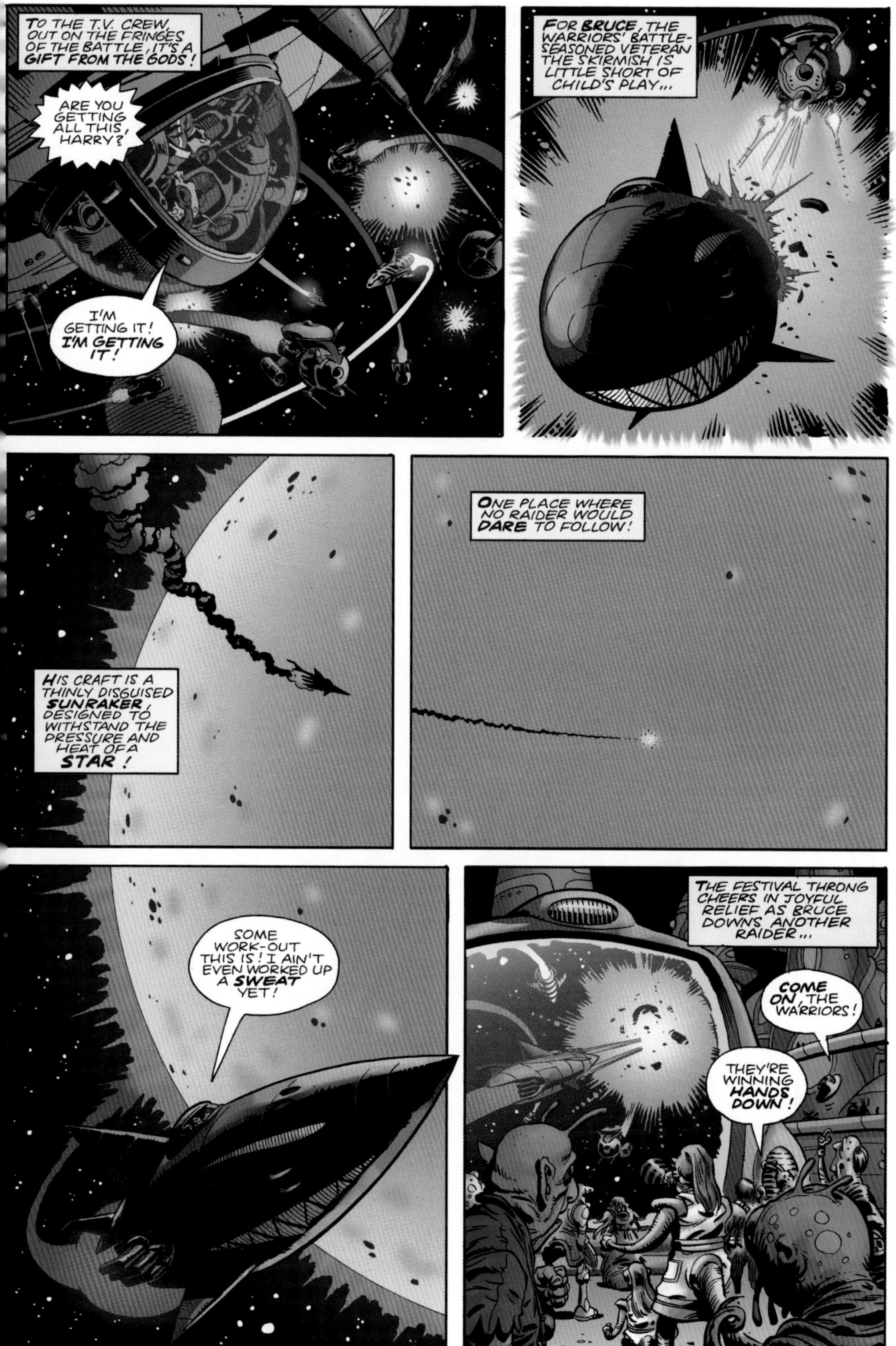
TO THE T.V. CREW, OUT ON THE FRINGES OF THE BATTLE, IT'S A GIFT FROM THE GODS!
ARE YOU GETTING ALL THIS, HARRY?
I'M GETTING IT! I'M GETTING IT!
FOR BRUCE, THE WARRIORS' BATTLE-SEASONED VETERAN THE SKIRMISH IS LITTLE SHORT OF CHILD'S PLAY...
HIS CRAFT IS A THINLY DISGUISED SUNRAKER, DESIGNED TO WITHSTAND THE PRESSURE AND HEAT OF A STAR!
ONE PLACE WHERE NO RAIDER WOULD DARE TO FOLLOW!
SOME WORK-OUT THIS IS! I AIN'T EVEN WORKED UP A SWEAT YET!
THE FESTIVAL THRONG CHEERS IN JOYFUL RELIEF AS BRUCE DOWNS ANOTHER RAIDER...
COME ON, THE WARRIORS!
THEY'RE WINNING HANDS DOWN!

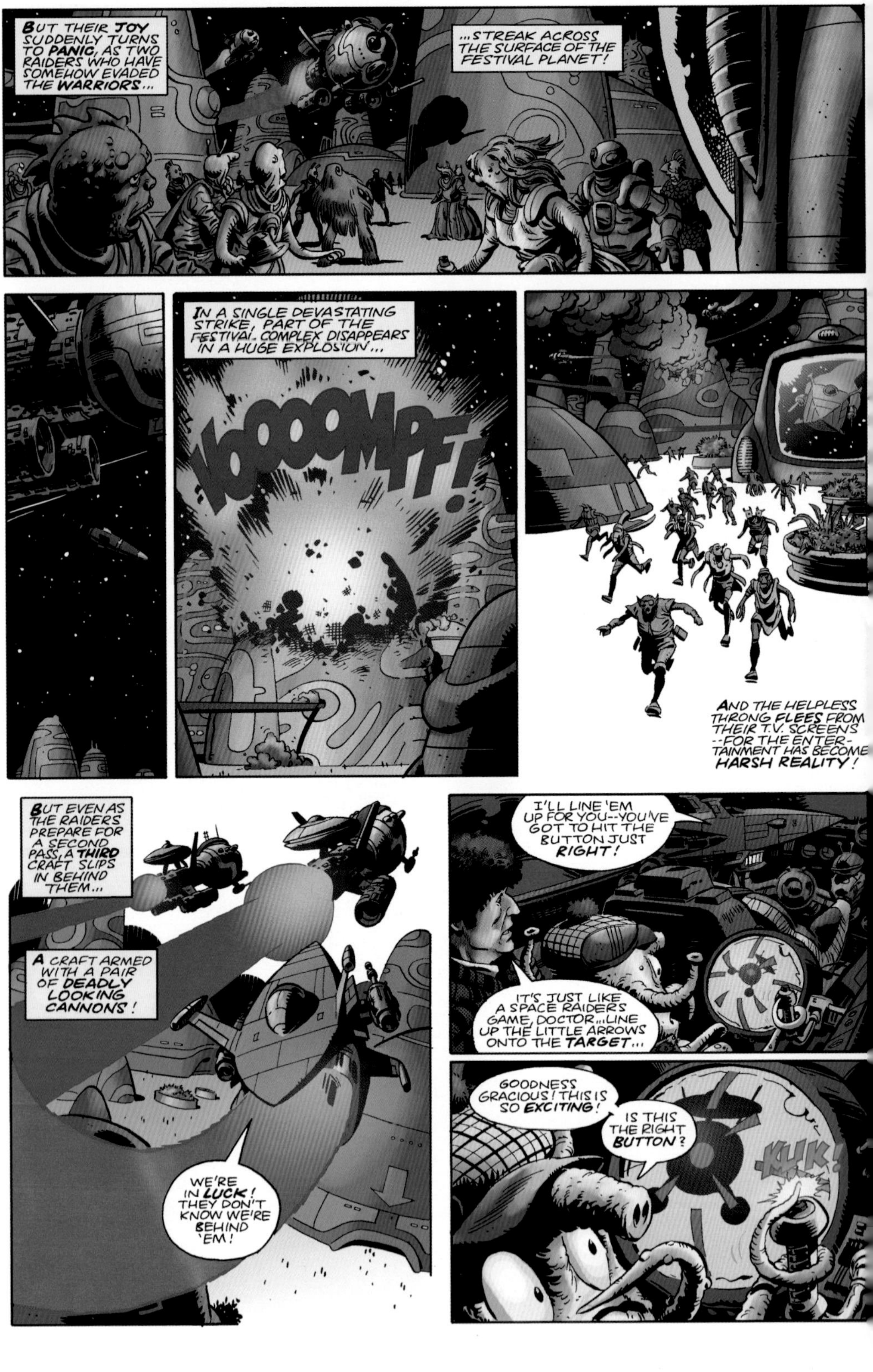

BUT THEIR JOY SUDDENLY TURNS TO PANIC, AS TWO RAIDERS WHO HAVE SOMEHOW EVADED THE WARRIORS...
...STREAK ACROSS THE SURFACE OF THE FESTIVAL PLANET!
IN A SINGLE DEVASTATING STRIKE, PART OF THE FESTIVAL COMPLEX DISAPPEARS IN A HUGE EXPLOSION...
VOOOOMPF!
AND THE HELPLESS THRONG FLEES FROM THEIR T.V. SCREENS --FOR THE ENTERTAINMENT HAS BECOME HARSH REALITY!
BUT EVEN AS THE RAIDERS PREPARE FOR A SECOND PASS, A THIRD CRAFT SLIPS IN BEHIND THEM...
A CRAFT ARMED WITH A PAIR OF DEADLY LOOKING CANNONS!
WE'RE IN LUCK! THEY DON'T KNOW WE'RE BEHIND 'EM!
I'LL LINE 'EM UP FOR YOU--YOU'VE GOT TO HIT THE BUTTON JUST RIGHT!
IT'S JUST LIKE A SPACE RAIDERS GAME, DOCTOR...LINE UP THE LITTLE ARROWS ONTO THE TARGET...
GOODNESS GRACIOUS! THIS IS SO EXCITING!
IS THIS THE RIGHT BUTTON?
KLIK!

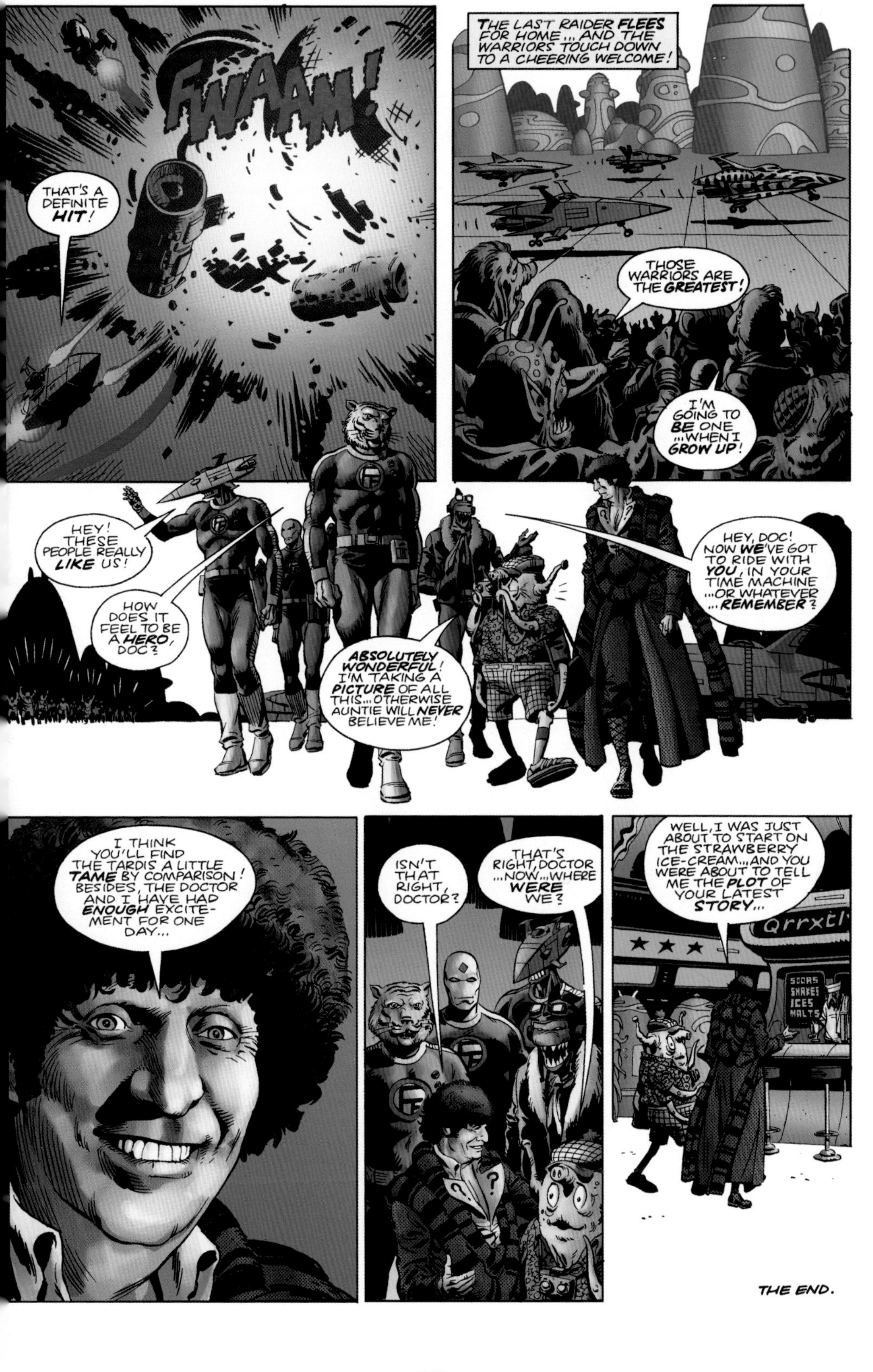
FWAAM!
THAT'S A DEFINITE HIT!
THE LAST RAIDER FLEES FOR HOME... AND THE WARRIORS TOUCH DOWN TO A CHEERING WELCOME!
THOSE WARRIORS ARE THE GREATEST!
I'M GOING TO BE ONE ...WHEN I GROW UP!
HEY! THESE PEOPLE REALLY LIKE US!
HOW DOES IT FEEL TO BE A HERO, DOC?
ABSOLUTELY WONDERFUL! I'M TAKING A PICTURE OF ALL THIS... OTHERWISE AUNTIE WILL NEVER BELIEVE ME!
HEY, DOC! NOW WE'VE GOT TO RIDE WITH YOU, IN YOUR TIME MACHINE ...OR WHATEVER ...REMEMBER?
I THINK YOU'LL FIND THE TARDIS A LITTLE TAME BY COMPARISON! BESIDES, THE DOCTOR AND I HAVE HAD ENOUGH EXCITE-MENT FOR ONE DAY...
ISN'T THAT RIGHT, DOCTOR?
THAT'S RIGHT, DOCTOR ...NOW... WHERE WERE WE?
WELL, I WAS JUST ABOUT TO START ON THE STRAWBERRY ICE-CREAM... AND YOU WERE ABOUT TO TELL ME THE PLOT OF YOUR LATEST STORY...
Qrrxtl
SODAS SHAKES ICES MALTS
THE END.

Art by **Charlie Kirchoff** over **Dave Gibbons**

ART GALLERY

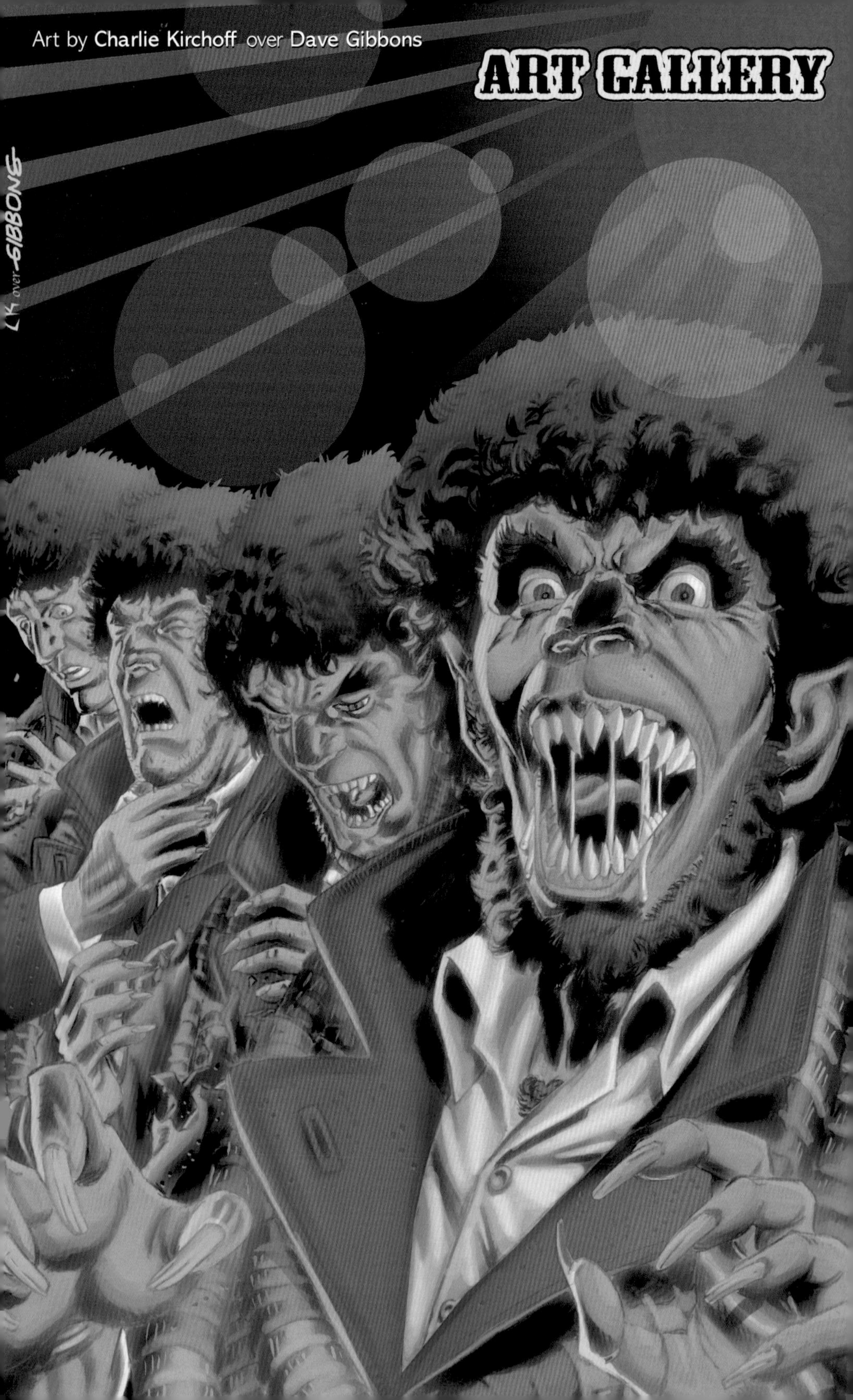
CK over GIBBONS

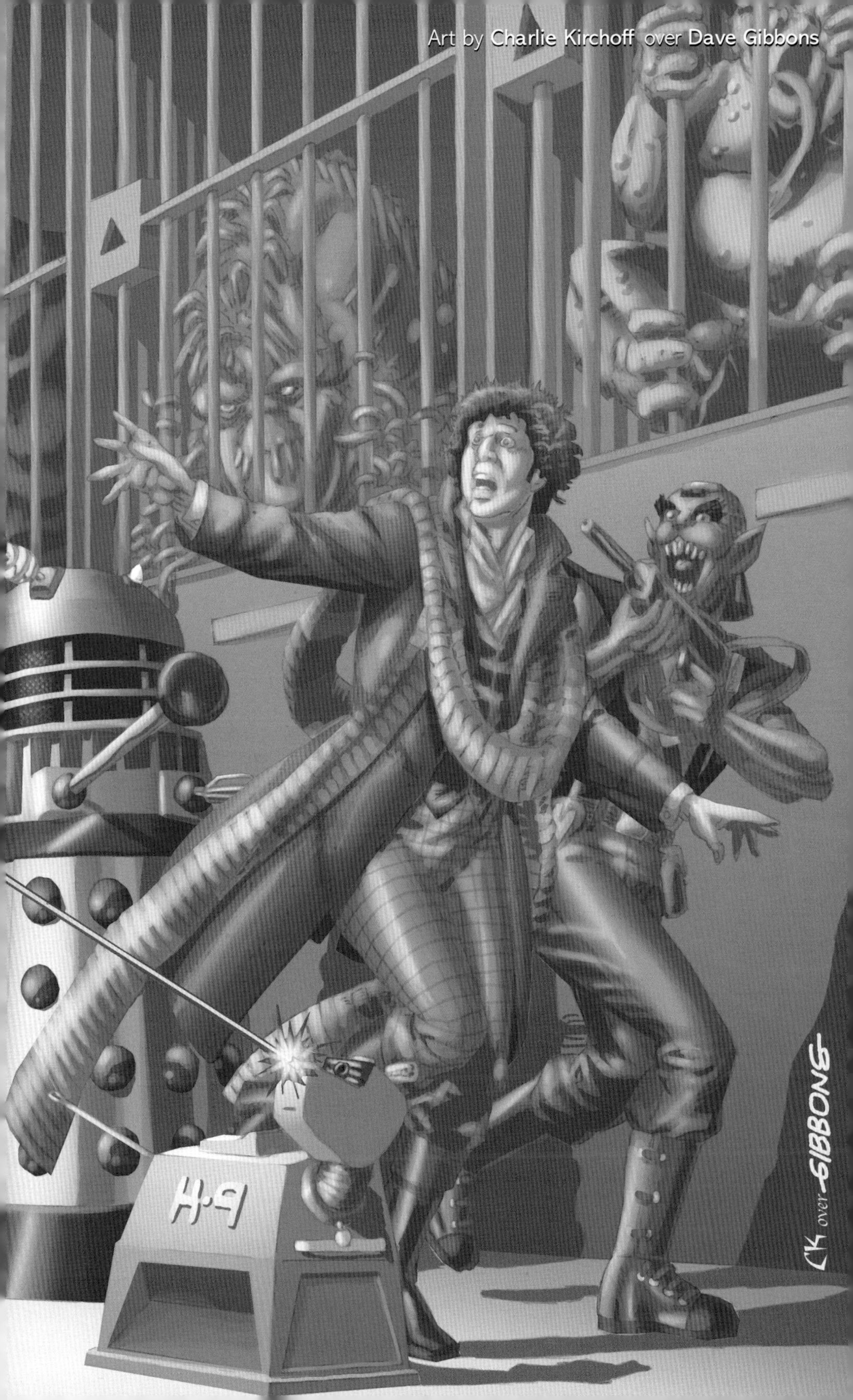
K-9
CK over GIBBONS

Art by **Charlie Kirchoff** over **Dave Gibbons**

Art by Charlie Kirchoff over Dave Gibbons

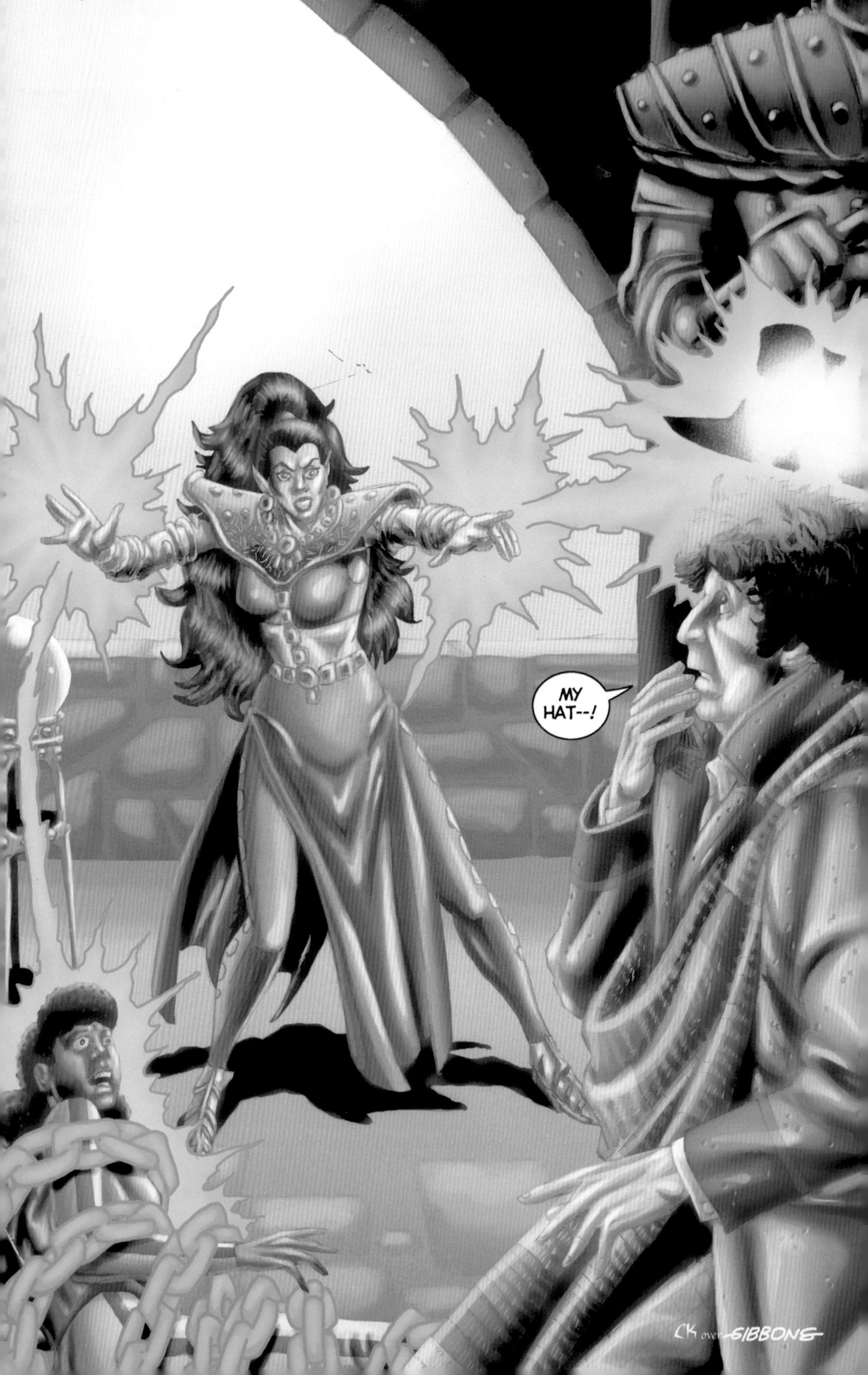
MY HAT--!
CK over GIBBONS

Art by **Charlie Kirchoff** over **Dave Gibbons**

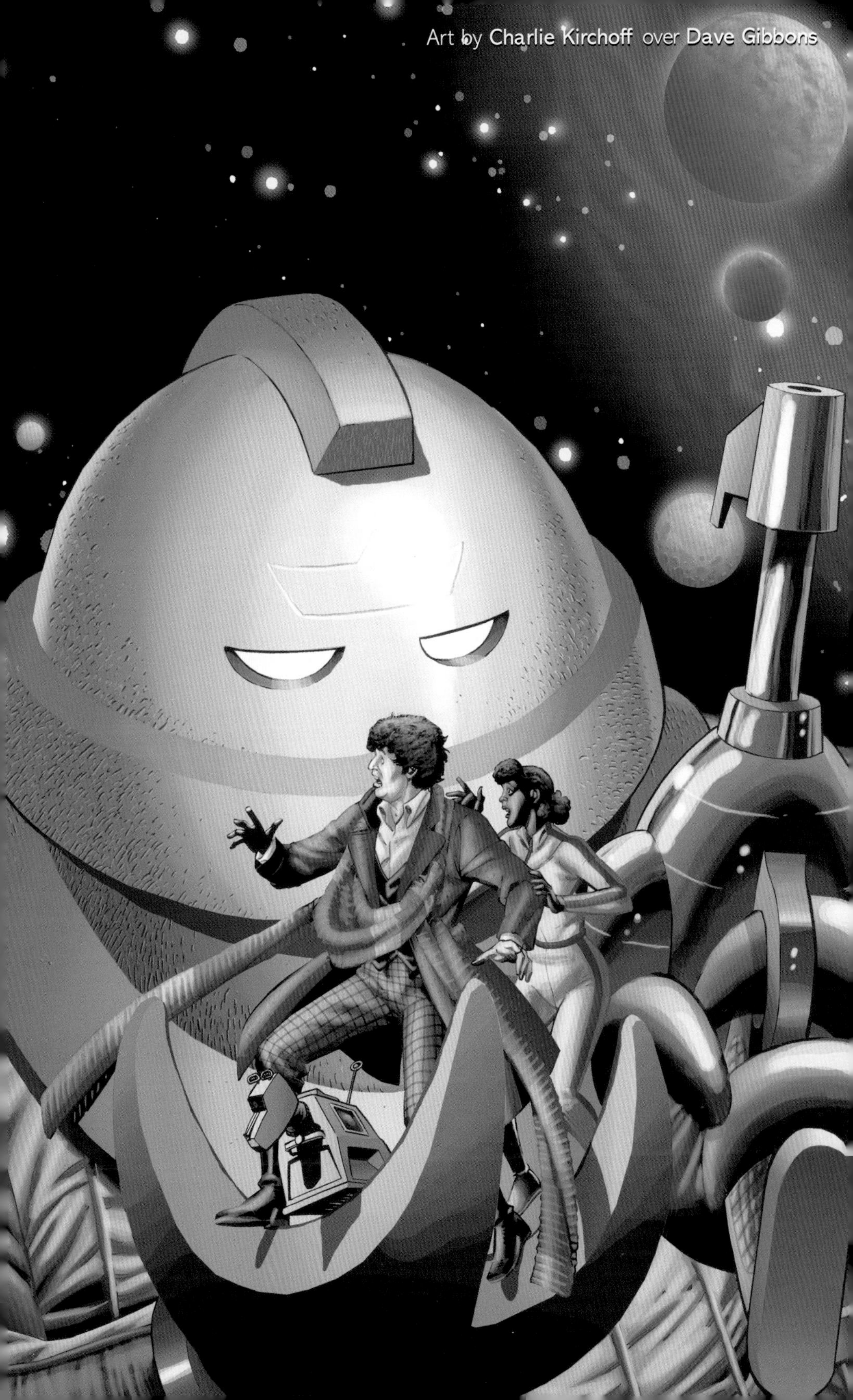

Art by **Robert Hack**
Colors by **Charlie Kirchoff**

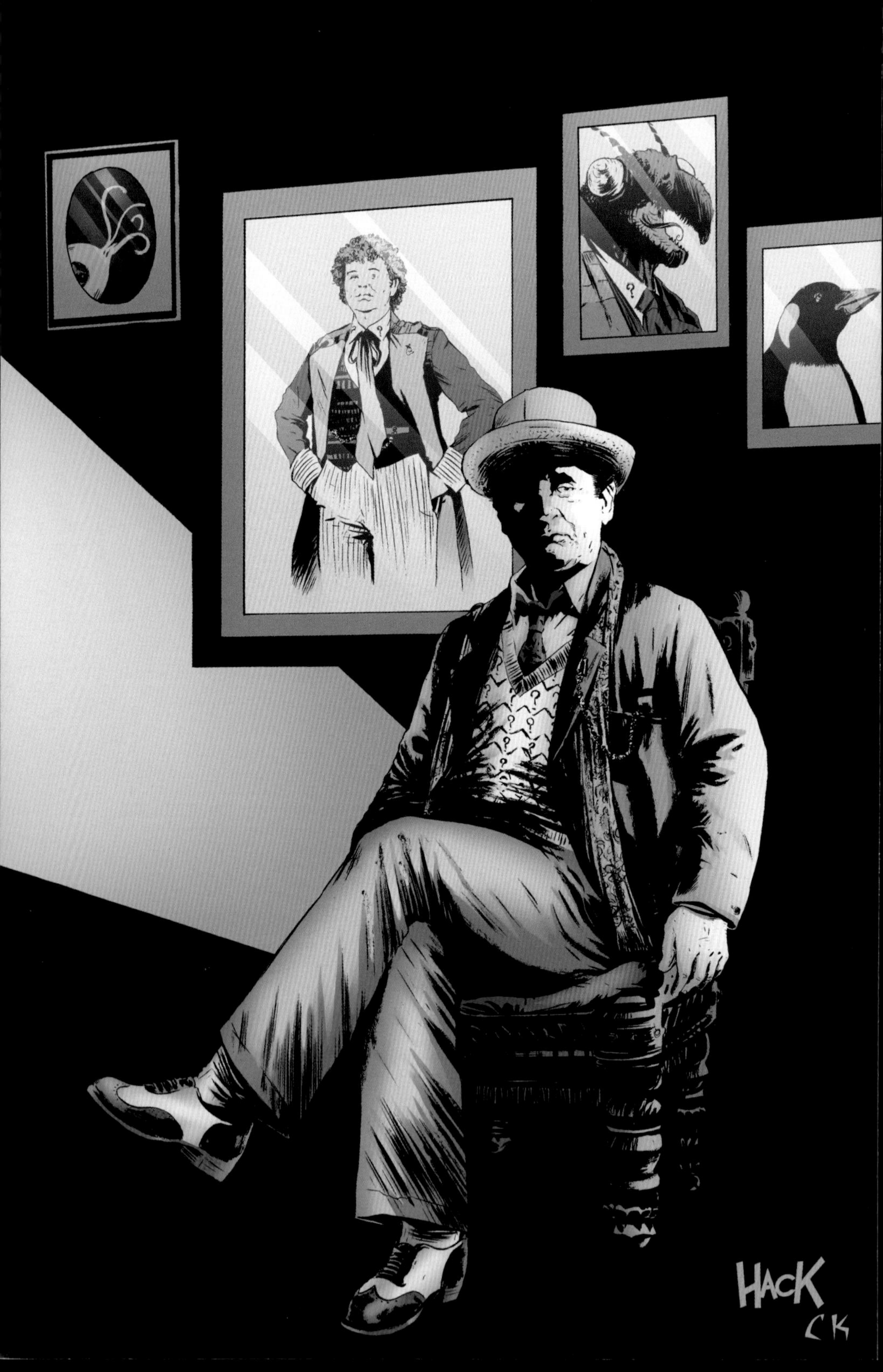
HACK
CK

Art by **Charlie Kirchoff** over **Dave Gibbons**

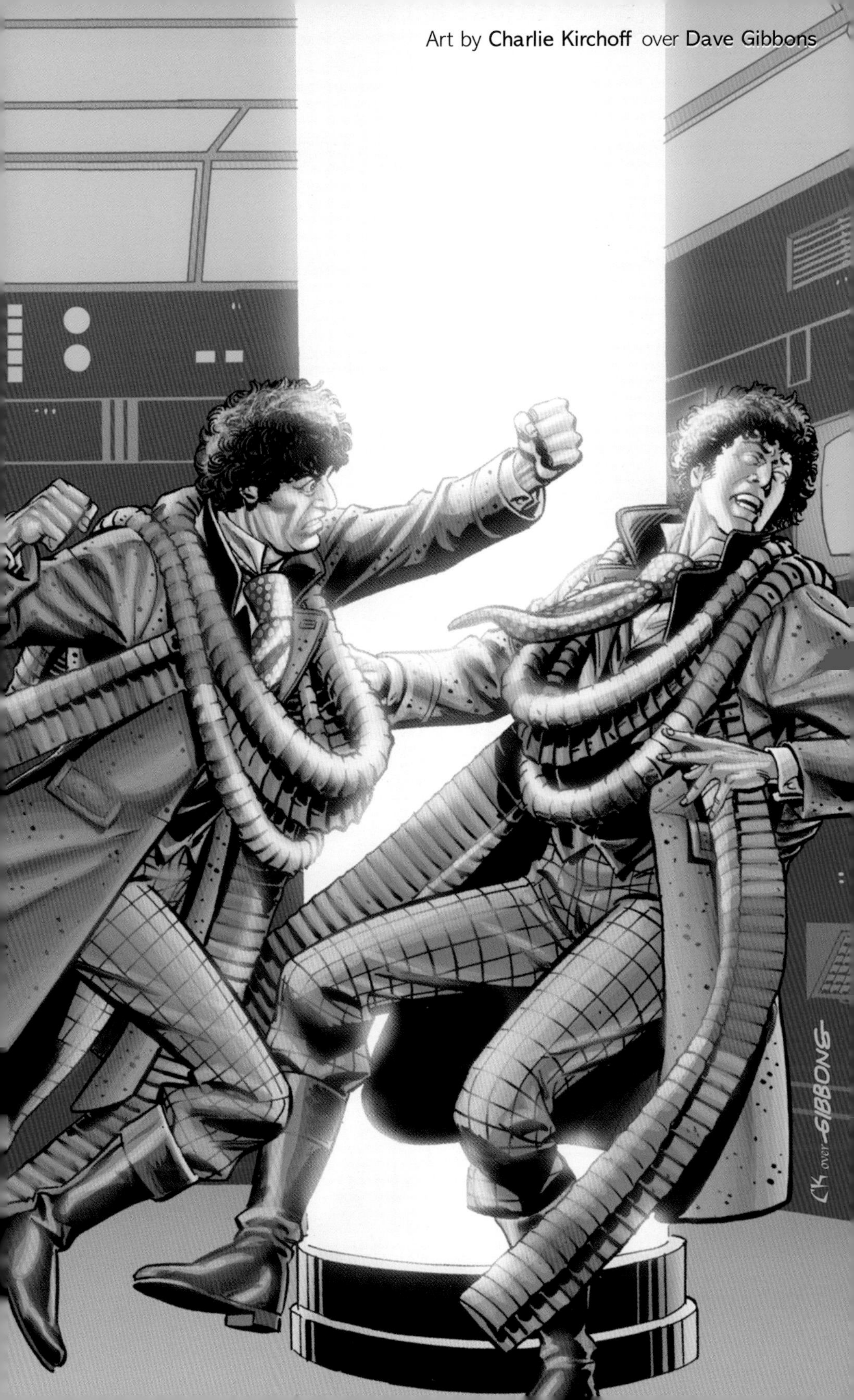
CK over GIBBONS

Art by Robert Hack
Colors by Charlie Kirchoff

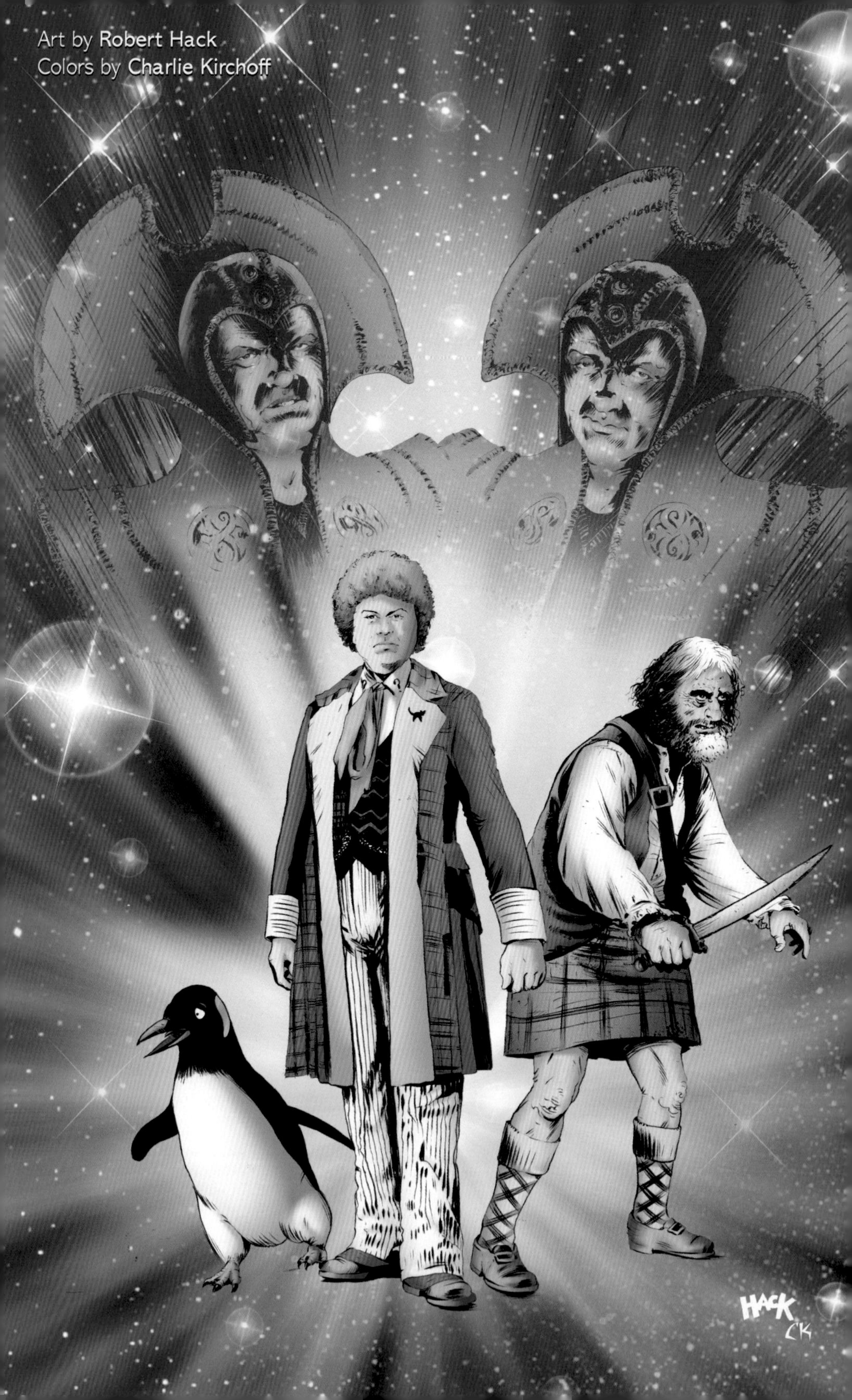
HACK
CK

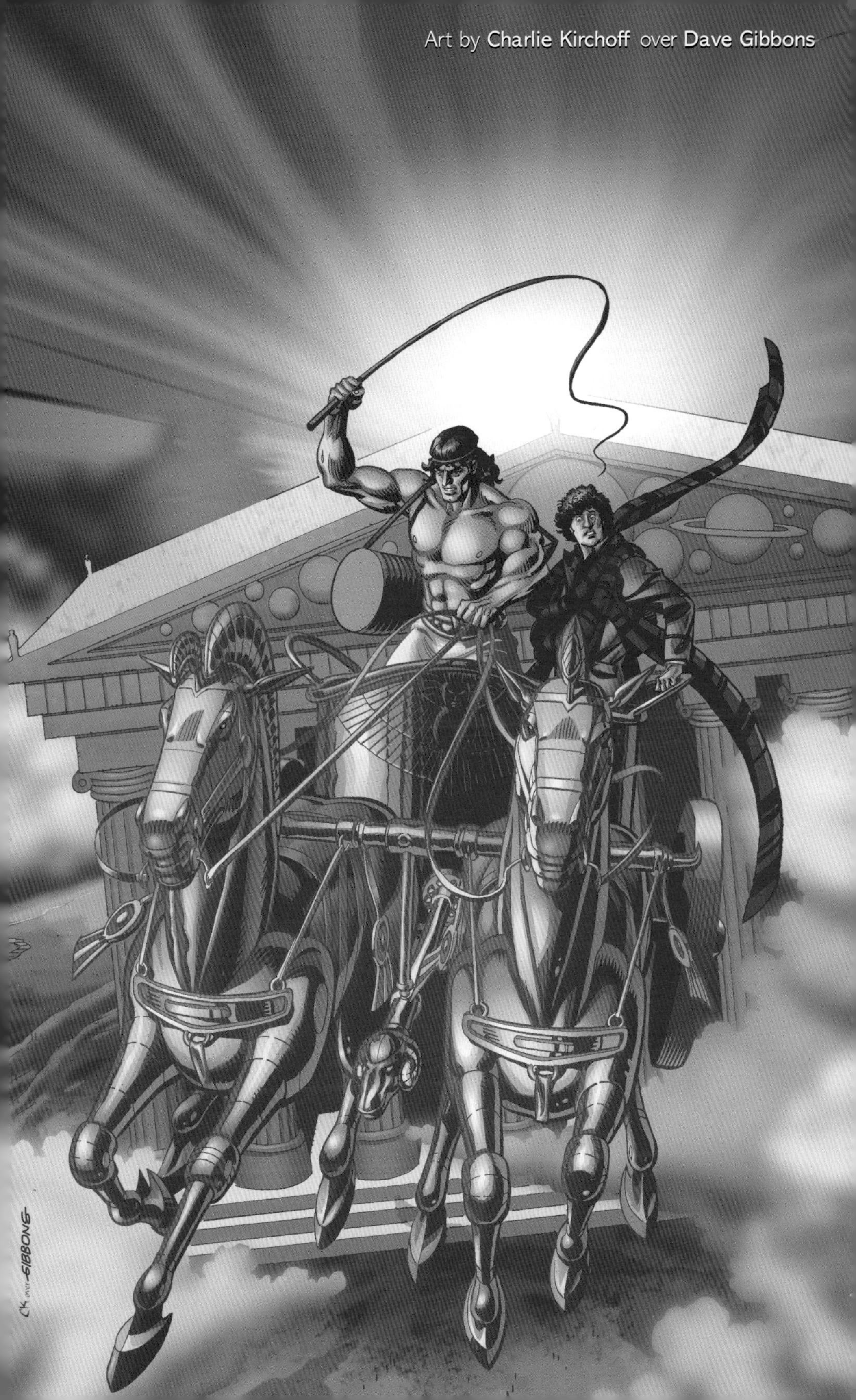
Art by **Charlie Kirchoff** over **Dave Gibbons**

Art by **Charlie Kirchoff** over **Dave Gibbons**

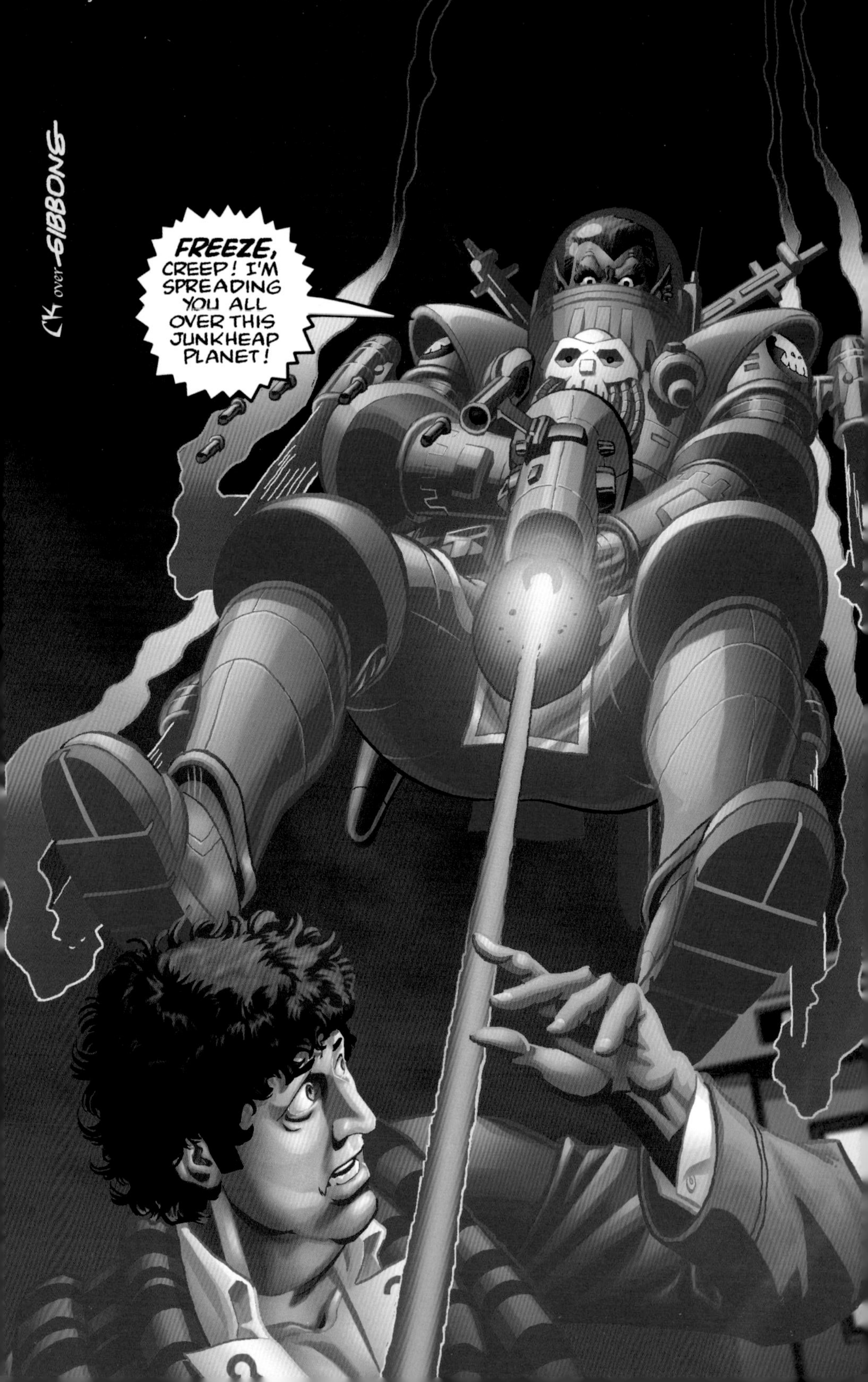
CK over GIBBONS
FREEZE, CREEP! I'M SPREADING YOU ALL OVER THIS JUNKHEAP PLANET!

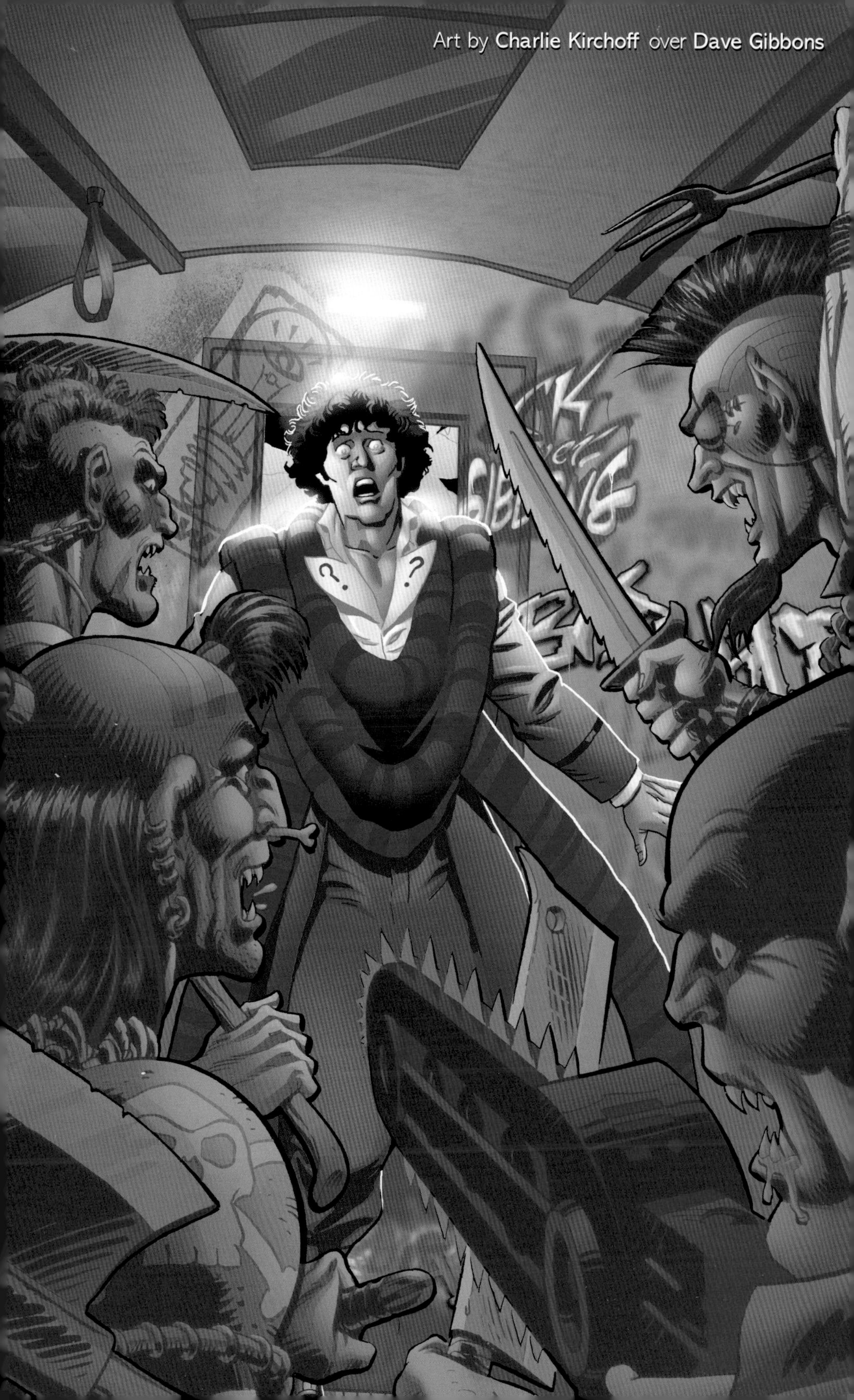

Art by **Charlie Kirchoff** over **Dave Gibbons**

Art by Joe Corroney

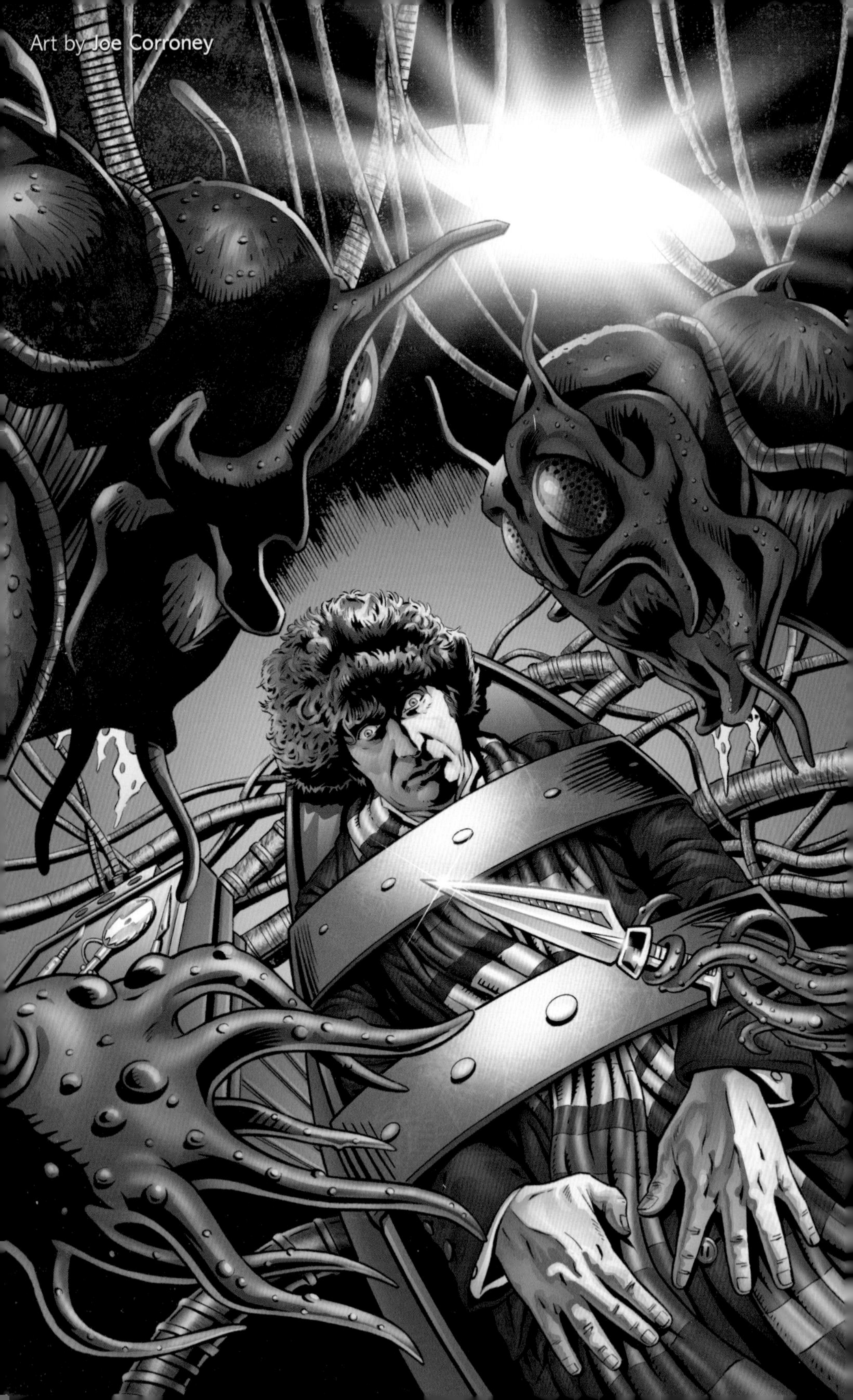